Browne, Sir Thomas
Religio Medici

RELIGIO MEDICI

AND OTHER WORKS

SIR THOMAS BROWNE

RELIGIO MEDICI

AND OTHER WORKS

EDITED BY L. C. MARTIN

OXFORD
AT THE CLARENDON PRESS
1964

Oxford University Press, Amen House, London E.C.4
GLASGOW NEW YORK TORONTO MELBOURNE WELLINGTON
BOMBAY CALCUTTA MADRAS KARACHI LAHORE DACCA
CAPE TOWN SALISBURY NAIROBI IBADAN ACCRA
KUALA LUMPUR HONG KONG

PRINTED IN GREAT BRITAIN

PREFACE

THE five works of Sir Thomas Browne included in this volume are those by which he is best known and they have often been reprinted, singly or in groups or in editions of the works as a whole. The first three have been edited very recently and their texts here and there considerably improved. The present aim, for all five works, is to carry this process a degree or two further, and to provide necessary annotation, both textual and explanatory. The pages of text have been kept as free from annotation as possible, by admitting editorial footnotes only to show where the basic originals have not been followed and by placing the main record of variant readings towards the end of the book.

The texts are based on the first (or the first authorized) edition of each work. To the rule that all departures from these must be shown there are the following exceptions: 's' replaces 'ſ'; abbreviated forms are expanded, and wrong founts, turned letters, and errors of spacing have been corrected silently. The same applies to the most obvious kinds of printer's error occurring in the marginal notes to the original editions. These notes are now placed at the foot of the pages, above the editor's notes on the text, where both kinds are present.

The variant readings recorded in the textual notes (pp. 261–88) are derived mainly from manuscripts, eight of which are contemporary copies of *Religio Medici*, not in Browne's hand but sometimes valuable for the establishment of the text or for their preservation of sentences omitted from the early printed versions. Thanks to some recent editors of *Religio Medici*, the merits and limitations of these manuscripts now stand clearly revealed. Less attention has been given to the manuscript material connected with *Hydriotaphia*, *The Garden of Cyrus*, *A Letter to a Friend*, and *Christian Morals*, and embedded in the mass of autograph writings by Browne now chiefly in the British Museum and Bodleian Libraries. Besides letters this collection contains memoranda filling hundreds of pages and greatly varying in length and legibility. Some of these memoranda were afterwards revised and incorporated in Browne's published works, especially *Christian Morals*; and it is thus possible fairly often to appreciate the differences between his sentences as they were first printed and as they exist in previous draftings; but too little of this material has been made generally available. As with *Religio Medici* some of the drafted passages were set aside and remained unpublished until long after. Simon Wilkin printed a number of them in his monumental edition of Browne's *Works* (1836); the same were reprinted by W. A. Greenhill and by Sir Geoffrey Keynes; and they now reappear with additions and with a selection of shorter variants not printed hitherto. It may well be long before Browne's autograph writings as a whole can be deciphered, co-ordinated, and fully described; nevertheless there is reason to believe that so far as the five works here reprinted are concerned most of the more important variants have been collected. In general, emendations or conjectures by previous editors are not noted save where a reading in the early texts can seem to be seriously challenged by them. In some places early readings which have been questioned or rejected are defended and retained.

The commentary at the end of the volume is designed chiefly to explain, so far as possible, the less obvious of Browne's allusions and to exemplify the kinds of material which enlarged his mind and stimulated his imagination. These fields have been already worked with valuable results, and yet many obscure passages and references have called in vain for elucidation. When the difficulties can be overcome it is most often in the light of literature with which Browne was certainly or probably acquainted, whether books which he mentions himself or others which were in the library formed by him and by his son, Dr. Edward Browne. This impressive collection was sold by auction in 1711, after the son's death, and fortunately two copies of the sale-catalogue are extant. It is much to be hoped that this document will soon be reprinted, as too little is known about the nature and extent of Browne's reading. A summary account of the catalogue is given in Appendix II (pp. 259–60). In the commentary '*SC*' attached to a book title indicates that the catalogue contains the work referred to.[1] Browne's own marginal notes frequently acknowledge his indebtedness to particular writers, but as this was done without system and the information is often very incomplete it has been supplemented at many points, either in the commentary or by means of additions in square brackets to the notes themselves.

Browne's Biblical quotations and echoings are very numerous and it has not seemed necessary to supply all of them with chapter and verse; but some of the more recondite ones have been pointed out. His quotations of classical literature are not always made at first hand, being often derived with other material from later writings in which the quotations were already provided; and

[1] The symbol is not as a rule attached to the titles of ancient classical works, the existence of which in the catalogue can generally be taken for granted.

where this is more or less clearly the case the immediate source is given as well as, or instead of, the ultimate one.

In preparing this volume I have had very great help from Browne's previous editors and from those many persons who have contributed, in books and articles, to the better understanding of his work; and I gratefully own a special debt to the comprehensive editions of Browne's works by Simon Wilkin (1835–6) and by Sir Geoffrey Keynes (1928–31), to Sir Geoffrey Keynes's *A Bibliography of Sir Thomas Browne* (1924), and to W. A. Greenhill, the most recent editor to supply (beginning in 1881) a commentary to all the five works chosen for the present edition.

I wish also to record my gratitude to the officials of many libraries where it has been necessary to seek out information hitherto unprovided, especially the British Museum, the Bodleian Library, the Castle Museum and the Public Library at Norwich, the Library of the Dean and Chapter, Norwich Cathedral, the libraries of St. John's College, Cambridge, of Pembroke College, Oxford, and of the universities of Edinburgh, Glasgow,[1] and Liverpool. Microfilms of manuscripts have been kindly supplied by the custodians of the Osler Library at Montreal and of the Library at Lehigh University. On two occasions valuable information was provided from the Department of Coins in the British Museum.

My thanks are also due, for various kindnesses, to Dr. T. J. Cadoux, Mr. John Carter, the Clarendon Press staff, Mr. J. B. Leishman, Mr. Paul Morgan, Mr. F. J. Routledge, Mr. D. A. F. M. Russell, Professor E. Scamuzzi, Mr. J. F. Soutter, Mr. John Sparrow, and above all to my wife, for her unfailing interest and for researches which have solved many problems and abbreviated many delays.

L. C. M.

[1] Copies of all the known editions of Browne's works save one were collected by Professor T. K. Munro, of Glasgow, and are now, since 1957, in the University Library there, by his bequest. The similar collection formerly in the Castle Museum, Norwich, is now in the Norwich Public Library.

CONTENTS

LIST OF ILLUSTRATIONS

INTRODUCTION

I. BRIEF LIST OF DATES

(*Chief authorities*: Life in *Posthumous Works*, 1712; Wood, *Athenae Oxonienses*; O. Leroy, *Le Chevalier Thomas Browne*, 1931).

1605 Born 19 October in London.

1616 Scholar of Winchester College.

1623 Matriculated at Oxford, Broadgates Hall (Pembroke College).

1626 Bachelor of Arts, Oxford.

1629 Master of Arts, Oxford.

?1631–?1634 Studied medicine at Montpellier, Padua, and Leyden.

1636 or 1637 Settled at Norwich.

1637 M.D., Oxford.

1641 Married Dorothy Mileham.

1642 *Religio Medici* published twice (editions unauthorized).

1643 Authorized edition of *Religio Medici*.

1646 *Pseudodoxia Epidemica* (also 1650, 1658, &c.).

1658 *Hydriotaphia* with *The Garden of Cyrus* (twice; also 1659 and 1669).

1664 Hon. Fellow, College of Physicians.

1671 Knighted by Charles II.

1682 Died 19 October.

1690 *A Letter to a Friend.*

1716 *Christian Morals.*

In the rest of this introduction the titles of the works mentioned above are abbreviated as follows:

RM = *Religio Medici*
PE = *Pseudodoxia Epidemica*
HGC = *Hydriotaphia* with *The Garden of Cyrus* (separately as *H* and *GC*)
LF = *A Letter to a Friend*
CM = *Christian Morals*

II. *RELIGIO MEDICI* (*RM*)

'This I confesse about seven yeares past . . . I had at leisurable houres composed' ('To the Reader', 1643).[1] The book was first published in 1642 in an unauthorized edition issued by Andrew Crooke, which was followed by a second unauthorized edition having the same date.[2] *RM*, however, had been for some time circulating in manuscript copies, eight of which are still extant. None of these is autograph and all are more or less corrupt. Two of them (the first two in the following list) represent the book in an earlier and shorter form than the rest.

1. Pembroke College, Oxford.[3] (*P.*)
2. British Museum, MS. Lansdowne 489 (incomplete, ending in Pt. I, Section 18, at 'all', p. 19. l. 4 below). (*L.*)
3. St. John's College, Cambridge (M. R. James, *Catalogue of the manuscripts in St. John's College, Cambridge*, no. 281). The best of the manuscripts in the longer version. (*J.*)
4. Norwich Public Library, MS. Wilkin 1 (formerly in Norwich Castle Museum). (*W.*)
5. Norwich Public Library, MS. Wilkin 2 (formerly in Norwich Castle Museum). (*N.*)
6. Bodleian Library, MS. Rawlinson D. 162. (*R.*)
7. The Osler Library, McGill University, Montreal, MS. 4417. (*O.*)
8. The Honeyman Collection, Lehigh University Library.[4] (*H.*)

The manuscript copy on which the editions of 1642 were based, and which has not been preserved, was evidently faithful in general to the author's intentions but also greatly marred by errors of detail such as are found in the extant manuscripts, especi-

[1] See p. 39, l. 33 for a sentence which must have been written before 19 October 1635. Four sections appeared for the first time in 1643.

[2] The first of these two editions has 190 pages; the second 159. Sir Geoffrey Keynes, whose earlier opinion about their relative order was the reverse of this (*A Bibliography of Sir Thomas Browne*, 1924, no. 1, p. 9) was led to change it by the arguments put forward in 1948 by Miss Elizabeth Cook, 'The first edition of Religio Medici' (*Harvard Library Bulletin*, ii, 1). See *TLS* 18 April 1952, p. 265.

[3] The importance of this manuscript, which contains a number of passages otherwise unrecorded, was first made sufficiently clear by M. Denonain in his edition of *RM* of 1953. M. Denonain has since edited the manuscript itself, *Une Version primitive de Religio Medici* (Presses Universitaires de France, 1958).

[4] A microfilm of this manuscript was very kindly presented to me by the Librarian, Mr. James D. Mack. The manuscript itself, which was formerly owned by Mr. de Havilland Hall, went out of his possession about 1928. In 1957 it was presented to Lehigh University by Mr. Robert B. Honeyman. For this last piece of information I am indebted to Miss Cécile Desbarats, Librarian of the Osler Library, Montreal.

ally in *W*. These errors were generously supplemented by the printer, some sentences as printed being unintelligible. The second edition, apart from some superficial improvements, was as defective as the first.

It was perhaps hardly to be expected that Andrew Crooke would greatly exert himself to secure a more accurate text. Once in rightful possession of the manuscript he was legally free to publish it without the author's permission. Had he known who the author was, and where to be found, he might well have felt obliged to seek an agreement with him, but probably the manuscript, like those extant today, gave no obvious clue to the author's identity. Any reasons Crooke may have had for refraining, as publishers often did, from registering the book with the Stationers' Company can only be surmised,[1] but they may have included a wish to leave the question of authorship undisturbed.

Browne seems at first not to have thought of any remedial action, but as he explains in his address 'To the Reader' (p. 1, ll. 12–13), the importunity of his friends and his own concern for the truth at length prevailed over the 'inactivity of his disposition' and he began to prepare a text which would do his work better justice. On 3 March 1642/3, having heard that Sir Kenelm Digby had written 'animadversions' on *RM* and that these were in the press, he wrote to Digby urging him to withhold publication until he could be in a position to judge the work more fairly. The 'true and intended Original' was to be delivered to the press in a few weeks and Digby could see it in the meantime if he wished (p. 76, ll. 26–27). Nothing came, however, of this request (see Digby's account of the matter, pp. 77–78), and *Observations upon Religio Medici* (1643) shows no acquaintance with *RM* as improved and amplified in the edition printed some time in 1643/4. The publisher of that edition was again Andrew Crooke, who presumably had undertaken to see that the faults of its predecessors were not repeated. But still the book went unregistered and there is no evidence that any attempt was made to secure the approval of the press censorship.[2]

How soon after 3 March 1642/3 the 'full and intended copy' reached the printer, in what shape, and how prepared, are problems still unsolved. It would not be surprising if months rather than 'a few weeks' went by before the copy was ready. Probably all or most of the new material (which includes four whole sections) was

[1] The circumstances in which *RM* was published are ably discussed by Professor V. Sanna in her edition of *RM* (Università di Cagliari, 1958).

[2] This had been in abeyance since 1641 but was reinstituted in the Puritan interests in June 1643.

written specially for the new edition; but there is no certainty that the printer's copy was entirely or even partly in Browne's own handwriting.

What happened to the manuscript in the printing-house is another open question; but it could soon have been realized there that large portions of the copy were identical, or almost so, with the corresponding passages in the otherwise very faulty editions of 1642, and that labour might be saved if one or other of those editions, corrected from the manuscript, could serve as working copy for the new one. Smaller emendations could be made in the margins of the printed sheets and it could also be made plain where, for more extensive improvements, the manuscript itself was to be followed. If this kind of procedure was adopted it could easily happen that a number of blemishes would be overlooked.

Some such hypothesis seems at any rate needed to account for the fact[1] that the 'authorized' edition of 1643 contains errors, not always small ones, found in the editions of 1642 but not in any of the extant manuscripts, though it also corrects many errors found in the manuscripts and again in the editions of 1642. Those of the faults in the new edition (including a number of its own misprints) which were observed when the sheets had been printed off were acknowledged in a list of errata. But the omissions from this list provide another sign that Browne was unable or unwilling to give the business all the attention it deserved. He may not even have had any hand in correcting the proofs or in drawing up the errata, which in one place propose altering a good Latin reading to a bad one (see p. 44, l. 37).

The edition dated 1643[2] is made up as follows:

Title. See plate facing p. xxviii.

Collation, 8°: π^1 A–M^8. \$1–4. Some copies have an additional A2–A7 after π or after M8.

Pages. (4) (A1^r–A2^v), 1–170, 171, 172, 171, 172, 173–83 (A3^r–M7^r).

Contents. π^r engraving serving as title, π^v blank, A1^r–A2^v To the Reader, A3^r–M7^r *Religio Medici*, M7^v–M8^v blank. Contents of additional A2–A7: A2^r–A3^r Letter to Digby, A1^r–A5^v Digby's reply, A6^r–A6^v Address by A. B., A7^r Errata, A7^v blank.

Running-titles. To the Reader. (on A1^v–A2^v) *Religio Medici.* (on A3^v–M7^r).

[1] As pointed out in M. Denonain's edition of 1953, pp. xxvi–xxvii.

[2] Copies used: Liverpool University Library; Public Library, Norwich (2); Library of the Dean and Chapter, Norwich Cathedral; Bodleian Library (2); British Museum.

Notes. (1) In the editions of 1642 the initial engraving carries the title 'Religio Medici.' in the space between the human figure and the sea. Below the engraving are the words '*Printed for Andrew Crooke* 1642. *Will. Marshall scu:*'. In *1643* the title is removed from the engraving (though retained elsewhere), and most of the sea at the foot of the page is replaced by the words '*A true and full copy* . . . 1643' (see engraving). It is thus uncertain whether the title had the author's approval. '*coelo*' in the engraving, 1642, becomes 'cælo', 1643, and the words '*Will. Marshall scu:*' are now omitted.

(2) In *1643* the work is divided into two parts as in *1642* and in the later extant manuscripts (i.e. all except *P* and *L*). It is also divided into sections, as is not the case in *1642* and the later manuscripts. *P* and *L* divide the work into sections but not at the same points as in *1643*. The numbering of the sections in *1643* is anomalous as follows:

(*a*) In Part I the numbers run 1–35, 35 is repeated, 36–46, 46 is repeated, 47–58. There are thus 60 sections in Part I.

(*b*) In Part II the numbers run 1–9, 10 is omitted, 11–14, 15, 15 is repeated. There are thus 15 sections in Part II. It may be, however, that Section 9 should have ended at p. 67, l. 39, where there is a rather sudden transition of thought, and that a Section 10 should have run from there to the end of the present Section 9.

(3) The following typographical variants have been noticed in different copies of *1643*: p. 29, l. 20 *Sect./ect. S* p. 30, note, appointed us/appointed a^s p. 32, l. 39 Habakkuk/Habakukk p. 33, l. 18 spirituall/spiritnall p. 45, l. 32 separation/eparation. Apart from these variants there are places where the printing is more or less distinct in some copies and invisible in others.

After 1643 *RM* was republished or reissued during Browne's lifetime nine times in English (counting the edition of 1682, the year of his death) seven times in Latin, once in Dutch, and once in French. The English editions, dated 1645 (twice), 1656, 1659 (twice), 1669, 1672, 1678, and 1682, give some new readings but these are generally unimportant and there is no clear evidence that the author supplied them. It is the less likely that he did as so many errors, some of them serious, were allowed to stand.[1] He seems, in fact, to have withdrawn his attention almost altogether from the text of *RM* once it had been given to the world in a fairly presentable shape.

Since the edition of 1643, with all its defects, is thus the only one that Browne is known to have sponsored it seems indispensable

[1] There are a few changes in the edition of 1678 which may be authorial and these are given in the Textual Notes.

as the foundation for a modern text, and in the present edition it is followed, wherever possible, in all its details. Where it fails, the manuscripts and the unauthorized texts of 1642 have to be consulted, for none of these is so corrupt that it can never furnish a trustworthy or at least an attractive emendation, and frequently when they are unanimous they are also convincing.

But the difficulties in the text of 1643 were not all of the printer's making. Browne himself was not uniformly careful to avoid awkwardness and obscurity, and some of his constructions must have troubled even contemporary readers. Misunderstanding can also arise today from usages in syntax, spelling, and punctuation which were more or less current in the seventeenth century but are now rare or obsolete; and in two very recent editions of *RM*, both by foreign editors well acquainted with present-day idioms, some of these earlier usages have been too confidently treated as 'mistakes', and the basic text at times needlessly corrected. The difficulty of distinguishing, in Browne, between misprints, solecisms, and archaisms increases the desirability of leaving the text of 1643 exactly as it stands save where the evidence against its readings is too strong to be resisted.

In the present edition all deviations from that text, including the correction of its most obvious misprints, are recorded in the footnotes. It has not, however, seemed necessary to cite once more the hundreds of manuscript and printed variants assembled by Professor Denonain and again, though more selectively, by Professor Sanna.[1] Many of these variants are worthless; others are interesting and not in themselves inferior to the printed readings. But since in all cases of doubt the 'authorized' readings must have the benefit the general rule observed here has been to admit to the textual notes (pp. 261–88) only such variants as have some special claim to consideration. The same notes also contain the following, of which at least the first two have the importance of throwing light on the development of Browne's mind and style:

1. Passages and phrases occurring in the earlier version of *RM* as represented by the manuscript at Pembroke College, Oxford, sometimes found also in the other manuscripts and in the editions of 1642, but not published in 1643. (Notes marked †.)

2. An indication of passages, phrases, and single words occurring neither in the manuscripts nor in the editions of 1642 and presumably added when the text of 1643 was in preparation or not long before. (Notes marked *.)

[1] It has not been found possible always to agree with these two editors in their recording of manuscript variants.

3. Marginal notes occurring in some of the manuscripts but not in the texts of 1642 and 1643.

The many editions of *RM* published between 1642 and 1924 are listed in Sir Geoffrey Keynes's *A Bibliography of Sir Thomas Browne*, which appeared in the latter year. The following is a *select* list of editions in English published between 1643 and 1960 (London and 8° except where stated otherwise):

1. 1656. With notes attributed to Thomas Keck.
2. 1678. With a few altered readings possibly supplied by Browne.
3. 1686, F°. In *Works* (the first collected edition).
4. 1754 (Edinburgh). With notes, partly those of Keck abridged.
5. [1835.] In vol. ii of *Works*, ed. S. Wilkin, 1836.
6. 1838. Ed. J. A. St. John. With *H*.
7. 1844. Ed. J. Peace. With *CM*.
8. 1845. Ed. H. Gardiner. With *LF* and *CM*.
9. 1869. Ed. J. W. Willis Bund. With *H* and *LF*.
10. 1881, &c. Ed. W. A. Greenhill. With *LF* and *CM* and many valuable notes.
11. 1883. Facsimile of first edition, 1642, with introduction by W. A. Greenhill.
12. 1886. Ed. J. Addington Symonds. With *H*, *LF*, *CM*, and *On Dreams*.
13. [1904.] In vol. i of *Works*, ed. C. Sayle, 1904–7.
14. [1906.] In Everyman's Library. With *H*, *GC*, *LF*, *CM*, and '*Brampton Urns*', and with introduction by C. H. Herford. Reprinted 1956, with introduction by H. Sutherland.
15. 1909 (Oxford). In Tudor and Stuart Library. With Digby's *Observations*. Follows text of 1643 'page for page and line for line'.
16. 1922. (Cambridge). Ed. W. Murison. With many useful notes.
17. [1928.] In vol. i of *Works*, ed. G. Keynes, 1928–31.
18. 1953 (Cambridge). Ed. J-J. Denonain. Plain text with very full textual notes and with introduction mainly on the manuscripts and early editions.
19. 1958 (Università di Cagliari). Ed. Vittoria Sanna (2 vols.) With substantial and valuable introductions and notes, in Italian; text in English with Italian translation.

Comment on *RM* began at once with Digby's *Observations*, 1643, followed in 1645 by Alexander Ross's *Medicus Medicatus*. For other references during Browne's lifetime see Keynes, *Bibliography*, pp. 140–58. Notes to *RM* (in Latin) were added in 1652 to the Latin translation by John Merryweather first published in 1644. The Preface in 1652 is signed 'L. N. M. E. M. ', identified by Placcius, *Theatrum anon.*, 1708, 861a, p. 161, as 'Eques Generosissimus Levinus Nicolaus Moltkius'. The English annotations attributed to Thomas Keck and first published in the edition of 1656 resemble those of Moltke in being concerned with points of religious and moral doctrine. Of the notes contained in later editions the most valuable are those of Wilkin, Greenhill, Murison, and Professor Sanna,[1] to all of whom, and especially to Greenhill, the present editor is in various ways indebted. Much useful information has also been derived from *The Common Expositor, An Account of the Commentaries on Genesis 1527–1633*, by Arnold Williams (1948).

III. *HYDRIOTAPHIA* AND *THE GARDEN OF CYRUS*

(*HGC*; separately, *H* and *GC*)

These two works were registered together 9 March 1657/8 (Roxburghe Club, ii, p. 168). As they both probably took their origin in isolated notes it is impossible to date their composition. One sentence in *H* must have been written in 1656 (see note to p. 99, ll. 10–12). A number of sentences in both works are found in manuscript (see pp. 268–70), but there appears to be no way of dating these.

HGC was first published in 1658 by Henry Brome in a small octavo volume made up as follows:[2]

Title and sub-title. Reproduced pp. 81 and 127.

Collation. 8°: A–O^8. \$1–4. Some copies have an additional leaf of Errata. See under Contents.

Pages [*1–16*], 1–84, [*85–88*], 89–202.

Contents. A1^r title, A1^v blank, A2^r–A4^v To . . . Thomas Le Gros, A5^r–A7^r To . . . Nicholas Bacon, A7^v–A8^r blank, A8^v engraving of urns, B1^r–G2^v *Hydriotaphia*, G3^r blank, G3^v engraving

[1] Miss Sanna quotes a large number of parallels from the works of Bacon, Burton, and Donne, in support of her opinion that Browne was specially influenced by these writers. In view, however, of Browne's wide learning, and as Miss Sanna herself allows, there is often, in the absence of close verbal correspondence, the possibility that Browne and these other authors were independently drawing upon sources available to them all.

[2] Copies used: Bodleian Library; National Library of Scotland (3 copies); British Museum.

of quincunx, G4r–O5r *The Garden of Cyrus*, O6 The Stationer to the Reader, O7r List of books printed for H. Broome, O7v blank, O8r label Dr. Brown's Garden of Cyrus, O8v blank. Separate leaf of Errata in some copies (of 18 or of 24 lines), either after O6 or pasted to O7v or O8v; longer version reproduced p. 176.

Running-titles. *The Epistle* (on A2v, A3v) / *Dedicatory.* (on A3r, A4r) *The Epistle*, &c. (on A4v) The Epistle (on A5v A6v) / Dedicatory. (on A6r, A7r) *Hydriotaphia*, (on versos B1–G2) / *Urne-Buriall.* (on rectos B2–G2) *Cyrus Garden*, Or (on versos G5–O5) / *The Quincunx.* (on rectos G6–H4) *The Quincunx Artificially Considered* (on rectos H6–I4) *The Quincunx Naturally Considered.* (on rectos I6–L8) *The Quincunx Mistically Considered.* (on rectos M2–O5).

Notes (1) O6 (The Stationer to the Reader) denies the statement on the title-page of *Nature's Cabinet Unlock'd* (1657) that 'Tho. Brown D. of Physick' was the author of that work.

(2) The marginal note on p. 138, l. 5 was misplaced. Other misplacings are pointed out in the footnotes.

The book was reprinted once in the same year (4°) and once in the next (F°), each time as an appendage to Browne's much more substantial work, *Pseudodoxia Epidemica, or Enquiries into Very many Received Tenents, And commonly Presumed Truths* (*PE*). The third edition of *PE* (revised) had been published in 1658 by Nathaniel Ekins, formerly in partnership with Edward Dod, the second edition (1650) bearing the imprint of both. In response to Ekins's edition of *PE* in 1658 (the third), Dod produced the quarto edition, including *HGC* as an added attraction. Ekins then retaliated by issuing in 1659 the unsold sheets of his own 1658 edition of *PE* with *HGC* and *RM* as well. Yet again, ten years later, *PE* with *HGC* was 'Printed for the Assigns of Edward Dod'.

The errata found in some copies of *HGC*, 8° 1658, are most often of 18 lines, but occasionally of 24 (see a note by Mr. John Carter in *The Library*, 1947, pp. 192–3). All that is in the shorter list is also in the longer one, which is reprinted on p. 176[1] and referred to in the present footnotes as *Er.* Most of the errors in the octavo edition reappear in the text of the quarto, together with a new list of errata. Some of the items in this list correct errors peculiar to the quarto, others repeat what was already in the octavo list; others again refer to errors which were not corrected in the octavo list; and these last alone are given in the present footnotes, with designation *Er(2)*. There is also in most copies of the quarto a list of 'Marginall Illustrations omitted, or to be added to the Discourses of *Urn-*

[1] From a photostat kindly lent by Mr. Carter.

Burial, and of the *Garden of Cyrus*'. In the present edition these supplementary notes are not listed but inserted in their places with designation [*Add.*]

In text of *HGC* has greatly benefited in recent years from the researches of Mr. John Carter. These have proved that in a greater degree than was already known Browne corrected copies of the 1658 octavo edition in his own handwriting, some of the corrections repeating those in the printed errata and others independent of them. Most are found in two or more copies, a few only in one. In Mr. Carter's edition of *HGC* (1932 and 1958) particulars are given of the corrected copies and the number of corrections which each contains. In the present edition the alterations are adopted almost without exception and noted (with designation *C*), but without specifying in which copies they occur. They include two[1] which are not in Browne's hand but which, as Mr. Carter argues, have probably been derived from autograph corrections occurring in a copy or copies whose location is not now known.

In the present edition two or three readings of the 1658 octavo volume which editors have emended or questioned are retained, the most important instance being in ll. 12–14 of p. 123, where Browne's drift seems to have been widely misinterpreted.

The textual notes on *H* (pp. 268–9) cite for the first time MS. Sloane 1862 to show how some of Browne's best-known sentences were initially drafted, or at least how they stood at some time previous to their final shaping.

A passage in MS. Sloane 1848, 'Large are the treasures of oblivion', printed by Wilkin, Greenhill, and Keynes as additional to *H* is now shown to belong rather to *CM* and is therefore printed in the notes to that work (see p. 284).

The marginal notes accompanying the editions of 1658[2] are generally helpful, but many of them need correction or enlargement. Browne so frequently owns his indebtedness to his authorities that when he fails to do so it is fairer to charge him with forgetfulness or 'inactivity' than with any intent to deceive (see note to p. 126 in Commentary); it is true, however, that his annotation is often sketchy or altogether lacking where it is greatly needed, and obscure allusions have to be traced before his meaning can be fully grasped. This applies especially to *GC*, which has hitherto

[1] See footnotes to p. 105, ll. 5 and 28.

[2] In the octavo edition these notes are usually attached to the relevant word or words either by raised letters or by asterisks, though in a few places neither letters nor asterisks are inserted. In the present edition raised numerals alone are used and the deficiencies are made up.

received much less elucidation than it calls for and now receives about as much as any other of the five works included in this volume.

The following is a select list of editions subsequent to those mentioned above. (Nos. 3, 5, 6, 7, 8, and 12 have *H* without *GC*). London and 8° except where stated otherwise.

1. 1686, F°. In *Works* (the first collected editions).
2. 1736. Printed for E. Curll. Omits chapters iv and v of *GC*.
3. 1822, 16°. In *Tracts*, ed. W. Crossley. With *LF* and *Musaeum Clausum*.
4. [1835.] In vol. iii of *Works*, ed. S. Wilkin, 1836.
5. 1838. Ed. J. A. St. John. With *RM*.
6. 1869. Ed. J. W. Willis Bund. With *RM* and *LF*.
7. 1886. Ed. J. Addington Symonds. With *RM*, *LF*, *CM*, and *On Dreams*.
8. 1893. Ed. Sir John Evans.
9. 1896. Ed. W. A. Greenhill. With many valuable notes.
10. [1906.] In Everyman's Library. With *RM*, *LF*, *CM*, and '*Brampton Urns*', and with introduction by C. H. Herford. Reprinted 1956, with introduction by H. Sutherland.
11. [1907.] In vol. iii of *Works*, ed. C. Sayle, 1904–7.
12. 1922. (Cambridge). Ed. W. Murison. With many valuable notes.
13. 1927. In Noel Douglas Replicas.
14. [1929.] In vol. ii of *Works*, ed. G. Keynes, 1928–31.
15. 1932, F°. Ed. J. Carter.
16. 1958 (Cambridge). Ed. J. Carter.

IV. *A LETTER TO A FRIEND* (*LF*)

This was published in 1690, eight years after Sir Thomas Browne's death, in the following form:[1]

Title. Reproduced p. 177.

Collation. F°: A–C^{2}. \$1.

Pages. 3–12.

Contents. A1^{r} title, A1^{v} blank, A2^{r}–C2^{v} text.

No running titles.

Note. The marginal note on p. 184, l. 22, was apparently misplaced.

According to an entry in the *Term Catalogues* (Arber, ii, 306) *LF* was to have been incorporated in a reprint of Browne's *Works* as

[1] Copies used: Bodleian Library; National Library of Scotland; British Museum.

published in 1686: 'Hilary Term Reprinted. The Works of the Learned Sir T. B. Knight. To which is added, A Letter to a Friend, never before published. Folio.' No such reprint is extant. One copy of *Works*, 1686 (British Museum, C. 118, g. 1), has *LF*, 1690, bound up with it.

In any attempt to date the composition of this work allowance has to be made, as usual, for the author's habit of accumulating notes which could afterwards be worked into a more coherent plan. But as *LF* refers to a particular occasion and is addressed to a particular person it seems likely that most of it was written about the same time. No obvious clue is given in *LF* itself to the identity of the addressee, or to that of his friend, who died of phthisis, and until recently the question was left unanswered. In 1951, however, Mr. F. L. Huntley in *Modern Philology*, xviii, 1950, pp. 157–71, argued cogently that the addressee was Sir John Pettus of Rockheath, near Norwich, and of Chediston Hall, East Suffolk; and that the other was Robert Loveday (1621–56), translator of La Calprenède's *Cléopâtre*, and author of *Loveday's Letters*, 1659, &c. Loveday belonged to Chediston and was well known to Pettus. (For both Pettus and Loveday, see *DNB.*) Sir Thomas Browne's acquaintance with Sir John and Lady Pettus is proved by several allusions to them in Browne's correspondence (*K*, vi). In some of *Loveday's Letters* the author, who is away from home and evidently suffering from phthisis, writes to his brother about his symptoms and mentions a 'Dr. B.' who has treated him unsuccessfully. This may be the 'Dr. Butler' referred to on p. 211 (ed. of 1659). Afterwards Loveday asks his brother to get advice from another 'Dr. B.', of Norwich, who can hardly have been anyone but Sir Thomas. From *LF* it appears that Browne attended his patient (presumably in Suffolk) during the last stages of the disease and that the patient was about 33 at his death. (See p. 189, l. 15 and note to *RM*, p. 40, ll. 7–8.) Loveday died at 35 in 1656. Pettus was probably away at that time, having been made deputy-governor of mines in 1655.

If these identifications are correct Browne must have begun to write *LF*, or at least the paragraphs relating to Loveday's death, much earlier than has commonly been supposed. Hitherto the date 1673 or thereabouts has been accepted because Browne alludes to a book published in 1654 as having appeared 'scarce twenty Years' (p. 184, l. 37) before; but this could easily have been a later interpolation. Support for the arguments which would make the first drafting of *LF* roughly contemporaneous with *Hydriotaphia* can be found in the fact that both works mention the same passage in Dante's *Purgatorio*, xxiii. 31–33 (see pp. 111, ll. 3–4 and 183, ll. 10–11).

The latter part of *LF* (p. 191, l. 5 to the end) consists of gnomic paragraphs (addressed to the recipient) which also occur in the much longer *Christian Morals*, mostly in a different order and with some differences of wording. It is arguable,[1] from considerations of style, that of the two versions of these paragraphs the one in *LF* was written first. In one place (p. 204, l. 9) *Christian Morals* refers to the 'sisters of Darius', who appear rightly in *LF* as the *daughters*; but the correction could have been made when *LF* was being prepared for publication, and the need for it could have been overlooked by the editor of *Christian Morals*.

The manuscript version of *LF* contained in MS. Sloane 1862, a shorter and evidently an earlier version than the printed one, has a few closing sentences in common with both *LF* and *CM*; and the fact that where there are differences between these two the manuscript more often agrees with *LF* than with *CM* favours the conclusion that *LF* preceded *CM*. The manuscript is printed in full in Appendix I (pp. 249–57).

The marginal notes in *1690* are not tied to particular words, either by raised letters or by asterisks. In the present edition the connexions are made and raised numerals are employed.

SELECT LIST OF EDITIONS SINCE 1690

1. 1712. In *Posthumous Works*.
2. 1822, 16°. In *Tracts*, ed. W. Crossley, With *H* and *Musaeum Clausum*.
3. [1835.] In vol. iv of *Works*, ed. S. Wilkin, 1836.
4. 1845. Ed. H. Gardiner. With *RM* and *CM*.
5. 1869. Ed. J. W. Willis Bund, With *RM* and *H*.
6. 1881. Ed. W. A. Greenhill. With *RM* and *CM* and with many valuable notes.
7. 1886. Ed. J. Addington Symonds. With *H*, *CM*, and *On Dreams*.
8. [1904.] In vol. iii of *Works*, ed. C. Sayle, 1904–7.
9. [1906.] In Everyman's Library. With *H*, *GC*, *CM*, and '*Brampton Urns*', and with introduction by C. H. Herford. Reprinted 1956, with introduction by H. Sutherland.
10. 1924, F°. Facsimile of *1690*. Haslewood Press.
11. [1928.] In vol. i of *Works*, ed. G. Keynes, 1928–31.

V. *CHRISTIAN MORALS* (*CM*)

This was first published in 1716, thirty-four years after Sir Thomas Browne's death. As stated by the editor, John Jeffery,

[1] See Mrs. J. Bennett, *Sir Thomas Browne*, 1962, pp. 230–40.

Archdeacon of Norwich, the original manuscript had been mislaid but was discovered among the papers of Dr. Tenison, Archbishop of Canterbury, to whom it had been lent. The manuscript has not been preserved, but Jeffery vouched for the fidelity with which it was copied for the press.

In her dedication of *CM* to the Earl of Buchan, Browne's daughter, Elizabeth Lyttelton, speaks of it as 'the Last Work of our Honoured and Learned Father'. Its connexion with *LF* has already been mentioned, together with the fact that one of the sentences common to both works was written about 1672; but the date when *CM* took on its final shape must remain uncertain. It was well printed in 1716 and presents hardly any textual difficulties. The first edition is made up as follows:[1]

Title. Reproduced p. 199.

Collation. 12°: π^6 A–E^{12} F^6. $AC 1–6, BD 1–5, E 1–6 (6 misprinted 5).

Pages 1–127.

Contents. π1 blank, $\pi 2^r$ half-title, $\pi 2^v$ blank, $\pi 3^r$ title, $\pi 3^v$ blank, $\pi 4^r$–$\pi 5^r$ Dedication, $\pi 5^v$–$\pi 6^v$ Preface, $A1^r$–$F4^r$ text, $F4^v$–$F5^v$ Publisher's list, F6 blank.

Running titles. $\pi 4^v$ $\pi 5^v$ *DEDICATION*. $\pi 6^r$ and ^{v} The PREFACE. No other running titles.

The Sloane manuscripts in the British Museum and Bodleian MS. Rawlinson D. 109 contain many sentences and paragraphs which, after revision, were printed in *CM*; and they also contain other sentences which, though connected in the manuscripts with passages in *CM*, are not found therein. A selection of the manuscript readings is given in the textual notes, where the discarded sentences printed by Wilkin and later editors are supplemented by others not printed before (marked *). Further, the same editors have printed certain passages in the manuscripts which although not appearing in conjunction with any parts of *CM* can be considered relevant to it; and these are included in the notes with the comment, however, that their connexion with *CM* has not been

[1] Copies used: Bodleian Library, National Library of Scotland, British Museum, Glasgow University Library. Facing the titlepage in the last mentioned copy there is an engraving of the mural memorial-stone in St. Peter Mancroft with inscription below as follows:

To the Reverend Arch-Deacon Nephew to my	Coat of Arms	Edw. Tenison LL.B. of Carmarthen Lady BROWNE

This Plate is most humbly inscrib'd.

established.[1] On the other hand there are two passages printed by Wilkin and Keynes as belonging to Browne's commonplace-books which in one manuscript or another appear in juxtaposition with parts of *CM* and for this reason these also are included in the present notes.

SELECT LIST OF EDITIONS SINCE 1716

1. 1756. Printed for J. Payne. With a life by Samuel Johnson; and explanatory notes.
2. [1835.] In vol. iv of *Works*, ed. S. Wilkin, 1836.
3. 1844. Ed. J. Peace. With *RM*.
4. 1845. Ed. J. A. St. John. With *RM* and *H*.
5. 1881. Ed. W. A. Greenhill. With *RM* and *LF*, and with many valuable notes.
6. 1886. Ed. J. Addington Symonds. With *H*, *LF*, and *On Dreams*.
7. [1904.] In vol. iii of *Works*, ed. C. Sayle.
8. [1906.] In Everyman's Library. See list on p. xvii.
9. 1927 (Cambridge). Ed. S. C. Roberts.
10. [1928.] In vol. i of *Works*, ed. G. Keynes, 1928–31.

VI. LIST OF ABBREVIATIONS

1. *Religio Medici* (*RM*).

   42 = the two editions of 1642, one of 190 and the other of 159 pages; distinguished as *42a* and *42b* respectively.
   43 = the edition of 1643.
   Er = Errata in the same.
   MSS. = all the manuscripts. For a list of these with abbreviations attached see p. xii.

2. *Pseudodoxia Epidemica* (*PE*).

3. *Hydriotaphia with The Garden of Cyrus* (*HGC*; separately *H* and *GC*).

   58 = the octavo edition of 1658.
   Er = Errata in the same.
   58(4°) = the quarto edition of 1658.
   Er (2) = Errata in the same.
   [*Add.*] = additional marginal notes in the same (see p. xx).

[1] The passages cited by Wilkin are not always to be found in the manuscript volumes to which he assigns them.

4. *A Letter to a Friend* (*LF*).
   90 = the edition of 1690.

5. *Christian Morals* (*CM*).
   16 = the edition of 1716.

6. *Manuscripts other than those of RM.*
   S43 = MS. Sloane 1843.
   S47 = MS. Sloane 1847.
   S48 = MS. Sloane 1848.
   S62 = MS. Sloane 1862.
   S66 = MS. Sloane 1866.
   S69 = MS. Sloane 1869.
   S82 = MS. Sloane 1882.
   S85 = MS. Sloane 1885.
   R = MS. Rawlinson D. 109.

7. *Later editions.*
   Gr = W. A. Greenhill in his editions of (*a*) *RM* with *LF* and *CM* (1881, &c.), and (*b*) *HGC* (1896, &c.; completed by E. H. Marshall).
   K = *The works of Sir Thomas Browne*, ed. Geoffrey Keynes (1928–31); the separate volumes, i–vi, referred to as *K*, i, &c.

8. *Miscellaneous.*
   HN = *Historia naturalis* (Pliny).
   Burton = *The Anatomy of Melancholy* (edition of 1638).
   G = Gerard's *Herbal*.
   SC = Sale-catalogue (1711) of books formerly owned by Sir Thomas Browne and his son.
   CE = *The Common Expositor*, by A. Williams (1948).

VII. NOTE ON THE PORTRAIT OF THOMAS AND DOROTHY BROWNE

(*Frontispiece*)

The various portraits of Sir Thomas Browne known before 1923 were listed and described by Miriam L. Tildesley in her monograph *Sir Thomas Browne: his skull, portraits, and ancestry*, published in that year (reprinted from *Biometrika*, 15). The small portrait of Thomas and Dorothy Browne did not come to Miss Tildesley's notice until her monograph had been printed off, but is reproduced and described in additional leaves attached thereto. It was in private hands before 1924, when it was acquired by the National Portrait Gallery. It is attributed to Jane Carlile and seems to have been painted at the time when Thomas and Dorothy Browne were married, or soon after. As an authentic likeness of Browne it stands very high among the extant portraits and Miss Tildesley gives good reasons for supposing it to be the most reliable of them all. It is reproduced by kind permission of the Trustees of the National Portrait Gallery.

TO THE READER.

CERTAINLY that man were greedy of life, who should desire to live when all the world were at an end; and he must needs be very impatient, who would repine at death in the societie of all things that suffer under it. Had not almost every man suffered by the presse; or were not the tyranny thereof become universall; I had not wanted reason for complaint: but in times wherein I have lived to behold the highest perversion of that excellent invention; the name of his Majesty defamed, the honour of Parliament depraved, the writings of both depravedly, anticipatively, counterfeitly imprinted; complaints may seeme ridiculous in private persons, and men of 10 *my condition may be as incapable of affronts, as hopelesse of their reparations. And truly had not the duty I owe unto the importunitie of friends, and the allegeance I must ever acknowledge unto truth prevayled with me; the inactivitie of my disposition might have made these sufferings continuall, and time that brings other things to light, should have satisfied me in the remedy of its oblivion. But because things evidently false are not onely printed, but many things of truth most falsly set forth; in this latter I could not but thinke my selfe engaged: for though we have no power to redresse the former, yet in the other the reparation being within our selves, I have at present represented unto the world a full and intended copy of* 20 *that Peece which was most imperfectly and surreptitiously published before.*

This I confesse about seven yeares past, with some others of affinitie thereto, for my private exercise and satisfaction, I had at leisurable houres composed; which being communicated unto one, it became common unto many, and was by transcription successively corrupted untill it arrived in a most depraved copy at the presse. He that shall peruse that worke, and shall take notice of sundry particularities and personall expressions therein, will easily discerne the intention was not publik: and being a private exercise directed to my selfe, what is delivered therein was rather a memoriall unto me then an example or rule unto any other: and therefore if there bee any 30 *singularitie therein correspondent unto the private conceptions of any man, it doth not advantage them; or if dissentaneous thereunto, it no way overthrowes them. It was penned in such a place and with such disadvantage, that (I protest) from the first setting of pen unto paper, I had not the assistance of any good booke, whereby to promote my invention or relieve my memory; and therefore there might be many reall lapses therein, which others might take notice of, and more that I suspected my selfe. It was set downe many yeares past, and was the sense of my conceptions at that time, not an immutable law unto my advancing judgement at all times, and therefore there might be many things therein plausible unto my passed* 40 *apprehension, which are not agreeable unto my present selfe. There are many things delivered Rhetorically, many expressions therein meerely Tropicall, and as they best illustrate my intention; and therefore also there are many things to be taken in a soft and flexible sense, and not to be called unto the rigid test of reason. Lastly all that is contained therein is in submission unto maturer discernments, and as I have declared shall no further father them then the best and learned judgements shall authorize them; under favour of which considerations I have made its secrecie publike and committed the truth thereof to every ingenuous Reader.*

10 THOMAS BROWNE.

RELIGIO MEDICI

SECT. I.

FOR my Religion, though there be severall circumstances that might perswade the world I have none at all, as the generall scandall of my profession, the naturall course of my studies, the indifferency of my behaviour, and discourse in matters of Religion, neither violently defending one, nor with that common ardour and contention opposing another; yet in despight hereof I dare, without usurpation, assume the honorable stile of a Christian: not that I meerely owe this title to the Font, my education, or Clime where- 10 in I was borne, as being bred up either to confirme those principles my Parents instilled into my unwary understanding; or by a generall consent proceed in the Religion of my Countrey: But having, in my riper yeares, and confirmed judgement, seene and examined all, I finde my selfe obliged by the principles of Grace, and the law of mine owne reason, to embrace no other name but this; neither doth herein my zeale so farre make me forget the generall charitie I owe unto humanity, as rather to hate then pity Turkes, Infidels, and (what is worse) Jewes, rather contenting my selfe to enjoy that happy stile, then maligning those who refuse so 20 glorious a title.

SECT. 2.

But because the name of a Christian is become too generall to expresse our faith, there being a Geography of Religions as well as Lands, and every Clime distinguished not onely by their lawes and limits, but circumscribed by their doctrines and rules of Faith; To be particular, I am of that reformed new-cast Religion, wherein I dislike nothing but the name, of the same beliefe our Saviour taught, the Apostles disseminated, the Fathers authorised, and the Martyrs confirmed; but by the sinister ends of Princes, the 30 ambition & avarice of Prelates, and the fatall corruption of times, so decaied, impaired, and fallen from its native beauty, that it required the carefull and charitable hand of these times to restore it to its primitive integrity: Now the accidentall occasion whereon, the slender meanes whereby, the low and abject condition of the person by whom so good a worke was set on foot, which in our adversaries begets contempt and scorn, fills me with wonder, and

37 begets *MSS.*: beget *42 43*

is the very same objection the insolent Pagans first cast at Christ and his Disciples.

SECT. 3.

Yet have I not so shaken hands with those desperate Resolutions, who had rather venture at large their decaied bottome, then bring her in to be new trim'd in the dock; who had rather promiscuously retaine all, then abridge any, and obstinately be what they are, then what they have beene, as to stand in diameter and swords point with them: we have reformed from them, not against them;
10 for omitting those improperations and termes of scurrility betwixt us, which onely difference our affections, and not our cause, there is between us one common name and appellation, one faith, and necessary body of principles common to us both; and therefore I am not scrupulous to converse and live with them, to enter their Churches in defect of ours, and either pray with them, or for them: I could never perceive any rationall consequence from those many texts which prohibite the children of Israel to pollute themselves with the Temples of the Heathens; we being all Christians, and not divided by such detested impieties as might prophane our
20 prayers, or the place wherein we make them; or that a resolved conscience may not adore her Creator any where, especially in places devoted to his service; where if their devotions offend him, mine may please him, if theirs prophane it, mine may hallow it; Holy water and Crucifix (dangerous to the common people) deceive not my judgement, nor abuse my devotion at all: I am, I confesse, naturally inclined to that, which misguided zeale termes superstition; my common conversation I do acknowledge austere, my behaviour full of rigour, sometimes not without morosity; yet at my devotion I love to use the civility of my knee, my hat, and
30 hand, with all those outward and sensible motions, which may expresse, or promote my invisible devotion. I should violate my owne arme rather then a Church window, nor willingly deface the memory of Saint or Martyr. At the sight of a Crosse or Crucifix I can dispence with my hat, but scarce with the thought or memory of my Saviour; I cannot laugh at but rather pity the fruitlesse journeys of Pilgrims, or contemne the miserable condition of Friers; for though misplaced in circumstance, there is something in it of devotion: I could never heare the **Ave Marie* Bell without an

* A Church Bell that tolls every day at 6. and 12. of the Clocke, at the hearing wherof every one in what place soever either of house or street betakes him to his prayer, which is commonly directed to the *Virgin*.

32 Church window *MSS.* / *42*: Church *43*

elevation, or thinke it a sufficient warrant, because they erred in one circumstance, for me to erre in all, that is in silence and dumbe contempt; whilst therefore they directed their devotions to her, I offered mine to God, and rectified the errours of their prayers by rightly ordering mine owne; At a solemne Procession I have wept abundantly, while my consorts, blinde with opposition and prejudice, have fallen into an accesse of scorne and laughter: There are questionlesse both in Greek, Roman, and African Churches, solemnities, and ceremonies, whereof the wiser zeales doe make a Christian use, and stand condemned by us; not as evill in themselves, but as allurements and baits of superstition to those vulgar heads that looke asquint on the face of truth, and those unstable judgements that cannot consist in the narrow point and centre of vertue without a reele or stagger to the circumference. 10

SECT. 4.

As there were many Reformers, so likewise many reformations; every Countrey proceeding in a particular way and Method, according as their nationall interest together with their constitution and clime inclined them, some angrily and with extremitie, others calmely, and with mediocrity, not rending, but easily dividing the community, and leaving an honest possibility of a reconciliation, which though peaceable Spirits doe desire, and may conceive that revolution of time, and the mercies of God may effect; yet that judgement that shall consider the present antipathies between the two extreames, their contrarieties in condition, affection and opinion, may with the same hopes expect an union in the poles of Heaven. 20

SECT. 5.

But to difference my self neerer, & draw into a lesser circle: There is no Church whose every part so squares unto my conscience, whose articles, constitutions, and customes seeme so consonant unto reason, and as it were framed to my particular devotion, as this whereof I hold my beliefe, the Church of *England*, to whose faith I am a sworne subject, and therefore in a double obligation, subscribe unto her Articles, and endeavour to observe her Constitutions: whatsoever is beyond, as points indifferent, I observe according to the rules of my private reason, or the humor and fashion of my devotion, neither believing this, because *Luther* affirmed it, or disproving that, because *Calvin* hath disavouched it. I condemne not all things in the Councell of *Trent*, nor approve all in the Synod of *Dort*. In briefe, where the Scripture is silent, the 30 40

Church is my Text; where that speakes, 'tis but my Comment; where there is a joynt silence of both, I borrow not the rules of my Religion from *Rome* or *Geneva*, but the dictates of my owne reason. It is an unjust scandall of our adversaries, and a grosse error in our selves, to compute the Nativity of our Religion from *Henry* the eight, who though he rejected the Pope, refus'd not the faith of *Rome*, and effected no more then what his owne Predecessors desired and assayed in ages past, and was conceived the State of *Venice* would have attempted in our dayes. It is as uncharitable a point in
10 us to fall upon those popular scurrilities and opprobrious scoffes of the Bishop of *Rome*, to whom as a temporall Prince, we owe the duty of good language: I confesse there is cause of passion betweene us; by his sentence I stand excommunicated, Heretick is the best language he affords me; yet can no eare witnesse I ever returned to him the name of Antichrist, Man of sin, or whore of *Babylon*; It is the method of charity to suffer without reaction: those usuall Satyrs, and invectives of the Pulpit may perchance produce a good effect on the vulgar, whose eares are opener to Rhetorick then Logick, yet doe they in no wise confirme the faith of wiser beleevers,
20 who know that a good cause needs not to be patron'd by a passion, but can sustaine it selfe upon a temperate dispute.

SECT. 6.

I could never divide my selfe from any man upon the difference of an opinion, or be angry with his judgement for not agreeing with mee in that, from which perhaps within a few dayes I should dissent my selfe: I have no Genius to disputes in Religion, and have often thought it wisedome to decline them, especially upon a disadvantage, or when the cause of truth might suffer in the weakenesse of my patronage: where wee desire to be informed, 'tis
30 good to contest with men above our selves; but to confirme and establish our opinions, 'tis best to argue with judgements below our own, that the frequent spoyles and victories over their reasons may settle in our selves an esteeme, and confirmed opinion of our owne. Every man is not a proper Champion for Truth, nor fit to take up the Gantlet in the cause of Veritie: Many from the ignorance of these Maximes, and an inconsiderate zeale unto Truth, have too rashly charged the troopes of error, and remaine as Trophees unto the enemies of Truth: A man may be in as just possession of Truth as of a City, and yet bee forced to surrender;
40 tis therefore farre better to enjoy her with peace, then to hazzard her on a battell: If therefore there rise any doubts in my way, I doe

11 to whom *MSS.* / *42*: whom *43*

forget them, or at least defer them, till my better setled judgement, and more manly reason be able to resolve them; for I perceive every mans owne reason is his best *Oedipus*, and will upon a reasonable truce, find a way to loose those bonds wherewith the subtilties of errour have enchained our more flexible and tender judgements. In Philosophy where truth seemes double-faced, there is no man more paradoxicall then my self; but in Divinity I love to keepe the road, and though not in an implicite, yet an humble faith, follow the great wheele of the Church, by which I move, not reserving any proper poles or motion from the epicycle of my 10 own braine; by this meanes I leave no gap for Heresies, Schismes, or Errors, of which at present, I hope I shall not injure Truth, to say, I have no taint or tincture; I must confesse my greener studies have beene polluted with two or three, not any begotten in the latter Centuries, but old and obsolete, such as could never have been revived, but by such extravagant and irregular heads as mine; for indeed Heresies perish not with their Authors, but like the River *Arethusa*, though they lose their currents in one place, they rise up againe in another: one generall Councell is not able to extirpate one single Heresie, it may be canceld for the present, but 20 revolution of time and the like aspects from Heaven, will restore it, when it will flourish till it be condemned againe; for as though there were a *Metempsuchosis*, and the soule of one man passed into another, opinions doe finde after certaine revolutions, men and mindes like those that first begat them. To see our selves againe wee neede not looke for *Platoes** yeare; every man is not onely himselfe; there have beene many *Diogenes*, and as many *Timons*, though but few of that name; men are lived over againe, the world is now as it was in ages past, there was none then, but there hath been some one since that parallels him, and is as it were his revived selfe. 30

SECT. 7.

Now the first of mine was that of the Arabians, that the soules of men perished with their bodies, but should yet bee raised againe at the last day; not that I did absolutely conceive a mortality of the soule, but if that were, which faith, not Philosophy hath yet throughly disproved, and that both entred the grave together, yet I held the same conceit thereof that wee all doe of the body, that it should rise againe. Surely it is but the merits of our unworthy

* A revolution of certaine thousand yeares when all things should returne unto their former estate and he be teaching againe in his schoole as when he delivered this opinion.

38 should rise *ErPL*: rise *43*: shall rise *42 and MSS. except PL*

natures, if wee sleepe in darkenesse, untill the last alarum: A serious reflex upon my owne unworthinesse did make me backward from challenging this prerogative of my soule; so I might enjoy my Saviour at the last, I could with patience be nothing almost unto eternity. The second was that of *Origen*, that God would not persist in his vengeance for ever, but after a definite time of his wrath hee would release the damned soules from torture; Which error I fell into upon a serious contemplation of the great attribute of God his mercy, and did a little cherish it in my selfe, 10 because I found therein no malice, and a ready weight to sway me from the other extream of despaire, wherunto melancholy and contemplative natures are too easily disposed. A third there is which I did never positively maintaine or practice, but have often wished it had been consonant to Truth, and not offensive to my Religion, and that is the prayer for the dead; whereunto I was inclined from some charitable inducements, whereby I could scarce containe my prayers for a friend at the ringing of a Bell, or behold his corpes without an oraison for his soule: 'Twas a good way me thought to be remembred by Posterity, and farre more noble then 20 an History. These opinions I never maintained with pertinacity, or endeavoured to enveagle any mans beliefe unto mine, nor so much as ever revealed or disputed them with my dearest friends; by which meanes I neither propagated them in others, nor confirmed them in my selfe, but suffering them to flame upon their owne substance, without addition of new fuell, they went out insensibly of themselves; therefore these opinions, though condemned by lawfull Councels, were not Heresies in me, but bare Errors, and single Lapses of my understanding, without a joynt depravity of my will: Those have not only depraved understand- 30 ings but diseased affections, which cannot enjoy a singularity without a Heresie, or be the author of an opinion, without they be of a Sect also; this was the villany of the first Schisme of *Lucifer*, who was not content to erre alone, but drew into his faction many Legions of Spirits; and upon this experience hee tempted only *Eve*, as well understanding the communicable nature of sin, and that to deceive but one, was tacitely and upon consequence to delude them both.

SECT. 8.

That Heresies should arise we have the prophecy of Christ, but 40 that old ones should be abolished wee hold no prediction. That there must be heresies, is true, not onely in our Church, but also

39 the] the the *43*

in any other: even in Doctrines hereticall there will be superheresies, and Arians not onely divided from their Church, but also among themselves: for heads that are disposed unto Schisme and complexionally propense to innovation, are naturally indisposed for a community, nor will ever be confined unto the order or œconomy of one body; and therefore when they separate from others they knit but loosely among themselves; nor contented with a generall breach or dichotomie with their Church, do subdivide and mince themselves almost into Atomes. 'Tis true, that men of singular parts and humors have not beene free from 10 singular opinions and conceits in all ages; retaining something not onely beside the opinion of his own Church or any other, but also any particular Author: which notwithstanding a sober judgement may doe without offence or heresie; for there is yet after all the decrees of counsells and the niceties of the Schooles, many things untouch'd, unimagin'd, wherein the libertie of an honest reason may play and expatiate with security and farre without the circle of an heresie.

SECT. 9.

As for those wingy mysteries in Divinity, and ayery subtilties in 20 Religion, which have unhindg'd the braines of better heads, they never stretched the *Pia Mater* of mine; me thinkes there be not impossibilities enough in Religion for an active faith; the deepest mysteries ours containes, have not only been illustrated, but maintained by syllogisme, and the rule of reason: I love to lose my selfe in a mystery to pursue my reason to an *oh altitudo*. 'Tis my solitary recreation to pose my apprehension with those involved ænigma's and riddles of the Trinity, with Incarnation and Resurrection. I can answer all the objections of Satan, and my rebellious reason, with that odde resolution I learned of *Tertullian*, *Certum est quia impossibile est*. I desire to exercise my faith in the difficultest points, for 30 to credit ordinary and visible objects is not faith, but perswasion. Some beleeve the better for seeing Christ his Sepulchre, and when they have seene the Red Sea, doubt not of the miracle. Now contrarily I blesse my selfe, and am thankefull that I lived not in the dayes of miracles, that I never saw Christ nor his Disciples; I would not have beene one of those Israelites that passed the Red Sea, nor one of Christs Patients, on whom he wrought his wonders; then had my faith beene thrust upon me, nor should I enjoy that greater blessing pronounced to all that believe & saw 40 not. 'Tis an easie and necessary beliefe to credit what our eye and

4 indisposed *Er*: disposed *43* 31 points *MSS.*: point *42 43*

sense hath examined: I believe he was dead, and buried, and rose againe; and desire to see him in his glory, rather then to contemplate him in his Cenotaphe, or Sepulchre. Nor is this much to beleeve, as we have reason, we owe this faith unto History: they only had the advantage of a bold and noble faith, who lived before his comming, who upon obscure prophesies and mysticall Types could raise a beliefe, and expect apparent impossibilities.

SECT. 10.

'Tis true, there is an edge in all firme beliefe, and with an easie
10 Metaphor wee may say the sword of faith; but in these obscurities I rather use it, in the adjunct the Apostle gives it, a Buckler; under which I perceive a wary combatant may lie invulnerable. Since I was of understanding to know we knew nothing, my reason hath beene more pliable to the will of faith; I am now content to understand a mystery without a rigid definition in an easie and Platonick description. That allegoricall description of *Hermes*,* pleaseth mee beyond all the Metaphysicall definitions of Divines; where I cannot satisfie my reason, I love to humour my fancy; I had as leive you tell me that *anima est angelus hominis, est Corpus Dei*, as *Entelechia*; *Lux*
20 *est umbra Dei*, as *actus perspicui:* where there is an obscurity too deepe for our reason, 'tis good to set downe with a description, periphrasis, or adumbration; for by acquainting our reason how unable it is to display the visible and obvious effects of nature, it becomes more humble and submissive unto the subtilties of faith: and thus I teach my haggard and unreclaimed reason to stoope unto the lure of faith. I believe there was already a tree whose fruit our unhappy parents tasted, though in the same Chapter, where God forbids it, 'tis positively said, the plants of the field were not yet growne; for God had not caused it to raine upon the earth.
30 I beleeve that the Serpent (if we shall literally understand it) from his proper forme and figure, made his motion on his belly before the curse. I find the triall of the Pucellage and Virginity of women, which God ordained the Jewes, is very fallible. Experience, and History informes me, that not onely many particular women, but likewise whole Nations have escaped the curse of childbirth, which God seemes to pronounce upon the whole Sex; yet doe I beleeve that all this is true, which indeed my reason would perswade me to be false; and this I think is no vulgar part of faith to

* *Sphæra, cujus centrum ubique, circumferentia nullibi.*

23 effects *MSS.*: effect *42 43* 27 where *MSS.*: when *42 43*

believe a thing not only above, but contrary to reason, and against the arguments of our proper senses.

SECT. 11.

In my solitary and retired imagination, (*Neque enim cum porticus aut me lectulus accepit, desum mihi*) I remember I am not alone, and therefore forget not to contemplate him and his attributes who is ever with mee, especially those two mighty ones, his wisedome and eternitie; with the one I recreate, with the other I confound my understanding: for who can speake of eternitie without a solœcisme, or thinke thereof without an extasie? Time we may comprehend, 10 'tis but five dayes elder then our selves, and hath the same Horoscope with the world; but to retire so farre backe as to apprehend a beginning, to give such an infinite start forward, as to conceive an end in an essence that wee affirme hath neither the one nor the other; it puts my reason to Saint *Pauls* Sanctuary; my Philosophy dares not say the Angells can doe it; God hath not made a creature that can comprehend him, 'tis the priviledge of his owne nature; *I am that I am*, was his owne definition unto *Moses*; and 'twas a short one, to confound mortalitie, that durst question God, or aske him what hee was; indeed he only is, all others have and shall be, 20 but in eternity there is no distinction of Tenses; and therefore that terrible terme *Predestination*, which hath troubled so many weake heads to conceive, and the wisest to explaine, is in respect to God no prescious determination of our estates to come, but a definitive blast of his will already fulfilled, and at the instant that he first decreed it; for to his eternitie which is indivisible, and altogether, the last Trumpe is already sounded, the reprobates in the flame, and the blessed in *Abrahams* bosome. Saint *Peter* speakes modestly, when hee saith, a thousand yeares to God are but as one day: for to speake like a Philosopher, those continued instances of time 30 which flow into thousand yeares, make not to him one moment; what to us is to come, to his Eternitie is present, his whole duration being but one permanent point without succession, parts, flux, or division.

SECT. 12.

There is no Attribute that adds more difficulty to the mystery of the Trinity, where though in a relative way of Father and Son, we must deny a priority. I wonder how *Aristotle* could conceive the world eternall, or how hee could make good two Eternities: his similitude of a Triangle, comprehended in a square, doth some- 40 what illustrate the Trinitie of our soules, and that the Triple Unity of God; for there is in us not three, but a Trinity of soules, because there is in us, if not three distinct soules, yet differing faculties, that can, and doe subsist apart in different subjects, and yet in us are so united as to make but one soule and substance; if one soule were so perfect as to informe three distinct bodies, that were a petty Trinity: conceive the distinct number of three, not divided nor separated by the intellect, but actually comprehended in its Unity, and that is a perfect Trinity. I have often admired the mysticall way of *Pythagoras*, and the secret Magicke of numbers; Beware of Philosophy, is a precept not to be received in too large a sense; for in this masse of nature there is a set of things that carry in their front, though not in capitall letters, yet in stenography, and short Characters, something of Divinitie, which to wiser reasons serve as Luminaries in the abysse of knowledge, and to judicious beliefes, as scales and roundles to mount the pinnacles and highest pieces of Divinity. The severe Schooles shall never laugh me out of the Philosophy of *Hermes*, that this visible world is but a picture of the invisible, wherein as in a pourtract, things are not truely, but in equivocall shapes; and as they counterfeit some more reall substance in that invisible fabrick.

SECT. 13.

That other attribute wherewith I recreate my devotion, is his wisedome, in which I am happy; and for the contemplation of this onely, do not repent me that I was bred in the way of study: The advantage I have of the vulgar, with the content and happinesse I conceive therein, is an ample recompence for all my endeavours, in what part of knowledg soever. Wisedome is his most beauteous attribute, no man can attaine unto it, yet *Solomon* pleased God when hee desired it. Hee is wise because hee knowes all things, and hee knoweth all things because he made them all, but his greatest knowledg is in comprehending that he made not, that is himselfe. And this is also the greatest knowledge in man. For this do I honour my own profession and embrace the counsell even of the Devill himselfe: had he read such a Lecture in Paradise as hee did at * *Delphos*, we had better knowne our selves, nor had we stood in feare to know him. I know he is wise in all, wonderfull in what we conceive, but far more in what we comprehend not, for we behold him but asquint upon reflex or shadow; our understanding is dimmer than *Moses* eye, we are ignorant of the backparts, or lower side of his Divinity; therefore to pry into the maze of his Counsels, is not onely folly in Man, but presumption even in Angels; like us,

* *γνῶθι σεαυτόν, nosce teipsum.*

they are his servants, not his Senators; he holds no Councell, but that mysticall one of the Trinity, wherein though there be three persons, there is but one minde that decrees, without contradiction; nor needs he any, his actions are not begot with deliberation, his wisedome naturally knowes what's best; his intellect stands ready fraught with the superlative and purest Idea's of goodnesse; consultation and election, which are two motions in us, make but one in him; his actions springing from his power, at the first touch of his will. These are Contemplations Metaphysicall, my humble speculations have another Method, and are content to trace and discover those expressions hee hath left in his creatures, and the obvious effects of nature; there is no danger to profound these mysteries, no *Sanctum sanctorum* in Philosophy: The world was made to be inhabited by beasts, but studied and contemplated by man: 'tis the debt of our reason wee owe unto God, and the homage wee pay for not being beasts; without this the world is still as though it had not been, or as it was before the sixt day when as yet there was not a creature that could conceive, or say there was a world. The wisedome of God receives small honour from those vulgar heads, that rudely stare about, and with a grosse rusticity admire his workes; those highly magnifie him whose judicious enquiry into his acts, and deliberate research into his creatures, returne the duty of a devout and learned admiration.

Therefore,

Search while thou wilt, and let thy reason goe
To ransome truth even to the Abysse below.
Rally the scattered causes, and that line
Which nature twists be able to untwine.
It is thy Makers will, for unto none
But unto reason can he ere be knowne. 30
The Devills doe know thee, but those damned meteours
Build not thy glory, but confound thy creatures.
Teach my endeavours so thy workes to read,
That learning them, in thee I may proceed.
Give thou my reason that instructive flight,
Whose weary wings may on thy hands still light.
Teach me to soare aloft, yet ever so,
When neare the Sunne, to stoope againe below.
Thus shall my humble feathers safely hover,
And though neere earth, more then the heavens discover. 40
And then at last, when homeward I shall drive

41 *homeward*] *holmeward* 43

Rich with the spoyles of nature to my hive,
There will I sit, like that industrious flye,
Buzzing thy prayses, which shall never die
Till death abrupts them, and succeeding glory
Bid me goe on in a more lasting story.

And this is almost all wherein an humble creature may endeavour to requite, and someway to retribute unto his Creator; for if not he that sayeth *Lord, Lord*; *but he that doth the will of the Father shall be saved*; certainely our wills must bee our performances, and our 10 intents make out our actions; otherwise our pious labours shall finde anxiety in their graves, and our best endeavours not hope, but feare a resurrection.

SECT. 14.

There is but one first cause, and foure second causes of all things; some are without efficient, as God, others without matter, as Angels, some without forme, as the first matter, but every Essence, created or uncreated, hath its finall cause, and some positive end both of its Essence and operation; This is the cause I grope after in the workes of nature, on this hangs the providence of God; to 20 raise so beauteous a structure, as the world and the creatures thereof, was but his Art, but their sundry and divided operations with their predestinated ends, are from the treasury of his wisedome. In the causes, nature, and affections of the Eclipse of Sunne and Moone, there is most excellent speculation; but to profound farther, and to contemplate a reason why his providence hath so disposed and ordered their motions in that vast circle, as to conjoyne and obscure each other, is a sweeter piece of reason, and a diviner point of Philosophy; therefore sometimes, and in some things there appeares to mee as much divinity in *Galen* his Books 30 *De usu partium*, as in *Suarez* Metaphysicks: Had *Aristotle* beene as curious in the enquiry of this cause as he was of the other, hee had not left behinde him an imperfect piece of Philosophy, but an absolute tract of Divinity.

SECT. 15.

Natura nihil agit frustra, is the onely indisputable axiome in Philosophy; there are no *Grotesques* in nature; nor any thing framed to fill up empty cantons, and unnecessary spaces; in the most imperfect creatures, and such as were not preserved in the Arke, but having their seeds and principles in the wombe of nature, are every-where where the power of the Sun is; in these is the wisedome of his hand discovered: Out of this ranke *Solomon* chose the object of his admiration, indeed what reason may not goe to Schoole to the wisedome of Bees, Aunts, and Spiders? what wise hand teacheth them to doe what reason cannot teach us? ruder heads stand amazed at those prodigious pieces of nature, Whales, Elephants, Dromidaries, and Camels; these I confesse, are the Colossus and Majestick pieces of her hand; but in these narrow Engines there is more curious Mathematicks, and the civilitie of these little Citizens, more neatly set forth the wisedome of their 10 Maker; Who admires not *Regio-Montanus* his Fly beyond his Eagle, or wonders not more at the operation of two soules in those little bodies, than but one in the trunck of a Cedar? I could never content my contemplation with those generall pieces of wonders, the flux and reflux of the sea, the encrease of Nile, the conversion of the Needle to the North, and have studied to match and parallel those in the more obvious and neglected pieces of Nature, which without further travell I can doe in the Cosmography of my selfe; wee carry with us the wonders, we seeke without us: There is all *Africa*, and her prodigies in us; we are that bold and adventurous 20 piece of nature, which he that studies wisely learnes in a *compendium*, what others labour at in a divided piece and endlesse volume.

SECT. 16.

Thus there are two bookes from whence I collect my Divinity; besides that written one of God, another of his servant Nature, that universall and publik Manuscript, that lies expans'd unto the eyes of all; those that never saw him in the one, have discovered him in the other: This was the Scripture and Theology of the Heathens; the naturall motion of the Sun made them more admire him, than its supernaturall station did the Children of Israel; the 30 ordinary effects of nature wrought more admiration in them, than in the other all his miracles; surely the Heathens knew better how to joyne and reade these mysticall letters, than wee Christians, who cast a more carelesse eye on these common Hieroglyphicks, and disdain to suck Divinity from the flowers of nature. Nor do I so forget God, as to adore the name of Nature; which I define not with the Schooles, the principle of motion and rest, but, that streight and regular line, that setled and constant course the wisedome of God hath ordained the actions of his creatures, according to their severall kinds. To make a revolution every day 40

21 studies *MSS.* / *42*: studies, *43* 31 effects *MSS.*: effect *42 43*

is the nature of the Sun, because that necessary course which God hath ordained it, from which it cannot swerve, but by a faculty from that voyce which first did give it motion. Now this course of Nature God seldome alters or perverts, but like an excellent Artist hath so contrived his worke, that with the selfe same instrument, without a new creation hee may effect his obscurest designes. Thus he sweetneth the water with a wood, preserveth the creatures in the Arke, which the blast of his mouth might have as easily created: for God is like a skilfull Geometrician, who when more easily, and with one stroke of his Compasse, he might describe, or divide a right line, had yet rather doe this in a circle or longer way, according to the constituted and forelaid principles of his art: yet this rule of his hee doth sometimes pervert, to acquaint the world with his prerogative, lest the arrogancy of our reason should question his power, and conclude he could not; & thus I call the effects of nature the works of God, whose hand & instrument she only is; and therefore to ascribe his actions unto her, is to devolve the honor of the principall agent, upon the instrument; which if with reason we may doe, then let our hammers rise up and boast they have built our houses, and our pens receive the honour of our writings. I hold there is a generall beauty in the works of God, and therefore no deformity in any kind or species of creature whatsoever: I cannot tell by what Logick we call a Toad, a Beare, or an Elephant, ugly, they being created in those outward shapes and figures which best expresse the actions of their inward formes, and having past that generall visitation of God, who saw that all that he had made was good, that is, conformable to his will, which abhors deformity, and is the rule of order and beauty; there is no deformity but in monstrosity, wherein notwithstanding there is a kind of beauty, Nature so ingeniously contriving the irregular parts, as they become sometimes more remarkable than the principall Fabrick. To speake yet more narrowly, there was never any thing ugly, or mis-shapen, but the Chaos; wherein notwithstanding to speake strictly, there was no deformity, because no forme, nor was it yet impregnate by the voyce of God: Now nature is not at variance with art, nor art with nature; they being both the servants of his providence: Art is the perfection of Nature: Were the world now as it was the sixt day, there were yet a Chaos: Nature hath made one world, and Art another. In briefe, all things are artificiall, for nature is the Art of God.

2 but by *Er*: by *43*
26 formes, and] formes. And *43 JW. Lighter punctuation in other MSS.*

SECT. 17.

This is the ordinary and open way of his providence, which art and industry have in a good part discovered, whose effects wee may foretell without an Oracle; To foreshew these is not Prophesie, but Prognostication. There is another way full of Meanders and Labyrinths, whereof the Devill and Spirits have no exact Ephemerides, and that is a more particular and obscure method of his providence, directing the operations of individualls and single Essences; this we call Fortune, that serpentine and crooked line, whereby he drawes those actions his wisedome intends in a more 10 unknowne and secret way; This cryptick and involved method of his providence have I ever admired, nor can I relate the history of my life, the occurrences of my dayes, the escapes of dangers, and hits of chance with a *Bezo las Manos*, to Fortune, or a bare Gramercy to my good starres: *Abraham* might have thought the Ram in the thicket came thither by accident; humane reason would have said that meere chance conveyed *Moses* in the Arke to the sight of *Pharaohs* daughter; what a Labyrinth is there in the story of *Joseph*, able to convert a Stoick? Surely there are in every mans life certaine rubs, doublings and wrenches which passe a while 20 under the effects of chance, but at the last, well examined, prove the meere hand of God: 'Twas not dumbe chance, that to discover the Fougade or Powder plot, contrived a miscarriage in the letter. I like the victory of 88. the better for that one occurrence which our enemies imputed to our dishonour, and the partiality of Fortune, to wit, the tempests and contrarietie of winds. King *Philip* did not detract from the Nation, when he said, he sent his Armado to fight with men, and not to combate with the winds. Where there is a manifest disproportion between the powers and forces of two severall agents, upon a maxime of reason wee may 30 promise the victory to the superiour; but when unexpected accidents slip in, and unthought of occurrences intervene, these must proceed from a power that owes no obedience to those axioms: where, as in the writing upon the wall, we behold the hand, but see not the spring that moves it. The successe of that pety Province of Holland (of which the Grand Seignieur proudly said, That if they should trouble him as they did the Spaniard, hee would send his men with shovels and pick-axes and throw it into the Sea) I cannot altogether ascribe to the ingenuity and industry of the people, but to the mercy of God, that hath disposed them 40 to such a thriving *Genius*; and to the will of his providence, that dispenseth her favour to each Countrey in their preordinate

42 dispenseth *MSS. except W*: disposeth *W42 43*

season. All cannot be happy at once, for because the glory of one State depends upon the ruine of another, there is a revolution and vicissitude of their greatnesse, and must obey the swing of that wheele, not moved by intelligences, but by the hand of God, whereby all Estates arise to their Zenith and verticall points, according to their predestinated periods. For the lives not onely of men, but of Commonweales, and the whole world, run not upon an Helix that still enlargeth, but on a Circle, where arriving to their Meridian, they decline in obscurity, and fall under the 10 Horizon againe.

SECT. 18.

These must not therefore bee named the effects of fortune, but in a relative way, and as we terme the workes of nature. It was the ignorance of mans reason that begat this very name, and by a carelesse terme miscalled the providence of God: for there is no liberty for causes to operate in a loose and stragling way, nor any effect whatsoever, but hath its warrant from some universall or superiour cause. 'Tis not a ridiculous devotion, to say a Prayer before a game at Tables; for even in *sortilegies* and matters of 20 greatest uncertainty, there is a setled and preordered course of effects; 'tis we that are blind, not fortune: because our eye is too dim to discover the mystery of her effects, we foolishly paint her blind, & hoodwink the providence of the Almighty. I cannot justifie that contemptible Proverb, *That fooles onely are fortunate*; or that insolent Paradox, *That a wise man is out of the reach of fortune*; much lesse those opprobrious Epithets of Poets, *Whore*, *Baud*, and *Strumpet*: 'Tis I confesse the common fate of men of singular gifts of mind, to be destitute of those of fortune; which doth not any way deject the spirit of wiser judgements, who throughly under- 30 stand the justice of this proceeding; and being enriched with higher donatives, cast a more carelesse eye on these vulgar parts of felicity. 'Tis a most unjust ambition, to desire to engrosse the mercies of the Almighty, nor to be content with the goods of mind, without a possession of those of body or fortune: and 'tis an errour worse than heresie, to adore these complementall & circum- stantiall pieces of felicity, and undervalue those perfections and essentiall points of happinesse, wherin we resemble our Maker. To wiser desires 'tis satisfaction enough to deserve, though not to enjoy the favours of fortune; let providence provide for fooles: 40 'tis not partiality, but equity in God, who deales with us but as our naturall parents; those that are able of body and mind, he leaves to their deserts; to those of weaker merits hee imparts a larger portion, and pieces out the defect of one by the excesse of the other. Thus have wee no just quarrell with Nature, for leaving us naked, or to envie the hornes, hoofs, skins, and furs of other creatures, being provided with reason, that can supply them all. Wee need not labour with so many arguments to confute judiciall Astrology; for if there be a truth therein, it doth not injure Divinity; if to be born under *Mercury* disposeth us to be witty, under *Iupiter* to be wealthy, I doe not owe a knee unto these, but unto that mercifull hand that hath ordered my indifferent and uncertaine nativity unto such benevolous aspects. Those that held that all things were governed by fortune had not erred, had they not persisted there: The Romans that erected a Temple to Fortune, acknowledged therein, though in a blinder way, somewhat of Divinity; for in a wise supputation all things begin and end in the Almighty. There is a neerer way to heaven than *Homers* chaine; an easie Logick may conjoyne heaven and earth in one argument, and with lesse than a Sorites resolve all things into God. For though wee Christen effects by their most sensible and nearest causes, yet is God the true and infallible cause of all, whose concourse though it be generall, yet doth it subdivide it selfe into the particular actions of everything, and is that spirit, by which each singular essence not onely subsists, but performes its operations.

SECT. 19.

The bad construction and perverse comment on these paire of second causes, or visible hands of God, have perverted the devotion of many unto Atheisme; who forgetting the honest advisoes of faith, have listened unto the conspiracie of Passion and Reason. I have therefore alwayes endeavoured to compose those fewds and angry dissentions between affection, faith, and reason: For there is in our soule a kind of Triumvirate, or Triple government of three competitors, which distract the peace of this our Common-wealth, not lesse than did that other the State of Rome.

As Reason is a rebell unto Faith, so passion unto Reason: As the propositions of Faith seeme absurd unto Reason, so the Theorems of Reason unto passion, and both unto Faith; yet a moderate and peaceable discretion may so state and order the matter, that they may bee all Kings, and yet make but one Monarchy, every one exercising his Soveraignty and Prerogative in a due time and

11 held *MSS.*: hold *42 43* 23 operations *MSS.*: operation *42 43*
36 Faith *P and N* (*margin*): *lacuna in O*: Reason *other MSS. 42 43* yet *Er*: yea *43*

place, according to the restraint and limit of circumstance. There is, as in Philosophy, so in Divinity, sturdy doubts, and boysterous objections, wherewith the unhappinesse of our knowledge too neerely acquainteth us. More of these no man hath knowne than my selfe, which I confesse I conquered, not in a martiall posture, but on my knees. For our endeavours are not onely to combate with doubts, but alwayes to dispute with the Devill; the villany of that spirit takes a hint of infidelity from our Studies, and by demonstrating a naturality in one way, makes us mistrust a miracle in 10 another. Thus having perus'd the Archidoxis and read the secret Sympathies of things, he would disswade my beliefe from the miracle of the Brazen Serpent, make me conceit that image work'd by Sympathie, and was but an Ægyptian tricke to cure their diseases without a miracle. Againe, having seene some experiments of *Bitumen*, and having read farre more of *Naptha*, he whispered to my curiositie the fire of the Altar might be naturall, and bid me mistrust a miracle in *Elias* when he entrench'd the Altar round with water; for that inflamable substance yeelds not easily unto water, but flames in the armes of its Antagonist: and thus would 20 hee inveagle my beliefe to thinke the combustion of *Sodom* might be naturall, and that there was an Asphaltick and Bituminous nature in that Lake before the fire of *Gomorrha*: I know that Manna is now plentifully gathered in *Calabria*, and *Josephus* tels me in his dayes 'twas as plentifull in *Arabia*; the Devill therefore made the *quere*, Where was then the miracle in the dayes of *Moses*? the *Israelites* saw but that in his time, the natives of those Countries behold in ours. Thus the Devill playd at Chesse with mee, and yeelding a pawne, thought to gaine a Queen of me, taking advantage of my honest endeavours; and whilst I labour'd to raise the structure of 30 my reason, hee striv'd to undermine the edifice of my faith.

SECT. 20.

Neither had these or any other ever such advantage of me, as to encline me to any point of infidelity or desperate positions of Atheisme; for I have beene these many yeares of opinion there was never any. Those that held Religion was the difference of man from beasts, have spoken probably, and proceed upon a principle as inductive as the other: That doctrine of *Epicurus*, that denied the providence of God, was no Atheism, but a magnificent and high-strained conceit of his Majesty, which hee deemed too sub- 40 lime to minde the triviall actions of those inferiour creatures: That fatall necessitie of the Stoickes, is nothing but the immutable Law of his will. Those that heretofore denied the Divinitie of the holy Ghost, have been condemned but as Heretickes; and those that now deny our Saviour (though more than Hereticks) are not so much as Atheists: for though they deny two persons in the Trinity, they hold as we do, there is but one God.

That villain and Secretary of Hell, that composed that miscreant piece of the three Impostors, though divided from all Religions, and was neither Jew, Turk, nor Christian, was not a positive Atheist. I confesse every Countrey hath its *Machiavell*, every age its *Lucian*, whereof common heads must not heare, nor more advanced judgements too rashly venture on: 'tis the Rhetorick 10 of Satan, and may pervert a loose or prejudicate beleefe.

SECT. 21.

I confesse I have perused them all, and can discover nothing that may startle a discreet beliefe: yet are there heads carried off with the wind and breath of such motives. I remember a Doctor in Physick of Italy, who could not perfectly believe the immortality of the soule, because *Galen* seemed to make a doubt thereof. With another I was familiarly acquainted in France, a Divine and man of singular parts, that on the same point was so plunged and gravelled with *three lines of *Seneca*, that all our Antidotes, drawne from 20 both Scripture and Philosophy, could not expell the poyson of his errour. There are a set of heads, that can credit the relations of Mariners, yet question the testimonies of Saint *Paul*; and peremptorily maintaine the traditions of *Ælian* or *Pliny*, yet in Histories of Scripture, raise Quere's and objections, beleeving no more than they can parallel in humane Authors. I confesse there are in Scripture stories that doe exceed the fables of Poets, and to a captious Reader sound like *Garagantua* or *Bevis*: Search all the Legends of times past, and the fabulous conceits of these present, and 'twill bee hard to find one that deserves to carry the buckler 30 unto *Sampson*, yet is all this of an easie possibility, if we conceive a divine concourse or an influence but from the little finger of the Almighty. It is impossible that either in the discourse of man, or in the infallible voyce of God, to the weakenesse of our apprehensions, there should not appeare irregularities, contradictions, and antinomies: my selfe could shew a catalogue of doubts, never yet

* *Post mortem nihil est, ipsaque mors nihil.*
Mors individua est noxia corpori,
Nec patiens animæ—
Toti morimur, nullaque pars manet Nostri—

27 fables *MSS.*: fable *42 43*

imagined nor questioned, as I know, which are not resolved at the first hearing, not fantastick Quere's, or objections of ayre: For I cannot heare of Atoms in Divinity. I can read the history of the Pigeon that was sent out of the Ark, and returned no more, yet not question how shee found out her mate that was left behind: That *Lazarus* was raised from the dead, yet not demand where in the interim his soule awaited; or raise a Law-case, whether his heire might lawfully detaine his inheritance, bequeathed unto him by his death; and he, though restored to life, have no Plea or title
10 unto his former possessions. Whether *Eve* was framed out of the left side of *Adam*, I dispute not; because I stand not yet assured which is the right side of a man, or whether there be any such distinction in Nature; that she was edified out of the ribbe of *Adam* I believe, yet raise no question who shall arise with that ribbe at the Resurrection. Whether *Adam* was an Hermaphrodite, as the Rabbines contend upon the letter of the Text; because it is contrary to reason, there should bee an Hermaphrodite before there was a woman, or a composition of two natures, before there was a second composed. Likewise, whether the world was created
20 in Autumne, Summer, or the Spring; because it was created in them all; for whatsoever Signe the Sun possesseth, those foure seasons are actually existent: It is the nature of this Luminary to distinguish the severall seasons of the yeare, all which it makes at one time in the whole earth, and successive in any part thereof. There are a bundle of curiosities, not onely in Philosophy but in Divinity, proposed and discussed by men of most supposed abilities, which indeed are not worthy our vacant houres, much lesse our serious studies; Pieces onely fit to be placed in **Pantagruels* Library, or bound up with *Tartaretus de modo Cacandi.*

30 SECT. 22.

These are niceties that become not those that peruse so serious a Mystery. There are others more generally questioned and called to the Barre, yet me thinkes of an easie, and possible truth. 'Tis ridiculous to put off, or drowne the generall Flood of *Noah* in that particular inundation of *Deucalion*: that there was a Deluge once, seemes not to mee so great a miracle, as that there is not one alwayes. How all the kinds of Creatures, not only in their owne bulks, but with a competency of food & sustenance, might be preserved in one Arke, and within the extent of three hundred

* In *Rabelais*.

35 particular *Er*: great particular *42 43*

cubits, to a reason that rightly examines it, will appeare very foesible. There is another secret, not contained in the Scripture, which is more hard to comprehend, & put the honest Father to the refuge of a Miracle; and that is, not onely how the distinct pieces of the world, and divided Ilands should bee first planted by men, but inhabited by Tygers, Panthers and Beares. How *America* abounded with beasts of prey, and noxious Animals, yet contained not in it that necessary creature, a Horse, is very strange. By what passage those, not onely Birds, but dangerous and unwelcome Beasts came over: How there bee creatures there, which are not 10 found in this triple Continent; all which must needs bee strange unto us, that hold but one Arke, and that the creatures began their progresse from the mountaines of *Ararat*. They who to salve this would make the Deluge particular, proceed upon a Principle that I can no way grant; not onely upon the negative of holy Scriptures, but of mine owne reason, whereby I can make it probable, that the world was as well peopled in the time of *Noah* as in ours, and fifteene hundred yeares to people the world, as full a time for them as foure thousand yeares since have beene to us. There are other assertions and common tenents drawn from Scrip- 20 ture, and generally beleeved as Scripture; whereunto, notwithstanding, I would never betray the libertie of my reason. 'Tis a postulate to me, that *Methusalem* was the longest liv'd of all the children of *Adam*, and no man will bee able to prove it; when from the processe of the Text I can manifest it may be otherwise. That *Judas* perished by hanging himself, there is no certainety in Scripture, though in one place it seemes to affirme it, and by a doubtfull word hath given occasion so to translate it; yet in another place, in a more punctuall description, it makes it improbable, and seemes to overthrow it. That our Fathers, after the Flood, erected 30 the Tower of *Babell*, to preserve themselves against a second Deluge, is generally opinioned and beleeved; yet is there another intention of theirs expressed in Scripture: Besides, it is improbable from the circumstance of the place, that is, a plaine in the land of *Shinar*. These are no points of Faith, and therefore may admit a free dispute. There are yet others, and those familiarly concluded from the Text, wherein (under favour) I see no consequence. The Church of Rome confidently proves the opinion of Tutelary Angels, from that answer when *Peter* knockt at the doore, *'Tis not he but his Angel*; that is, might some say, his Messenger, or some 40 body from him; for so the Originall signifies, and is as likely to be

23 postulate *Er and MSS.*: Paradoxe *42 43* 28 so to *HJNW*: to *OR 42 43* (*not in P*)

the doubtfull Families meaning. This exposition I once suggested to a young Divine, that answered upon this point, to which I remember the *Franciscan* Opponent replyed no more, but, That it was a new and no authentick interpretation.

SECT. 23.

These are but the conclusions, and fallible discourses of man upon the word of God, for such I doe beleeve the holy Scriptures; yet were it of man, I could not choose but say, it was the singularest, and superlative Piece that hath been extant since the Creation;
10 were I a Pagan, I should not refraine the Lecture of it; and cannot but commend the judgement of *Ptolomy*, that thought not his Library compleate without it: the Alcoran of the Turks (I speake without prejudice) is an ill composed Piece, containing in it vaine and ridiculous errours in Philosophy, impossibilities, fictions, and vanities beyond laughter, maintained by evident and open Sophismes, the policy of Ignorance, deposition of Universities, and banishment of Learning. That hath gotten foot by armes and violence; This without a blow hath disseminated it selfe through the whole earth. It is not unremarkable what *Philo* first observed,
20 That the Law of *Moses* continued two thousand yeares without the least alteration; whereas, we see, the Lawes of other Commonweales doe alter with occasions; and even those that pretended their originall from some Divinity, to have vanished without trace or memory. I beleeve, besides *Zoroaster*, there were divers that writ before *Moses*, who notwithstanding have suffered the common fate of time. Mens Workes have an age like themselves; and though they out-live their Authors, yet have they a stint and period to their duration: This onely is a Worke too hard for the teeth of time, and cannot perish but in the generall flames, when all things
30 shall confesse their ashes.

SECT. 24.

I have heard some with deepe sighs lament the lost lines of *Cicero*; others with as many groanes deplore the combustion of the Library of *Alexandria*; for my owne part, I thinke there be too many in the world, and could with patience behold the urne and ashes of the *Vatican*, could I with a few others recover the perished leaves of *Solomon*. I would not omit a Copy of *Enochs* Pillars, had they many neerer Authors than *Josephus*, or did not relish some-

17 Learning. That *RW*: Learning, that *42 43. The punctuation of the other MSS. varies, but all except O capitalize* That *even when it is preceded by a comma. P has* Learning, This *and* that *for* This *in l.*18.

what of the Fable. Some men have written more than others have spoken; **Pineda* quotes more Authors in one worke, than are necessary in a whole world. Of those three great inventions in *Germany*, there are two which are not without their incommodities, and 'tis disputable whether they exceed not their use and commodities. 'Tis not a melancholy *Utinam* of mine owne, but the desire of better heads, that there were a generall Synod; not to unite the incompatible differences of Religion, but for the benefit of learning, to reduce it as it lay at first in a few and solid Authours; and to condemne to the fire those swarms and millions of *Rhapsodies*, begotten onely to distract and abuse the weaker judgements of Scholars, and to maintaine the Trade and Mystery of Typographers.

SECT. 25.

I cannot but wonder with what exceptions the *Samaritanes* could confine their beliefe to the *Pentateuch*, or five Books of *Moses*. I am ashamed at the Rabbinicall Interpretations of the Jews, upon the Old Testament, as much as their defection from the New: and truely it is beyond wonder, how that contemptible and degenerate issue of *Jacob*, once so devoted to Ethnick Superstition, and so easily seduced to the Idolatry of their Neighbours, should now in such an obstinate and peremptory beliefe, adhere unto their owne Doctrine, expect impossibilities, and in the face and eye of the Church persist without the least hope of conversion: This is a vice in them, that were a vertue in us; for obstinacy in a bad cause, is but constancy in a good. And herein I must accuse those of my own Religion; for there is not any of such a fugitive faith, such an unstable belief, as a Christian; none that do so oft transforme themselves, not unto severall shapes of Christianity and of the same Species, but unto more unnaturall and contrary formes, of Jew and Mahometan, that from the name of Saviour can descend to the bare terme of Prophet; and from an old beliefe that he is come, fall to a new expectation of his comming: It is the promise of Christ to make us all one flock; but how and when this union shall be, is as obscure to me as the last day. Of those foure members of Religion wee hold a slender proportion; there are I confesse some new additions, yet small to those which accrew to our

* *Pineda* in his *Monarchia Ecclesiastica* quotes one thousand and fortie Authors.

7 desire *MSS.*: desires *42 43* 8 differences *MSS.*: difference *42 43*
17 Interpretations *MSS.*: Interpretation *42 43* 31 descend *MSS.*: condescend *42 43*

Adversaries, and those onely drawne from the revolt of Pagans, men but of negative impieties, and such as deny Christ, but because they never heard of him: But the Religion of the Jew is expresly against the Christian, and the Mahometan against both; for the Turke, in the bulke hee now stands, he is beyond all hope of conversion; if hee fall asunder there may be conceived hopes, but not without strong improbabilities. The Jew is obstinate in all fortunes; the persecution of fifteene hundred yeares hath but confirmed them in their errour: they have already endured what-
10 soever may be inflicted, and have suffered, in a bad cause, even to the condemnation of their enemies. Persecution is a bad and indirect way to plant Religion; It hath beene the unhappy method of angry devotions, not onely to confirme honest Religion, but wicked Heresies, and extravagant opinions. It was the first stone and Basis of our Faith, none can more justly boast of persecutions, and glory in the number and valour of Martyrs; For, to speake properly, those are true and almost onely examples of fortitude: Those that are fetch'd from the field, or drawne from the actions of the Campe, are not oft-times so truely precedents of valour as
20 audacity, and at the best attaine but to some bastard piece of fortitude: If wee shall strictly examine the circumstances and requisites which *Aristotle* requires to true and perfect valour, we shall finde the name onely in his Master *Alexander*, and as little in that Romane Worthy, *Julius Cæsar*; and if any, in that easie and active way, have done so nobly as to deserve that name, yet in the passive and more terrible piece these have surpassed, and in a more heroicall way may claime the honour of that Title. 'Tis not in the power of every honest faith to proceed thus farre, or passe to Heaven through the flames; every one hath it not in that full
30 measure, nor in so audacious and resolute a temper, as to endure those terrible tests and trialls, who notwithstanding in a peaceable way doe truely adore their Saviour, and have (no doubt) a faith acceptable in the eyes of God.

SECT. 26.

Now as all that die in warre are not termed Souldiers, so neither can I properly terme all those that suffer in matters of Religion Martyrs. The Councell of *Constance* condemnes *John Husse* for an Heretick, the Stories of his owne party stile him a Martyr; He must needs offend the Divinity of both, that sayes hee was neither
40 the one nor the other: There are many (questionlesse) canonized on earth, that shall never be Saints in Heaven; and have their

29 that *ErPNOR*: the *HJW 42 43*

names in Histories and Martyrologies, who in the eyes of God, are not so perfect Martyrs as was that wise Heathen *Socrates*, that suffered on a fundamentall point of Religion, the Unity of God. I have often pitied the miserable Bishop that suffered in the cause of *Antipodes*, yet cannot choose but accuse him of as much madnesse, for exposing his living on such a trifle, as those of ignorance and folly that condemned him. I think my conscience will not give me the lie, if I say, there are not many extant that in a noble way feare the face of death lesse than my selfe, yet from the morall duty I owe to the Commandement of God, and the naturall re- 10 spect that I tender unto the conservation of my essence and being, I would not perish upon a Ceremony, Politick point, or indifferency: nor is my beleefe of that untractable temper, as not to bow at their obstacles, or connive at matters wherein there are not manifest impieties: The leaven therefore and ferment of all, not onely Civill, but Religious actions, is wisedome; without which, to commit our selves to the flames is Homicide, and (I feare) but to passe through one fire into another.

SECT. 27.

That Miracles are ceased, I can neither prove, nor absolutely deny, 20 much lesse define the time and period of their cessation; that they survived Christ, is manifest upon record of Scripture; that they out-lived the Apostles also, and were revived at the conversion of Nations, many yeares after, we cannot deny, if wee shall not question those Writers whose testimonies wee doe not controvert, in points that make for our owne opinions; therefore that may have some truth in it that is reported by the Jesuites of their Miracles in the Indies, I could wish it were true, or had any other testimony then their owne Pennes: they may easily beleeve those Miracles abroad, who daily conceive a greater at home; the transmutation 30 of those visible elements into the body and blood of our Saviour: for the conversion of water into wine, which he wrought in *Cana*, or what the Devill would have had him done in the wildernesse, of stones into Bread, compared to this, will scarce deserve the name of a Miracle: Though indeed, to speake properly, there is not one Miracle greater than another, they being the extraordinary effects of the hand of God, to which all things are of an equall facility; and to create the world as easie as one single creature. For this is also a miracle, not onely to produce effects against, or above Nature, but before Nature; and to create Nature as great a miracle, 40

10 respect *MSS. except O*: respects *O 42 43* 12 point *MSS.*: points *42 43* 27 Jesuites] Jesu-suites *43* 36 effects *MSS.*: effect *42 43*

as to contradict or transcend her. Wee doe too narrowly define the power of God, restraining it to our capacities. I hold that God can doe all things, how he should work contradictions I do not understand, yet dare not therefore deny. I cannot see why the Angel of God should question *Esdras* to recall the time past, if it were beyond his owne power; or that God should pose mortalitie in that, which hee was not able to performe himselfe. I will not say God cannot, but hee will not performe many things, which wee plainely affirme he cannot: this I am sure is the mannerliest
10 proposition, wherein notwithstanding I hold no Paradox. For strictly his power is the same with his will, and they both with all the rest doe make but one God.

SECT. 28.

Therefore that Miracles have beene I doe beleeve, that they may yet bee wrought by the living I doe not deny: but have no confidence in those which are fathered on the dead; and this hath ever made me suspect the efficacy of reliques, to examine the bones, question the habits and appertinencies of Saints, and even of Christ himselfe: I cannot conceive why the Crosse that *Helena* found and
20 whereon Christ himself died should have power to restore others unto life; I excuse not *Constantine* from a fall off his horse, or a mischiefe from his enemies, upon the wearing those nayles on his bridle which our Saviour bore upon the Crosse in his hands: I compute among your *Piæ fraudes*, nor many degrees before consecrated swords and roses, that which *Baldwin* King of Jerusalem return'd the *Genovese* for their cost and paines in his warre, to wit the ashes of *John* the Baptist. Those that hold the sanctitie of their soules doth leave behind a tincture and sacred facultie on their bodies, speake naturally of Miracles, and doe not salve the doubt.
30 Now one reason I tender so little devotion unto reliques is, I think, the slender and doubtfull respect I have alwayes held unto Antiquities: for that indeed which I admire is farre before antiquity, that is Eternity, and that is God himselfe; who though hee be stiled the Antient of dayes, cannot receive the adjunct of antiquity, who was before the world, and shall be after it, yet is not older then it: for in his yeares there is no Climacter, his duration is eternity, and farre more venerable then antiquitie.

SECT. 29.

But above all things, I wonder how the curiositie of wiser heads
40 could passe that great and indisputable miracle, the cessation of Oracles: and in what swoun their reasons lay, to content them-

selves and sit downe with such far-fetch't and ridiculous reasons as *Plutarch* alleadgeth for it. The Jewes that can beleeve the supernaturall solstice of the Sunne in the days of *Joshua*, have yet the impudence to deny the Eclipse, which even Pagans confessed at his death: but for this, it is evident beyond all contradiction, *the Devill himselfe confessed it. Certainly it is not a warrantable curiosity, to examine the verity of Scripture by the concordance of humane history, or seek to confirme the Chronicle of *Hester* or *Daniel*, by the authority of *Megasthenes* or *Herodotus*. I confesse I have had an unhappy curiosity this way, till I laughed my selfe out **10** of it with a piece of *Justine*, where hee delivers that the children of *Israel* for being scabbed were banished out of Egypt. And truely since I have understood the occurrences of the world, and know in what counterfeit shapes & deceitfull vizzards times present represent on the stage things past; I doe beleeve them little more than things to come. Some have beene of my opinion, and endevoured to write the History of their own lives; wherein *Moses* hath outgone them all, and left not onely the story of his life, but as some will have it of his death also.

SECT. 30. **20**

It is a riddle to me, how this story of Oracles hath not worm'd out of the world that doubtfull conceit of Spirits and Witches; how so many learned heads should so farre forget their Metaphysicks, and destroy the Ladder and scale of creatures, as to question the existence of Spirits: for my part, I have ever beleeved, and doe now know, that there are Witches; they that doubt of these, doe not onely deny them, but Spirits; and are obliquely and upon consequence a sort, not of Infidels, but Atheists. Those that to confute their incredulity desire to see apparitions, shall questionlesse never behold any, nor have the power to be so much as Witches; **30** the Devill hath them already in a heresie as capitall as Witchcraft, and to appeare to them, were but to convert them: Of all the delusions wherewith he deceives mortalitie, there is not any that puzleth mee more than the Legerdemain of *Changelings*; I doe not credit those transformations of reasonable creatures into beasts, or that the Devill hath a power to transpeciate a man into a horse, who tempted Christ (as a triall of his Divinitie) to convert but

* In his Oracle to *Augustus*.

4 even Pagans *MSS.*: every Pagan *42 43* 9 *Megasthenes*] *Magasthenes 43 only* *Herodotus.*] *Herodotus 43* 14 times present represent *Er and MSS. except W*: the time represents *W 42 43*

stones into bread. I could beleeve that Spirits use with man the act of carnality, and that in both sexes; I conceive they may assume, steale, or contrive a body, wherein there may be action enough to content decrepit lust, or passion to satisfie more active veneries; yet in both, without a possibility of generation: and therefore that opinion, that Antichrist should be borne of the Tribe of *Dan* by conjunction with the Devill, is ridiculous, and a conceit fitter for a Rabbin than a Christian. I hold that the Devill doth really possesse some men, the spirit of melancholy others, the
10 spirit of delusion others; that as the Devill is concealed and denyed by some, so God and good Angels are pretended by others, whereof the late detection of the Maid of Germany hath left a pregnant example.

SECT. 31.

Againe, I beleeve that all that use sorceries, incantations, and spells, are not Witches, or as we terme them, Magicians; I conceive there is a traditionall Magicke, not learned immediately from the Devill, but at second hand from his Schollers; who having once the secret betrayed, are able, and doe emperically practice
20 without his advice, they both proceeding upon the principles of nature: where actives aptly conjoyned to disposed passives, will under any Master produce their effects. Thus I thinke at first a great part of Philosophy was Witchcraft, which being afterward derived to one another, proved but Philosophy, and was indeed no more but the honest effects of Nature: What invented by us is Philosophy, learned from him is Magicke. Wee doe surely owe the honour of many secrets to the discovery of good and bad Angels. I could never passe that sentence of *Paracelsus* without an asterisk or annotation; * *Ascendens constellatum multa revelat, quærentibus magnalia*
30 *naturæ*, i.e. *opera Dei*. I doe thinke that many mysteries ascribed to our owne inventions, have beene the courteous revelations of Spirits; for those noble essences in heaven beare a friendly regard unto their fellow-natures on earth; and therefore beleeve that those many prodigies and ominous prognostickes which fore-run the ruines of States, Princes, and private persons, are the charitable premonitions of good Angels, which more carelesse enquiries terme but the effects of chance and nature.

* Thereby is meant our good Angel appointed us from our nativity.

---

12 detection *MSS.*: defection *42 43* 27 honour *MSS. except W*: discovery *W 42 43*

SECT. 32.

Now besides these particular and divided Spirits, there may be (for ought I know) an universall and common Spirit to the whole world. It was the opinion of *Plato*, and it is yet of the *Hermeticall* Philosophers; if there be a common nature that unites and tyes the scattered and divided individuals into one species, why may there not bee one that unites them all? However, I am sure there is a common Spirit that playes within us, yet makes no part of us, and that is the Spirit of God, the fire and scintillation of that noble and mighty Essence, which is the life and radicall heat of spirits, and those 10 essences that know not the vertue of the Sunne, a fire quite contrary to the fire of Hell: This is that gentle heate that brooded on the waters, and in six dayes hatched the world; this is that irradiation that dispells the mists of Hell, the clouds of horrour, feare, sorrow, despaire; and preserves the region of the mind in serenity: whosoever feels not the warme gale and gentle ventilation of this Spirit (though I feele his pulse) I dare not say he lives; for truely without this, to mee there is no heat under the Tropick; nor any light, though I dwelt in the body of the Sunne.

As when the labouring Sun hath wrought his track, 20
Vp to the top of lofty Cancers *back,*
The ycie Ocean cracks, the frozen pole
Thawes with the heat of the Celestiall coale;
So when thy absent beames begin t' impart
Againe a Solstice on my frozen heart,
My winters ov'r, my drooping spirits sing,
And every part revives into a Spring.
But if thy quickning beames a while decline,
And with their light blesse not this Orbe of mine,
A chilly frost surpriseth every member, 30
And in the midst of Iune I feele December.
O how this earthly temper doth debase
The noble Soule, in this her humble place!
Whose wingy nature ever doth aspire,
To reach that place whence first it tooke its fire.
These flames I feele, which in my heart doe dwell,
Are not thy beames, but take their fire from Hell:
O quench them all, and let thy light divine
Be as the Sunne to this poore Orbe of mine.
And to thy sacred Spirit convert those fires, 40
Whose earthly fumes choake my devout aspires.

SECT. 33.

Therefore for Spirits I am so farre from denying their existence, that I could easily beleeve, that not onely whole Countries, but particular persons have their Tutelary, and Guardian Angels: It is not a new opinion of the Church of *Rome*, but an old one of *Pythagoras* and *Plato*; there is no heresie in it, and if not manifestly defin'd in Scripture, yet is it an opinion of a good and wholesome use in the course and actions of a mans life, and would serve as an *Hypothesis* to salve many doubts, whereof common Philosophy 10 affordeth no solution: Now if you demand my opinion and Metaphysicks of their natures, I confesse them very shallow, most of them in a negative way, like that of God; or in a comparative, between our selves and fellow creatures; for there is in this Universe a Staire, or manifest Scale of creatures, rising not disorderly, or in confusion, but with a comely method and proportion: betweene creatures of meere existence and things of life, there is a large disproportion of nature; betweene plants and animals or creatures of sense, a wider difference; between them and man, a farre greater: and if the proportion hold on, betweene man and 20 Angels there should bee yet a greater. We doe not comprehend their natures, who retaine the first definition of *Porphyry*, and distinguish them from our selves by immortality; for before his fall, man also was immortall; yet must wee needs affirme that he had a different essence from the Angels: having therefore no certaine knowledge of their natures, 'tis no bad method of the Schooles, whatsoever perfection we finde obscurely in our selves, in a more compleate and absolute way to ascribe unto them. I beleeve they have an extemporary knowledge, and upon the first motion of their reason doe what we cannot without study or deliberation; 30 that they know things by their formes, and define by specificall differences, what we describe by accidents and properties; and therefore probabilities to us may bee demonstrations unto them; that they have knowledge not onely of the specificall, but numericall formes of individualls, and understand by what reserved difference each single *Hypostasis* (besides the relation to its species) becomes its numericall selfe. That as the Soule hath a power to move the body it informes, so there's a Faculty to move any, though informe none; ours upon restraint of time, place, and distance; but that invisible hand that conveyed *Habakkuk* to the Lions den, or 40 *Philip* to *Azotus*, infringeth this rule, and hath a fecret conveyance, wherewith mortality is not acquainted; if they have that intuitive

31 differences *MSS.*: difference *42 43* properties] porpeties *43*

knowledge, whereby as in reflexion they behold the thoughts of one another, I cannot peremptorily deny but they know a great part of ours. They that to refute the Invocation of Saints, have denied that they have any knowledge of our affaires below, have proceeded too farre, and must pardon my opinion, till I can thoroughly answer that piece of Scripture, *At the conversion of a sinner the Angels of heaven rejoyce.* I cannot with those in that great Father securely interpret the worke of the first day, *Fiat lux*, to the creation of Angels, though (I confesse) there is not any creature that hath so neare a glympse of their nature, as light in the Sunne and 10 Elements; we stile it a bare accident, but where it subsists alone, 'tis a spirituall Substance, and may bee an Angel: in briefe, conceive light invisible, and that is a Spirit.

SECT. 34.

These are certainly the Magisteriall & master pieces of the Creator, the Flower (or as we may say) the best part of nothing, actually existing, what we are but in hopes, and probabilitie, we are onely that amphibious piece betweene a corporall and spirituall essence, that middle forme that linkes those two together, and makes good the method of God and nature, that jumps not from extreames, but 20 unites the incompatible distances by some middle and participating natures; that wee are the breath and similitude of God, it is indisputable, and upon record of holy Scripture, but to call our selves a Microcosme, or little world, I thought it onely a pleasant trope of Rhetorick, till my neare judgement and second thoughts told me there was a reall truth therein: for first wee are a rude masse, and in the ranke of creatures, which only are, and have a dull kinde of being not yet priviledged with life, or preferred to sense or reason; next we live the life of plants, the life of animals, the life of men, and at last the life of spirits, running on in one mysterious 30 nature those five kinds of existences, which comprehend the creatures not onely of the world, but of the Universe; thus is man that great and true *Amphibium*, whose nature is disposed to live not onely like other creatures in divers elements, but in divided and distinguished worlds; for though there bee but one world to sense, there are two to reason; the one visible, the other invisible, whereof *Moses* seemes to have left noe description, and of the other so obscurely, that some parts thereof are yet in controversie; and truely for the first chapters of *Genesis*, I must confesse a great deale of obscurity, though Divines have to the power of humane reason 40

35 one world *MSS.*: one *42 43* 37 left noe *P*: least *O*: left *other MSS. 42 43*

endeavoured to make all goe in a literall meaning, yet those allegoricall interpretations are also probable, and perhaps the mysticall method of *Moses* bred up in the Hieroglyphicall Schooles of the Egyptians.

SECT. 35.

Now for that immateriall world, me thinkes wee need not wander so farre as the first moveable, for even in this materiall fabricke the spirits walke as freely exempt from the affection of time, place, and motion, as beyond the extreamest circumference: doe but extract
10 from the corpulency of bodies, or resolve things beyond their first matter, and you discover the habitation of Angels, which if I call the ubiquitary, and omnipresent essence of God, I hope I shall not offend Divinity; for before the Creation of the world God was really all things. For the Angels hee created no new world, or determinate mansion, and therefore they are every where where is his essence, and doe live at a distance even in himselfe: that God made all things for man, is in some sense true, yet not so farre as to subordinate the creation of those purer creatures unto ours, though as ministring spirits they doe, and are willing to fulfill the
20 will of God in these lower and sublunary affaires of man; God made all things for himself, and it is impossible hee should make them for any other end than his owne glory; it is all he can receive, and all that is without himselfe; for honour being an externall adjunct, and in the honourer rather than in the person honoured, it was necessary to make a creature, from whom hee might receive this homage, and that is in the other world Angels, in this, man; which when we neglect, we forget the very end of our creation, and may justly provoke God, not onely to repent that hee hath made the world, but that hee hath sworne hee would not destroy
30 it. That there is but one world, is a conclusion of faith. *Aristotle* with all his Philosophy hath not beene able to prove it, and as weakely that the world was eternall; that dispute much troubled the pennes of the antient Philosophers, but *Moses* decided that question, and all is salved with the new terme of a creation, that is, a production of something out of nothing; and what is that? Whatsoever is opposite to something or more exactly, that which is truely contrary unto God: for he onely is, all others have an existence with dependency and are something but by a distinction; and herein is Divinity conformant unto Philosophy, and genera-
40 tion not onely founded on contrarieties, but also creation; God being all things is contrary unto nothing out of which were made all

33 pennes *MSS.*: penne *42 43* 38 existence *MSS.*: existence, *42 43*

things, and so nothing became something, and *Omneity* informed *Nullity* into an essence.

SECT. 36.

The whole Creation is a mystery, and particularly that of man, at the blast of his mouth were the rest of the creatures made, and at his bare word they started out of nothing: but in the frame of man (as the text describes it) he played the sensible operator, and seemed not so much to create, as make him; when hee had separated the materials of other creatures, there consequently resulted a forme and soule, but having raised the wals of man, he was driven 10 to a second and harder creation of a substance like himselfe, an incorruptible and immortall soule. For these two affections we have the Philosophy, and opinion of the Heathens, the flat affirmative of *Plato*, and not a negative from *Aristotle*: there is another scruple cast in by Divinity (concerning its production) much disputed in the *Germane* auditories, and with that indifferency and equality of arguments, as leave the controversie undetermined. I am not of *Paracelsus* minde that boldly delivers a receipt to make a man without conjunction, yet cannot but wonder at the multitude of heads that doe deny traduction, having 20 no other argument to confirme their beliefe, then that Rhetoricall sentence, and *Antimetathesis* of *Augustine*, *Creando infunditur, infundendo creatur*: either opinion will consist well enough with religion, yet I should rather incline to this, did not one objection haunt mee, not wrung from speculations and subtilties, but from common sense, and observation, not pickt from the leaves of any author, but bred amongst the weeds and tares of mine owne braine. And this is a conclusion from the equivocall and monstrous productions in the copulation of man with beast; for if the soule of man bee not transmitted and transfused in the seed of the parents, 30 why are not those productions meerely beasts, but have also an impression and tincture of reason in as high a measure as it can evidence it selfe in those improper organs? Nor truely can I peremptorily deny, that the soule in this her sublunary estate, is wholly and in all acceptions inorganicall, but that for the performance of her ordinary actions, is required not onely a symmetry and proper disposition of Organs, but a Crasis and temper correspondent to its operations; yet is not this masse of flesh and visible structure the instrument and proper corps of the soule, but rather of sense, and that the hand of reason. In our study of Anatomy 40 there is a masse of mysterious Philosophy, and such as reduced the very Heathens to Divinitie; yet amongst all those rare discoveries, and curious pieces I finde in the fabricke of man, I doe not so much content my selfe, as in that I finde not, that is no Organe or instrument for the rationall soule; for in the braine, which wee tearme the seate of reason, there is not any thing of moment more than I can discover in the cranie of a beast: and this is a sensible and no inconsiderable argument of the inorganity of the soule, at least in that sense we usually so receive it. Thus we are men, and we know not how, there is something in us, that can be without us, and will be after us, though it is strange that it hath no history, what it was 10 before us, nor cannot tell how it entred in us.

SECT. 37.

Now for these wals of flesh, wherein the soule doth seeme to be immured before the Resurrection, it is nothing but an elementall composition, and a fabricke that must fall to ashes; *All flesh is grasse*, is not onely metaphorically, but literally true, for all those creatures we behold, are but the hearbs of the field, digested into flesh in them, or more remotely carnified in our selves. Nay further, we are what we all abhorre, *Anthropophagi* and Cannibals, devourers not onely of men, but of our selves; and that not in an 20 allegory, but a positive truth; for all this masse of flesh which wee behold, came in at our mouths: this frame wee looke upon, hath beene upon our trenchers; In briefe, we have devoured our selves. I cannot beleeve the wisedome of *Pythagoras* did ever positively, and in a literall sense, affirme his *Metempsychosis*, or impossible transmigration of the soules of men into beasts: of all Metamorphoses or transmigrations, I beleeve onely one, that is of *Lots* wife, for that of *Nabuchodonosor* proceeded not so farre; In all others I conceive there is no further verity then is contained in their implicite sense and morality: I beleeve that the whole frame of 30 a beast doth perish, and is left in the same state after death, as before it was materialled unto life; that the soules of men know neither contrary nor corruption, that they subsist beyond the body, and outlive death by the priviledge of their proper natures, and without a miracle; that the soules of the faithfull, as they leave earth, take possession of Heaven: that those apparitions, and ghosts of departed persons are not the wandring soules of men, but the unquiet walkes of Devils, prompting and suggesting us unto mischiefe, bloud, and villany, instilling, & stealing into our hearts, that the blessed spirits are not at rest in their graves, but wander

14 must *Er MSS.*: may *42 43* 18 *Anthropophagi HJNOR 42b*: *Antropophagi O 42a* (*not in P*) 39 at *Er*: a *43*

solicitous of the affaires of the world. That those phantasmes appeare often, and doe frequent Cemiteries, charnall houses, and Churches, it is because those are the dormitories of the dead, where the Devill like an insolent Champion beholds with pride the spoyles and Trophies of his victory in *Adam*.

SECT. 38.

This is that dismall conquest we all deplore, that makes us so often cry (O) *Adam, quid fecisti?* I thanke God I have not those strait ligaments, or narrow obligations to the world, as to dote on life, or be convulst and tremble at the name of death: Not that I am insensible of the dread and horrour thereof, or by raking into the bowells of the deceased, continuall sight of Anatomies, Skeletons, or Cadaverous reliques, like Vespilloes, or Grave-makers, I am become stupid, or have forgot the apprehension of mortality, but that marshalling all the horrours, and contemplating the extremities thereof, I finde not any thing therein able to daunt the courage of a man, much lesse a well resolved Christian. And therefore am not angry at the errour of our first parents, or unwilling to beare a part of this common fate, and like the best of them to dye, that is, to cease to breathe, to take a farewell of the elements, to be a kinde of nothing for a moment, to be within one instant of a spirit. When I take a full view and circle of my selfe, without this reasonable moderator, and equall piece of justice, Death, I doe conceive my selfe the miserablest person extant; were there not another life that I hope for, all the vanities of this world should not intreat a moments breath from me; could the Devill worke my beliefe to imagine I could never dye, I would not out-live that very thought; I have so abject a conceit of this common way of existence, this retaining to the Sunne and Elements, I cannot thinke this is to be a man, or to live according to the dignitie of humanity; in expectation of a better I can with patience embrace this life, yet in my best meditations doe often desire death; I honour any man that contemnes it, nor can I highly love any that is afraid of it; this makes me naturally love a Souldier, and honour those tattered and contemptible Regiments that will die at the command of a Sergeant. For a Pagan there may bee some motives to bee in love with life, but for a Christian to be amazed at death, I see not how hee can escape this Dilemma, that he is too sensible of this life, or hopelesse of the life to come.

1 world. That] world; that *Er 42*: world; but *43*. *See Commentary*.
27 never *MSS.* / *42*: ever *43* 32 desire *MSS.* / *42*: defie *43*

SECT. 39.

Some Divines count *Adam* 30. yeares old at his creation, because they suppose him created in the perfect age and stature of man; and surely wee are all out of the computation of our age, and every man is some moneths elder than hee bethinkes him; for we live, move, have a being, and are subject to the actions of the elements, and the malice of diseases in that other world, the truest Microcosme, the wombe of our mother; for besides that generall and common existence wee are conceived to hold in our Chaos, and 10 whilst wee sleepe within the bosome of our causes, wee enjoy a being and life in three distinct worlds, wherein we receive most manifest graduations: In that obscure world and wombe of our mother, our time is short, computed by the Moone; yet longer than the dayes of many creatures that behold the Sunne, our selves being not yet without life, sense, and reason, though for the manifestation of its actions, it awaits the opportunity of objects; and seemes to live there but in its roote and soule of vegetation: entring afterwards upon the scene of the world, wee arise up and become another creature, performing the reasonable actions of 20 man, and obscurely manifesting that part of Divinity in us, but not in complement and perfection, till we have once more cast our secondine, that is, this slough of flesh, and are delivered into the last world, that is, that ineffable place of *Paul*, that proper *ubi* of spirits. The smattering I have of the Philosophers stone, (which is something more then the perfect exaltation of gold) hath taught me a great deale of Divinity, and instructed my beliefe, how that immortall spirit and incorruptible substance of my soule may lye obscure, and sleepe a while within this house of flesh. Those strange and mysticall transmigrations that I have observed in 30 Silkewormes, turn'd my Philosophy into Divinity. There is in these workes of nature, which seeme to puzle reason, something Divine, and hath more in it then the eye of a common spectator doth discover.

SECT. 40.

I am naturally bashfull, nor hath conversation, age, or travell, beene able to effront, or enharden me, yet I have one part of modesty, which I have seldome discovered in another, that is (to speake truly) I am not so much afraid of death, as ashamed thereof; tis the very disgrace and ignominy of our natures, that in a 40 moment can so disfigure us that our nearest friends, Wife, and Children stand afraid and start at us. The Birds and Beasts of the field that before in a naturall feare obeyed us, forgetting all allegiance begin to prey upon us. This very conceite hath in a tempest disposed and left me willing to be swallowed up in the abysse of waters; wherein I had perished unseene, unpityed, without wondring eyes, teares of pity, Lectures of mortality, and none had said, *quantum mutatus ab illo*! Not that I am ashamed of the Anatomy of my parts, or can accuse nature for playing the bungler in any part of me, or my owne vitious life for contracting any shamefull disease upon me, whereby I might not call my selfe as wholesome a morsell for the wormes as any.

SECT. 41. 10

Some upon the courage of a fruitfull issue, wherein, as in the truest Chronicle, they seem to outlive themselves, can with greater patience away with death. This conceit and counterfeit subsisting in our progenies seemes to mee a meere fallacy, unworthy the desires of a man, that can but conceive a thought of the next world; who, in a nobler ambition, should desire to live in his substance in Heaven rather than his name and shadow in the earth. And therefore at my death I meane to take a totall adieu of the world, not caring for a Monument, History, or Epitaph, not so much as the bare memory of my name to be found any where but in the 20 universall Register of God: I am not yet so Cynicall, as to approve the *Testament of *Diogenes*, nor doe I altogether allow that *Rodomontado* of *Lucan*;

——Cœlo tegitur, qui non habet urnam.
He that unburied lies wants not his Herse,
For unto him a tombe's the Vniverse.

But commend in my calmer judgement, those ingenuous intentions that desire to sleepe by the urnes of their Fathers, and strive to goe the nearest way unto corruption. I doe not envie the temper of Crowes and Dawes, nor the numerous and weary dayes 30 of our Fathers before the Flood. If there bee any truth in Astrology, I may outlive a Jubilee, as yet I have not seene one revolution of *Saturne*, nor hath my pulse beate thirty yeares, and yet excepting one, have seene the Ashes, and left under ground, all the Kings of *Europe*, have beene contemporary to three Emperours, foure Grand Signiours, and as many Popes; mee thinkes I have outlived my selfe, and begin to bee weary of the Sunne, I have shaked hands

* Who willed his friend not to bury him, but to hang him up with a staffe in his hand to fright away the Crowes.

---

29 nearest *MSS.* / *42*: neatest *43*

with delight in my warme blood and Canicular dayes, I perceive I doe Anticipate the vices of age, the world to mee is but a dreame, or mockshow, and wee all therein but Pantalones and Antickes to my severer contemplations.

SECT. 42.

It is not, I confesse, an unlawfull Prayer to desire to surpasse the dayes of our Saviour, or wish to out-live that age wherein he thought fittest to dye, yet, if (as Divinity affirmes) there shall be no gray hayres in Heaven, but all shall rise in the perfect state of
10 men, we doe but out-live those perfections in this world, to be recalled unto them, by a greater miracle in the next, and run on here but to be retrograde hereafter. Were there any hopes to out-live vice, or a point to be super-annuated from sin, it were worthy our knees to implore the dayes of *Methuselah*. But age doth not rectifie, but incurvate our natures, turning bad dispositions into worser habits, and (like diseases) brings on incurable vices; for every day as we grow weaker in age, we grow stronger in sinne, and the number of our dayes doth but make our sinnes innumerable. The same vice committed at sixteene, is not the same, though
20 it agree in all other circumstances, at forty, but swels and doubles from the circumstance of our ages, wherein besides the constant and inexcusable habit of transgressing, the maturity of our Judgement cuts off pretence unto excuse or pardon: every sin, the oftner it is committed, the more it acquireth in the quality of evill; as it succeeds in time, so it precedes in degrees of badnesse, for as they proceed they ever multiply, and like figures in Arithmeticke, the last stands for more than all that went before it: And though I thinke no man can live well once but hee that could live twice, yet for my owne part, I would not live over my houres past, or be-
30 ginne againe the thred of my dayes: not upon *Cicero's* ground, because I have lived them well, but for feare I should live them worse: I find my growing Judgement dayly instruct me how to be better, but my untamed affections and confirmed vitiosity makes mee dayly doe worse; I finde in my confirmed age the same sinnes I discovered in my youth, I committed many then because I was a child, and because I commit them still I am yet an Infant. Therefore I perceive a man may bee twice a child before the dayes of dotage, and stand in need of *Æsons* bath before threescore.

SECT. 43.

40 And truely there goes a great deale of providence to produce a mans life unto threescore; there is more required than an able

temper for those yeeres; though the radicall humour containe in it sufficient oyle for seventie, yet I perceive in some it gives no light past thirtie; men assigne not all the causes of long life that write whole bookes thereof. They that found themselves on the radicall balsome or vitall sulphur of the parts, determine not why *Abel* liv'd not so long as *Adam*. There is therefore a secret glome or bottome of our dayes; 'twas his wisedome to determine them, but his perpetuall and waking providence that fulfils and accomplisheth them, wherein the spirits, our selves, and all the creatures of God in a secret and disputed way doe execute his will. Let them 10 not therefore complaine of immaturitie that die about thirty, they fall but like the whole world, whose solid and well composed substance must not expect the duration and period of its constitution, when all things are compleated in it, its age is accomplished, and the last and generall fever may as naturally destroy it before six thousand, as me before forty; there is therfore some other hand that twines the thread of life than that of nature; wee are not onely ignorant in Antipathies and occult qualities, our ends are as obscure as our beginnings, the line of our dayes is drawne by night, and the various effects therein by a pencill that is 20 invisible; wherein though wee confesse our ignorance, I am sure we doe not erre, if wee say, it is the hand of God.

SECT. 44.

I am much taken with two verses of *Lucan*, since I have beene able not onely, as we doe at Schoole, to construe, but understand:

Victurosque Dei celant ut vivere durent,
Felix esse mori.
We're all deluded, vainely searching wayes,
To make us happy by the length of dayes;
For cunningly to make's protract this breath, 30
The Gods conceale the happines of Death.

There be many excellent straines in that Poet, wherewith his Stoicall Genius hath liberally supplyed him; and truely there are singular pieces in the Philosophy of *Zeno*, and doctrine of the Stoickes, which I perceive, delivered in a Pulpit, passe for currant Divinity: yet herein are they in extreames, that can allow a man to be his owne *Assassine*, and so highly extoll the end and suicide of *Cato*; this is indeed not to feare death, but yet to bee afraid of life. It is a brave act of valour to contemne death, but where life is

16 forty ;] *The semicolon is not clear in all copies.* 35 passe for *Er*: passe or *43* 39 of] of of *43*

more terrible than death, it is then the truest valour to dare to live, and herein Religion hath taught us a noble example: For all the valiant acts of *Curtius*, *Scevola* or *Codrus*, do not parallel or match that one of *Job*; and sure there is no torture to the racke of a disease, nor any Poynyards in death it selfe like those in the way or prologue unto it. *Emori nolo, sed me esse mortuum nihil curo*, I would not die, but care not to be dead. Were I of *Cæsars* Religion I should be of his desires, and wish rather to goe off at one blow, then to be sawed in peeces by the grating torture of a disease. Men that 10 looke no further than their outsides thinke health an appertinance unto life, and quarrell with their constitutions for being sick; but I that have examined the parts of man, and know upon what tender filaments that Fabrick hangs, doe wonder that we are not alwayes so; and considering the thousand dores that lead to death doe thanke my God that we can die but once. 'Tis not onely the mischiefe of diseases, and the villanie of poysons that make an end of us, we vainly accuse the fury of Gunnes, and the new inventions of death; 'tis in the power of every hand to destroy us, and wee are beholding unto every one wee meete hee doth not kill us. There is 20 therefore but one comfort left, that though it be in the power of the weakest arme to take away life, it is not in the strongest to deprive us of death: God would not exempt himselfe from that, the misery of immortality in the flesh, he undertooke not that was in it immortall. Certainly there is no happinesse within this circle of flesh, nor is it in the Opticks of these eyes to behold felicity; the first day of our Jubilee is death; the devill hath therefore fail'd of his desires; wee are happier with death than we should have beene without it: there is no misery but in himselfe where there is no end of misery; and so indeed in his own sense, the Stoick is in 30 the right. Hee forgets that hee can die who complaines of misery, wee are in the power of no calamitie while death is in our owne.

SECT. 45.

Now besides this literall and positive kinde of death, there are others whereof Divines make mention, and those I thinke, not meerely Metaphoricall, as Mortification, dying unto sin and the world; therefore, I say, every man hath a double Horoscope, one of his humanity, his birth; another of his Christianity, his baptisme, and from this doe I compute or calculate my Nativitie, not reckoning those *Horæ combustæ*, and odde dayes, or esteeming my selfe 40 any thing, before I was my Saviours, and inrolled in the Register of Christ: Whosoever enjoyes not this life, I count him but an apparition, though he weare about him the sensible affections of flesh. In these morall acceptions, the way to be immortall is to die daily, nor can I thinke I have the true Theory of death, when I contemplate a skull, or behold a Skeleton with those vulgar imaginations it casts upon us; I have therefore enlarged that common *Memento mori*, into a more Christian memorandum, *Memento quatuor novissima*, those foure inevitable points of us all, Death, Judgement, Heaven, and Hell. Neither did the contemplations of the Heathens rest in their graves, without a further thought of *Radamanth* or some judiciall proceeding after death, though in another way, and upon suggestion of their naturall reasons. I 10 cannot but marvaile from what *Sibyll* or Oracle they stole the prophesy of the worlds destruction by fire, or whence *Lucan* learned to say,

> *Communis mundo superest rogus, ossibus astra Misturus.*——
> *There yet remaines to th' world one common fire,*
> *Wherein our bones with stars shall make one pyre.*

I beleeve the world growes neare its end, yet is neither old nor decayed, nor will ever perish upon the ruines of its owne principles. As the worke of Creation was above nature, so is its adversary, annihilation; without which the world hath not its end, but its 20 mutation. Now what force should bee able to consume it thus farre, without the breath of God, which is the truest consuming flame, my Philosophy cannot informe me. Some beleeve there went not a minute to the worlds creation, nor shal there go to its destruction; those six dayes so punctually described, make not to them one moment, but rather seem to manifest the method and Idea of that great worke in the intellect of God, than the manner how hee proceeded in its operation. I cannot dreame that there should be at the last day any such Judiciall proceeding, or calling to the Barre, as indeed the Scripture seemes to imply, and 30 the literall commentators doe conceive: for unspeakable mysteries in the Scriptures are often delivered in a vulgar and illustrative way, and being written unto man, are delivered, not as they truely are, but as they may bee understood; wherein notwithstanding the different interpretations according to different capacities may stand firme with our devotion, nor bee any way prejudiciall to each single edification.

SECT. 46.

Now to determine the day and yeare of this inevitable time, is not onely convincible and statute madnesse, but also manifest 40

27 that *MSS.*: the *42 43* in the *MSS.*: of the *42 43*

impiety; How shall we interpret *Elias* 6000. yeares, or imagine the secret communicated to a Rabbi, which God hath denyed unto his Angels? It had beene an excellent quære, to have posed the devill of *Delphos*, and must needs have forced him to some strange amphibology; it hath not onely mocked the predictions of sundry Astrologers in ages past, but the prophecies of many melancholy heads in these present, who neither understanding reasonably things past or present, pretend a knowledge of things to come, heads ordained onely to manifest the incredible effects of melan-
10 choly, and to fulfill *old prophesies, rather than be the authors of new. [In those dayes there shall come warres and rumours of warres,] to me seemes no prophesie, but a constant truth, in all times verified since it was pronounced: There shall bee signes in the Moone and Starres, how comes he then like a theefe in the night, when he gives an item of his comming? That common signe drawne from the revelation of Antichrist is as obscure as any; in our common compute he hath beene come these many yeares, but for my owne part to speake freely, I am halfe of opinion that Antichrist is the Philosophers stone in Divinity, for the discovery
20 and invention whereof, though there be prescribed rules, and probable inductions, yet hath hardly any man attained the perfect discovery thereof. That generall opinion that the world growes neere its end, hath possessed all ages past as neerely as ours; I am afraid that the Soules that now depart, cannot escape that lingring expostulation of the Saints under the Altar, *Quousque Domine? How long, O Lord?* and groane in the expectation of the great Jubilee.

SECT. 47.

This is the day that must make good that great attribute of God, his Justice, that must reconcile those unanswerable doubts that
30 torment the wisest understandings, and reduce those seeming inequalities, and respective distributions in this world, to an equality and recompensive Justice in the next. This is that one day, that shall include and comprehend all that went before it, wherein as in the last scene, all the Actors must enter to compleate and make up the Catastrophe of this great peece. This is the day whose memory hath onely power to make us honest in the darke, and to bee vertuous without a witnesse. *Ipsa sui pretium virtus sibi*, that vertue is her owne reward, is but a cold principle, and not able to maintaine our variable resolutions in a constant and setled way of

* In those dayes there shall come lyers and false prophets.

---

37 *sui*] *suæ Er. See Commentary.*

goodnesse. I have practised that honest artifice of *Seneca*, and in my retired and solitary imaginations, to detaine me from the foulenesse of vice, have fancyed to my selfe the presence of my deare and worthiest friends, before whom I should lose my head, rather than be vitious, yet herein I found that there was nought but morall honesty, and this was not to be vertuous for his sake who must reward us at the last. I have tryed if I could reach that great resolution of his, to be honest without a thought of Heaven or Hell; and indeed I found upon a naturall inclination, and inbred loyalty unto vertue, that I could serve her without a livery, yet not in that 10 resolved and venerable way, but that the frailty of my nature, upon an easie temptation, might be induced to forget her. The life therefore and spirit of all our actions, is the resurrection, and stable apprehension, that our ashes shall enjoy the fruit of our pious endeavours; without this, all Religion is a Fallacy, and those impieties of *Lucian*, *Euripedes*, and *Julian* are no blasphemies, but subtile verities, and Atheists have beene the onely Philosophers.

SECT. 48.

How shall the dead arise, is no question of my faith; to beleeve onely possibilities, is not faith, but meere Philosophy; many things 20 are true in Divinity, which are neither inducible by reason, nor confirmable by sense, and many things in Philosophy confirmable by sense, yet not inducible by reason. Thus it is impossible by any solid or demonstrative reasons to perswade a man to beleeve the conversion of the Needle to the North; though this be possible, and true, and easily credible, upon a single experiment unto the sense. I beleeve that our estranged and divided ashes shall unite againe, that our separated dust after so many pilgrimages and transformations into the parts of mineralls, Plants, Animals, Elements, shall at the voyce of God returne into their primitive shapes; and joyne 30 againe to make up their primary and predestinate formes. As at the Creation, there was a separation of that confused masse into its species, so at the destruction thereof there shall bee a separation into its distinct individuals. As at the Creation of the world, all the distinct species that wee behold, lay involved in one masse, till the fruitfull voyce of God separated this united multitude into its severall species: so at the last day, when these corrupted reliques shall be scattered in the wildernesse of formes, and seeme to have forgot their proper habits, God by a powerfull voyce shall command them backe into their proper shapes, and call them out 40 by their single individuals: Then shall appeare the fertilitie of

9 and *MSS.* / *42*: an *43*

Adam, and the magicke of that sperme that hath dilated into so many millions. I have often beheld as a miracle, that artificiall resurrection and revivification of *Mercury*, how being mortified into thousand shapes, it assumes againe its owne, and returns into its numericall selfe. Let us speake naturally, and like Philosophers, the formes of alterable bodies in these sensible corruptions perish not; nor, as wee imagine, wholly quit their mansions, but retire and contract themselves into their secret and unaccessible parts, where they may best protect themselves from the action of their 10 Antagonist. A plant or vegetable consumed to ashes, to a contemplative and schoole Philosopher seemes utterly destroyed, and the forme to have taken his leave for ever: But to a sensible Artist the formes are not perished, but withdrawne into their incombustible part, where they lie secure from the action of that devouring element. This is made good by experience, which can from the ashes of a plant revive the plant, and from its cinders recall it into its stalk and leaves againe. What the Art of man can doe in these inferiour pieces, what blasphemy is it to affirme the finger of God cannot doe in these more perfect and sensible structures? This is 20 that mysticall Philosophy, from whence no true Scholler becomes an Atheist, but from the visible effects of nature, growes up a reall Divine, and beholds not in a dreame, as *Ezekiel*, but in an ocular and visible object the types of his resurrection.

SECT. 49.

Now, the necessary Mansions of our restored selves are those two contrary and incompatible places wee call Heaven and Hell; to define them, or strictly to determine what and where these are, surpasseth my Divinity. That elegant Apostle which seemed to have a glimpse of Heaven, hath left but a negative description 30 thereof; Which neither eye hath seen, nor eare hath heard, nor can enter into the heart of man: he was translated out of himself to behold it, but being returned into himselfe could not expresse it. Saint *Johns* description by Emeralds, Chrysolites, and pretious stones, is too weake to expresse the materiall Heaven we behold. Briefely therefore, where the soule hath the full measure, and complement of happinesse, where the boundlesse appetite of that spirit remaines compleatly satisfied, that it can neither desire addition nor alteration, that I thinke is truely Heaven: and this can onely be in the enjoyment of that essence, whose infinite good-40 nesse is able to terminate the desires of it selfe, and the unsatiable wishes of ours; where-ever God will thus manifest himselfe, there is

33 Saint] Saints *43*

Heaven, though within the circle of this sensible world. Thus the soule of man may bee in Heaven any where, even within the limits of his owne proper body, and when it ceaseth to live in the body, it may remaine in its owne soule, that is its Creator. And thus wee may say that Saint *Paul*, whether in the body, or out of the body, was yet in Heaven. To place it in the Empyreall, or beyond the tenth Spheare, is to forget the worlds destruction; for when this sensible world shall bee destroyed, all shall then be here as it is now there, an Empyreall Heaven, a *quasi* vacuitie, when to aske where Heaven is, is to demand where the presence of God is, or 10 where wee have the glory of that happy vision. *Moses* that was bred up in all the learning of the *Egyptians*, committed a grosse absurdity in Philosophy, when with these eyes of flesh he desired to see God, and petitioned his Maker, that is truth it selfe, to a contradiction. Those that imagine Heaven and Hell neighbours, and conceive a vicinity between those two extreames, upon consequence of the Parable, where *Dives* discoursed with *Lazarus* in *Abrahams* bosome, do too grossely conceive of those glorified creatures, whose eyes shall easily out-see the Sunne, and behold without a Perspective, the extremest distances: for if there shall be 20 in our glorified eyes, the faculty of sight & reception of objects I could thinke the visible species there to be in as unlimitable a way as now the intellectuall. I grant that two bodies placed beyond the tenth Spheare, or in a vacuity, according to *Aristotles* Philosophy, could not behold each other, because there wants a body or Medium to hand and transport the visible rayes of the object unto the sense; but when there shall be a generall defect of either Medium to convey, or light to prepare & dispose that Medium, and yet a perfect vision, wee must suspend the rules of our Philosophy, and make all good by a more absolute piece of Opticks. 30

SECT. 50.

I cannot tell how to say that fire is the essence of hell, I know not what to make of Purgatory, or conceive a flame that can either prey upon, or purifie the substance of a soule; those flames of sulphure mentioned in the Scriptures, I take not to be understood of this present Hell, but of that to come, where fire shall make up the complement of our tortures, & have a body or subject wherein to manifest its tyranny: Some who have had the honour to be textuarie in Divinity, are of opinion it shall be the same specificall fire with ours. This is hard to conceive, yet can I make good how 40 even that may prey upon our bodies, and yet not consume us: for

34 or *PJNOR*: nor *HW* 43

in this materiall world, there are bodies that persist invincible in the powerfullest flames, and though by the action of fire they fall into ignition and liquation, yet will they never suffer a destruction: I would gladly know how *Moses* with an actuall fire calcin'd, or burnt the golden Calfe into powder: for that mysticall mettle of gold, whose solary and celestiall nature I admire, exposed unto the violence of fire, grows onely hot and liquifies, but consumeth not: so when the consumable and volatile pieces of our bodies shall be refined into a more impregnable and fixed temper like gold, though 10 they suffer from the action of flames, they shall never perish, but lie immortall in the armes of fire. And surely if this frame must suffer onely by the action of this element, there will many bodies escape, and not onely Heaven, but earth will not bee at an end, but rather a beginning; For at present it is not earth, but a composition of fire, water, earth, and aire; but at that time spoyled of these ingredients, it shall appeare in a substance more like it selfe, its ashes. Philosophers that opinioned the worlds destruction by fire, did never dreame of annihilation, which is beyond the power of sublunary causes; for the last and proper action of that element 20 is but vitrification or a reduction of a body into Glasse; & therefore some of our Chymicks facetiously affirm, that at the last fire all shall be crystallized & reverberated into glasse, which is the utmost action of that element. Nor need we fear this term [annihilation] or wonder that God will destroy the workes of his Creation: for man subsisting, who is, and will then truely appeare a Microcosme, the world cannot bee said to be destroyed. For the eyes of God, and perhaps also of our glorified selves, shall as really behold and contemplate the world in its Epitome or contracted essence, as now it doth at large and in its dilated substance. In the 30 seed of a Plant to the eyes of God, and to the understanding of man, there exists, though in an invisible way, the perfect leaves, flowers, and fruit thereof: (for things that are in *posse* to the sense, are actually existent to the understanding.) Thus God beholds all things, who contemplates as fully his workes in their Epitome, as in their full volume, and beheld as amply the whole world in that little compendium of the sixth day, as in the scattered and dilated pieces of those five before.

SECT. 51.

Men commonly set forth the torments of Hell by fire, and the 40 extremity of corporall afflictions, and describe Hell in the same method that *Mahomet* doth Heaven. This indeed makes a noyse, and drums in popular eares: but if this be the terrible piece thereof, it is not worthy to stand in diameter with Heaven, whose happinesse consists in that part that is best able to comprehend it, that immortall essence, that translated divinity and colony of God, the soule. Surely though wee place Hell under earth, the Devils walke and purlue is about it; men speake too popularly who place it in those flaming mountaines, which to grosser apprehensions represent Hell. The heart of man is the place the devill dwels in; I feele somtimes a hell within my selfe, *Lucifer* keeps his court in my brest, *Legion* is revived in me. There are as many hels as *Anaxagoras* conceited worlds; there was more than one hell in *Magdalen*, 10 when there were seven devils; for every devill is an hell unto himselfe: hee holds enough of torture in his owne *ubi*, and needs not the misery of circumference to afflict him, and thus a distracted conscience here is a shadow or introduction unto hell hereafter; Who can but pity the mercifull intention of those hands that doe destroy themselves? the devill were it in his power would doe the like, which being impossible his miseries are endlesse, and he suffers most in that attribute wherein he is impassible, his immortality.

SECT. 52.

I thanke God, and with joy I mention it, I was never afraid of Hell, 20 nor never grew pale at the description of that place; I have so fixed my contemplations on Heaven, that I have almost forgot the Idea of Hell, and am afraid rather to lose the joyes of the one than endure the misery of the other; to be deprived of them is a perfect hell, & needs me thinkes no addition to compleate our afflictions; that terrible terme hath never detained me from sin, nor do I owe any good action to the name thereof: I feare God, yet am not afraid of him, his mercies make me ashamed of my sins, before his judgements afraid thereof: these are the forced and secondary method of his wisedome, which he useth but as the last remedy, and upon 30 provocation, a course rather to deterre the wicked, than incite the vertuous to his worship. I can hardly thinke there was ever any scared into Heaven, they goe the fairest way to Heaven, that would serve God without a Hell, other Mercenaries that crouch unto him in feare of Hell, though they terme themselves the servants, are indeed but the slaves of the Almighty.

SECT. 53.

And to be true, and speake my soule, when I survey the occurrences of my life, and call into account the finger of God, I can perceive nothing but an abysse and masse of mercies, either in generall 40 to mankind, or in particular to my selfe; and whether out of the

prejudice of my affection, or an inverting and partiall conceit of his mercies, I know not, but those which others terme crosses, afflictions, judgements, misfortunes, to me who enquire farther into them than their visible effects, they both appeare, and in event have ever proved the secret and dissembled favours of his affection. It is a singular piece of wisedome to apprehend truly, and without passion the workes of God, and so well to distinguish his justice from his mercy, as not to miscall those noble attributes; yet it is likewise an honest piece of Logick so to dispute and
10 argue the proceedings of God, as to distinguish even his judgements into mercies. For God is mercifull unto all, because better to the worst, than the best deserve, and to say he punisheth none in this world, though it be a Paradox, is no absurdity. To one that hath committed murther, if the Judge should onely ordaine a Fine, it were a madnesse to call this a punishment, and to repine at the sentence, rather than admire the clemency of the Judge. Thus our offences being mortall, and deserving not onely death, but damnation, if the goodnesse of God be content to traverse and passe them over with a losse, misfortune, or disease; what frensie were it
20 to terme this a punishment, rather than an extremity of mercy, and to groane under the rod of his judgements, rather than admire the Scepter of his mercies? Therefore to adore, honour, and admire him, is a debt of gratitude due from the obligation of our nature, states, and conditions; and with these thoughts, he that knowes them best, will not deny that I adore him; that I obtaine Heaven, and the blisse thereof, is accidentall, and not the intended worke of my devotion, it being a felicitie I can neither thinke to deserve, nor scarse in modesty to expect. For these two ends of us all, either as rewards or punishments, are mercifully
30 ordained and disproportionally disposed unto our actions, the one being so far beyond our deserts, the other so infinitely below our demerits.

SECT. 54.

There is no salvation to those that beleeve not in Christ, that is, say some, since his Nativity, and as Divinity affirmeth, before also; which makes me much apprehend the end of those honest Worthies and Philosophers which died before his Incarnation. It is hard to place those soules in Hell whose worthy lives doe teach us vertue on earth; methinks amongst those many subdivisions of
40 hell, there might have bin one Limbo left for these: What a strange vision will it be to see their poeticall fictions converted into verities,

8 not to *Er*: not *42 43* 14 should *Er*: should say *42 43*

& their imagined & fancied Furies, into reall Devils? how strange to them will sound the History of *Adam*, when they shall suffer for him they never heard of? when they that derive their Genealogy from the Gods, shall know they are the unhappy issue of sinfull man? It is an insolent part of reason to controvert the works of God, or question the justice of his proceedings; Could humility teach others, as it hath instructed me, to contemplate the infinite and incomprehensible distance betwixt the Creator and the creature, or did wee seriously perpend that one Simile of Saint *Paul*, *Shall the vessell say to the Potter*, *Why hast thou made me thus*? it would prevent these arrogant disputes of reason, nor would wee argue the definitive sentence of God, either to Heaven or Hell. Men that live according to the right rule and law of reason, live but in their owne kinde, as beasts doe in theirs; who justly obey the prescript of their natures, and therefore cannot reasonably demand a reward of their actions, as onely obeying the naturall dictates of their reason. It will therefore, and must at last appeare, that all salvation is through Christ; which verity I feare these great examples of vertue must confirme, and make it good, how the perfectest actions of earth have no title or claime unto Heaven.

SECT. 55.

Nor truely doe I thinke the lives of these or of any other were ever correspondent, or in all points conformable unto their doctrines; it is evident that *Aristotle* transgressed the rule of his owne Ethicks; the Stoicks that condemne passion, and command a man to laugh in *Phalaris* his Bull, could not endure without a groane a fit of the stone or collick. The *Scepticks* that affirmed they knew nothing, even in that opinion confuted themselves, and thought they knew more than all the world beside. *Diogenes* I hold to bee the most vaineglorious man of his time, and more ambitious in refusing all honours, than *Alexander* in rejecting none. Vice and the Devill put a fallacie upon our reasons and provoking us too hastily to run from it, entangle and profound us deeper in it. The Duke of *Venice*, that weds himselfe unto the Sea, by a ring of Gold, I will not argue of prodigality, because it is a solemnity of good use and consequence in the State. But the Philosopher that threw his money into the Sea to avoyd avarice, was a notorious prodigal. There is no road or ready way to vertue, it is not an easie point of art to disentangle our selves from this

3 when they that *MSS.* / *42*: when they *43* 28 knew *MSS.* / *42*: know *43* (*corrected Er*) confuted *POR*: confute *HJNW 42 43* 32–33 reasons . . . to] *line repeated 43*

riddle, or web of sin: To perfect vertue, as to Religion, there is required a Panoplia or compleat armour, that whilst we lye at close ward against one vice we lye not open to the vennie of another: And indeed wiser discretions that have the thred of reason to conduct them, offend without a pardon; whereas under heads may stumble without dishonour. There goe so many circumstances to piece up one good action, that it is a lesson to be good, and wee are forced to be vertuous by the booke. Againe, the practice of men holds not an equall pace, yea, and often runnes counter to their 10 Theory; we naturally know what is good, but naturally pursue what is evill: the Rhetoricke wherewith I perswade another cannot perswade my selfe: there is a depraved appetite in us, that will with patience heare the learned instructions of Reason; but yet performe no farther than agrees to its owne irregular Humour. In briefe, we all are monsters, that is, a composition of man and beast, wherein we must endeavour to be as the Poets fancy that wise man *Chiron*, that is, to have the Region of Man above that of Beast, and sense to sit but at the feete of reason. Lastly, I doe desire with God, that all, but yet affirme with men, that few shall 20 know salvation, that the bridge is narrow, the passage straite unto life; yet those who doe confine the Church of God, either to particular Nations, Churches, or Families, have made it farre narrower than our Saviour ever meant it.

SECT. 56.

The vulgarity of those judgements that wrap the Church of God in *Strabo's* cloake and restraine it unto Europe, seeme to mee as bad Geographers as *Alexander*, who thought hee had conquer'd all the world when hee had not subdued the halfe of any part thereof: For wee cannot deny the Church of God both in Asia and Africa, if we 30 doe not forget the peregrinations of the Apostles, the death of their Martyrs, the sessions of many, and even in our reformed judgement lawfull councells held in those parts in the minoritie and nonage of ours: nor must a few differences more remarkable in the eyes of man than perhaps in the judgement of God, excommunicate from heaven one another, much lesse those Christians who are in a manner all Martyrs, maintaining their faith in the noble way of persecution, and serving God in the fire, whereas we honour him but in the Sunshine. 'Tis true we all hold there is a number of Elect and many to be saved, yet take our opinions together, and 40 from the confusion thereof there will be no such thing as salvation, nor shall any one be saved; for first the Church of *Rome* condemneth

3 lye not *MSS. except W*: lye *W 42 43* 28 had not] not *43*

us, wee likewise them, the Sub-reformists and Sectaries sentence the Doctrine of our Church as damnable, the Atomist, or Familist reprobates all these, and all these them againe. Thus whilst the mercies of God doth promise us heaven, our conceits and opinions exclude us from that place. There must be therefore more than one Saint *Peter*, particular Churches and Sects usurpe the gates of heaven, and turne the key against each other, and thus we goe to heaven against each others wills, conceits and opinions, and with as much uncharity as ignorance, doe erre I feare in points, not onely of our own, but on anothers salvation. 10

SECT. 57.

I beleeve many are saved who to man seeme reprobated, and many are reprobated, who in the opinion and sentence of man, stand elected; there will appeare at the last day, strange, and unexpected examples, both of his justice and his mercy, and therefore to define either is folly in man, and insolency, even in the devils; those acute and subtill spirits, in all their sagacity, can hardly divine who shall be saved, which if they could prognostick, their labour were at an end; nor need they compasse the earth, seeking whom they may devoure. Those who upon a rigid application of 20 the Law, sentence *Solomon* unto damnation, condemne not onely him, but themselves, and the whole world; for by the letter, and written Word of God, we are without exception in the state of death, but there is a prerogative of God, and an arbitrary pleasure above the letter of his owne Law, by which alone wee can pretend unto salvation, and through which *Solomon* might be as easily saved as those who condemne him.

SECT. 58.

The number of those who pretend unto salvation, and those infinite 30 swarmes who thinke to passe through the eye of this Needle, have much amazed me. That name and compellation of *little Flocke*, doth not comfort but deject my devotion, especially when I reflect upon mine owne unworthinesse, wherein, according to my humble apprehensions, I am below them all. I beleeve there shall never be an Anarchy in Heaven, but as there are Hierarchies amongst the Angels, so shall there be degrees of priority amongst the Saints. Yet is it (I protest) beyond my ambition to aspire unto the first rankes, my desires onely are, and I shall be happy therein, to be but the last man, and bring up the Rere in Heaven.

SECT. 59.

Againe, I am confident, and fully perswaded, yet dare not take my oath of my salvation; I am as it were sure, and do beleeve, without all doubt, that there is such a City as *Constantinople*, yet for me to take my oath thereon, were a kinde of perjury, because I hold no infallible warrant from my owne sense to confirme me in the certainty thereof. And truely, though many pretend an absolute certainty of their salvation, yet when an humble soule shall contemplate her owne unworthinesse, she shall meete with many
10 doubts and suddainely finde how little wee stand in need of the precept of Saint *Paul*, *Worke out your salvation with feare and trembling*. That which is the cause of my election, I hold to be the cause of my salvation, which was the mercy, and beneplacit of God, before I was, or the foundation of the world. *Before Abraham was, I am*, is the saying of Christ, yet is it true in some sense if I say it of my selfe, for I was not onely before my selfe, but *Adam*, that is, in the Idea of God, and the decree of that Synod held from all Eternity. And in this sense, I say, the world was before the Creation, and at an end before it had a beginning; and thus was I dead before I was
20 alive, though my grave be *England*, my dying place was Paradise, and *Eve* miscarried of mee before she conceiv'd of *Cain*.

SECT. 60.

Insolent zeales that doe decry good workes and rely onely upon faith, take not away merit: for depending upon the efficacy of their faith, they enforce the condition of God, and in a more sophisticall way doe seeme to challenge Heaven. It was decreed by God, that onely those that lapt in the water like dogges, should have the honour to destroy the *Midianites*, yet could none of those justly challenge, or imagine hee deserved that honour thereupon. I doe
30 not deny, but that true faith, and such as God requires, is not onely a marke or token, but also a meanes of our Salvation, but where to finde this, is as obscure to me, as my last end. And if our Saviour could object unto his owne Disciples, & favourites, a faith, that to the quantity of a graine of Mustard seed, is able to remove mountaines; surely that which wee boast of, is not any thing, or at the most, but a remove from nothing. This is the Tenor of my beleefe, wherein, though there be many things singular, and to the humour of my irregular selfe, yet, if they square not with maturer Judgements, I disclaime them, and doe no further father
40 them, than the learned and best Judgements shall authorize them.

THE SECOND PART.

SECT. 1.

NOW for that other Vertue of Charity, without which Faith is a meer notion, and of no existence, I have ever endeavoured to nourish the mercifull disposition, and humane inclination I borrowed from my Parents, and regulate it to the written and prescribed Lawes of Charity; and if I hold the true Anatomy of my selfe, I am delineated & naturally framed to such a piece of vertue: for I am of a constitution so generall, that it consorts, and sympathizeth with all things; I have no antipathy, or rather Idio- 10 syncrasie, in dyet, humour, ayre, any thing; I wonder not at the *French*, for their dishes of frogges, snailes, and toadstooles, nor at the Jewes for Locusts and Grasse-hoppers, but being amongst them, make them my common viands; and I finde they agree with my stomach as well as theirs; I could digest a Sallad gathered in a Church-yard, as well as in a Garden. I cannot start at the presence of a Serpent, Scorpion, Lizard, or Salamander; at the sight of a Toad, or Viper, I finde in me no desire to take up a stone to destroy them. I feele not in my selfe those common antipathies that I can discover in others: Those nationall repugnances doe not touch 20 me, nor doe I behold with prejudice the *French*, *Italian*, *Spaniard*, or *Dutch*; but where I finde their actions in ballance with my Countreymens, I honour, love, and embrace them in the same degree; I was borne in the eighth Climate, but seeme for to bee framed, and constellated unto all; I am no Plant that will not prosper out of a Garden. All places, all ayres make unto me one Country; I am in *England*, every where, and under any meridian; I have beene shipwrackt, yet am not enemy with the sea or winds; I can study, play, or sleepe in a tempest. In briefe, I am averse from nothing, my conscience would give mee the lie if I should say I absolutely detest or hate any 30 essence but the Devill, or so at least abhorre any thing but that wee might come to composition. If there be any among those common objects of hatred I doe contemne and laugh at, it is that great enemy of reason, vertue and religion, the multitude, that numerous piece of monstrosity, which taken asunder seeme men, and the reasonable creatures of God; but confused together, make but one great beast, & a monstrosity more prodigious than Hydra; it is no breach of Charity to call these fooles, it is the stile all holy Writers have afforded them, set downe by *Solomon* in canonicall Scripture, and a point of our faith to beleeve so. Neither in the name of multitude 40

23 the same *Er*: some *42 43*

doe I onely include the base and minor sort of people; there is a rabble even amongst the Gentry, a sort of Plebeian heads, whose fancy moves with the same wheele as these; men in the same Levell with Mechanickes, though their fortunes doe somewhat guild their infirmities, and their purses compound for their follies. But as in casting account, three or foure men together come short in account of one man placed by himself below them: So neither are a troope of these ignorant Doradoes, of that true esteeme and value, as many a forlorne person, whose condition doth place them below 10 their feet. Let us speake like Politicians, there is a Nobility without Heraldry, a naturall dignity, whereby one man is ranked with another, another Filed before him, according to the quality of his desert, and preheminence of his good parts. Though the corruption of these times, and the byas of present practise wheele another way, thus it was in the first and primitive Common-wealths, and is yet in the integrity and Cradle of well-ordered polities, till corruption getteth ground, ruder desires labouring after that which wiser considerations contemn, every one having a liberty to amasse & heape up riches, and they a license or faculty to doe or 20 purchase any thing.

SECT. 2.

This generall and indifferent temper of mine, doth more neerely dispose mee to this noble vertue. It is a happinesse to be borne and framed unto vertue, and to grow up from the seeds of nature, rather than the inoculation and forced graffes of education; yet if we are directed only by our particular Natures, and regulate our inclinations by no higher rule than that of our reasons, we are but Moralists; Divinity will still call us Heathens. Therfore this great worke of charity, must have other motives, ends, and 30 impulsions: I give no almes to satisfie the hunger of my Brother, but to fulfill and accomplish the Will and Command of my God; I draw not my purse for his sake that demands it, but his that enjoyned it; I relieve no man upon the Rhetorick of his miseries, nor to content mine own commiserating disposition, for this is still but morall charity, and an act that oweth more to passion than reason. Hee that relieves another upon the bare suggestion and bowels of pity, doth not this so much for his sake as for his own: for by compassion we make anothers misery our own, & so by relieving them, we relieve our selves also. It is as erroneous a conceite to 40 redresse other mens misfortunes upon the common considerations of mercifull natures, that it may bee one day our own case, for this is a sinister and politick kind of charity, wherby we seem to bespeak the pities of men, in the like occasions; and truly I have observed that those professed Eleemosynaries, though in a croud or multitude, doe yet direct and place their petitions on a few and selected persons; there is surely a Physiognomy, which those experienced and Master Mendicants observe, whereby they instantly discover a mercifull aspect, and will single out a face, wherein they spy the signatures and markes of mercy: for there are mystically in our faces certaine characters which carry in them the motto of our Soules, wherein he that cannot read *A.B.C.* may read our natures. I hold moreover that there is a Phytognomy, or 10 Physiognomy, not onely of men, but of Plants, and Vegetables; and in every one of them, some outward figures which hang as signes or bushes of their inward formes. The finger of God hath left an inscription upon all his workes, not graphicall or composed of Letters, but of their severall formes, constitutions, parts, and operations, which aptly joyned together doe make one word that doth expresse their natures. By these Letters God cals the Starres by their names, and by this Alphabet *Adam* assigned to every creature a name peculiar to its Nature. Now there are besides these Characters in our faces, certaine mysticall figures in our 20 hands, which I dare not call meere dashes, strokes, *a la volee*, or at randome, because delineated by a pencill, that never workes in vaine; and hereof I take more particular notice, because I carry that in mine owne hand, which I could never read of, nor discover in another. *Aristotle*, I confesse, in his acute, and singular booke of Physiognomy, hath made no mention of Chiromancy, yet I beleeve the *Egyptians*, who were neerer addicted to those abstruse and mysticall sciences, had a knowledge therein, to which those vagabond and counterfeit *Egyptians* did after pretend, and perhaps retained a few corrupted principles, which sometimes might 30 verifie their prognostickes.

It is the common wonder of all men, how among so many millions of faces, there should be none alike; Now contrary, I wonder as much how there should be any; he that shall consider how many thousand severall words have beene carelesly and without study composed out of 24. Letters; withall how many hundred lines there are to be drawn in the fabrick of one man; shall easily finde that this variety is necessary: And it will bee very hard that they shall so concur as to make one portract like another. Let a Painter carelesly limbe out a Million of faces, and you shall finde 40 them all different, yea let him have his copy before him, yet after all his art there will remaine a sensible distinction; for the patterne

9 cannot *Er and MSS. except W*: can *W 42 43*

or example of every thing is the perfectest in that kind, whereof wee still come short, though wee transcend or goe beyond it, because herein it is wide and agrees not in all points unto its Copy. Nor doth the similitude of creatures disparage the variety of nature, nor any way confound the workes of God. For even in things alike, there is diversitie, and those that doe seeme to accord, doe manifestly disagree. And thus is Man like God, for in the same things that wee resemble him, wee are utterly different from him. There was never any thing so like another, as in all 10 points to concurre, there will ever some reserved difference slip in, to prevent the Identity, without which, two severall things would not be alike, but the same, which is impossible.

SECT. 3.

But to returne from Philosophy to Charity, I hold not so narrow a conceit of this vertue, as to conceive that to give almes, is onely to be Charitable, or thinke a piece of Liberality can comprehend the Totall of Charity; Divinity hath wisely divided the acts thereof into many branches, and hath taught us in this narrow way, many pathes unto goodnesse; as many wayes as we may doe good, 20 so many wayes we may bee Charitable; there are infirmities, not onely of body, but of soule, and fortunes, which doe require the mercifull hand of our abilities. I cannot contemn a man for ignorance but behold him with as much pity as I doe *Lazarus*. It is no greater Charity to cloath his body, than apparell the nakednesse of his Soule. It is an honourable object to see the reasons of other men weare our Liveries, and their borrowed understandings doe homage to the bounty of ours. It is the cheapest way of beneficence, and like the naturall charity of the Sunne illuminates another without obscuring it selfe. To be reserved and caitif in this part of 30 goodnesse, is the sordidest piece of covetousnesse, and more contemptible than the pecuniary avarice. To this (as calling my selfe a Scholler) I am obliged by the duty of my condition, I make not therefore my head a grave, but a treasure of knowledge; I intend no Monopoly, but a Community in learning; I study not for my owne sake onely, but for theirs that study not for themselves. I envy no man that knowes more than my selfe, but pity them that know lesse. I instruct no man as an exercise of my knowledge, or with an intent rather to nourish and keepe it alive in mine owne head, than beget and propagate it in his; and in the 40 midst of all my endeavours there is but one thought that dejects me, that my acquired parts must perish with my selfe, nor can bee

7 accrod] ac-accord *43* 17 acts *MSS. except W*: act *W 42 43*

Legacyed among my honoured Friends. I cannot fall out or contemne a man for an errour, or conceive why a difference in opinion should divide an affection: for controversies, disputes, and argumentations, both in Philosophy, and in Divinity, if they meete with discreet and peaceable natures, doe not infringe the Lawes of Charity. In all disputes so much as there is of passion, so much there is of nothing to the purpose, for then reason like a bad hound spends upon a false sent, and forsakes the question first started. And this is one reason why controversies are never determined, for though they be amply proposed, they are scarse at all 10 handled, they doe so swell with unnecessary Digressions, and the Parenthesis on the party, is often as large as the maine discourse upon the Subject. The Foundations of Religion are already established, and the principles of Salvation subscribed unto by all, there remaines not many controversies worth a passion, and yet never any disputed without, not onely in Divinity, but in inferiour Arts: What a Βατραχομυομαχία, and hot skirmish is betwixt S. and *T.* in *Lucian?* How doth Grammarians hack and slash for the Genitive case in * *Jupiter.* How doe they breake their owne pates to salve that of *Priscian? Si foret in terris, rideret Democritus.* Yea, even 20 amongst wiser militants, how many wounds have beene given, and credits slaine for the poore victory of an opinion or beggerly conquest of a distinction? Schollers are men of peace, they beare no armes, but their tongues are sharper then *Actius* his razor, their pens carry farther, and give a lowder report than thunder; I had rather stand in the shock of a Basilisco than in the fury of a mercilesse Pen. It is not meere zeale to Learning, or devotion to the Muses, that wiser Princes Patron the Arts, and carry an indulgent aspect unto Schollers, but a desire to have their names eternized by the memory of their writings, and a feare of the revengefull pen 30 of succeeding ages: for these are the men, that when they have played their parts, and had their *exits*, must step out and give the morall of their Scenes, and deliver unto posterity an Inventory of their vertues and vices. And surely there goes a great deale of conscience to the compiling of an History, and there is no reproach to the scandall of a Story; It is such an Authenticke kinde of falsehood that with authority belies our good names to all Nations and Posteritie.

* Whether *Jovis* or *Jupiteris.*

---

6 Charity. In all disputes] Charity in all disputes; *42 43. The weight of the MS. evidence is in favour of the punctuation adopted here.* 35 and there *MSS.* | *42*: there *43*

SECT. 4.

There is another offence unto Charity, which no Author hath ever written of, and few take notice of, and that's the reproach, not of whole professions, mysteries and conditions, but of whole nations, wherein by opprobrious Epithets wee miscall each other, and by an uncharitable Logicke from a disposition in a few conclude a habit in all.

Le mutin Anglois, et le bravache Escossois;
Le bougre Italien, et le fol Francois;
10 *Le poultron Romain, le larron de Gascongne,*
L'Espagnol superbe, et l' Aleman yurongne.

Saint *Paul* that cals the *Cretians* lyers, doth it but indirectly and upon quotation of their owne Poet. It is as bloody a thought in one way as *Neroes* was in another. For by a word wee wound a thousand, and at one blow assassine the honour of a Nation. It is as compleate a piece of madnesse to miscall and rave against the times, or thinke to recall men to reason, by a fit of passion: *Democritus* that thought to laugh the times into goodnesse, seemes to mee as deepely Hypochondriack, as *Heraclitus* that bewailed them; it 20 moves not my spleene to behold the multitude in their proper humours, that is, in their fits of folly and madnesse, as well understanding that Wisedome is not prophan'd unto the World, and 'tis the priviledge of a few to be vertuous. They that endeavour to abolish vice destroy also vertue, for contraries, though they destroy one another, are yet the life of one another. Thus vertue (abolish vice) is an Idea; againe, the communitie of sinne doth not disparage goodnesse; for when vice gaines upon the major part, vertue, in whom it remaines, becomes more excellent, and being lost in some, multiplies its goodnesse in others which remaine 30 untouched, and persists intire in the generall inundation. I can therefore behold vice without a Satyre, content onely with an admonition, or instructive reprehension; for Noble natures, and such as are capable of goodnesse, are railed into vice, that might as easily bee admonished into vertue; and we should be all so farre the Orators of goodnesse, as to protect her from the power of vice, and maintaine the cause of injured truth. No man can justly censure or condemne another, because indeed no man truely knowes another. This I perceive in my selfe, for I am in the darke to all the world, and my nearest friends behold mee but in a cloud,

25 the life *Er*: in life *42 43* 31 Satyre, content onely *MSS.*: Satyre content onely, *43*

those that know mee but superficially, thinke lesse of me than I doe of my selfe; those of my neere acquaintance thinke more; God, who truely knowes me, knowes that I am nothing, for hee onely beholds me, and all the world, who lookes not on us through a derived ray, or a trajection of a sensible species, but beholds the substance without the helpe of accidents, and the formes of things, as wee their operations. Further, no man can judge another, because no man knowes himselfe, for we censure others but as they disagree from that humour which wee fancy laudable in our selves, and commend others but for that wherein they seeme to quadrate 10 and consent with us. So that in conclusion, all is but that we all condemne, selfe-love. 'Tis the generall complaint of these times, and perhaps of those past, that charity growes cold; which I perceive most verified in those which most doe manifest the fires and flames of zeale; for it is a vertue that best agrees with coldest natures, and such as are complexioned for humility: But how shall we expect charity towards others, when we are uncharitable to our selves? Charity begins at home, is the voyce of the world, yet is every man his owne greatest enemy, and as it were, his owne executioner. *Non occides*, is the Commandement of God, yet 20 scarse observed by any man; for I perceive every man is his owne *Atropos*, and lends a hand to cut the thred of his owne dayes. *Cain* was not therefore the first murtherer, but *Adam*, who brought in death; whereof hee beheld the practise and example in his owne sonne *Abel*, and saw that verified in the experience of another; which faith could not perswade him in the Theory of himselfe.

SECT. 5.

There is I thinke no man that apprehends his owne miseries lesse than my selfe, and no man that so neerely apprehends anothers. I could lose an arme without a teare, and with few groans, mee 30 thinkes, be quartered into pieces; yet can I weepe most seriously at a Play, and receive with a true passion, the counterfeit griefes of those knowne and professed impostures. It is a barbarous part of inhumanity to adde unto any afflicted parties misery, or endeavour to multiply in any man, a passion, whose single nature is already above his patience; this was the greatest affliction of *Job*, and those oblique expostulations of his friends a deeper injury than the downe-right blowes of the Devill. It is not the teares of our owne eyes onely, but of our friends also, that doe exhaust the current of our sorrowes, which falling into many streames, runnes more 40

6 helpe *MSS.*: helpes *42 43* 19 his owne *MSS.* / *42*: his *43*
21 his owne *Er*: her owne *43* 40 runnes *P*: runne *other MSS.* *42 43*

peaceably, and is contented with a narrower channel. It is an act within the power of charity, to translate a passion out of one breast into another, and to divide a sorrow almost out of it selfe; for an affliction like a dimension may be so divided, as if not indivisible, at least to become insensible. Now with my friend I desire not to share or participate, but to engrosse his sorrowes, that by making them mine owne, I may more easily discusse them; for in mine owne reason, and within my selfe I can command that, which I cannot entreate without my selfe, and within the circle of
10 another. I have often thought those Noble paires and examples of friendship not so truely Histories of what had beene, as fictions of what should be, but I now perceive nothing in them, but possibilities, nor any thing in the Heroick examples of *Damon* and *Pythias*, *Achilles* and *Patroclus*, which mee thinkes upon some grounds I could not performe within the narrow compasse of my selfe. That a man should lay down his life for his friend, seemes strange to vulgar affections, and such as confine themselves within that worldly principle, Charity beginnes at home. For mine owne part I could never remember the relations that I hold unto my selfe, nor
20 the respect that I owe unto mine owne nature, in the cause of God, my Country, and my Friends. Next to these three, I doe embrace my selfe; I confesse I doe not observe that order that the Schooles ordaine our affections, to love our Parents, Wifes, Children, and then our Friends, for excepting the injunctions of Religion, I doe not find in my selfe such a necessary and indissoluble Sympathy to all those of my bloud. I hope I doe not breake the fifth Commandement, if I conceive I may love my friend before the nearest of my bloud, even those to whom I owe the principles of life; I never yet cast a true affection on a Woman, but I have loved my Friend as I
30 do vertue, my soule, my God. From hence me thinkes I doe conceive how God loves man, what happinesse there is in the love of God. Omitting all other, there are three most mysticall unions; Two natures in one person; three persons in one nature; one soule in two bodies. For though indeed they bee really divided, yet are they so united, as they seeme but one, and make rather a duality then two distinct soules.

SECT. 6.

There are wonders in true affection, it is a body of *Ænigmaes*, mysteries and riddles, wherein two so become one, as they both
40 become two; I love my friend before my selfe, and yet me thinkes I do not love him enough; some few months hence my multiplyed

19 hold *MSS.*: held *42 43*

affection will make me beleeve I have not loved him at all, when I am from him, I am dead till I bee with him, when I am with him, I am not satisfied, but would still be nearer him: united soules are not satisfied with embraces, but desire to be truely each other, which being impossible, their desires are infinite, and must proceed without a possibility of satisfaction. Another misery there is in affection, that whom we truely love like our owne selves, wee forget their lookes, nor can our memory retaine the Idea of their faces; and it is no wonder, for they are our selves, and our affections make their lookes our owne. This noble affection fals not on 10 vulgar and common constitutions, but on such as are mark'd for vertue; he that can love his friend with this noble ardour, will in a competent degree affect all. Now if wee can bring our affections to looke beyond the body, and cast an eye upon the soule, wee have found out the true object, not onely of friendship but charity; and the greatest happinesse that wee can bequeath the soule, is that wherein we all doe place our last felicity, Salvation, which though it bee not in our power to bestow, it is in our charity, and pious invocations to desire, if not procure, and further. I cannot contentedly frame a Prayer for my selfe in particular, without a 20 catalogue for my friends, nor request a happinesse wherein my sociable disposition doth not desire the fellowship of my neighbour. I never heare the Toll of a passing Bell, though in my mirth, without my prayers and best wishes for the departing spirit; I cannot goe to cure the body of my Patient, but I forget my profession, and call unto God for his soule; I cannot see one say his Prayers, but in stead of imitating him, I fall into a supplication for him, who perhaps is no more to mee than a common nature: and if God hath vouchsafed an eare to my supplications, there are surely many happy that never saw me, and enjoy the blessing of 30 mine unknowne devotions. To pray for enemies, that is, for their salvation, is no harsh precept, but the practise of our daily and ordinary devotions. I cannot beleeve the story of the Italian, our bad wishes and uncharitable desires proceed no further than this life; it is the Devill, and the uncharitable votes of Hell, that desire our misery in the world to come.

SECT. 7.

To doe no injury, nor take none, was a principle, which to my former yeares, and impatient affections, seemed to containe enough of morality, but my more setled yeares and Christian 40

7 owne selves *HJW 42*: owne *P43*: selves *NOR* 9–10 our affections make *JNOW*: our affections makes *H 42 43*: affection makes *P*: affections make *R*

constitution have fallen upon severer resolutions. I can hold there is no such thing as injury, that if there be, there is no such injury as revenge, and no such revenge as the contempt of an injury; that to hate another, is to maligne himselfe, that the truest way to love another, is to despise our selves. I were unjust unto mine owne conscience, if I should say I am at variance with any thing like my selfe, I finde there are many pieces in this one fabricke of man; this frame is raised upon a masse of Antipathies: I am one mee thinkes, but as the world; wherein notwithstanding there are a
10 swarme of distinct essences, and in them another world of contrarieties; wee carry private and domesticke enemies within, publike and more hostile adversaries without. The Devill that did but buffet Saint *Paul*, playes mee thinkes at sharpe with me: Let mee be nothing if within the compasse of my selfe, I doe not find the battell of *Lepanto*, passion against reason, reason against faith, faith against the Devill, and my conscience against all. There is another man within mee that's angry with mee, rebukes, commands, and dastards mee. I have no conscience of Marble to resist the hammer of more heavie offences, nor yet so soft and waxen, as
20 to take the impression of each single peccadillo or scape of infirmity: I am of a strange beliefe, that it is as easie to be forgiven some sinnes, as to commit some others. For my originall sinne, I hold it to be washed away in my Baptisme; for my actuall transgressions, I compute and reckon with God, but from my last repentance, Sacrament or generall absolution: And therefore am not terrified with the sinnes or madnesse of my youth. I thanke the goodnesse of God I have no sinnes that want a name, I am not singular in offences, my transgressions are Epidemicall, and from the common breath of our corruption. For there are certaine
30 tempers of body, which matcht with an humorous depravity of mind, doe hatch and produce viciosities, whose newnesse and monstrosity of nature admits no name; this was the temper of that Lecher that carnald with a Statua, and the constitution of *Nero* in his Spintrian recreations. For the heavens are not onely fruitfull in new and unheard of starres, the earth in plants and animals, but mens minds also in villany and vices; now the dulnesse of my reason, and the vulgarity of my disposition, never prompted my invention, nor sollicited my affection unto any of these; yet even those common and *quotidian* infirmities that so necessarily attend
40 me, and doe seeme to bee my very nature, have so dejected me,

6 should] shoul *43* 15 passion against reason *Er P*: passion against passion *42 43 and MSS. except P* 19 so *Er*: too *43* 25 or generall *Er*: or *42 43 and MSS.*

so broken the estimation that I should have otherwise of my selfe, that I repute my selfe the most abjectest piece of mortality: Divines prescribe a fit of sorrow to repentance, there goes indignation, anger, contempt and hatred, into mine, passions of a contrary nature, which neither seeme to sute with this action, nor my proper constitution. It is no breach of charity to our selves to be at variance with our vices, nor to abhorre that part of us, which is an enemy to the ground of charity, our God; wherein wee doe but imitate our great selves the world, whose divided Antipathies and contrary faces doe yet carry a charitable regard unto the whole, by their particular discords preserving the common harmony, and keeping in fetters those powers, whose rebellions once Masters, might bee the ruine of all.

SECT. 8.

I thanke God, amongst those millions of vices I doe inherit and hold from *Adam*, I have escaped one, and that a mortall enemy to charity, the first and father sin, not only of man, but of the devil, Pride, a vice whose name is comprehended in a Monosyllable, but in its nature not circumscribed with a world; I have escaped it in a condition that can hardly avoid it: those petty acquisitions and reputed perfections that advance and elevate the conceits of other men, adde no feathers unto mine; I have seene a Grammarian toure, and plume himselfe over a single line in *Horace*, and shew more pride in the construction of one Ode, than the Author in the composure of the whole book. For my owne part, besides the *Jargon* and *Patois* of severall Provinces, I understand no lesse then six Languages, yet I protest I have no higher conceit of my selfe than had our Fathers before the confusion of *Babel*, when there was but one Language in the world, and none to boast himselfe either Linguist or Criticke. I have not onely seene severall Countries, beheld the nature of their climes, the Chorography of their Provinces, Topography of their Cities, but understood their severall Lawes, Customes and Policies; yet cannot all this perswade the dulnesse of my spirit unto such an opinion of my self, as I behold in nimbler & conceited heads, that never looked a degree beyond their nests. I know the names, and somewhat more, of all the constellations in my Horizon, yet I have seene a prating Mariner that could onely name the Poynters and the North Starre, out-talke

1 otherwise of my selfe *Er P*: otherwise *42 43 and MSS. except P*
4 contempt and *MSS. except W*: sorrow, *W 42 43* 11 whole, . . . discords] whole . . . discords, *42 43. The weight of the MS. evidence is in favour of the punctuation adopted.* 19 nature not *Er*: nature *43*

mee, and conceit himselfe a whole Spheare above mee. I know most of the Plants of my Country and of those about mee; yet me thinkes I do not know so many as when I did but know an hundred, and had scarcely ever Simpled further than Cheap-side: for indeed heads of capacity, and such as are not full with a handfull, or easie measure of knowledg, thinke they know nothing, till they know all, which being impossible, they fall upon the opinion of *Socrates*, and onely know they know not any thing. I cannot thinke that *Homer* pin'd away upon the riddle of the Fisherman,
10 or that *Aristotle*, who understood the uncertainty of knowledge, and confessed so often the reason of man too weake for the workes of nature, did ever drowne himselfe upon the flux and reflux of *Euripus*: wee doe but learne to day, what our better advanced judgements will unteach us to morrow: and *Aristotle* doth but instruct us as *Plato* did him; that is, to confute himselfe. I have runne through all sects, yet finde no rest in any, though our first studies & *junior* endeavors may stile us Peripateticks, Stoicks, or Academicks, yet I perceive the wisest heads prove at last, almost all Scepticks, and stand like *Janus* in the field of knowledge. I have
20 therefore on common and authentick Philosophy I learned in the Schooles, whereby I discourse and satisfie the reason of other men, another more reserved and drawne from experience, whereby I content mine owne. *Solomon* that complained of ignorance in the height of knowledge, hath not onely humbled my conceits, but discouraged my endeavours. There is yet another conceit that hath sometimes made me shut my bookes; which tels mee it is a vanity to waste our dayes in the blind pursuit of knowledge, it is but attending a little longer, and wee shall enjoy that by instinct and infusion which we endeavour at here by labour and inquisition:
30 it is better to sit downe in a modest ignorance, & rest contented with the naturall blessing of our owne reasons, then buy the uncertaine knowledge of this life, with sweat and vexation, which death gives every foole gratis, and is an accessary of our glorification.

SECT. 9.

I was never yet once, and commend their resolutions who never marry twice, not that I disallow of second marriage; as neither in all cases of Polygamy, which considering some times and the unequall number of both sexes may bee also necessary. The whole

14 unteach us *P*: teach us *other MSS.*: teach *42*: unteach *43* 16 sects *MSS.* (*R has* sexts): sorts *42 43* 29 at *Er*: all *43* 36 commend *Er*: commend not *43*

world was made for man, but the twelfth part of man for woman: man is the whole world and the breath of God, woman the rib and crooked piece of man. I could be content that we might procreate like trees, without conjunction, or that there were any way to perpetuate the world without this triviall and vulgar way of coition; It is the foolishest act a wise man commits in all his life, nor is there any thing that will more deject his coold imagination, when hee shall consider what an odde and unworthy piece of folly hee hath committed; I speake not in prejudice, nor am averse from that sweet sexe, but naturally amorous of all that is beautifull; I can looke a whole day with delight upon a handsome picture, though it be but of an Horse. It is my temper, & I like it the better, to affect all harmony, and sure there is musicke even in the beauty, and the silent note which *Cupid* strikes, farre sweeter than the sound of an instrument. For there is a musicke where-ever there is a harmony, order or proportion; and thus farre we may maintain the musick of the spheares; for those well ordered motions, and regular paces, though they give no sound unto the eare, yet to the understanding they strike a note most full of harmony. Whatsoever is harmonically composed, delights in harmony; which makes me much distrust the symmetry of those heads which declaime against all Church musicke. For my selfe, not only from my obedience but my particular genius, I doe imbrace it; for even that vulgar and Taverne Musicke, which makes one man merry, another mad, strikes in mee a deepe fit of devotion, and a profound contemplation of the first Composer, there is something in it of Divinity more than the eare discovers. It is an Hieroglyphicall and shadowed lesson of the whole world, and Creatures of God, such a melody to the eare, as the whole world well understood, would afford the understanding. In briefe, it is a sensible fit of that Harmony, which intellectually sounds in the eares of God. I will not say with *Plato*, the Soule is an Harmony, but harmonicall, and hath its neerest sympathy unto musicke: thus some, whose temper of body agrees, and humours the constitution of their soules, are borne Poets, though indeed all are naturally inclined unto Rhythme. *This made *Tacitus* in the very first line of his Story, fall upon a verse; and *Cicero*, the worst of Poets, but *declayming for a Poet, falls in the very first sentence upon a perfect *Hexameter. I feele not in me those sordid, and unchristian

* *Vrbem Romam in principio Reges habuere.* * *Pro Archia Poeta.*
* *In qua me non inficior mediocriter esse.*

7 coold imagination *Er*: imagination coold *43*

desires of my profession, I doe not secretly implore and wish for Plagues, rejoyce at Famines, revolve Ephemerides, and Almanacks, in expectation of malignant Aspects, fatall conjunctions, and Eclipses: I rejoyce not at unwholsome Springs, nor unseasonable Winters; my Prayer goes with the Husbandmans; I desire every thing in its proper season, that neither men nor the times bee out of temper. Let mee be sicke my selfe, if sometimes the malady of my patient be not a disease unto me, I desire rather to cure his infirmities than my owne necessities, where I do him no good me
10 thinkes it is scarce honest gaine, though I confesse 'tis but the worthy salary of our well-intended endeavours: I am not onely ashamed, but heartily sorry, that besides death, there are diseases incurable, yet not for my own sake, or that they be beyond my art, but for the general cause & sake of humanity whose common cause I apprehend as mine own: And to speak more generally, those three Noble professions which all civil Common wealths doe honour, are raised upon the fall of *Adam*, & are not any exempt from their infirmities; there are not onely diseases incurable in Physicke, but cases indissoluble in Lawe, Vices incorrigible in
20 Divinity: if general Councells may erre, I doe not see why particular Courts should be infallible, their perfectest rules are raised upon the erroneous reason of Man, and the Lawes of one, doe but condemn the rules of another; as *Aristotle* oft-times the opinions of his predecessours, because, though agreeable to reason, yet were not consonant to his owne rules, and the Logicke of his proper principles. Againe, to speake nothing of the sinne against the Holy Ghost, whose cure not onely, but whose nature is unknowne; I can cure the gout or stone in some, sooner than Divinity, Pride, or Avarice in others. I can cure vices by Physicke, when they
30 remaine incurable by Divinity, and shall obey my pils, when they contemne their precepts. I boast nothing, but plainely say, we all labour against our owne cure, for death is the cure of all diseases. There is no Catholicon or universall remedy I know but this, which thogh nauseous to queasie stomachs, yet to prepared appetites is Nectar and a pleasant potion of immortality.

SECT. 10.

For my conversation, it is like the Sunne's with all men, and with a friendly aspect to good and bad. Me thinkes there is no man bad, and the worst, best; that is, while they are kept within the circle
40 of those qualities, wherein they are good: there is no mans minde

16 all] al *43* 19 Lawe *MSS.*: Lawes *42 43* 22 reason *MSS. except W*: reasons *W 42 43*

of such discordant and jarring a temper to which a tuneable disposition may not strike a harmony. *Magnæ virtutes nec minora vitia*, it is the posie of the best natures, and may bee inverted on the worst; there are in the most depraved and venemous dispositions, certaine pieces that remaine untoucht; which by an Antiperistasis become more excellent, or by the excellency of their antipathies are able to preserve themselves from the contagion of their enemy vices, and persist entire beyond the generall corruption. For it is also thus in nature. The greatest Balsames doe lie enveloped in the bodies of most powerfull Corrosives; I say moreover, and I ground 10 upon experience, that poysons containe within themselves their owne Antidote, and that which preserves them from the venom of themselves; without which they were not deleterious to others onely, but to themselves also. But it is the corruption that I feare within me, not the contagion of commerce without me. 'Tis that unruly regiment within me that will destroy me, 'tis I that doe infect my selfe, the man without a Navell yet lives in me; I feele that originall canker corrode and devoure me, and therefore *Defenda me Dios de me*, Lord deliver me from my selfe, is a part of my Letany, and the first voyce of my retired imaginations. There 20 is no man alone, because every man is a *Microcosme*, and carries the whole world about him; *Nunquam minus solus quam cum solus*, though it bee the Apophthegme of a wise man, is yet true in the mouth of a foole; for indeed, though in a Wildernesse, a man is never alone, not onely because hee is with himselfe, and his owne thoughts, but because he is with the devill, who ever consorts with our solitude, and is that unruly rebell that musters up those disordered motions, which accompany our sequestred imaginations: And to speake more narrowly, there is no such thing as solitude, nor any thing that can be said to be alone, and by it selfe, 30 but God, who is his owne circle, and can subsist by himselfe, all others besides their dissimilary and Heterogeneous parts, which in a manner multiply there natures, cannot subsist without the concourse of God, and the society of that hand which doth uphold their natures. In briefe, there can be nothing truely alone, and by its self, which is not truely one, and such is onely God: All others doe transcend an unity, and so by consequence are many.

SECT. II.

Now for my life, it is a miracle of thirty yeares, which to relate, were not a History, but a peece of Poetry, and would sound to 40

9 nature *MSS.*: natures *42 43* 13 deleterious] deletorious *HRW 42 43*
33 there *Er*: the *43*

common eares like a fable; for the world, I count it not an Inne, but an Hospitall, and a place, not to live, but to die in. The world that I regard is my selfe, it is the Microcosme of mine owne frame, that I cast mine eye on; for the other, I use it but like my Globe, and turne it round sometimes for my recreation. Men that look upon my outside, perusing onely my condition, and fortunes, do erre in my altitude; for I am above *Atlas* his shoulders. The earth is a point not onely in respect of the heavens above us, but of that heavenly and celestial part within us: that masse of flesh that 10 circumscribes me, limits not my mind: that surface that tells the heavens it hath an end, cannot perswade me I have any; I take my circle to be above three hundred and sixty, though the number of the Arke do measure my body, it comprehendeth not my minde: whilst I study to finde how I am a Microcosme or little world, I finde my selfe something more than the great. There is surely a peece of Divinity in us, something that was before the Elements, and owes no homage unto the Sun. Nature tels me I am the Image of God as well as Scripture; he that understands not thus much, hath not his introduction or first lesson, and is yet to begin the 20 Alphabet of man. Let me not injure the felicity of others, if I say I am as happy as any, *Ruat cœlum Fiat voluntas tua*, salveth all; so that whatsoever happens, it is but what our daily prayers desire. In briefe, I am content, and what should providence adde more? Surely this is it wee call Happinesse, and this doe I enjoy, with this I am happy in a dreame, and as content to enjoy a happinesse in a fancie as others in a more apparent truth and reality. There is surely a neerer apprehension of any thing that delights us in our dreames, than in our waked senses; without this I were unhappy, for my awaked judgement discontents me, ever whispering unto 30 me, that I am from my friend, but my friendly dreames in the night requite me, and make me thinke I am within his armes. I thanke God for my happy dreames, as I doe for my good rest, for there is a satisfaction in them unto reasonable desires, and such as can be content with a fit of happinesse; and surely it is not a melancholy conceite to thinke we are all asleepe in this world, and that the conceits of this life are as meare dreames to those of the next, as the Phantasmes of the night, to the conceits of the day. There is an equall delusion in both, and the one doth but seeme to bee the embleme or picture of the other; we are somewhat more 40 than our selves in our sleepes, and the slumber of the body seemes to bee but the waking of the soule. It is the ligation of sense, but the liberty of reason, and our awaking conceptions doe not match

37 conceits *MSS. except R*: conceit *R 42 43*

the fancies of our sleepes. At my Nativity, my ascendant was the watery signe of *Scorpius*, I was borne in the Planetary houre of *Saturne*, and I think I have a peece of that Leaden Planet in me. I am no way facetious, nor disposed for the mirth and galliardize of company, yet in one dreame I can compose a whole Comedy, behold the action, apprehend the jests, and laugh my selfe awake at the conceits thereof; were my memory as faithfull as my reason is then fruitfull, I would never study but in my dreames, and this time also would I chuse for my devotions, but our grosser memories have then so little hold of our abstracted understandings, that 10 they forget the story, and can only relate to our awaked soules, a confused & broken tale of that that hath passed. *Aristotle*, who hath written a singular tract of sleepe, hath not me thinkes throughly defined it, nor yet *Galen*, though hee seeme to have corrected it; for those *Noctambuloes* or night-walkers, though in their sleepe, doe yet enjoy the action of their senses: wee must therefore say that there is something in us that is not in the jurisdiction of *Morpheus*; and that those abstracted and ecstaticke soules doe walke about in their owne corps, as spirits with the bodies they assume, wherein they seeme to heare, see, and feele, 20 though indeed the organs are destitute of sense, and their natures of those faculties that should informe them. Thus it is observed that men sometimes upon the houre of their departure, doe speake and reason above themselves. For then the soule begins to bee freed from the ligaments of the body, begins to reason like her selfe, and to discourse in a straine above mortality.

SECT. 12.

We tearme sleepe a death, and yet it is waking that kils us, and destroyes those spirits that are the house of life. Tis indeed a part of life that best expresseth death, for every man truely lives so 30 long as hee acts his nature, or someway makes good the faculties of himselfe: *Themistocles* therefore that slew his Souldier in his sleepe was a mercifull executioner, 'tis a kinde of punishment the mildnesse of no lawes hath invented; I wonder the fancy of *Lucan* and *Seneca* did not discover it. It is that death by which we may be literally said to die daily, a death which *Adam* died before his mortality; a death whereby we live a middle and moderating point betweene life and death; in fine, so like death, I dare not trust it without my prayers, and an halfe adiew unto the world, and take my farewell in a Colloquy with God. 40

2 watery *Er*: earthly *42 43*: earthie [*or* earthly] *MSS.* 15 or night-walkers *P*: *phrase not in other MSS. nor in 42*: and night-walkers *43*

The night is come like to the day,
Depart not thou great God away.
Let not my sinnes, blacke as the night,
Eclipse the lustre of thy light.
Keepe still in my Horizon, for to me,
The Sunne makes not the day, but thee.
Thou whose nature cannot sleepe,
On my temples centry keepe;
Guard me 'gainst those watchfull foes,
10 *Whose eyes are open while mine close.*
Let no dreames my head infest,
But such as Jacobs *temples blest.*
While I doe rest, my soule advance,
Make my sleepe a holy trance:
That I may, my rest being wrought,
Awake into some holy thought.
And with as active vigour runne
My course, as doth the nimble Sunne.
Sleepe is a death, O make me try,
20 *By sleeping what it is to die.*
And as gently lay my head
On my Grave, as now my bed.
How ere I rest, great God let me
Awake againe at last with thee.
And thus assur'd, behold I lie
Securely, or to wake or die.
These are my drowsie dayes, in vaine
I doe now wake to sleepe againe.
O come that houre, when I shall never
30 *Sleepe againe, but wake for ever!*

This is the dormitive I take to bedward, I need no other *Laudanum* than this to make me sleepe; after which I close mine eyes in security, content to take my leave of the Sunne, and sleepe unto the resurrection.

SECT. 13.

The method I should use in distributive justice, I often observe in commutative, and keepe a Geometricall proportion in both, whereby becomming equable to others, I become unjust to my selfe, and supererogate in that common principle, Doe unto others 40 as thou wouldest be done unto thy selfe. I was not borne unto riches, neither is it I thinke my Starre to be wealthy; or if it were,

36 should *Er*: would *HO 42 43* 40–41 unto riches *Er*: unto *43*

the freedome of my minde, and franknesse of my disposition, were able to contradict and crosse my fates: for to me avarice seemes not so much a vice, as a deplorable piece of madnesse; to conceive our selves Urinals, or bee perswaded that wee are dead, is not so ridiculous, nor so many degrees beyond the power of Hellebore, as this. The opinions of theory and positions of men are not so voyd of reason as their practised conclusions: some have held that Snow is blacke, that the earth moves, that the soule is ayre, fire, water, but all this is Philosophy, and there is no *delirium*, if we doe but speculate the folly and indisputable dotage of avarice. To 10 that subterraneous Idoll, and God of the earth, I doe confesse I am an Atheist, I cannot perswade my selfe to honour that the world adores; whatsoever vertue its prepared substance may have within my body, it hath no influence nor operation without; I would not entertaine a base designe, or an action that should call mee villaine, for the Indies, and for this onely doe I love and honour my owne soule, and have mee thinkes, two armes too few to embrace my selfe. *Aristotle* is too severe, that will not allow us to bee truely liberall without wealth, and the bountifull hand of fortune; if this be true, I must confesse I am charitable onely in my liberall 20 intentions, and bountifull well-wishes. But if the example of the Mite bee not onely an act of wonder, but an example of the noblest charity, surely poore men may also build Hospitals, and the rich alone have not erected Cathedralls. I have a private method which others observe not, I take the opportunity of my selfe to do good, I borrow occasion of charity from mine owne necessities, and supply the wants of others, when I am in most neede my selfe; for it is an honest stratagem to take advantage of our selves, and so to husband the acts of vertue, that where they are defective in one circumstance, they may repay their want, and 30 multiply their goodnesse in another. I have not *Peru* in my desires, but a competence, and abilitie to performe those good workes to which hee hath inclined my nature. Hee is rich, who hath enough to bee charitable, and it is hard to bee so poore, that a noble minde may not finde a way to this piece of goodnesse. *Hee that giveth to the poore lendeth to the Lord*; there is more Rhetorick in that one sentence than in a Library of Sermons, and indeed if those sentences were understood by the Reader, with the same Emphasis as they are delivered by the Author, wee needed not those Volumes of instructions, but might bee honest by an Epitome. 40

7 conclusions *MSS.*: conclusion *42 43* 8 fire, *MSS.* / *42*: fire *43*
10–11 avarice. To . . . earth,] avarice to . . . earth. *42 43*. *The weight of the MS. evidence favours the punctuation adopted.* 29 acts *MSS.* / *42*: act *43*

Upon this motive onely I cannot behold a Begger without relieving his necessities with my purse, or his soule with my prayers; these scenicall and accidentall differences betweene us cannot make mee forget that common and untoucht part of us both; there is under these *Centoes* and miserable outsides, these mutilate and semi-bodies, a soule of the same alloy with our owne, whose Genealogy is God as well as ours, and in as faire a way to salvation, as our selves. Statists that labour to contrive a Common-wealth without poverty, take away the object of charity, not understanding
10 only the Common-wealth of a Christian, but forgetting the prophecy of Christ.

SECT. 14.

Now there is another part of charity, which is the Basis and Pillar of this, and that is the love of God, for whom wee love our neighbour: for this I thinke charity, to love God for himselfe, and our neighbour for God. All that is truely amiable is God, or as it were a divided piece of him, that retaines a reflex or shadow of himselfe. Nor is it strange that wee should place affection on that which is invisible, all that wee truely love is thus, what wee adore under
20 affection of our senses, deserves not the honour of so pure a title. Thus wee adore vertue, though to the eyes of sense shee bee invisible. Thus that part of our noble friends that wee love, is not that part that we embrace, but that insensible part that our armes cannot embrace. God being all goodnesse, can love nothing but himselfe, hee loves us but for that part which is as it were himselfe, and the traduction of his holy Spirit. Let us call to assize the love of our parents, the affection of our wives and children, and they are all dumbe showes, and dreames, without reality, truth, or constancy; for first there is a strong bond of affection betweene us and
30 our parents, yet how easily dissolved? We betake our selves to a woman, forgetting our mothers in a wife, and the wombe that bare us in that that shall beare our image. This woman blessing us with children, our affection leaves the levell it held before, and sinkes from our bed unto our issue and picture of posterity, where affection holds no steady mansion. They growing up in yeares desire our ends, or applying themselves to a woman, take a lawfull way to love another better than our selves. Thus I perceive a man may bee buried alive, and behold his grave in his owne issue.

22 noble *ErP*: loving *42 43 and MSS. except P* 26 the love *P*: the loves *other MSS. and Er*: the lives *42 43* 33 affection *MSS. except HR*: affections *HR 42 43*

SECT. 15.

I conclude therefore and say, there is no happinesse under (or as *Copernicus* will have it, above) the Sunne, nor any Crambe in that repeated veritie and burthen of all the wisedom of *Solomon*, *All is vanitie and vexation of spirit:* there is no felicity in that the world adores. *Aristotle* whilst hee labours to refute the Idea's of *Plato*, fals upon one himselfe: for his *summum bonum*, is a *Chimæra*, and there is no such thing as his Felicity. That wherein God himselfe is happy, the holy Angels are happy, in whose defect the Devils are unhappy; that dare I call happinesse: whatsoever conduceth unto 10 this, may with an easie Metaphor deserve that name; whatsoever else the world termes happines, is to me a story out of *Pliny*, an apparition, or neat delusion, wherin there is no more of happinesse than the name. Blesse mee in this life with but the peace of my conscience, command of my affections, the love of thy selfe and my dearest friends, and I shall be happy enough to pity *Cæsar*. These are O Lord the humble desires of my most reasonable ambition and all I dare call happinesse on earth: wherein I set no rule or limit to thy hand or providence, dispose of me according to the wisedome of thy pleasure. Thy will bee done, though in my owne 20 undoing.

FINIS.

A LETTER

sent upon the Information of Animadversions to come forth, upon the imperfect and surreptitious Copy of *Religio Medici*; whilst this true one was going to the Presse.

Honourable Sir,

GIVE *your Servant who hath ever honour'd you, leave to take notice of a Booke at present in the Presse, Intituled (as I am informed)* Animadversions *upon a Treatise lately Printed under the Name of* Religio Medici; *hereof I am advertised you have descended to be the Author. Worthy Sir, permit your Servant to affirme there is contain'd therein nothing that can deserve the Reason of your contradictions, much lesse the candor of your* Animadversions: *and to certifie the truth thereof; that Booke (whereof I doe acknowledge my self the Author) was pen'd many yeers past, and (what cannot escape your apprehension) with no intention for the Presse, or the least desire to obliege the Faith of any man to its assertions. But what hath more especially emboldened my Pen unto you at present is, that the same piece contrived in my private Study, and as an exercise unto my self, rather then exercitation for any other, having past from my hand under a broken and imperfect Copy, by frequent transcription it still run forward in corruption, and after the addition of some things, omission of others, and transposition of many, without my assent or privacy, the liberty of these times committed it unto the Presse, from whence it issued so disguised, the Author without distinction could not acknowledg it. Having thus miscarried, within a few Weekes I shall, God willing, deliver unto the Presse the true and intended Originall (wherof in the meane time your Worthy selfe may command a view) otherwise when ever that Copy shall be extant, it will most cleerly appeare how farre the Text hath been mistaken, and all observations, glosses, or exercitations thereon will in a great part impugne the Printer or transcriber, rather then the Author. If after that you shall esteem it worth your vacant houres to discourse thereon, you shall but take that liberty which I assume my selfe, that is freely to abound in your sense, as I have done in my own. However you shall determine, you shall sufficiently honour me in the vouchsafe of your refute, and I obliege the whole World in the occasion of your Pen.*

Norwich,
March 3.
1642.

Your Servant,
T. B.

Worthy Sir,

SPEEDILY *upon the Receipt of your Letter of the third Current, I sent to find out the Printer that Mr.* CROOKE *(who delivered mee yours) told mee was Printing something under my Name, concerning your Treatise of* 10 Religio Medici, *and to forbid him any further proceeding therein; But my Servant could not meete with him; Whereupon I have left with Mr.* Crooke *a Note to that purpose, entreating him to deliver it to the Printer. I verily beleeve there is some mistake in the information given you, and that what is Printing must bee from some other Pen then mine, for such reflections as I made upon your learned and ingenuous Discourse, are so farre from meriting the Presse, as they can tempt no body to a serious reading of them: They were Notes hastily set downe, as I suddenly ran over your excellent Piece, which is of so weighty Subject, and so strongly Penned, as requireth much time, and sharpe attention but to comprehend it;* 20 *Whereas what I writ was the imployment but of one sitting; and there was not twenty foure houres betweene my receiving my Lord of* DORSETS *Letter that occasioned what I said, and the finishing my Answer to him; and yet part of that time was taken up in procuring your Booke, which hee desired mee to read, and give him an accompt of, for till then I was so unhappy as never to have heard of that worthy Discourse. If that Letter ever come to your view, you will see the high value I set upon your great parts: And if it should bee thought I have beene something too bold in differing from your sense, I hope I shall easily obtaine pardon when it shall bee considered that his Lordship assigned it mee as an exercitation to oppose in it for his entertain-* 30 *ment, such passages as I might judge capable thereof; wherein what liberty I tooke, is to bee attributed to the security of a private Letter, and to my not knowing (nor my Lords) the person whom it concerned.*

But Sir, now that I am so happy as to have that knowledge, I dare assure you, that nothing shall ever issue from mee, but savouring of all Honour, Esteem, and Reverence both to your selfe, and that Worthy Production of yours. If I had the vanity to give my selfe reputation by entring the lists in publike with so eminent and learned a Man as you are, yet I know right well, I am no wayes able to doe it, it would be a very unequall congresse: I pretend not to Learning, those slender notions I have are but dis-jointed 40 *pieces I have by chance gleaned up here and there: To encounter such a sinewy Opposite, or make Animadversions upon so smart a piece as yours is, requireth a solid stocke and exercise in Schoole Learning. My superficiall besprinkling will serve onely for a private Letter, or familiar discourse with Lay auditors. With longing I expect the comming abroad of the true Copy of that Booke, whose false and stollen one hath already given me so much delight. And so assuring you I shall deeme it a great good fortune to deserve your favour and friendship, I kisse your hand and rest.*

Winchester
10 House the
20 of March
1642.

Your most humble
Servant,
Kenelme Digby.

To such as have, or shall peruse the Observations upon a former corrupt Copy of this Booke.

THERE *are some men that* Politian *speakes of*, Cui quam recta manus, tam fuit & facilis: *and it seemes the Author to the observations upon this book, would arrogate as much to himselfe; for they were by his owne confession, but the conceptions of one night; a hasty birth; and so it proves: for what is really controullable, he generally omitteth; and what is false upon the error of the Copy, he doth not alwayes take notice of; and wherein he would contradict, he mistaketh, or traduceth the intention, and (besides a parenthesis sometimes upon the Authour) onely medleth* 10 *with those points from whence he takes a hint to deliver his prepar'd conceptions: But the grosse of his Booke is made out by discourses collaterall, and digressions of his own, not at all emergent from this Discourse; which is easily perceptible unto the intelligent Reader. Thus much I thought good to let thee understand, without the Authours knowledge, who slighting the refute hath inforcedly published (as a sufficient confutation) his owne Booke: and in this I shall not make so bold with him, as the Observator hath done with that noble Knight, whose name he hath wrongfully prefixed, as I am informed, to his slight Animadversions: but I leave him to repentance, and thee to thy satisfaction.* 20

Farewell
Yours A. B.

16 *inforcedly*] *insorcedly 43*

ERRATA.

PAGE 13.l.6. r. that it should, p. 16.l.12. r. indisposed, p. 33.l.13. r. swerve, but, p. 43.l.11. for yea, r. yet, p. 50.l.20. dele great, p. 52.l.15. r. postulate, p. 60.l.8. for the, r. that, p. 67.l.3. r. times present, p. 84.l.15. for may, r. must, p. 86.l.6. for a, r. at, l.8. for but, r. that, p. 98.l.11. r. for, p. 106.l.7. r. *suæ*, p. 119.l.23. r. not to, p. 120.l.8. dele say, p. 123. dele the last line, p. 133.l.23. r. in the fame degree, p. 138.l.5. r. cannot, p. 146.l.26. for in, r. the, p. 149.l.8 r. his, p. 156.l.18. r. against reason, l.25. for too, r. so, p. 157.l.9. r. or generall, p. 158.l.10. r. otherwise of my selfe, p. 159.l.12. 10 r. not, p. 162. l. 17. for all, r. at, p. 163.l. 2. dele not, l. 19. r. coold imagination, p. 170.l.15. for the, r. there, p. 171.l.23. for earthly, r. watery, p. 175. l.23. r. should, p. 176.l.7. unto riches, p. 180.l.21. r. noble friends, p. 181. l.5. r. the loves.

Errata. Some stops, missing in *43*, have been supplied. The page-numbers and line-numbers are those of *43*. The corresponding numbers in the present edition are 7.37–38, 9.3, 16.2, 19.36, 22.35, 23.23, 26.29, 29.14, 36.14, 36.39, 37.1, 41.35, 44.51, 50.8, 50.14, 51.32–33, 55.23, 57.9, 60.25, 61.21, 64.15, 64.19, 64.25, 65.1, 65.19, 66.29, 66.36, 67.7, 69.33, 71.2, 72.36, 72.40–41, 74.22, 74.26.

3 84.l.15] 84.l 5 *43* 4 p. 8] p. 89 *43*
6 say] sav *43*

HYDRIOTAPHIA,

URNE-BURIALL,

OR,

A Discourse of the Sepulchrall Urnes lately found in

NORFOLK.

Together with

The Garden of *CYRUS,*

OR THE

Quincunciall, Lozenge, or Net-work Plantations of the Ancients, Artificially, Naturally, Mystically Considered.

With Sundry Observations.

By *Thomas Browne* D. of Physick.

LONDON,

Printed for *Hen. Brome* at the Signe of the Gun in *Ivy-lane.* 1658.

To My Worthy and Honoured Friend THOMAS Le GROS of *Crostwick* Esquire.

WHEN the Funerall pyre was out, and the last valediction over, men took a lasting adieu of their interred Friends, little expecting the curiosity of future ages should comment upon their ashes, and having no old experience of the duration of their Reliques, held no opinion of such after-considerations.

But who knows the fate of his bones, or how often he is to be buried? who hath the Oracle of his ashes, or whether they are to be scattered? The Reliques of many lie like the ruines of [1]*Pompeys*, in all parts of the earth; And when they arrive at your hands, these may seem to have wandred far, who in a direct[2] and *Meridian* Travell, have but few miles of known Earth between your self and the Pole.

That the bones of *Theseus* should be seen again [3]in *Athens*, was not beyond conjecture, and hopeful expectation; but that these should arise so opportunely to serve your self, was an hit of fate and honour beyond prediction.

We cannot but wish these Urnes might have the effect of Theatrical vessels, and great [4]*Hippodrome* Urnes in *Rome*; to resound the acclamations and honour due unto you. But these are sad and sepulchral Pitchers, which have no joyful voices; silently expressing old mortality, the ruines of forgotten times, and can only speak with life, how long in this corruptible frame, some parts may be uncorrupted; yet able to out-last bones long unborn, and noblest pyle [5]among us.

We present not these as any strange sight or spectacle unknown to your eyes who have beheld the best of Urnes, and noblest variety of Ashes; Who are your self no slender master of Antiquities, and can daily command the view of so many Imperiall faces; Which raiseth your thoughts unto old things, and con-

[1] *Pompeios juvenes Asia, atque Europa, sed ipsum terra tegit* Lybica. [Martial, v. 74. 1–2.]

[2] Little directly, but Sea between your house and *Greenland*.

[3] Brought back by *Cimon*. Plutarch. [*Cimon*, 8.]

[4] The great Urnes in the *Hippodrome* at *Rome* conceived to resound the voices of people at their shows.

[5] Worthily possessed by that true Gentleman Sir *Horatio Townshend* my honored Friend.

sideration of times before you, when even living men were Antiquities; when the living might exceed the dead, and to depart this world, could not be properly said, to go unto the [1]greater number. And so run up your thoughts upon the ancient of dayes, the Antiquaries truest object, unto whom the eldest parcels are young, and earth it self an Infant; and without [2]Ægyptian account makes but small noise in thousands.

We were hinted by the occasion, not catched the opportunity to write of old things, or intrude upon the Antiquary. We are coldly 10 drawn unto discourses of Antiquities, who have scarce time before us to comprehend new things, or make out learned Novelties. But seeing they arose as they lay, almost in silence among us, at least in short account suddenly passed over; we were very unwilling they should die again, and be buried twice among us.

Beside, to preserve the living, and make the dead to live, to keep men out of their Urnes, and discourse of humane fragments in them, is not impertinent unto our profession; whose study is life and death, who daily behold examples of mortality, and of all men least need artificial *memento's*, or coffins by our bed side, to minde 20 us of our graves.

'Tis time to observe Occurrences, and let nothing remarkable escape us; The Supinity of elder dayes hath left so much in silence, or time hath so martyred the Records, that the most [3]industrious heads do finde no easie work to erect a new *Britannia*.

'Tis opportune to look back upon old times, and contemplate our Forefathers. Great examples grow thin, and to be fetched from the passed world. Simplicity flies away, and iniquity comes at long strides upon us. We have enough to do to make up our selves from present and passed times, and the whole stage of things 30 scarce serveth for our instruction. A compleat peece of vertue must be made up from the *Centos* of all ages, as all the beauties of *Greece* could make but one handsome *Venus*.

When the bones of King *Arthur* were digged up[4], the old Race might think, they beheld therein some Originals of themselves; Unto these of our Urnes none here can pretend relation, and can only behold the Reliques of those persons, who in their life giving the Law unto their predecessors, after long obscurity, now lye at

[1] *Abiit ad plures*. [Petronius, 42. 5.]

[2] Which makes the world so many years old.

[3] Wherein M. *Dugdale* hath excellently well endeavoured, and worthy to be countenanced by ingenuous and noble persons.

[4] In the time of *Henry* the second, *Cambden*.

37 Law *C*: Laws *58*

their mercies. But remembring the early civility they brought upon these Countreys, and forgetting long passed mischiefs; We mercifully preserve their bones, and pisse not upon their ashes.

In the offer of these Antiquities we drive not at ancient Families, so long out-lasted by them; We are farre from erecting your worth upon the pillars of your Fore-fathers, whose merits you illustrate. We honour your old Virtues, conformable unto times before you, which are the Noblest Armoury. And having long experience of your friendly conversation, void of empty Formality, full of freedome, constant and Generous Honesty. I look upon you as a 10 Gemme of the [1]Old Rock, and must professe my self even to Urne and Ashes,

Norwich
May 1.

Your ever faithfull Friend,
and Servant,
Thomas Browne.

[1] *Adamas de rupe veteri præstantissimus.*

To My Worthy and Honored Friend
NICHOLAS BACON
of Gillingham Esquire.

HAD *I not observed that* [1]*Purblinde men have discoursed well of sight, and some*[2] *without issue, excellently of Generation; I that was never master of any considerable garden, had not attempted this Subject. But the Earth is the Garden of Nature, and each fruitfull Countrey a Paradise.* Dioscorides *made most of his Observations in his march about with* Antonius; *and* Theophrastus *raised his generalities chiefly from the*
10 *field.*

Beside we write no Herball, nor can this Volume deceive you, who have handled the [3]*massiest thereof: who know that three* [4]*Folio's are yet too little, and how New Herbals fly from* America *upon us; from persevering Enquirers, and* [5]*old in those singularities, we expect such Descriptions. Wherein* [6]England *is now so exact, that it yeelds not to other Countreys.*

We pretend not to multiply vegetable divisions by Quincuncial and Reticulate plants; or erect a new Phytology. The Field of knowledge hath been so traced, it is hard to spring any thing new. Of old things we write something new, If truth may receive addition, or envy will have anything
20 *new; since the Ancients knew the late Anatomicall discoveries, and* Hippocrates *the Circulation.*

You have been so long out of trite learning, that 'tis hard to finde a subject proper for you; and if you have met with a Sheet upon this, we have missed our intention. In this multiplicity of writing, bye and barren Themes are best fitted for invention; Subjects so often discoursed confine the Imagination, and fix our conceptions unto the notions of fore-writers. Beside, such Discourses allow excursions, and venially admit of collaterall truths, though at some distance from their principals. Wherein if we sometimes take wide liberty, we are not single, but erre by great [7]*example.*
30 *He that will illustrate the excellency of this order, may easily fail upon*

[1] *Plempius, Cabeus,* &c. [2] D. *Harvy.*
[3] Besleri *Hortus Eystetensis.* [4] Bauhini *Theatrum Botanicum,* &c.
[5] My worthy friend M. *Goodier* an ancient and learned Botanist.
[6] As in *London* and divers parts, whereof we mention none, lest we seem to omit any.
[7] *Hippocrates de superfœtatione, de dentitione.*

---

13 *us;*] *us,* 58

so spruce a Subject, wherein we have not affrighted the common Reader with any other Diagramms, then of it self; and have industriously declined illustrations from rare and unknown plants.

Your discerning judgement so well acquainted with that study, will expect herein no mathematicall truths, as well understanding how few generalities and [1]V finita's *there are in nature. How* Scaliger *hath found exceptions in most Universals of* Aristotle *and* Theophrastus. *How Botanicall Maximes must have fair allowance, and are tolerably currant, if not intolerably over-ballanced by exceptions.*

You have wisely ordered your vegetable delights, beyond the reach of exception. The Turks who passt their dayes in Gardens here, will have Gardens also hereafter, and delighting in Flowers on earth, must have Lillies and Roses in Heaven. In Garden Delights 'tis not easie to hold a Mediocrity; that insinuating pleasure is seldome without some extremity. The Antients venially delighted in flourishing Gardens; Many were Florists that knew not the true use of a Flower; And in Plinies *dayes none had directly treated of that Subject. Some commendably affected Plantations of venemous Vegetables, some confined their delights unto single plants, and* Cato *seemed to dote upon Cabbadge; While the Ingenuous delight of Tulipists, stands saluted with hard language, even by their own* [2]*Professors.*

That in this Garden Discourse, we range into extraneous things, and many parts of Art and Nature, we follow herein the example of old and new Plantations, wherein noble spirits contented not themselves with Trees, but by the attendance of Aviaries, Fish Ponds, and all variety of Animals, they made their gardens the Epitome of the earth, and some resemblance of the secular shows of old.

That we conjoyn these parts of different Subjects, or that this should succeed the other; Your judgement will admit without impute of incongruity; Since the delightfull World comes after death, and Paradise succeeds the Grave. Since the verdant state of things is the Symbole of the Resurrection, and to flourish in the state of Glory, we must first be sown in corruption. Beside the ancient practise of Noble Persons, to conclude in Garden-Graves, and Urnes themselves of old, to be wrapt up in flowers and garlands.

Nullum sine venia placuisse eloquium, *is more sensibly understood by Writers, then by Readers; nor well apprehended by either, till works have hanged out like* Apelles *his Pictures; wherein even common eyes will finde something for emendation.*

To wish all Readers of your abilities, were unreasonably to multiply the

[1] Rules without exceptions.

[2] *Tulipomania, Narrencruiid, Laurenberg. Pet. Hondius in lib.* Belg.

24 *of Aviaries*] *ef Aviaries 58*   33 *up in Er*: *up 58*

number of Scholars beyond the temper of these times. But unto this ill-judging age, we charitably desire a portion of your equity, judgement, candour, and ingenuity; wherein you are so rich, as not to lose by diffusion. And being a flourishing branch of that [1]*Noble Family, unto which we owe so much observance, you are not new set, but long rooted in such perfection; whereof having had so lasting confirmation in your worthy conversation, constant amity, and expression; and knowing you a serious Student in the highest* arcana's *of Nature; with much excuse we bring these low delights, and poor maniples to your Treasure.*

10 *Norwich* May 1.

Your affectionate Friend
and Servant,
Thomas Browne.

[1] Of the most worthy S[r] *Edmund Bacon* prime Baronet, my true and noble friend.

[*See p.* 94, *l.* 34 *sqq.*]

HYDRIOTAPHIA
Urne-Buriall.

OR,

A Brief Discourse of the Sepulchrall Urnes lately found in NORFOLK.

CHAPTER I.

IN the deep discovery of the Subterranean world, a shallow part would satisfie some enquirers; who, if two or three yards were open about the surface, would not care to rake the bowels of *Potosi*[1] and regions towards the Centre. Nature hath furnished 10 one part of the Earth, and man another. The treasures of time lie high, in Urnes, Coynes, and Monuments, scarce below the roots of some vegetables. Time hath endlesse rarities, and shows of all varieties; which reveals old things in heaven, makes new discoveries in earth, and even earth it self a discovery. That great Antiquity *America* lay buried for thousands of years; and a large part of the earth is still in the Urne unto us.

Though if *Adam* were made out of an extract of the Earth, all parts might challenge a restitution, yet few have returned their bones farre lower then they might receive them; not affecting the 20 graves of Giants, under hilly and heavy coverings, but content with lesse then their owne depth, have wished their bones might lie soft, and the earth be light upon them; Even such as hope to rise again, would not be content with centrall interrment, or so desperately to place their reliques as to lie beyond discovery, and in no way to be seen again; which happy contrivance hath made communication with our forefathers, and left unto our view some parts, which they never beheld themselves.

Though earth hath engrossed the name yet water hath proved the smartest grave; which in forty dayes swallowed almost 30 mankinde, and the living creation; Fishes not wholly escaping, except the Salt Ocean were handsomely contempered by a mixture of the fresh Element.

[1] The rich Mountain of *Peru*.

16 thousands of *Er C*: a thousand *58*

Many have taken voluminous pains to determine the state of the soul upon disunion; but men have been most phantasticall in the singular contrivances of their corporall dissolution: whilest the sobrest Nations have rested in two wayes, of simple inhumation and burning.

That carnall interment or burying, was of the elder date, the old examples of *Abraham* and the Patriarchs are sufficient to illustrate; And were without competition, if it could be made out, that *Adam* was buried near *Damascus*, or Mount *Calvary*, according to
10 some Tradition. God himself, that buried but one, was pleased to make choice of this way, collectible from Scripture-expression, and the hot contest between Satan and the Arch-Angel, about discovering the body of *Moses*. But the practice of Burning was also of great Antiquity, and of no slender extent. For (not to derive the same from *Hercules*) noble descriptions there are hereof in the Grecian Funerals of *Homer*, In the formall Obsequies of *Patroclus*, and *Achilles*; and somewhat elder in the *Theban* warre, and solemn combustion of *Meneceus*, and *Archemorus*, contemporary unto *Jair* the Eighth Judge of *Israel*. Confirmable also among the *Trojans*,
20 from the Funerall Pyre of *Hector*, burnt before the gates of *Troy*, And the [1]burning of *Penthisilea* the *Amazonean Queen*: and long continuance of that practice, in the inward Countries of *Asia*; while as low as the Reign of *Julian*, we finde that the King of *Chionia*[2] burnt the body of his Son, and interred the ashes in a silver Urne.

The same practice extended also farre West[3], and besides *Herulians*, *Getes*, and *Thracians*, was in use with most of the *Celtæ*, *Sarmatians*, *Germans*, *Gauls*, *Danes*, *Swedes*, *Norwegians*; not to omit some use thereof among *Carthaginians* and *Americans*: Of greater
30 Antiquity among the *Romans* then most opinion, or *Pliny* seems to allow. For (beside the old Table Laws of burning[4] or burying within the City, of making the Funerall fire with plained wood, or quenching the fire with wine.) *Manlius* the Consul burnt the body of his Son: *Numa* by speciall clause of his Will, was not burnt but buried;

[1] Q. Calaber. lib. 1. [*Posthomerica*, i. 789–94.]

[2] Ammianus Marcellinus [xix. 2], Gumbrates [*for* Grumbates] King of *Chionia* a Countrey near *Persia*.

[3] Arnoldus Montanus, not. in Cæs. Commentar. L. L. Gyraldus. Kirkmannus.

[4] 12. Tabul. part. 1. de jure sacro. Hominem mortuum in urbe ne sepelito, neve urito. tom 2. Rogum asciâ ne polito. to. 4. Item Vigeneri Annotat. in Livium. & Alex. ab Alex. cum Tiraquello. Roscinus cum Dempstero.

---

3 contrivances] contrivancss *58*

And *Remus* was solemnly burned, according to the description of *Ovid*.[1]

Cornelius Sylla was not the first whose body was burned in *Rome*, but of the *Cornelian* Family, which being indifferently, not frequently used before; from that time spread, and became the prevalent practice. Not totally pursued in the highest runne of Cremation; For when even Crows were funerally burnt, *Poppæa* the Wife of *Nero* found a peculiar grave enterment. Now as all customes were founded upon some bottome of Reason, so there wanted not grounds for this; according to severall apprehensions of the most 10 rationall dissolution. Some being of the opinion of *Thales*, that water was the originall of all things, thought it most equall to submit unto the principle of putrefaction, and conclude in a moist relentment. Others conceived it most natural to end in fire, as due unto the master principle in the composition, according to the doctrine of *Heraclitus*. And therefore heaped up large piles, more actively to waft them toward that Element, whereby they also declined a visible degeneration into worms, and left a lasting parcell of their composition.

Some apprehended a purifying virtue in fire, refining the grosser 20 commixture, and firing out the Æthereall particles so deeply immersed in it. And such as by tradition or rationall conjecture held any hint of the finall pyre of all things; or that this Element at last must be too hard for all the rest; might conceive most naturally of the fiery dissolution. Others pretending no natural grounds, politickly declined the malice of enemies upon their buried bodies. Which consideration led *Sylla* unto this practise; who having thus served the body of *Marius*, could not but fear a retaliation upon his own; entertained after in the Civill wars, and revengeful contentions of *Rome*. 30

But as many Nations embraced, and many left it indifferent, so others too much affected, or strictly declined this practice. The *Indian Brachmans* seemed too great friends unto fire, who burnt themselves alive, and thought it the noblest way to end their dayes in fire; according to the expression of the Indian, burning himself at *Athens*[2], in his last words upon the pyre unto the amazed spectators, *Thus I make my selfe Immortall*.

1 Ultima prolato subdita flamma rogo. De Fast. lib. 4. cum Car. Neapol. anaptyxi.

2 And therefore the Inscription of his Tomb was made accordingly. *Nic. Damasc.*

---

1 burned *Er(2)*: buried *58* 24 naturally] na-naturally *58*

But the *Chaldeans* the great Idolaters of fire, abhorred the burning of their carcasses, as a pollution of that Deity. The *Persian Magi* declined it upon the like scruple, and being only sollicitous about their bones, exposed their flesh to the prey of Birds and Dogges. And the *Persees* now in *India*, which expose their bodies unto Vultures, and endure not so much as *feretra* or Beers of Wood, the proper Fuell of fire, are led on with such niceties. But whether the ancient *Germans* who burned their dead, held any such fear to pollute their Deity of *Herthus*, or the earth, we have no Authentick conjecture.

The Ægyptians were afraid of fire, not as a Deity, but a devouring Element, mercilesly consuming their bodies, and leaving too little of them; and therefore by precious Embalments, depositure in dry earths, or handsome inclosure in glasses, contrived the notablest wayes of integrall conservation. And from such Ægyptian scruples imbibed by *Pythagoras*, it may be conjectured that *Numa* and the Pythagoricall Sect first waved the fiery solution.

The *Scythians* who swore by winde and sword, that is, by life and death, were so farre from burning their bodies, that they declined all interrment, and made their graves in the ayr: And the *Ichthyophagi* or fish-eating Nations about Ægypt, affected the Sea for their grave: Thereby declining visible corruption, and restoring the debt of their bodies. Whereas the old Heroes in *Homer*, dreaded nothing more than water or drowning; probably upon the old opinion of the fiery substance of the soul, only extinguishable by that Element; And therefore the Poet emphatically implieth the totall destruction in this kinde of death, which happened to *Ajax Oileus*[1].

The old [2]*Balearians* had a peculiar mode, for they used great Urnes and much wood, but no fire in their burials, while they bruised the flesh and bones of the dead, crowded them into Urnes, and laid heapes of wood upon them. And the [3]*Chinois* without cremation or urnall interrment of their bodies, make use of trees and much burning, while they plant a Pine-tree by their grave, and burn great numbers of printed draughts of slaves and horses over it, civilly content with their companies in effigie, which barbarous Nations exact unto reality.

Christians abhorred this way of obsequies, and though they stickt not to give their bodies to be burnt in their lives, detested that mode after death; affecting rather a depositure than absumption, and properly submitting unto the sentence of God, to return

[1] Which *Magius* reades ἐξαπόλωλε.
[2] *Diodorus Siculus*. [v. 18.]
[3] *Ramusius* in *Navigat*.

not unto ashes but unto dust againe, conformable unto the practice of the Patriarchs, the interrment of our Saviour, of *Peter*, *Paul*, and the ancient Martyrs. And so farre at last declining promiscuous enterrment with Pagans, that some[1] have suffered Ecclesiastical censures, for making no scruple thereof.

The *Musselman* beleevers will never admit this fiery resolution. For they hold a present trial from their black and white Angels in the grave; which they must have made so hollow, that they may rise upon their knees.

The Jewish Nation, though they entertained the old way of 10 inhumation, yet sometimes admitted this practice. For the men of *Jabesh* burnt the body of *Saul*. And by no prohibited practice to avoid contagion or pollution, in time of pestilence, burnt the bodies of their friends[2]. And when they burnt not their dead bodies yet sometimes used great burnings neare and about them, deducible from the expressions concerning *Jehoram*, *Sedechias*, and the sumptuous pyre of *Asa*: And were so little averse from [3]Pagan burning, that the Jews lamenting the death of *Cæsar* their friend, and revenger on *Pompey*, frequented the place where his body was burnt for many nights together. And as they raised noble Monu- 20 ments and *Mausolæums* for their own Nation[4], so they were not scrupulous in erecting some for others, according to the practice of *Daniel*, who left that lasting sepulchrall pyle in *Echbatana*, for the *Medean* and *Persian* Kings[5].

But even in times of subjection and hottest use, they conformed not unto the *Romane* practice of burning; whereby the Prophecy was secured concerning the body of Christ, that it should not see corruption, or a bone should not be broken; which we beleeve was also providentially prevented, from the Souldiers spear and nails that past by the little bones both in his hands and feet: Nor of 30 ordinary contrivance, that it should not corrupt on the Crosse, according to the Laws of *Romane* Crucifixion, or an hair of his head perish, though observable in Jewish customes, to cut the hairs of Malefactors.

[1] Martialis the Bishop. *Cyprian*. [2] Amos 6. 10.
[3] Sueton. in vita. *Jul. Cæs*. [84.]
[4] As that magnificent sepulchral Monument erected by Simon. Mach. [1Macc.] 1. 13.
[5] *Κατασκεύασμα θαυμασίως πεποιημένον*, whereof a Jewish Priest had alwayes the custody unto *Josephus* his dayes. *Jos*. Lib. 10. Antiq. [x. 11. 7.]

30 Nor *C*: Not *58*

Nor in their long co-habitation with Ægyptians, crept into a custome of their exact embalming, wherein deeply slashing the muscles, and taking out the brains and entrails, they had broken the subject of so entire a Resurrection, nor fully answered the types of *Enoch*, *Eliah*, or *Jonah*, which yet to prevent or restore, was of equall facility unto that rising power, able to break the fasciations and bands of death, to get clear out of the Cere-cloth, and an hundred pounds of oyntment, and out of the Sepulchre before the stone was rolled from it.

10 But though they embraced not this practice of burning, yet entertained they many ceremonies agreeable unto *Greeke* and *Romane* obsequies. And he that observeth their funerall Feasts, their Lamentations at the grave, their musick, and weeping mourners; how they closed the eyes of their friends, how they washed, anointed, and kissed the dead; may easily conclude these were not meere Pagan-Civilities. But whether that mournfull burthen, and treble calling out after *Absalom*[1], had any reference unto the last conclamation, and triple valediction, used by other Nations, we hold but a wavering conjecture.

20 *Civilians* make sepulture but of the Law of Nations, others doe naturally found it and discover it also in animals. They that are so thick skinned as still to credit the story of the *Phœnix*, may say something for animall burning: More serious conjectures finde some examples of sepulture in Elephants, Cranes, the Sepulchrall Cells of Pismires and practice of Bees; which civill society carrieth out their dead, and hath exequies, if not interrments.

CHAP. II

THE Solemnities, Ceremonies, Rites of their Cremation or enterrment, so solemnly delivered by Authours, we shall not 30 disparage our Reader to repeat. Only the last and lasting part in their Urns, collected bones and Ashes, we cannot wholly omit, or decline that Subject, which occasion lately presented, in some discovered among us.

In a Field of old *Walsingham*, not many moneths past, were digged up between fourty and fifty Vrnes, deposited in a dry and sandy soile, not a yard deep, nor farre from one another: Not all strictly of one figure, but most answering these described: Some containing two pounds of bones, distinguishable in skulls, ribs, jawes, thigh-bones, and teeth, with fresh impressions of their combustion.

[1] O Absolom, Absolom, Absolom. Sam. 2. 18. [*Add.*]

Besides the extraneous substances, like peeces of small boxes, or combes handsomely wrought, handles of small brasse instruments, brazen nippers, and in one some kinde of *Opale*[1].

Near the same plot of ground, for about six yards compasse were digged up coals and incinerated substances, which begat conjecture that this was the *Ustrina* or place of burning their bodies, or some sacrificing place unto the *Manes*, which was properly below the surface of the ground, as the *Aræ* and Altars unto the gods and *Heroes* above it.

That these were the Vrnes of *Romanes* from the common custome 10 and place where they were found, is no obscure conjecture, not farre from a *Romane* Garrison, and but five Miles from *Brancaster*, set down by ancient Record under the name of *Brannodunum*. And where the adjoyning Towne, containing seven Parishes, in no very different sound, but Saxon Termination, still retains the Name of *Burnham*, which being an early station, it is not improbable the neighbour parts were filled with habitations, either of *Romanes* themselves, or *Brittains Romanised*, which observed the *Romane* customes.

Nor is it improbable that the *Romanes* early possessed this 20 Countrey; for though we meet not with such strict particulars of these parts, before the new Institution of *Constantine*, and military charge of the Count of the *Saxon* shore, and that about the *Saxon* Invasions, the *Dalmatian* Horsemen were in the Garrison of *Brancaster*: Yet in the time of *Claudius*, *Vespasian*, and *Severus*, we finde no lesse then three Legions dispersed through the Province of *Brittain*. And as high as the Reign of *Claudius* a great overthrow was given unto the *Iceni*, by the *Romane* Lieutenant *Ostorius*. Not long after the Countrey was so molested, that in hope of a better state, *Prasutagus* bequeathed his Kingdome unto *Nero* and his 30 Daughters; and *Boadicea* his Queen fought the last decisive Battle with *Paulinus*. After which time and Conquest of *Agricola* the Lieutenant of *Vespasian*, probable it is they wholly possessed this Countrey, ordering it into Garrisons or Habitations, best suitable with their securities. And so some *Romane* Habitations, not improbable in these parts, as high as the time of *Vespasian*, where the *Saxons* after seated, in whose thin-fill'd Mappes we yet finde the Name of *Walsingham*. Now if the *Iceni* were but *Gammadims*, *Anconians*, or men that lived in an Angle wedge or Elbow of *Brittain*, according to the Originall Etymologie, this countrey will challenge 40

[1] In one sent me by my worthy friend Dr *Thomas Witherley* of *Walsingham*.

---

30 *Prasutagus Er(2) C*: *Prasatagus Er*: *Prastaagus 58*

the Emphaticall appellation, as most properly making the Elbow or Iken of *Icenia*.

That *Britain* was notably populous is undeniable, from that expression of *Cæsar*[1]. That the *Romans* themselves were early in no small Numbers, Seventy Thousand with their associats slain by *Boadicea*, affords a sure account. And though many *Roman* habitations are now unknowne, yet some by old works, Rampiers, Coynes, and Urnes doe testifie their Possessions. Some Urnes have been found at *Castor*, some also about *Southcreake*, and not many 10 years past, no lesse then ten in a Field at *Buxton*[2], not near any recorded Garison. Nor is it strange to finde *Romane* Coynes of Copper and Silver among us; of *Vespasian*, *Trajan*, *Adrian*, *Commodus*, *Antoninus*, *Severus*, &c. But the greater number of *Dioclesian*, *Constantine*, *Constans*, *Valens*, with many of *Victorinus*, *Posthumius*, *Tetricus*, and the thirty Tyrants in the Reigne of *Gallienus*; and some as high as *Adrianus* have been found about *Thetford*, or *Sitomagus*, mentioned in the itinerary of *Antoninus*, as the way from *Venta* or *Castor* unto *London*[3]. But the most frequent discovery is made at the two *Casters* by *Norwich* and *Yarmouth*[4], at *Burghcastle* 20 and *Brancaster*[5].

Besides, the *Norman*, *Saxon* and *Danish* peeces of *Cuthred*, *Canutus*, *William*, *Matilda*[6], and others, som Brittish Coynes of gold have been dispersedly found; And no small number of silver peeces near [7]*Norwich*; with a rude head upon the obverse, and an ill formed horse on the reverse, with Inscriptions *Ic. Duro. T.* whether implying *Iceni*, *Durotriges*, *Tascia*, or *Trinobantes*, we leave

[1] *Hominum infinita multitudo est, creberrimaque ædificia ferè Gallicis consimilia.* Cæs. *de bello Gal.* l. 5. [12.]

[2] In the ground of my worthy Friend *Rob Jegon* Esq. wherein some things contained were preserved by the most worthy Sir *William Paston* B[t].

[3] From *Castor* to *Thetford* the Romanes accounted thirty two miles, and from thence observed not our common road to *London*, but passed by *Combretonium ad Ansam*, *Canonium*, *Cæsaromagus*, &c. by *Bretenham*, *Coggeshall*, *Chelmeford*, *Burntwood*, &c.

[4] Most at *Caster* by *Yarmouth*, found in a place called *East-bloudy-burgh furlong*, belonging to Mr *Thomas Wood*, a person of civility, industry and knowledge in this way, who hath made observation of remarkable things about him, and from whom we have received divers Silver and Copper Coynes.

[5] Belonging to that Noble Gentleman, and true example of worth Sir *Ralph Hare* Baronet, my honoured Friend.

[6] A peece of *Maud* the Empresse said to be found in *Buckenham* Castle with this Inscription, *Elle n'a elle.*

[7] At *Thorpe*.

---

7 unknown(e) *Er C*: knowne *58* 14 *Victorinus,*] *Victorinus 58* 22 *William, C*: *William 58*

to higher conjecture. Vulgar Chronology will have *Norwich* Castle as old as *Julius Cæsar*; but his distance from these parts, and its *Gothick* form of structure, abridgeth such Antiquity. The *British* Coyns afford conjecture of early habitation in these parts, though the City of *Norwich* arose from the ruines of *Venta*, and though perhaps not without some habitation before, was enlarged, builded, and nominated by the *Saxons*. In what bulk or populosity it stood in the old East-angle Monarchy, tradition and history are silent. Considerable it was in the *Danish* Eruptions, when *Sueno* burnt *Thetford* and *Norwich*[1], and *Ulfketel* the Governour thereof, 10 was able to make some resistance, and after endeavoured to burn the *Danish* Navy.

How the *Romanes* left so many Coynes in Countreys of their Conquests, seems of hard resolution, except we consider how they buried them under ground, when upon barbarous invasions they were fain to desert their habitations in most part of their Empire; and the strictnesse of their laws forbidding to transfer them to any other uses; Wherein the [2]*Spartans* were singular, who to make their Copper money uselesse, contempered it with vinegar. That the *Brittains* left any, some wonder; since their money was iron, 20 and Iron rings before *Cæsar*; and those of after stamp by permission, and but small in bulk and bignesse. That so few of the *Saxons* remain, because overcome by succeeding Conquerours upon the place, their Coynes by degrees passed into other stamps, and the marks of after ages.

Then the time of these Urnes deposited, or precise Antiquity of these Reliques, nothing of more uncertainty. For since the Lieutenant of *Claudius* seems to have made the first progresse into these parts, since *Boadicea* was overthrown by the Forces of *Nero*, and *Agricola* put a full end to these Conquests; it is not probable 30 the Countrey was fully garrison'd or planted before; and therefore however these Urnes might be of later date, not likely of higher Antiquity.

And the succeeding Emperours desisted not from their Conquests in these and other parts; as testified by history and medall inscription yet extant. The Province of *Brittain* in so divided a distance from *Rome*, beholding the faces of many Imperiall persons, and in large account no fewer then *Cæsar*, *Claudius*, *Britannicus*, *Vespasian*, *Titus*, *Adrian*, *Severus*, *Commodus*, *Geta*, and *Caracalla*.

A great obscurity herein, because no medall or Emperours 40

[1] *Brampton* [*for Brompton*] *Abbas Jorrnallensis* [*for Jorruallensis*].
[2] Plut. *in vita Lycurg.* [9.]

16 Empire; *C*: Empire, *58* 22 bignesse. That *C*: bignesse; that *58*

Coyne enclosed, which might denote the date of their enterrments. observable in many Urnes, and found in those of *Spittle* Fields[1] by *London*, which contained the Coynes of *Claudius*, *Vespasian*, *Commodus*, *Antoninus*, attended with Lacrymatories, Lamps, Bottles of Liquor, and other appurtenances of affectionate superstition, which in these rurall interrements were wanting.

Some uncertainty there is from the period or term of burning, or the cessation of that practise. *Macrobius* affirmeth it was disused in his dayes. But most agree, though without authentick record, 10 that it ceased with the *Antonini*. Most safely to be understood after the Reigne of those Emperours, which assumed the name of *Antoninus*, extending unto *Heliogabalus*. Not strictly after *Marcus*; For about fifty years later we finde the magnificent burning, and consecration of *Severus*; and if we so fix this period or cessation, these Urnes will challenge above thirteen hundred years.

But whether this practise was onely then left by Emperours and great persons, or generally about *Rome*, and not in other Provinces, we hold no authentick account. For after *Tertullian*, in the dayes of *Minucius* it was obviously objected upon Christians, that they 20 condemned the practise of burning[2]. And we finde a passage in *Sidonius*[3], which asserteth that practise in *France* unto a lower account. And perhaps not fully disused till Christianity fully established, which gave the finall extinction to these sepulchrall Bonefires.

Whether they were the bones of men or women or children, no authentick decision from ancient custome in distinct places of buriall. Although not improbably conjectured, that the double[4] Sepulture or burying place of *Abraham*, had in it such intension. But from exility of bones, thinnesse of skulls, smallnesse of teeth, 30 ribbes, and thigh-bones; not improbable that many thereof were persons of *minor* age, or women. Confirmable also from things contained in them: In most were found substances resembling Combes, Plates like Boxes, fastened with Iron pins, and handsomely overwrought like the necks or Bridges of Musicall Instruments, long brasse plates overwrought like the handles of neat implements, brazen nippers to pull away hair, and in one a kinde of *Opale* yet maintaining a blewish colour.

Now that they accustomed to burn or bury with them, things wherein they excelled, delighted, or which were dear unto them,

1 *Stowes* Survey of *London*.
2 *Execrantur rogos, & damnant ignium sepulturam.* Min. in Oct.
3 *Sidon. Apollinaris.* [*Ep.* iii. 3.]
4 *Det mihi speluncam duplicem.* Gen. 23 [9.] [*Add.*]

either as farewells unto all pleasure, or vain apprehension that they might use them in the other world, is testified by all Antiquity. Observable from the Gemme or Berill Ring upon the finger of *Cynthia*, the Mistresse of *Propertius*, when after her Funerall Pyre her Ghost appeared unto him. And notably illustrated from the Contents of that *Romane* Urne preserved by Cardinall *Farnese*[1], wherein besides great number of Gemmes with heads of Gods and Goddesses, were found an Ape of *Agath*, a Grashopper, an Elephant of Ambre, a Crystall Ball, three glasses, two Spoones, and six Nuts of Crystall. And beyond the content of Urnes, in the Monument of *Childerick* the first[2], and fourth King from *Pharamond*, casually discovered three years past at *Tournay*, restoring unto the world much gold richly adorning his Sword, two hundred Rubies, many hundred Imperial Coyns, three hundred golden Bees, the bones and horseshoe of his horse enterred with him, according to the barbarous magnificence of those dayes in their sepulchral Obsequies. Although if we steer by the conjecture of many and Septuagint expression; some trace thereof may be found even with the ancient Hebrews, not only from the Sepulcrall treasure of *David*, but the circumcision knives which *Josuah* also buried.

Some men considering the contents of these Vrnes, lasting peeces and toyes included in them, and the custome of burning with many other Nations, might somewhat doubt whether all Vrnes found among us, were properly *Romane* Reliques, or some not belonging unto our *Brittish*, *Saxon*, or *Danish* Forefathers.

In the form of Buriall among the ancient *Brittains*, the large Discourses of *Cæsar*, *Tacitus*, and *Strabo* are silent: For the discovery whereof, with other particulars, we much deplore the losse of that Letter which *Cicero* expected or received from his Brother *Quintus*, as a resolution of *Brittish* customes; or the account which might have been made by *Scribonins Largus* the Physician, accompanying the Emperour *Claudius*, who might have also discovered that frugall Bit[3] of the Old *Brittains*, which in the bignesse of a Bean could satisfie their thirst and hunger.

But that the *Druids* and ruling Priests used to burn and bury, is expressed by *Pomponius*; That *Bellinus* the Brother of *Brennus*, and King of *Brittains* was burnt, is acknowledged by *Polydorus*.[4]

[1] *Vigeneri Annot. in* 4. *Liv.* [2] *Chifflet in Anast. Childer.*

[3] *Dionis excerpta per Xiphilin. in Severo.*

[4] As also by *Amandus Zierexensis* in *Historia,* and *Pineda* in his *Universa historia.* Spanish.

note 4 above: As also .. Spanish. *Part of the text in 58, which reads Polydorus,* as also &c. *Transferred to margin C*

That they held that practise in *Gallia*, *Cæsar* expresly delivereth. Whether the *Brittains* (probably descended from them, of like Religion, Language and Manners) did not sometimes make use of burning; or whether at least such as were after civilized unto the *Romane* life and manners, conformed not unto this practise, we have no historicall assertion or deniall. But since from the account of *Tacitus* the *Romanes* early wrought so much civility upon the Brittish stock, that they brought them to build Temples, to wear the Gowne, and study the *Romane* Laws and language, that they 10 conformed also unto their religious rites and customes in burials, seems no improbable conjecture.

That burning the dead was used in *Sarmatia*, is affirmed by *Gaguinus*, that the *Sueons* and *Gothlanders* used to burne their Princes and great persons, is delivered by *Saxo* and *Olaus*; that this was the old *Germane* practise, is also asserted by *Tacitus*. And though we are bare in historicall particulars of such obsequies in this Island, or that the *Saxons*, *Jutes*, and *Angles* burnt their dead, yet came they from parts where 'twas of ancient practise; the *Germanes* using it, from whom they were descended. And even in 20 *Jutland* and *Sleswick* in *Anglia Cymbrica*, Vrnes with bones were found not many years before us.

But the *Danish* and Northern Nations have raised an *Æra*[1] or point of compute from their Custome of burning their dead: Some deriving it from *Unguinus*, some from *Frotho* the great; who ordained by Law, that Princes and Chief Commanders should be committed unto the fire, though the common sort had the common grave enterrment. So *Starkatterus* that old *Heroe* was burnt, and *Ringo* royally burnt the body of *Harald* the King slain by him.

30 What time this custome generally expired in that Nation, we discern no assured period; whether it ceased before Christianity, or upon their Conversion, by *Ansgarius* the Gaul in the time of *Ludovicus Pius* the Sonne of *Charles* the great, according to good computes; or whether it might not be used by some persons, while for a hundred and eighty years Paganisme and Christianity were promiscuously embraced among them, there is no assured conclusion. About which times the *Danes* were busie in *England*, and particularly infested this Countrey: Where many Castles and strong holds, were built by them, or against them, and great number 40 of names and Families still derived from them. But since this

1 *Roisold, Brendetiide. Ildtyde.*

32 *Ansgarius Er* (2) *C*: *Ausgarius Er: Ausgurius 58* 39 against them] against rhem *58*

custome was probably disused before their Invasion or Conquest, and the *Romanes* confessedly practised the same, since their possession of this Island, the most assured account will fall upon the *Romanes*, or *Brittains Romanized*.

However certain it is, that Vrnes conceived of no *Romane* Originall, are often digged up both in *Norway*, and *Denmark*, handsomely described, and graphically represented by the Learned Physician *Wormius*[1], And in some parts of *Denmark* in no ordinary number, as stands delivered by Authours exactly describing those Countreys[2]. And they contained not only bones, but many other 10 substances in them, as Knives, peeces of Iron, Brasse and Wood, and one of *Norwaye* a brasse guilded Jewes-harp.

Nor were they confused or carelesse in disposing the noblest sort, while they placed large stones in circle about the Vrnes, or bodies which they interred: Somewhat answerable unto the Monument of *Rollrich* stones in *England*[3], or sepulcrall Monument probably erected by *Rollo*, who after conquered *Normandy*. Where 'tis not improbable somewhat might be discovered. Mean while to what Nation or person belonged that large Vrne found at *Ashburie*,[4] containing mighty bones, and a Buckler; What those large Vrnes 20 found at little *Massingham*,[5] or why the *Anglesea* Urnes[6] are placed with their mouths downward, remains yet undiscovered.

CHAP. III.

PLAYSTERED and whited Sepulchres, were anciently affected in cadaverous, and corruptive Burials; And the rigid Jews were wont to garnish the Sepulchres of the [7]righteous; *Ulysses* in *Hecuba*[8] cared not how meanly he lived, so he might finde a noble Tomb after death. Great persons affected great Monuments, And the fair and larger Urnes contained no vulgar ashes, which makes that disparity in those which time discovereth among us. The present 30 Urnes were not of one capacity, the largest containing above a gallon, Some not much above half that measure; nor all of one figure,

[1] *Olai Wormii monumenta & Antiquitat. Dan.*
[2] *Adolphus Cyprius in Annal. Sleswic. urnis adeo abundabat collis; &c.*
[3] In Oxfordshire; *Cambden.*
[4] In Cheshire, *Twinus de rebus Albionicis.*
[5] In Norfolk.
[6] *Hollingshead.*
[7] Mat. 23. [29.]
[8] *Euripides.* [*Hecuba*, 317–20.]

17 probably] probaby *58* 28 persons *Er(2) C*: Princes *58*

wherein there is no strict conformity, in the same or different Countreys; Observable from those represented by *Casalius*, *Bosio*, and others, though all found in *Italy*: While many have handles, ears, and long necks, but most imitate a circular figure, in a sphericall and round composure; whether from any mystery, best duration or capacity, were but a conjecture. But the common form with necks was a proper figure, making our last bed like our first; nor much unlike the Urnes of our Nativity, while we lay in the nether part of the Earth[1], and inward vault of our Microcosme. Many Urnes are
10 red, these but of a black colour, somewhat smooth, and dully sounding, which begat some doubt, whether they were burnt, or only baked in Oven or Sunne: According to the ancient way, in many bricks, tiles, pots, and testaceous works; and as the word *testa* is properly to be taken, when occurring without addition: And chiefly intended by *Pliny*, when he commendeth bricks and tiles of two years old, and to make them in the spring. Nor only these concealed peeces, but the open magnificence of Antiquity, ran much in the Artifice of Clay. Hereof the house of *Mausolus* was built, thus old *Jupiter* stood in the Capitoll, and the *Statua* of
20 *Hercules* made in the Reign of *Tarquinius Priscus*, was extant in *Plinies* dayes. And such as declined burning or Funerall Urnes, affected Coffins of Clay, according to the mode of *Pythagoras*, and way preferred by *Varro*. But the spirit of great ones was above these circumscriptions, affecting copper, silver, gold, and *Porphyrie* Urnes, wherein *Severus* lay, after a serious view and sentence on that which should contain him[2]. Some of these Urnes were thought to have been silvered over, from sparklings in several pots, with small Tinsell parcels; uncertain whether from the earth, or the first mixture in them.

30 Among these Urnes we could obtain no good account of their coverings; Only one seemed arched over with some kinde of brick-work. Of those found at *Buxton* some were covered with flints, some in other parts with tiles, those at *Yarmouth Caster*, were closed with *Romane* bricks. And some have proper earthen covers adapted and fitted to them. But in the *Homericall* Urne of *Patroclus*, whatever was the solid Tegument, we finde the immediate covering to be a purple peece of silk: And such as had no covers might have the earth closely pressed into them, after which disposure were probably some of these, wherein we found the bones and

[1] Psa. 63.

[2] *Χωρήσεις τὸν ἄνθρωπον, ὃν ἡ οἰκουμένη οὐκ ἠχώρησεν. Dion.*

---

22 and *Er C*: a *58*

ashes half mortered unto the sand and sides of the Urne; and some long roots of Quich, or Dogs-grass wreathed about the bones.

No Lamps, included Liquors, Lachrymatories, or Tear-bottles attended these rurall Urnes, either as sacred unto the *Manes*, or passionate expressions of their surviving friends. While with rich flames, and hired tears they solemnized their Obsequies, and in the most lamented Monuments made one part of their Inscriptions[1]. Some finde sepulchrall Vessels containing liquors, which time hath incrassated into gellies. For beside these Lachrymatories, notable Lamps, with Vessels of Oyles and Aromaticall Liquors attended noble Ossuaries. And some yet retaining a [2]Vinosity and spirit in them, which if any have tasted they have farre exceeded the Palats of Antiquity. Liquors not to be computed by years of annuall Magistrates, but by great conjunctions and the fatall periods of Kingdomes[3]. The draughts of Consulary date, were but crude unto these, and *Opimian*[4] Wine but in the must unto them.

In sundry Graves and Sepulchres, we meet with Rings, Coynes, and Chalices; Ancient frugality was so severe, that they allowed no gold to attend the Corps, but only that which served to fasten their teeth[5]. Whether the *Opaline* stone in this Urne were burnt upon the finger of the dead, or cast into the fire by some affectionate friend, it will consist with either custome. But other incinerable substances were found so fresh, that they could feel no sindge from fire. These upon view were judged to be wood, but sinking in water and tried by the fire, we found them to be bone or Ivory. In their hardnesse and yellow colour they most resembled Box, which in old expressions found the Epithete[6] of Eternall, and perhaps in such conservatories might have passed uncorrupted.

That Bay-leaves were found green in the Tomb of S. *Humbert*[7], after an hundred and fifty years, was looked upon as miraculous. Remarkable it was unto old Spectators, that the Cypresse of the Temple of *Diana*, lasted so many hundred years: The wood of the Ark and Olive Rod of *Aaron* were older at the Captivity. But the Cypresse of the Ark of *Noah*, was the greatest vegetable Antiquity, if *Josephus* were not deceived, by some fragments of it in his dayes. To omit the Moore-logs, and Firre-trees found under-ground in many parts of *England*; the undated ruines of windes, floods or

1 *Cum lacrymis posuere.* 2 *Lazius.*

3 About five hundred years. *Plato.*

4 *Vinum Opiminianum* [Opimianum] *annorum centum.* Petron. [34. 6.]

5 12. *Tabul.* l. xi. *de Jure sacro. Neve aurum addito, ast quoi auro dentes vincti erunt, im cum illo sepelire & urere, se fraude esto.*

6 Plin. l. xvi. [78.] *Inter* ξύλα ἀσαπῆ *numerat Theophrastus.* [*Enquiry into plants,* v. 4. 2.] 7 *Surius.*

earthquakes; and which in *Flanders* still shew from what quarter they fell, as generally lying in a North-East position[1].

But though we found not these peeces to be Wood, according to first apprehenion, yet we missed not altogether of some woody substance; For the bones were not so clearly pickt, but some coals were found amongst them; A way to make wood perpetuall, and a fit associat for metall, whereon was laid the foundation of the great *Ephesian* Temple, and which were made the lasting tests of old boundaries and Landmarks; Whilest we look on these, we admire 10 not Observations of Coals found fresh, after four hundred years[2]. In a long deserted habitation[3], even Egge-shels have been found fresh, not tending to corruption.

In the Monument of King *Childerick*, the Iron Reliques were found all rusty and crumbling into peeces. But our little Iron pins which fastened the Ivory works, held well together, and lost not their Magneticall quality, though wanting a tenacious moisture for the firmer union of parts, although it be hardly drawn into fusion, yet that metall soon submitteth unto rust and dissolution. In the brazen peeces we admired not the duration but the freedome 20 from rust, and ill savour, upon the hardest attrition; but now exposed unto the piercing Atomes of ayre, in the space of a few moneths, they begin to spot and betray their green entrals. We conceive not these Urnes to have descended thus naked as they appear, or to have entred their graves without the old habit of flowers. The Urne of *Philopœmen* was so laden with flowers and ribbons, that it afforded no sight of it self. The rigid *Lycurgus* allowed Olive and Myrtle. The *Athenians* might fairly except against the practise of *Democritus* to be buried up in honey; as fearing to embezzle a great commodity of their Countrey, and the 30 best of that kinde in *Europe*. But *Plato* seemed too frugally politick, who allowed no larger Monument then would contain four Heroick Verses, and designed the most barren ground for sepulture: Though we cannot commend the goodnesse of that sepulchrall ground, which was set at no higher rate then the mean salary of *Judas*. Though the earth had confounded the ashes of these Ossuaries, yet the bones were so smartly burnt, that some thin plates of brasse were found half melted among them: whereby we

[1] *Gorop. Becanus in Niloscopio.*
[2] Of *Beringuccio nella pyrotechnia.*
[3] At *Elmeham.*

---

14 peeces] peecees *58* 18 rust *Er C*: rest *58* 20 savour,] savour; *58* attrition;] attrition, *58* 21 ayre,] ayre; *58* 31 four *Er C*: for *58*

apprehend they were not of the meanest carcasses, perfunctorily fired as sometimes in military, and commonly in pestilence, burnings; or after the manner of abject corps, hudled forth and carelesly burnt, without the Esquiline Port at *Rome*; which was an affront contriued upon *Tiberius*, while they but half burnt his body[1], and in the Amphitheatre, according to the custome in notable Malefactors; whereas *Nero* seemed not so much to feare his death, as that his head should be cut off, and his body not burnt entire.

Some finding many fragments of sculs in these Urnes, suspected a mixture of bones; In none we searched was there cause of such conjecture, though sometimes they declined not that practise; The ashes of [2]*Domitian* were mingled with those of *Julia*, of *Achilles* with those of *Patroclus*: All Urnes contained not single ashes; Without confused burnings they affectionately compounded their bones; passionately endeavouring to continue their living Unions. And when distance of death denied such conjunctions, unsatisfied affections, conceived some satisfaction to be neighbours in the grave, to lye Urne by Urne, and touch but in their names. And many were so curious to continue their living relations, that they contrived large, and family Urnes, wherein the Ashes of their nearest friends and kindred might successively be received[3], at least some parcels thereof, while their collaterall memorials lay in *minor* vessels about them.

Antiquity held too light thoughts from Objects of mortality, while some drew provocatives of mirth from Anatomies[4], and Juglers shewed tricks with Skeletons. When Fidlers made not so pleasant mirth as Fencers, and men could sit with quiet stomacks while hanging was plaied[5] before them. Old considerations made few *memento's* by sculs and bones upon their monuments. In the Ægyptian Obelisks and Hieroglyphicall figures, it is not easie to meet with bones. The sepulchrall Lamps speak nothing lesse then sepulture; and in their literall draughts prove often obscene and

[1] Sueton. *in vitâ Tib.* [75] & *in Amphitheatro semiustulandum*, not. *Casaub.*

[2] *Sueton. in vitâ Domitian.* [17.]

[3] S. the most learned and worthy Mr *M. Casaubon* upon *Antoninus*.

[4] *Sic erimus cuncti, &c. Ergo dum vivimus vivamus.*

[5] *'Ανχώνην* [*for ἀγχόνην*] *παίζειν*. A barbarous pastime at Feasts, when men stood upon a rolling Globe, with their necks in a Rope fastned to a beame, and a knife in their hands, ready to cut it when the stone was rolled away, wherein if they failed, they lost their lives to the laughter of their spectators. *Athenæus.* [iv. 155.]

---

5 contriued *C* (*see Commentary*) *St. John &c.*: continued *58*
7 Malefactors] Malefactore *58* *note 5 above*: fastned to a beame *C*: *not in 58*

antick peeces: Where we finde *D. M*[1]. it is obvious to meet with sacrificing *patera's*, and vessels of libation, upon old sepulchrall Monuments. In the Jewish *Hypogæum*[2] and subterranean Cell at *Rome*, was little observable beside the variety of Lamps, and frequent draughts of the holy Candlestick. In authentick draughts of *Anthony* and *Jerome*, we meet with thigh-bones and deaths heads; but the cemiteriall Cels of ancient Christians and Martyrs, were filled with draughts of Scripture Stories; not declining the flourishes of Cypresse, Palmes, and Olive; and the mysticall Figures of Pea-
10 cocks, Doves and Cocks. But iterately affecting the pourtraits of *Enoch*, *Lazarus*, *Jonas*, and the Vision of *Ezechiel*, as hopefull draughts, and hinting imagery of the Resurrection; which is the life of the grave, and sweetens our habitations in the Land of Moles and Pismires.

Gentile Inscriptions precisely delivered the extent of mens lives, seldome the manner of their deaths, which history it self so often leaves obscure in the records of memorable persons. There is scarce any Philosopher but dies twice or thrice in *Laertius*; Nor almost any life without two or three deaths in *Plutarch*; which
20 makes the tragicall ends of noble persons more favourably resented by compassionate Readers, who finde some relief in the Election of such differences.

The certainty of death is attended with uncertainties, in time, manner, places. The variety of Monuments hath often obscured true graves: and *Cenotaphs* confounded Sepulchres. For beside their reall Tombs, many have found honorary and empty Sepulchres. The variety of *Homers* Monuments made him of various Countreys. *Euripides*[3] had his Tomb in *Attica*, but his sepulture in *Macedonia*. And *Severus*[4] found his real Sepulchre in *Rome*, but his empty grave
30 in *Gallia*.

He that lay in a golden Urne[5] eminently above the Earth, was not like to finde the quiet of these bones. Many of these Urnes were broke by a vulgar discoverer in hope of inclosed treasure. The ashes of *Marcellus*[6] were lost above ground, upon the like account. Where profit hath prompted, no age hath wanted such miners. For which the most barbarous Expilators found the most civill Rhetorick.[7] Gold once out of the earth is no more due unto it;

[1] *Diis manibus.* [2] *Bosio.* [3] *Pausan. in Atticis.* [i. 21.]
[4] Lamprid. *in vit. Alexand. Severi.* [5] Trajanus. *Dion.*
[6] Plut. *in vit. Marcelli.* [30. 2–3.]
[7] The Commission of the *Gothish* King *Theodoric* for finding out sepulchrall treasure. *Cassiodor. Var.* l. 4.

28 *Attica*] *Africa* 58

What was unreasonably committed to the ground is reasonably resumed from it: Let Monuments and rich Fabricks, not Riches adorn mens ashes. The commerce of the living is not to be transferred unto the dead: It is no injustice to take that which none complains to lose, and no man is wronged where no man is possessor.

What virtue yet sleeps in this *terra damnata* and aged cinders, were petty magick to experiment; These crumbling reliques and long-fired particles superannate such expectations: Bones, hairs, nails, and teeth of the dead, were the treasures of old Sorcerers. In 10 vain we revive such practices; Present superstition too visibly perpetuates the folly of our Fore-fathers, wherein unto old Observation[1] this Island was so compleat, that it might have instructed *Persia*.

Plato's historian of the other world, lies twelve dayes incorrupted, while his soul was viewing the large stations of the dead. How to keep the corps seven dayes from corruption by anointing and washing, without exenteration, were an hazardable peece of art, in our choisest practise. How they made distinct separation of bones and ashes from fiery admixture, hath found no historicall solution. 20 Though they seemed to make a distinct collection, and overlooked not *Pyrrhus* his toe[2]. Some provision they might make by fictile Vessels, Coverings, Tiles, or flat stones, upon and about the body. And in the same Field, not farre from these Urnes, many stones were found under ground, as also by carefull separation of extraneous matter, composing and raking up the burnt bones with forks, observable in that notable lamp of *Galuanus*[3]. *Marlianus*[4], who had the sight of the *Vas Ustrinum*, or vessell wherein they burnt the dead, found in the Esquiline Field at *Rome*, might have afforded clearer solution. But their insatisfaction herein begat that re- 30 markable invention in the Funerall Pyres of some Princes, by incombustible sheets made with a texture of *Asbestos*, incremable flax, or Salamanders wool, which preserved their bones and ashes incommixed.

[1] *Britannia hodie eam attonitè celebrat tantis ceremoniis, ut dedisse Persis videri possit*. Plin. l. 29. [30. 4.]

[2] Which could not be burnt. [*Add.*]

[3] To be seen in *Licet. de reconditis veterum lucernis*.

[4] *Topographia Romæ ex Marliano. Erat & vas ustrinum appellatum quod in eo cadavera comburerentur*. Cap. *de Campo Esquilino*. (In *58* this note and the preceding one are printed in reverse order. Browne calls attention to this in *Add.*)

3–4 transferred] trrnsferred *58* 4 no *C*: not *58* 27 lamp *Er C*: lump *58* *Galuanus*. *Er*: *Galuanus 58* *Marlianus Er*(2) *C*: *Martianus 58* 33 ashes] ashes[c] *58* (*no note attached*). *See Commentary*.

How the bulk of a man should sink into so few pounds of bones and ashes, may seem strange unto any who considers not its constitution, and how slender a masse will remain upon an open and urging fire of the carnall composition. Even bones themselves reduced into ashes, do abate a notable proportion. And consisting much of a volatile salt, when that is fired out, make a light kind of cinders. Although their bulk be disproportionable to their weight, when the heavy principle of Salt is fired out, and the Earth almost only remaineth; Observable in sallow, which makes
10 more Ashes then Oake; and discovers the common fraud of selling Ashes by measure, and not by ponderation.

Some bones make best Skeletons[1], some bodies quick and speediest ashes: Who would expect a quick flame from Hydropicall *Heraclitus?* The poysoned Souldier when his Belly brake, put out two pyres in *Plutarch*[2]. But in the plague of *Athens*[3], one private pyre served two or three Intruders; and the *Saracens* burnt in large heaps, by the King of *Castile*[4], shewed how little Fuell sufficeth. Though the Funerall pyre of *Patroclus* took up an hundred foot[5], a peece of an old boat burnt *Pompey*; And if the burthen of *Isaac*
20 were sufficient for an holocaust, a man may carry his owne pyre.

From animals are drawn good burning lights, and good medicines[6] against burning; Though the seminall humour seems of a contrary nature to fire, yet the body compleated proves a combustible lump, wherein fire findes flame even from bones, and some fuell almost from all parts. Though the [7]Metropolis of humidity seems least disposed unto it, which might render the sculls of these Urnes lesse burned then other bones. But all flies or sinks before fire almost in all bodies: When the common ligament is dissolved, the attenuable parts ascend, the rest subside in coal,
30 calx or ashes.

To burn the bones of the King of[8] *Edom* for Lyme, seems no irrationall ferity; But to drink of the ashes of dead relations[9], a passionate prodigality. He that hath the ashes of his friend, hath an everlasting treasure: where fire taketh leave, corruption slowly

[1] Old bones according to *Lyserus*. Those of young persons not tall nor fat according to *Columbus*.
[2] *In vita* Gracc. [13.]
[3] *Thucydides*. [ii. 52.]
[4] *Laurent. Valla*.
[5] Ἑκατόμπεδον ἔνθα ἢ ἔνθα.
[6] *Sperm. ran. Alb. Ovorum*.
[7] The brain. *Hippocrates*.
[8] Amos 2. 1.
[9] As *Artemisia* of her Husband *Mausolus*.

---

16 *Castile*] *Gastile 58*

note 6 above: sperm. ran. Er: Sperma ranarum C: Speran. 58 Ovorum. C: Ovor. 58. In 58 the note is placed at the beginning of the paragraph, without a definite reference. See Commentary.

enters; In bones well burnt, fire makes a wall against it self; experimented in copels, and tests of metals, which consist of such ingredients. What the Sun compoundeth, fire analyseth, not transmuteth. That devouring agent leaves almost allwayes a morsell for the Earth, whereof all things are but a colonie; and which, if time permits, the mother Element will have in their primitive masse again.

He that looks for Urnes and old sepulchrall reliques, must not seek them in the ruines of Temples: where no Religion anciently placed them. These were found in a Field, according to ancient 10 custome, in noble or private buriall; the old practise of the *Canaanites*, the Family of *Abraham*, and the burying place of *Josua*, in the borders of his possessions; and also agreeable unto *Roman* practice to bury by high-wayes, whereby their Monuments were under eye: Memorials of themselves, and *memento's* of mortality into living passengers; whom the Epitaphs of great ones were fain to beg to stay and look upon them. A language though sometimes used, not so proper in Church-Inscriptions[1]. The sensible Rhetorick of the dead, to exemplarity of good life, first admitted the bones of pious men, and Martyrs within Church-wals; which in 20 succeeding ages crept into promiscuous practise. While *Constantine* was peculiarly favoured to be admitted unto the Church Porch; and the first thus buried in *England* was in the dayes of *Cuthred*.

Christians dispute how their bodies should lye in the grave. In urnall enterrment they clearly escaped this Controversie: Though we decline the Religious consideration, yet in cemiteriall and narrower burying places, to avoid confusion and crosse position, a certain posture were to be admitted; Which even Pagan civility observed[2], The *Persians* lay North and South, The *Megarians* and 30 *Phœnicians* placed their heads to the East: The *Athenians*, some think, towards the West, which Christians still retain. And *Beda* will have it to be the posture of our Saviour. That he was crucified with his face towards the West, we will not contend with tradition and probable account; But we applaud not the hand of the Painter, in exalting his Crosse so high above those on either side; since hereof we finde no authentick account in history, and even the crosses found by *Helena* pretend no such distinction from longitude or dimension.

To be gnaw'd out of our graves, to have our sculs made drinking- 40

1 *Siste viator.* 2 *Kirckmannus de funer.* (*See Commentary.*)

40 gnaw'd *C*: gnawd *Er*: knav'd *58*

bowls, and our bones turned into Pipes, to delight and sport our Enemies, are Tragicall abominations, escaped in burning Burials.

Urnall enterrments, and burnt Reliques lye not in fear of worms, or to be an heritage for Serpents; In carnall sepulture, corruptions seem peculiar unto parts, and some speak of snakes out of the spinall marrow. But while we suppose common wormes in graves, 'tis not easie to finde any there; few in Church-yards above a foot deep, fewer or none in Churches, though in fresh decayed bodies. Teeth, bones, and hair, give the most lasting defiance to corrup-
10 tion. In an Hydropicall body ten years buried in a Church-yard, we met with a fat concretion, where the nitre of the Earth, and the salt and lixivious liquor of the body, had coagulated large lumps of fat, into the consistence of the hardest castle-soap; whereof part remaineth with us. After a battle with the *Persians* the *Roman* Corps decayed in few dayes, while the *Persian* bodies remained dry and uncorrupted. Bodies in the same ground do not uniformly dissolve, nor bones equally moulder; whereof in the opprobrious disease we expect no long duration. The body of the Marquesse of *Dorset* seemed sound and handsomely cereclothed, that after
20 seventy eight years was found uncorrupted.[1] Common Tombs preserve not beyond powder: A firmer consistence and compage of parts might be expected from Arefaction, deep buriall or charcoal. The greatest Antiquities of mortall bodies may remain in petrified bones, whereof, though we take not in the pillar of *Lots* wife, or Metamorphosis of *Ortelius*[2], some may be older then Pyramids, in the petrified Reliques of the generall inundation. When *Alexander* opened the Tomb of *Cyrus*, the remaining bones discovered his proportion, whereof urnall fragments afford but a bad conjecture, and have this disadvantage of grave enterrments, that they leave
30 us ignorant of most personall discoveries. For since bones afford not only rectitude and stability, but figure unto the body; It is no impossible Physiognomy to conjecture at fleshy appendencies; and after what shape the muscles and carnous parts might hang in their full consistences. A full spread *Cariola*[3] shews a well-shaped horse behinde, handsome formed sculls, give some analogie of

[1] Of *Thomas* Marquesse of *Dorset*, whose body being buried 1530 was 1608 upon the cutting open of the Cerecloth found perfect and nothing corrupted, the flesh not hardened, but in colour, proportion, and softnesse like an ordinary corps newly to be interred. *Burtons* descript. of *Leicestershire*.

[2] In his Map of *Russia*.

[3] That part in the Skeleton of an Horse, which is made by the hanch-bones. [*Add.*]

---

23 *and* 26 petrified *Er C*: putrefied *58*

fleshy resemblance. A criticall view of bones makes a good distinction of sexes. Even colour is not beyond conjecture; since it is hard to be deceived in the distinction of *Negro's*[1] sculls. [2]*Dantes* Characters are to be found in sculls as well as faces. *Hercules* is not onely known by his foot. Other parts make out their comproportions, and inferences upon whole or parts. And since the dimensions of the head measure the whole body, and the figure thereof gives conjecture of the principall faculties; Physiognomy outlives our selves, and ends not in our graves.

Severe contemplators observing these lasting reliques, may 10 think them good monuments of persons past, little advantage to future beings. And considering that power which subdueth all things unto it self, that can resume the scattered Atomes, or identifie out of any thing, conceive it superfluous to expect a resurrection out of Reliques. But the soul subsisting, other matter clothed with due accidents, may salve the individuality: Yet the Saints we observe arose from graves and monuments, about the holy City. Some think the ancient Patriarchs so earnestly desired to lay their bones in *Canaan*, as hoping to make a part of that Resurrection, and though thirty miles from Mount *Calvary*, at 20 least to lie in that Region, which should produce the first-fruits of the dead. And if according to learned conjecture, the bodies of men shall rise where their greatest Reliques remain, many are not like to erre in the Topography of their Resurrection, though their bones or bodies be after translated by Angels into the field of *Ezechiels*[3] vision, or as some will order it, into the Valley of Judgement, or *Jehosaphat*.

CHAP. IV.

CHRISTIANS have handsomely glossed the deformity of death, by careful consideration of the body, and civil rites which take 30

[1] For their extraordinary thicknesse. [*Add.*]

[2] The Poet *Dante* in his view of Purgatory, found gluttons so meagre, and extenuated, that he conceited them to have been in the Siege of *Jerusalem*, and that it was easie to have discovered *Homo* or *Omo* in their faces: M being made by the two lines of their cheeks, arching over the Eye brows to the nose, and their sunk eyes making O O which makes up *Omo*.

Parean l'occhiaie anella senza gemme
Che nel viso de gli huomini legge huomo
Ben'hauria quiui conosciuto l'emme.

[*Purgatorio*, xxiii. 31–33.]

[3] *Tirin.* in Ezek.

---

note 3 above: in 58 the note is placed against l. 24.

of brutall terminations. And though they conceived all reparable by a resurrection, cast not off all care of enterrment. For since the ashes of Sacrifices burnt upon the Altar of God, were carefully carried out by the Priests, and deposed in a clean field; since they acknowledged their bodies to be the lodging of Christ, and temples of the holy Ghost, they devolved not all upon the sufficiency of soul existence; and therefore with long services and full solemnities concluded their last Exequies, wherein[1] to all distinctions the Greek devotion seems most pathetically ceremonious.

10 Christian invention hath chiefly driven at Rites, which speak hopes of another life, and hints of a Resurrection. And if the ancient Gentiles held not the immortality of their better part, and some subsistence after death; in severall rites, customes, actions and expressions, they contradicted their own opinions: wherein *Democritus* went high, even to the thought of a resurrection[2], as scoffingly recorded by *Pliny*. What can be more expresse than the expression of *Phocyllides*[3]? Or who would expect from *Lucretius*[4] a sentence of *Ecclesiastes*? Before *Plato* could speak, the soul had wings in *Homer*, which fell not, but flew out of the body into the 20 mansions of the dead; who also observed that handsome distinction of *Demas* and *Soma*, for the body conjoyned to the soul and body separated from it. *Lucian* spoke much truth in jest, when he said, that part of *Hercules* which proceeded from *Alchmena* perished, that from *Jupiter* remained immortall. Thus [5]*Socrates* was content that his friends should bury his body, so they would not think they buried *Socrates*, and regarding only his immortall part, was indifferent to be burnt or buried. From such Considerations *Diogenes* might contemn Sepulture. And being satisfied that the soul could not perish, grow carelesse of corporall enterrment. The *Stoicks* who 30 thought the souls of wise men had their habitation about the *moon*, might make slight account of subterraneous deposition; whereas the *Pythagorians* and transcorporating Philosophers, who were to be often buried, held great care of their enterrment. And the Platonicks rejected not a due care of the grave, though they

[1] *Rituale Græcum opera J. Goar in officio exequiarum.*

[2] *Similis reviviscendi promissa Democrito vanitas, qui non revixit ipse. Quæ, malùm, ista dementia est; iterari vitam morte.* Plin. l. 7. c. 55.

[3] Καὶ τάχα δ' ἐκ γαίης ἐλπίζομεν ἐς φάον ἐλθεῖν
Λείψαν' ἀποιχομένων.
& deinceps.

[4] *Cedit enim retro de terrâ quod fuit ante In terram,* &c. Lucret.

[5] *Plato* in *Phæd.* [64 (115E).]

---

2 For *C*: And *58*

put their ashes to unreasonable expectations, in their tedious term of return and long set revolution.

Men have lost their reason in nothing so much as their religion, wherein stones and clouts make Martyrs; and since the religion of one seems madnesse unto another, to afford an account or rationall of old Rites, requires no rigid Reader; That they kindled the pyre aversly, or turning their face from it, was an handsome Symbole of unwilling ministration; That they washed their bones with wine and milk, that the mother wrapt them in Linnen, and dryed them in her bosome, the first fostering part, and place of their nourish- 10 ment; That they opened their eyes towards heaven, before they kindled the fire, as the place of their hopes or originall, were no improper Ceremonies. Their last valediction[1] thrice uttered by the attendants was also very solemn, and somewhat answered by Christians, who thought it too little, if they threw not the earth thrice upon the enterred body. That in strewing their Tombs the *Romans* affected the Rose, the Greeks *Amaranthus* and myrtle; that the Funerall pyre consisted of sweet fuell, Cypresse, Firre, Larix, Yewe, and Trees perpetually verdant, lay silent expressions of their surviving hopes: Wherein Christians which deck their 20 Coffins with Bays have found a more elegant Embleme. For that tree seeming dead, will restore it self from the root, and its dry and exuccous leaves resume their verdure again; which if we mistake not, we have also observed in furze. Whether the planting of yewe in Churchyards, hold not its originall from ancient Funerall rites, or as an Embleme of Resurrection from its perpetual verdure, may also admit conjecture.

They made use of Musick to excite or quiet the affections of their friends, according to different harmonies. But the secret and symbolicall hint was the harmonical nature of the soul; which delivered 30 from the body, went again to enjoy the primitive harmony of heaven, from whence it first descended; which according to its progresse traced by antiquity, came down by *Cancer*, and ascended by *Capricornus*.

They burnt not children before their teeth appeared as apprehending their bodies too tender a morsell for fire, and that their gristly bones would scarce leave separable reliques after the pyrall combustion. That they kindled not fire in their houses for some dayes after, was a strict memoriall of the late afflicting fire. And mourning without hope, they had an happy fraud against 40

[1] *Vale, vale, nos te ordi*[*ne*] *quo natura permittet sequemur.*

22 tree *Er C*: he *58* 24 furze *Er C*: fures *58*

excessive lamentation, by a common opinion that deep sorrows disturbed their ghosts[1].

That they buried their dead on their backs, or in a supine position, seems agreeable unto profound sleep, and common posture of dying; contrary to the most naturall way of birth; Nor unlike our pendulous posture, in the doubtfull state of the womb. *Diogenes* was singular, who preferred a prone situation in the grave, and some Christians[2] like neither, who decline the figure of rest, and make choice of an erect posture.

10 That they carried them out of the world with their feet forward, not inconsonant unto reason: As contrary unto the native posture of man, and his production first into it. And also agreeable unto their opinions, while they bid adieu unto the world, not to look again upon it; whereas *Mahometans* who think to return to a delightfull life again, are carried forth with their heads forward, and looking toward their houses.

They closed their eyes as parts which first die or first discover the sad effects of death. But their iterated clamations to excitate their dying or dead friends, or revoke them unto life again, was a
20 vanity of affection; as not presumably ignorant of the criticall tests of death, by apposition of feathers, glasses, and reflexion of figures, which dead eyes represent not; which however not strictly verifiable in fresh and warm *cadavers*, could hardly elude the test, in corps of four or five dayes.[3]

That they suck'd in the last breath of their expiring friends, was surely a practice of no medicall institution, but a loose opinion that the soul passed out that way, and a fondnesse of affection from some [4]*Pythagoricall* foundation, that the spirit of one body passed into another; which they wished might be their own.

30 That they powred oyle upon the pyre, was a tolerable practise, while the intention rested in facilitating the accension; But to place good *Omens* in the quick and speedy burning, to sacrifice unto the windes for a dispatch in this office, was a low form of superstition.

The *Archimime* or *Jester* attending the Funerall train, and imitating the speeches, gesture, and manners of the deceased, was too light for such solemnities, contradicting their Funerall Orations, and dolefull rites of the grave.

That they buried a peece of money with them as a Fee of the

[1] *Tu manes ne læde meos.* [Tibullus, i. 1. 67.]
[2] *Russians*, &c.
[3] At least by some difference from living Eyes. [*Add.*]
[4] *Francesco Perucci. Pompe funebri.*

Elysian Ferriman, was a practise full of folly. But the ancient custome of placing coynes in considerable Urnes, and the present practise of burying medals in the Noble Foundations of *Europe*, are laudable wayes of historicall discoveries, in actions, persons, Chronologies; and posterity will applaud them.

We examine not the old Laws of Sepulture, exempting certain persons from buriall or burning. But hereby we apprehend that these were not the bones of persons Planet-struck or burnt with fire from Heaven: No Reliques of Traitors to their Countrey, Self-killers, or Sacrilegious Malefactors; Persons in old apprehen- 10 sion unworthy of the *earth*; condemned unto the *Tartara's* of Hell, and bottomlesse pit of *Pluto*, from whence there was no redemption.

Nor were only many customes questionable in order to their Obsequies, but also sundry practises, fictions, and conceptions, discordant or obscure, of their state and future beings; whether unto eight or ten bodies of men to adde one of a woman, as being more inflammable, and unctuously constituted for the better pyrall combustion, were any rationall practise: Or whether the complaint of *Perianders* Wife be tolerable, that wanting her Funerall 20 burning she suffered intolerable cold in Hell, according to the constitution of the infernall house of *Pluto*, wherein cold makes a great part of their tortures; it cannot passe without some question.

Why the Female Ghosts appear unto *Ulysses*, before the *Heroes* and masculine spirits? Why the *Psyche* or soul of *Tiresias* is of the masculine gender[1]; who being blinde on earth sees more then all the rest in hell; Why the Funerall Suppers consisted of Egges, Beans, Smallage, and Lettuce, since the dead are made to eat *Asphodels*[2] about the *Elyzian* medows? Why since there is no Sacrifice acceptable, nor any propitiation for the Covenant of the grave; 30 men set up the Deity of *Morta*, and fruitlesly adored Divinities without ears? it cannot escape some doubt.

The dead seem all alive in the humane *Hades* of *Homer*, yet cannot well speak, prophesie, or know the living, except they drink bloud, wherein is the life of man. And therefore the souls of *Penelope*'s Paramours conducted by *Mercury* chirped like bats, and those which followed *Hercules* made a noise but like a flock of birds.

[1] In *Homer*, ψυχὴ Θηβαίου Τειρεσίαο σκῆπτρον ἔχων. [*Od.* xi. 90.] [*Add.*]
[2] In *Lucian*. [*Cataplus*, 2.] [*Add.*]

---

12 *Pluto C 58* (*4°*): *Plato 58* 22 *Pluto C 58* (*4°*): *Plato 58 Er*(*2*) *correcting Pluto*

The departed spirits know things past and to come, yet are ignorant of things present. *Agamemnon* foretels what should happen unto *Ulysses*, yet ignorantly enquires what is become of his own Son. The Ghosts are afraid of swords in *Homer*, yet *Sybilla* tels *Æneas* in *Virgil*, the thin habit of spirits was beyond the force of weapons. The spirits put off their malice with their bodies, and *Cæsar* and *Pompey* accord in Latine Hell, yet *Ajax* in *Homer* endures not a conference with *Ulysses*: And *Deiphobus* appears all mangled in *Virgils* Ghosts, yet we meet with perfect shadows among the
10 wounded ghosts of *Homer*.

Since *Charon* in *Lucian* applauds his condition among the dead, whether it be handsomely said of *Achilles*, that living contemner of death, that he had rather be a Plowmans servant then Emperour of the dead? How *Hercules* his soul is in hell, and yet in heaven, and *Julius* his soul in a Starre, yet seen by *Æneas* in hell, except the Ghosts were but Images and shadows of the soul, received in higher mansions, according to the ancient division of body, soul, and image or *simulachrum* of them both. The particulars of future beings must needs be dark unto ancient Theories, which Christian
20 Philosophy yet determines but in a Cloud of opinions. A Dialogue between two Infants in the womb concerning the state of this world, might handsomely illustrate our ignorance of the next, whereof methinks we yet discourse in *Platoes* denne, and are but *Embryon* Philosophers.

Pythagoras escapes in the fabulous hell of *Dante*[1], among that swarm of Philosophers, wherein whilest we meet with *Plato* and *Socrates*, *Cato* is to be found in no lower place then Purgatory. Among all the set, *Epicurus* is most considerable, whom men make honest without an *Elyzium*, who contemned life without en-
30 couragement of immortality, and making nothing after death, yet made nothing of the King of terrours.

Were the happinesse of the next world as closely apprehended as the felicities of this, it were a martyrdome to live; and unto such as consider none hereafter, it must be more then death to dye, which makes us amazed at those audacities, that durst be nothing, and return into their *Chaos* again. Certainly such spirits as could contemn death, when they expected no better being after, would have scorned to live had they known any. And therefore we applaud not the judgment of *Machiavel*, that Christianity makes
40 men cowards, or that with the confidence of but half dying, the despised virtues of patience and humility, have abased the spirits of men, which Pagan principles exalted, but rather regulated the

[1] *Del inferno*. cant. 4.

wildenesse of audacities, in the attempts, grounds, and eternall sequels of death; wherein men of the boldest spirits are often prodigiously temerarious. Nor can we extenuate the valour of ancient Martyrs, who contemned death in the uncomfortable scene of their lives, and in their decrepit Martyrdomes did probably lose not many moneths of their dayes, or parted with life when it was scarce worth the living. For (beside that long time past holds no consideration unto a slender time to come) they had no small disadvantage from the constitution of old age, which naturally makes men fearfull; complexionally superannuated from the bold 10 and couragious thoughts of youth and fervent years. But the contempt of death from corporall animosity, promoteth not our felicity. They may set in the *Orchestra*, and noblest Seats of Heaven, who have held up shaking hands in the fire, and humanely contended for glory.

Mean while *Epicurus* lyes deep in *Dante*'s hell, wherein we meet with Tombs enclosing souls which denied their immortalities. But whether the virtuous heathen, who lived better then he spake, or erring in the principles of himself, yet lived above Philosophers of more specious Maximes, lye so deep as he is placed; at least so low 20 as not to rise against Christians, who beleeving or knowing that truth, have lastingly denied it in their practise and conversation, were a quæry too sad to insist on.

But all or most apprehensions rested in Opinions of some future being, which ignorantly or coldly beleeved, begat those perverted conceptions, Ceremonies, Sayings, which Christians pity or laugh at. Happy are they, which live not in that disadvantage of time, when men could say little for futurity, but from reason. Whereby the noblest mindes fell often upon doubtfull deaths, and melancholly Dissolutions; With these hopes *Socrates* warmed his doubt- 30 full spirits, against that cold potion, and *Cato* before he durst give the fatall stroak spent part of the night in reading the immortality of *Plato*, thereby confirming his wavering hand unto the animosity of that attempt.

It is the heaviest stone that melancholy can throw at a man, to tell him he is at the end of his nature; or that there is no further state to come, unto which this seemes progressionall, and otherwise made in vaine; Without this accomplishment the naturall expectation and desire of such a state, were but a fallacy in nature; unsatisfied Considerators would quarrell the justice of their 40

10 complexionally *Er*(*2*): And complexionally *58* superannuated] superannua-ated *58* 23 on.] on, *58* 39 nature; *C*: nature, *58* 40 Considerators *C*: Considerators; *58*

constitutions, and rest content that *Adam* had fallen lower, whereby by knowing no other Originall, and deeper ignorance of themselves, they might have enjoyed the happinesse of inferiour Creatures; who in tranquility possesse their Constitutions, as having not the apprehension to deplore their own natures. And being framed below the circumference of these hopes, or cognition of better being, the wisedom of God hath necessitated their Contentment: But the superiour ingredient and obscured part of our selves, whereto all present felicities afford no resting contentment, 10 will be able at last to tell us we are more then our present selves; and evacuate such hopes in the fruition of their own accomplishments.

CHAP. V.

NOW since these dead bones have already out-lasted the living ones of *Methuselah*, and in a yard under ground, and thin walls of clay, out-worn all the strong and specious buildings above it; and quietly rested under the drums and tramplings of three conquests; What Prince can promise such diuturnity unto his Reliques, or might not gladly say,

20 [1]*Sic ego componi versus in ossa velim.*

Time which antiquates Antiquities, and hath an art to make dust of all things, hath yet spared these *minor* Monuments. In vain we hope to be known by open and visible conservatories, when to be unknown was the means of their continuation and obscurity their protection: If they dyed by violent hands, and were thrust into their Urnes, these bones become considerable, and some old Philosophers would honour[2] them, whose souls they conceived most pure, which were thus snatched from their bodies; and to retain a stronger propension unto them: whereas they weariedly 30 left a languishing corps, and with faint desires of re-union. If they fell by long and aged decay, yet wrapt up in the bundle of time, they fall into indistinction, and make but one blot with Infants. If we begin to die when we live, and long life be but a prolongation of death; our life is a sad composition; We live with death, and die not in a moment. How many pulses made up the life of *Methuselah*,

1 *Tibullus.* [iii. 2. 26.]

2 *Oracula Chaldaica cum scholiis Pselli & Plethonis.* Βίῃ λιπόντων σῶμα ψυχαὶ καθαρώταται. *Vi corpus relinquentium animæ purissimæ.*

note 2 above: Καθαρώταται *Er* (*shorter list* καθαρώτατας): καθαρώτεται *58*

29 stronger *Er C*: stranger *58*

were work for *Archimedes*: Common Counters summe up the life of *Moses* his man[1]. Our dayes become considerable like petty sums by minute accumulations; where numerous fractions make up but small round numbers; and our dayes of a span long make not one little finger[2].

If the nearnesse of our last necessity, brought a nearer conformity unto it, there were a happinesse in hoary hairs, and no calamity in half senses. But the long habit of living indisposeth us for dying; When Avarice makes us the sport of death; When even *David* grew politickly cruell; and *Solomon* could hardly be said to be 10 the wisest of men. But many are too early old, and before the date of age. Adversity stretcheth our dayes, misery makes [3]*Alcmenas* nights, and time hath no wings unto it. But the most tedious being is that which can unwish it self, content to be nothing, or never to have been, which was beyond the *male*-content of *Job*, who cursed not the day of his life, but his Nativity: Content to have so farre been, as to have a Title to future being; Although he had lived here but in an hidden state of life, and as it were an abortion.

What Song the *Syrens* sang, or what name *Achilles* assumed when 20 he hid himself among women, though puzling Questions[4] are not beyond all conjecture. What time the persons of these Ossuaries entred the famous Nations of the dead[5], and slept[6] with Princes and Counsellours, might admit a wide solution. But who were the proprietaries of these bones, or what bodies these ashes made up, were a question above Antiquarism. Not to be resolved by man, nor easily perhaps by spirits, except we consult the Provinciall Guardians, or tutellary Observators. Had they made as good provision for their names, as they have done for their Reliques, they had not so grosly erred in the art of perpetuation. But to 30 subsist in bones, and be but Pyramidally extant, is a fallacy in duration. Vain ashes, which in the oblivion of names, persons, times, and sexes, have found unto themselves, a fruitlesse continuation, and only arise unto late posterity, as Emblemes of mortall vanities; Antidotes against pride, vain-glory, and madding vices. Pagan vain-glories which thought the world might last for

[1] In the Psalme of *Moses*. [xc. 10.]

[2] According to the ancient Arithmetick of the hand wherein the little finger of the right hand contracted, signified an hundred. *Pierius in Hieroglyph.*

[3] One night as long as three.

[4] The puzling questions of *Tiberius* unto *Grammarians. Marcel. Donatus in Suet.* [*Tiberius*, 70.]

[5] *Κλυτὰ ἔθνεα νεκρῶν Hom.* [*Od.* x. 526.]

[6] *Job.* [iii. 13–15.]

ever, had encouragement for ambition, and finding no *Atropos* unto the immortality of their Names, were never dampt with the necessity of oblivion. Even old ambitions had the advantage of ours, in the attempts of their vain-glories, who acting early, and before the probable Meridian of time, have by this time found great accomplishment of their designes, whereby the ancient *Heroes* have already out-lasted their Monuments, and Mechanicall preservations. But in this latter Scene of time we cannot expect such Mummies unto our memories, when ambition may fear the
10 Prophecy of *Elias*[1], and *Charles* the fifth can never hope to live within two *Methusela's* of *Hector*[2].

And therefore restlesse inquietude for the diuturnity of our memories unto present considerations, seems a vanity almost out of date, and superanuated peece of folly. We cannot hope to live so long in our names, as some have done in their persons, one face of *Janus* holds no proportion unto the other. 'Tis too late to be ambitious. The great mutations of the world are acted, or time may be too short for our designes. To extend our memories by Monuments, whose death we dayly pray for, and whose duration
20 we cannot hope, without injury to our expectations, in the advent of the last day, were a contradiction to our beliefs. We whose generations are ordained in this setting part of time, are providentially taken off from such imaginations. And being necessitated to eye the remaining particle of futurity, are naturally constituted unto thoughts of the next world, and cannot excusably decline the consideration of that duration, which maketh Pyramids pillars of snow, and all that's past a moment.

Circles and right lines limit and close all bodies, and the mortall right-lined circle[3], must conclude and shut up all. There is no
30 antidote against the *Opium* of time, which temporally considereth all things; Our Fathers finde their graves in our short memories, and sadly tell us how we may be buried in our Survivors. Gravestones tell truth scarce fourty years[4]: Generations passe while some trees stand, and old Families last not three Oaks. To be read by bare Inscriptions like many in *Gruter*[5], to hope for Eternity by Ænigmaticall Epithetes, or first letters of our names, to be

1 That the world may last but six thousand years.

2 Hectors fame lasting above two lives of *Methuselah,* before that famous Prince was extant.

3 ⊖ The character of death.

4 Old ones being taken up, and other bodies laid under them.

5 *Gruteri Inscriptiones Antiquæ.*

---

6 designes] ddsignes *58*

studied by Antiquaries, who we were, and have new Names given us like many of the Mummies[1], are cold consolations unto the Students of perpetuity, even by everlasting Languages.

To be content that times to come should only know there was such a man, not caring whether they knew more of him, was a frigid ambition in *Cardan*[2]*:* disparaging his horoscopal inclination and judgement of himself. Who cares to subsist like *Hippocrates* Patients, or *Achilles* horses in *Homer*, under naked nominations, without deserts and noble acts, which are the balsame of our memories, the *Entelechia* and soul of our subsistences. To be 10 namelesse in worthy deeds exceeds an infamous history. The *Canaanitish* woman lives more happily without a name, then *Herodias* with one. And who had not rather have been the good theef, then *Pilate*?

But the iniquity of oblivion blindely scattereth her poppy, and deals with the memory of men without distinction to merit of perpetuity. Who can but pity the founder of the Pyramids? *Herostratus* lives that burnt the Temple of *Diana*, he is almost lost that built it; Time hath spared the Epitaph of *Adrians* horse, confounded that of himself. In vain we compute our felicities by the 20 advantage of our good names, since bad have equall durations; and *Thersites* is like to live as long as *Agamemnon*. Who knows whether the best of men be known? or whether there be not more remarkable persons forgot, then any that stand remembred in the known account of time? without the favour of the everlasting Register the first man had been as unknown as the last, and *Methuselahs* long life had been his only Chronicle.

Oblivion is not to be hired: The greater part must be content to be as though they had not been, to be found in the Register of God, not in the record of man. Twenty seven Names make up the first 30 story[3], and the recorded names ever since contain not one living Century. The number of the dead long exceedeth all that shall live. The night of time far surpasseth the day, and who knows when was the Æquinox? Euery houre addes unto that current Arithmetique,

[1] Which men show in several Countries, giving them what Names they please; and unto some the Names of the old Ægyptian Kings out of *Herodotus*. [*Add.*]

[2] *Cuperem notum esse quod sim, non opto ut sciatur qualis sim.* Card. *in vita propria.*

[3] Before the flood [*Add.*]

---

7 himself. Who] himself, who *58* 17 perpetuity.] perpetuity, *58*
22 *Agamemnon*. Who *Er C*: *Agamemnon*, without the favour of the everlasting Register: Who *58* (*Er directs that the words* without . . . Register *are to be placed after* account of time)

which scarce stands one moment. And since death must be the *Lucina* of life, and even Pagans could doubt[1] whether thus to live, were to dye. Since our longest Sunne sets at right descensions, and makes but winter arches, and therefore it cannot be long before we lie down in darknesse, and have our light in ashes[2]. Since the brother of death daily haunts us with dying *memento*'s, and time that grows old it self, bids us hope no long duration: Diuturnity is a dream and folly of expectation.

Darknesse and light divide the course of time, and oblivion 10 shares with memory, a great part even of our living beings; we slightly remember our felicities, and the smartest stroaks of affliction leave but short smart upon us. Sense endureth no extremities, and sorrows destroy us or themselves. To weep into stones are fables. Afflictions induce callosities, miseries are slippery, or fall like snow upon us, which notwithstanding is no unhappy stupidity. To be ignorant of evils to come, and forgetfull of evils past, is a mercifull provision in nature, whereby we digest the mixture of our few and evil dayes, and our delivered senses not relapsing into cutting remembrances, our sorrows are not kept raw by the edge 20 of repetitions. A great part of Antiquity contented their hopes of subsistency with a transmigration of their souls. A good way to continue their memories, while having the advantage of plurall successions, they could not but act something remarkable in such variety of beings, and enjoying the fame of their passed selves, make accumulation of glory unto their last durations. Others rather then be lost in the uncomfortable night of nothing, were content to recede into the common being, and make one particle of the publick soul of all things, which was no more then to return into their unknown and divine Originall again. Ægyptian inge- 30 nuity was more unsatisfied, contriving their bodies in sweet consistences, to attend the return of their souls. But all was vanity, feeding[3] the winde, and folly. The Ægyptian Mummies, which *Cambyses* or time hath spared, avarice now consumeth. Mummie is become Merchandise, *Mizraim* cures wounds, and *Pharaoh* is sold for balsoms.

In vain do individuals hope for Immortality, or any patent from

[1] *Euripides*. [*Add.*]

[2] According to the custome of the Jewes, who place a lighted wax-candle in a pot of ashes by the Corps. *Leo*. [*Add.*]

[3] *Omnia vanitas & pastio venti*, *νομὴ ἀνέμου*, *βόσκησις ut olim Aquila & Symmachus*. V. Drus. *Eccles.*

---

8 dream] drean *58* *note 3 above*: *νομὴ Er*: *νημὴ 58*

oblivion, in preservations below the Moon: Men have been deceived even in their flatteries above the Sun, and studied conceits to perpetuate their names in heaven. The various Cosmography of that part hath already varied the names of contrived constellations; *Nimrod* is lost in *Orion*, and *Osyris* in the Dogge-starre. While we look for incorruption in the heavens, we finde they are but like the Earth; Durable in their main bodies, alterable in their parts: whereof beside Comets and new Stars, perspectives begin to tell tales. And the spots that wander about the Sun, with *Phaetons* favour, would make clear conviction. 10

There is nothing strictly immortall, but immortality; whatever hath no beginning may be confident of no end. All others have a dependent being, and within the reach of destruction, which is the peculiar of that necessary essence that cannot destroy it self; And the highest strain of omnipotency to be so powerfully constituted, as not to suffer even from the power of it self. But the sufficiency of Christian Immortality frustrates all earthly glory, and the quality of either state after death, makes a folly of posthumous memory. God who can only destroy our souls, and hath assured our resurrection, either of our bodies or names hath directly promised 20 no duration. Wherein there is so much of chance that the boldest Expectants have found unhappy frustration; and to hold long subsistence, seems but a scape in oblivion. But man is a Noble Animal, splendid in ashes, and pompous in the grave, solemnizing Nativities and Deaths with equall lustre, nor omitting Ceremonies of bravery, in the infamy of his nature.

Life is a pure flame, and we live by an invisible Sun within us. A small fire sufficeth for life, great flames seemed too little after death, while men vainly affected precious pyres, and to burn like *Sardanapalus*, but the wisedom of funerall Laws found the folly of 30 prodigall blazes, and reduced undoing fires, unto the rule of sober obsequies, wherein few could be so mean as not to provide wood, pitch, a mourner, and an Urne[1].

Five Languages secured not the Epitaph of *Gordianus*[2]; The man of God lives longer without a Tomb then any by one, invisibly

[1] According to the Epitaph of Rufus and Beronica in Gruterus,

—nec ex
Eorum bonis plus inventum est, quam
Quod sufficeret ad emendam pyram
Et picem quibus corpora cremarentur,
Et præfica conducta & olla empta. [*Add.*]

[2] In Greek, Latine, Hebrew, Ægyptian, Arabick, defaced by *Licinius* the Emperour. [*Add.*]

interred by Angels, and adjudged to obscurity, though not without some marks directing humane discovery. *Enoch* and *Elias* without either tomb or buriall, in an anomalous state of being, are the great Examples of perpetuity, in their long and living memory, in strict account being still on this side death, and having a late part yet to act upon this stage of earth. If in the decretory term of the world we shall not all dye but be changed, according to received translation; the last day will make but few graves; at least quick Resurrections will anticipate lasting Sepultures; Some Graves will 10 be opened before they be quite closed, and *Lazarus* be no wonder. When many that feared to dye shall groane that they can dye but once, the dismall state is the second and living death, when life puts despair on the damned; when men shall wish the coverings of Mountaines, not of Monuments, and annihilation shall be courted.

While some have studied Monuments, others have studiously declined them: and some have been so vainly boisterous, that they durst not acknowledge their Graves; wherein[1] *Alaricus* seems most subtle, who had a River turned to hide his bones at the bottome. Even *Sylla* that thought himself safe in his Urne, could 20 not prevent revenging tongues, and stones thrown at his Monument. Happy are they whom privacy makes innocent, who deal so with men in this world, that they are not afraid to meet them in the next, who when they dye, make no commotion among the dead, and are not toucht with that poeticall taunt of *Isaiah*[2].

Pyramids, *Arches*, *Obelisks*, were but the irregularities of vainglory, and wilde enormities of ancient magnanimity. But the most magnanimous resolution rests in the Christian Religion, which trampleth upon pride, and sets on the neck of ambition, humbly pursuing that infallible perpetuity, unto which all others must 30 diminish their diameters, and be poorly seen in Angles of contingency[3].

Pious spirits who passed their dayes in raptures of futurity, made little more of this world, then the world that was before it, while they lay obscure in the Chaos of pre-ordination, and night of their fore-beings. And if any have been so happy as truly to understand Christian annihilation, extasis, exolution, liquefaction, transformation, the kisse of the Spouse, gustation of God, and ingression into the divine shadow, they have already had an handsome anti-

[1] *Jornandes de rebus Geticis.* [xxx, 1597, p. 87.]

[2] Isa. 14. [4–17.]

[3] *Angulus contingentiæ*, the least of Angles.

---

6 stage *Er C*: staye *58*

cipation of heaven; the glory of the world is surely over, and the earth in ashes unto them.

To subsist in lasting Monuments, to live in their productions, to exist in their names, and prædicament of *Chymera's*, was large satisfaction unto old expectations, and made one part of their *Elyziums*. But all this is nothing in the Metaphysicks of true belief. To live indeed is to be again our selves, which being not only an hope but an evidence in noble beleevers; 'Tis all one to lye in St *Innocents*[1] Church-yard, as in the Sands of *Ægypt*: Ready to be any thing, in the extasie of being ever, and as content with six 10 foot as the Moles of *Adrianus*[2].

Lucan
——*Tabesne cadavera solvat*
An rogus haud refert.——

[1] In *Paris* where bodies soon consume.

[2] A stately *Mausoleum* or sepuchral pyle built by *Adrianus* in *Rome*, where now standeth the Castle of St. *Angelo*.

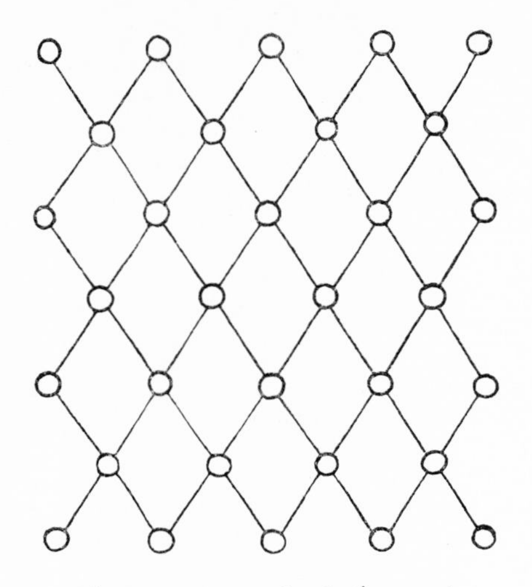

Quid Quincunce speciosius, qui, in quam cunque partem spectaueris, rectus est. Quintilian:

THE GARDEN OF CYRUS.

OR,

The Quincunciall, Lozenge, or Net-work Plantations of the Ancients, Artificially Naturally, Mystically Considered.

BY

Thomas Brown D. of Physick

Printed in the Year, 1658.

THE GARDEN OF CYRUS.

OR,

The Quincunciall, Lozenge, or Net-work Plantations of the Ancients, Artificially, Naturally, Mystically considered.

CHAPTER I.

THAT *Vulcan* gave arrows unto *Apollo* and *Diana* the fourth day after their Nativities, according to Gentile Theology, may passe for no blinde apprehension of the Creation of the Sunne and Moon, in the work of the fourth day; When the diffused light 10 contracted into Orbes, and shooting rayes, of those Luminaries. Plainer Descriptions there are from Pagan pens, of the creatures ot the fourth day; While the [1]divine Philosopher unhappily omitteth the noblest part of the third; And *Ovid* (whom many conceive to have borrowed his description from *Moses*) coldly deserting the remarkable account of the text, in three words,[2] describeth this work of the third day; the vegetable creation, and first ornamentall Scene of nature; the primitive food of animals, and first story of Physick, in Dietetical conservation.

For though Physick may pleade high, from that medicall act of 20 God, in casting so deep a sleep upon our first Parent; And Chirurgery[3] finde its whole art, in that one passage concerning the Rib of *Adam*, yet is there no rivality with Garden contrivance and Herbery. For if Paradise were planted the third day of the Creation, as wiser Divinity concludeth, the Nativity thereof was too early for Horoscopie; Gardens were before Gardiners, and but some hours after the earth.

Of deeper doubt is its Topography, and locall designation, yet being the primitive garden, and without much[4] controversie seated in the East; it is more then probable the first curiosity, and 30 cultivation of plants, most flourished in those quarters. And

[1] *Plato in Timæo.* [2] *fronde tegi silvas.*

[3] διαίρεσις, in opening the flesh. ἐξαίρεσις, in taking out the rib. σύνθεσις in closing up the part again.

[4] For some there is from the ambiguity of the word *Mikedem*, whether *ab oriente* or *a principio.*

since the Ark of *Noah* first toucht upon some mountains of *Armenia*, the planting art arose again in the East, and found its revolution not far from the place of its Nativity, about the Plains of those Regions. And if *Zoroaster* were either *Cham*, *Chus*, or *Mizraim*, they were early proficients therein, who left (as *Pliny* delivereth) a work of Agriculture.

However the account of the Pensill or hanging gardens of *Babylon*, if made by *Semiramis*, the third or fourth from *Nimrod*, is of no slender antiquity; which being not framed upon ordinary levell 10 of ground, but raised upon pillars, admitting under-passages, we cannot accept as the first *Babylonian* Gardens; But a more eminent progress and advancement in that art, then any that went before it: Somewhat answering or hinting the old Opinion concerning Paradise itself, with many conceptions elevated, above the plane of the Earth.

Nebuchodonosor whom some will have to be the famous *Syrian* King of *Diodorus*, beautifully repaired that City; and so magnificently built his [1]hanging gardens; that from succeeding Writers he had the honour of the first. From whence over-looking *Babylon*, 20 and all the Region about it, he found no circumscription to the eye of his ambition, till over-delighted with the bravery of this Paradise; in his melancholy metamorphosis, he found the folly of that delight, and a proper punishment, in the contrary habitation, in wilde plantations and wandrings of the fields.

The *Persian* Gallants who destroyed this Monarchy, maintained their Botanicall bravery. Unto whom we owe the very name of Paradise: wherewith we meet not in Scripture before the time of *Solomon*, and conceived originally *Persian*. The word for that disputed Garden, expressing in the Hebrew no more then a Field 30 enclosed, which from the same Root is content to derive a garden and a Buckler.

Cyrus the elder brought up in Woods and Mountains, when time and power enabled, pursued the dictate of his education, and brought the treasures of the field into rule and circum-scription. So nobly beautifying the hanging Gardens of *Babylon*, that he was also thought to be the authour thereof.

Ahasuerus (whom many conceive to have been *Artaxerxes Longimanus*) in the [2]Countrey and City of Flowers, and in an open Garden, entertained his Princes and people, while *Vasthi* more 40 modestly treated the Ladies within the Palace thereof.

[1] *Josephus*. [2] *Sushan in Susiana*. [Esther i. 2, &c.]

7 gardens of] gardens yf *58* 11 first] fitst *58*

But if (as some opinion) King *Ahasuerus* were *Artaxerxes Mnemon*, that found a life and reign answerable unto his great memory, our magnified *Cyrus* was his second Brother[1]: who gave the occasion of that memorable work, and almost miraculous retrait of *Xenophon*. A person of high spirit and honour, naturally a King, though fatally prevented by the harmlesse chance of *post*-geniture: Not only a Lord of Gardens, but a manuall planter thereof: disposing his trees like his armies in regular ordination. So that while old *Laertes* hath found a name in *Homer* for pruning hedges, and clearing away thorns and bryars; while King *Attalus* lives for his poysonous plantations of *Aconites*, Henbane, Hellebore, and plants hardly admitted within the walls of Paradise; While many of the Ancients do poorly live in the single names of Vegetables; All stories do look upon *Cyrus*, as the splendid and regular planter.

According whereto *Xenophon*[2] describeth his gallant plantation at *Sardis*, thus rendred by *Strebæus*. [3]*Arbores pari intervallo sitas, rectos ordines, & omnia perpulchrè in Quincuncem directa.* Which we shall take for granted as being accordingly rendred by the most elegant of the [4]*Latines*; and by no made term, but in use before by *Varro*. That is the rows and orders so handsomly disposed; or five trees so set together, that a regular angularity, and through prospect, was left on every side, Owing this name not only unto the Quintuple number of Trees, but the figure declaring that number. which being doubled at the angle, makes up the Letter χ, that is the Emphaticall decussation, or fundamentall figure.

Now though in some ancient and modern practice the *area* or decussated plot, might be a perfect square, answerable to a *Tuscan Pedestall*, and the *Quinquernio* or Cinque-point of a dye; wherein by Diagonall lines the intersection was rectangular; accomodable unto Plantations of large growing Trees; and we must not deny our selves the advantage of this order; yet shall we chiefly insist upon that of [5]*Curtius* and *Porta*, in their brief description hereof. Wherein the *decussis* is made within a longilaterall square, with opposite angles,

1 *Plutarch* in the life of *Artaxerxes*.[*See Commentary*.]

2 *Xenophon in Oeconomico*. [iv. 21.]

3 *Καλὰ μὲν τά δένδρα, δί ἴσου δὲ τὰ πεφυτευμένα, ὀρθοὶ δὲ οἱ στίχοι τῶν δένδρων, εὐγώνια δὲ πάντα καλῶς.*

4 *Cicero in Cat. Major*. [17.]

5 *Benedict Curtius de Hortis. Bapt. Porta in Villa.*

3 Brother[1]] Brother *58* 9 *Laertes*] *Laertas 58* 19 being] heing *58* *note 3 above* ἐυγώνια *Er*: ἐυδώνια *58* 25 doubled *Er C*: doubted *58* 30 rectangular *Er*(*2*): regular *58*

acute and obtuse at the intersection; and so upon progression making a *Rhombus* or Lozenge figuration, which seemeth very agreeable unto the Originall figure; Answerable whereunto we observe the decussated characters in many consulary Coynes, and even in those of *Constantine* and his Sons, which pretend their pattern in the Sky; the crucigerous Ensigne carried this figure, not transversly or rectangularly intersected, but in a decussation, after the form of an *Andrean* or *Burgundian* cross, which answereth this description.

10 Where by the way we shall decline the old Theme, so traced by antiquity of crosses and crucifixion: Whereof some being right, and of one single peece without traversion or transome, do little advantage our subject. Nor shall we take in the mysticall *Tau*, or the Crosse of our blessed Saviour, which having in some descriptions an *Empedon* or crossing foot-stay, made not one single transversion. And since the Learned *Lipsius* hath made some doubt even of the Crosse of St *Andrew*, since some Martyrologicall Histories deliver his death by the generall Name of a crosse, and *Hippolitus* will have him suffer by the sword; we should have 20 enough to make out the received Crosse of that Martyr. Nor shall we urge the *labarum*, and famous Standard of *Constantine*, or make further use thereof, then as the first Letters in the Name of our Saviour Christ, in use among Christians, before the dayes of *Constantine*, to be observed in [1]Sepulchral Monuments of Martyrs, in the Reign of *Adrian*, and *Antoninus*; and to be found in the Antiquities of the Gentiles, before the advent of Christ, as in the Medall of King *Ptolomy*, signed with the same characters, and might be the beginning of some word or name, which Antiquaries have not hit on.

30 We will not revive the mysterious crosses of *Ægypt*, with circles on their heads, in the breast of *Serapis*, and the hands of their Geniall spirits, not unlike the character of *Venus*, and looked on by ancient Christians, with relation unto Christ. Since however they first began, the Ægyptians thereby expressed the processe and motion of the spirit of the world, and the diffusion thereof upon the Celestiall and Elementall nature; implyed by a circle and right-lined intersection. A secret in their Telesmes and magicall Characters among them. Though he that considereth the [2]plain crosse

[1] Of *Marius, Alexander, Roma Sotterranea.*

[2] Wherein the lower part is somewhat longer, as defined by *Upton de studio militari*, and *Johannes de Bado Aureo, cum comment. clariss. & doctiss. Bissæi.*

---

7 transversly] transverly *58*

upon the head of the Owl in the Laterane Obelisk, or the [1]crosse erected upon a picher diffusing streams of water into two basins, with sprinkling branches in them, and all described upon a two-footed Altar, as in the Hieroglyphicks of the brasen Table of *Bembus*; will hardly decline all thought of Christian signality in them.

We shall not call in the Hebrew *Tenupha*, or ceremony of their Oblations, waved by the Priest unto the four quarters of the world, after the form of a cross; as in the peace-offerings. And if it were clearly made out what is remarkably delivered from the Traditions 10 of the Rabbins, that as the Oyle was powred coronally or circularly upon the head of Kings, so the High-Priest was anointed decussatively or in the form of a X; though it could not escape a typicall thought of Christ, from mysticall considerators; yet being the conceit is Hebrew, we should rather expect its verification from Analogy in that language, then to confine the same unto the unconcerned Letters of *Greece*, or make it out by the characters of *Cadmus* or *Palamedes*.

Of this Quincunciall Ordination the Ancients practised much discoursed little; and the Moderns have nothing enlarged; which 20 he that more nearly considereth, in the form of its square *Rhombus*, and decussation, with the severall commodities, mysteries, parallelismes, and resemblances, both in Art and Nature, shall easily discern the elegancy of this order.

That this was in some wayes of practice in diverse and distant Nations, hints or deliveries there are from no slender Antiquity. In the hanging Gardens of *Babylon*, from *Abydenus*, *Eusebius*, and others, [2]*Curtius* describeth this rule of decussation. In the memorable Garden of *Alcinous* anciently conceived an originall phancy, from Paradise, mention there is of well contrived order; For so 30 hath *Didymus* and *Eustachius* expounded the emphatical word. *Diomedes* describing the Rurall possessions of his father, gives account in the same Language of Trees orderly planted. And *Ulysses* being a boy was promised by his Father fourty Figge-trees, and fifty[3] rows of Vines producing all kinde of grapes.

That the Eastern Inhabitants of *India*, made use of such order, even in open Plantations, is deducible from *Theophrastus*; who

[1] *Casal. de Ritibus. Bosio nella Trionfante croce.*

[2] *Decussatio ipsa jucundum ac peramænum conspectum præbuit*. Curt. *Hortor*. l. 6.

[3] *ὄρχοι, στίχοι αμπέλων, φυτῶν στίχος ἡ κατὰ τάξιν φυτέια*. Phavorinus [*Lexicon*]. Philoxenus [*Lexicon*].

7 *Tenupha Er*(2): *Tenapha 58* 11 circularly] circularlly *58*

describing the trees whereof they made their garments, plainly delivereth that they were planted κατ' ὄρχους, and in such order that at a distance men would mistake them for Vineyards. The same seems confirmed in *Greece* from a singular expression in [1]*Aristotle* concerning the order of Vines, delivered by a military term representing the orders of Souldiers, which also confirmeth the antiquity of this form yet used in vineall plantations.

That the same was used in Latine plantations is plainly confirmed from the commending penne of *Varro*, *Quintilian*, and
10 handsome Description of [2]*Virgil*.

That the first Plantations not long after the Floud were disposed after this manner, the generality and antiquity of this order observed in Vineyards, and Wine plantations, affordeth some conjecture. And since from judicious enquiry, *Saturn* who divided the world between his three sonnes, who beareth a Sickle in his hand, who taught the plantations of Vines, the setting, grafting of trees, and the best part of Agriculture, is discovered to be *Noah*, whether this early dispersed Husbandry in Vineyards, had not its Originall in that Patriarch, is no such Paralogicall doubt.

20 And if it were clear that this was used by *Noah* after the Floud, I could easily beleeve it was in use before it; Not willing to fix to such ancient inventions no higher originall then *Noah*; Nor readily conceiving those aged *Heroes*, whose diet was vegetable, and only, or chiefly consisted in the fruits of the earth, were much deficient in their splendid cultivations; or after the experience of fifteen hundred years, left much for future discovery in Botanicall Agriculture. Nor fully perswaded that Wine was the invention of *Noah*, that fermented Liquors, which often make themselves, so long escaped their Luxury or experience; that the first sinne of the new world
30 was no sin of the old. That *Cain* and *Abel* were the first that offered Sacrifice; or because the Scripture is silent that *Adam* or *Isaac* offered none at all.

Whether *Abraham* brought up in the first planting Countrey, observed not some rule hereof, when he planted a grove at *Beersheba*; or whether at least a like ordination were not in the Garden of *Solomon*, probability may contest. Answerably unto the wisedom of that eminent Botanologer, and orderly disposer of all his other

[1] συστάδας αμπέλων. Polit. 7. [10.]

[2] *Indulge ordinibus, nec secius omnis in unguem*
Arboribus positis, secto via limite quadret.
Georg. 2. [277–8.]

1 describing] descrribing *58* 4 *Greece*] *Creece 58* 15 sonnes *Er C*: stones *58* 21 fix to *Works, 1686*: fix *58*

works. Especially since this was one peece of Gallantry, wherein he pursued the specious part of felicity, according to his own description[1]. I made me Gardens and Orchards, and planted Trees in them of all kindes of fruit. I made me Pools of water, to water therewith the wood that bringeth forth Trees, which was no ordinary plantation, if according to the *Targum*, or *Chaldee Paraphrase*, it contained all kindes of Plants, and some fetched as far as *India*; And the extent thereof were from the wall of *Jerusalem* unto the water of *Siloah*.

And if *Jordan* were but *Jaar Eden*, that is, the Riuer of *Eden*, 10 *Genesar* but *Gansar* or the Prince of Gardens; and it could be made out, that the Plain of *Jordan* were watered not comparatively, but causally, and because it was the Paradise of God, as the Learned [2]*Abramas* hinteth, he was not far from the Prototype and originall of Plantations. And since even in Paradise it self, the tree of knowledge was placed in the middle of the Garden, whatever was the ambient figure, there wanted not a centre and rule of decussation. Whether the groves and sacred Plantations of Antiquity, were not thus orderly placed, either by *quaternio's*, or quintuple ordinations, may favourably be doubted. For since they were so methodicall in 20 the constitutions of their temples, as to observe the due scituation, aspect, manner, form, and order in Architectonicall relations, whether they were not as distinct in their groves and Plantations about them, in form and *species* respectively unto their Deities, is not without probability of conjecture. And in their groves of the Sunne this was a fit number, by multiplication to denote the dayes of the year; and might Hieroglyphically speak as much, as the mysticall *Statua* of [3]*Janus* in the Language of his fingers. And since they were so criticall in the number of his horses, the strings of his Harp, and rayes about his head, denoting the orbes of heaven, the 30 Seasons and Moneths of the Yeare; witty Idolatry would hardly be flat in other appropriations.

CHAP. II.

NOR was this only a form of practise in Plantations, but found imitation from high Antiquity, in sundry artificiall contrivances

[1] Eccles. 2. [5.]

[2] *Vet. Testamenti Pharus.*

[3] Which King *Numa* set up with his fingers so disposed that they numerically denoted 365. *Pliny*. [*HN*, xxxiv (xvi) 33.]

35 Antiquity,] Antiquity. *58*

and manuall operations. For to omit the position of squared stones, *cuneatim* or *wedgwise* in the Walls of *Roman* and *Gothick* buildings; and the *lithostrata* or figured pavements of the ancients, which consisted not all of square stones, but were divided into triquetrous segments, honey-combs, and sexangular figures, according to *Vitruvius*; The squared stones and bricks in ancient fabricks, were placed after this order. And two above or below conjoyned by a middle stone or *Plinthus*, observable in the ruines of *Forum Nervæ*, the *Mausoleum* of *Augustus*, the Pyramid of *Cestius*, 10 and the sculpture draughts of the larger Pyramids of Ægypt. And therefore in the draughts of eminent fabricks, Painters do commonly imitate this order in the lines of their description.

In the Laureat draughts of sculpture and picture, the leaves and foliate works are commonly thus contrived, which is but in imitation of the *Pulvinaria*, and ancient pillow-work, observable in *Ionick* peeces, about columns, temples and altars. To omit many other analogies, in Architectonicall draughts, which art it self is founded upon [1]fives, as having its subject, and most gracefull peeces divided by this number.

20 The Triumphal Oval, and Civicall Crowns of Laurel, Oake, and Myrtle, when fully made, were pleated after this order. And to omit the crossed Crowns of Christian Princes; what figure that was which *Anastatius* described upon the head of *Leo* the third; or who first brought in the Arched Crown; That of Charles the great, (which seems the first remarkably closed Crown,) was framed after this [2]manner; with an intersection in the middle from the main crossing barres, and the interspaces unto the frontal circle, continued by handsome network-plates, much after this order. Whereon we shall not insist, because from greater Antiquity, and 30 practice of consecration, we meet with the radiated, and starry Crown, upon the head of *Augustus*, and many succeeding Emperors. Since the Armenians and Parthians had a peculiar royall Capp; And the Grecians from *Alexander* another kinde of diadem. And even Diadems themselves were but fasciations, and handsome ligatures, about the heads of Princes; nor wholly omitted in the mitrall Crown, which common picture seems to set too upright and forward upon the head of *Aaron*: Worne sometimes singly, or

[1] Of a structure five parts, *Fundamentum, parietes, Aperturæ, Compartitio, tectum*, Leo. Alberti. Five Columes, *Tuscan, Dorick, Ionick, Corinthian, Compound*. Five different intercolumniations, *Pycnostylos, dystylos, Systylos, Areostylos, Eustylos*. Vitru. [iii. 3.]

[2] *Vti constat ex pergamena apud Chifflet*; *in* B. R. *Bruxelli*, & *Icon*. f. *Stradæ*.

27 interspaces *C*: interspaces, *58*

doubly by Princes, according to their Kingdomes; and no more to be expected from [1]two Crowns at once, upon the head of *Ptolomy*. And so easily made out when historians tell us, some bound up wounds, some hanged themselves with diadems.

The beds of the antients were corded somewhat after this fashion: That is not directly, as ours at present, but obliquely, from side to side, and after the manner of network; whereby they strengthened the spondæ or bedsides, and spent less cord in the work: as is demonstrated by [2]*Blancanus*.

And as they lay in crossed beds, so they sat upon seeming crosselegg'd seats: in which form the noblest thereof were framed: Observable in the triumphall seats, the *sella curulis*, or *Ædyle Chayres*, in the coyns of *Cestius*, *Sylla*, and *Julius*. That they sat also crosse legg'd many noble draughts declare; and in this figure the sitting gods and goddesses are drawn in medalls and medallions[3]. And beside this kinde of work in Retiarie and hanging textures, in embroderies, and eminent needle-works; the like is obvious unto every eye in glass-windows. Nor only in Glassie contrivances, but also in Lattice and Stone-work, conceived in the Temple of *Solomon*; wherein the windows are termed *fenestræ reticulatæ*[4], or lights framed like nets. And agreeable unto the Greek expression concerning Christ in the [5]Canticles, looking through the nets, which ours hath rendered, he looketh forth at the windows, shewing himself through the lattesse; that is, partly seen and unseen, according to the visible and invisible side of his nature. To omit the noble reticulate work, in the chapiters of the pillars of *Solomon*, with Lillies, and Pomegranats upon a network ground; and the *Craticula* or grate through which the ashes fell in the altar of burnt offerings.

That the networks and nets of antiquity were little different in the form from ours at present, is confirmable from the nets in the hands of the Retiarie gladiators, the proper combatants with the secutores. To omit the ancient Conopeion or gnatnet, of theÆgyptians, the inventors of that Artifice: the rushey labyrinths of *Theocritus*; the nosegay nets, which hung from the head under the nostrils of Princes; and that uneasie metaphor of *Reticulum Jecoris*,[6] which some expound the lobe, we the caule above the liver. As

[1] Macc. i. 11. [1 Macc. 11. 13.]
[2] *Aristot. Mechan. Quæst.*
[3] The larger sort of Medals. [*Add.*]
[4] δικτυωτά.
[5] Cant. 2.
[6] In *Leviticus* [iii. 4 &c.] [*Add.*]

2 *Ptolomy*] *Ptlomy 58* 13 *Cestius*] *Cestuis 58* 26 chapiters *Er C*: chapters *58*

for that famous network of *Vulcan*, which inclosed *Mars* and *Venus*, and caused that unextinguishable[1] laugh in heaven; since the gods themselves could not discern it, we shall not prie into it; Although why *Vulcan* bound them, *Neptune* loosed them, and *Apollo* should first discover them, might afford no vulgar mythologie. Heralds[2] have not omitted this order or imitation thereof, whiles they Symbollically adorn their Scuchions with Mascles Fusils and Saltyrs, and while they disposed the figures of Ermins, and vaired coats in this Quincuncial method.

10 The same is not forgot by Lapidaries while they cut their gemms pyramidally, or by æquicrural triangles. Perspective picturers, in their Base, Horison, and lines of distances, cannot escape these Rhomboidall decussations. Sculptors in their strongest shadows, after this order do draw their double Haches. And the very *Americans* do naturally fall upon it, in their neat and curious textures, which is also observed in the elegant artifices of *Europe*. But this is no law unto the woof of the neat *Retiarie* Spider, which seems to weave without transversion, and by the union of right lines to make out a continued surface, which is beyond the com-20 mon art of Textury, and may still nettle *Minerva*[3] the Goddesse of that mystery. And he that shall hatch the little seeds, either found in small webs, or white round Egges, carried under the bellies of some Spiders, and behold how at their first production in boxes, they will presently fill the same with their webbs, may observe the early, and untaught finger of nature, and how they are natively provided with a stock, sufficient for such Texture.

The Rurall charm against *Dodder*, *Tetter*, and strangling weeds, was contrived after this order, while they placed a chalked Tile at the four corners, and one in the middle of their fields, which 30 though ridiculous in the intention, was rationall in the contrivance, and a good way to diffuse the magick through all parts of the *Area*.

Somewhat after this manner they ordered the little stones in the old game of *Pentalithismus*, or casting up five stones to catch them on the back of their hand. And with some resemblance hereof, the *Proci* or Prodigall Paramours disposed their men, when

[1] Ἄσβεστος δ ἀρ ἐνῶρτο γέλως. *Hom.* [*Od.* viii. 326.]

[2] *De armis Scaccatis, masculatis, invectis fuselatis vide Spelm. Aspilog. & Upton. cum erudit. Bissæo.*

[3] As in the contention between *Minerva* and *Arachne*. [Ovid, *Met.* vi. 5–145.]

---

note 2 above: *De armis* &c. *In 58 the note is placed against* 136.38–137.3. *The mistake is corrected in Add.* 11 picturers *C*: pictures *58*

they played at [1]*Penelope*. For being themselves an hundred and eight, they set fifty four stones on either side, and one in the middle, which they called *Penelope*, which he that hit was master of the game.

In Chesse-boards and Tables we yet finde Pyramids and Squares, I wish we had their true and ancient description, farre different from ours, or the *Chet mat* of the *Persians*, which might continue some elegant remarkables, as being an invention as High as *Hermes*[2] the Secretary of *Osyris*, figuring the whole world, the motion of the Planets, with Eclipses of Sunne and Moon.

Physicians are not without the use of this decussation in severall operations, in ligatures and union of dissolved continuities. Mechanicks make use hereof in forcipall Organs, and Instruments of Incision; wherein who can but magnifie the power of decussation, inservient to contrary ends, solution and consolidation, union, and division, illustrable from *Aristotle* in the old *Nucifragium* or Nutcracker, and the Instruments of Evulsion, compression or incision; which consisting of two *Vectes* or armes, converted towards each other, the innitency and stresse being made upon the *hypomochlion* or fulciment in the decussation, the greater compression is made by the union of two impulsors.

The *Roman*[3] *Batalia* was ordered after this manner, whereof as sufficiently known *Virgil* hath left but an hint, and obscure intimation. For thus were the maniples and cohorts of the *Hastati*, *Principes* and *Triarii* placed in their bodies, wherein consisted the strength of the *Roman* battle. By this Ordination they readily fell

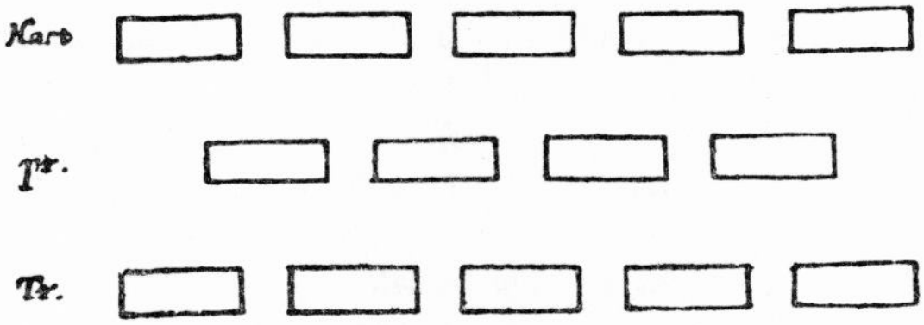

Hast.

Pr.

Tr.

into each other; the *Hastati* being pressed, handsomely retired into

[1] In *Eustathius* his Comment upon *Homer*. [*Add.*]

[2] *Plato.*

[3] In the disposure of the Legions in the Wars of the Republike, before the division of the Legion into ten Cohorts by the Emperours. *Salmas.* in his Epistle a Mounsieur de Peyresc & de Re militari Romanorum.

---

note 1 above: In *Eustathius* . . . *Homer*. *Add.*: In *Eustachius*. *58* 7 which *Er*(*2*): and *58* *note 2 above*: *Plato.*] *In 58 the note is not attached to any word in the sentence. See Commentary.*

the intervalls of the *principes*, these into that of the *Triarii*, which making as it were a new body, might joyntly renew the battle, wherein consisted the secret of their successes. And therefore it was remarkably [1]singular in the battle of *Africa*, that *Scipio* fearing a rout from the Elephants of the Enemy, left not the *Principes* in their alternate distances, whereby the Elephants passing the vacuities of the *Hastati*, might have run upon them, but drew his battle into right order, and leaving the passages bare, defeated the mischief intended by the Elephants. Out of this figure were made 10 too remarkable forms of Battle, the *Cuneus* and *Forceps*, or the sheare and wedge battles, each made by half a *Rhombus*, and but differenced by position. The wedge invented to break or work into a body, the *forceps* to environ and defeat the power thereof, composed out of the selectest Souldiery and disposed into the form of an V, wherein receiving the wedge, it inclosed it on both sides. After this form the famous [2]*Narses* ordered his battle against the *Franks*, and by this figure the *Almans* were enclosed, and cut in peeces.

The *Rhombus* or Lozenge figure so visible in this order, was also 20 a remarkable form of battle in the *Grecian*[3] Cavalry, observed by the *Thessalians*, and *Philip* King of *Macedon*, and frequently by the *Parthians*, As being most ready to turn every way, and best to be commanded, as having its ductors, or Commanders at each Angle.

The *Macedonian Phalanx* (a long time thought invincible) consisted of a long square. For though they might be sixteen in Rank and file, yet when they shut close, so that the sixt pike advanced before the first ranck, though the number might be square, the figure was oblong, answerable unto the Quincunciall quadrate of *Curtius*. 30 According to this square *Thucydides* delivers, the *Athenians* disposed their battle against the *Lacedemonians*[4] brickwise, and by the same word the Learned *Guellius* expoundeth the quadrate of [5]*Virgil*, after the form of a brick or tile.

And as the first station and position of trees, so was the first habitation of men, not in round Cities, as of later foundation; For the form of *Babylon* the first City was square, and so shall also be the last, according to the description of the holy City in the Apocalyps. The famous pillars of *Seth* before the floud, had also the

[1] *Polybius. Appianus.*
[2] *Agathius.* [*Hist.* ii. 8.] *Ammianus.* [xvi. 11.3]
[3] *Ælian. Tact.*
[4] ἐν πλαισίῳ.
[5] *Secto via limite quadret.* Comment. *in Virgil.*

16 *Narses C*: nurses *Er(2)*: *Nasses 58* 28 first ranck *Er(2)*: first *58*

like foundation, if they were but *antidiluvian* Obelisks[1], and such as *Cham* and his *Ægyptian* race, imitated after the Floud.

But *Nineveh* which Authours acknowledge to have exceeded *Babylon*, was of a [2]longilaterall figure, ninety five Furlongs broad, and an hundred and fifty long, and so making about sixty miles in circuit, which is the measure of three dayes journey, according unto military marches, or castrensiall mansions. So that if *Jonas* entred at the narrower side, he found enough for one dayes walk to attain the heart of the City, to make his Proclamation. And if we imagine a City extending from *Ware* to *London*, the expression 10 will be moderate of six score thousand Infants, although we allow vacuities, fields, and intervals of habitation, as there needs must be when the monument of *Ninus* took up no lesse then ten furlongs.

And, though none of the seven wonders, yet a noble peece of Antiquity, and made by a Copy exceeding all the rest, had its principall parts disposed after this manner, that is, the Labyrinth of *Crete*, built upon a long quadrate, containing five large squares, communicating by right inflections, terminating in the centre of the middle square, and lodging of the *Minotaur*, if we conform unto the description of the elegant medall thereof in [3]*Agostino*. 20 And though in many accounts we reckon grosly by the square, yet is that very often to be accepted as a long-sided quadrate, which was the figure of the Ark of the Covenant, the table of the Shew-bread, and the stone wherein the names of the twelve Tribes were engraved, that is, three in a row, naturally making a longilaterall Figure, the perfect quadrate being made by nine.

What figure the stones themselves maintained, tradition and Scripture are silent, yet Lapidaries in precious stones affect a Table or long square, and in such proportion, that the two laterall, and also the three inferiour Tables are equall unto the superiour, 30 and the angles of the laterall Tables, contain and constitute the *hypothenusæ*, or broader sides subtending.

That the Tables of the Law were of this figure, general imitation and tradition hath confirmed; yet are we unwilling to load the shoulders of *Moses* with such massie stones, as some pictures lay upon them, since 'tis plainly delivered that he came down with them in his hand; since the word strictly taken implies no such massie hewing, but cutting, and fashioning of them into shape and surface; since some will have them Emeralds, and if they

[1] Obelisks being erected upon a square base. [*Add.*]

[2] *Diod. Sic.* [ii. 3. 2–3.]

[3] *Antonio Agostino delle medaglie.*

39 surface] furface *58*

were made of the materials of Mount *Sina*, not improbable that they were marble: Since the words were not many, the letters short of seven hundred, and the Tables written on both sides required no such capacity.

The beds of the Ancients were different from ours at present, which are almost square, being framed ob-long, and about a double unto their breadth; not much unlike the *area*, or bed of this Quincuncial quadrate. The single beds of *Greece* were [1]six foot, and a little more in length, three in breadth; the Giantlike bed of *Og*, 10 which had four cubits of bredth, nine and a half in length, varied not much from this proportion. The Funeral bed of King *Cheops*, in the greater Pyramid, which holds seven in length, and four foot in bredth, had no great difformity from this measure; And whatsoever were the bredth, the length could hardly be lesse, of the tyrannical bed of *Procrustes*, since in a shorter measure he had not been fitted with persons for his cruelty of extension. But the old sepulchral bed, or *Amazonian*[2] Tomb in the market-place of *Megara*, was in the form of a Lozenge; readily made out by the composure of the body. For the arms not lying fasciated or wrapt 20 up after the *Grecian* manner, but in a middle distention, the including Lines will strictly make out that figure.

CHAP. III.

NOW although this elegant ordination of vegetables, hath found coincidence or imitation in sundry works of Art, yet is it not also destitute of naturall examples, and though overlooked by all, was elegantly observable, in severall works of nature.

Could we satisfie our selves in the position of the lights above, or discover the wisedome of that order so invariably maintained in the fixed Stars of heaven; Could we have any light, why the stellary 30 part of the first masse, separated into this order, that the Girdle of *Orion* should ever maintain its line, and the two Starres in *Charles*'s Wain never leave pointing at the Pole-Starre, we might abate the *Pythagoricall* Musick of the Spheres, the sevenfold Pipe of *Pan*; and the strange Cryptography of *Gaffarell* in his Starrie Booke of Heaven.

But not to look so high as Heaven or the single Quincunx of the *Hyades* upon the head of *Taurus*, the Triangle, and remarkable

1 *Aristot. Mechan.* [26.]

2 Plut. *in vit. Thes.* [28.]

3 seven *Er C*: five *58* 19 fasciated] sasciated *58* 21 figure.] figure, *58* 37 head *Er C* (front *in some C copies*): neck *58*

Crusero about the foot of the *Centaur*; observable rudiments there are hereof in subterraneous concretions, and bodies in the Earth; in the *Gypsum* or *Talcum Rhomboides*, in the Favaginites or honey-comb-stone, in the *Asteria* and *Astroites*, and in the crucigerous stone of S. *Iago* of *Gallicia*.

The same is observably effected in the *Julus*, *Catkins*, or pendulous excrescencies of severall Trees, of Wallnuts, Alders, and Hazels, which hanging all the Winter, and maintaining their Net-worke close, by the expansion thereof are the early foretellers of the Spring, discoverable also in long Pepper, and elegantly in the 10 *Julus* of *Calamus Aromaticus*, so plentifully growing with us in the first palmes of Willowes, and in the Flowers of Sycamore, Petasites, Asphodelus, and *Blattaria*, before explication. After such order stand the flowery Branches in our best spread *Verbascum*, and the seeds about the spicous head or torch of *Tapsas Barbatus*, in as fair a regularity as the circular and wreathed order will admit, which advanceth one side of the square, and makes the same Rhomboidall.

In the squamous heads of *Scabious*, *Knapweed*, and the elegant *Jacea Pinea*, and in the Scaly composure of the [1] *Oak-Rose*, which 20 some years most aboundeth. After this order hath Nature planted the Leaves in the Head of the common and prickled Artichoak; wherein the black and shining Flies do shelter themselves, when they retire from the purple Flower about it; The same is also found in the pricks, sockets, and impressions of the seeds, in the pulp or bottome thereof; wherein do elegantly stick the Fathers of their Mother[2]. To omit the Quincunciall Specks on the top of the Miscle-berry, especially that which grows upon the *Tilia* or Lime-Tree. And the remarkable disposure of those yellow fringes about the purple Pestill of *Aaron*, and elegant clusters of Dragons, 30 so peculiarly secured by nature, with an *umbrella* or skreening Leaf about them.

The Spongy leaves of some Seawracks, Fucus, Oaks, in their severall kindes,[3] found about the Shoar, with ejectments of the Sea, are over-wrought with Net-work elegantly containing this

[1] *Capitula squammata Quercum Bauhini*, whereof though he saith *perraro reperiuntur bis tantum invenimus*, yet we finde them commonly with us and in great numbers.

[2] *Antho. Græc.* [xiv. 58] *inter Epigrammata* γριφώδη Ἐνδὸν ἐμῶν λαγόνων μητρὸς ἔχω πατέρα.

[3] Especially the *porus cervinus Imperati*, *Sporosa*, or *Alga* πλατύκερως. *Bauhini*.

---

note 2 above: λαγόνων μητρὸς *Er Add.*: μετρὸς λαγώναν *58* (*the note is misplaced in 58 against ll. 28–32*)

order, which plainly declareth the naturality of this texture; And how the needle of nature delighteth to work, even in low and doubtful vegetations.

The *Arbustetum* or Thicket on the head of the Teasel, may be observed in this order: And he that considereth that fabrick so regularly palisadoed, and stemm'd with flowers of the royall colour; in the house of the solitary maggot[1], may finde the Seraglio of *Solomon*. And contemplating the calicular shafts, and uncous disposure of their extremities, so accommodable unto the office of 10 abstersion, not condemne as wholly improbable the conceit of those who accept it, for the herbe [2]*Borith*. Where by the way, we could with much inquiry never discover any transfiguration, in this abstemious insect, although we have kept them long in their proper houses, and boxes. Where some wrapt up in their webbs, have lived upon their own bowels, from September unto July.

In such a grove doe walke the little creepers about the head of the burre. And such an order is observed in the aculeous prickly plantation, upon the heads of several common thistles, remarkably in the notable palisados about the flower of the milk-Thistle; 20 and he that inquireth into the little bottome of the globe-thistle, may finde that gallant bush arise from a scalpe of like disposure.

The white umbrella or medicall bush of Elder, is an Epitome of this order: arising from five main stemms Quincuncially disposed, and tollerably maintained in their subdivisions. To omit the lower observations in the seminal spike of Mercurie, weld, and Plantane.

Thus hath nature ranged the flowers of Santfoyne, and French honey suckle; and somewhat after this manner hath ordered the bush in *Jupiters* beard, or houseleek; which old superstition set 30 on the tops of houses, as a defensative against lightening, and thunder. The like in Fenny Sengreen or the water [3]Souldier; which, though a militarie name from Greece, makes out the Roman order.

A like ordination there is in the favaginous Sockets, and Lozenge seeds of the noble flower of the Sunne. Wherein in Lozenge figured boxes nature shuts up the seeds, and balsame which is about them.

But the Firre and Pinetree from their fruits doe naturally dictate

[1] There being a single Maggot found almost in every head. [*Add.*]
[2] Ier. 2. 22.
[3] *Stratiotes.*

---

4 Teasel *Er C*: Tearell *58* 25 Mercurie, *C*: Mercurie *58* 31 Sengreen *C*: Seagreen *58* *note 3 above*: *stratiotes Er*: *Strutiotes 58*.

this position. The Rhomboidall protuberances in Pineapples maintaining this Quincuncial order unto each other, and each Rhombus in it selfe. Thus are also disposed the triangular foliations, in the conicall fruit of the firre tree, orderly shadowing and protecting the winged seeds below them.

The like so often occurreth to the curiosity of observers, especially in spicated seeds and flowers, that we shall not need to take in the single Quincunx of Fuchsius in the grouth of the masle fearn, the seedie disposure of Gramen Ischemon, and the trunk or neat Reticulate work in the codde of the Sachell palme. 10

For even in very many round stalk plants, the leaves are set after a Quintuple ordination, the first leaf answering the fifth, in lateral disposition. Wherein the leaves successively rounding the stalke, in foure at the furthest the compass is absolved, and the fifth leafe or sprout, returns to the position of the other fift before it; as in accounting upward is often observable in furze, pellitorye, Ragweed, the sproutes of Oaks, and thorns upon pollards[1], and very remarkably in the regular disposure of the rugged excrescencies in the yearly shoots of the Pine.

But in square stalked plants, the leaves stand respectively unto 20 each other, either in crosse or decussation to those above or below them, arising at crosse positions; whereby they shadow not each other, and better resist the force of winds, which in a parallel situation, and upon square stalkes would more forcibly bear upon them.

And to omit, how leaves and sprouts which compasse not the stalk, are often set in a Rhomboides, and making long, and short Diagonals, doe stand like the leggs of Quadrupeds when they goe: Nor to urge the thwart enclosure and furdling of flowers, and blossomes, before explication, as in the multiplyed leaves of 30 Pionie; And the Chiasmus in five leaved flowers, while one lies wrapt about the staminous beards, the other foure obliquely shutting and closing upon each other; and how even flowers which consist of foure leaves, stand not ordinarily in three and one, but two and two, crossewise unto the Stylus; even the Autumnal budds, which awaite the returne of the sun, doe after the winter solstice multiply their calicular leaves, making little Rhombuses, and network figures, as in the Sycamore and Lilac.

[1] Upon pollard Oaks and Thorns. [*Add.*]

5 them.] them, *58* 16 in] in in *58* furze *Er C* (*adding comma*): furre *58*
23 better] bettter *58* 35 two and two,] two, and two *58*

The like is discoverable in the original production of plants, which first putting forth two leaves, those which succeed, bear not over each other, but shoot obliquely or crossewise, untill the stalke appeareth; which sendeth not forth its first leaves without all order unto them; and he that from hence can discover in what position the two first leaves did arise, is no ordinary observator.

Where by the way, he that observeth the rudimental spring of seeds, shall finde strict rule, although not after this order. How little is required unto effectual generation, and in what diminutives 10 the plastick principle lodgeth, is exemplified in seeds, wherein the greater mass affords so little comproduction. In Beanes the leaf and root sprout from the Germen, the main sides split, and lye by, and in some pull'd up near the time of blooming, we have found the pulpous sides intire or little wasted. In Acorns the nebb dilating splitteth the two sides. which sometimes lye whole, when the Oak is sprouted two handfuls. In Lupins these pulpy sides do sometimes arise with the stalk in a resemblance of two fat leaves. Wheat and Rye will grow up, if after they have shot some tender Roots, the adhering pulp be taken from them. Beanes will prosper 20 though a part be cut away, and so much set as sufficeth to contain and keep the Germen close. From this superfluous pulp in unkindely, and wet years, may arise that multiplicity of little insects, which infest the Roots and Sprouts of tender Graines and pulses.

In the little nebbe or fructifying principle, the motion is regular, and not transvertible, as to make that ever the leaf, which nature intendeth the root; observable from their conversion, until they attain their right position, if seeds be set inversedly.

In vain we expect the production of plants from different parts of the seed, from the same *corculum* or little original proceed both 30 germinations; and in the power of this slender particle lye many Roots and sprouts, that though the same be pull'd away, the generative particle will renew them again, and proceed to a perfect plant; And malt may be observed to grow, though the Cummes be fallen from it.

The seminall nebbe hath a defined and single place, and not extended unto both extremes. And therefore many too vulgarly conceive that Barley and Oats grow at both ends; For they arise from one *punctilio* or generative nebbe, and the Speare sliding under the husk, first appeareth nigh the toppe. But in Wheat 40 and Rye being bare the sprouts are seen together. If Barley unhulled would grow, both would appear at once. But in this and

21 Germen *Er C*: German *58* 31 Roots and sprouts *Er*(*2*): Roots and sproutings (*or* sprouts) *C*: Roots *58* same] fame *58*

Oat-meal the nebbe is broken away, which makes them the milder food, and lesse apt to raise fermentation in Decoctions.

Men taking notice of what is outwardly visible, conceive a sensible priority in the Root. But as they begin from one part, so they seem to start and set out upon one signall of nature. In Beans yet soft, in Pease while they adhere unto the Cod, the rudimentall Leafe and Root are discoverable. In the Seeds of Rocket and Mustard, sprouting in Glasses of water, when the one is manifest the other is also perceptible. In muddy waters apt to breed *Duckweed*, and Periwinkles, if the first and rudimentall stroaks of Duckweed be observed, the Leaves and Root anticipate not each other. But in the Date-stone the first sprout is neither root nor leaf distinctly, but both together; For the Germination being to passe through the narrow Navell and hole about the midst of the stone, the generative germ is faine to enlengthen it self, and shooting out about an inch, at that distance divideth into the ascending and descending portion.

And though it be generally thought that Seeds will root at that end, where they adhere to their Originals, and observable it is that the nebbe sets most often next the stalk, as in Grains, Pulses, and most small Seeds, yet is it hardly made out in many greater plants. For in Acornes, Almonds, Pistachios, Wallnuts, and accuminated shells, the germ puts forth at the remotest part of the pulp. And therefore to set Seeds in that posture, wherein the Leaf and Roots may shoot right without contortion, or forced circumvolution, which might render them strongly rooted, and straighter, were a Criticisme in Agriculture. And nature seems to have made some provision hereof in many from their figure, that as they fall from the tree they may lye in Positions agreeable to such advantages.

Beside the open and visible Testicles of plants, the seminall powers lie in great part invisible, while the Sun findes polypody in stone-wals, the little stinging Nettle, and nightshade in barren sandy High-wayes, *Scurvy-grasse* in *Greeneland*, and unknown plants in earth brought from remote Countries. Beside the known longevity of some Trees, what is the most lasting herb, or seed, seems not easily determinable. Mandrakes upon known account have lived near an hundred yeares. Seeds found in Wilde-Fowls Gizards have sprouted in the earth. The Seeds of Marjorane and *Stramonium* carelesly kept, have grown after seven years. Even in Garden-plots long fallow, and digged up, the seeds of *Blattaria* and yellow

9 perceptible] peeceptible *58* 13 both] borh *58* 14 the narrow] the the narrow *58* 32 powers *Er C*: pores *58*

henbane, after twelve years burial have produced themselves a-gain.

That bodies are first spirits *Paracelsus* could affirm, which in the maturation of Seeds and fruits, seems obscurely implied by [1]*Aristotle*, when he delivereth, that the spirituous parts are converted into water, and the water into earth, and attested by observation in the maturative progresse of Seeds, wherein at first may be discerned a flatuous distension of the husk, afterwards a thin liquor, which longer time digesteth into a pulp or kernell
10 observable in Almonds and large Nuts. And some way answered in the progressionall perfection of animall semination, in its spermaticall maturation, from crude pubescency unto perfection. And even that seeds themselves in their rudimentall discoveries, appear in foliaceous surcles, or sprouts within their coverings, in a diaphonous gellie, before deeper incrassation, is also visibly verified in Cherries, Acorns, Plums.

From seminall considerations, either in reference unto one another, or distinction from animall production, the holy Scripture describeth the vegetable creation; And while it divideth
20 plants but into Herb and Tree, though it seemeth to make but an accidental division, from magnitude, it tacitely containeth the naturall distinction of vegetables, observed by Herbarists, and comprehending the four kinds. For since the most naturall distinction is made from the production of leaf or stalk, and plants after the two first seminall leaves, do either proceed to send forth more leaves, or a stalk, and the folious and stalky emission distinguisheth herbs and trees; in a large acception it compriseth all Vegetables, for the frutex and suffrutex are under the progression of trees, and stand Authentically differenced, but from the acci-
30 dents of the stalk.

The Æquivocall production of things under undiscerned principles, makes a large part of generation, though they seem to hold a wide univocacy in their set and certain Originals, while almost every plant breeds its peculiar insect, most a Butterfly, moth or fly, wherein the Oak seems to contain the largest seminality, while the Julus, [2]Oak-apple, pill, woolly tuft, foraminous roundles

[1] *In met. cum Cabeo.*

[2] These and more to be found upon our Oaks; not well described by any till the Edition of *Theatrum Botanicum* [Bauhin]. [*Add.*]

1 after *Er*(*2*) *C*: and after *58* 11 perfection] perfectlon *58* 15 incrassation] incr-ssation *58* 18 another *58* (*4°*): mother *58* (*8°*)
25 proceed] proceeed *58* 27 trees; *eds.*: trees, *58* *27-29* in a large . . . of trees, *Er C* (*in some copies C has* 'see errata'): *omitted in 58* 36 Oak-apple *C*: Oak, apple *58* pill *Er C*: dill *58*

upon the leaf, and grapes under ground make a Fly with some difference. The great variety of Flyes lyes in the variety of their originals, in the seeds of Caterpillars or Cankers there lyeth not only a Butterfly or Moth, but if they be sterill or untimely cast, their production is often a Fly, which we have also observed from corrupted and mouldred Egges, both of Hens and Fishes; To omit the generation of Bees out of the bodies of dead Heifers, or what is strange yet well attested, the production of Eeles[1] in the backs of living Cods and Perches.

The exiguity and smallnesse of some seeds extending to large 10 productions is one of the magnalities of nature, somewhat illustrating the work of the Creation, and vast production from nothing. The true [2]seeds of Cypresse and Rampions are indistinguishable by old eyes. Of the seeds of Tobacco a thousand make not one grain, The disputed seeds of Harts tongue, and Maidenhair, require a greater number. From such undiscernable seminalities arise spontaneous productions. He that would discern the rudimentall stroak of a plant, may behold it in the Originall of Duckweed, at the bignesse of a pins point, from convenient water in glasses, wherein a watchfull eye may also discover the puncticular 20 Originals of Periwincles and Gnats.

That seeds of some Plants are lesse then any animals, seems of no clear decision; That the biggest of Vegetables exceedeth the biggest of Animals, in full bulk, and all dimensions, admits exception in the Whale, which in length and above ground measure, will also contend with tall Oakes. That the richest odour of plants, surpasseth that of Animals, may seem of some doubt, since animall-musk, seems to excell the vegetable, and we finde so noble a sent in the Tulip-Fly, and [3]Goat-Beetle.

Now whether seminall nebbes hold any sure proportion unto 30 seminall enclosures, why the form of the germe doth not answer the figure of the enclosing pulp, why the nebbe is seated upon the solid, and not the channeld side of the seed as in grains, why since we often meet with two yolks in one shell, and sometimes one Egge within another, we do not oftener meet with two nebbes in one distinct seed: why since the Egges of a Hen laid at one course, do commonly out-weigh the bird, and some moths coming out of their cases, without assistance of food, will lay so many Egges as to out-weigh their bodies, trees rarely bear their fruit,

[1] *Schoneveldus de Pisc.* [2] *Doctissim. Laurenburg hort.*

[3] The long and tender green *Capricornus* rarely found, we could never meet with but two.

29 sent *C*: scent *58*

in that gravity or proportion: Whether in the germination of seeds according to *Hippocrates*, the lighter part ascendeth, and maketh the sprout, the heaviest tending downward frameth the root; Since we observe that the first shoot of seeds in water, will sink or bow down at the upper and leafing end: Whether it be not more rational Epicurisme to contrive whole dishes out of the nebbes and spirited particles of plants, then from the Gallatures and treddles of Egges; since that part is found to hold no seminal share in Oval Generation, are quæries which might enlarge but must conclude 10 this digression.

And though not in this order, yet how nature delighteth in this number, and what consent and coordination there is in the leaves and parts of flowers, it cannot escape our observation in no small number of plants. For the calicular or supporting and closing leaves, do answer the number of the flowers, especially in such as exceed not the number of Swallows Egges[1]; as in Violets, Stichwort, Blossomes, and flowers of one leaf have often five divisions, answered by a like number of calicular leaves; as *Gentianella*, *Convolvulus*, Bell-flowers. In many the flowers, blades, or staminous 20 shootes and leaves are all equally five, as in cockle, mullein and *Blattaria*; Wherein the flowers before explication are pentagonally wrapped up, with some resemblance of the *blatta* or moth from whence it hath its name: But the contrivance of nature is singular in the opening and shutting of Bindeweeds, performed by five inflexures, distinguishable by pyramidall figures, and also different colours.

The rose at first is thought to have been of five leaves, as it yet groweth wilde among us; but in the most luxuriant, the calicular leaves do still maintain that number. But nothing is more admired 30 then the five Brethren of the Rose, and the strange disposure of the Appendices or Beards, in the calicular leaves thereof, which in despair of resolution is tolerably salved from this contrivance, best ordered and suited for the free closure of them before explication. For those two which are smooth, and of no beard are contrived to lye undermost, as without prominent parts, and fit to be smoothly covered; the other two which are beset with Beards on either side, stand outward and uncovered, but the fifth or half-bearded leaf is covered on the bare side but on the open side stands free, and bearded like the other.

[1] Which exceed not five. [*Add.*]

13 escape] eseape *58* 14 closing *Er C*: dosing *58* 25 pyramidall *C*: pyramidicall *58* (*4°*): pyramidcall *58*

Besides a large number of leaves have five divisions, and may be circumscribed by a *Pentagon* or figure of five Angles, made by right lines from the extremity of their leaves, as in Maple, Vine, Figge-Tree: But five-leaved flowers are commonly disposed circularly about the *Stylus*; according to the higher Geometry of nature, dividing a circle by five *radii*, which concurre not to make Diameters, as in Quadrilaterall and sexangular Intersections.

Now the number of five is remarkable in every circle, not only as the first sphærical number, but the measure of sphærical motion. For sphærical bodies move by fives, and every globular figure placed 10 upon a plane, in direct volutation, returns to the first point of contaction in the fifth touch, accounting by the Axes of the Diameters or Cardinall points of the four quarters thereof. And before it arriveth unto the same point again, it maketh five circles equall unto it self, in each progresse from those quarters, absolving an equall circle.

By the same number doth nature divide the circle of the Sea-Starre, and in that order and number disposeth those elegant Semi-circles, or dentall sockets and egges in the Sea Hedgehogge. And no mean Observations hereof there is in the Mathematicks of 20 the neatest Retiary Spider, which concluding in fourty four Circles, from five Semidiameters beginneth that elegant texture.

And after this manner doth lay the foundation of the circular branches of the Oak, which being five-cornered, in the tender annual sprouts, and manifesting upon incision the signature of a Starre, is after made circular, and swel'd into a round body: Which practice of nature is become a point of art, and makes two Problemes[1] in *Euclide*. But the Bramble which sends forth shoots and prickles from its angles, maintains its pentagonall figure, and the unobserved signature of a handsome porch within it. To omit the 30 five small buttons dividing the Circle of the Ivy-berry, and the five characters in the Winter stalk of the Walnut, with many other Observables, which cannot escape the eyes of signal discerners; Such as know where to finde *Ajax* his name in *Delphinium*, or *Aarons* Mitre in Henbane.

Quincuncial forms and ordinations, are also observable in animal figurations. For to omit the hioides or throat-bone of animals, the *furcula* or *merry-thought* in birds, which supporteth the *scapulæ*, affording a passage for the windepipe and the gullet, the wings of

[1] *Elem.* li. 4. [11 and 14.]

12 fifth *Er C*: first *58* 28 Bramble *Er* (2): Bryar *58* 29 its] itt *58*
34 *Delphinium Er*(2): *Gallitricum 58* (*for Callitricum*?)

Flyes, and disposure of their legges in their first formation from maggots, and the position of their horns, wings and legges, in their *Aurelian* cases and swadling clouts: The back of the *Cimex Arboreus*, found often upon Trees and lesser plants, doth elegantly discover the *Burgundian* decussation; And the like is observable in the belly of the *Notonecton*, or water-Beetle, which swimmeth on its back, and the handsome Rhombusses of the Sea-poult, or Weazell, on either side the Spine.

The sexangular Cels in the Honey-combs of Bees, are disposed 10 after this order, much there is not of wonder in the confused Houses of Pismires, though much in their busie life and actions, more in the edificial Palaces of Bees and Monarchical spirits; who make their combs six-corner'd, declining a circle, whereof many stand not close together, and compleatly fill the *area* of the place; But rather affecting a six-sided figure, whereby every cell affords a common side unto six more, and also a fit receptacle for the Bee it self, which gathering into a Cylindrical Figure, aptly enters its sexangular house, more nearly approaching a circular Figure, then either doth the Square or Triangle. And the Combes themselves 20 so regularly contrived, that their mutual intersections make three Lozenges at the bottome of every Cell; which severally regarded make three Rows of neat Rhomboidall Figures, connected at the angles, and so continue three several chains throughout the whole comb.

As for the *Favago* found commonly on the Sea shoar, though named from an honey-comb, it but rudely makes out the resemblance, and better agrees with the round Cels of humble Bees. He that would exactly discern the shop of a Bees mouth, need observing eyes, and good augmenting glasses; wherein is discoverable one 30 of the neatest peeces in nature, and must have a more piercing eye then mine; who findes out the shape of Buls heads, in the guts of Drones pressed out behinde, according to the experiment of *Gomesius*;[1] wherein notwithstanding there seemeth somewhat which might incline a pliant fancy to credulity of similitude.

A resemblance hereof there is in the orderly and rarely disposed Cels, made by Flyes and Insects, which we have often found fastened about small sprigs, and in those cottonary and woolly pillows, which sometimes we meet with fastened unto Leaves, there is included an elegant Net-work Texture, out of which come 40 many small Flies. And some resemblance there is of this order in

[1] *Gom. de Sale.*

8 Weazell *Er C*: Werrell *58* 25 Sea] 8ea *58*

the Egges of some Butterflies and moths, as they stick upon leaves, and other substances; which being dropped from behinde, nor directed by the eye, doth neatly declare how nature Geometrizeth, and observeth order in all things.

A like correspondency in figure is found in the skins and outward teguments of animals, whereof a regardable part are beautiful by this texture. As the backs of several Snakes and Serpents, elegantly remarkable in the *Aspis*, and the Dart-snake, in the Chiasmus and larger decussations upon the back of the Rattle-snake, and in the close and finer texture of the *Mater formicarum*, 10 or snake that delights in Ant-hils; whereby upon approach of outward injuries, they can raise a thicker Phalanx on their backs, and handsomely contrive themselves into all kindes of flexures: Whereas their bellies are commonly covered with smooth semicircular divisions, as best accommodable unto their quick and gliding motion.

This way is followed by nature in the peculiar and remarkable tayl of the Bever, wherein the scaly particles are disposed, somewhat after this order, which is the plainest resolution of the wonder of *Bellonius*, while he saith, with incredible Artifice hath Nature 20 framed the tayl or Oar of the Bever: where by the way we cannot but wish a model of their houses, so much extolled by some Describers: wherein since they are so bold as to venture upon three stages, we might examine their Artifice in the contignations, the rule and order in the compartitions; or whether that magnified structure be any more then a rude rectangular pyle or meer hovell-building.

Thus works the hand of nature in the feathery plantation about birds. Observable in the skins of the [1]breast, legs and Pinions of Turkies, Geese, and Ducks, and the Oars or finny feet of Water- 30 Fowl: And such a naturall Net is the scaly covering of Fishes, of Mullets, Carps, Tenches, &c. even in such as are excoriable and consist of smaller scales, as Bretts, Soals, and Flounders. The like Reticulate grain is observable in some *Russia* Leather. To omit the ruder Figures of the ostracion, the triangular or cunny fish, or the pricks of the Sea-Porcupine.

The same is also observable in some part of the skin of man, in habits of neat texture, and therefore not unaptly compared unto a Net: We shall not affirm that from such grounds, the Ægyptian Embalmers imitated this texture, yet in their linnen folds the same 40 is still observable among their neatest Mummies, in the figures of

[1] Elegantly conspicuous on the inside of the stripped skins of Dive-Fowl, of the Cormorant, Goshonder, Weasell, Loon, &c.

Isis and *Osyris*, and the Tutelary spirits in the Bembine Table. Nor is it to be over-looked how *Orus*, the Hieroglyphick of the world is described in a Net-work covering, from the shoulder to the foot. And (not to enlarge upon the cruciated character of *Trismegistus*, or handed crosses[1], so often occurring in the Needles of *Pharaoh*, and Obelisks of Antiquity) the *Statuæ Isiacæ*, Teraphims, and little Idols, found about the Mummies, do make a decussation or *Jacobs* Crosse, with their armes, like that on the head of *Ephraim* and *Manasses*, and this *decussis* is also graphically described between 10 them.

This Reticulate or Net-work was also considerable in the inward parts of man, not only from the first *subtegmen* or warp of his formation, but in the netty *fibres* of the veins and vessels of life; wherein according to common Anatomy the right and transverse *fibres* are decussated, by the oblique *fibres*; and so must frame a Reticulate and Quincunciall Figure by their Obliquations, Emphatically extending that Elegant expression of Scripture. Thou hast curiously embroydered me, thou hast wrought me up after the finest way of texture, and as it were with a Needle.

20 Nor is the same observable only in some parts, but in the whole body of man, which upon the extension of arms and legges, doth make out a square, whose intersection is at the genitals. To omit the phantastical Quincunx in *Plato* of the first Hermaphrodite or double man, united at the Loynes, which *Jupiter* after divided.

A rudimentall resemblance hereof there is in the cruciated and rugged folds of the *Reticulum*, or Net-like Ventricle of ruminating horned animals, which is the second in order, and culinarily called the Honey-comb. For many divisions there are in the stomack of severall animals; what number they maintain in the *Scarus* and 30 ruminating Fish, common description, or our own experiment hath made no discovery. But in the Ventricle of *Porpuses* there are three divisions. In many Birds a crop, Gizard, and little receptacle before it; but in Cornigerous animals, which chew the cudd, there are no less then four[2] of distinct position and office.

The *Reticulum* by these crossed eels, makes a further digestion, in the dry and exuccous part of the Aliment received from the first Ventricle. For at the bottome of the gullet there is a double Orifice; What is first received at the mouth descendeth into the

[1] *Cruces ansatæ*, being held by a finger in the circle. [*Add.*]

[2] *μεγάλη κοιλία, κεκρύφαλος ἐχῖνος ἤνυστρον*. Arist. *magnus venter, Reticulum, omasus, abomasus*. Gaza. [*Add.*]

6 *Isiacæ*] *Isiicæ 58*   23 Quincunx] Quincunx, *58*

first and greater stomack, from whence it is returned into the mouth again; and after a fuller mastication, and salivous mixture, what part thereof descendeth again, in a moist and succulent body, it slides down the softer and more permeable Orifice, into the Omasus or third stomack; and from thence conveyed into the fourth, receives its last digestion. The other dry and exuccous part after rumination by the larger and stronger orifice beareth into the first stomack, from thence into the *Reticulum*, and so progressively into the other divisions. And therefore in Calves newly calved, there is little or no use of the two first Ventricles, for 10 the milk and liquid aliment slippeth down the softer Orifice, into the third stomack; where making little or no stay, it passeth into the fourth, the seat of the *Coagulum*, or Runnet, or that division of stomack which seems to bear the name of the whole, in the Greek translation of the Priests Fee, in the Sacrifice of Peace-offerings.

As for those Rhomboidal Figures made by the Cartilagineous parts of the Wezon, in the Lungs of great Fishes, and other animals, as *Rondeletius* discovered, we have not found them so to answer our figure as to be drawn into illustration; Something we expected in the more discernable texture of the lungs of frogs, which 20 notwithstanding being but two curious bladders not weighing above a grain, we found interwoven with veins, not observing any just order. More orderly situated are those cretaceous and chalky concretions found sometimes in the bignesse of a small fech on either side their spine; which being not agreeable unto our order, nor yet observed by any, we shall not here discourse on.

But had we found a better account and tolerable Anatomy, of that prominent jowle of the [1]*Sperma Ceti* Whale, then questuary operation, or the stench of the last cast upon our shoar, permitted, we might have perhaps discovered some handsome order in those 30 Net-like seases and sockets, made like honey-combs, containing that medicall matter.

Lastly, The incession or locall motion of animals is made with analogy unto this figure, by decussative diametrals, Quincunciall Lines and angles. For to omit the enquiry how Butterflies and breezes move their four wings, how birds and fishes in ayre and water move by joynt stroaks of opposite wings and Finnes, and how salient animals in jumping forward seem to arise and fall upon a square base; As the station of most Quadrupeds, is made upon a long square, so in their motion they make a Rhomboides; their 40 common progression being performed Diametrally, by decussation and crosse advancement of their legges, which not observed

[1] 1652. described in our *Pseudo. Epidem.* Edit. 3. [iii. 26.]

begot that remarkable absurdity in the position of the legges of *Castors* horse in the Capitol. The Snake which moveth circularly makes his spires in like order, the convex and concave spirals answering each other at alternate distances; In the motion of man the armes and legges observe this thwarting position, but the legges alone do move Quincuncially by single angles with some resemblance of an V measured by successive advancement from each foot, and the angle of indenture great or lesse, according to the extent or brevity of the stride.

10 Studious Observators may discover more analogies in the orderly book of nature, and cannot escape the Elegancy of her hand in other correspondencies. The Figures of nails and crucifying appurtenances, are but precariously made out in the *Granadilla* or flower of Christs passion: And we despair to behold in these parts that handsome draught of crucifixion in the fruit of the *Barbado* Pine. The seminal Spike of *Phalaris*, or great shaking grasse, more nearly answers the tayl of a Rattle-Snake, then many resemblances in *Porta*: And if the man [1]*Orchis* of *Columna* be well made out, it excelleth all analogies. In young Wallnuts cut athwart, it is not 20 hard to apprehend strange characters; and in those of somewhat elder growth, handsome ornamental draughts about a plain crosse. In the root of *Osmond* or Water fern, every eye may discern the form of a Half Moon, Rain-bow, or half the character of Pisces. Some finde Hebrew, Arabick, Greek, and Latine Characters in Plants; In a common one among us we seem to reade *Aiaia*, *Viviu*, *Lilil*.

Right lines and circles make out the bulk of plants; In the parts thereof we finde Helicall or spirall roundles, voluta's, conicall Sections, circular Pyramids, and frustums of *Archimedes*; And 30 cannot overlook the orderly hand of nature, in the alternate succession of the flat and narrower sides in the tender shoots of the Ashe, or the regular inequality of bignesse in the five-leaved flowers of Henbane, and something like in the calicular leaves of *Tutson*. How the spots of *Persicaria* do manifest themselves between the sixt and tenth ribbe. How the triangular capp in the stemme or *stylus* of Tuleps doth constantly point at three outward leaves. That spicated flowers do open first at the stalk[2]. That white flowers have yellow thrums or knops. That the nebbe of Beans and Pease do all look downward, and so presse not upon each other;

[1] *Orchis Anthropophora, Fabii Columnæ.*
[2] Below. [*Add.*]

25 *Aiaia C*: *Aiain Er*(2): *Acaia 58*

And how the seeds of many pappous or downy flowers lockt up in sockets after a gomphosis or *mortis*-articulation, diffuse themselves circularly into branches of rare order, observable in *Tragopogon* or Goats-beard, conformable to the Spiders web, and the *Radii* in like manner telarely inter-woven.

And how in animall natures, even colours hold correspondencies, and mutuall correlations. That the colour of the Caterpillar will shew again in the Butterfly, with some latitude is allowable. Though the regular spots in their wings seem but a mealie adhesion, and such as may be wiped away, yet since they come in this variety, out of their cases, there must be regular pores in those parts and membranes, defining such Exudations. 10

That [1]*Augustus* had native notes on his body and belly, after the order and number in the Starres of *Charles wayne*, will not seem strange unto astral Physiognomy, which accordingly considereth moles in the body of man, or Physicall Observators, who from the position of moles in the face, reduce them to rule and correspondency in other parts. Whether after the like method medicall conjecture may not be raised, upon parts inwardly affected; since parts about the lips are the critical seats of Pustules discharged in Agues; And scrophulous tumours about the neck do so often speak the like about the Mesentery, may also be considered. 20

The russet neck[2] in young Lambs seems but adventitious, and may owe its tincture to some contaction in the womb; But that if sheep have any black or deep russet in their faces, they want not the same about their legges and feet; That black Hounds have mealy mouths and feet; That black Cows which have any white in their tayls, should not misse of some in their bellies; and if all white in their bodies, yet if black-mouth'd, their ears and feet maintain the same colour, are correspondent tinctures not ordinarily failing in nature, which easily unites the accidents of extremities, since in some generations she transmutes the parts themselves, while in the *Aurelian Metamorphosis* the head of the canker becomes the Tayl of the Butterfly. Which is in some way not beyond the contrivance of Art, in submersions and Inlays, inverting the extremes of the plant, and fetching the root from the top, and also imitated in handsome columnary work, in the inversion of the extremes; wherein the Capitel, and the Base, hold such near correspondency. 30

[1] *Suet. in vit. Aug.* [80.]

[2] To be observed in white young Lambs, which afterward vanisheth. [*Add.*]

---

14 Starres *Er C*: Starre *58*

In the motive parts of animals may be discovered mutuall proportions; not only in those of Quadrupeds, but in the thigh-bone, legge, foot-bone, and claws of Birds. The legs of Spiders are made after a sesqui-tertian proportion, and the long legs of some locusts, double unto some others. But the internodial parts of Vegetables, or spaces between the joints, are contrived with more uncertainty; though the joints themselves in many plants, maintain a regular number.

In vegetable composure, the unition of prominent parts seems most to answer the *Apophyses* or processes of Animall bones, whereof they are the produced parts or prominent explantations. And though in the parts of plants which are not ordained for motion, we do not expect correspondent Articulations; yet in the setting on of some flowers, and seeds in their sockets, and the lineal commissure of the pulpe of severall seeds, may be observed some shadow of the Harmony; some show of the Gomphosis or *mortis*-articulation.

As for the Diarthrosis or motive Articulation, there is expected little Analogy, though long-stalked leaves doe move by long lines, and have observable motions, yet are they made by outward impulsion, like the motion of pendulous bodies, while the parts themselves are united by some kinde of *symphysis* unto the stock.

But standing vegetables, void of motive-Articulations, are not without many motions. For beside the motion of vegetation upward, and of radiation unto all quarters, that of contraction, dilatation, inclination, and contortion, is discoverable in many plants. To omit the rose of *Jericho*, the ear of Rye, which moves with change of weather, and the Magical spit, made of no rare plants, which windes before the fire, and rosts the bird without turning.

Even Animals near the Classis of plants, seem to have the most restlesse motions. The Summer-worm of Ponds and plashes makes a long waving motion; the hair-worm seldome lies still. He that would behold a very anomalous motion, may observe it in the Tortile and tiring stroaks of [1]Gnatworms.

CHAP. IIII.

As for the delights, commodities, mysteries, with other concernments of this order, we are unwilling to fly them over, in the short

[1] Found often in some form of red maggot in the standing waters of Cisterns in the Summer.

deliveries of *Virgil*, *Varro*, or others, and shall therefore enlarge with additionall ampliations.

By this position they had a just proportion of Earth, to supply an equality of nourishment. The distance being ordered, thick or thin, according to the magnitude or vigorous attraction of the plant, the goodnesse, leannesse, or propriety of the soyle, and therefore the rule of *Solon*, concerning the territory of *Athens*, not extendible unto all; allowing the distance of six foot unto common Trees, and nine for the Figge and Olive.

They had a due diffusion of their roots on all or both sides, whereby they maintained some proportion to their height, in Trees of large radication. For that they strictly make good their profundeur or depth unto their height, according to common conceit, and that expression of [1]*Virgil*, though confirmable from the plane Tree in *Pliny*, and some few examples, is not to be expected from the generallitie of Trees almost in any kinde, either of side-spreading, or tap-roots: Except we measure them by lateral and opposite diffusions; nor commonly to be found in *minor* or hearby plants; If we except Sea-holly, Liquorish, Sea-rush, and some others.

They had a commodious radiation in their growth; and a due expansion of their branches, for shadow or delight. For trees thickly planted, do runne up in height and branch with no expansion, shooting unequally or short, and thinne upon the neighbouring side. And therefore Trees are inwardly bare, and spring, and leaf from the outward and Sunny side of their branches.

Whereby they also avoided the perill of συνολεθρία or one tree perishing with another, as it happeneth oft-times from the sick *effluviums* or entanglements of the roots, falling foul with each other. Observable in Elmes set in hedges, where if one dieth the neighbouring Tree prospereth not long after.

In this situation divided into many intervals and open unto six passages, they had the advantage of a fair perflation from windes, brushing and cleansing their surfaces, relaxing and closing their pores unto due perspiration. For that they afford large *effluviums* perceptible from odours, diffused at great distances, is observable from Onyons out of the earth; which though dry, and kept until the spring, as they shoot forth large and many leaves, do notably

1 *Quantum vertice ad auras*
Æthereas, tantum radice ad tartara tendit.
[*Aen.* iv. 445–6.]

12 their] theit *58* 16 generallitie *ErC*: generation *58* 27 συνολεθρία *C*: συνολεθρισμὸς *58*

abate of their weight. And mint growing in glasses of water, until it arriveth unto the weight of an ounce, in a shady place, will sometimes exhaust a pound of water.

And as they send forth much, so may they receive somewhat in: For beside the common way and road of reception by the root, there may be a refection and imbibition from without; For gentle showrs refresh plants, though they enter not their roots; And the good and bad *effluviums* of Vegetables, promote or debilitate each other. So *Epithymum* and *Dodder*, rootlesse and out of the ground,
10 maintain themselves upon Thyme, Savory, and plants, whereon they hang. And *Ivy* divided from the root, we have observed to live some years, by the cirrous parts commonly conceived but as tenacles and holdfasts unto it. The stalks of mint cropt from the root stripped from the leaves, and set in *glasses* with the root end upward, & out of the water, we have observed to send forth sprouts and leaves without the aid of roots, and *scordium* to grow in like manner, the leaves set downward in water. To omit severall Sea-plants, which grow on single roots from stones, although in very many there are side-shoots and *fibres*, beside the
20 fastening root.

By this open position they were fairly exposed unto the rayes of Moon and Sunne, so considerable in the growth of Vegetables. For though Poplars, Willows, and severall Trees be made to grow about the brinks of *Acharon*, and dark habitations of the dead; Though some plants are content to grow in obscure Wells; wherein also old Elme pumps afford sometimes long bushy sprouts, not observable in any above-ground: And large fields of Vegetables are able to maintain their verdure at the bottome and shady part of the Sea; yet the greatest number are not content without the
30 actual rayes of the Sunne, but bend, incline, and follow them; As large lists of solisequious and Sun-following plants. And some observe the method of its motion in their owne growth and conversion twining towards the West by the South, as Bryony, Hops, Woodbine, and several kindes of Bindeweed, which we shall more admire; when any can tell us, they observe another motion, and Twist by the North at the *Antipodes*. The same plants rooted against an erect North-wall full of holes, will finde a way through them to look upon the Sunne. And in tender plants from mustard-seed, sown in the winter, and in a pot of earth placed inwardly
40 in a chamber against a South-window, the tender stalks of two leaves arose not erect, but bending towards the window, nor looking much higher then the Meridian Sun. And if the pot were

39 pot *Er C*: plot *58*   40 in a chamber *C*: *omitted in 58*

turned they would work themselves into their former declinations, making their conversion by the East. That the Leaves of the Olive and some other Trees solstitially turn, and precisely tell us, when the Sun is entred *Cancer*, is scarce expectable in any Climate; and *Theophrastus* warily observes it; Yet somewhat thereof is observable in our own, in the leaves of Willows and Sallows, some weeks after the Solstice. But the great *Convolvulus* or white-flower'd *Bindweed* observes both motions of the Sunne, while the flower twists Æquinoctionally from the left hand to the right, according to the daily revolution; The stalk twineth ecliptically from the right to 10 the left, according to the annual conversion.

Some commend the exposure of these orders unto the Western gales, as the most generative and fructifying breath of heaven. But we applaud the Husbandry of *Solomon*, whereto agreeth the doctrine of *Theophrastus*. Arise O North-winde, and blow thou South upon my garden, that the spices thereof may flow out; For the North-winde closing the pores, and shutting up the *effluviums*, when the South doth after open and relax them; the Aromatical gummes do drop, and sweet odours fly actively from them. And if his garden had the same situation, which mapps, and charts 20 afford it, on the East side of *Jerusalem*, and having the wall on the West; these were the windes, unto which it was well exposed.

By this way of plantation they encreased the number of their trees, which they lost in *Quaternio's*, and square-orders, which is a commodity insisted on by *Varro*, and one great intent of nature, in this position of flowers and seeds in the elegant formation of plants, and the former Rules observed in naturall and artificiall Figurations.

Whether in this order and one Tree in some measure breaking the cold, and pinching gusts of windes from the other, trees will 30 not better maintain their inward circles, and either escape or moderate their excentricities, may also be considered. For the circles in Trees are naturally concentricall, parallell unto the bark, and unto each other, till frost and piercing windes contract and close them on the weatherside, the opposite semicircle widely enlarging, and at a comely distance, which hindreth ofttimes the beauty and roundnesse of Trees, and makes the Timber lesse serviceable; whiles the ascending juyce not readily passing, settles in knots and inequalities. And therefore it is no new course of Agriculture, to observe the native position of Trees according to 40 North and South in their transplantations.

The same is also observable underground in the circinations and sphærical rounds of Onyons, wherein the circles of the Orbes are ofttimes larger, and the meridionall lines stand wider upon one side then the other. And where the largenesse will make up the number of planetical Orbes, that of *Luna*, and the lower planets excede the dimensions of *Saturne*, and the higher: Whether the like be not verified in the Circles of the large roots of Briony and Mandrakes, or why in the knotts of Deale or Firre the Circles are often eccentricall, although not in a plane, but vertical and right position, deserves a further enquiry.

Whether there be not some irregularity of roundnesse in most 10 plants according to their position? Whether some small compression of pores be not perceptible in parts which stand against the current of waters, as in Reeds, Bullrushes, and other vegetables toward the streaming quarter, may also be observed, and therefore such as are long and weak, are commonly contrived into a roundnesse of figure, whereby the water presseth lesse, and slippeth more smoothly from them, and even in flags of flat-figured leaves, the greater part obvert their sharper sides unto the current in ditches.

But whether plants which float upon the surface of the water, 20 be for the most part of cooling qualities, those which shoot above it of heating vertues, and why? whether *Sargasso* for many miles floating upon the Western Ocean, or Sea-lettuce, and Phasganium at the bottome of our Seas, make good the like qualities? Why Fenny waters afford the hottest and sweetest plants, as Calamus, Cyperus, and Crowfoot, and mudd cast out of ditches most naturally produceth Arsmart, Why plants so greedy of water so little regard oyl? Why since many seeds contain much oyle within them, they endure it not well without, either in their growth or production? Why since Seeds shoot commonly under ground, and 30 out of the ayre, those which are let fall in shallow glasses, upon the surface of the water, will sooner sprout then those at the bottome? And if the water be covered with oyle, those at the bottome will hardly sprout at all, we have not room to conjecture.

Whether Ivy would not lesse offend the Trees in this clean ordination, and well kept paths, might perhaps deserve the question. But this were a quæry only unto some habitations, and little concerning *Cyrus* or the Babylonian territory; wherein by no industry *Harpalus* could make Ivy grow: And *Alexander* hardly found it about those parts to imitate the pomp of *Bacchus*. And 40 though in these Northern Regions we are too much acquainted with one Ivy, we know too little of another, whereby we apprehend not the expressions of Antiquity, the [1]Splenetick medicine

[1] *Galen. de med. secundum loc.*

of *Galen*, and the Emphasis of the Poet, in the [1]beauty of the white Ivy.

The like concerning the growth of Misseltoe, which dependeth not only of the *species*, or kinde of Tree, but much also of the Soil. And therefore common in some places, not readily found in others, frequent in *France*, not so common in *Spain*, and scarce at all in the Territory of *Ferrara*: Nor easily to be found where it is most required upon Oaks, lesse on Trees continually verdant. Although in some places the Olive escapeth it not, requiting its detriment, in the delightfull view of its red Berries; as *Clusius* observed in *Spain*, and *Bellonius* about *Hierusalem*. But this Parasiticall plant suffers nothing to grow upon it, by any way of art; nor could we ever make it grow where nature had not planted it; as we have in vain attempted by inocculation and incision, upon its native or forreign stock. And though there seem nothing improbable in the seed, it hath not succeeded by sation in any manner of ground, wherein we had no reason to despair, since we reade of vegetable horns, and how Rams horns[2] will root about *Goa*.

But besides these rurall commodities, it cannot be meanly delectable in the variety of Figures, which these orders open, and closed do make. Whilest every inclosure makes a *Rhombus*, the figures obliquely taken a Rhomboides, the intervals bounded with parallell lines, and each intersection built upon a square, affording two Triangles or Pyramids vertically conjoyned; which in the strict Quincunciall order doe oppositely make acute and blunt Angles.

And though therein we meet not with right angles, yet every Rhombus containing four Angles equall unto four right, it virtually contains four right. Nor is this strange unto such as observe the naturall lines of Trees, and parts disposed in them. For neither in the root doth nature affect this angle, which shooting downward for the stability of the plant, doth best effect the same by Figures of Inclination; Nor in the Branches and stalky leaves, which grow most at acute angles; as declining from their head the root, and diminishing their Angles with their altitude: Verified also in lesser Plants, whereby they better support themselves, and bear not so heavily upon the stalk: So that while near the root they often make an Angle of seventy parts, the sprouts near the top will often come short of thirty. Euen in the nerves and master

[1] *Hedera formosior alba* [Virg. *Ecl.* vii. 38.]

[2] *Linschoten.*

28–29 unto four . . . four *Er C*: unto two . . . two *58* 29 right. *Er C*: right in every one. *58*

veins of the leaves the acute angle ruleth; the obtuse but seldome found, and in the backward part of the leaf, reflecting and arching about the stalk. But why ofttimes one side of the leaf is unequall unto the other, as in Hazell and Oaks, why on either side the master vein the lesser and derivative channels stand not directly opposite, nor at equall angles, respectively unto the adverse side, but those of one part do often exceed the other, as the Wallnut and many more, deserves another enquiry.

Now if for this order we affect coniferous and tapering Trees, 10 particularly the Cypresse, which grows in a conicall figure; we have found a Tree not only of great Ornament, but in its Essentials of affinity unto this order. A solid Rhombus being made by the conversion of two Equicrurall Cones, as *Archimedes* hath defined. And these were the common Trees about *Babylon*, and the East, whereof the Ark was made; and *Alexander* found no Trees so accomodable to build his Navy; And this we rather think to be the Tree mentioned in the Canticles, which stricter Botanology will hardly allow to be Camphire.

And if delight or ornamentall view invite a comely disposure by 20 circular amputations, as is elegantly performed in Hawthorns; then will they answer the figures made by the conversion of a Rhombus, which maketh two concentricall Circles; the greater circumference being made by the lesser angles, the lesser by the greater.

The Cylindrical figure of Trees is virtually contained and latent in this order. A Cylinder or long round being made by the conversion or turning of a Parallelogram, and most handsomely by a long square, which makes an equall, strong, and lasting figure in Trees, agreeable unto the body and motive parts of animals, the 30 greatest number of Plants, and almost all roots, though their stalks be angular, and of many corners, which seem not to follow the figure of their Seeds; Since many angular Seeds send forth round stalks, and sphæricall seeds arise from angular spindles, and many rather conform unto their Roots, as the round stalks of bulbous Roots, and in tuberous Roots stemmes of like figure. But why since the largest number of Plants maintain a circular Figure, there are so few with teretous or longround leaves; why coniferous Trees are tenuifolious or narrowleafed, why Plants of few or no joynts have commonly round stalks, why the greatest 40 number of hollow stalks are round stalks; or why in this variety of angular stalks the quadrangular most exceedeth, were too long a speculation; Mean while obvious experience may finde, that in

5 stand not *Er*(*2*) *C*: not *58*   8 more,] more *58*

Plants of divided leaves above, nature often beginneth circularly in the two first leaves below, while in the singular plant of Ivy, she exerciseth a contrary Geometry, and beginning with angular leaves below, rounds them in the upper branches.

Nor can the rows in this order want delight, as carrying an aspect answerable unto the *dipteros hypæthros*, or double order of columns open above; the opposite ranks of Trees standing like pillars in the *Cavedia* of the Courts of famous buildings, and the *Portico*'s of the *Templa subdialia* of old; Somewhat imitating the *Peristylia* or Cloyster buildings, and the *Exedræ* of the Ancients, 10 wherein men discoursed, walked and exercised; For that they derived the rule of Columnes from Trees, especially in their proportionall diminutions, is illustrated by *Vitruvius* from the shafts of Firre and Pine. And though the inter-arborations do imitate the *Areostylos*, or thin order, not strictly answering the proportion of intercolumniations; yet in many Trees they will not exceed the intermission of the Columnes in the Court of the Tabernacle; which being an hundred cubits long, and made up by twenty pillars, will afford no lesse then intervals of five cubits.

Beside, in this kinde of aspect the sight being not diffused but 20 circumscribed between long parallels and the ἐπισκιάσμὸς and adumbration from the branches, it frameth a penthouse over the eye, and maketh a quiet vision: And therefore in diffused and open aspects, men hollow their hand above their eye, and make an artificiall brow, whereby they direct the dispersed rayes of sight, and by this shade preserve a moderate light in the chamber of the eye; keeping the *pupilla* plump and fair, and not contracted or shrunk as in light and vagrant vision.

And therefore providence hath arched and paved the great house of the world, with colours of mediocrity, that is, blew and 30 green, above and below the sight, moderately terminating the *acies* of the eye. For most plants, though green above ground, maintain their Originall white below it, according to the candour of their seminall pulp, and the rudimental leaves do first appear in that colour; observable in Seeds sprouting in water upon their first foliation. Green seeming to be the first supervenient, or above-ground complexion of Vegetables, separable in many upon ligature or inhumation, as Succory, Endive, Artichoaks, and which is also lost upon fading in the Autumn.

And this is also agreeable unto water it self, the alimental 40 vehicle of plants, which first altereth into this colour; And containing many vegetable seminalities, revealeth their Seeds by

14 inter-arborations *C*: inter-arboration *58* 16 exceed] exeeed *58*

greennesse; and therefore soonest expected in rain or standing water, not easily found in distilled or water strongly boiled; wherein the Seeds are extinguished by fire and decoction, and therefore last long and pure without such alteration, affording neither uliginous coats, gnatworms, Acari, hair-worms, like crude and common water; And therefore most fit for wholsome beverage, and with malt makes Ale and Beer without boyling. What large water-drinkers some Plants are, the Canary-Tree and Birches in some Northern Countries, drenching the Fields about them do
10 sufficiently demonstrate. How water it self is able to maintain the growth of Vegetables, and without extinction of their generative or medicall vertues; Beside the experiment of *Helmonts* tree, we have found in some which have lived six years in glasses. The seeds of Scurvy-grasse growing in waterpots, have been fruitfull in the Land; And *Asarum* after a years space, and once casting its leaves in water, in the second leaves, hath handsomely performed its vomiting operation.

Nor are only dark and green colors, but shades and shadows contrived through the great Volume of nature, and trees ordained
20 not only to protect and shadow others, but by their shades and shadowing parts, to preserve and cherish themselves. The whole radiation or branchings shadowing the stock and the root, the leaves, the branches and fruit, too much exposed to the windes and scorching Sunne. The calicular leaves inclose the tender flowers, and the flowers themselves lye wrapt about the seeds, in their rudiment and first formations, which being advanced the flowers fall away; and are therefore contrived in variety of figures, best satisfying the intention; Handsomely observable in hooded and gaping flowers, and the Butterfly bloomes of leguminous
30 plants, the lower leaf closely involving the rudimental Cod, and the alary or wingy divisions embracing or hanging over it.

But Seeds themselves do lie in perpetual shades, either under the leaf, or shut up in coverings; And such as lye barest, have their husks, skins, and pulps about them, wherein the nebbe and generative particle lyeth moist and secured from the injury of Ayre and Sunne. Darknesse and light hold interchangeable dominions, and alternately rule the seminal state of things. Light unto [1]*Pluto* is darknesse unto *Jupiter*. Legions of seminall *Idæa's* lye in their second Chaos and *Orcus* of *Hipocrates*; till putting
40 on the habits of their forms, they shew themselves upon the stage

[1] *Lux orco, tenebræ Jovi, tenebræ orco, lux Jovi.* Hippocr. *de diæta.* [i. 5.]

---

38 *Pluto Er C*: *Plato 58*

of the world, and open dominion of *Jove*. They that held the Stars of heaven were but rayes and flashing glimpses of the Empyreall light, through holes and perforations of the upper heaven, took of the natural shadows of stars, while according to better discovery[1] the poor Inhabitants of the Moone have but a polary life, and must passe half their dayes in the shadow of that Luminary.

Light that makes things seen, makes some things invisible, were it not for darknesse and the shadow of the earth, the noblest part of the Creation had remained unseen, and the Stars in heaven as invisible as on the fourth day, when they were created above 10 the Horizon, with the Sun, or there was not an eye to behold them. The greatest mystery of Religion is expressed by adumbration, and in the noblest part of Jewish Types, we finde the Cherubims shadowing the Mercy-seat: Life it self is but the shadow of death, and souls departed but the shadows of the living: All things fall under this name. The Sunne it self is but the dark *simulachrum*, and light but the shadow of God.

Lastly, It is no wonder that this Quincunciall order was first and still affected as gratefull unto the Eye: For all things are seen Quincuncially; For at the eye the Pyramidal rayes from the object, 20 receive a decussation, and so strike a second base upon the *Retina* or hinder coat, the proper organ of Vision; wherein the pictures from objects are represented, answerable to the paper, or wall in the dark chamber; after the decussation of the rayes at the hole of the hornycoat, and their refraction upon the Christalline humour, answering the *foramen* of the window, and the *convex* or burning-glasses, which refract the rayes that enter it. And if ancient Anatomy would hold, a like disposure there was of the optick or visual nerves in the brain, wherein Antiquity conceived a concurrence by decussation. And this not only observable in the Laws 30 of direct Vision, but in some part also verified in the reflected rayes of sight. For making the angle of incidence equal to that of reflexion, the visuall raye returneth Quincuncially, and after the form of a V, and the line of reflexion being continued unto the place of vision, there ariseth a semi-decussation, which makes the object seen in a perpendicular unto it self, and as farre below the reflectent, as it is from it above; observable in the Sun and Moon beheld in water.

And this is also the law of reflexion in moved bodies and sounds, which though not made by decussation, observe the rule of 40 equality between incidence and reflexion; whereby whispering places are framed by Ellipticall arches laid side-wise; where the

[1] *S. Hevelii Selenographia.*

voice being delivered at the *focus* of one extremity, observing an equality unto the angle of incidence, it will reflect unto the *focus* of the other end, and so escape the ears of the standers in the middle.

A like rule is observed in the reflection of the vocall and sonorous line in Ecchoes, which cannot therefore be heard in all stations. But happening in woody plantations, by waters, and able to return some words; if reacht by a pleasant and well-dividing voice, there may be heard the softest notes in nature.

And this not only verified in the way of sence, but in animall 10 and intellectuall receptions. Things entring upon the intellect by a Pyramid from without, and thence into the memory by another from within, the common decussation being in the understanding as is delivered by [1]*Bovillus.* Whether the intellectual and phantastical lines be not thus rightly disposed, but magnified diminished, distorted, and ill placed in the Mathematicks of some brains, whereby they have irregular apprehensions of things, perverted notions, conceptions, and incurable hallucinations, were no unpleasant speculation.

And if Ægyptian Philosophy may obtain, the scale of influences 20 was thus disposed, and the geniall spirits of both worlds, do trace their way in ascending and descending Pyramids, mystically apprehended in the Letter X, and the open Bill and stradling Legges of a Stork, which was imitated by that Character.

Of this Figure *Plato* made choice to illustrate the motion of the soul, both of the world and man; while he delivereth that God divided the whole conjunction length-wise, according to the figure of a Greek X, and then turning it about reflected it into a circle; By the circle implying the uniform motion of the first Orb, and by the right lines, the planetical and various motions within 30 it. And this also with application unto the soul of man, which hath a double aspect, one right, whereby it beholdeth the body, and objects without; another circular and reciprocal, whereby it beholdeth it self. The circle declaring the motion of the indivisible soul, simple, according to the divinity of its nature, and returning into it self; the right lines respecting the motion pertaining unto sense, and vegetation, and the central decussation, the wondrous connexion of the severall faculties conjointly in one substance. And so conjoyned the unity and duality of the soul, and made out the three substances so much considered by him; That is, the 40 indivisible or divine, the divisible or corporeal, and that third, which was the *Systasis* or harmony of those two, in the mystical decussation.

[1] *Car. Bovillus de intellectu.*

And if that were clearly made out which *Justin Martyr* took for granted, this figure hath had the honour to characterize and notifie our blessed Saviour, as he delivereth in that borrowed expression from *Plato*; *Decussavit eum in universo*,[1] the hint whereof he would have *Plato* derive from the figure of the brazen Serpent, and to have mistaken the Letter X for T, whereas it is not improbable, he learned these and other mystical expressions in his Learned Observations of Ægypt, where he might obviously behold the Mercurial characters, the handed crosses, and other mysteries not throughly understood in the sacred Letter X, which being derivative from the Stork, one of the ten sacred animals, might be originally Ægyptian, and brought into *Greece* by *Cadmus* of that Countrey.

CHAP. V.

TO enlarge this contemplation unto all the mysteries and secrets, accomodable unto this number, were inexcusable Pythagorisme, yet cannot omit the ancient conceit of five surnamed the number of [2]justice; as justly dividing between the digits, and hanging in . . . the centre of Nine, described by square numeration, which angu- . . . larly divided will make the decussated number; and so agreeable . . . unto the Quincunciall Ordination, and rowes divided by Equality, and just *decorum*, in the whole com-plantation; And might be the Originall of that common game among us, wherein the fifth place is Soveraigne, and carrieth the chief intention. The Ancients wisely instructing youth, even in their recreations unto virtue, that is, early to drive at the middle point and Central Seat of justice.

Nor can we omit how agreeable unto this number an handsome division is made in Trees and Plants, since *Plutarch*, and the Ancients have named it the Divisive Number, justly dividing the Entities of the world, many remarkable things in it, and also comprehending the [3]generall division of Vegetables. And he that considers how most blossomes of Trees, and greatest number of Flowers, consist of five leaves; and therein doth rest the setled rule of nature; So that in those which exceed there is often found, or

[1] *ἐχῖασεν ἀυτὸν ἐν τῷ παντὶ*. [*Add.*] [2] *δίκη*.

[3] *Δένδρον, Θάμνος, Φρύγανον, Πόα, Arbor, frutex, suffrutex, herba*, and that fifth which comprehendeth the *fungi* and *tubera*, whether to be named *Ἄσχιον* or *γύμνον*, comprehending also *conferva marina salsa*, and Sea-cords, of so many yards length.

easily made a variety; may readily discover how nature rests in this number, which is indeed the first rest and pause of numeration in the fingers, the naturall Organs thereof. Nor in the division of the feet of perfect animals doth nature exceed this account. And even in the joints of feet, which in birds are most multiplied, surpasseth not this number; So progressionally making them out in many[1], that from five in the fore-claw she descendeth unto two in the hindemost; And so in fower feet makes up the number of joynts, in the five fingers or toes of man.

10 Not to omit the Quintuple Section of a [2]Cone, of handsome practise in Ornamentall Garden-plots, and in some way discoverable in so many works of Nature; In the leaves, fruits, and seeds of Vegetables, and scales of some Fishes, so much considerable in glasses, and the optick doctrine; wherein the learned may consider the Crystalline humour of the eye in the cuttle fish and *Loligo.*

He that forgets not how Antiquity named this the Conjugall or wedding number, and made it the Embleme of the most remarkable conjunction, will conceive it duely appliable unto this handsome Oeconomy, and vegetable combination; May hence apprehend 20 the allegoricall sence of that obscure expression of [3]*Hesiod*, and afford no improbable reason why *Plato* admitted his Nuptiall guests by fives, in the kindred of the [4]married couple.

And though a sharper mystery might be implied in the Number of the five wise and foolish Virgins, which were to meet the Bridegroom, yet was the same agreeable unto the Conjugall Number, which ancient Numerists made out by two and three, the first parity and imparity, the active and passive digits, the materiall and formall principles in generative Societies. And not discordant even from the customes of the *Romans*, who admitted 30 but [5]five Torches in their Nuptiall solemnities. Whether there were any mystery or not implied, the most generative animals were created on this day, and had accordingly the largest benediction: And under a Quintuple consideration, wanton Antiquity considered the Circumstances of generation, while by this number of five they naturally divided the Nectar of the fifth Planet.[6]

1 As Herns, Bitterns, and long claw-d Fowls. [*Add.*]
2 *Elleipsis, parabola, Hyperbole, Circulus, Triangulum.*
3 *πέμπτας id est nuptias multas.* Rhodig.
4 Plato *de leg.* 6. [775.]
5 *Plutarch problem. Rom.* 1. [2.]
6 *Oscula quæ Venus*
Quinta parte sui Nectaris imbuit.
[Hor. *Od.* 1. 13. 15–16.] [*Add.*]

35 Planet.] Planet, *58*

The same number in the Hebrew mysteries and Cabalistical accounts was the [1]character of Generation; declared by the Letter *He*, the fifth in their Alphabet; According to that Cabalisticall *Dogma*: If *Abram* had not had this Letter added unto his Name, he had remained fruitlesse, and without the power of generation: Not onely because hereby the number of his Name attained two hundred fourty eight, the number of the affirmative precepts, but because as in created natures there is a male and female, so in divine and intelligent productions, the mother of Life and Fountain of souls in Cabalisticall Technology is called *Binah*; whose Seal 10 and Character was *He*. So that being sterill before, he recived the power of generation from that measure and mansion in the Archetype; and was made conformable unto *Binah*. And upon such involved considerations, the [2]ten of *Sarai* was exchanged into five. If any shall look upon this as a stable number, and fitly appropriable unto Trees, as Bodies of Rest and Station, he hath herein a great Foundation in nature, who observing much variety in legges and motive Organs of Animals, as two, four, six, eight, twelve, fourteen, and more, hath passed over five and ten, and assigned them unto none[3]. And for the stability of this Number, 20 he shall not want the sphericity of its nature, which multiplied in it self, will return into its own denomination, and bring up the reare of the account. Which is also one of the Numbers that makes up the mysticall Name of God, which consisting of Letters denoting all the sphæricall Numbers, ten, five, and six; Emphatically sets forth the Notion of *Trismegistus*, and that intelligible Sphere, which is the Nature of God.

Many Expressions by this Number occurre in Holy Scripture, perhaps unjustly laden with mysticall Expositions, and little concerning our order. That the Israelites were forbidden to eat the 30 fruit of their new planted Trees, before the fifth yeare, was very agreeable unto the naturall Rules of Husbandry: Fruits being unwholsome and lash, before the fourth, or fifth Yeare. In the second day or Feminine part of five, there was added no approbation. For in the third or masculine day, the same is twice repeated; and a double benediction inclosed both Creations, whereof the one, in some part was but an accomplishment of the other. That

[1] *Archang. dog. Cabal.* [2] *Jod* into *He*.

[3] Or very few, as the *Phalangium monstrosum Brasilianum, Clusii & Jac. de Laet. Cur. poster. Americæ Descript.* If perfectly described.

---

15 five.] five, *58* 20 none.] none, *58* *note 3 above*: Or ... described.] *Part of the text in 58, which reads* none, or very few *&c. Transferred to margin C.*

the [1]Trespasser was to pay a fifth part above the head or principall, makes no secret in this Number, and implied no more then one part above the principall; which being considered in four parts, the additionall forfeit must bear the Name of a fift. The five golden mice had plainly their determination from the number of the Princes; That five should put to flight an hundred might have nothing mystically implyed; considering a rank of Souldiers could scarce consist of a lesser number. Saint *Paul* had rather speak five words in a known then ten thousand in an unknowne tongue:
10 That is as little as could well be spoken. A simple proposition consisting of three words and a complexed one not ordinarily short of five.

More considerable there are in this mysticall account, which we must not insist on. And therefore why the radicall Letters in the Pentateuch, should equall the number of the Souldiery of the Tribes; Why our Saviour in the Wildernesse fed five thousand persons with five Barley Loaves, and again, but four thousand with no lesse then seven of Wheat? Why *Joseph* designed five changes of Rayment unto *Benjamin*? and *David* took just five pibbles out of
20 the Brook against the Pagan Champion? We leave it unto Arithmeticall Divinity, and Theologicall explanation.

Yet if any delight in new Problemes, or think it worth the enquiry, whether the Criticall Physician hath rightly hit the nominall notation of Quinque[2]; Why the Ancients mixed five or three but not four parts of water unto their Wine: And *Hippocrates* observed a fifth proportion in the mixture of water with milk, as in *Dysenteries* and bloudy fluxes. Under what abstruse foundation Astrologers do Figure the good or bad Fate from our Children, in [3]good Fortune, or the fifth house of their Celestiall
30 Schemes. Whether the Ægyptians described a Starre by a Figure of five points, with reference unto the [4]five Capitall aspects, whereby they transmit their Influences, or abstruser Considerations? Why the Cabalisticall Doctors, who conceive the whole *Sephiroth*, or divine emanations to have guided the ten-stringed Harp of *David*, whereby he pacified the evil spirit of *Saul*, in strict numeration doe begin with the Perihypate Meson, or si fa ut, and so place the Tiphereth answering C sol fa ut, upon the fifth string: Or

[1] Lev. 6. [5.]
[2] τέσσαρα ἕνκε four and one, or five. *Scalig.*
[3] Ἀγαθὴ τυχὴ, or *bona fortuna* the name of the fifth house.
[4] Conjunct, opposite, sextile, trigonal, tetragonal.

---

note 2 τέσσαρα *&c. In 58 note 2 is placed against ll. 19–21* 36 si] ff *58*

whether this number be oftner applied unto bad things and ends, then good in holy Scripture, and why? He may meet with abstrusities of no ready resolution.

If any shall question the rationality of that Magick, in the cure of the blind man by *Serapis*, commanded to place five fingers on his Altar, and then his hand on his Eyes? Why since the whole Comœdy is primarily and naturally comprised in [1]four parts, and Antiquity permitted not so many persons to speak in one Scene, yet would not comprehend the same in more or lesse then five acts? Why amongst Sea-starres nature chiefly delighteth in five points? And since there are found some of no fewer then twelve, and some of seven, and nine, there are few or none discovered of six or eight? If any shall enquire why the Flowers of *Rue* properly consist of four Leaves, The first and third Flower have five? Why since many Flowers have one leaf or [2]none, as *Scaliger* will have it, diverse three, and the greatest number consist of five divided from their bottomes; there are yet so few of two: or why nature generally beginning or setting out with two opposite leaves at the Root, doth so seldome conclude with that order and number at the Flower? he shall not passe his hours in vulgar speculations.

If any shall further quæry why magneticall Philosophy excludeth decussations, and needles transversly placed do naturally distract their verticities? Why Geomancers do imitate the Quintuple Figure, in their Mother Characters of Acquisition and Amission, *&c.* somewhat answering the Figures in the Lady or speckled Beetle? With what Equity, Chiromantical conjecturers decry these decussations in the Lines and Mounts of the hand? What that decussated Figure intendeth in the medall of *Alexander* the Great? Why the Goddesses sit commonly crosse-legged in ancient draughts, Since *Juno* is described in the same as a veneficial posture to hinder the birth of *Hercules*? If any shall doubt why at the Amphidromicall Feasts, on the fifth day after the Childe was born, presents were sent from friends, of *Polipusses*, and Cuttle-fishes? Why five must be only left in that Symbolicall mutiny among the men of *Cadmus*? Why *Proteus* in *Homer* the Symbole of the first matter, before he setled himself in the midst of his Sea-monsters, doth place them out by fives? Why the fifth years Oxe was acceptable Sacrifice unto *Jupiter*? Or why the Noble *Antoninus* in some sence doth call the soul it self a Rhombus? He shall not fall on trite or triviall disquisitions. And these we invent and propose unto acuter enquirers, nauseating crambe verities and

[1] *Πρότασις, ἐπίτασις, κατάστασις, καταστροφή.*

[2] *Unifolium, nullifolium.*

questions over-queried. Flat and flexible truths are beat out by every hammer; But *Vulcan* and his whole forge sweat to work out *Achilles* his armour. A large field is yet left unto sharper discerners to enlarge upon this order, to search out the *quaternio's* and figured draughts of this nature, and moderating the study of names, and meer nomenclature of plants, to erect generalities, disclose unobserved proprieties, not only in the vegetable shop, but the whole volume of nature; affording delightful Truths, confirmable by sense and ocular Observation, which seems to me the
10 surest path, to trace the Labyrinth of Truth. For though discursive enquiry and rationall conjecture, may leave handsome gashes and flesh-wounds; yet without conjunction of this expect no mortal or dispatching blows unto errour.

But the [1]Quincunx of Heaven runs low, and 'tis time to close the five ports of knowledge; We are unwilling to spin out our awaking thoughts into the phantasmes of sleep, which to often continueth præcogitations; making Cables of Cobwebbes and Wildernesses of handsome Groves. Beside [2]*Hippocrates* hath spoke so little and the [3]Oneirocriticall Masters, have left such frigid
20 Interpretations from plants, that there is little encouragement to dream of Paradise it self. Nor will the sweetest delight of Gardens afford much comfort in sleep; wherein the dulnesse of that sense shakes hands with delectable odours; and though in the [4]Bed of *Cleopatra*, can hardly with any delight raise up the ghost of a Rose.

Night which Pagan Theology could make the daughter of *Chaos*, affords no advantage to the description of order: Although no lower then that Masse can we derive its Genealogy. All things began in order, so shall they end, and so shall they begin again;
30 according to the ordainer of order and mystical Mathematicks of the City of Heaven.

Though *Somnus* in *Homer* be sent to rowse up *Agamemnon*, I finde no such effects in the drowsy approaches of sleep. To keep our eyes open longer were but to act our *Antipodes*. The Huntsmen are up in *America*, and they are already past their first sleep in

[1] *Hyades* near the Horizon about midnight, at that time.
[2] *De Insomniis*.
[3] *Artemodorus*. & *Apomazar*.
[4] Strewed with roses.

---

16 to often *C*: often *58*   33 the *C*: these *58*

Persia. But who can be drowsie at that howr which freed us from everlasting sleep? or have slumbring thoughts at that time, when sleep it self must end, and as some conjecture all shall awake again?

FINIS.

ERRATA

EPIST. 2. pag. *ult.* l. 1. *wraps up* adde *in.* p. 2. l. 10. read *thousands of yeares.* p. 16. line 14. for *Prastaagus* read *Prasatagus.* p. 17. l. 14. r. *unknown.* p. 27. l. 16. r. *Ausgarius.* p. 32. l. 4. for *a* r. *and.* p. 36. l. 15. for *rest* r. *rust.* p. 37. l. 9. for *for* r. *four.* p. 43. l. 11. for *lump* r. *lamp.* l. 10. *Galvanus.* full point. *p.* 45. *m.* for *speran.* r. *sperm. ran.* p. 48. l. 3. for *knav'd* r. *gnawd.* p. 49. l. 16. & 20. for *putrified* r. *petrified.* p. 56. l. 23. for *be* r. *tree.* l. 27. r. *furze.* p. 69. m. r. καθαρώταται. p. 70. l. 3. for *stranger* r. *stronger.* p. 76. l. 7. these words [*without the favour of the everlasting Register*] to come in l. 13. after [*account of time*]. p. 78. m. for νημη r. νομὴ. p. 81. l. 18. for *stay* r. *stage.* p. 94. m. for ἐυδωνια r. ἐυγώνια. l. 27. for *doubted* r. *doubled.* p. 100. l. 23. for *stones* r. *sonnes.* p. 109. l. 9. r. *chapiters.* p. 119. l. 8. for *five* r. *seven.* p. 122. l. 3. for *neck* r. *bead.* p. 123. m. for μετρος λαγωναν r. λαγόνων μητρὸς. p. 124. l. 13. r. *Teasel.* p. 126. m. r. *stratiotes.* p. 127. l. 14. r. *furze.* p. 130. l. 5. r. *germen.* p. 133. l. 10. for *pores* r. *powers.* p. 135. l. 15. after [*trees*] adde [*in a large acception it compriseth all Vegetables, for the frutex and suffrutex are under the progression of trees*] l. ult. for *dill* r. *pill.* p. 139. l. 7. for *dosing* r. *closing.* p. 141. l. 14. for *first* r. *fifth.* p. 143. l. 19. r. *weazel.* p. 156. l. 17. r. *starres.* p. 162. l. 8. r. *generallitie.* p. 166. l. 4. r. *pot.* p. 173. l. 8. and 9. for *two* r. *four.* l. 10. dele *in every one.* 181. l. 14. r. *Pluto.*

Errata. The page-numbers and line-numbers are those of *58*. The corresponding numbers in the present edition are 87.33, 89.16, 95.30, 96.7, 100.32, 102.22, 104.18, 104.31, 107.27, 107.27, 108 note 6, 109.40, 110.23 & 26, 113.22, 113.24, 118.29, 118, note 2, 121.22–25, 122, note 3, 124.6, 131, note 3, 131.25, 134.15, 137.25, 142.3, 142.37, 143, note 2, 144.4, 144, note 3, 145.16, 146.21, 147.32, 148.27–29, 148.36, 150.14, 151.12, 152.8, 157.14, 159.16, 160.39, 163.29–30, 163.30, 166.38.

ADDITIONAL FOOTNOTE

136.27 interspaces *C*: interspaces, 58. *The correction* was reported by Mr. John Carter in *The Library*, 1947, pp. 191–2.

A
LETTER
TO A
FRIEND,
Upon occasion of the
DEATH
OF HIS
Intimate Friend.

By the Learned
Sir *THOMAS BROWN*, Knight,
Doctor of Physick, late of *Norwich*.

LONDON:
Printed for *Charles Brome* at the *Gun* in the West-End
of S. *Paul*'s Church-yard. 1690.

TO A FRIEND,
Upon occasion of the Death of his Intimate Friend.

GIVE me leave to wonder that News of this nature should have such heavy Wings, that you should hear so little concerning your dearest Friend, and that I must make that unwilling Repetition to tell you, *Ad portam rigidos calces extendit*, that he is Dead and Buried, and by this time no Puny among the mighty Nations of the Dead; for tho he left this World not very many days past, yet every hour you know largely addeth unto that dark Society; and considering the incessant Mortality of Mankind, you cannot conceive 10 there dieth in the whole Earth so few as a thousand an hour.

Altho at this distance you had no early Account or Particular of his Death; yet your Affection may cease to wonder that you had not some secret Sense or Intimation thereof by Dreams, thoughtful Whisperings, Mercurisms, Airy Nuncio's, or sympathetical Insinuations, which many seem to have had at the Death of their dearest Friends: for since we find in that famous Story, that Spirits themselves were fain to tell their Fellows at a distance, that the great *Antonio* was dead; we have a sufficient Excuse for our Ignorance in such Particulars, and must rest content with the common 20 Road, and *Appian* way of Knowledge by Information. Tho the uncertainty of the End of this World hath confounded all Humane Predictions; yet they who shall live to see the Sun and Moon darkned, and the Stars to fall from Heaven, will hardly be deceived in the Advent of the last Day; and therefore strange it is, that the common Fallacy of consumptive Persons, who feel not themselves dying, and therefore still hope to live, should also reach their Friends in perfect Health and Judgment. That you should be so little acquainted with *Plautus*'s sick Complexion, or that almost an *Hippocratical* Face should not alarum you to higher fears, or 30 rather despair of his Continuation in such an emaciated State, wherein medical Predictions fail not, as sometimes in acute Diseases, and wherein 'tis as dangerous to be sentenced by a Physician as a Judge.

Upon my first Visit I was bold to tell them who had not let fall all hopes of his Recovery, That in my sad Opinion he was not like to behold a Grashopper, much less to pluck another Fig; and in no long time after seemed to discover that odd mortal Symptom in him not mention'd by *Hippocrates*, that is, to lose his own Face and look like some of his near Relations; for he maintained not his proper Countenance, but looked like his Uncle, the Lines of whose Face lay deep and invisible in his healthful Visage before; for as from our beginning we run through variety of Looks, before we come to consistent and settled Faces; so before our End, by sick and languishing Alterations, we put on new Visages: and in our Retreat to Earth, may fall upon such Looks which from community of seminal Originals were before latent in us.

He was fruitlesly put in hope of advantage by change of Air, 10 and imbibing the pure Aerial Nitre of these Parts; and therefore being so far spent, he quickly found *Sardinia* in *Tivoli*[1], and the most healthful Air of little effect, where Death had set her Broad Arrow[2]; for he lived not unto the middle of *May*, and confirmed the Observation of [3]*Hippocrates* of that mortal time of the Year when the Leaves of the Fig-tree resemble a Daw's Claw. He is happily seated who lives in Places whose Air, Earth, and Water, promote not the Infirmities of his weaker Parts, or is early removed into Regions that correct them. He that is tabidly inclined, were unwise to pass his days in *Portugal*: Cholical Persons will find little 20 Comfort in *Austria* or *Vienna*: He that is Weak-legg'd must not be in Love with *Rome*, nor an infirm Head with *Venice* or *Paris*. Death hath not only particular Stars in Heaven, but malevolent Places on Earth, which single out our Infirmities, and strike at our weaker Parts; in which Concern, passager and migrant Birds have the great Advantages; who are naturally constituted for distant Habitations, whom no Seas nor Places limit, but in their appointed Seasons will visit us from *Greenland* and Mount *Atlas*, and as some think, even from the *Antipodes*[4].

Tho we could not have his Life, yet we missed not our desires in 30 his soft Departure, which was scarce an Expiration; and his End not unlike his Beginning, when the salient Point scarce affords a sensible motion, and his Departure so like unto Sleep, that he scarce needed the civil Ceremony of closing his Eyes; contrary unto the common way wherein Death draws up, Sleep lets fall the Eye-lids. With what strift and pains we came into the World

[1] *Cum mors venerit, in medio Tibure Sardinia est.* [Martial, iv. 60. 5–6.]

[2] In the King's Forests they set the Figure of a broad Arrow upon Trees that are to be cut down.

[3] *Hippoc. Epidem.* [vi. 7. 9.]

[4] Bellonius *de Avibus*.

32 Sleep] Sheep *90*   34 Sleep lets] Sheep let *90*

we know not; but 'tis commonly no easie matter to get out of it: yet if it could be made out, that such who have easie Nativities have commonly hard Deaths, and contrarily; his Departure was so easie, that we might justly suspect his Birth was of another nature, and that some *Juno* sat cross-legg'd at his Nativity.

Besides his soft Death, the incurable state of his Disease might somewhat extenuate your Sorrow, who know that Monsters[1] but seldom happen, Miracles more rarely, in Physick. *Angelus Victorius*[2] gives a serious Account of a Consumptive, Hectical, Pthysical Woman, who was suddenly cured by the Intercession of *Ignatius*. 10 We read not of any in Scripture who in this case applied unto our Saviour, tho some may be contained in that large Expression, That he went about *Galilee* healing all manner of Sickness, and all manner of Diseases[3]. Amulets, Spells, Sigils and Incantations, practised in other Diseases, are seldom pretended in this; and we find no Sigil in the Archidoxis of *Paracelsus* to cure an extreme Consumption or *Marasmus*, which if other Diseases fail, will put a period unto long Livers, and at last make dust of all. And therefore the *Stoicks* could not but think that the firy Principle would wear out all the rest, and at last make an end of the World, which not- 20 withstanding without such a lingring period the Creator may effect at his Pleasure: and to make an end of all things on Earth, and our Planetical System of the World, he need but put out the Sun.

I was not so curious to entitle the Stars unto any concern of his Death, yet could not but take notice that he died when the Moon was in motion from the Meridian; at which time, an old *Italian* long ago would persuade me, that the greatest part of Men died: but herein I confess I could never satisfie my Curiosity; altho from the time of Tides in Places upon or near the Sea, there may be 30 considerable Deductions; and *Pliny*[4] hath an odd and remarkable Passage concerning the Death of Men and Animals upon the Recess or Ebb of the Sea. However, certain it is he died in the dead and deep part of the Night, when *Nox* might be most apprehensibly said to be the Daughter of Chaos, the Mother of Sleep and Death, according to old Genealogy; and so went out of this World about that hour when our blessed Saviour entred it,

[1] *Monstra contingunt in medicina. Hippoc.* Strange and rare Escapes there happen sometimes in Physick.

[2] *Angeli Victorii Consultationes.* [83; 1640, pp. 381–4.]

[3] Matth. iv. 25.

[4] *Aristoteles nullum animal nisi æstu recedente expirare affirmat: observatum id multum in Gallico Oceano & duntaxat in Homine compertum,* [*HN*] lib. 2. cap. 101.

and about what time many conceive he will return again unto it. *Cardan* hath a peculiar and no hard Observation from a Man's Hand, to know whether he was born in the day or night, which I confess holdeth in my own. And *Scaliger*[1] to that purpose hath another from the tip of the Ear. Most Men are begotten in the Night, most Animals in the Day; but whether more Persons have been born in the Night or the Day, were a Curiosity undecidable, tho more have perished by violent Deaths in the Day; yet in natural Dissolutions both Times may hold an Indifferency, at least 10 but contingent Inequality. The whole course of Time runs out in the Nativity and Death of Things; which whether they happen by Succession or Coincidence, are best computed by the natural, not artificial Day.

That *Charles* the Fifth was Crowned upon the day of his Nativity, it being in his own power so to order it, makes no singular Animadversion; but that he should also take King *Francis* Prisoner upon that day, was an unexpected Coincidence, which made the same remarkable. *Antipater* who had an Anniversary Fever every Year upon his Birthday, needed no Astrological Revolution to know 20 what day he should dye on. When the fixed Stars have made a Revolution unto the points from whence they first set out, some of the Ancients thought the World would have an end; which was a kind of dying upon the day of its Nativity. Now the Disease prevailing and swiftly advancing about the time of his Nativity, some were of Opinion, that he would leave the World on the day he entred into it: but this being a lingring Disease, and creeping softly on, nothing critical was found or expected, and he died not before fifteen days after. Nothing is more common with Infants than to dye on the day of their Nativity, to behold the worldly 30 Hours and but the Fractions thereof; and even to perish before their Nativity in the hidden World of the Womb, and before their good Angel is conceived to undertake them. But in Persons who out-live many Years, and when there are no less than three hundred sixty five days to determine their Lives in every Year; that the first day should make the last, that the Tail of the Snake should return into its Mouth[2] precisely at that time, and they should wind up upon the day of their Nativity, is indeed a remarkable

[1] *Auris pars pendula Lobus dicitur, non omnibus ea pars est auribus; non enim iis qui noctu nati sunt, sed qui interdiu, maxima ex parte. Com. in Aristot. de Animal.* lib. I. [lxxvi; 1619, p. 73.]

[2] According to the *Egyptian* Hieroglyphick.

5 Ear. Most] Ear, most *90* 18 Fever] Feast *90*. *See Commentary.*

Coincidence, which tho Astrology hath taken witty pains to salve, yet hath it been very wary in making Predictions of it.

In this consumptive Condition and remarkable Extenuation he came to be almost half himself, and left a great part behind him which he carried not to the Grave. And tho that Story of Duke *John Ernestus Mansfield*[1] be not so easily swallowed, that at his Death his Heart was found not to be so big as a Nut; yet if the Bones of a good Sceleton weigh little more than twenty pounds, his Inwards and Flesh remaining could make no Bouffage, but a light bit for the Grave. I never more lively beheld the starved Characters of *Dante*[2] in any living Face; an Aruspex might have read a Lecture upon him without Exenteration, his Flesh being so consumed that he might, in a manner, have discerned his Bowels without opening of him: so that to be carried *sextâ cervice* to the Grave, was but a civil unnecessity; and the Complements of the Coffin might outweigh the Subject of it.

Omnibonus Ferrarius[3] in mortal Dysenteries of Children looks for a Spot behind the Ear; in consumptive Diseases some eye the Complexion of Moals; *Cardan* eagerly views the Nails, some the Lines of the Hand, the Thenar or Muscle of the Thumb; some are so curious as to observe the depth of the Throat-pit, how the proportion varieth of the Small of the Legs unto the Calf, or the compass of the Neck unto the Circumference of the Head: but all these, with many more, were so drowned in a mortal Visage and last Face of *Hippocrates*, that a weak Physiognomist might say at first eye, This was a Face of Earth, and that *Morta*[4] had set her Hard-Seal upon his Temples, easily perceiving what *Caricatura*[5] Draughts Death makes upon pined Faces, and unto what an unknown degree a Man may live backward.

Tho the Beard be only made a distinction of Sex and sign of masculine Heat by *Ulmus*,[6] yet the Precocity and early growth thereof in him, was not to be liked in reference unto long Life. *Lewis*, that virtuous but unfortunate King of *Hungary*, who lost his Life at the Battel of *Mohacz*, was said to be born without a Skin, to have bearded at Fifteen, and to have shewn some gray Hairs about Twenty; from whence the Diviners conjectured, that he would be spoiled of his Kingdom, and have but a short Life:

1 *Turkish* History.

2 In the Poet *Dante* his Description.

3 *De morbis Puerorum.*

4 *Morta*, the Deity of Death or Fate.

5 When Mens Faces are drawn with resemblance to some other Animals, the *Italians* call it, to be drawn in *Caricatura*.

6 *Ulmus de usu barbæ humanæ.*

But Hairs make fallible Predictions, and many Temples early gray have out-lived the Psalmist's Period[1]. Hairs which have most amused me have not been in the Face or Head but on the Back, and not in Men but Children, as I long ago observed in that Endemial Distemper of little Children in *Languedock*, called the *Morgellons*, wherein they critically break out with harsh Hairs on their Backs, which takes off the unquiet Symptoms of the Disease, and delivers them from Coughs and Convulsions.

The *Egyptian* Mummies that I have seen, have had their Mouths 10 open, and somewhat gaping, which affordeth a good opportunity to view and observe their Teeth, wherein 'tis not easie to find any wanting or decayed: and therefore in *Egypt*, where one Man practised but one Operation, or the Diseases but of single Parts, it must needs be a barren Profession to confine unto that of drawing of Teeth, and little better than to have been Tooth-drawer unto King *Pyrrhus*, who had but two in his Head[2]. How the *Bannyans* of *India* maintain the Integrity of those Parts, I find not particularly observed; who notwithstanding have an Advantage of their Preservation by abstaining from all Flesh, and employing their 20 Teeth in such Food unto which they may seem at first framed, from their Figure and Conformation: but sharp and corroding Rheums[3] had so early mouldred those Rocks and hardest parts of his Fabrick, that a Man might well conceive that his Years were never like to double or twice tell over his Teeth[4]. Corruption had dealt more severely with them, than sepulchral Fires and smart Flames with those of burnt Bodies of old; for in the burnt Fragments of Urns which I have enquired into, altho I seem to find few Incisors or Shearers, yet the Dog Teeth and Grinders do notably resist those Fires.

30 In the Years of his Childhood he had languished under the Disease of his Country, the Rickets; after which notwithstanding many have been become strong and active Men; but whether any have attained unto very great Years the Disease is scarce so old as to afford good Observation. Whether the Children of the *English* Plantations be subject unto the same Infirmity, may be worth the observing. Whether Lameness and Halting do still encrease among the Inhabitants of *Rovigno* in *Istria*, I know not; yet scarce twenty

[1] The Life of a Man is Threescore and Ten.

[2] His upper and lower Jaw being solid, and without distinct rows of Teeth.

[3] See *Picotus de Rheumatismo*.

[4] Twice tell over his Teeth never live to threescore Years.

---

note 3 above: See **Picotus** &c.] *In 90 the note is placed against ll. 5–6. See Commentary.*

Years ago Monsieur *du Loyr* observed, that a third part of that People halted: but too certain it is, that the Rickets encreaseth among us; the Small-Pox grows more pernicious than the Great: the Kings Purse knows that the King's Evil grows more common. *Quartan* Agues are become no Strangers in *Ireland*; more common and mortal in *England*: and tho the Ancients gave that Disease very good Words[1], yet now that Bell[2] makes no strange sound which rings out for the Effects thereof.

Some think there were few Consumptions in the Old World, when Men lived much upon Milk; and that the ancient Inhabitants of this Island were less troubled with Coughs when they went naked, and slept in Caves and Woods, than Men now in Chambers and Feather-beds. *Plato* will tell us, that there was no such Disease as a Catarrh in *Homer*'s time, and that it was but new in *Greece* in his Age. *Polydore Virgil* delivereth that Pleurisies were rare in *England*, who lived but in the days of *Henry* the Eighth. Some will allow no Diseases to be new, others think that many old ones are ceased; and that such which are esteemed new, will have but their time: However, the Mercy of God hath scattered the great heap of Diseases, and not loaded any one Country with all: some may be new in one Country which have been old in another. New Discoveries of the Earth discover new Diseases: for besides the common swarm, there are endemial and local Infirmities proper unto certain Regions, which in the whole Earth make no small number: and if *Asia*, *Africa*, and *America* should bring in their List, *Pandoras* Box would swell, and there must be a strange Pathology.

Most Men expected to find a consumed Kell, empty and bladder-like Guts, livid and marbled Lungs, and a withered *Pericardium* in this exuccous Corps: but some seemed too much to wonder that two Lobes of his Lungs adhered unto his side; for the like I had often found in Bodies of no suspected Consumptions or difficulty of Respiration[3]. And the same more often happeneth in Men than other Animals; and some think, in Women than in Men: but the most remarkable I have met with, was in a Man, after a Cough of almost fifty Years, in whom all the Lobes adhered unto the Pleura, and each Lobe unto another; who having also been much troubled with the Gout, brake the Rule of *Cardan*,[4] and died of the Stone in

[1] *Ἀσφαλέστατος καὶ ῥήιστος, securissima & facillima,* Hippocrat. [*Epid.* i. 3. 11.]

[2] Pro febre quartana raro sonat campana.

[3] So *A. F.*

[4] *Cardan* in his *Encomium Podagræ* reckoneth this among the *Dona Podagræ* that they are delivered thereby from the Pthysis and Stone in the Bladder.

the Bladder. *Aristotle* makes a Query, Why some Animals cough as Man, some not, as Oxen. If coughing be taken as it consisteth of a natural and voluntary motion, including Expectoration and spitting out, it may be as proper unto Man as bleeding at the Nose; otherwise we find that *Vegetius* and Rural Writers have not left so many Medicines in vain against the Coughs of Cattel; and Men who perish by Coughs dye the Death of Sheep, Cats and Lyons: and tho Birds have no Midriff, yet we meet with divers Remedies in *Arrianus* against the Coughs of Hawks. And tho it
10 might be thought, that all Animals who have Lungs do cough; yet in cetaceous Fishes, who have large and strong Lungs, the same is not observed; nor yet in oviparous Quadrupeds: and in the greatest thereof, the Crocodile, altho we read much of their Tears, we find nothing of that motion.

From the Thoughts of Sleep, when the Soul was conceived nearest unto Divinity, the Ancients erected an Art of Divination, wherein while they too widely expatiated in loose and inconsequent Conjectures, *Hippocrates*[1] wisely considered Dreams as they presaged Alterations in the Body, and so afforded hints to-
20 ward the preservation of Health, and prevention of Diseases; and therein was so serious as to advise Alteration of Diet, Exercise, Sweating, Bathing, and Vomiting; and also so religious, as to order Prayers and Supplications unto respective Deities, in good Dreams unto *Sol*, *Jupiter cœlestis*, *Jupiter opulentus*, *Minerva*, *Mercurius*, and *Apollo*; in bad unto *Tellus* and the Heroes.

And therefore I could not but take notice how his Female Friends were irrationally curious so strictly to examine his Dreams, and in this low state to hope for the Fantasms of Health. He was now past the healthful Dreams of the Sun, Moon, and
30 Stars in their Clarity and proper Courses. 'Twas too late to dream of Flying, of Limpid Fountains, smooth Waters, white Vestments, and fruitful green Trees, which are the Visions of healthful Sleeps, and at good distance from the Grave.

And they were also too deeply dejected that he should dream of his dead Friends, inconsequently divining, that he would not be long from them; for strange it was not that he should sometimes dream of the dead whose Thoughts run always upon Death: beside, to dream of the dead, so they appear not in dark Habits, and take nothing away from us, in *Hippocrates*[2] his Sense was of good significa-
40 tion: for we live by the dead, and every thing is or must be so before it becomes our Nourishment. And *Cardan*, who dream'd that he discoursed with his dead Father in the Moon, made thereof no

[1] *Hippoc. de Insomniis.*

[2] *Hippoc. de Insomniis.*

mortal Interpretation: and even to dream that we are dead, was no condemnable Fantasm in old *Oneirocriticism*, as having a signification of Liberty, vacuity from Cares, exemption and freedom from Troubles, unknown unto the dead.

Some Dreams I confess may admit of easie and feminine Exposition: he who dream'd that he could not see his right Shoulder, might easily fear to lose the sight of his right Eye; he that before a Journey dream'd that his Feet were cut off, had a plain warning not to undertake his intended Journey. But why to dream of Lettuce should presage some ensuing Disease, why to eat Figs should signifie foolish Talk, why to eat Eggs great Trouble, and to dream of Blindness should be so highly commended, according to the *Oneirocritical* Verses of *Astrampsychus* and *Nicephorus*, I shall leave unto your Divination.

He was willing to quit the World alone and altogether, leaving no Earnest behind him for Corruption or Aftergrave, having small content in that common satisfaction to survive or live in another, but amply satisfied that his Disease should dye with himself, nor revive in a Posterity to puzzle Physick, and make sad *Memento*'s of their Parent hereditary. Leprosie awakes not sometimes before Forty, the Gout and Stone often later; but consumptive and tabid Roots sprout more early, and at the fairest make seventeen[1] Years of our Life doubtful before that Age. They that enter the World with original Diseases as well as Sin, have not only common Mortality but sick Traductions to destroy them, make commonly short Courses, and live not at length but in Figures; so that a sound *Cæsarean* Nativity[2] may out-last a natural Birth, and a Knife may sometimes make way for a more lasting fruit than a Midwife; which makes so few Infants now able to endure the old Test of the River[3], and many to have feeble Children who could scarce have been married at *Sparta*, and those provident States who studied strong and healthful Generations; which happen but contingently in mere *pecuniary* Matches, or Marriages made by the Candle, wherein notwithstanding there is little redress to be hoped from an Astrologer or a Lawyer, and a good discerning Physician were like to prove the most successful Counsellor.

Julius Scaliger, who in a sleepless Fit of the Gout could make two hundred Verses in a Night, would have but five plain Words

[1] *Tabes maxime contingunt ab anno decimo octavo ad trigesimum quintum*, Hippoc. [*Aphor*. v. 9.]

[2] A sound Child cut out of the Body of the Mother.

[3] *Natos ad flumina primum*
deferimus sævoque gelu duramus & undis. [Virg. *Aen*. ix. 603–4.]

upon his Tomb[1]. And this serious Person, tho no *minor* Wit, left the Poetry of his Epitaph unto others; either unwilling to commend himself, or to be judged by a Distich, and perhaps considering how unhappy great Poets have been in versifying their own Epitaphs; wherein *Petrarcha*, *Dante*, and *Ariosto*, have so unhappily failed, that if their Tombs should out-last their Works, Posterity would find so little of *Apollo* on them, as to mistake them for Ciceronian Poets.

In this deliberate and creeping progress unto the Grave, he was 10 somewhat too young, and of too noble a mind, to fall upon that stupid Symptom observable in divers Persons near their Journeys end, and which may be reckoned among the mortal Symptoms of their last Disease; that is, to become more narrow minded, miserable and tenacious, unready to part with any thing when they are ready to part with all, and afraid to want when they have no time to spend; mean while Physicians, who know that many are mad but in a single depraved Imagination, and one prevalent Decipiency; and that beside and out of such single Deliriums a Man may meet with sober Actions and good Sense in *Bedlam*; 20 cannot but smile to see the Heirs and concerned Relations, gratulating themselves in the sober departure of their Friends; and tho they behold such mad covetous Passages, content to think they dye in good Understanding, and in their sober Senses.

Avarice, which is not only Infidelity but Idolatry, either from covetous Progeny or questuary Education, had no Root in his Breast, who made good Works the Expression of his Faith, and was big with desires unto publick and lasting Charities; and surely where good Wishes and charitable Intentions exceed Abilities, Theorical Beneficency may be more than a Dream. They 30 build not Castles in the Air who would build Churches on Earth; and tho they leave no such Structures here, may lay good Foundations in Heaven. In brief, his Life and Death were such, that I could not blame them who wished the like, and almost to have been himself; almost, I say; for tho we may wish the prosperous Appurtenances of others, or to be an other in his happy Accidents; yet so intrinsecal is every Man unto himself, that some doubt may be made, whether any would exchange his Being, or substantially become another Man.

He had wisely seen the World at home and abroad, and thereby 40 observed under what variety Men are deluded in the pursuit of that which is not here to be found. And altho he had no Opinion of reputed Felicities below, and apprehended Men widely out in the

[1] *Julii Cæsaris Scaligeri quod fuit. Joseph. Scaliger in vita patris.* [1594, p. 52.]

estimate of such Happiness; yet his sober contempt of the World wrought no *Democratism* or *Cynicism*, no laughing or snarling at it, as well understanding there are not Felicities in this World to satisfie a serious Mind; and therefore to soften the stream of our Lives, we are fain to take in the reputed Contentations of this World, to unite with the Crowd in their Beatitudes, and to make our selves happy by Consortion, Opinion, or Co-existimation: for strictly to separate from received and customary Felicities, and to confine unto the rigor of Realities, were to contract the Consolation of our Beings unto too uncomfortable Circumscriptions. 10

Not to fear Death, nor desire it[1], was short of his Resolution: to be dissolved, and be with Christ, was his dying ditty. He conceived his Thred long, in no long course of Years, and when he had scarce out-lived the second Life of *Lazarus*[2]; esteeming it enough to approach the Years of his Saviour, who so ordered his own humane State, as not to be old upon Earth.

But to be content with Death may be better than to desire it: a miserable Life may make us wish for Death, but a virtuous one to rest in it; which is the Advantage of those resolved Christians, who looking on Death not only as the sting, but the period and end of 20 Sin, the Horizon and Isthmus between this Life and a better, and the Death of this World but as a Nativity of another, do contentedly submit unto the common Necessity, and envy not *Enoch* or *Elias*.

Not to be content with Life is the unsatisfactory state of those which destroy themselves; who being afraid to live, run blindly upon their own Death, which no Man fears by Experience: and the *Stoicks* had a notable Doctrine to take away the fear thereof; that is, In such Extremities to desire that which is not to be avoided[3], and wish what might be feared; and so made Evils voluntary, and 30 to suit with their own Desires, which took off the terror of them.

But the ancient Martyrs were not encouraged by such Fallacies; who, tho they feared not Death, were afraid to be their own Executioners; and therefore thought it more Wisdom to crucifie their Lusts than their Bodies, to circumcise than stab their Hearts, and to mortifie than kill themselves.

[1] *Summum ne metuas diem nec optes*. [Martial, x. 47. 13.]

[2] Who upon some Accounts, and Tradition, is said to have lived 30 Years after he was raised by our Saviour. *Baronius*.

[3] In the Speech of *Vulteius in Lucan* [iv. 486–7], animating his Souldiers in a great struggle to kill one another.

Decernite Lethum
& metus omnis abest, cupias quodcumque necesse est.

All fear is over do but resolve to dye, and make your Desires meet Necessity.

His willingness to leave this World about that Age when most Men think they may best enjoy it, tho paradoxical unto worldly Ears, was not strange unto mine, who have so often observed, that many, tho old, oft stick fast unto the World, and seem to be drawn like *Cacus*'s Oxen, backward with great strugling and reluctancy unto the Grave. The long habit of Living makes meer Men more hardly to part with Life, and all to be nothing, but what is to come. To live at the rate of the old World, when some could scarce remember themselves young, may afford no better digested Death than a more moderate period. Many would have thought it an Happiness to have had their lot of Life in some notable Conjunctures of Ages past; but the uncertainty of future Times hath tempted few to make a part in Ages to come. And surely, he that hath taken the true Altitude of Things, and rightly calculated the degenerate state of this Age, is not like to envy those that shall live in the next, much less three or four hundred Years hence, when no Man can comfortably imagine what Face this World will carry: and therefore since every Age makes a step unto the end of all things, and the Scripture affords so hard a Character of the last Times; quiet Minds will be content with their Generations, and rather bless Ages past than be ambitious of those to come.

Tho Age had set no Seal upon his Face, yet a dim Eye might clearly discover Fifty in his Actions; and therefore since Wisdom is the gray Hair, and an unspotted Life old Age; altho his Years came short, he might have been said to have held up with longer Livers, and to have been *Solomon*'s Old Man[1]. And surely if we deduct all those days of our Life which we might wish unlived, and which abate the comfort of those we now live; if we reckon up only those days which God hath accepted of our Lives, a Life of good Years will hardly be a span long: the Son in this sense may out-live the Father, and none be climaterically old. He that early arriveth unto the Parts and Prudence of Age, is happily old without the uncomfortable Attendants of it; and 'tis superfluous to live unto gray Hairs, when in a precocious Temper we anticipate the Virtues of them. In brief, he cannot be accounted young who outliveth the old Man. He that hath early arrived unto the measure of a perfect Stature in Christ, hath already fulfilled the prime and longest Intention of his Being: and one day lived after the perfect Rule of Piety, is to be preferred before sinning Immortality.

Altho he attained not unto the Years of his Predecessors, yet he wanted not those preserving Virtues which confirm the thread of

[1] *Wisdom* cap. iv. [9.]

weaker Constitutions. Cautelous Chastity and crafty Sobriety were far from him; those Jewels were Paragon, without Flaw, Hair, Ice, or Cloud in him: which affords me an hint to proceed in these good Wishes and few *Memento's* unto you.

Tread softly and circumspectly in this funambulous Track and narrow Path of Goodness: pursue Virtue virtuously; be sober and temperate, not to preserve your Body in a sufficiency to wanton Ends; not to spare your Purse; not to be free from the Infamy of common Transgressors that way, and thereby to ballance or palliate obscure and closer Vices; nor simply to enjoy Health: by 10 all which you may leaven good Actions, and render Virtues disputable: but in one Word, that you may truly serve God; which every Sickness will tell you, you cannot well do without Health. The sick mans Sacrifice is but a lame Oblation. Pious Treasures laid up in healthful days, excuse the defect of sick Non-performances; without which we must needs look back with Anxiety upon the lost opportunities of Health; and may have cause rather to envy than pity the Ends of penitent Malefactors, who go with clear parts unto the last Act of their Lives; and in the integrity of their Faculties return their Spirit unto God that gave it. 20

Consider whereabout thou art in *Cebes* his Table, or that old philosophical Pinax of the Life of Man; whether thou art still in the Road of Uncertainties; whether thou hast yet entred the narrow Gate, got up the Hill and asperous way which leadeth unto the House of Sanity, or taken that purifying Potion from the hand of sincere Erudition, which may send thee clear and pure away unto a virtuous and happy Life.

In this virtuous Voyage let not disappointment cause Despondency, nor difficulty Despair: think not that you are sailing from *Lima* to *Manillia*[1], wherein thou may'st tye up the Rudder, and 30 sleep before the Wind; but expect rough Seas, Flaws, and contrary Blasts; and 'tis well if by many cross Tacks and Verings thou arrivest at thy Port. Sit not down in the popular Seats and common Level of Virtues, but endeavour to make them Heroical. Offer not only Peace-Offerings but Holocausts unto God. To serve him singly to serve our selves, were too partial a piece of Piety, nor likely to place us in the highest Mansions of Glory.

He that is chaste and continent, not to impair his Strength, or terrified by Contagion, will hardly be heroically virtuous. Adjourn not that Virtue unto those Years when *Cato* could lend out 40 his Wife, and impotent Satyrs write Satyrs against Lust: but be chaste in thy flaming days, when *Alexander* dared not trust his

[1] Through the Pacifick Sea, with a constant Gale from the East.

Eyes upon the fair Daughters of *Darius*, and when so many Men think there is no other way but *Origen*'s[1].

Be charitable before Wealth makes thee covetous, and lose not the Glory of the Mite. If Riches increase, let they Mind hold pace with them; and think it not enough to be liberal, but munificent. Tho a Cup of cold Water from some hand may not be without its Reward; yet stick not thou for Wine and Oyl for the Wounds of the distressed: and treat the Poor as our Saviour did the Multitude, to the Relicks of some Baskets.

10 Trust not to the Omnipotency of Gold, or say unto it, Thou art my Confidence: kiss not thy Hand when thou beholdest that terrestrial Sun, nor bore thy Ear unto its Servitude. A Slave unto Mammon makes no Servant unto God: Covetousness cracks the Sinews of Faith, numbs the Apprehension of any thing above Sense, and only affected with the certainty of things present, makes a peradventure of Things to come; lives but unto one World, nor hopes but fears another; makes our own Death sweet unto others, bitter unto our selves; gives a dry Funeral, Scenical Mourning, and no wet Eyes at the Grave.

20 If Avarice be thy Vice, yet make it not thy Punishment: miserable Men commiserate not themselves, bowelless unto others, and merciless unto their own Bowels. Let the fruition of Things bless the possession of them, and take no satisfaction in dying but living rich: for since thy good Works, not thy Goods, will follow thee; since Riches are an Appurtenance of Life, and no dead Man is rich, to famish in Plenty, and live poorly to dye rich, were a multiplying improvement in Madness, and Use upon Use in Folly.

Persons lightly dip'd, not grain'd in generous Honesty, are but 30 pale in Goodness, and faint hued in Sincerity: but be thou what thou virtuously art, and let not the Ocean wash away thy Tincture: stand magnetically upon that Axis where prudent Simplicity hath fix'd thee, and let no Temptation invert the Poles of thy Honesty: and that Vice may be uneasie, and even monstrous unto thee, let iterated good Acts, and long confirmed Habits, make Vertue natural, or a second Nature in thee. And since few or none prove eminently vertuous but from some advantageous Foundations in their Temper and natural Inclinations; study thy self betimes, and early find, what Nature bids thee to be, or tells thee what 40 thou may'st be. They who thus timely descend into themselves,

[1] Who is said to have castrated himself.

4 Mite] Mitre *90* 21 unto others *16*: unto themselves *90*

cultivating the good Seeds which Nature hath set in them, and improving their prevalent Inclinations to Perfection, become not Shrubs, but Cedars in their Generation; and to be in the form of the best of the Bad, or the worst of the Good, will be no satisfaction unto them.

Let not the Law of thy Country be the *non ultra* of thy Honesty, nor think that always good enough which the Law will make good. Narrow not the Law of Charity, Equity, Mercy; joyn Gospel Righteousness with Legal Right; be not a meer *Gamaliel* in the Faith; but let the Sermon in the Mount be thy *Targum* unto the Law of *Sinai*.

Make not the Consequences of Vertue the Ends thereof: be not beneficent for a Name or Cymbal of Applause, nor exact and punctual in Commerce, for the Advantages of Trust and Credit, which attend the Reputation of just and true Dealing; for such Rewards, tho unsought for, plain Virtue will bring with her, whom all Men honour, tho they pursue not. To have other bye ends in good Actions, sowers laudable Performances, which must have deeper Roots, Motions, and Instigations, to give them the Stamp of Vertues.

Tho humane Infirmity may betray thy heedless days into the popular ways of Extravagancy, yet let not thine own depravity, or the torrent of vicious Times, carry thee into desperate Enormities in Opinions, Manners, or Actions: if thou hast dip'd thy foot in the River, yet venture not over *Rubicon*; run not into Extremities from whence there is no Regression, nor be ever so closely shut up within the holds of Vice and Iniquity, as not to find some Escape by a Postern of Recipiscency.

Owe not thy Humility unto Humiliation by Adversity, but look humbly down in that State when others look upward upon thee: be patient in the Age of Pride and days of Will and Impatiency, when Men live but by Intervals of Reason, under the Sovereignty of Humor and Passion, when 'tis in the Power of every one to transform thee out of thy self, and put thee into the short Madness[1]. If you cannot imitate *Job*, yet come not short of *Socrates*, and those patient Pagans, who tired the Tongues of their Enemies, while they perceiv'd they spet their Malice at brazen Walls and Statues.

Let Age, not Envy, draw Wrinkles on thy Cheeks: be content to be envied, but envy not. Emulation may be plausible, and Indignation allowable; but admit no Treaty with that Passion which no Circumstance can make good. A Displacency at the good of

[1] *Ira furor brevis est*. [Hor. *Ep*. i. 2. 62.]

others, because they enjoy it, altho we do not want it, is an absurd Depravity, sticking fast unto humane Nature from its primitive Corruption; which he that can well subdue, were a Christian of the first Magnitude, and for ought I know, may have one foot already in Heaven.

While thou so hotly disclaimst the Devil, be not guilty of Diabolism; fall not into one Name with that unclean Spirit, nor act his Nature whom thou so much abhorrest; that is, to accuse, calumniate, backbite, whisper, detract, or sinistrously interpret others;
10 degenerous Depravities and narrow-minded Vices, not only below S. *Paul*'s noble Christian, but *Aristotle*'s true Gentleman.[1] Trust not with some, that the Epistle of S. *James* is Apocryphal, and so read with less fear that stabbing truth, that in company with this Vice thy Religion is in vain. *Moses* broke the Tables without breaking of the Law; but where Charity is broke the Law it self is shattered, which cannot be whole without Love, that is the fulfilling of it. Look humbly upon thy Virtues, and tho thou art rich in some, yet think thy self poor and naked without that crowning Grace, which thinketh no Evil, which envieth not, which beareth,
20 believeth, hopeth, endureth all things. With these sure Graces, while busie Tongues are crying out for a drop of cold Water, Mutes may be in Happiness, and sing the *Trisagium*[2] in Heaven.

Let not the Sun in *Capricorn*[3] go down upon thy Wrath, but write thy Wrongs in Water; draw the Curtain of Night upon Injuries; shut them up in the Tower of Oblivion[4], and let them be as tho they had not been. Forgive thine Enemies totally, and without any Reservé of hope, that however, God will revenge thee.

Be substantially great in thy self, and more than thou appearest unto others; and let the World be deceived in thee, as they are in
30 the Lights of Heaven. Hang early Plummets upon the Heels of Pride, and let Ambition have but an Epicycle or narrow Circuit in thee. Measure not thy self by thy Morning shadow, but by the Extent of thy Grave; and reckon thy self above the Earth by the Line thou must be contented with under it. Spread not into bound-

[1] See *Arist. Ethicks* Chapt. of Magnanimity. [iv. 5.]

[2] Holy, Holy, Holy.

[3] Even when the days are shortest.

[4] Alluding to the Tower of Oblivion mentioned by *Procopius* [*De bello Pers.* i. 4–5], which was the name of a Tower of Imprisonment among the *Persians*: whosoever was put therein, he was as it were buried alive, and it was Death for any but to name him.

---

31 Epicycle] Epicyche *90*

less Expansions either of Designs or Desires. Think not that Mankind liveth but for a few, and that the rest are born but to serve the Ambition of those, who make but Flies of Men, and Wildernesses of whole Nations. Swell not into Actions which embroil and confound the Earth; but be one of those violent ones which force the Kingdom of Heaven[1]. If thou must needs reign, be *Zeno*'s King, and enjoy that Empire which every Man gives himself. Certainly the iterated Injunctions of Christ unto Humility, Meekness, Patience, and that despised Train of Virtues, cannot but make pathetical Impressions upon those who have well considered 10 the Affairs of all Ages, wherein Pride, Ambition, and Vain-glory, have led up the worst of Actions, and whereunto Confusion, Tragedies, and Acts denying all Religion, do owe their Originals.

Rest not in an Ovation[2], but a Triumph over thy Passions; chain up the unruly Legion of thy Breast; behold thy Trophies within thee, not without thee: Lead thine own Captivity captive, and be *Cæsar* unto thy self.

Give no quarter unto those Vices which are of thine inward Family; and having a Root in thy Temper, plead a Right and Propriety in thee. Examine well thy complexional Inclinations. 20 Raise early Batteries against those strong-holds built upon the Rock of Nature, and make this a great part of the Militia of thy Life. The politick Nature of Vice must be opposed by Policy, and therefore wiser Honesties Project, and plot against Sin; wherein notwithstanding we are not to rest in Generals, or the trite Stratagems of Art: that may succeed with one Temper which may prove successless with another. There is no Community or Commonwealth of Virtue; every Man must study his own OEconomy, and erect these Rules unto the Figure of himself.

Lastly, If length of Days be thy Portion, make it not thy Ex- 30 pectation: reckon not upon long Life, but live always beyond thy Account. He that so often surviveth his Expectation, lives many Lives, and will hardly complain of the shortness of his Days. Time past is gone like a shadow; make Times to come, present; conceive that near which may be far off; approximate thy last Times by present Apprehensions of them: live like a Neighbour unto Death, and think there is but little to come. And since there is something in us that must still live on, joyn both Lives together;

[1] Matthew xi. [12.]   [2] Ovation a petty and minor kind of Triumph.

1 of *16*: to *90*   *note 1 above*: Matthew xi.] Matthew xl. *90*   7 *Zeno*'s *16*: *Zeno*, *90*

unite them in thy Thoughts and Actions, and live in one but for the other. He who thus ordereth the Purposes of this Life, will never be far from the next; and is in some manner already in it, by an happy Conformity, and close Apprehension of it.

FINIS.

Sir *THOMAS BROWN*'s

CHRISTIAN

MORALS.

CHRISTIAN
MORALS,

BY

Sr THOMAS BROWN,

Of NORWICH, *M. D.*

And AUTHOR of

RELIGIO MEDICI.

Publiſhed from the Original and Correct Manuſcript of the Author; by *JOHN JEFFERY*, D.D. ARCH-DEACON of NORWICH.

CAMBRIDGE:

Printed at the UNIVERSITY-PRESS, For *Cornelius Crownfield* Printer to the UNIVERSITY; And are to be Sold by Mr. *Knapton* at the Crown in St. *Paul*'s Church-yard; and Mr. *Morphew* near Stationers-Hall, *LONDON*, 1716.

To the Right Honourable DAVID

Earl of Buchan
Viscount Auchterhouse,
Lord Cardross
and Glendovachie,

One of the
LORDS COMMISSIONERS
of POLICE, and
LORD LIEUTENANT
of the Counties of 10
STIRLING and CLACKMANNAN
in NORTH-BRITTAIN.

MY LORD,

THE Honour you have done our Family Obligeth us to make all just Acknowledgments of it: & there is no Form of Acknowledgment in our power, more worthy of Your Lordship's Acceptance, than this Dedication of the Last Work of our Honoured and Learned Father. Encouraged hereunto by the Knowledge we have of Your Lordship's Judicious Relish of universal Learning, and sublime Virtue; we beg the Favour of Your Acceptance of it, 20 which will very much Oblige our Family in general, and Her in particular, who is,

My Lord,
Your Lordship's
most humble Servant,
ELIZABETH LITTELTON.

THE PREFACE.

IF *any One, after he has read* Religio Medici *and the ensuing Discourse, can make Doubt whether the same Person was the Author of them both, he may be Assured by the Testimony of Mrs* LITTELTON, *Sr.* THOMAS BROWN'S *Daughter, who Lived with her Father, when it was composed by Him; and who, at the time, read it written by his own Hand: and also by the Testimony of Others, (of whom I am One) who read the MS. of the Author, immediately after his Death, and who have since Read the Same; from which it hath been faithfully and exactly Transcribed for the Press.*
10 *The Reason why it was not Printed sooner is, because it was unhappily Lost, by being Mislay'd among Other MSS for which Search was lately made in the Presence of the Lord Arch-Bishop of Canterbury, of which his Grace, by Letter, Informed Mrs* LITTELTON, *when he sent the MS to Her. There is nothing printed in the Discourse, or in the short notes, but what is found in the Original MS of the Author, except only where an Oversight had made the Addition or Transposition of some words necessary.*

JOHN JEFFERY

Arch-Deacon *of* Norwich.

PART I.

SECT. I.

TREAD softly and circumspectly in this funambulatory Track and narrow Path of Goodness: Pursue Virtue virtuously: Leven not good Actions nor render Virtues disputable. Stain not fair Acts with foul Intentions: Maim not Uprightness by halting Concomitances, nor circumstantially deprave substantial Goodness.

Consider where about thou art in *Cebes*'s Table, or that old Philosophical Pinax of the Life of Man: whether thou art yet in the 10 Road of uncertainties; whether thou hast yet entred the narrow Gate, got up the Hill and asperous way, which leadeth unto the House of Sanity, or taken that purifying Potion from the hand of sincere Erudition, which may send Thee clear and pure away unto a virtuous and happy Life.

In this virtuous Voyage of thy Life hull not about like the Ark without the use of Rudder, Mast, or Sail, and bound for no Port. Let not Disappointment cause Despondency, nor difficulty despair. Think not that you are Sailing from *Lima* to *Manillia*, when you may fasten up the Rudder, and sleep before the Wind; but 20 expect rough Seas, Flaws, and contrary Blasts, and 'tis well if by many cross Tacks and Veerings you arrive at the Port; for we sleep in Lyons Skins in our Progress unto Virtue, and we slide not, but climb unto it.

Sit not down in the popular Forms and common Level of Virtues. Offer not only Peace Offerings but Holocausts unto God: where all is due make no reserve, and cut not a Cummin Seed with the Almighty: To serve Him singly to serve our selves were too partial a piece of Piety, not like to place us in the illustrious Mansions of Glory. 30

SECT. II.

REST not in an *Ovation but a Triumph over thy Passions. Let Anger walk hanging down the head: Let Malice go Manicled, and Envy fetter'd after thee. Behold within thee the long train of thy Trophies not without thee. Make the quarrelling Lapithytes sleep, and Centaurs within lye quiet. Chain up the unruly Legion

* Ovation a petty and minor Kind of Triumph.

---

16 hull *1756*: hall *16*

of thy breast. Lead thine own captivity captive, and be *Cæsar* within thy self.

SECT. III.

HE that is Chast and Continent not to impair his strength, or honest for fear of Contagion, will hardly be Heroically virtuous. Adjourn not this virtue untill that temper, when *Cato* could lend out his Wife, and impotent Satyrs write Satyrs upon Lust: But be chast in thy flaming Days, when *Alexander* dar'd not trust his eyes upon the fair Sisters of *Darius*, and when so many think 10 there is no other way but *Origen's*.*

SECT. IV.

SHOW thy Art in Honesty, and loose not thy Virtue by the bad Managery of it. Be Temperate and Sober, not to preserve your body in an ability for wanton ends, not to avoid the infamy of common transgressors that way, and thereby to hope to expiate or palliate obscure and closer vices, not to spare your purse, nor simply to enjoy health; but in one word that thereby you may truly serve God, which every sickness will tell you you cannot well do without health. The sick Man's Sacrifice is but a lame 20 Oblation. Pious Treasures lay'd up in healthful days plead for sick non-performances: without which we must needs look back with anxiety upon the lost opportunities of health, and may have cause rather to envy than pity the ends of penitent publick Sufferers, who go with healthfull prayers unto the last Scene of their lives, and in the Integrity of their faculties return their Spirit unto God that gave it.

SECT. V.

BE Charitable before wealth make thee covetous, and loose not the glory of the Mite. If Riches encrease, let thy mind hold 30 pace with them, and think it not enough to be Liberal, but Munificent. Though a Cup of cold water from some hand may not be without it's reward, yet stick not thou for Wine and Oyl for the Wounds of the Distressed, and treat the poor, as our Saviour did the Multitude, to the reliques of some baskets. Diffuse thy beneficence early, and while thy Treasures call thee Master: there may be an Atropos of thy Fortunes before that of thy Life, and thy wealth cut off before that hour, when all Men shall be poor; for the Justice of Death looks equally upon the dead, and *Charon* expects no more from *Alexander* than from *Irus*.

* Who is said to have Castrated himself.

SECT. VI.

GIVE not only unto seven, but also unto eight, *that is unto more than many. Though to give unto every one that asketh† may seem severe advice, yet give thou also before asking, that is, where want is silently clamorous, and mens Necessities not their Tongues do loudly call for thy Mercies. For though sometimes necessitousness be dumb, or misery speak not out, yet true Charity is sagacious, and will find out hints for beneficence. Acquaint thy self with the Physiognomy of Want, and let the Dead colours and first lines of necessity suffise to tell thee there is 10 an object for thy bounty. Spare not where thou canst not easily be prodigal, and fear not to be undone by mercy. For since he who hath pity on the poor lendeth unto the Almighty Rewarder, who observes no Ides but every day for his payments; Charity becomes pious Usury, Christian Liberality the most thriving industry, and what we adventure in a Cockboat may return in a Carrack unto us. He who thus casts his bread upon the Water shall surely find it again; for though it falleth to the bottom, it sinks but like the Ax of the Prophet, to arise again unto him.

SECT. VII. 20

IF Avarice be thy Vice, yet make it not thy Punishment. Miserable men commiserate not themselves, bowelless unto others, and merciless unto their own bowels. Let the fruition of things bless the possession of them, and think it more satisfaction to live richly than dye rich. For since thy good works, not thy goods, will follow thee; since wealth is an appertinance of life, and no dead Man is Rich; to famish in Plenty, and live poorly to dye Rich, were a multiplying improvement in Madness, and use upon use in Folly.

SECT. VIII. 30

TRUST not to the Omnipotency of Gold, and say not unto it Thou art my Confidence. Kiss not thy hand to that Terrestrial Sun, not bore thy ear unto its servitude. A Slave unto Mammon makes no servant unto God. Covetousness cracks the sinews of Faith; nummes the apprehension of any thing above sense, and only affected with the certainty of things present makes a peradventure of things to come; lives but unto one World, nor hopes but fears another; makes their own death sweet unto others,

* Ecclesiasticus [*for* Ecclesiastes]. [xi. 2.]
† Luke [vi. 30]

bitter unto themselves; brings formal sadness, scenical mourning, and no wet eyes at the grave.

SECT. IX.

PERSONS lightly dipt, not grain'd in generous Honesty, are but pale in Goodness, and faint hued in Integrity. But be thou what thou vertuously art, and let not the Ocean wash away thy Tincture. Stand magnetically upon that Axis, where prudent simplicity hath fixt thee; and let no attraction invert the Poles of thy Honesty. That Vice may be uneasy and even monstrous unto 10 thee, let iterated good Acts and long confirmed habits make Virtue almost natural, or a second nature in thee. Since virtuous superstructions have commonly generous foundations, dive into thy inclinations, and early discover what nature bids thee to be, or tells thee thou may'st be. They who thus timely descend into themselves, & cultivate the good seeds which nature hath set in them, prove not shrubs but Cedars in their generation. And to be in the form of the best of the Bad, or the worst of the Good,* will be no satisfaction unto them.

SECT. X.

20 MAKE not the consequence of Virtue the ends thereof. Be not beneficent for a name or Cymbal of applause, nor exact and just in Commerce for the advantages of Trust and Credit, which attend the reputation of true and punctual dealing. For these Rewards, though unsought for, plain Virtue will bring with her. To have other by-ends in good actions sowers Laudable performances, which must have deeper roots, motives, and instigations, to give them the stamp of Virtues.

SECT. XI.

LET not the Law of thy Country be the non ultra of thy Honesty; 30 nor think that always good enough which the Law will make good. Narrow not the Law of Charity, Equity, Mercy. Joyn Gospel Righteousness with Legal Right. Be not a mere *Gamaliel* in the Faith, but let the Sermon in the Mount be thy *Targum* unto the Law of *Sinah*.

SECT. XII.

LIVE by old Ethicks and the classical Rules of Honesty. Put no new names or notions upon Authentick Virtues and Vices.

* *Optimi malorum pessimi bonorum.*

---

7 where *90*: when *16* 8 thee *90*: there *16*

Think not that Morality is Ambulatory; that Vices in one age are not Vices in another; or that Virtues, which are under the everlasting Seal of right Reason, may be Stamped by Opinion. And therefore though vicious times invert the opinions of things, and set up a new Ethicks against Virtue, yet hold thou unto old Morality; and rather than follow a multitude to do evil, stand like *Pompey's* Pillar conspicuous by thy self, and single in Integrity. And since the worst of times afford imitable Examples of Virtue; since no Deluge of Vice is like to be so general, but more than eight will escape; Eye well those Heroes who have held their Heads 10 above Water, who have touched Pitch, and not been defiled, and in the common Contagion have remained uncorrupted.

SECT. XIII.

LET Age not Envy draw wrinkles on thy cheeks, be content to be envy'd, but envy not. Emulation may be plausible and Indignation allowable, but admit no treaty with that passion which no circumstance can make good. A displacency at the good of others because they enjoy it, though not unworthy of it, is an absurd depravity, sticking fast unto corrupted nature, and often too hard for Humility and Charity, the great Suppressors of Envy. 20 This surely is a Lyon not to be strangled but by *Hercules* himself, or the highest stress of our minds, and an Atom of that power which subdueth all things unto it self.

SECT. XIV.

OWE not thy Humility unto humiliation from adversity, but look humbly down in that State when others look upwards upon thee. Think not thy own shadow longer than that of others, nor delight to take the Altitude of thy self. Be patient in the age of Pride, when Men live by short intervals of Reason under the dominion of Humor and Passion, when it's in the Power of every 30 one to transform thee out of thy self, and run thee into the short madness. If you cannot imitate *Job*, yet come not short of *Socrates*, and those patient Pagans who tired the Tongues of their Enemies, while they perceived they spit their malice at brazen Walls and Statues.

SECT. XV.

LET not the Sun in Capricorn* go down upon thy wrath, but write thy wrongs in Ashes. Draw the Curtain of night upon

* Even when the Days are shortest.

injuries, shut them up in the Tower of Oblivion* and let them be as though they had not been. To forgive our Enemies, yet hope that God will punish them, is not to forgive enough. To forgive them our selves, and not to pray God to forgive them, is a partial piece of Charity. Forgive thine enemies totally, and without any reserve, that however God will revenge thee.

SECT. XVI.

WHILE thou so hotly disclaimest the Devil, be not guilty of Diabolism. Fall not into one name with that unclean Spirit, nor 10 act his nature whom thou so much abhorrest; that is to Accuse, Calumniate, Backbite, Whisper, Detract, or sinistrously interpret others. Degenerous depravities, and narrow minded vices! not only below St. *Paul*'s noble Christian but *Aristotle*'s true Gentleman.† Trust not with some that the Epistle of St. *James* is Apocryphal, and so read with less fear that Stabbing Truth, that in company with this vice thy Religion is in vain. *Moses* broke the Tables without breaking of the Law; but where Charity is broke, the Law it self is shattered, which cannot be whole without Love, which is the fulfilling of it. Look humbly upon thy Virtues, and 20 though thou art Rich in some, yet think thy self Poor and Naked without that Crowning Grace, which thinketh no evil, which envieth not, which beareth, hopeth, believeth, endureth all things. With these sure Graces, while busy Tongues are crying out for a drop of cold Water, mutes may be in happiness, and sing the *Trisagion*‡ in Heaven.

SECT. XVII.

HOWEVER thy understanding may waver in the Theories of True and False, yet fasten the Rudder of thy Will, steer strait unto good and fall not foul on evil. Imagination is apt to rove 30 and conjecture to keep no bounds. Some have run out so far, as to fancy the Stars might be but the light of the Crystalline Heaven shot through perforations on the bodies of the Orbs. Others more Ingeniously doubt whether there hath not been a vast tract of Land in the *Atlantick* Ocean, which Earthquakes and violent causes have long ago devoured. Speculative Misapprehensions

* Alluding unto the Tower of Oblivion mentioned by *Procopius* [*De bello Pers.* i. 4–5], which was the name of a Tower of Imprisonment among the *Persians*; whoever was put therein was as it were buried alive, and it was death for any but to name him.

† See *Aristotle*'s Ethicks, chapter of Magnanimity. [iv. 5.]

‡ Holy, Holy, Holy.

may be innocuous, but immorality pernicious; Theorical mistakes and Physical Deviations may condemn our Judgments, not lead us into Judgment. But perversity of Will, immoral and sinfull enormities walk with *Adraste* and *Nemesis* at their Backs, pursue us unto Judgment, and leave us viciously miserable.

SECT. XVIII.

BID early defiance unto those Vices which are of thine inward Family, and having a root in thy Temper plead a right and propriety in thee. Raise timely batteries against those strong holds built upon the Rock of Nature, and make this a great part of 10 the Militia of thy life. Delude not thy self into iniquities from participation or community, which abate the sense but not the obliquity of them. To conceive sins less, or less of sins, because others also Transgress, were Morally to commit that natural fallacy of Man, to take comfort from Society, and think adversities less, because others also suffer them. The politick nature of Vice must be opposed by Policy. And therefore wiser Honesties project and plot against it. Wherein notwithstanding we are not to rest in generals, or the trite Stratagems of Art. That may succeed with one which may prove succesless with another: There is no com- 20 munity or commonweal of Virtue: Every man must study his own oeconomy, and adapt such rules unto the figure of himself.

SECT. XIX.

BE substantially great in thy self, and more than thou appearest unto others; and let the World be deceived in thee, as they are in the Lights of Heaven. Hang early plummets upon the heels of Pride, and let Ambition have but an Epicycle and narrow circuit in thee. Measure not thy self by thy morning shadow, but by the extent of thy grave, and Reckon thy self above the Earth by the line thou must be contented with under it. Spread not into 30 boundless Expansions either of designs or desires. Think not that mankind liveth but for a few, and that the rest are born but to serve those Ambitions, which make but flies of Men and wildernesses of whole Nations. Swell not into vehement actions which imbroil and confound the Earth; but be one of those violent ones which force* the Kingdom of Heaven. If thou must needs Rule, be *Zeno*'s King, and enjoy that Empire which every Man gives himself. He who is thus his own Monarch contentedly sways the Scepter of himself, not envying the Glory of Crowned Heads and Elohims

* Matthew xi. [12.]

of the Earth. Could the World unite in the practise of that despised train of Virtues, which the Divine Ethicks of our Saviour hath so inculcated unto us, the furious face of things must disappear, Eden would be yet to be found, and the Angels might look down not with pity, but Joy upon us.

SECT. XX.

THOUGH the Quickness of thine Ear were able to reach the noise of the Moon, which some think it maketh in it's rapid revolution; though the number of thy Ears should equal *Argus* his Eyes;
10 yet stop them all with the wise man's wax, and be deaf unto the suggestions of Talebearers, Calumniators, Pickthank or Malevolent Delators, who while quiet Men sleep, sowing the Tares of discord and division, distract the tranquillity of Charity and all friendly Society. These are the Tongues that set the world on fire, cankers of reputation, and, like that of *Jonas* his Gourd, wither a good name in a night. Evil Spirits may sit still while these Spirits walk about, and perform the business of Hell. To speak more strictly, our corrupted hearts are the Factories of the Devil, which may be at work without his presence. For when that circumvent-
20 ing Spirit hath drawn Malice, Envy, and all unrighteousness unto well rooted habits in his disciples, iniquity then goes on upon its own legs, and if the gate of Hell were shut up for a time, Vice would still be fertile and produce the fruits of Hell. Thus when God forsakes us, Satan also leaves us. For such offenders he looks upon as sure and sealed up, and his temptations then needless unto them.

SECT. XXI.

ANNIHILATE not the Mercies of God by the Oblivion of Ingratitude. For Oblivion is a kind of Annihilation, and for things to
30 be as though they had not been is like unto never being. Make not thy Head a Grave, but a Repository of God's mercies. Though thou hadst the Memory of *Seneca*, or *Simonides*, and Conscience, the punctual Memorist within us, yet trust not to thy Remembrance in things which need Phylacteries. Register not only strange but merciful occurrences: Let *Ephemerides* not *Olympiads* give thee account of his mercies. Let thy Diaries stand thick with dutiful Mementos and Asterisks of acknowledgment. And to be compleat and forget nothing, date not his mercy from thy nativity, Look beyond the World, and before the *Æra* of *Adam*.

11 Calumniators] Caluminiators *16*

SECT. XXII.

PAINT not the Sepulcher of thy self, and strive not to beautify thy corruption. Be not an Advocate for thy Vices, nor call for many Hour-Glasses to justify thy imperfections. Think not that always good which thou thinkest thou canst always make good, nor that concealed which the Sun doth not behold. That which the Sun doth not now see will be visible when the Sun is out, and the Stars are fallen from Heaven. Mean while there is no darkness unto Conscience, which can see without Light, and in the deepest obscurity give a clear Draught of things, which the Cloud of 10 dissimulation hath conceal'd from all eyes. There is a natural standing Court within us, examining, acquitting, and condemning at the Tribunal of our selves, wherein iniquities have their natural Theta's, and no nocent is absolved by the verdict of himself. And therefore although our transgressions shall be tryed at the last bar, the process need not be long: for the Judge of all knoweth all, and every Man will nakedly know himself. And when so few are like to plead not Guilty, the Assize must soon have an end.

SECT. XXIII.

COMPLY with some humors, bear with others, but serve none. 20 Civil complacency consists with decent honesty: Flattery is a Juggler, and no Kin unto Sincerity. But while thou maintainest the plain path, and scornest to flatter others, fall not into self Adulation, and become not thine own Parasite. Be deaf unto thy self, and be not betrayed at home. Self-credulity, pride, and levity lead unto self-Idolatry. There is no *Damocles* like unto self opinion, nor any *Siren* to our own fawning Conceptions. To magnify our minor things, or hug our selves in our apparitions; to afford a credulous Ear unto the clawing suggestions of fancy; to pass our days in painted mistakes of our selves; and though we behold our 30 own blood, to think our selves the Sons of *Jupiter**; are blandishments of self love, worse than outward delusion. By this Imposture Wise Men sometimes are Mistaken in their Elevation, and look above themselves. And Fools, which are Antipodes unto the Wise, conceive themselves to be but their *Periœci*, and in the same parallel with them.

SECT. XXIV.

BE not a *Hercules furens* abroad, and a Poltron within thy self. To chase our Enemies out of the Field, and be led captive by out

* As *Alexander* the Great did.

Vices; to beat down our Foes, and fall down to our Concupiscences; are Solecisms in Moral Schools, and no Laurel attends them. To well manage our Affections, and wild Horses of *Plato*, are the highest Circenses; and the noblest Digladiation is in the Theater of our selves: for therein our inward Antagonists, not only like common Gladiators, with ordinary Weapons and down right Blows make at us, but also like Retiary and Laqueary Combatants, with Nets, Frauds, and Entanglements fall upon us. Weapons for such combats are not to be forged at *Lipara*: *Vulcan's* Art doth
10 nothing in this internal Militia: wherein not the Armour of *Achilles*, but the Armature of St. *Paul*, gives the Glorious day, and Triumphs not Leading up into Capitols, but up into the highest Heavens. And therefore while so many think it the only valour to command and master others, study thou the Dominion of thy self, and quiet thine own Commotions. Let Right Reason be thy *Lycurgus*, and lift up thy hand unto the Law of it; move by the Intelligences of the superiour Faculties, not by the Rapt of Passion, not merely by that of Temper and Constitution. They who are merely carried on by the Wheel of such Inclinations, with-
20 out the Hand and Guidance of Sovereign Reason, are but the Automatous part of mankind, rather lived than living, or at least underliving themselves.

SECT. XXV.

LET not Fortune, which hath no name in Scripture, have any in thy Divinity. Let Providence, not Chance, have the honour of thy acknowledgments, and be thy *Oedipus* in Contingences. Mark well the Paths and winding Ways thereof; but be not too wise in the Construction, or sudden in the Application. The Hand of Providence writes often by Abbreviatures, Hieroglyphicks or short
30 Characters, which, like the Laconism on the Wall, are not to be made out but by a Hint or Key from that Spirit which indited them. Leave future occurrences to their uncertainties, think that which is present thy own; And since 'tis easier to foretell an Eclipse, than a foul Day at some distance, Look for little Regular below. Attend with patience the uncertainty of Things, and what lieth yet unexerted in the Chaos of Futurity. The uncertainty and ignorance of Things to come makes the World new unto us by unexpected Emergences, whereby we pass not our days in the trite road of affairs affording no Novity; for the novellizing Spirit
40 of Man lives by variety, and the new Faces of Things.

SECT. XXVI.

THOUGH a contented Mind enlargeth the dimension of little things, and unto some 'tis Wealth enough not to be Poor, and others are well content, if they be but Rich enough to be Honest, and to give every Man his due: yet fall not into that obsolete Affectation of Bravery to throw away thy Money, and to reject all Honours or Honourable stations in this courtly and splendid World. Old Generosity is superannuated, and such contempt of the World out of date. No Man is now like to refuse the favour of great ones, or be content to say unto Princes, stand out of my Sun. 10
And if any there be of such antiquated Resolutions, they are not like to be tempted out of them by great ones; and 'tis fair if they escape the name of Hypocondriacks from the Genius of latter times, unto whom contempt of the World is the most contemptible opinion, and to be able, like *Bias*, to carry all they have about them were to be the eighth Wise-man. However, the old tetrick Philosophers look'd always with Indignation upon such a Face of Things, and observing the unnatural current of Riches, Power, and Honour in the World, and withall the imperfection and demerit of persons often advanced unto them, were tempted unto 20
angry Opinions, that Affairs were ordered more by Stars than Reason, and that things went on rather by Lottery, than Election.

SECT. XXVII.

IF thy Vessel be but small in the Ocean of this World, if Meanness of Possessions be thy allotment upon Earth, forget not those Virtues which the great disposer of all bids thee to entertain from thy Quality and Condition, that is, Submission, Humility, Content of mind, and Industry. Content may dwell in all Stations. To be low, but above contempt, may be high enough to be Happy. But many of low Degree may be higher than computed, and some 30
Cubits above the common Commensuration; for in all States Virtue gives Qualifications, and Allowances, which make out defects. Rough Diamonds are sometimes mistaken for Pebbles, and Meanness may be Rich in Accomplishments, which Riches in vain desire. If our merits be above our Stations, if our intrinsecal Value be greater than what we go for, or our Value than our Valuation, and if we stand higher in God's, than in the Censor's Book; it may make some equitable balance in the inequalities of this World, and there may be no such vast Chasm or Gulph between disparities as common Measures determine. The Divine Eye looks 40
upon high and low differently from that of Man. They who seem

28 Stations] Sations *16*

to stand upon *Olympus*, and high mounted unto our eyes, may be but in the Valleys, and low Ground unto his; for he looks upon those as highest who nearest approach his Divinity, and upon those as lowest, who are farthest from it.

SECT. XXVIII.

WHEN thou lookest upon the Imperfections of others, allow one Eye for what is Laudable in them, and the balance they have from some excellency, which may render them considerable. While we look with fear or hatred upon the Teeth of the Viper, we may be-
10 hold his Eye with love. In venemous Natures something may be amiable: Poysons afford Antipoysons: nothing is totally, or altogether uselesly bad. Notable Virtues are sometimes dashed with notorious Vices, and in some vicious tempers have been found illustrious Acts of Virtue; which makes such observable worth in some actions of King *Demetrius*, *Antonius*, and *Ahab*, as are not to be found in the same kind in *Aristides*, *Numa*, or *David*. Constancy, Generosity, Clemency, and Liberality have been highly conspicuous in some Persons not markt out in other concerns for Example or Imitation. But since Goodness is exemplary in all, if others have
20 not our Virtues, let us not be wanting in theirs, nor scorning them for their Vices whereof we are free, be condemned by their Virtues, wherein we are deficient. There is Dross, Alloy, and Embasement in all human Temper; and he flieth without Wings, who thinks to find Ophyr or pure Metal in any. For perfection is not like Light center'd in any one Body, but like the dispersed Seminalities of Vegetables at the Creation scattered through the whole Mass of the Earth, no place producing all and almost all some. So that 'tis well, if a perfect Man can be made out of many Men, and to the perfect Eye of God even out of Mankind. Time, which perfects
30 some Things, imperfects also others. Could we intimately apprehend the Ideated Man, and as he stood in the intellect of God upon the first exertion by Creation, we might more narrowly comprehend our present Degeneration, and how widely we are fallen from the pure Exemplar and Idea of our Nature: for after this corruptive Elongation from a primitive and pure Creation, we are almost lost in Degeneration; and *Adam* hath not only fallen from his Creator, but we our selves from *Adam*, our Tycho and primary Generator.

SECT. XXIX.

40 QUARREL not rashly with Adversities not yet understood; and overlook not the Mercies often bound up in them. For we consider

not sufficiently the good of Evils, nor fairly compute the Mercies of Providence in things afflictive at first hand. The famous *Andreas Doria* being invited to a Feast by *Aloysio Fieschi* with design to Kill him, just the night before, fell mercifully into a fit of the Gout and so escaped that mischief. When *Cato* intended to Kill himself, from a blow which he gave his servant, who would not reach his Sword unto him, his Hand so swell'd that he had much ado to Effect his design. Hereby any one but a resolved Stoick might have taken a fair hint of consideration, and that some mercifull Genius would have contrived his preservation. To be sagacious in 10 such intercurrences is not Superstition, but wary and pious Discretion, and to contemn such hints were to be deaf unto the speaking hand of God, wherein *Socrates* and *Cardan* would hardly have been mistaken.

SECT. XXX.

BREAK not open the gate of Destruction, and make no haste or bustle unto Ruin. Post not heedlesly on unto the *non ultra* of Folly, or precipice of Perdition. Let vicious ways have their Tropicks and Deflexions, and swim in the Waters of Sin but as in the *Asphaltick* Lake, though smeared and defiled, not to sink to the 20 bottom. If thou hast dipt thy foot in the Brink, yet venture not over *Rubicon*. Run not into Extremities from whence there is no regression. In the vicious ways of the World it mercifully falleth out that we become not extempore wicked, but it taketh some time and pains to undo our selves. We fall not from Virtue, like *Vulcan* from Heaven, in a day. Bad Dispositions require some time to grow into bad Habits, bad Habits must undermine good, and often repeated acts make us habitually evil: so that by gradual depravations, and while we are but staggeringly evil, we are not left without Parentheses of considerations, thoughtful rebukes, 30 and merciful interventions, to recal us unto our selves. For the Wisdom of God hath methodiz'd the course of things unto the best advantage of goodness, and thinking Considerators overlook not the tract thereof.

SECT. XXXI.

SINCE Men and Women have their proper Virtues and Vices, and even Twins of different sexes have not only distinct coverings in the Womb, but differing qualities and Virtuous Habits after; transplace not their Proprieties and confound not their Distinctions. Let Masculine and feminine accomplishments shine in their 40 proper Orbs, and adorn their Respective subjects. However unite not the Vices of both Sexes in one; be not Monstrous in Iniquity, nor Hermaphroditically Vitious.

SECT. XXXII.

IF generous Honesty, Valour, and plain Dealing, be the Cognisance of thy Family or Characteristick of thy Country, hold fast such inclinations suckt in with thy first Breath, and which lay in the Cradle with thee. Fall not into transforming degenerations, which under the old name create a new Nation. Be not an Alien in thine own Nation; bring not *Orontes* into *Tiber*; learn the Virtues not the
10 Vices of thy foreign Neighbours, and make thy imitation by discretion not contagion. Feel something of thy self in the noble Acts of thy Ancestors, and find in thine own Genius that of thy Predecessors. Rest not under the Expired merits of others, shine by those of thy own. Flame not like the central fire which enlightneth no Eyes, which no Man seeth, and most men think there's no such thing to be seen. Add one Ray unto the common Lustre; add not only to the Number but the Note of thy Generation; and prove not a Cloud but an Asterisk in thy Region.

SECT. XXXIII.

20 SINCE thou hast an Alarum in thy Breast, which tells thee thou hast a Living Spirit in thee above two thousand times in an hour; dull not away thy Days in slothful supinity and the tediousness of doing nothing. To strenuous Minds there is an inquietude in overquietness, and no laboriousness in labour; and to tread a mile after the slow pace of a Snail, or the heavy measures of the Lazy of Brazilia, were a most tiring Pennance, and worse than a Race of some furlongs at the Olympicks. The rapid courses of the heavenly bodies are rather imitable by our Thoughts than our corporeal Motions; yet the solemn motions of our lives amount unto a
30 greater measure than is commonly apprehended. Some few men have surrounded the Globe of the Earth; yet many in the set Locomotions and movements of their days have measured the circuit of it, and twenty thousand miles have been exceeded by them. Move circumspectly not meticulously, and rather carefully sollicitous than anxiously sollicitudinous. Think not there is a Lyon in the way, nor walk with Leaden Sandals in the paths of Goodness; but in all Virtuous motions let Prudence determine thy measures. Strive not to run like *Hercules* a furlong in a breath: Festination may prove Precipitation: Deliberating delay may be wise cuncta-
40 tion, and slowness no sloathfulness.

SECT. XXXIV.

SINCE Virtuous Actions have their own Trumpets, and without any noise from thy self will have their resound abroad; busy not thy best Member in the Encomium of thy self. Praise is a debt we owe unto the Virtues of others, and due unto our own from all, whom Malice hath not made Mutes, or Envy struck Dumb. Fall not however into the common prevaricating way of self commendation and boasting, by denoting the imperfections of others. He who discommendeth others obliquely commendeth himself. He who whispers their infirmities proclaims his own Exemption 10 from them, and consequently says, I am not as this Publican, or *Hic Niger*,* whom I talk of. Open ostentation and loud vain-glory is more tolerable than this obliquity, as but containing some Froath, no Ink, as but consisting of a personal piece of folly, nor complicated with uncharitableness. Superfluously we seek a precarious applause abroad: every good Man hath his plaudite within himself; and though his Tongue be silent, is not without loud Cymbals in his Breast. Conscience will become his Panegyrist, and never forget to crown and extol him unto himself.

SECT. XXXV. 20

BLESS not thy self only that thou wert born in *Athens*;† but among thy multiplyed acknowledgments lift up one hand unto Heaven, that thou wert born of Honest Parents, that Modesty, Humility, Patience, and Veracity lay in the same Egg, and came into the World with thee. From such foundations thou may'st be Happy in a Virtuous precocity, and make an early and long walk in Goodness; so may'st thou more naturally feel the contrariety of Vice unto Nature, and resist some by the Antidote of thy Temper. As Charity covers, so Modesty preventeth a multitude of sins; withholding from noon day Vices and brazen-brow'd Iniquities, 30 from sinning on the house top, and painting our follies with the rays of the Sun. Where this Virtue reigneth, though Vice may show its Head, it cannot be in its Glory: where shame of sin sets, look not for Virtue to arise; for when Modesty taketh Wing, *Astræa*‡ goes soon after.

SECT. XXXVI.

THE Heroical vein of Mankind runs much in the Souldiery, and couragious part of the World; and in that form we oftenest find

* *Hic Niger est, hunc tu Romane caveto*. Horace. [Sat. i. 4. 85.]
† As *Socrates* did. *Athens* a place of Learning and Civility.
‡ *Astræa* Goddess of Justice and consequently of all Virtue.

Men above Men. History is full of the gallantry of that Tribe; and when we read their notable Acts, we easily find what a difference there is between a Life in *Plutarch* and in *Laërtius*. Where true Fortitude dwells, Loyalty, Bounty, Friendship, and Fidelity, may be found. A man may confide in persons constituted for noble ends, who dare do and suffer, and who have a Hand to burn for their Country and their Friend. Small and creeping things are the product of petty Souls. He is like to be mistaken, who makes choice of a covetous Man for a Friend, or relieth upon the Reed of
10 narrow and poltron Friendship. Pityful things are only to be found in the cottages of such Breasts; but bright Thoughts, clear Deeds, Constancy, Fidelity, Bounty, and generous Honesty are the Gems of noble Minds; wherein, to derogate from none, the true Heroick English Gentleman hath no Peer.

PART II.

SECT. I.

PUNISH not thy self with Pleasure; Glut not thy sense with palative Delights; nor revenge the contempt of Temperance by the penalty of Satiety. Were there an Age of delight or any pleasure
20 durable, who would not honour *Volupia*? but the Race of Delight is short, and Pleasures have mutable faces. The pleasures of one age are not pleasures in another, and their Lives fall short of our own. Even in our sensual days the strength of delight is in its seldomness or rarity, and sting in its satiety: Mediocrity is its Life, and immoderacy its Confusion. The Luxurious Emperors of old inconsiderately satiated themselves with the Dainties of Sea and Land, till, wearied through all varieties, their refections became a study unto them, and they were fain to feed by Invention. Novices in true Epicurism! which by mediocrity, paucity,
30 quick and healthful Appetite, makes delights smartly acceptable; whereby *Epicurus* himself found *Jupiter*'s brain* in a piece of Cytheridian Cheese, and the Tongues of Nightingals in a dish of Onyons. Hereby healthful and temperate poverty hath the start of nauseating Luxury; unto whose clear and naked appetite every meal is a feast, and in one single dish the first course of *Metellus*;† who are cheaply hungry, and never loose their hunger, or advantag of a craving appetite, because obvious food contents it; while *Nero*‡

* *Cerebrum Jovis,* for a Delicious bit.

† *Metellus* his riotous Pontificial Supper, the great variety whereat is to be seen in *Macrobius*. [Sat. iii. 13. 10.]

‡ *Nero* in his flight. *Sueton*.

half famish'd could not feed upon a piece of Bread, and lingring after his snowed water, hardly got down an ordinary cup of Calda.* By such circumscriptions of pleasure the contemned Philosophers reserved unto themselves the secret of Delight, which the *Helluo*'s of those days lost in their exorbitances. In vain we study Delight: It is at the command of every sober Mind, and in every sense born with us: but Nature, who teacheth us the rule of pleasure, instructeth also in the bounds thereof, and where its line expireth. And therefore Temperate Minds, not pressing their pleasures until the sting appeareth, enjoy their contentations contentedly, 10 and without regret, and so escape the folly of excess, to be pleased unto displacency.

SECT. II.

BRING candid Eyes unto the perusal of mens works, and let not *Zoilism* or Detraction blast well intended labours. He that endureth no faults in mens writings must only read his own ,wherein for the most part all appeareth White. Quotation mistakes, inadvertency, expedition, and human Lapses may make not only Moles but Warts in Learned Authors, who notwithstanding being judged by the capital matter admit not of disparagement. I should 20 unwillingly affirm that *Cicero* was but slightly versed in *Homer*, because in his Work *de Gloria* he ascribed those verses unto *Ajax*, which were delivered by *Hector*. What if *Plautus* in the account of *Hercules* mistaketh nativity for conception? Who would have mean thoughts of *Apollinaris Sidonius*, who seems to mistake the River *Tigris* for *Euphrates*, and though a good Historian and learned Bishop of *Auvergne* had the misfortune to be out in the Story of *David*, making mention of him when the Ark was sent back by the *Philistins* upon a Cart; which was before his time. Though I have no great opinion of *Machiavel*'s Learning, yet I 30 shall not presently say, that he was but a Novice in Roman History, because he was mistaken in placing *Commodus* after the Emperour *Severus*. Capital Truths are to be narrowly eyed, collateral Lapses and circumstantial deliveries not to be too strictly sifted. And if the substantial subject be well forged out, we need not examine the sparks, which irregularly fly from it.

SECT. III.

LET well weighed Considerations, not stiff and peremptory Assumptions, guide thy discourses, Pen, and Actions. To begin or

* *Caldæ gelidæque* Minister. [Juvenal, v. 63.]

2 Calda.] Calda 16

continue our works like *Trismegistus* of old, *verum certè verum atque verissimum est*,* would sound arrogantly unto present Ears in this strict enquiring Age, wherein, for the most part, Probably, and Perhaps, will hardly serve to mollify the Spirit of captious Contradictors. If *Cardan* saith that a Parrot is a beautiful Bird, *Scaliger* will set his Wits o' work to prove it a deformed Animal. The Compage of all Physical Truths is not so closely jointed, but opposition may find intrusion, nor always so closely maintained, as not to suffer attrition. Many Positions seem quodlibetically constituted, and like a *Delphian* Blade will cut on both sides. Some Truths seem almost Falshoods, and some Falshoods almost Truths; wherein Falshood and Truth seem almost æquilibriously stated, and but a few grains of distinction to bear down the ballance. Some have digged deep, yet glanced by the Royal Vein; and a Man may come unto the *Pericardium*, but not the Heart of Truth. Besides, many things are known, as some are seen, that is by Parallaxis, or at some distance from their true and proper beings, the superficial regard of things having a different aspect from their true and central Natures. And this moves sober Pens unto suspensory and timorous assertions, nor presently to obtrude them as *Sibyls* leaves, which after considerations may find to be but folious apparences, and not the central and vital interiours of Truth.

SECT. IV.

VALUE the Judicious, and let not mere acquests in minor parts of Learning gain thy preexistimation. 'Tis an unjust way of compute to magnify a weak Head for some Latin abilities, and to undervalue a solid Judgment, because he knows not the genealogy of *Hector*. When that notable King of *France*† would have his Son to know but one sentence in Latin, had it been a good one, perhaps it had been enough. Natural parts and good Judgments rule the World. States are not governed by Ergotisms. Many have Ruled well who could not perhaps define a Commonwealth, and they who understand not the Globe of the Earth command a great part of it. Where natural Logick prevails not, Artificial too often faileth. Where Nature fills the Sails, the Vessel goes smoothly on, and when Judgment is the Pilot, the Ensurance need not be high. When Industry builds upon Nature, we may exspect Pyramids: where that foundation is wanting, the structure must be low. They do most by Books, who could do much without them, and he that chiefly ows himself unto himself is the substantial Man.

* *In Tabula Smaragdina.*

‡ Lewis the Eleventh. *Qui nescit dissimulare nescit Regnare.*

SECT. V.

LET thy Studies be free as thy Thoughts and Contemplations: but fly not only upon the wings of Imagination; Joyn Sense unto Reason, and Experiment unto Speculation, and so give life unto Embryon Truths, and Verities yet in their Chaos. There is nothing more acceptable unto the Ingenious World, than this noble Eluctation of Truth; wherein, against the tenacity of Prejudice and Prescription, this Century now prevaileth. What Libraries of new Volumes aftertimes will behold, and in what a new World of Knowledge the eyes of our Posterity may be happy, a few Ages 10 may joyfully declare; and is but a cold thought unto those, who cannot hope to behold this Exantlation of Truth, or that obscured Virgin half out of the Pit. Which might make some content with a commutation of the time of their lives, and to commend the Fancy of the *Pythagorean* metempsychosis; whereby they might hope to enjoy this happiness in their third or fourth selves, and behold that in *Pythagoras*, which they now but foresee in *Euphorbus*.* The World, which took but six days to make, is like to take six thousand years to make out: mean while old Truths voted down begin to resume their places, and new ones arise upon us; wherein 20 there is no comfort in the happiness of *Tully*'s Elizium,† or any satisfaction from the Ghosts of the Ancients, who knew so little of what is now well known. Men disparage not Antiquity, who prudently exalt new Enquiries, and make not them the Judges of Truth, who were but fellow Enquirers of it. Who can but magnify the Endeavors of *Aristotle*, and the noble start which Learning had under him; or less than pitty the slender progression made upon such advantages? While many Centuries were lost in repetitions and transcriptions sealing up the Book of Knowledge. And therefore rather than to swell the leaves of Learning by fruitless Repeti- 30 tions, to sing the same Song in all Ages, nor adventure at Essays beyond the attempt of others, many would be content that some would write like *Helmont* or *Paracelsus*; and be willing to endure the monstrosity of some opinions, for divers singular notions requiting such aberrations.

* *Ipse ego, nam memini, Trojani in tempore belli*
Panthoides Euphorbus eram.
[Ovid, *Metamorph* xv. 160–1.]

† Who comforted himself that he should there converse with the old Philosophers. [*De Senectute*, 84.]

---

19 thousand years] thousand *16*. *See Commentary.*

SECT. VI.

DESPISE not the obliquities of younger ways, nor despair of better things whereof there is yet no prospect. Who would imagine that *Diogenes*, who in his younger days was a falsifier of Money, should in the after course of his Life be so great a contemner of Metal? Some Negros, who believe the Resurrection, think that they shall Rise white.* Even in this life Regeneration may imitate Resurrection, our black and vitious tinctures may wear off, and goodness cloath us with candour. Good Admonitions Knock not
10 always in vain. There will be signal Examples of God's mercy, and the Angels must not want their charitable Rejoyces for the conversion of lost Sinners. Figures of most Angles do nearest approach unto Circles, which have no Angles at all. Some may be near unto goodness, who are conceived far from it, and many things happen, not likely to ensue from any promises of Antecedencies. Culpable beginnings have found commendable conclusions, and infamous courses pious retractations. Detestable Sinners have proved exemplary Converts on Earth, and may be Glorious in the Apartment of *Mary Magdalen* in Heaven. Men are not the same
20 through all divisions of their Ages. Time, Experience, self Reflexions, and God's mercies make in some well-temper'd minds a kind of translation before Death, and Men to differ from themselves as well as from other Persons. Hereof the old World afforded many Examples to the infamy of latter Ages, wherein Men too often live by the rule of their inclinations; so that, without any Astral prediction, the first day gives the last,† Men are commonly as they were, or rather, as bad dispositions run into worser habits, the Evening doth not crown, but sowerly conclude the Day.

SECT. VII.

30 IF the Almighty will not spare us according to his merciful capitulation at *Sodom*, if his Goodness please not to pass over a great deal of Bad for a small pittance of Good, or to look upon us in the Lump; there is slender hope for Mercy, or sound presumption of fulfilling half his Will, either in Persons or Nations: they who excel in some Virtues being so often defective in others; few Men driving at the extent and amplitude of Goodness, but computing themselves by their best parts, and others by their worst, are content to rest in those Virtues, which others commonly want. Which makes this speckled Face of Honesty in the World; and which was the im-

* *Mandelslo.*

† *Primusque dies dedit extremum.* [Seneca, *Oedipus*, 988.]

perfection of the old Philosophers and great pretenders unto Virtue, who well declining the gaping Vices of Intemperance, Incontinency, Violence and Oppression, were yet blindly peccant in iniquities of closer faces, were envious, malicious, contemners, scoffers, censurers, and stufft with Vizard Vices, no less depraving the Ethereal particle and diviner portion of Man. For Envy, Malice, Hatred are the qualities of *Satan*, close and dark like himself; and where such brands smoak the Soul cannot be White. Vice may be had at all prices; expensive and costly iniquities, which make the noise, cannot be every Man's sins: but the soul may be 10 foully inquinated at a very low rate, and a Man may be cheaply vitious, to the perdition of himself.

SECT. VIII.

OPINION rides upon the neck of Reason, and Men are Happy, Wise, or Learned, according as that Empress shall set them down in the Register of Reputation. However weigh not thy self in the scales of thy own opinion, but let the Judgment of the Judicious be the Standard of thy Merit. Self-estimation is a flatterer too readily intitling us unto Knowledge and Abilities, which others sollicitously labour after, and doubtfully think they attain. Surely 20 such confident tempers do pass their days in best tranquility, who, resting in the opinion of their own abilities, are happily gull'd by such contentation; wherein Pride, Self-conceit, Confidence, and Opiniatrity will hardly suffer any to complain of imperfection. To think themselves in the right, or all that right, or only that, which they do or think, is a fallacy of high content; though others laugh in their sleeves, and look upon them as in a deluded state of Judgment. Wherein notwithstanding 'twere but a civil piece of complacency to suffer them to sleep who would not wake, to let them rest in their securities, nor by dissent or opposition to stagger 30 their contentments.

SECT. IX.

SINCE the Brow speaks often true, since Eyes and Noses have Tongues, and the countenance proclaims the Heart and inclinations; let observation so far instruct thee in Physiognomical lines, as to be some Rule for thy distinction, and Guide for thy affection unto such as look most like Men. Mankind, methinks, is comprehended in a few Faces, if we exclude all Visages, which any way participate of Symmetries and Schemes of Look common unto other Animals. For as though Man were the extract of the World, 40

in whom all were *in coagulato*, which in their forms were *in soluto* and at Extension; we often observe that Men do most act those Creatures, whose constitution, parts, and complexion do most predominate in their mixtures. This is a corner-stone in Physiognomy, and holds some Truth not only in particular Persons but also in whole Nations. There are therefore Provincial Faces, National Lips and Noses, which testify not only the Natures of those Countries, but of those which have them elsewhere. Thus we may make *England* the whole Earth, dividing it not only into
10 *Europe*, *Asia*, *Africa*, but the particular Regions thereof, and may in some latitude affirm, that there are *Ægyptians*, *Scythians*, *Indians* among us; who though born in *England*, yet carry the Faces and Air of those Countries, and are also agreeable and correspondent unto their Natures. Faces look uniformly unto our Eyes: How they appear unto some Animals of a more piercing or differing sight, who are able to discover the inequalities, rubbs, and hairiness of the Skin, is not without good doubt. And therefore in reference unto Man, *Cupid* is said to be blind. Affection should not be too sharp-Eyed, and Love is not to be made by magnifying Glasses. If
20 things were seen as they truly are, the beauty of bodies would be much abridged. And therefore the wise Contriver hath drawn the pictures and outsides of things softly and amiably unto the natural Edge of our Eyes, not leaving them able to discover those uncomely asperities, which make Oyster-shells in good Faces, and Hedghoggs even in *Venus*'s moles.

SECT. X.

COURT not Felicity too far, and weary not the favorable hand of Fortune. Glorious actions have their times, extent and *non ultra*'s. To put no end unto Attempts were to make prescription
30 of Successes, and to bespeak unhappiness at the last. For the Line of our Lives is drawn with white and black vicissitudes, wherein the extremes hold seldom one complexion. That *Pompey* should obtain the sirname of Great at twenty five years, that Men in their young and active days should be fortunate and perform notable things, is no observation of deep wonder, they having the strength of their fates before them, nor yet acted their parts in the World, for which they were brought into it: whereas Men of years, matured for counsels and designs, seem to be beyond the vigour of their active fortunes, and high exploits of life, providentially
40 ordained unto Ages best agreeable unto them. And therefore many brave men finding their fortune grow faint, and feeling its declination, have timely withdrawn themselves from great attempts,

and so escaped the ends of mighty Men, disproportionable to their beginnings. But magnanimous Thoughts have so dimmed the Eyes of many, that forgetting the very essence of Fortune, and the vicissitude of good and evil, they apprehend no bottom in felicity; and so have been still tempted on unto mighty Actions, reserved for their destructions. For Fortune lays the Plot of our Adversities in the foundation of our Felicities, blessing us in the first quadrate, to blast us more sharply in the last. And since in the highest felicities there lieth a capacity of the lowest miseries, she hath this advantage from our happiness to make us truly miser- 10 able. For to become acutely miserable we are to be first happy. Affliction smarts most in the most happy state, as having somewhat in it of *Bellisarius* at Beggers bush, or *Bajazet* in the grate. And this the fallen Angels severely understand, who having acted their first part in Heaven, are made sharply miserable by transition, and more afflictively feel the contrary state of Hell.

SECT. XI.

CARRY no careless Eye upon the unexpected scenes of things; but ponder the acts of Providence in the publick ends of great and notable Men, set out unto the view of all for no common 20 *memorandums*. The Tragical Exits and unexpected periods of some eminent Persons cannot but amuse considerate Observators; wherein notwithstanding most Men seem to see by extramission, without reception or self-reflexion, and conceive themselves unconcerned by the fallacy of their own Exemption: Whereas the Mercy of God hath singled out but few to be the signals of his Justice, leaving the generality of Mankind to the pædagogy of Example. But the inadvertency of our Natures not well apprehending this favorable method and merciful decimation, and that he sheweth in some what others also deserve; they entertain no 30 sense of his Hand beyond the stroak of themselves. Whereupon the whole becomes necessarily punished, and the contracted Hand of God extended unto universal Judgments: from whence nevertheless the stupidity of our tempers receives but faint impressions, and in the most Tragical state of times holds but starts of good motions. So that to continue us in goodness there must be iterated returns of misery, and a circulation in afflictions is necessary. And since we cannot be wise by warnings, since Plagues are insignificant, except we be personally plagued, since also we cannot be punish'd unto Amendment by proxy or commutation, nor by 40 vicinity, but contaction; there is an unhappy necessity that we must smart in our own Skins, and the provoked arm of the Almighty must fall upon our selves. The capital sufferings of others are rather our monitions than acquitments. There is but one who dyed salvifically for us, and able to say unto Death, hitherto shalt thou go and no farther; only one enlivening Death, which makes Gardens of Graves, and that which was sowed in Corruption to arise and flourish in Glory: when Death it self shall dye, and living shall have no Period, when the damned shall mourn at the funeral of Death, when Life not Death shall be the wages of sin, when the 10 second Death shall prove a miserable Life, and destruction shall be courted.

SECT. XII.

ALTHOUGH their Thoughts may seem too severe, who think that few ill natur'd Men go to Heaven; yet it may be acknowledged that good natur'd Persons are best founded for that place; who enter the World with good Dispositions, and natural Graces, more ready to be advanced by impressions from above, and christianized unto pieties; who carry about them plain and down right dealing Minds, Humility, Mercy, Charity, and Virtues 20 acceptable unto God and Man. But whatever success they may have as to Heaven, they are the acceptable Men on Earth, and happy is he who hath his quiver full of them for his Friends. These are not the Dens wherein Falshood lurks, and Hypocrisy hides its Head, wherein Frowardness makes its Nest, or where Malice, Hardheartedness, and Oppression love to dwell; not those by whom the Poor get little, and the Rich some times loose all; Men not of retracted Looks, but who carry their Hearts in their Faces, and need not to be look'd upon with perspectives; not sordidly or mischievously ingrateful; who cannot learn to ride 30 upon the neck of the afflicted, nor load the heavy laden, but who keep the Temple of *Janus* shut by peaceable and quiet tempers; who make not only the best Friends, but the best Enemies, as easier to forgive than offend, and ready to pass by the second offence, before they avenge the first; who make natural Royalists, obedient Subjects, kind and merciful Princes, verified in our own, one of the best natur'd Kings of this Throne. Of the old Roman Emperours the best were the best natur'd; though they made but a small number, and might be writ in a Ring. Many of the rest were as bad Men as Princes; Humorists rather than of good 40 humors, and of good natural parts, rather than of good natures: which did but arm their bad inclinations, and make them wittily wicked.

SECT. XIII.

WITH what strift and pains we come into the World we remember not; but 'tis commonly found no easy matter to get out of it. Many have studied to exasperate the ways of Death, but fewer hours have been spent to soften that necessity. That the smoothest way unto the grave is made by bleeding, as common opinion presumeth, beside the sick and fainting Languors which accompany that effusion, the experiment in *Lucan* and *Seneca* will make us doubt; under which the noble Stoick so deeply laboured, that, to conceal his affliction, he was fain to retire from the sight of his Wife, and not ashamed to implore the merciful hand of his Physician to shorten his misery therein. *Ovid** the old Heroes, and the Stoicks, who were so afraid of drowning, as dreading thereby the extinction of their Soul, which they conceived to be a Fire, stood probably in fear of an easier way of Death; wherein the Water, entring the possessions of Air, makes a temperate suffocation, and kills as it were without a Fever. Surely many, who have had the Spirit to destroy themselves, have not been ingenious in the contrivance thereof. 'Twas a dull way practised by *Themistocles*† to overwhelm himself with Bulls-blood, who, being an *Athenian*, might have held an easier Theory of Death from the state potion of his Country; from which *Socrates* in *Plato* seemed not to suffer much more than from the fit of an Ague. *Cato* is much to be pitied, who mangled himself with poyniards; And *Hannibal* seems more subtle, who carried his delivery not in the point, but the pummel‡ of his Sword.

The *Egyptians* were merciful contrivers, who destroyed their malefactors by Asps, charming their senses into an invincible sleep, and killing as it were with *Hermes* his Rod. The Turkish Emperour,§ odious for other Cruelty, was herein a remarkable Master of Mercy, killing his Favorite in his sleep, and sending him from the shade into the house of darkness. He who had been thus destroyed would hardly have bled at the presence of his destroyer; when Men are already dead by metaphor, and pass but from one sleep unto another, wanting herein the eminent part of severity, to feel themselves to dye, and escaping the sharpest attendant of

* *Demito naufragium, mors mihi munus erit.* [*Trist.* i. 2. 52.]

† *Plutarch.* [*Themistocles*, 31.]

‡ Pummel, wherein he is said to have carried something, whereby upon a struggle or despair he might deliver himself from all misfortunes.

§ *Solyman* Turkish History.

---

2 strift *90, p. 180, l. 35 and MS. of LF, p. 251, l. 24*: shift *16, &c See Commentary.*

Death, the lively apprehension thereof. But to learn to dye is better than to study the ways of dying. Death will find some ways to unty or cut the most Gordian Knots of Life, and make men's miseries as mortal as themselves: whereas evil Spirits, as undying Substances, are unseparable from their calamities; and therefore they everlastingly struggle under their *Angustia's*, and bound up with immortality can never get out of themselves.

PART III.

SECT. I.

10 'TIS hard to find a whole Age to imitate, or what Century to propose for Example. Some have been far more approveable than others: but Virtue and Vice, Panegyricks and Satyrs, scatteringly to be found in all. History sets down not only things laudable, but abominable; things which should never have been or never have been known: So that noble patterns must be fetched here and there from single Persons, rather than whole Nations, and from all Nations, rather than any one. The World was early bad, and the first sin the most deplorable of any. The younger World afforded the oldest Men, and perhaps the Best and the
20 Worst, when length of days made virtuous habits Heroical and immoveable, vitious, inveterate and irreclaimable. And since 'tis said that the imaginations of their hearts were evil, only evil, and continually evil; it may be feared that their sins held pace with their lives; and their Longevity swelling their Impieties, the Longanimity of God would no longer endure such vivacious abominations. Their Impieties were surely of a deep dye, which required the whole Element of Water to wash them away, and overwhelmed their memories with themselves; and so shut up the first Windows of Time, leaving no Histories of those longevous
30 generations, when Men might have been properly Historians, when *Adam* might have read long Lectures unto *Methuselah*, and *Methuselah* unto *Noah*. For had we been happy in just Historical accounts of that unparallel'd World, we might have been acquainted with Wonders, and have understood not a little of the Acts and undertakings of *Moses* his mighty Men, and Men of renown of old; which might have enlarged our Thoughts, and made the World older unto us. For the unknown part of time shortens the estimation, if not the compute of it. What hath escaped our Knowledge falls not under our Consideration, and what is and will be latent is
40 little better than non existent.

SECT. II.

SOME things are dictated for our Instruction, some acted for our Imitation, wherein 'tis best to ascend unto the highest conformity, and to the honour of the Exemplar. He honours God who imitates him. For what we virtuously imitate we approve and Admire; and since we delight not to imitate Inferiors, we aggrandize and magnify those we imitate; since also we are most apt to imitate those we love, we testify our affection in our imitation of the Inimitable. To affect to be like may be no imitation. To act, and not to be what we pretend to imitate, is but a mimical conformation, and carrieth no Virtue in it. *Lucifer* imitated not God, when he said he would be like the Highest, and he imitated not *Jupiter*, who counterfeited Thunder. Where Imitation can go no farther, let Admiration step on, whereof there is no end in the wisest form of Men. Even Angels and Spirits have enough to admire in their sublimer Natures, Admiration being the act of the Creature and not of God, who doth not Admire himself. Created Natures allow of swelling Hyperboles; nothing can be said Hyperbolically of God, nor will his Attributes admit of expressions above their own Exuperances. *Trismegistus* his Circle, whose center is every where, and circumference no where, was no Hyperbole. Words cannot exceed, where they cannot express enough. Even the most winged Thoughts fall at the setting out, and reach not the portal of Divinity.

SECT. III.

IN Bivious Theorems and *Janus*-faced Doctrines let Virtuous considerations state the determination. Look upon Opinions as thou doest upon the Moon, and chuse not the dark hemisphere for thy contemplation. Embrace not the opacous and blind side of Opinions, but that which looks most Luciferously or influentially unto Goodness. 'Tis better to think that there are Guardian Spirits, than that there are no Spirits to Guard us; that vicious Persons are Slaves, than that there is any servitude in Virtue; that times past have been better than times present, than that times were always bad, and that to be Men it suffiseth to be no better than Men in all Ages, and so promiscuously to swim down the turbid stream, and make up the grand confusion. Sow not thy understanding with Opinions, which make nothing of Iniquities, and fallaciously extenuate Transgressions. Look upon Vices and vicious Objects with Hyperbolical Eyes, and rather enlarge their dimensions, that their unseen Deformities may not escape thy sense, and their Poysonous parts and stings may appear massy and monstrous unto thee; for the undiscerned Particles and Atoms of Evil deceive us, and we are undone by the Invisibles of seeming Goodness. We are only deceived in what is not discerned, and to Err is but to be Blind or Dim-sighted as to some Perceptions.

SECT. IV.

TO be Honest in a right Line,* and Virtuous by Epitome, be firm unto such Principles of Goodness, as carry in them Volumes of instruction and may abridge thy Labour. And since instructions are many, hold close unto those, whereon the rest depend. So may 10 we have all in a few, and the Law and the Prophets in a Rule, the Sacred Writ in Stenography, and the Scripture in a Nut-Shell. To pursue the osseous and solid part of Goodness, which gives Stability and Rectitude to all the rest; To settle on fundamental Virtues, and bid early defiance unto Mother-vices, which carry in their Bowels the seminals of other Iniquities, makes a short cut in Goodness, and strikes not off an Head but the whole Neck of *Hydra.* For we are carried into the dark Lake, like the *Ægyptian* River into the Sea, by seven principal Ostiaries. The Mother-Sins of that number are the Deadly engins of Evil Spirits that undo us, 20 and even evil Spirits themselves, and he who is under the Chains thereof is not without a possession. *Mary Magdalene* had more than seven Devils, if these with their Imps were in her, and he who is thus possessed may literally be named *Legion.* Where such Plants grow and prosper, look for no Champian or Region void of Thorns, but productions like the Tree of *Goa,*† and Forrests of abomination.

SECT. V.

GUIDE not the Hand of God, nor order the Finger of the Almighty, unto thy will and pleasure; but sit quiet in the soft 30 showers of Providence, and Favorable distributions in this World, either to thy self or others. And since not only Judgments have their Errands, but Mercies their Commissions; snatch not at every Favour, nor think thy self passed by, if they fall upon thy Neighbour. Rake not up envious displacences at things successful unto others, which the wise Disposer of all thinks not fit for thy self. Reconcile the events of things unto both beings, that is, of this World and the next: So will there not seem so many Riddles in

* *Linea Recta brevissima.*

† *Arbor Goa de Ruyz* or *ficus Indica,* whose branches send down shoots which root in the ground, from whence there successively rise others, till one Tree becomes a wood.

Providence, nor various inequalities in the dispensation of things below. If thou doest not anoint thy Face, yet put not on sackcloth at the felicities of others. Repining at the Good draws on rejoicing at the evils of others, and so falls into that inhumane Vice,* for which so few Languages have a name. The blessed Spirits above rejoice at our happiness below; but to be glad at the evils of one another is beyond the malignity of Hell, and falls not on evil Spirits, who, though they rejoice at our unhappiness, take no pleasure at the afflictions of their own Society or of their fellow Natures. Degenerous Heads! who must be fain to learn from such 10 Examples, and to be Taught from the School of Hell.

SECT. VI.

GRAIN not thy vicious stains, nor deepen those swart Tinctures, which Temper, Infirmity, or ill habits have set upon thee; and fix not by iterated depravations what time might Efface, or Virtuous washes expunge. He who thus still advanceth in Iniquity deepneth his deformed hue, turns a Shadow into Night, and makes himself a *Negro* in the black Jaundice; and so becomes one of those Lost ones, the disproportionate pores of whose Brains afford no entrance unto good Motions, but reflect and frustrate all Counsels, Deaf 20 unto the Thunder of the Laws, and Rocks unto the Cries of charitable Commiserators. He who hath had the Patience of *Diogenes*, to make Orations unto Statues, may more sensibly apprehend how all Words fall to the Ground, spent upon such a surd and Earless Generation of Men, stupid unto all Instruction, and rather requiring an Exorcist, than an Orator for their Conversion.

SECT. VII.

BURDEN not the back of *Aries*, *Leo*, or *Taurus*, with thy faults, nor make *Saturn*, *Mars*, or *Venus*, guilty of thy Follies. Think not to 30 fasten thy imperfections on the Stars, and so despairingly conceive thy self under a fatality of being evil. Calculate thy self within, seek not thy self in the Moon, but in thine own Orb or Microcosmical Circumference. Let celestial aspects admonish and advertise, not conclude and determine thy ways. For since good and bad Stars moralize not our Actions, and neither excuse or commend, acquit or condemn our Good or Bad Deeds at the present or last Bar, since some are Astrologically well disposed who are morally highly vicious; not Celestial Figures, but Virtuous

* *'Επικαιρεκακία* [*for* *'Επιχαιρεκακία*].

Schemes must denominate and state our Actions. If we rightly understood the Names whereby God calleth the Stars, if we knew his Name for the Dog-Star, or by what appellation *Jupiter*, *Mars*, and *Saturn* obey his Will, it might be a welcome accession unto Astrology, which speaks great things, and is fain to make use of appellations from Greek and Barbarick Systems. Whatever Influences, Impulsions, or Inclinations there be from the Lights above, it were a piece of wisdom to make one of those Wise men who overrule their Stars,* and with their own Militia contend with the
10 Host of Heaven. Unto which attempt there want not Auxiliaries from the whole strength of Morality, supplies from Christian Ethicks, influences also and illuminations from above, more powerfull than the Lights of Heaven.

SECT. VIII.

CONFOUND not the distinctions of thy Life which Nature hath divided: that is, Youth, Adolescence, Manhood, and old Age, nor in these divided Periods, wherein thou art in a manner Four, conceive thy self but One. Let every division be happy in its proper Virtues, nor one Vice run through all. Let each distinction
20 have its salutary transition, and critically deliver thee from the imperfections of the former, so ordering the whole, that Prudence and Virtue may have the largest Section. Do as a Child but when thou art a Child, and ride not on a Reed at twenty. He who hath not taken leave of the follies of his Youth, and in his maturer state scarce got out of that division, disproportionately divideth his Days, crowds up the latter part of his Life, and leaves too narrow a corner for the Age of Wisdom, and so hath room to be a Man scarce longer than he hath been a Youth. Rather than to make this confusion, anticipate the Virtues of Age, and live long
30 without the infirmities of it. So may'st thou count up thy Days as some do *Adams*,† that is, by anticipation; so may'st thou be coetaneous unto thy Elders, and a Father unto thy contemporaries.

SECT. IX.

WHILE others are curious in the choice of good Air, and chiefly sollicitous for healthful habitations, Study thou Conversation, and be critical in thy Consortion. The aspects, conjunctions, and

* *Sapiens dominabitur Astris.*

† *Adam* thought to be created in the State of Man, about thirty years Old.

---

32 contemporaries.] contemporaries *58*

configurations of the Stars, which mutually diversify, intend, or qualify their influences, are but the varieties of their nearer or farther conversation with one another, and like the Consortion of Men, whereby they become better or worse, and even Exchange their Natures. Since Men live by Examples, and will be imitating something; order thy imitation to thy Improvement, not thy Ruin. Look not for Roses in *Attalus** His Garden, or wholsome Flowers in a venemous Plantation. And since there is scarce any one bad, but some others are the worse for him; tempt not Contagion by proximity, and hazard not thy self in the shadow of 10 Corruption. He who hath not early suffered this Shipwrack, and in his Younger Days escaped this *Charybdis*, may make a happy Voyage, and not come in with black Sails into the port. Self conversation, or to be alone, is better than such Consortion. Some School-men tell us, that he is properly alone, with whom in the same place there is no other of the same Species. *Nabuchodonozor* was alone, though among the Beasts of the Field, and a Wise Man may be tolerably said to be alone though with a Rabble of People, little better than Beasts about him. Unthinking Heads, who have not learn'd to be alone, are in a Prison to themselves, if they be not 20 also with others: Whereas on the contrary, they whose thoughts are in a fair, and hurry within, are sometimes fain to retire into Company, to be out of the crowd of themselves. He who must needs have Company, must needs have sometimes bad Company. Be able to be alone. Loose not the advantage of Solitude, and the Society of thy self, nor be only content, but delight to be alone and single with Omnipresency. He who is thus prepared, the Day is not uneasy nor the Night black unto him. Darkness may bound his Eyes, not his Imagination. In his Bed he may ly, like *Pompey* and his Sons,† in all quarters of the Earth, may speculate the Universe, 30 and enjoy the whole World in the Hermitage of himself. Thus the old *Ascetick* Christians found a Paradise in a Desert, and with little converse on Earth held a conversation in Heaven; thus they Astronomiz'd in Caves, and though they beheld not the Stars, had the Glory of Heaven before them.

SECT. X.

LET the Characters of good things stand indelibly in thy Mind, and thy Thoughts be active on them. Trust not too much unto suggestions from Reminiscential Amulets, or Artificial *Memorandums*.

* *Attalus* made a Garden which contained only venemous Plants.

† *Pompeios Juvenes Asia atque Europa, sed ipsum*
Terra tegit Libyes. [Martial, v. 74. 1–2.]

Let the mortifying *Janus* of *Covarrubias** be in thy daily Thoughts, not only on thy Hand and Signets. Rely not alone upon silent and dumb remembrances. Behold not Death's Heads till thou doest not see them, nor look upon mortifying Objects till thou overlook'st them. Forget not how assuefaction unto any thing minorates the passion from it, how constant Objects loose their hints, and steal an inadvertisement upon us. There is no excuse to forget what every thing prompts unto us. To thoughtful Observators the whole World is a Phylactery, and every thing we 10 see an Item of the Wisdom, Power, or Goodness of God. Happy are they who verify their Amulets, and make their Phylacteries speak in their Lives and Actions. To run on in despight of the Revulsions and Pul-backs of such Remora's aggravates our transgressions. When Death's Heads on our Hands have no influence upon our Heads, and fleshless Cadavers abate not the exorbitances of the Flesh; when Crucifixes upon Mens Hearts suppress not their bad commotions, and his Image who was murdered for us with-holds not from Blood and Murder; Phylacteries prove but formalities, and their despised hints sharpen our condemnations.

20 SECT. XI.

LOOK not for *Whales* in the *Euxine* Sea, or expect great matters where they are not to be found. Seek not for Profundity in Shallowness, or Fertility in a Wilderness. Place not the expectation of great Happiness here below, or think to find Heaven on Earth; wherein we must be content with Embryon-felicities, and fruitions of doubtful Faces. For the Circle of our felicities makes but short Arches. In every clime we are in a periscian state, and with our Light our Shadow and Darkness walk about us. Our Contentments stand upon the tops of Pyramids ready to fall off, and the 30 insecurity of their enjoyments abrupteth our Tranquilities. What we magnify is Magnificent, but like to the *Colossus*, noble without, stuft with rubbidge and course Metal within. Even the Sun, whose Glorious outside we behold, may have dark and smoaky Entrails. In vain we admire the Lustre of any thing seen: that which is truly glorious is invisible. *Paradise* was but a part of the Earth, lost not only to our Fruition but our Knowledge. And if, according to old Dictates, no Man can be said to be happy before Death, the

* *Don Sebastian de Covarrubias* writ 3 Centuries of moral Emblems in *Spanish*. In the 88*th* of the second Century he sets down two Faces averse, and conjoined *Janus*-like, the one a Gallant Beautiful Face, the other a Death's Head Face, with this Motto out of Ovid's *Metamorphosis* [ii. 551.],

Quid fuerim quid simque vide.

happiness of this Life goes for nothing before it be over, and while we think our selves happy we do but usurp that Name. Certainly true Beatitude groweth not on Earth, nor hath this World in it the Expectations we have of it. He Swims in Oyl, and can hardly avoid sinking, who hath such light Foundations to support him. 'Tis therefore happy that we have two Worlds to hold on. To enjoy true happiness we must travel into a very far Countrey, and even out of our selves; for the Pearl we seek for is not to be found in the *Indian*, but in the *Empyrean* Ocean.

SECT. XII. 10

ANSWER not the Spur of Fury, and be not prodigal or prodigious in Revenge. Make not one in the *Historia Horribilis*;* Flay not thy Servant for a broken Glass, nor pound him in a Mortar who offendeth thee; supererogate not in the worst sense, and overdo not the necessities of evil; humour not the injustice of Revenge. Be not Stoically mistaken in the equality of sins, nor commutatively iniquous in the valuation of transgressions; but weigh them in the Scales of Heaven, and by the weights of righteous Reason. Think that Revenge too high, which is but level with the offence. Let thy Arrows of Revenge fly short, or be 20 aimed like those of *Jonathan*, to fall beside the mark. Too many there be to whom a Dead Enemy smells well, and who find Musk and Amber in Revenge. The ferity of such minds holds no rule in Retaliations, requiring too often a Head for a Tooth, and the Supreme revenge for trespasses, which a night's rest should obliterate. But patient Meekness takes injuries like Pills, not chewing but swallowing them down, Laconically suffering, and silently passing them over, while angred Pride makes a noise, like *Homerican Mars*,† at every scratch of offences. Since Women do most delight in Revenge, it may seem but feminine manhood to 30 be vindicative. If thou must needs have thy Revenge of thine Enemy, with a soft Tongue break his Bones,‡ heap Coals of Fire on his Head, forgive him, and enjoy it. To forgive our Enemies is a charming way of Revenge, and a short *Cæsarian* Conquest overcoming without a blow; laying our Enemies at our Feet, under sorrow, shame, and repentance; leaving our Foes our Friends, and solicitously inclined to grateful Retaliations. Thus to Return upon our Adversaries is a healing way of Revenge, and to do

* A Book so entituled wherein are sundry horrid accounts.

† *Tu tamen exclamas ut Stentora vincere possis*
Vel saltem quantum Gradivus Homericus. Juvenal. [xiii. 112–13.]

‡ A soft Tongue breaketh the bones. *Proverbs* 25. 15. [*A.V.* 'bone'.]

good for evil a soft and melting ultion, a method Taught from Heaven to keep all smooth on Earth. Common forceable ways make not an end of Evil, but leave Hatred and Malice behind them. An Enemy thus reconciled is little to be trusted, as wanting the foundation of Love and Charity, and but for a time restrained by disadvantage or inability. If thou hast not Mercy for others, yet be not Cruel unto thy self. To ruminate upon evils, to make critical notes upon injuries, and be too acute in their apprehensions, is to add unto our own Tortures, to feather the Arrows of our Enemies, 10 to lash our selves with the Scorpions of our Foes, and to resolve to sleep no more. For injuries long dreamt on take away at last all rest; and he sleeps but like *Regulus*, who busieth his Head about them.

SECT. XIII.

AMUSE not thy self about the Riddles of future things. Study Prophecies when they are become Histories, and past hovering in their causes. Eye well things past and present, and let conjectural sagacity suffise for things to come. There is a sober Latitude for prescience in contingences of discoverable Tempers, whereby discerning Heads see sometimes beyond their Eyes, and Wise Men 20 become Prophetical. Leave Cloudy predictions to their Periods, and let appointed Seasons have the lot of their accomplishments. 'Tis too early to study such Prophecies before they have been long made, before some train of their causes have already taken Fire, laying open in part what lay obscure and before buryed unto us. For the voice of Prophecies is like that of Whispering-places: They who are near or at a little distance hear nothing, those at the farthest extremity will understand all. But a Retrograde cognition of times past, and things which have already been, is more satisfactory than a suspended Knowledge of what is yet unexistent. 30 And the Greatest part of time being already wrapt up in things behind us; it's now somewhat late to bait after things before us; for futurity still shortens, and time present sucks in time to come. What is Prophetical in one Age proves Historical in another, and so must hold on unto the last of time; when there will be no room for Prediction, when *Janus* shall loose one Face, and the long beard of time shall look like those of *David*'s Servants, shorn away upon one side, and when, if the expected *Elias* should appear, he might say much of what is past, not much of what's to come.

SECT. XIV.

40 LIVE unto the Dignity of thy Nature, and leave it not disputable at last, whether thou hast been a Man, or since thou art a composi-

tion of Man and Beast, how thou hast predominantly passed thy days, to state the denomination. Un-man not therefore thy self by a Beastial transformation, nor realize old Fables. Expose not thy self by four-footed manners unto monstrous draughts, and *Caricatura* representations. Think not after the old *Pythagorean* conceit, what Beast thou may'st be after death. Be not under any Brutal *metempsychosis* while thou livest, and walkest about erectly under the scheme of Man. In thine own circumference, as in that of the Earth, let the Rational Horizon be larger than the sensible, and the Circle of Reason than of Sense. Let the Divine part be upward, 10 and the Region of Beast below. Otherwise, 'tis but to live invertedly, and with thy Head unto the Heels of thy *Antipodes*. Desert not thy title to a Divine particle and union with invisibles. Let true Knowledge and Virtue tell the lower World thou art a part of the higher. Let thy Thoughts be of things which have not entred into the Hearts of Beasts: Think of things long past, and long to come: Acquaint thy self with the *Choragium* of the Stars, and consider the vast expansion beyond them. Let Intellectual Tubes give thee a glance of things, which visive Organs reach not. Have a glimpse of incomprehensibles, and Thoughts of things, which 20 Thoughts but tenderly touch. Lodge immaterials in thy Head: ascend unto invisibles: fill thy Spirit with Spirituals, with the mysteries of Faith, the magnalities of Religion, and thy Life with the Honour of God; without which, though Giants in Wealth and Dignity, we are but Dwarfs and Pygmies in Humanity, and may hold a pitiful rank in that triple division of mankind into Heroes, Men, and Beasts. For though human Souls are said to be equal, yet is there no small inequality in their operations; some maintain the allowable Station of Men; many are far below it; and some have been so divine, as to approach the *Apogeum* of their Natures, 30 and to be in the *Confinium* of Spirits.

SECT. XV.

BEHOLD thy self by inward Opticks and the Crystalline of thy Soul. Strange it is that in the most perfect sense there should be so many fallacies, that we are fain to make a doctrine, and often to see by Art. But the greatest imperfection is in our inward sight, that is, to be Ghosts unto our own Eyes, and while we are so sharp-sighted as to look thorough others, to be invisible unto our selves; for the inward Eyes are more fallacious than the outward. The Vices we scoff at in others laugh at us within our selves. Avarice, 40

Pride, Falshood lye undiscerned and blindly in us, even to the Age of blindness: and therefore, to see our selves interiourly, we are fain to borrow other Mens Eyes; wherein true Friends are good Informers, and Censurers no bad Friends. Conscience only, that can see without Light, sits in the *Areopagy* and dark Tribunal of our Hearts, surveying our Thoughts and condemning their obliquities, Happy is that state of vision that can see without Light, though all should look as before the Creation, when there was not an Eye to see, or Light to actuate a Vision: wherein 10 notwithstanding obscurity is only imaginable respectively unto Eyes; for unto God there was none, Eternal Light was ever, created Light was for the creation, not himself, and as he saw before the Sun, may still also see without it. In the City of the new *Jerusalem* there is neither Sun nor Moon; where glorifyed Eyes must see by the *Archetypal* Sun, or the Light of God, able to illuminate Intellectual Eyes, and make unknown Visions. Intuitive perceptions in Spiritual beings may perhaps hold some Analogy unto Vision: but yet how they see us, or one another, what Eye, what Light, or what perception is required unto their intuition, is yet dark unto our apprehen- 20 sion; and even how they see God, or how unto our glorified Eyes the Beatifical Vision will be celebrated, another World must tell us, when perceptions will be new, and we may hope to behold invisibles.

SECT. XVI.

WHEN all looks fair about, and thou seest not a cloud so big as a Hand to threaten thee, forget not the Wheel of things: Think of sullen vicissitudes, but beat not thy brains to fore-know them. Be armed against such obscurities rather by submission than fore-knowledge. The Knowledge of future evils mortifies present 30 felicities, and there is more content in the uncertainty or ignorance of them. This favour our Saviour vouchsafed unto *Peter*, when he fore-told not his Death in plain terms, and so by an ambiguous and cloudy delivery dampt not the Spirit of his Disciples. But in the assured fore-knowledge of the Deluge *Noah* lived many Years under the affliction of a Flood, and *Jerusalem* was taken unto *Jeremy* before it was besieged. And therefore the Wisdom of Astrologers, who speak of future things, hath wisely softned the severity of their Doctrines; and even in their sad predictions, while they tell us of inclination not coaction from the Stars, they 40 Kill us not with *Stygian* Oaths and merciless necessity, but leave us hopes of evasion.

SECT. XVII.

IF thou hast the brow to endure the Name of Traytor, Perjur'd, or Oppressor, yet cover thy Face when Ingratitude is thrown at thee. If that degenerous Vice possess thee, hide thy self in the shadow of thy shame, and pollute not noble society. Grateful Ingenuities are content to be obliged within some compass of Retribution, and being depressed by the weight of iterated favours may so labour under their inabilities of Requital, as to abate the content from Kindnesses. But narrow self-ended Souls make prescription of good Offices, and obliged by often favours think others still due unto them: whereas, if they but once fail, they prove so perversely ungrateful, as to make nothing of former courtesies, and to bury all that's past. Such tempers pervert the generous course of things; for they discourage the inclinations of noble minds, and make Beneficency cool unto acts of obligation, whereby the grateful World should subsist, and have their consolation. Common gratitude must be kept alive by the additionary fewel of new courtesies: but generous Gratitudes, though but once well obliged, without quickening repetitions or expectation of new Favours, have thankful minds for ever; for they write not their obligations in sandy but marble memories, which wear not out but with themselves.

SECT. XVIII.

THINK not Silence the wisdom of Fools, but, if rightly timed, the honour of Wise Men, who have not the Infirmity, but the Virtue of Taciturnity, and speak not out of the abundance, but the well weighed thoughts of their Hearts. Such Silence may be Eloquence, and speak thy worth above the power of Words. Make such a one thy friend, in whom Princes may be happy, and great Councels successful. Let him have the Key of thy Heart, who hath the Lock of his own, which no Temptation can open; where thy Secrets may lastingly ly, like the Lamp in *Olybius* his Urn,* alive, and light, but close and invisible.

SECT. XIX.

LET thy Oaths be sacred and Promises be made upon the Altar of thy Heart. Call not *Jove*† to witness with a Stone in one Hand, and a Straw in another, and so make Chaff and Stubble of thy

* Which after many hundred years was found burning under ground, and went out as soon as the air came to it.

† *Jovem lapidem jurare.*

Vows. Worldly Spirits, whose interest is their belief, make Cobwebs of Obligations, and, if they can find ways to elude the Urn of the *Prætor*, will trust the Thunderbolt of *Jupiter*: And therefore if they should as deeply swear as *Osman** to *Bethlem Gabor*; yet whether they would be bound by those chains, and not find ways to cut such *Gordian* Knots, we could have no just assurance. But Honest Mens Words are *Stygian* Oaths, and Promises inviolable. These are not the Men for whom the fetters of Law were first forged: they needed not the solemness of Oaths; by keeping their 10 Faith they swear,† and evacuate such confirmations.

SECT. XX.

THOUGH the World be Histrionical, and most Men live Ironically, yet be thou what thou singly art, and personate only thy self. Swim smoothly in the stream of thy Nature, and live but one Man. To single Hearts doubling is discruciating: such tempers must sweat to dissemble, and prove but hypocritical Hypocrites. Simulation must be short: Men do not easily continue a counterfeiting Life, or dissemble unto Death. He who counterfeiteth, acts a part, and is as it were out of himself: which, if long, proves so 20 ircksome, that Men are glad to pull of their Vizards, and resume themselves again; no practice being able to naturalize such unnaturals, or make a Man rest content not to be himself. And therefore since Sincerity is thy Temper, let veracity be thy Virtue in Words, Manners, and Actions. To offer at iniquities, which have so little foundations in thee, were to be vitious up hill, and strain for thy condemnation. Persons vitiously inclined want no Wheels to make them actively vitious, as having the Elater and Spring of their own Natures to facilitate their Iniquities. And therefore so many, who are sinistrous unto Good Actions, are Ambi-dexterous 30 unto bad, and *Vulcans* in virtuous Paths, *Achilleses* in vitious motions.

SECT. XXI.

REST not in the high strain'd Paradoxes of old Philosophy supported by naked Reason, and the reward of mortal Felicity, but labour in the Ethicks of Faith, built upon Heavenly assistance, and the happiness of both beings. Understand the Rules, but swear not unto the Doctrines of *Zeno* or *Epicurus*. Look beyond

* See the Oath of *Sultan Osman* in his life, in the addition to *Knolls* his Turkish history.

† *Colendo fidem jurant.* [Quintus] Curtius. [vii. 8. 29.]

Antoninus, and terminate not thy Morals in *Seneca* or *Epictetus*. Let not the twelve, but the two Tables be thy Law: Let *Pythagaras* be thy Remembrancer, not thy textuary and final Instructer; and learn the Vanity of the World rather from *Solomon* than *Phocylides*. Sleep not in the Dogma's of the *Peripatus*, Academy, or *Porticus*. Be a moralist of the Mount, an *Epictetus* in the Faith, and christianize thy Notions.

SECT. XXII.

IN seventy or eighty years a Man may have a deep Gust of the World, Know what it is, what it can afford, and what 'tis to have been a Man. Such a latitude of years may hold a considerable corner in the general Map of Time; and a Man may have a curt Epitome of the whole course thereof in the days of his own Life, may clearly see he hath but acted over his Fore-fathers, what it was to live in Ages past, and what living will be in all ages to come.

He is like to be the best judge of Time who hath lived to see about the sixtieth part thereof. Persons of short times may Know what 'tis to live, but not the life of Man, who, having little behind them, are but *Januses* of one Face, and Know not singularities enough to raise Axioms of this World: but such a compass of Years will show new Examples of old Things, Parallelisms of occurrences through the whole course of Time, and nothing be monstrous unto him; who may in that time understand not only the varieties of Men, but the variation of himself, and how many Men he hath been in that extent of time.

He may have a close apprehension what it is to be forgotten, while he hath lived to find none who could remember his Father, or scarce the friends of his youth, and may sensibly see with what a face in no long time oblivion will look upon himself. His Progeny may never be his Posterity; he may go out of the World less related than he came into it, and considering the frequent mortality in Friends and Relations, in such a Term of Time, he may pass away divers years in sorrow and black habits, and leave none to mourn for himself; Orbity may be his inheritance, and Riches his Repentance.

In such a thred of Time, and long observation of Men, he may acquire a *Physiognomical* intuitive Knowledge, Judge the interiors by the outside, and raise conjectures at first sight; and knowing what Men have been, what they are, what Children probably will be, may in the present Age behold a good part, and the temper of the next; and since so many live by the Rules of Constitution, and so few overcome their temperamental Inclinations, make no improbable predictions.

Such a portion of Time will afford a large prospect backward, and Authentick Reflections how far he hath performed the great intention of his Being, in the Honour of his Maker; whether he hath made good the Principles of his Nature and what he was made to be; what Characteristick and special Mark he hath left, to be observable in his Generation; whether he hath Lived to purpose or in vain, and what he hath added, acted, or performed, that 10 might considerably speak him a Man.

In such an Age Delights will be undelightful and Pleasures grow stale unto him; Antiquated Theorems will revive, and *Solomon*'s Maxims be Demonstrations unto him; Hopes or presumptions be over, and despair grow up of any satisfaction below. And having been long tossed in the Ocean of this World, he will by that time feel the In-draught of another, unto which this seems but preparatory, and without it of no high value. He will experimentally find the Emptiness of all things, and the nothing of what is past; and wisely grounding upon true Christian Expectations, finding so 20 much past, will wholly fix upon what is to come. He will long for Perpetuity, and live as though he made haste to be happy. The last may prove the prime part of his Life, and those his best days which he lived nearest Heaven.

SECT. XXIII.

LIVE happy in the *Elizium* of a virtuously composed Mind, and let Intellectual Contents exceed the Delights wherein mere Pleasurists place their Paradise. Bear not too slack reins upon Pleasure, nor let complexion or contagion betray thee unto the exorbitancy of Delight. Make Pleasure thy Recreation or inter- 30 missive Relaxation, not thy *Diana*, Life and Profession. Voluptuousness is as insatiable as Covetousness. Tranquility is better than Jollity, and to appease pain than to invent pleasure. Our hard entrance into the World, our miserable going out of it, our sicknesses, disturbances, and sad Rencounters in it, do clamorously tell us we come not into the World to run a Race of Delight, but to perform the sober Acts and serious purposes of Man; which to omit were foully to miscarry in the advantage of humanity, to play away an uniterable Life, and to have lived in vain. Forget not the capital end, and frustrate not the opportunity of once Living. 40 Dream not of any kind of *Metempsychosis* or transanimation, but into thine own body, and that after a long time, and then also unto wail or bliss, according to thy first and fundamental Life.

Upon a curricle in this World depends a long course of the next, and upon a narrow Scene here an endless expansion hereafter. In vain some think to have an end of their Beings with their Lives. Things cannot get out of their natures, or be or not be in despite of their constitutions. Rational existences in Heaven perish not at all, and but partially on Earth: That which is thus once will in some way be always: The first Living human Soul is still alive, and all *Adam* hath found no Period.

SECT. XXIV.

SINCE the Stars of Heaven do differ in Glory; since it hath pleased the Almighty hand to honour the North Pole with Lights above the South; since there are some Stars so bright, that they can hardly be looked on, some so dim that they can scarce be seen, and vast numbers not to be seen at all even by Artificial Eyes; Read thou the Earth in Heaven, and things below from above. Look contentedly upon the scattered difference of things, and expect not equality in lustre, dignity, or perfection, in Regions or Persons below; where numerous numbers must be content to stand like *Lacteous* or *Nebulous* Stars, little taken notice of, or dim in their generations. All which may be contentedly allowable in the affairs and ends of this World, and in suspension unto what will be in the order of things hereafter, and the new Systeme of Mankind which will be in the World to come; when the last may be the first and the first the last; when *Lazarus* may sit above *Cæsar*, and the just obscure on Earth shall shine like the Sun in Heaven; when personations shall cease, and Histrionism of happiness be over; when Reality shall rule, and all shall be as they shall be for ever.

SECT. XXV.

WHEN the *Stoick* said that life would not be accepted, if it were offered unto such as knew it,* he spoke too meanly of that state of being which placeth us in the form of Men. It more depreciates the value of this life, that Men would not live it over again; for although they would still live on, yet few or none can endure to think of being twice the same Men upon Earth, and some had rather never have lived than to tread over their days once more. *Cicero* in a prosperous state had not the patience to think of beginning in a cradle again. *Job* would not only curse the day of his Nativity, but also of his Renascency, if he were to act over his Disasters, and the miseries of the Dunghil. But the greatest underweening of this

* *Vitam nemo acciperet si daretur scientibus*. Seneca. [*Consol. ad Marc*. 22. 3.]

Life is to undervalue that, unto which this is but Exordial or a Passage leading unto it. The great advantage of this mean life is thereby to stand in a capacity of a better; for the Colonies of Heaven must be drawn from Earth, and the Sons of the first *Adam* are only heirs unto the second. Thus *Adam* came into this World with the power also of another, nor only to replenish the Earth, but the everlasting Mansions of Heaven. Where we were when the foundations of the Earth were lay'd, when the morning Stars sang together* and all the Sons of God shouted for
10 Joy, He must answer who asked it; who understands Entities of preordination, and beings yet unbeing; who hath in his Intellect the Ideal Existences of things, and Entities before their Extances. Though it looks but like an imaginary kind of existency to be before we are; yet since we are under the decree or prescience of a sure and Omnipotent Power, it may be somewhat more than a non-entity to be in that mind, unto which all things are present.

SECT. XXVI.

If the end of the World shall have the same foregoing Signs, as the period of Empires, States, and Dominions in it, that is, Corrup-
20 tion of Manners, inhuman degenerations, and deluge of iniquities; it may be doubted whether that final time be so far of, of whose day and hour there can be no prescience. But while all men doubt and none can determine how long the World shall last, some may wonder that it hath spun out so long and unto our days. For if the Almighty had not determin'd a fixed duration unto it, according to his mighty and merciful designments in it, if he had not said unto it, as he did unto a part of it, hitherto shalt thou go and no farther; if we consider the incessant and cutting provocations from the Earth, it is not without amazement how his patience
30 hath permitted so long a continuance unto it, how he, who cursed the Earth in the first days of the first Man, and drowned it in the tenth Generation after, should thus lastingly contend with Flesh and yet defer the last flames. For since he is sharply provoked every moment, yet punisheth to pardon, and forgives to forgive again; what patience could be content to act over such vicissitudes, or accept of repentances which must have after penitences, his goodness can only tell us. And surely if the patience of Heaven were not proportionable unto the provocations from Earth; there needed an Intercessor not only for the sins, but the duration of this
40 World, and to lead it up unto the present computation. Without such a merciful Longanimity, the Heavens would never be so aged

* *Job* 38. [4, 7.]

as to grow old like a Garment; it were in vain to infer from the Doctrine of the Sphere, that the time might come when *Capella*, a noble Northern Star, would have its motion in the *Æquator*, that the Northern *Zodiacal* Signs would at length be the Southern, the Southern the Northern, and *Capricorn* become our *Cancer*. However therefore the Wisdom of the Creator hath ordered the duration of the World, yet since the end thereof brings the accomplishment of our happiness, since some would be content that it should have no end, since Evil Men and Spirits do fear it may be too short, since Good Men hope it may not be too long; the prayer of the 10 Saints under the Altar will be the supplication of the Righteous World. That his mercy would abridge their languishing Expectation and hasten the accomplishment of their happy state to come.

SECT. XXVII.

THOUGH Good Men are often taken away from the Evil to come, though some in evil days have been glad that they were old, nor long to behold the iniquities of a wicked World, or Judgments threatened by them; yet is it no small satisfaction unto honest minds to leave the World in virtuous well temper'd times, under a prospect of good to come, and continuation of worthy ways 20 acceptable unto God and Man. Men who dye in deplorable days, which they regretfully behold, have not their Eyes closed with the like content; while they cannot avoid the thoughts of proceeding or growing enormities, displeasing unto that Spirit unto whom they are then going, whose honour they desire in all times and throughout all generations. If *Lucifer* could be freed from his dismal place, he would little care though the rest were left behind. Too many there may be of *Nero*'s mind, who, if their own turn were served, would not regard what became of others, and, when they dye themselves, care not if all perish. But good Mens wishes 30 extend beyond their lives, for the happiness of times to come, and never to be known unto them. And therefore while so many question prayers for the dead, they charitably pray for those who are not yet alive; they are not so enviously ambitious to go to Heaven by themselves; they cannot but humbly wish, that the little Flock might be greater, the narrow Gate wider, and that, as many are called, so not a few might be chosen.

SECT. XXVIII.

THAT a greater number of Angels remained in Heaven, than fell from it, the School-men will tell us; that the number of blessed 40 Souls will not come short of that vast number of fallen Spirits, we have the favorable calculation of others. What Age or Century hath sent most Souls unto Heaven, he can tell who vouchsafeth that honour unto them. Though the Number of the blessed must be compleat before the World can pass away, yet since the World it self seems in the wane, and we have no such comfortable prognosticks of Latter times, since a greater part of time is spun than is to come, and the blessed Roll already much replenished; happy are those pieties, which solicitously look about, and hasten to make one of that already much filled and abbreviated List to come.

10 SECT. XXIX.

THINK not thy time short in this World since the World it self is not long. The created World is but a small *Parenthesis* in Eternity, and a short interposition for a time between such a state of duration, as was before it and may be after it. And if we should allow of the old Tradition that the World should last Six Thousand years, it could scarce have the name of old, since the first Man lived near a sixth part thereof, and seven *Methusela*'s would exceed its whole duration. However to palliate the shortness of our Lives, and somewhat to compensate our brief term in this World, 20 it's good to know as much as we can of it, and also so far as possibly in us lieth to hold such a *Theory* of times past, as though we had seen the same. He who hath thus considered the World, as also how therein things long past have been answered by things present, how matters in one Age have been acted over in another, and how there is nothing new under the Sun, may conceive himself in some manner to have lived from the beginning, and to be as old as the World; and if he should still live on 'twould be but the same thing.

SECT. XXX.

30 LASTLY, if length of Days be thy Portion, make it not thy Expectation. Reckon not upon long Life: think every day the last, and live always beyond thy account. He that so often surviveth his Expectation lives many Lives, and will scarce complain of the shortness of his days. Time past is gone like a Shadow; make time to come present. Approximate thy latter times by present apprehensions of them: be like a neighbour unto the Grave, and think there is but little to come. And since there is something of us that will still live on, join both lives together, and live in one but for the other. He who thus ordereth the purposes of this Life 40 will never be far from the next, and is in some manner already

15 that] rhat *58*

in it, by a happy conformity, and close apprehension of it. And if, as we have elsewhere declared, any have been so happy as personally to understand Christian Annihilation, Extasy, Exolution, Transformation, the Kiss of the Spouse, and Ingression into the Divine Shadow, according to Mystical Theology, they have already had an handsome Anticipation of Heaven; the World is in a manner over, and the Earth in Ashes unto them.

FINIS.

APPENDIX I

THE VERSION OF *A LETTER TO A FRIEND* IN SLOANE MS. 1862 (BRITISH MUSEUM)

This version runs from f. 8 to f. 25 of the manuscript, and the leaves are also numbered separately 1–18, f. 13 being written on both sides. The first leaf, down to 'information', ll. 34–35, has a diagonal line drawn across it, as for erasure. There is no title.

See below, p. 270, for a note on the differences between this version and the printed one. The numbers in square brackets in the margin of this 10 transcription are those of the pages in the printed text where corresponding passages will be found. Some small erasures are disregarded.

*marks the beginning and † the end of passages omitted from the printed version.

Sr

I am sorry you vnderstood so litle concerning that worthy gentleman your deare freind & that I must also performe that vnwelcome office to tell you Ad portam rigidos calces extendit, hee is dead & buried & by this time no punie in the famous nations of the dead. for though hee left this world not many dayes ago, yet 20 euery hower largely addeth vnto that Dark societie. & considering the incessant mortallity of mankind you cannot well conceaue there dyeth in the whole world [*erasure followed by* so *erased*] fewer then a thousand an hower. [179]

Though at this distance you had no particular information of his death yet your affection may cease to wonder you had nott some sense or intimation thereof by dreames, visions, sympathicall communications or thoughtfull whisperings which diuers seeme to haue had at the death of their dearest freinds. for since wee read in that famous story that spirits themselues were fayne to 30 tell their [*erasure*] fellowes at a distance that the great Antonio was comming; wee haue sufficient excuse for our ignorance in such poynts, nor can wee well looke for such secret insinuations butt must rest content in the vsuall way of knowledge by information.

Though the incertainty of the worlds end hath confounded all

36 *On blank leaf opposite*: this Letter may bee added to the Letters in the folio with red leaues.

human prediction yet they which shall liue to see the sunne & moone darkened & the starres to fall from heauen will hardly bee deceaued in the approach of the last daye. And therefore somewhat strange it is that the common fallacy of consumptiue persons who feele not them selues to dye & therefore still hope for life should also reach their freinds in perfect health & judgement that you should bee to [*? read* so] litle acquainted with Plautus sick complexion or that an Hippocraticall face could not alarum you vnto higher feares or rather despayre of his continuance among us vnder 10 such languishing emaciations, wherin medicall predictions fayle not as sometimes in acute diseases, and wherin tis as dangerous to bee condemned by a physitian as a judge.

[180.9] Hee was fruitlesly putt in hope of aduantage by change of ayre and therefore being so farre spent hee quickly found Sardinia in Tibur & the most healthfull ayre of litle effect where death had set his broad arrowe, for hee liued not vnto the middle of May & confirmed the obseruation of Hippocrates of that mortall time of the yeare when the figge tree putts forth [leaues *erased*] his leaf like vnto a choughs clawe ⌐X

[181.8] Angelus victorius giues a serious account of a consumptiue tabid [& *erased*] hecticall & pthysicall woeman who was suddenly cured by the intercession of Ignatius wee read not of any in Scripture who in this case applyed vnto our Sauiour, though some might bee contained in that expression, that hee went about Galilie healing all manner of sicknesse and all manner of disease. Amulets, spells sigills & incantations [vs *erased*] commended in other diseases are seldom or neuer pretended agaynst this, and wee find no Sigill in the Archidoxis of Paracelsus to cure or consumption or Marasmus. which if other diseases fayle must make an end of 30 the longest liuers & putt a period vnto [euen *written above*] [the duration *erased*] of oakes and cedars. so that the stoicks could not butt think the firy principle would [at last *erased*] weare out all the rest and at last make an end of the world. which without such a lingring-period the Creatour may do at his pleasure and to make an end of all things on earth & the planeticall systeme of the world hee need not [butt *written below*] putt out the sunne

[179.35] At my first visit of him I was bold to tell his freinds who had not lett fall all hope of his recouery that in my sad opinion hee was not like to behold a grassehopper agayne much lesse to tast another

20 Angel victorii consultationes 24–25 m. Mathewe 4 23

of the sprouts of that mortall time of the yeare
when the figge tree putts forth branches & its leaf
like unto the choughs claw X

Angelus victorius giues a serious account
of a consumptive tabid & hecticall pthysi-
sicall woeman who was suddenly cured
by the intercession of Ignatius. wee read not
of any in scripture who in this case applyed
unto our saviour, though some might bee
contained in that expression, that hee went
about Galilee healing all manner of sicknesse
and all manner of disease. Amuletts, spells
sigills & incantations recommended in other
diseases are seldome or neuer pretended
agaynst this, and wee find no sigill in the
Archidoxis of paracelsus to cure an extreme consumption or marasmus. which if other diseases
fayle must make an end of the longest livers &
shall a period unto of oakes and
cedars. so that the stoicks could not but thinke
the fiery principle would at last weare out all
things and at last make an end of the world.
which without such a lingring period the creator
may effect at his pleasure and to make an end

From MS. Sloane 1862; f. 10 [3]

(Lines 17–35 opposite)

figge and though it bee not vsuall with mee to forgett the face of freinds yet to knowe him without doubt I was fayne to looke twice upon him & withall I seemd to discouer in him that odde mortall symptome not mentiond by Hippocrates. for hee maintained not his owne countenance butt looked like his grandmother the lines of whose face lay deep & inuisibly in his [before *erased*] healthfull face before.

In this consumptiue condition & remarkable emaciation hee came [183.3] to bee almost half himself and left a great part behind him which hee caryed not to the graue: And though it bee not easie to 10 [assent *erased*] giue a full assent vnto the account [story *written above*] of Count Ernestus mansfeild that after his death his heart was found [to bee *erased*] not to bee [so *erased*] no bigger [as *erased*] then a wallnutt, yet if the bones of a good Sceleton waigheth litle more then twentie pounds, surely his bowells & flesh remaining could make butt a light course & a short bitt for curruption in st Innocents churchyard. I neuer more liuely beheld the starued characters of Dante in any liuing face. an Aruspex might haue read a Lecture upon him without exenturation. so that to bee caryed sexta ceruice to the graue was butt a ciuill vnnecessity; 20 and the complements of the coffin might outwaigh the subject of it.

Though wee could not haue his life yet wee had our desires in his [180.29] soft departure, which was scarce an expiration. with what strift and paynes wee come into the world wee knowe not and tis commonly no easie matter to get out of it. butt if it could bee made out, that such as haue an easie natiuity haue commonly a hard death and contrarily, his departure was so easie, that wee might iustly suspect his birth was of another nature and that some Juno satt crosse legd at his natiuity. 30

I was not so curious to intitle the fixed starres to any concerne [181.25] in his death yet could not butt obserue that hee dyed when the moone was descending from the meridian at which time an old Italian long ago would persuade mee that the greatest part of men dyed. butt herin I confesse I could neuer satisfie my curiositie. allthough from the time of tides in places upon or neere the sea there may bee considerable deductions.

In the yeares of his childhood hee had languished vnder the disease [184.30] of his country the Rickets. after which notwithstanding I haue seen many to haue become strong & actiue men. butt whether 40

any who haue had the same attained vnto very great yeares, the disease is not yet so old as to afford good obseruation. whether Lamenesse & halting still encreaseth among the inhabitants of Rouigno in Istria I do not vnderstand, yet not twentie yeares ago Monsr de Loyre obserued upon the place that a third part of the inhabitants halted butt to certaine it is that the Rickets encreaseth among us, the small pox growes more pernicious then the great, the kings purse knoweth that the kings euell growes more common and though the ancients giue that disease good words, it
10 is not now rare to heare the bell ring out for [Quartans *erased*] such as dye of Quartans. yet the sound of a bell is not strange that rings out for a Quartan ague. [*Cramped insertion of about two lines, not deciphered.*]

*Some I obserued to wonder how in his tabid consumptiue state his hayre held on so well without that considerable defluuium which is one of the last symptomes in such diseases butt they tooke not notice of a mark in his face which if hee had liued was a probable security agaynst baldnesse if the obseruation of Aristotle will hold that persons are lesse apt to bee bald who are double
20 chinnd, [*erasure*] nor of the varices or knotted veynes in his legge which they that haue, in the same authors assertions are lesse disposed to baldnesse.†

[183.30] Though the beard bee onely made a distinction of sex and signe of masculine heat by Vlmus yet the precocitie & early comming thereof in him was not to bee liked in reference vnto long life. Lewis that virtuous butt vnhappy King of Hungary who was lost at the battail of Mohacz was sayd to bee borne without a skinne, to haue bearded at fifteen & to haue [*erasure*] begunne to showe some gray hayres [at *erased*] about twentie whereby the Diuiners
30 coniectured that hee should bee spoyled of his kingdom and haue butt a short life. butt many persons wee haue knowne early graye who haue outliued Davids period. *Though hayres afford butt fallible coniectures yet wee cannot butt take notice of them. They growe not equally in bodyes after death. woemens sculls afford mosse as well as mens. and the best I haue seen was upon a woemans scull taken up and layd in a roome after 25 yeares buriall. Though the skinne bee made the place of hayres, yet sometimes they are found on the heart and inward parts. The plica or elues locks happen vnto both sexes & being cutt of will
40 come agayne. butt they are wary in cutting the same, for feare of

10 m. *Ασφαλέστατος και ῥήιστος*. febrium securissima et facillima. Hippocrates

20–21 m. according as Theodorus Gaza renders it though Scaliger reades the text otherwise. (See Commentary, p. 289.)

headach & other diseases.† Hayres which most amused mee were those in the Morgellons an endemicall disease of litle children in Languedoc which some times in sharp distempers breake out with harsh hayres on their backs which takes of the vnquiet symptomes of the disease & preserues from conuulsions & coughs.

That Charles the fift was crowned upon the daye of his natiuity, it [182.14] being in his power to order it so makes no singular animaduersion; butt that hee should also take King Francis prisoner upon that day was a notable coincidence that made the same obseruable. King Antipater who had an anniuersary feuer euery yeare on his 10 birthday and dyed at last on the same day needed not an Astrologicall reuolution to knowe what day hee should dye on. when the fixed starres haue made a reuolution vnto the place from whence they first sett out, [many *erased*] some of the Antients thought the world would haue an end, which was a kind of dying upon the daye of its natiuity. Now the disease preuayling about the time of his birth [day *erased*] many were of opinion that hee would leaue the world on the daye hee entred into it. butt this being a lingring disease and creeping softly on, nothing criticall was expected or found on that daye, and hee dyed fifteen dayes 20 after. To dye upon the day and euen hower of their natiuity is ordinarie in many Ephemerous children and such as see butt one day. butt in those who outliue many yeares and when there are 3 hundred sixtie fiue dayes to determine our liues in euery yeare; that the first day should make the last that the tayle of the snake should returne into its mouth precisely at that time and, wee should wind up upon the day of our birth is indeed a remarkable coincidence and such which though Astrologie hath taken witty paynes to resolue, yet hath it been very warie in making predictions of it 30

*Affection had so blinded some of his neerest relations as to retaine some hope of a postliminious life and that hee might come to life agayne and therefore would [hau *erased*] not haue had him coffind before the third daye. Some such Virbiusses I confesse wee find in Story and one or two I remember my self butt they liued not long after⟨.⟩ Such contingent reuiuictions are to bee hoped in diseases wherein the lamp of life is butt puft out or seemingly choaked, & not where the oyle is quite spent & exhausted. Though Nonnus will haue it a feuer, yet what disease Lazarus first dyed of is as vncertaine from the text as his second 40 death from good Authentick history. butt since some persons

conceaued to bee dead do sometimes returne agayne vnto euidence of life. that miracle was wisely managed by our Sauiour. for had hee not been dead 4 dayes & vnder corruption, there had not wanted enough who would haue cauilled the same. which the scripture now putts out of doubt & tradition also confirmeth. That hee liued thirtie yeares after and being [*erasure*] pursued by the Iewes came by sea into [vnto (?)] prouence by marseilles with marie magdalen maximinus & others where [vnto this day *erased*] remarkable places carry their names or memories vnto this daye⟨.⟩
10 butt to arise from the graue to returne agayne vnto it is butt an vnconfortable [is no satisfactory *written above*] reuiuiction⟨.⟩ few men would bee content to cradle it once agayne. [*insertion not deciphered*] except a man could lead his second life better then the first a man may bee doubly condemned for [*erasure* (?) 2 euell] liuing euelly twice. which were butt to make the second death in scripture the third and to accumulate in the punishment of 2 bad liuers at the last daye. To haue performed the duty of corruption in the graue, to [aris *erased*] liue agayne as farre from sinne as death and arise like our Sauiour for euer, are the [confortable *erased*] only
20 satisfactio ns ofwell wayghed expectations.†

[188.9] In this deliberate & creeping progresse vnto his end, hee was somewhat to yong and of to noble a mind to fall into that stupid accident [symptome *written above*] obseruable in diuers [toward *erased*] neere their iourneys end & proues a mortall symptome [signe *written above*] in their last sicknesse that is to bee narrowe minded parsimonious miserable & tenacious, vnready to part with anything when they are ready to part with all and afrayd to want when they haue butt a few dayes [of *erased*] or howers of life to spend any thing they haue [when they haue no time to spend
30 *written below*] meanewhile physitians who knowe that many are made butt in a single depraued imagination and one preualent delirium [dicipiency *written above*] and that [men *erased*] out of this single delirium, a man may meet with sober actions & good sense in Bedlam cannot butt smile to see the heirs & concerned relations [grat *erased*] to gratulate themselues in the sober departure of their freinds and though they behold such [irrationall *erased*] couetous & mad passages are content to think they dye in good vnderstanding & in their [*erasure*] sober senses. Auarice which is not only Idolatrie butt infidelity, nether from couetous progenie or questuary
40 education had no root in his [christian *erased*] brest, who made good works the expression of his fayth and was bigge with desires to publick & lasting charities. & surely where good wishes and

charitable intentions exceed abillities, Theoricall beneficency may bee more then a dreame. They build not castles in the ayre who would build churches upon earth & though they leaue no such structures [on earth *erased*] heere may lay good foundations in heauen.

Iulius Scaliger who in a sleepelesse fitt of the goutc could make [187.37] 2 hundred verses in a night would haue butt fiue plaine words upon his tomb, and this serious person though [hee were *erased*] no minor poet [left the poetry of his epithite vnto others yet vnwilling *erased*] left the poetrie of his epitaph vnto others ether 10 vnwilling to commend himself, or to bee iudged by a distich, and perhaps considering how vnhappy great poets haue been in versifiyng their owne epitaphs, wherin petrarcha Dante & Ariosto haue so vnhappily fayled that if their [epitaphs *erased*] tombs should outlast their works posterity would find so litle of Apollo in them as to mistake them butt for Ciceronian poets.

[Not *erased*] Nether to feare death nor desire it was not his resolu- [189.11] tion, to bee dissolued & bee with Christ was his sick dittie—though his yeares were not many yet would hee oft complayne nimio de stamine and thought hee had liued to long to see on 20 earth one Lustre more then his Sauiour. his life and death were [188.32] such that I would not blame them who wished [to *erased*] the like [him *inserted*] and almost to haue been himself. almost I say; for though wee may wish the [happy *erased*] prosperous appurtenances of others, or to bee an other in his happy accidents, yet so intrinsecall is euery man vnto himself, that some doubt may bee made whether any one would exchange his being or substantially become another man

Hee had wisely seen the world at home and abroad and therin obserued vnder what varietie men are deluded in the pursuit of 30 that which is not heare to bee found⟨.⟩ And though hee [held *erased*] had no opinion of [(?) reputed] felicities belowe & thought men were widely out in the estimate of such happinesse, yet his sober contempt of the world wrought no democritisme or cynicisme no laughing or snarling at it. There are not reall felicities enough in nature to satisfie a serious mind. and therefore to soften the streame of our liues, wee are fayne to take in the receaued contentations of the world, to vnite with the crowd in their beatitudes, & so make ourselues happy by consortion, opinion, & coimagination. for strictly to [confine *erased*] separate from 40 reputed and customarie felicities and to confine vnto the rigour

8 m. Iulii Ca'saris Scaligeri quod fuit

of reallities were to contract the consolation of our beings vnto confortlesse circumscriptions.

[190.23] Though age had not set his seale of yeares upon his face yet [a man *erased*] a dimme sight [(?) eye] might haue cleerely discouered threescore in his Actions & so [*erasure*] although his yeares were not many hee might bee sayd to haue equalld the dayes of longer liuers, since in the [iudgment] compute of Solomon wisedome is the gray hayre vnto men and an vnspotted life is old age. And certainly if wee deduct all those dayes which wee might wish 10 vnliued, & which take away the confort of those wee now liue: if wee Reckon only those dayes which god hath accepted of our liues the thred of our dayes at fourscore will hardly bee a spanne long, the sonne in this sence may bee elder then the father, and none bee climacterically old. hee that early arriueth vnto the parts and prudence of age is happily old without the vnconfortable marks of it. tis superfluous to liue vnto gray hayres, when in a timely [precocious *written above*] complexion wee anticipate the virtues of them. hee cannot bee accounted yong who outliueth the old man. hee that [arriveth *erased*] hath early arrived vnto the 20 measure of a perfect stature in Christ hath fullfilled the best & longest intention of his being. and one day liued after the perfect rule of pietie is to bee preferred before peccant [sinning *written above*] immortallity⟨.⟩ [Lastly *inserted*] Though hee attained not vnto the yeares of his predecessors yet hee wanted not those preseruing virtus which confirmes & strengthens the thred of doubtfull constitutions. Cautelous chastitie & cunning sobrietie were far from him. These virtues were paragon without hayre Ice spot or blemish in him which affords mee a hint to conclude in these good wishes vnto you. Tread softly and circumspectly in this 30 [funamb, narrow tract *erased*] funambulatory tract and [funambulatory *erased*] narrowe path of goodnesse. pursue virtue virtuously. bee sober and temperat, not to preserue your body in a sufficiency for wanton ends, not to spare your purse, not to bee out of the obliquie of common transgressors that way, or thereby to balance or palliat obscure and closer vices, nor simply to enioy health. by all which you may leuen good actions and [make *erased*] render virtues disputable; butt in one word that you may truly serue god, which euery sicknesse will tell you cannot well do without it [health *written above*]; The sick mans sacrifice is butt a Leane 40 [lame *written above*] offering. treasures of pietie layd up in healthfull dayes excuse the defect and impotency of sick performances; with

7–8 m. wisedome 4 (*See note on 190.27.*)

out which wee must needs looke back with anxietie [and impotency *erased*] upon the lost opportunities of health and may haue cause [more *erased*] rather to enuy then pitty the ends of pa'nitent malefactors, who come with cleare parts vnto their last act, and in the integrity of their faculties returne their spirit vnto god that gaue it.

CATALOGUE

Of the Libraries of the Learned

Sir *Thomas Brown*,

AND

Dr. *Edward Brown*, his Son,

Late Preſident of the College of Phyſicians.

Conſiſting of many very Valuable and Uncommon Books, in moſt *Faculties* and *Languages*, Chiefly in

PHYSICK,	DIVINITY,
CHIRURGERY,	PHILOLOGY,
CHYMISTRY,	HISTORY,

And other Polite Parts of *Learning*.

Moſt of the Claſſics *Not Varior.* Old *Elzevir*'s, and other Choice Editions, well Bound, and very Fair.

ALSO

BOOKS of SCULPTURE & PAINTING,

with Choice Manuſcripts.

WHICH

Will begin to be Sold by AUCTION, at the *Black-boy* Coffee-houſe in *Ave-Mary-Lane*, near *Ludgate*, on MONDAY the 8th Day of *January*, 17$\frac{10}{11}$, beginning every Evening at Four of the Clock, till the Sale is finiſh'd.

By **Thomas Ballard**, Bookſeller, at the *Riſing-Sun* in *Little-Britain*.

Where Catalogues may be had; as alſo of Mr. *King* in *Weſtminſter-hall*, Mr. *Stokoe* againſt the Mews Gate, Mr. *Vaillant* againſt *Bedford*-buildings in the *Strand*, Mr. *Brown* without *Temple-bar*, Mr. *Clements* in St. *Paul*'s Church-yard, Mr. *Strahan* in *Cornhill*, Bookſellers, at both Univerſities, and at the Place of Sale. *Pr.* 6*d.*

APPENDIX II

SIR THOMAS BROWNE'S LIBRARY

THE library of books collected by Browne and by his son Dr. Edward Browne was sold by auction in 1711. The title-page of the sale-catalogue is reproduced opposite.

Relatively few of the books have dates later than 1682, the year of Sir Thomas Browne's death, and it can be assumed that most of those dated earlier than 1660 were acquired by him. His son Edward was born in 1644 and died in 1708.

The Catalogue has 60 pages, numbered 1–17, 16 and 17 repeated, 18–58. There are 2,352 items and about 2,890 volumes. The Catalogue is divided into sections according to languages. Ancient languages (mostly Latin) are treated for this purpose as one language and subdivided according to book-sizes and class of subjects; books in modern languages are divided according to book-sizes only.

A. GREEK, LATIN, ETC.

Pp. 1–5. *Libri Theologici.* F°, pp. 1–2, items 1–36; 4°, pp. 2–3, items 1–29; 8°, pp. 3–4, items 1–48; 12°, &c., pp. 4–5, items 1–21.

Pp. 5–17. 16^2–17^2, *Libri Historici, Philologici.* F°, pp. 5–8, items 1–105; 4°, pp. 8–12, items 1–145; 8°, pp. 13–17, items 1–218; 12°, pp. 16^2–17^2, items 1–42; 24°, p. 17^2, items 1–9.

Pp. 17^2–27. *Libri Medici, Philosophici.* F°, pp. 17^2–19, items 1–96; 4°, pp. 19–22, items 1–133; 8°, pp. 23–26, items 1–144; 12° and 24°, pp. 26–27, items 1–69.

Pp. 28–30. *Libri Mathematici.* F°, p. 28, items 1–20; 4°, pp. 28–30, items 1–58; 8°, p. 30, items 1–17; 12°, p. 30, items 1–3.

B. MODERN LANGUAGES

Pp. 31–38. *Livres Francois.* F°, pp. 31–32, items 1–19; 4°, pp. 39–40, items 1–38; 8°, pp. 40–41, items 1–23; 12°, p. 41, items 1–14.

Pp. 41–42. *Libros Espannolos.* F°, p. 41, items 1–3; 4°, p. 42, items 1–9; 8° and 12°, p. 42, items 1–7.

Pp. 42–43. *Libri Teutonicè & Belgicè.* F°, pp. 42–43, items 1–13; 4°, p. 43, items 1–5; 8°, p. 43, items 1–10; 12°, p. 43, items 1–14.

Pp. 44–56. *English Books*. F°, pp. 44–46; items 1–112; 4°, pp. 46–48, items 1–89; 8° and 12°, pp. 48–56, items 1–382.

C. OMISSIONS

Pp. 57–58. *Libri Omissi.* F°, p. 57, items 1–11; 4°, p. 57, items 1–30; 8° and 12°, pp. 57–58, items 1–44; F°, p. 58 (*English Folio's Omitted*), items 1–7.

TEXTUAL NOTES

(The transcriptions from the manuscripts are unmodernized as regards both spelling and punctuation. In some places they differ verbally from those of previous editors.)

RELIGIO MEDICI

Notes marked * record passages, phrases, and single words occurring neither in the manuscripts nor in the editions of 1642, and appearing for the first time in that of 1643.

Notes marked † record passages, &c., not published in 1643 but contained in the earlier version of *RM* as represented by the manuscript at Pembroke College, Oxford (*P*). Some of them are found in other manuscripts and in the editions of 1642. The text of all these passages is taken from *P*.

3. 5. and] of *42 and MSS. except L* (*P has* and *corrected to* of). 18–21. *Facing the end of Section 1 R has on fly-leaf*:

Quousque patiere bone Jesu!
Judæi te semel, Ego Sæpius Crucifixi
Illi in Asia, Ego in Europa,
Illi in Judæa, Ego in Britania
Gallia Germania
Bone Jesu Miscrere mei, et
Judæorum.

31. Prelates] Presbyters *42 and MSS. except PL.*

4. 30–31. violate . . . deface] loose mine arme rather then violate a church window, demolish an image, or deface *P* (*other MSS. and 42 similar*). 33. or] and *MSS.* / *42.* *34. but rather pity *43.*

5. 7. accesse] excesse *PLHJW42b* extasie *NOR.* 17. particular way and] peculiar *MSS.* 18. nationall] naturall *or* their naturall *MSS.* / *42.* *18. together *43.* †35–36. Constitutions:] *MSS.* / *42 add:* Noe man shall wreath my faith to another article, or command my obedience to a cañon more.

6. 8. State of Venice] *Marginal note in HJW*: In theire quarrells with Pope Paul the first [*read* fift]. 11. whom] to whom *MSS.* / *42.* †13. excommunicated] *PL add*: and my posterity

***7.** 7–8. love to *43.* *13. I hope *43.* 13. not] *omitted LW.* 18. *Arethusa*] *Marginal note in HJW*: That looseth it selfe in Greece and riseth againe in Sicilie.

8. 5. *Origen*] the Originists or [and *L*] Chiliasts *PL* the Chiliasts *HJNORW* the *Chiliast 42.* 16–17. from some . . . contain] by an excesse of charity, whereby I thought the number of the liueing too small an obiect for my deuotion; I could scarce [not *PL*] containe *MSS.* / *42.* 17. ringing] ringing out *MSS. except W.*

***8.** 38–**9.** 18. *Section* 8 *added in 43.*

9. 40. believe] believed *MSS. except LW.*

10. 13. knew] know *PL.* 16. *Footnote: Sphæra*] Deus est Sphæra *HJW.*

11. 4. imagination] imaginations *P. See Commentary.* 15. Saint *Paul's* Sanctuary] *Marginal note in PL*: o altitudo 20. have and] haue beene, or *PL.* 24. prescious] previous *PLW.* 25. blast] placet *PL.* 28. *Peter*] Paul *MSS.* instances] instants *MSS. / 42.* 31. thousand] a thousand *MSS. / 42.*

***12.** 27–36. Wisedome . . . know him. *43.* †41. Angels;] *PL add*: there is noe threed or line to guide vs in this Labyrinth;

13. 7. make but] are but *PLO* (but *altered from* not?) *RW42* are not *HJN.* 11. expressions . . . in] impressions . . . on *MSS.* 12. profound] propound *MSS. / 42.* (*Cf.* 14. 24.) *17. still *43.* *18. as yet *43.* 19. small] no *MSS. / 42.* 21. highly] onely *MSS. / 42.*

***13.** 24–**14.** 12. Therefore . . . resurrection. *43.*

14. 24. profound] propound *MSS. / 42.* *28–29. sometimes, and in some things *43.*

15. 10. set] sets *OW 42.* 14. wonders] wonder *PHLO.* 16. have] have therefore *MSS. except W.* 39. ordained] ordained to regulate *P* ordained to guide *42.*

16. 1. because] because it is *PLNORW.* 26. past] past with approbation *HJNRW not in PL* past y[t] approbation *O.* 29. is] is therefore *MSS. except W.*

17. 10. actions] actions that *MSS. / 42.*

18. 3. and] which *PL* and they *NOR.* 29. spirit] spirits *MSS. except W.*

***20.** 6–30. For our . . . my faith. *43.* 22. *Gomorrha*:] *Gomorrha. catchword 43.* *32. or any other *43.*

21. 6. three Impostors] *Marginal note in HJW*: Moses, Christ, and Mahomet.

***22.** 13–15. that she . . . Resurrection. *43.* 24. successive] successively *MSS. / 42.*

22. *Footnote*: In Rabelais] *HJW add*: the French [*or* a ffrench] author.

23. 2. foesible] forcible *P* difficult *or* difficile *other MSS. and 42.* *8. is very strange *43.* †25–35. That Judas . . . land of *Shinar*. These] *P* (*alone*) *reads*: That Judas hanged himselfe tis an absurdity & an affirmative that is not expressed in the text, but quite contrarie to the words & their externall construction; with this paradoxe I remember I netled an angrie Jesuite who had that day let this fall in his sermon, who afterwards vpon a serious perusall of the text, confessed my opinion, & prooved a courteous friend to mee a stranger, and noe enemy; These 27. one

place] *Marginal note in H*: Math. 27. 5. 28–29. another place] *Marginal note in H*: Acts 1. 18. †37. consequence.] *P adds*: to instance in one, or two, as to proove the Trinity from that speech of God in the plurall number faciamus hominem Lett us make man, which is but the common style of princes, and men of eminency; hee that shall reade one of his Ma[ties]. proclamations, may with the same Logicke conclude there bee two Kings in England. To inferre the obedient respect of wiues to their husbands from the example of Sarah, who usually called her husband Lord, which if you examine, you shall finde to be noe more then Seignior, or Mounsieur, which are the ordinarie languages all ciuill nations use in their familiar compellations, not to their superiors or equalls, but to their inferiours allso and persons of Lower condition.

24. 22. doe] to *P* (*cf. l.* 5). †37. *Solomon.*] *P adds*: the sayings of the Seers, and the chronicles of the Kings of Judah; 38. many neerer Authors] anie other author *P* any better author *42 and MSS. except P.*

24. 38–**25.** 1. somewhat] too much *MSS.* / *42.*

25. 3. three great inventions] *Marginal note in HJW*: Gunnes printing. The Mariners compasse. 17. ashamed] amazed *42 and MSS. except W.*

26. 16. valour] nature *P* (*but cf. H*, 117. 3). 17. true] the true *MSS. except JW.* 38–39. He must . . . sayes] What false divinity is it if I say *P*. Is it [*or* It is] false divinity if I say *42 and other MSS.* 41. be] be called *42 and MSS. except W.*

27. 2. *Socrates*] *In marginal note instead of in text HJW; in other MSS. neither in text nor in margin.* 4. Bishop] *Marginal note in HJW*: Virgilius 6. living] life *MSS.* / *42.* 8–9. are not many . . . feare] is not a man . . . feares *MSS.* / *42.* 27. by] of *MSS. except W.* of] and *MSS. except W.* 33. had him] him have *P.* done] do *1764.*

28. 3. things] things but sinne *MSS.* / *42.* *13–37. *Section 28 added in 43.*

***29.** 19. as some will have it *43.* 21. this] this very *MSS.* 30. be] see *P.* 36. a power] the power *MSS.* / *42.*

30. 12. Maid of Germany] *Marginal note in HJW*: That liued without meate vpon the smell of a rose. 24. derived] diuined *JNOW.* to one] from one to *P* to *other MSS. and 42.* 27. of good] both of good *P.*

***31.** 2. and *43.* 12–13. This . . . waters] *Marginal note in HJW*: Spiritus domini incubabat acquis Gen: 1.
15. despaire] and despaire *MSS.* / *42.* 31, 32. *Between these two lines MSS.* / *42 have the two following lines*:

> Keepe still in my Horizon, for to mee,
> Tis not the Sunne that makes the day, but thee. (*Text of 42*)

Cf. 72. 5–6.

***32.** 4. an old one *43.* 21. definition of *Porphyry*] *Marginal note in HJW*: Essentia rationalis immortalis 23. man] tis thought, man *1678.*

33. 4. denied . . . knowledge of] denied that they know *MSS.* deemed that they know not *42.* 5–6. thoroughly] truly *MSS.* / *42.* 7. *of*] in *MSS. except W.* *7. those in *43.* 8. worke] words *P.* 17. probabilitie] probabilities *MSS.* / *42.* 19. forme] frame *MSS. except W.* 25. neare] nearer *MSS. except W.* 38. some parts] *Marginal note in HJW*: The element of fire.

34. 7. as] as beyond *1678.* 8. affection] affections *MSS. except W.* †33. Philosophers,] *P adds*: who saw noe further then the first matter 34. all is salved] has [*or* hath] salved all *MSS. except W* salv'd all *W 42.*

***34.** 39–**35.** 2. and herein . . . essence *43.*

35. 13. have the] have in *HJW sentence not in NOR.* 22. *Antimetathesis*] *not in O*: Antanaclasis *other MSS. and 42 with marginal note in HJW*: A figure in Rhetorick, where one word is inverted upon an other. *35. and in all acceptions *43.* 40. hand] nearer Ubi *MSS.* / *42.*

***36.** 5–7. and this . . . receive it. *43.* 13. Resurrection] Restauration *MSS.* / *42.* 19. selves.] selves, and yet do live and remaine our selves *MSS.* (*added in W*); *passage not in P.*

37. 19. of this] in this *HJNR* (*not in O*). 21. of a] a *W 42.* †**37.** 22. death;] *MSS. add*: It is a symptome of Melancholy to be afraid of death; and yet sometimes to desire it, this latter I have often discouered in my selfe, and thinke noe man euer desired life as I have sometimes death; *33. highly *43.* 39. hopelesse] too careless [*or* careless] *MSS.* / *42.*

38. 25. something more then] nothing else but *MSS.* / *42.* perfect] perfectest *PHJNOR.* gold] god *PJNOR.* †33. discover.] *P adds*: I haue therefore forsaken those strict definitions of Death, by priuation of life, extinction of naturall heate, separation &c. of soule & body, & have fram'd one in an hermiticall way unto mine owne fancie; est mutatio ultima, quâ perficitur nobile illud extractum Microcosmi, for to mee that consider things in a naturall and experimentall way, man seemes to bee but a digestion or a preparatiue way unto that last and glorious Elixar which lies imprison'd in the chaines of flesh &c 40. Wife] wives *MSS. except P.*

39. 32. Jubilee] *Marginal note—HJW*: The Jewish computacion for 50 [500 *H*] yeares 33. *Saturne*] *Marginal note in HJW*: The planet of Saturne makes his revolution once in 30 yeares. 37. shaked] shaken *MSS.* / *42.*

40. 1. delight] delight: *1678.* dayes,] dayes. *HJ* daies: *R.* 3. Pantalones] *Marginal note in HJW*: A french word for Anticks. 25. precedes] proceeds *MSS.* / *42.* †27–38. And though . . . threescore.] *This replaces the following sentences occurring in MSS.* / *42* (*P also omits*

Section 42 up to this point): the course & order of my life would bee a verie death unto others, I use my selfe to all diets, aires, humours, hunger, thirst, heate; cold, I cure not my selfe by heate; when sicke, not by physicke; those that understand how I liue may iustly say I regard not life, nor stand in feare of Death. (*The text of P, with amended punctuation.*) 32. instruct] instructs *1672*.

***40. 40–41.** 22. *Section 43 added in 43*.

41. 25. understand] understand them *MSS.* understand it *42*. *37. and suicide *43*.

42. 4. sure] surely *MSS. except HW*. *9–31. Men that looke . . . our owne *43*. 39. *Horæ combustæ*] *Marginal note in HJW*: That tyme when the moone is in coniunction and obscured by the Sunne, the Astrologers call horæ combustæ

43. 21. force] fire *MSS. except W*. 23. Some] I *MSS. / 42*. 26. them] me *MSS. / 42*. 29. any such] any *MSS. except P*.

44. 3–4. devill of *Delphos*] *Marginal note in HJW*: The Oracle of Apollo †11. of new.] *P adds*: those prognostickes of Scripture are obscure, I know not how to construe them; †17. these many yeares] manie hundreds of yeares allready and hath outliud his daies *P*. †18. freely,] *MSS. add*: omitting those ridiculous Anagrams *Marginal note to this in HJW*: whereby men laboure to proue the Pope Antichrist from theire names making the number of the beast. †opinion] Paracelsus opinion and thinke *MSS.* (*not in 42*). 18–19. that Antichrist is] Antichrist *MSS. except W* (*not in 42*). 21. hardly any] no *MSS. / 42*.

45. 3–4. deare] dearest *P*. 14. fruit] fruits *MSS.*

†46. 2. millions.] *MSS. / 42 add*: what is made to be immortall, nature cannot nor will the voice of god destroy; these bodies wee behold to perish were in their created natures immortall, and liable to death but accidentally, & upon forfeit; therefore they owe not that naturall homage unto death, as other creatures but may bee restored to immortality by a lesser miracle, and by a bare and easie reuocation of the curse returne immortall 4. thousand] a thousand *MSS. / 42*. 12. sensible] suttle *HW 42*. 15. is made] I make *MSS. / 42*. which] and *MSS. / 42*. 26. to] for to *MSS.*

†47. 9. vacuitie,] *P adds*: or place exempt from the naturall affection of bodies,

48. 4. calcin'd] *Marginal note in HJW*: Calcination a chymicall terme for the reduction of a minerall into powder. 6. admire] adore *MSS. / 42*. †7. consumeth not] *P adds*: neither in its substance, weight or vertue 19. proper] powerfullest *MSS. except W*. †21. affirm,] *MSS. / 42 add*: yea & urge scripture for it, 27. selves] senses *MSS. except HW*. 29. it doth] they doe *P*.

***49.** 4–18. Surely . . . immortality. *43*. 32. can hardly] cannot *MSS. / 42*. 33. fairest] surest *MSS. except W*.

†**50.** 8. attributes] *P adds*: of the Allmighty 14. Fine] boxe of the ear *P lacuna in other MSS.* whipping *in margin of N.* *21. and *43.* 23. nature] natures *MSS. except W.* 28. to expect] expect *MSS. except W.*

***51.** 29. beside *43.*

52. 17. *Chiron*] *Marginal note in HJ*: Chiron a Centaure

***52.** 24–**53.** 10. *Section 56 added in 43.*

53. 17. can hardly] cannot *MSS. / 42.* 23. Word] Law *MSS. except W.*

54. 10. little] much *PH* little *corrected to* much *W.* *15. in some sense *43.* *19–21. and thus . . . *Cain. 43.* *23. onely *43.* 24. merit] merits *MSS.*

55. 24. for to] to *P*; *corruptions of* for to *in other MSS. and 42.* †29. nothing,] *MSS. / 42 add*: neither plant, animal, or spirit, *30–31. any essence but *43.* 31. any thing] him *MSS. / 42.* †33. hatred] hatred which [that] I can safely say *MSS.*

56. 6–7. in account of] of *JNRO* (*passage not in P*). 9. them] him *1672 &c.* 12. another Filed] and filed *MSS. / 42* (*not in P*). 19. they] that *HJNORW* (*not in P*) therewith *42.* †23. noble vertue] *P adds*: that with an easier measure of grace I maie obtaine it. 30. to] only to 1678. 38. anothers] others *42 and MSS. except P.* 39. as erroneous a] an erroneous *MSS. / 42.* conceit] course *MSS.*

†**57.** 1. occasions;] *P adds*: buy out of God a facultie to bee exempted from it. 16. doe make] make *MSS. / 42.* †20. figures] lines and figures *PHJNW.* 29. did after] doe yet *MSS. / 42.* 30. retained] retaine *MSS. / 42.* might] maie *MSS. / 42.*

†**58.** 3. Copy.] *P adds*: I rather wonder how allmost all plants being of one colour yet should bee all different herein, and their seuerall kinds distinguished in one accident of Vert. 33. treasure] treasurie *42 and MSS. except P.*

59. 3. an affection] our affections *MSS. / 42.* 15. remaines] remaine *MSS. / 42.* many controversies] one [*or* a] controversie *MSS. / 42.* 18. How doth] How doe *P* so doe *other MSS.* so doth *42.* †19. Jupiter.] *MSS. / 42 add*: how manie Synods haue beene assembled, and angerly broken up about a line in propria quae maribus? **Footnote 43.* 22. slaine] stained *JNORW* strained *H* shamed *42.* 24. *Actius* his razor] *Marginal note in HJ*: that cutt a whetstone in two 26. in the shock] the shock *P* shock] stroke *42 and MSS. except P.* in the fury] the fury *PHJNOR.*

60. 2. few] as few *MSS.* (*sentence not in P*). 16. rave] raile *MSS. / 42.* 22. prophan'd] hereditary *JNRO lacuna in HW* common *42* (*passage not in P*). 30. persists] persist *1669–1685.*

***61.** 28. I thinke *43.*

†62. 1. peaceably] *P adds* within its owne bankes, is] are *MSS. except P.* †12–13. possibilities] easie possibilities *MSS. / 42.* †13. examples of] *P adds*: Nisus & Euryalus, *14. mee thinkes . . . grounds *43.* 23. Wifes] Wives *MSS.* 27 conceive I may love] confesse [*or* confesse that] I love *MSS. / 42.* †30–32. From hence . . . love of God.] *This replaces the following sentence found in P*: These indiuiduall sympathies are stronger, & from a more powerfull hand, then those specificall Vnions.

63. 12. he that . . . will] he cannot love . . . ardour, that will *42 and MSS. except P.* *19–20. contentedly *43.* 21. for] of *OW.* †23. mirth] *MSS. / 42 add*: & at Tauerne [*or* and at a Tavern] 27. supplication] zealous orizon *P* zealous oration *other MSS. and 42.* 34. uncharitable] malevolous *MSS. except W.*

***64.** 1. can *43.* 8. this] and that this *PHJNOW* and this *R 42.* 22. some others] them *P* others *MSS. except W.* *29–38. For there are . . . any of these *43.*

†65. 2. mortality:] *P adds*: I detest my owne nature, and in my retir'd meditation, cannot withold my hands from violence on my selfe, 6–7. constellations] starres *MSS. / 42.*

66. 1–2. most of] almost all *MSS. / 42.* 9. Fisherman] Fishermen *1682.* 36–37. commend . . . twice] am resolved never to be married twice *MSS. / 42.* *38. some times and *43.*

67. 1. world] woman *PHJNOR.* †2. rib] rib onely *MSS. / 42.* 3. be content] wish *MSS. / 42.* 13. musicke] a musicke *MSS. except W.* 13. the beauty] beauty *P.* †15. sound] vocall sound *MSS. / 42.* 22. all] our *MSS. / 42.* †23. obedience] Catholicke obedience *MSS. / 42.* 23. doe imbrace] am obliged to maintaine *MSS. / 42.* 26. the first Composer] my Maker *MSS. 42.* †31–32. eares of God.] *MSS. / 42 add*: it unties [vnites *P*] the ligaments of my frame, takes mee to peeces, dilates mee out of my selfe, and by degrees (Mee thinkes) resolues mee into heauen. (*In P this sentence follows* musique, *l. 12.*) 8. falls] fall *42 and MSS. except O* fell *O.*

68. 7. sometimes] oftentimes *MSS. except W.* 10. scarce] no [*or* not] *42 and MSS. except P* an *P.* 17. any] any way *NOR.* 23–24. ofttimes . . . predecessours] the [*or* did the] 4th figure *MSS. / 42.* 28. Divinity] Divinity can *PH.* 30. shall] they shall *P.*

69. 10. of most] of the most *P* of *other MSS. and 42.* 17. man without a Navell] Marginal note in *HJW*: Adam. whom I conceaue to want a navill, because he was not borne of a woman.

†70. 7. shoulders.] *P adds*: & though I seeme on earth to [*read* do] stand on tiptoe in heauen. *7–20. The earth . . . Alphabet of man. *43.* †21–22. I am as happy . . . desire] *This replaces the following found in MSS. / 42*: I am the happiest man aliue, I haue that in mee can conuert pouerty into riches, transforme aduersity into prosperity; I am more invulnerable then Achilles, fortune hath not one place to hit mee; †28 senses;]

MSS. / *42 add*: with this I can bee a king without a crowne, rich without a stiver [Royalty *42 and MSS. except P*], in heauen though on earth enioy my friend, and embrace him at a distance when I cannot behold him;

***71.** 13. me thinkes *43.* 22–23. it is . . . sometimes] I observe that men oftentimes *MSS.* / *42.* 25. begins] beginning *P* being *NOR with the text in the following order*: beginnes to reason like it selfe, (And being to be freed from the Ligaments of the body) to discourse . . . (*text of N.*). *29–35. Tis indeed . . . discover it. *43.* †39. world,] *P adds*: And truly tis a fit time for our deuotion, & therefore I cannot laie downe my head without an Orizon, 31. dormitive] *Marginal note in HJ*: The name of an extract, wherewith wee use to provoke sleepe. 36. often] also *MSS.* / *42.* *41. I thinke *43.*

73. 9–10. if we doe but speculate] *bracketed in P.* 9–10. speculate] speculate) to *P.* 13 substance] sublime *42 and MSS. except P.* 23–24. surely . . . have not] I can justly boast I am as charitable as some who have built Hospitals, or *MSS.* / *42.* †28. my selfe;] *MSS.* / *42 add*: when I am reduc'd to the last tester, I loue to diuide it to the poore.

74. 11. prophecy of Christ] *Marginal note in HW*: The poore ye shall haue alwayes with you.

75. 3. *Copernicus*] *Marginal note in JW*: Who holds the Sunne is the center of the World. 12. *Pliny*,] *Pliny*, a tale of *Boccace* or *Malizspini*, *1678.* *15. thy selfe and *43.* 20. wisedome] justice *MSS. 42.* 21. undoing] damnation *42 and PHW*; *sentence omitted in other MSS.* †22. FINIS.] *P subjoins*: Triuni Deo sit gloria in æternum Amen.

HYDRIOTAPHIA

107. 23–24. body. And] *? read* body, and (*see Commentary*).

114. 5. unlike] like *editors* (*see Commentary*).

115. 11. *Tartara's*] *Tartarus 58* (4°).

116. 3–5. Were the . . . dye,] *In S62, f. 48*: Could wee truly apprehend heauen or were they [*read* the] happinesse of the next world as sensible as that of this it were a martyrdome to liue, & to those who conceue noe life after death it is an hell to dye.

117. 35–**118.** 5. It is the . . . natures.] *In S62, f. 3*: Tis the coldest thought that melancholy can cast upon the spirit of a man to tis the [col *erased*] heauiest stone that melancholy can throwe at [the spirit of *erased*] a man to tell him hee is at the end of his nature or that there is noe higher state of being to come vnto which this [seemes *erased*] is progressionall & without which this seemes to be made in uayne without which it [were butt *erased?*] might seeme butt rationall madnesse to murmur at this condition to wish that Adam had fallen lower, wherein [? whereby] [we might haue had the happinesse *erased*] by knowing noe higher creation & deeper ignorance of our selues [*replacing* natures *erased*] wee [were *erased*] might haue enioyned [*read* enioyed] the happinesse of inferior creatures, whoe [*two lines erased*] whoe in tranqullity [enioy *erased*] possesse theire constitutions, as hauing not the apprehension to deplore theire owne natures.

120. 8–21. But in . . . last day] *In S62, f. 78*^{v}: Whereas in this later scene of time wee cannot [with Christianity *erased*] expect such durable mumies of our names. tis [to late to bee ambitious *erased*] the great mutations of the [earth *erased*] are acted the time of its destruction dayly hoped, inuayne wee study monuments whose continuance wee must not hope: [*all from* to late *above to* hope *crossed out*] tis to late to bee ambitious [*erasure*] tis to late to bee ambitious the great mutations of the world are acted the time of its destruction dayly hoped, our memorys must bee disproport [? ionable] to our designes & the world world may bee to short for our designes it is a folly to build pyramids or expect the preseruation of [our li *erased*] the life of our memories by monuments whose death wee pray for & whose whose duration [? durition] must whose [deaths wee not *erased*] wee cannot hope, without iniurie of our expectation in the aduent of ye last [happy *written below*] day (*Some abbreviated words expanded; two or three readings uncertain.*) 17. or time] our time *conj. J. Sparrow.*

120. 26. Pyramids . . . snow] Christian ambition . . . looking on the [?] butt as a candle & the pyramids as a pillar of snowe. *S62, f. 81.*

121. 15–17. But . . . Pyramids?] the ill successe of our ambitions and the vnconfortable thought that time may soe obscure us, as euen to question the most reuered existences, is able to cast ice upon our flames & choake the [? flames] of all vayn glories who can butt pitty the founder of the pyramids *S62, f. 81.*

122. 30. contriving] continuing *conj. J. Sparrow.*

123. 5. and *Osyris* in the Dogge starre.] & Noahs Arck in [Argus *erased*] in the shipp of Argos *S62, f. 79*^{v} (*part of isolated note*). 11–13. There is . . . destruction,] *In S62, f. 80*^{v}: in breif there is nothing truly immortal butt immortallity [? the] what euer had noe beginyng may bee confident of noe end all others hold there duration with depending and are butt precariously immortall Aristotle therefore who held the world had noe beginning is not to bee condemned for affirming it had noe end [*two lines erased*] (*The last sentence,* 'Aristotle . . . noe end', *apparently not published before.*)

125. 8–11. 'Tis all one . . . Adrianus.] whereby men are contented with six foote of any & [*erasure*] & rest as satisfactory rest in a church yard as under the Moles & ambitious pyle of Adrianus *S62, f. 81*^{v} (*isolated*).

THE GARDEN OF CYRUS

Manuscript material for this work is generally of less interest than that for *H*, *LF*, and *CM*. See *K*, v, pp. 203–5, and J. S. Finch, *Publications of the Modern Language Association*, 55/2, 1940, pp. 742–7, 'Early Drafts of *The Garden of Cyrus*'. The following notes perhaps indicate the most important correspondences.

129. 7–27. That *Vulcan* . . . the earth.] *There is a rough draft of this in S82, f. 4*^{v}*. See Finch, p. 745.*

129. 26–**130.** 15. Gardens . . . the Earth.] *Wilkin and later editors have connected with this a passage in S47, f. 48ᵛ, which although concerned with ancient gardens seems not certainly to have been intended for GC. See K, iv, p. 126.*

131. 17. *Strebæus*] *altered (incorrectly) in two copies of 58 to* Stebæus

136. 28. continued] *? read* contained *See Commentary.*

139. 7. *Chet mat*] chec-mate *1669.* continue] *? read* containe 16. division] divisions *C (one copy).*

148. 3–6. That bodies . . . earth] *In S82, f. 1.* 3 That bodies . . . spirits] That euery body is first a spirit *S82.* 4 seems . . . by] is also verified from the exp⟨r⟩ession of *S82 (see Finch, p. 744).*

152. 10–24. much . . . comb] *Cf. S66, ff. 4, 5, and 4ᵛ; K, v, pp. 203–4.* 25–27. *Favago* . . . resemblance] *Cf. S66, f. 6; K, v, p. 204.* 27–30. He that . . . nature] *Cf. S66, f. 5; K, v, p. 204.*

156. 22–23. *Osmond* . . . Pisces] *Cf. R, f. 24; K, v, p. 205.*

168. 13–18. Whether . . . speculation] *In S82, f. 1, in two drafts, the first rough and the second much the same as the printed version. See Finch, pp. 743–4.*

173. 13. why] *? read* why since *(cf. l. 15).*

A LETTER TO A FRIEND

See Appendix I (pp. 249–57) for the autograph version of this work in its earlier and shorter form (British Museum, MS. Sloane 1862), containing many variant readings and three passages not included in the printed version. In order that the differences between the two texts may be easily found the passages common to both are indicated in the margins of the Appendix. The three passages peculiar to the manuscript are also marked off. Those peculiar to the printed version are the following: 180. 3–8, 180. 15–28, 181. 6–8, 181. 31–182. 13, 183. 17–29, 184. 9–29, 185. 9–187. 36, 189. 25–end. The passages which (with variants) are common to *LF* and *CM* are indicated in the notes below.

182. 14–20. That *Charles* . . . dye on.] *In S69, f. 12ᵛ (see K, v, p. 242).* 15. makes . . . Animadversion] caryeth no unmachable consideration *S69.* 17. unexpected Coincidence] concurrence of accidents 18–20. *Antipater* . . . dye on] Antipater that dyed on his birthdaye & had an Anniuersary feuer all his life vpon the day of his natiuitie, needed not an Astrologicall reuolution of his natiuitie to knowe the day of his death.

184. 32. have been become] have become *Wilkin, Gardiner* I have seen become *Hazlewood Reprint, Keynes* I haue seen many to haue become *S62.*

189. 3–10. There are not . . . Circumscriptions] *As well as in S62, f. 22 (see 255. 27–256. 3), this passage occurs on f. 43 of the same manuscript and in S69, f. 16. It may have been in error that the word* enough *was omitted after* Felicities *in the printed text* (l. 3). 4. soften] sweeten *S62, f. 43, S69.* 5–6. to unite . . . Beatitudes] & to [?] opinions into reallities

S62, f. 43. 7. for strictly to] To *S62, f. 43.* 10. unto too uncomfortable] into to narrowe [comfortlesse *written above*] *S62, f. 43.*

191. 5–6. Tread . . . virtuously: *CM*, 203. 3–4. 6. virtuously] for itself or at least for the noblest ends that attend it *S69.* 6–16. pursue . . . Non-performances;] *In S69*, ff. 25–26 (*see K, v, p. 251*). 6–10. be sober . . . Health, *CM*, 204. 13–17. 8–9. not to . . . Transgressors] not to procure the name of a sober & temperate person & so to bee out of the list of common offenders *S69.* 10. palliate . . . closer] obscure thy closer & hidden *S69.* 10–12. by all . . . disputable. *CM*, 203. 4–5. 11–12. render Virtues disputable] tread away from true virtue *S69.* 12–20. but in . . . gave it. *CM*, 204. 17–26. 12–13. which every . . . Health] which in sicknesse you will easily find you cannot doe *S69.* 14. Oblation.] offering. Remember thy creator in the dayes of thy youth & lay up a treasure of pietie in thy healthfull dayes. & conserue thy heath [*read* health] in the first place for that intention. *S69, f. 26.* 21–37. Consider . . . Glory. *CM*, 203. 9–30.

191. 38–**192.** 2. He that . . . *Origen*'s. *CM*, 204. 4–10.

192. 3–9. Be charitable . . . Baskets. *CM*, 204. 28–34. 10–19. Trust not . . . Grave. *CM*, 205. 31–206. 2. 20–28. If Avarice . . . Folly. *CM*, 205. 21–29.

192. 29–**193.** 5. Persons . . . unto them. *CM*, 206. 4–18.

193. 6–11. Let not . . . *Sinai.* *CM*, 206. 29–34. 12–20. Make not . . . Vertues. *CM*, 206. 20–27. 21–26. Tho humane . . . Regression. *CM*, 215. 16–23. 29–38. Owe not . . . Statues. *CM*, 207. 25–35.

193. 39–**194.** 5. Let Age . . . in Heaven. *CM*, 207. 14–23.

194. 6–23. While thou . . . in Heaven. *CM*, 208. 8–26. 23–27. Let not . . . revenge thee. *CM*, 207. 37–208. 6.

194. 28–**195.** 8. Be substantially . . . himself. *CM*, 209. 24–37.

195. 14–17. Rest not . . . thy self. *CM*, 203. 32–204. 2. 18–23. Give no . . . of himself. *CM*, 209. 7–11. 23–29. The politick . . . himself. *CM*, 209. 16–22.

195. 30–**196.** 4. Lastly . . . of it. *CM*, 246. 30–247. 1.

Additional Note

Sir Geoffrey Keynes (*K*, i, pp. 188–9) cites from The Commonplace Book of Elizabeth Lyttelton some observations on consumption perhaps intended for *LF* but not obviously connected with any part of it.

CHRISTIAN MORALS

* marks the beginning and † the end of sentences in the notes apparently not published before. [. . .] indicates a word or words not deciphered. The passages which (with variants) are common to *CM* and *LF* are indicated in the notes below. A number of unimportant erasures and alterations are not recorded.

203. 3–4. Tread softly . . . virtuously: *LF*, 191. 5–6. 4–5. Leven . . . disputable. *LF*, 191. 10–12. 9–30. Consider . . . Glory. *LF*, 191. 21–37.

203. 32–**204.** 2. Rest not . . . thy self. *LF*, 195. 14–17.

204. 2. within thy self.] *The following has been printed by Wilkin and others as from S48, with the suggestion that it could appropriately have been inserted here. It is not, however, conjoined in the manuscript with any part of CM and may not have been intended for this work. Text from S48, f. 161*:

To restrayne the Rise of extrauagances and timely to ostracize the most ouergrowing enormities makes a calme and quiet state in the dominion of our selues. for vices haue their ambitions and will bee aboue on another butt though many may possesse us yet is there commonly one that hath [possession of us *erased*] the dominion ouer us, one that lordeth ouer all & the rest remaine butt slaues vnto the humor of it. such towring iniquities are not to bee temporally exostracized, butt perpetually exild or rather to bee serued like the ranck poppies in Tarquins garden & made shorter by the head for the sharpest arrowes are to be lett flye agaynst [at *written above*] all such imperious vices who [ich *written above*] nether enduring priority or equallity Caesarean or Pompeian primity must command [bee absolute *written above*] ouer all for these opprobiously dominate us here and cheifly condemne us hereafter and must [will *written above*] stand in capitall letters ouer our heads as the titles of our sufferings 4–10. He that . . . *Origen's*. *LF*, 191. 38–192. 2. 13–26. Be Temperate . . . gave it. *LF*, 191. 6–10, 12–20. 28–34. Be Charitable . . . baskets. *LF*, 192. 3–9. 36–38. there may . . . poor; *In S43, f. 14 (isolated)*: There is an Atropos of fortune as well as of fate which often cutts of our felicities before our liues whereby so many before old age arrive vnto [their *erased*] euill dayes, and such as they may iustly say, they haue no pleasure in them.

205. 2–6. Give . . . Mercies.] *In R, f. 37*. 12–18. For since . . . again.] *R, f. 37*: Since hee who hath mercy on the poore lendeth vnto the mightie Rewarder christian liberallity is the most thriving policy and charity may proue more then centesimall vsurie. hee who thus casteth his bread upon the waters though it may seeme to bee lost will surely find it agayne and what hee aduentures in a Cockboat may returne in a Carrack vnto him 21–29. If Avarice . . . Folly. *LF*, 192. 20–28.

205. 31–**206.** 2. Trust not . . . grave. *LF*, 192. 10–19.

206. 4–18. Persons . . . unto them. *LF*, 192. 29–193. 5. 20–27. Make not . . . Virtues. *LF*, 193. 12–20. 29–34. Let not the Law . . . *Sinah*. *LF*, 193. 6–11.

206. 36–**207.** 2. Live by . . . another.] *In S47, f. 196, which adds*: modestie will neuer quitt its title fortitude will not bee degraded into Audacitie & foolhardinesse, continency will neuer endure the name [*half-line blank*] liberallity will not bee putt of with the [*erasure*] of prodallity [*read* prodigallity] nor frugallity [*erasure*] exchange its name with Auarice &

sordid parsimonie nor vrbanitie [with scurrillity *erased*] bee swallowd in scurrillity or veracity [. . .] [*erasure*] nor [*erasure*] our vices bee exalted into virtues & to bee stamped by opinion & not the euerlasting rule of right reason. [*no continuation.*]

207. 4–12. though . . . uncorrupted] *As follows in R, f. 41, after* men of all ages (*see note to 229. 33–36*): if [though *written above*] [. . .] of inquty [*read* iniquity] bee generall stand single in goodnesse & followe [rather then *written above*] not a multitude to do euell stand single in Integritie & adde one [bring not *written above*] not one stone vnto the heap of transgression [iniquity *written above*]. the worst times afford some imitable example of virtue, and there canne bee no such deluge of vice butt some may [more then 8 persons *written above*] escape the Flood & the best may bee gathered from times of such tempers [. . .] that haue persisted sound amidst the generall coruption & haue [can *written above*] touched pich & not bee defiled & haue persisted sound in the generall corruption. 14–23. Let Age . . . it self. *LF*, 193. 39–194. 5. 25–35. Owe not . . . Statues. *LF*, 193. 29–38.

207. 37–**208.** 6. Let not . . . revenge thee. *LF*, 194. 23–27.

208. 8–26. While thou . . . in Heaven. *LF*, 194. 6–23.

208. 27–**209.** 5. However . . . miserable.] *In R, ff. 22–21*ᵛ, *with little difference except that after* devoured *there is the following addition*: whether there hath not been a passage from the mediterranean into the read sea & whether the ocean at first had a passage into the mediterranean by the strayghts of Hercules.

209. 7–11. Bid early . . . thy life. *LF*, 195. 18–23. 16–22. The politick . . . himself. *LF*, 195. 23–29. 24–37. Be substantially . . . himself. *LF*, 194. 28–195. 8.

210. 7–17. Though . . . business of Hell.] *In R, f. 21*ᵛ: Though the quicknesse of thy eare were able to heare the noyse made by the motion of the moone in her rapid reuolution. Though thou hadst as many eares as Argus had eyes yett stoppe them all and bee deaf vnto the whisperings of Talebearers tatling sycophants officious calum⟨n⟩iators, & pickthank delators who while qu⟨i⟩et persons sleepe sowe [sowing *written above*] the tares of disquietnesse Jelousie & [discord *erased*] diuision distract the tranquill⟨it⟩y of charity and euen of frend⟨l⟩y societie Cankers of reputations and like that of Jonas able to eat up a good name in a night. Euell spirits may sitt still while such spirits walk about & performe the work of hell. these are the tongues which sett the world on fire 30–31. Make . . . mercies.] *In R, f. 40*ᵛ, *which adds*: that no obligation call thee vngratefull 31–39. Though . . . Adam.] *In R, f. 40*ᵛ *as follows*: Thou thou hast the memorie of concience that punctuall [witnesse *erased*] iudge & witnesse within us yet trust not vnto thy remembrance in things wherin most need phylacteries Register the remarkable indulgences of god *make Epochas from his mercies & æras from his fauors† summ up thy dayes [by the *erased*] not by Lustrums or Olympiads butt by [diaries *erased*] Ephemerides of his mercies lett thy diaries stand thick with dutifull mementos & asterisks of his obligations write his mercies in marble & forgett thy own name before that of thy maker. [*space*] Looke beyond [the world *erased*] & date not his mercies to mankind [from thy natiuity *written below* date not] Looke not only before thy natiuity butt that of [. . .] & before the race of Adame. *write his mercies not in dust butt marble & forgett thy owne name before that of thy maker†

211. 2–16. Paint not . . . last bar] *Parts of this passage are variously drafted in R, ff.* 36^{v} *and 66; f.* 36^{v} *is nearest to the printed version. F. 66 begins*: paynt not thy sepulcher of thy self nor beautifie thy corruption *hide [cover *written above*] not butt abolish thy vices skinne not ouer thy vlcers, by deceatfull palliations & the fallacies of interest & affection.† plead not the cause of thy vnrighteousnesse & think not to make good thy iniquities or iustifie thy self by many howerglasses by arguments which will not hold water at the last barre. thinck not that good, which thou thinckest thou makest good nor iustifie thy self by many howerglasses by arguments which will nott hold good at the last barre. bee not an aduocat to thy iniquities nor call for many howerglasses to *This draft is repeated with slight variants and continued thus*: what the sunne doth not yet see that [? starre] of time will discouer make ugly when the sunne & stars are fallen from Heauen. there is no darknesse vnto consience which can see without light and euen in obscurity present a liuely [& iust *written above*] portrayal of that [vnto thy self *written above*] which the cloud of dissimulation hath concealed from others [appearance *written below*] what [that which *written above*] the sune doth not see will bee visible without the sune when the sunne & starres are fallen from heven beside [*end of f. 66*]. *On f.* 36^{v} *the sentence continues*: beside there is no darknesse *&c. ending* concealed from appearance. 20–22. Comply . . . Sincerity.] *In S48, f. 157; also in R in three drafts, f.* 29^{v}, *f.* 32^{v} *and f. 34. F* 29^{v}: Comply with some humors butt serue none. genuine [free *written above*] complacency is better then acted [fallacious *written above*] flatterie *& to lett them fayrly bee what they are then to make them beleaue they are what they are not [*space*] to hinder their understanding of themselues. & more [? charitable] to lett them fayrly appeare what they are then to cast a mist upon their understandings & make them beleeue they are what they are not.† *f.* 32^{v}: comply with some humors beare with others butt serue none. a ciuill complacencie consists with honestie flatterie is a Jugler & no kinne vnto synceritie *f. 34*: beare with some humors comply with others butt serue none Free complacency is better then close flattery. 22–32. while . . . delusion] *In R, f. 28, with hardly any variants.*

211. 37–**212.** 22. Be not . . . themselves] *In R, ff. 36 and 38; as follows in f. 38*: While boysterous spirits thinck it the only valour to vanquish & master others studdy thou inward self [inward *written above*] fortitude & learne to subdue thyself make temperance a great peece of thy valour to quiet thyne owne commotions To well manage our affections & wild horses of Plato is the highest Olympicks and the noblest digladiation is in the Theater of ourselues *Thus to mortifie ourselues is no suicide butt the destruction of our destroyers.† to beat our enemies out of the feild & bee led captiue by our vices to chase our foes and fall downe to our concupiscences is to be Hercules furens abroad & [? poultrons] in our owne circumference They who are thus merely led by the wheele of their owne inclinations without the hand of virtue & guidance of soueraigne reason are butt the Automata of man⟨k⟩ind, *& at the best the prone part of the creation †*f. 36 generally follows this version but ends*: and though erect in figure are [. . .] the brutall & prone part of the creation.

212. 24–32. Let not . . . indited them.] *In R, f. 67, the first sentences, down to* Contingencies, *as printed, except that the MS. reads* obscurities *for* Contingencies. *The MS. continues*: mark well the paths thereof butt bee not sudden in the construction of euents ether as to iudgments or mercies, in such affayres [the hand of god *erased*] though the hand bee seen yett the [letters *erased*] writing ar is hardly construed & sometimes butt by himself. *that which is intended upon one being interpreted upon another & [men *erased*] euery [man *erased*] commonly putting [. . .] and like pythagoras in the Moone can read [? sure] iudgments at a distance upon others, butt are in the dark vnto them selues & seeke out with alertnesse the faults & blotts of others.† 32–36. *Leave . . . Futurity.*] *In R, f. 67* as follows: Leaue future occurencies to their vncertainties thinck only that which is past thy owne and since tis easier to foretell an Eclips at a distance of time then a fayre [black *written above*] daye Looke for litle regular belowe entertaine with patience the instabilities of Earth & the chaos of futurities.

213. 8–22. Old Generosity . . . Election] *In S85, ff. 31–32.* 8. such contempt] contempt *S85.* 9. favour] fauors 11. And if] If 13. name] obloquie latter] present 16. Wise-man.] *Insertion in S85*: *It were a successelesse peece of Rhetorick to saye that Gold were butt a piece of earth vnto such a one as commandeth the earth by it, or that the earth itself is butt a poynt in respect of the whole world, vnto a person who cannot looke ouer his owne Lands† tetrick] despised 17. such a] this 18. and] who 18–19. unnatural . . . World] paradoxicall distribution & vnnaturall current of power Riches & honor in the word [*read* world] 19. imperfection] iniquitie, imperfection 20. unto them] therin *The first two sentences of this passage are also on f. 21 of the same MS., as follows*: The old humors of generositie are superannated & contempt of the world out of date. no man is now like to refuse the fauors of princes [great ones *written above*], or bee content [? confident *written above*] to saye vnto Great ones [princes *written below*] stand out of his my sunne [*these sentences scored out*].

213. 40–**214.** 4. The Divine . . . from it. *In R, ff. 30 and 33*v *(the nearer to the printed version); f. 30 as follows*: for the diuine eye lookes upon high & lowe differently from that of man they who stand [upon Oly *erased*] seeme lowe & are butt in the valley vnto our apprehension may stand upon Olympus & high ground vnto his. for hee lookes upon them as lowe who are most remoud from his will & nature & those highest who neerest approach vnto it.

214. 30. Could we . . . Nature] *In S85, f. 24; also in S69, f. 26 (see K, v, p. 251).* 31. and as he stood] or [and *S69*] as it primatiuely stood *S85, S69.* 33. our present] our great *S85.* 34. our Nature] our selues *S85.* 34–38. for after . . . Generator] *as follows in S85, ff. 24–25*: butt at this distance and elongation wee dearly knowe that deprauity hath ouerspred us, & corruption entred like oyle into our bones. imperfection vpprayds us at all hands, and ignorance stands poynting at us in euery corner in nature wee are vnknowing in things which fall vnder cognition yet driue at that which is aboue our comprehension wee haue a slender knowledge of ourselues, and much lesse of god wherein wee are like to rest vntill the aduantage of another being, and therefore in uayne wee seeke to satisfie our souls in close [*replacing* narrowe *erased*] apprehensions & piercing theories of the diuinity [*replacing* diuine esse *erased* (? essence)] euen from the diuine word. meanwhile we haue an happy sufficiency in our own natures, to apprehend his good will and pleasure it beeing not of our concern or capacity from thence to apprehend or reach his nature the diuine Reuelation in such poynts being not framed vnto intellectualls of earth. Euen the Angels and Spirits haue enough to admire in their sublimer created natures. Admiration being the act of the creature and not of god, who doth not admire himself. *Cf.* 229. 15–17: 'Even Angels . . . himself.'

214. 41–**215.** 14. we consider . . . mistaken] *In S85, f. 16*; we consider . . . preservation *also in S69, f. 23.* 2. afflictive] that are afflictiue *S85.* 4. kill] haue despached mercifully] opportunely 6. from] upon 6–7. his Sword unto him] him his sword 8. his design] it Hereby] whereby but] beside 10. in] upon 11. wary and pious] pious & wary 12. hints] ominous hints 12–13. were . . . God] is to ouerlooke the mercifull hand of prouidence 13. and *Cardan*] or Cardan

215. 16–23. Break not open . . . regression. *LF*, 193. 21–26.

217. 2–9. Since . . . himself.] *Apparently developed from the following in R, f. 64*: *men take too much notice of their owne virtues & [? tacitly] [obliquely *written above*] speake ther owne perfections while they commonly condemne others. & make ther common discourse a censuring of those vices wherin they are free themselues. Reioyce in such exemptions from such iniquities butt possesse thy virtues with charity charitably loose not charity for self Loue. [*line space*] Reioyce in thy exemption from clamorous & vulgar vices butt possesse thy virtue charitably nether reuiling others nor magnifying thyself according ⟨to⟩ that deluding mode whereby men take pleasure to magnifye themselues & condemne others splitting on the rock of self loue & making shipwrack of charitie.† *The following at foot of page*: yett fall not into that common [vncharitable *written above*] fallacy to prayse thy self by discommending others. 15. uncharitableness.] *Wilkin and later editors here quote the following from S47, f. 228. The passage would also be appropriate to i, 20, after 'business of Hell.' (210. 17), but may not have been intended for CM.*

They who thus closely and whisperingly calumniat the absent liuing will stayne [*read* strayne] their voyce and bee apt to bee loud enough in infamy of the dead wherein there should bee a ciuill amnestie and an obliteration concerning those who are in a state where all things are forgotten butt Solon will make us ashamed to speake euell of the dead. a crime though not actionable in Xtien goverments yet hath been prohibited by pagan lawes and the old sanctions of Athens. [*isolated.*]

Wilkin and later editors here add the following passage, which in the manuscript (ff. 227–227v) precedes the foregoing and which does not seem very appropriate either here or elsewhere in CM (unless perhaps i. 25 or iii. 13):

many persons are like those many riuers whose mouths are at a vast distance from their heads. for their words are as farre from their thoughts as Canopus from the head of Nilus. These are of the forme of those men whose punish⟨m⟩ent in Dantes hell is to looke euerlastingly backward [*end of f. 227r; the rest is on f. 227v and is probably a separate note*] if you haue a mind to laugh at a man or disparage the iudgement of any one sett him a talking of things to come or euent of hereafter [? contingencies] which elude the [? science *erased*] cognition of such as arrogate the knowledge of them whereto the ignorant pretend not and the learned imprudently fayle wherein men seeem to talk butt as babes would do in the womb of their mother of the things of the world which they are entring into.

218. 19–**219.** 12. Were there . . . displacency] *In S85, ff. 5–6; also in S62, ff. 38–39.* 20. durable] continuall [perpetuall *written above*] *S85* honour *Volupia*] bee an Epicure *S85.* 20–21. the Race of Delight is short] there is noe longeuitie in voluptuousnesse *S62.* 21. and Pleasures] pleasures *S85.* 21–25. have mutable . . . Confusion] *of [our *erased?*] youthfull dayes drawe sowr faces on our elder browes. man is butt weakely constituted for sensuallitie whose strongest sense is weakened with satietie.† the strength of pleasure being placed in its raritie, & delight by continuation becomming its owne destruction, mediocrity is its life & immoderacy its destruction *S85.* 25–26. of old] *omitted* 27. all] all their 28. fain] fayne *underlined and* driuen *written above* 29. Invention.] *S85 inserts*: *& nauseating partriges & phaisants were fayne to descend vnto despised dishes & proue tasters vnto common palates of the flesh of colts & Asses† 29–30. mediocrity . . . Appetite] wch by paucitie Raritie & healthfull appetite 31. *Epicurus* himself] old Epicurus brain] braines 32–33. and the Tongues . . . Onyons.] and in a dish of onyons the braines of peacocks & nightingales. 33–34. Hereby . . . nauseating] whereby [*replacing* By such circumscriptions *erased*] healthfull pouertie hath the aduantage of satiated 34. and naked] vntired & naked 36. one single] each common 36–37. who . . . contents it] *omitted*

219. 1. feed upon] deale with   2. hardly] butt coldly   Calda] caldo [*as also in S62*]   3. such circumscriptions] this circumscription   pleasure] *replacing* delight *erased*   4. Delight] delight (*the final choice, replacing* voluptuousnesse delight pleasure *in that order*)   5. days] times   lost in] quite lost by   7. but Nature, who] Nature wch   pleasure] *replacing* delight   8. bounds thereof] circumference   its line] the line [*replacing* rule] thereof   9. not pressing] *replacing* pressing not   10. contentedly] quietly   11. and so . . . excess] wch is one of the rewards of virtue, & the naturall punishment of excesse   17–36. Quotation . . . fly from it.] *Similar material in S62, f. 52; also in S69, f. 13 (K, v, p. 243). For 24–29,* Who would . . . his time., *S69 has*: Plinie who was well seen in Homer denyeth the Art of picture in the Troian warre Iliad. Σ vers. 483 whereas it is playnly sayd that Vulcan engraued in the armes of Achilles the earth & starres of heauen. *S62 adds*: Plautus mistakes natiuity for conception Homer makes Aginour able to foretell things vnto Vlysses & euen to tell him where his wife was & yet enquire of him what was become of his own sone Orestes. *For 30–32,* Though . . . because, *S69 has*: And though I haue no great opinion of Machiauells learning yet am I unwilling to say hee was butt [Nor will I presently say that Machiauell was butt *written above*] a weake historian because hee commonly exemplified in Caesar Borgia & the pettie princes of Italie, or that hee had butt a slight knowledge in Roman storie because

219. 39–**220.** 15. To begin . . . Heart of Truth] *In S85, ff. 29–30*; To begin . . . both sides] *also in S69, ff. 21 and 20*v.   39–1. or continue] *omitted MSS.*

220. 1. works] discourses   2. present] newe   3. enquiring Age] enquirie of things   4. to mollify] the turne *written above S85* the turne or mollify *S69.*   4. Spirit] spirits *MSS.*   4. captious] positiue   6. o' work] on work   7. all Physical Truths] things *S69.*   8. always] commonly *S85* closely . . . attrition] close as not to admitt of object *S69.*   closely] well *S85.*   9–10 Many . . . Blade] Many things seeme quodlibetically stated in nature & may bee many truths seeme quodlibetically constituted & like a Delphian sword *S69.*   12–13. Falshood . . . ballance] *In S69, f. 20*v *thus*: Truth & falshood hang almost equilibriously in some assertions and a few grains of truth wh bear doune the balance   14. may come] come *S85.*   15. but not] yet missed *S85.*   15–19. Besides . . . Natures] *In S69, f. 15.*   15. many] most *S69.*   16. some] many   18. having a] being of a   18–19. true and central] centrall *S69.*   19. Natures] *S69* continues (*K, v, pp. 244–5*): wch long search & deepe enquirie is only able to discern & therefore following the common vewe & liuing by the obuious track of sense, wee are insensibly imposed upon by consuetude & only wise or happy by coestimation. The receaued apprehensions of true or good, hauing widely confounded the substantiall [*?* vse] & inward veritie thereof. wch now subsisting in the theorie & acknowledgment of some fewe wise or good men, are lookd upon as Antiquated paradoxes or sullen

Theoremes of the old world [*on f. 14*^{v} *opposite*: wee liue, iudge & commonly knowe by Appearances.]. wheras indeed truth wch is sayd not to seeke corners, lyes in the center of things. the area & exterous part being only ouerspred with legionary varieties of error or stuffed with the meteors & imperfect mixtures of truth. hee that found out the line of the middle motion of the planets holds an higher mansion in my thoughts then hee that discouered the Indies, and ptolomie that sawe no farther then the feet of The Centaur, then hee that beheld the Snake by the southern pole. the rationall discouerie of things transcends their simple detections whose inuentions are often casuall, & secondarie vnto intention. [*no continuation.*] *The latter part of this passage*, 'hee that found . . . intention', *is also in S48, f. 195.* 19–22. And this . . . Truth] *In S85, f. 30.* 20. nor presently to obtrude] not obtruding *S85.* 21. after considerations may] time may hereafter *S85.*

221. 5–35. There is nothing . . . aberrations] *In S85, ff. 17–18* (*part also in S62, f. 42*). 6 Ingenious] Ingenuous *S85.* 8. Libraries] vaticans 9. Volumes] bookes aftertimes] the next ages 10. may be] will bee 10–11. a few Ages may joyfully declare] were half a resurrection to behold 11. but a cold] a cold [*replacing* sober] 12. behold] see 13. content with] men desire 14. the time of their lives] their beings 14–15. and . . . metempsychosis] or not content with the fauor of a metempsuchosis 16. to enjoy] for 18. but six] six is like to] doth [*replacing* will] plainly 19. mean while] *omitted* 20. resume] take 21. there is] wee haue or any] & cold 22. from] like to bee had from 22–23. Ancients . . . well known] Aristotle or the Ancients 24. prudently] *omitted* Enquiries] enquirie 25. were but] are butt magnify] honour 26. Endeavors] endeauours *replacing* know *erased* Learning] learning & Arts 27–28. made . . . advantages] thereof upon that notable aduantage 30. swell] continue this tautologie in writing & meerely to swell 30. fruitless Repetitions] trite & fruitless repetition 31. sing the same Song] cuckoe out the same note 32. attempt] leaues many . . . some] some [*replacing* I] had rather men 33. be willing to] could 34. monstrosity] monstrosities 34. divers] many 35. aberrations.] *S85, with a fresh line, adds*: *And therefore to iudge of mens workes which are written at distant times of their liues & make them out as genuine or spurious according as they containe repugnant or congruous conceptions is to forget the difference† [*end of page; no continuation*]. *Cf.* 222, *especially* 19–23, 'Men are not . . . Persons'.

222. 12–13. Figures . . . at all] *In S85, f. 21, scored out.* 12. do nearest approach] approach neerest 13–16. Some . . . Antecedencies] many things happen from causes most vnlikely to ensue improbable to ensue & most vnlike vnto their causes. (*scored out.*)

222. 30–**223.** 6. If the Almighty . . . portion of Man] *In S85, f. 15–15*^{v}. If . . . want] *S85 reads*: If the mercy of god will not [agregrately *read* agregately] accept the obedience & duty of his seruants there is litle plea for mercy or sound pretence of fullfilling half the Law in persons, churches, or nations. They which are singularly obseruant of some Christian dutyes being notoriously defectiue in others. persons sects & nations mainly settling upon some Christian particulars which they conceaue acceptable vnto god & promoting the interest of their [diuisions or *erased*] inclinations & diuisions. every one reckoning & preferring himself by the particulars wherein hee excelleth & condemning all others though [more *erased*] highly eminent in other Christian virtues 39. speckled] Spotted Honesty] pietie in the World] throughout the church of god *S85 inserts*: whereas if men would not seeke themselues abroad [*opposite on f. 14*ᵛ: persius nec te qua'siueris extra] if euery one would iudge and reckon himself by his worst & others by their better parts this deception must needs vanish [charitie *erased*] humillitie would gayne ground, charitie would ouerspred the face of the church and the fruits of the spirits not bee so thinnly found among us 39 and which] This was

223. 1. pretenders unto] pursuers of 3. Violence] ambition violence 4. iniquities] *replacing* vices 5. censurers,] censurers, backbiters, depraving] imparing portion] parcell

223. 37–**224.** 25. Mankind . . . moles] *In S85, f. 10–f. 9*ᵛ. 18–25. Cupid . . . moles] *Also in S69, f. 15*ᵛ.

223. 37–**224.** 14. Mankind . . . Natures] *Similar material in S62, ff. 67–68.*

223. 39. Symmetries] *replacing* shapes *written twice and erased the first time S85.* Schemes] *replacing* figures 40. World] whole world

224. 1. forms were] proper formes are 2. most act] much act 3. parts] *omitted* do most] doth much 5. some Truth not only] not only some truth 7–8. Natures of those] nature of their owne 8. which have] that weare Thus] And thus 9. Earth] world 10–11. in some latitude] *omitted* 13. Countries] nations and are . . . correspondent] & doe no lesse agree & correspond 15. a more] more or differing] *omitted* 16. rubbs] webbs 17. doubt] question 18. said] iustly said 19. is not] not 20. truly are] are 21. wise Contriver] wisedome of god 22. outsides] outside 23. not . . . discover] not able to discover

224. 30–**225.** 16. the Line . . . state of Hell] *In S85, ff. 11–14; cf. also S62, ff. 72*ᵛ*–75.* 33–35. that Men . . . is no] That yong men are fortunate & perform the notablest actions is no *S85.* 36. their parts] their [eminent *erased*] parts 37. were brought] were cheifly brought 37. Men of years] old men 38. matured . . . designs] *omitted* to be beyond] beyond 39. active fortunes] fates [destinies *written above, no erasure*] high exploits] the high designes 40. ordained] disposed 41. brave] wise *The passage thus far reads as follows in S62*: that young men are fortunate & performe the notablest actions is noe poynt of deepe wonder. they hauing [before them *erased*] the strength of their fates before them nor yett acted the parts of [time *erased*] the world for which they were made far from the accomplishment of their destinies, whereas old men haue acted the desinges of their life. & passed the vigor of fates prouidentialy determined to ages best agreable vnto them 41. finding . . . declination] discerning their fates grewe faynt or feeling their declinations *S85*.

225. 1. so escaped] escaped 2. beginnings.] *S85 inserts*: wisely stopping about the meridian of their felicities or vnwilling to hazard the fauors of the descending wheele or to fight downeward in the setting arch of fortune *and opposite, on f. 10*^{v}: Lucan 7

sic Longius a'uum
destruit ingentes animos, et vita superstes
fortuna'. nisi summa dies cum fine bonorum
affluit et celeri pra'uertit tristia letho
dedecori est fortuna prior, quisquamne secundis
tradere se fatis audet nisi morte paratâ?

2. magnanimous] confident ambition & high flowne 4. the vicissitude] vicissitude evil] bad apprehend] conceaue 5. have been still] are on unto] vnto 6. destructions.] *S85 inserts*: whereof I that haue not seen the sixtieth part of time haue beheld great examples. Then the incomparable Montrosse no man acted a more fortunate part in the first scene of his aduentures. butt courageous Loyaltie continuing his attempts hee quickly felt that fortunes fauors were out & fell upon miseries smartly answering his felicities which was the only accomplishment wanting before, to make him fitt for Plutarchs [luies *erased*] pen & to parallel the liues of his Heroick [*replacing* many worthy *erased*] Captaines. For] Thus 7. in] on blessing us] blessing 8. to] & [bla *erased*] to 9. a capacity] the capacitie lowest] sharpest 10. from our] of our precedent 11–16. For to become . . . state of Hell] *As follows in S85, ff. 13–14, in this order, not the order followed by Wilkin and later editors*: wherin notwithstanding if swelling beginnings haue found unconfortable conclusions [*replacing* beginnings *erased*] it is by the method & justice of prouidence equalizing one with the other, & reducing the [summe of *erased*] whole vnto a mediocrity by the balance of extremities. so [*replacing* whereby *erased*] that in the summe the felicitie of great ones holds a leuell and paritie with most [*replacing* of most *erased*] that are belowe them. whereby the minor fauorites of fortune wch incurre not such sharpe transitions haue no cause to repine, nor men of middle fates to murmur at their indifferences And this is the obseruable cours not only in this visible stage of things butt may bee feared in our second beings & euerlasting selues wherin the good things past are seconded by the bad to come, and many vnto whom [*replacing* who haue *erased*] the [open *erased*] embraces of fortune are open heere, may find Abrahams armes shutt vnto them hereafter, which makes serious contemplators not so much to pitty as enuie some infelicities, wherin considering the circle of both our beings and the succession of good vnto euell tyranny may sometimes proue courteous & malice mercifully cruell.

By this method of prouidence the Deuill is deluded who maligning us at all poynts and beating felicity from us euen in this vncertain being [*replacing* place world thereof *erased*] hee becomes assistant vnto our future happynesse & blessed vicissitude of the next. And this is also the vnhappinesse of [the next *erased*] himself who hauing acted his first part in heauen is made sharpely miserable by transition & more afflictiuely feels the contrarie state of hell. 21–37. The Tragical . . . necessary] *In S85, ff. 19–20; also in S62, f. 7–7*v*, which mostly agrees with S85.* 21. Exits] periods unexpected periods] irreconcilable ends 21–22. some eminent] many excellent 22. amuse] amaze (*as also S62*) 24. without . . . self-reflexion] & beholding them without reflexion and conceive] conceaue 24–25. unconcerned . . . Exemption] absolued by the fallacy of exemption 26. but few] some [*replacing* some butt *erased*] 28. inadvertency] stupiditie well] *omitted* 30. he] god some] some Jewe others also deserve] all deserue in themselues 31. sense] sensible apprehension stroak] sphere 33. from whence] wherin 33–34. nevertheless . . . tempers] notwithstanding the deprauitie of our natures [tempers *S62*] 36. must be] are required 37. afflictions] infelicities necessary.] *S85 inserts*: which is the amazing part of that incomprehensible goodnesse content to act ouer these vicissitudes euen in the despayre of our betterments, or [*written above* &] how that omnipotent spirit that would not bee exasperated by our forefathers beyond sixteen hundred yeares should thus lastingly endure our succeeding transgressions & still contend with flesh. & truly how he can forgiue those sins who knowes it is not long before they will bee committed agayne or accept of repentancies which must haue after-penitencies, is the riddle of his mercies. (*no continuation.*) *This material was developed into a part of iii. 26* (244. 24–37), 'For if . . . tell us', *where it is fused with a sentence from the manuscript quoted in the note to* 244. 24–37 ('If God . . . continued it.')

227. 3–228. 1. Many . . . apprehension thereof.] *In R, ff. 45 and 44, almost exactly as in the printed version; in S85, ff. 7–9, with variants as below; part also in S62, f. 46.* Many . . . therein.] *S85 has*: Many haue been earnest [studious *written above*] in the inuention of the miserablest deaths butt few howers haue been spent to [find out wayes that might *underlined, ? for deletion*] sweeten [death *erased*] the same & extenuate the last necessitie. That the smoothest way vnto the Graue is made by bleeding as [the *erased*] common opinion presumeth the experiment of Seneca & Lucan will make us doubt vnder wch the noble Stoick so mightily [smartly *written above*] laboured, that hee was fayne to retire from the sight of his wife to conceale the affliction thereof and was [fayne *erased*] not ashamed to require the mercifull hand of his physitian to shorten his miserie therin. Nor can wee readily beleif it who behold the sick & fainting languors which accompany the effusion of blood when it proceedeth vnto death. [*Some interlined words not fully deciphered and not included.*] 12. Ovid] *opposite, on f. 6*v*:* Demito naufragium mors mihi munus erit 13. who were so] wch were 14. Soul] soules a Fire] fire 14–15. probably in fear] surely in feare [afrayd *written above*] 16. Air] ayer & passages of respiration temperate] coole 19. thereof] *omitted* 21. potion] poyson *S85 S62* potion *R.* 22–23. much more than from] so much as *S85.* 25–26. his Sword] *opposite, on f.* 7v: m pummell. wherin hee is sayd to haue caryed a litle medicine wch at any time might free him from [misfortune *or* misfortunes *erased*] might dispach him from all [*?* misfortues]. 27. merciful contrivers] mercifully witty *S62.* 28. invincible] irrecouerable *S85 S62* vnexcitable [insuperable *written above*] *R.* 30. Emperour] Seignor *S85.* was herein] herin was 31. killing] *replacing* strangling 32. He who] hee that 34. when Men] wherin men 35. severity] malice 36. feel themselves to die] bee made to feele themselues dye

228. 10–40. 'Tis hard . . . non existent.] *Numerous portions of this section (iii. 1) are scattered in R and only a summary account of their location, nature, and variant readings is attempted here.*

(1) *What appears to be the germ of the section is on f. 36v as follows*: *while wee commend ages past and magnifie the goodnesse of the first times wee find no times acquitt the wickednesse of man the yong world was so abominable that they tempted the mercie [patience *written above*] of god vnto a deluge, the earth was full of violence and the heart of man corrupted.†

(2) *The whole section, with hardly any variation from the printed text, appears on ff. 31v–32, followed, after a space, by the passage given under* (10).

(3) 10–17. 'Tis hard . . . any one.] *Drafted variously on ff. 29 and 34v.*

(4) 18–28. The younger World . . . with themselves] *On f. 29, ending* water which destroyed ouerwhelmd man & beast & left so few to beginne the world agayne.

(5) 18–21. The younger World . . . irreclaimable] *On f. 33v.*

(6) 24–26. their Longevity . . . abominations] *Roughly drafted on f. 42.*

(7) 18–26. tis said . . . abominations] *In R, f. 30, without material difference.*

(8) 28–32. their memories . . . Noah] *On f. 34v*: the memorie of the [An⟨te⟩deluian] times was drowned with themselues and litle sayd of that wherof [time world *written above*] men might haue been lively historians when Methuselah might haue told what Adam sayd & told vnto Noah what hee had seen himself whey [*read* when they] were so old they scarce remembered [*continued as under* (9), *with variants suggesting that the version on f. 34v is the earlier; ending* would kill him]

(9) *See (8). F. 33v gives the continuation as a separate unit as follows*: when they liued so long that they scarce remembred themselues yong & ancient men were Antiquities when men feard not palsies & Apoplexies till 7 or 8 hundred yeares when homicide & the cutting of the probable hopes of so long a life & to kill one another was the transcendent crime & when life was so highly valued & life was so well worth the liuing that no man would kill himself. yet since it is sayd that (*foot of f. 33v; no continuation found.*) *Comparison of the last six words with ll.* 21–22 *shows that the passage was to*

follow irreclaimable. (8) *shows that an alternative place for it was after* Noah (*l.* 32); *but the passage has no place in CM as printed in 1716. For its further history see* (10).

(10) *See* (2). *The passage appearing, after a space, at the end of the section* (*ff.* 31^v–32) *is as follows*: *this makes historicall losses greater then any other [. . .] & industrie these wrapt vp in the night of obliuion must [can *written above*] expect to no light to relieue them & euen those heads which pretend to knowe things to come attempt [pretend *written beneath*] not to [?vntie] [to reuiue *written beneath*] what is [?soberly] past.† *This passage, although not printed in CM, was developed and combined with a revised from of the passage given under* (9) *to form a paragraph beginning* Large are the treasures of oblivion. *This paragraph again was not printed in CM but Browne wrote it out several times. It occurs three times in MS. Sloane 1848, ff. 162, 165^v, and 167^v. Wilkin and other editors have printed the version on f. 162* (*formerly 194*) *and have supposed the passage to be an addendum to Hydriotaphia* (122. 8, *after* expectation). *There are three versions also in R, ff. 42^v, 43, and 44^v, that on f. 42^v apparently the latest, and as follows*: Large are the treasures of obliuion and heapes of things next to nothing allmost numberlesse much more remaineth in silence then is recorded The account of time began with night & darknesse still attendeth it the world is not half itself & a [. . .] of affayrs lost in it some things neuer come to light more lyeth swallowed in obscuritie & the cauerns of obliuion much lyeth in uacuo [as it were *written above*] & can neuer bee raysed up of that long liuing age when men could scarce [were so old . . . *partly erased*] remember themselues yong & men to us seem not Ancient butt Antiquities when wee cannot now hope to subsist in our Memories so long as they did in their liues when men feard Apoplexies & palsies at [after *written above*] 7 or 8 hundred yeares when liuing was so lasting that homicide might admitt distinctiue qualifications & it might seeme a lesser offence to kill a man at eight hundred then then at fortie & when life was so well worth the liuing that fewe or none could kill themselues. [*on a fresh line*: when they subsisted longer in their liues then [*erasure*] can now hope to do in our memories] *With this last clause and that which it replaces cf. H,* 120. 14–15. *The sentence* The world is not half itself *occurs with an extension in S48, f. 161^v, as follows*: The world is not half itself nor the moyetie known of its occurrencies of what hath been acted [*isolated*]

229. 15–17. Even Angels . . . himself.] *See note to* 214. 34–38 (*end of passage quoted*). 17–24. Created . . . Divinity] *In S48, f. 157; in R, ff. 29^v; 32^v; and 34, the last the most rudimentary, as follows*: where wee canot say enough wee cannot exceed. where wee canot exceed wee cannot say enough euen our sublimest thought tire at the setting out & wee enter not the portall of his diuinity 17. Created Natures] Expressions concerning the creatures *R, ff. 29^v, 32^v.* 33–36. that times past . . . Ages] *In R, f. 41, as follows*: *Though the satyrists thought that corruption of manners was in its Apogee & hight in his time & that no addition could bee made by succeeding deprauities iniquities.† yett thinck thou times past better then the present & [theorems *partly erased*] a venerable error [mistake of *written above*] to haue [languist in *written above*] that opinion of them that so wee may liue up vnto ther virtues nor think it enough to erre with our forefathers & that if times were allways bad wee are butt in the same forme, and to [*erasure*] and to bee men [in our age *written above*] it suffiseth to bee no better then men of all ages. [*Immediately followed by the passage quoted in note to* 207. 4–12.]

230. 34–35. Rake not . . . thy self.] *Wilkin cites S47 (where the passage has not been found) as follows (one phrase incorrectly transcribed?)*: So mayst thou carry a smooth face, and sit down in contentation, without those cancerous commotions which take up every suffering, displeasing [*cf.* Rake not up envious displacences] at things successful unto others, which the arch-disposer of all things thinks not fit for ourselves. To rejoice only in thine [own] good, exclusively to that of others, is a stiff piece of self-love, wanting the supplying oil of benevolence and charity.

231. 13–18. *Grain . . . Jaundice;*] *In R, ff. 37–37ᵛ and 67ᵛ; 67ᵛ as follows*: Grayne not thy vicious dyes & deepen not the bad tinctures which temper infirmitie or ill habits haue sett upon thee nor fix by iterated habits what time & virtuous washes might efface & expunge upon thee. hee who thus aduanceth in obscuritie & dark deformities turnes a shadowe vnto night of a gypsie becomes a blackmore and is to mee a negro in the black jandis. *Ending on ff. 37–37ᵛ*: hee who thus blindly plungeth in iniquitie [aduanceth *erased*] in wildly aduanceth [ing *written above*] in obscurity & dark deformities turnes a shaddowe into night and is to mee a negro in the black Jaundis *Each of these versions is followed, after a one-line space, by the following unpublished passage, of which there is a third transcription on ff. 65–64ᵛ. Thus on 37ᵛ*: *Though long habits leaue deepe traces & hee in a manner whitens a blackmore that can get fayrely out of them yet enslaue not thyself vnto vices which though thou wouldst vertuously ouercome yet you cannot safely leaue Intemperance in many becomes their very temper that without their health [without (the) hazard of health *ff. 65 and 67ᵛ*] & almost at the rate of life they cannot at last forsake it which is a captiuity beyond the bonds of other iniquities & euen that of the graue from whence there may bee an aduantageous redemption and the longer wee haue been vnder it the nearer wee are from the captivity & fetters of it.† *Beginning on f. 67ᵛ*: Though long habits leaue deepe dyes & tis next to washing of a brick that can get fayrly out of them yett enslaue not thy self vnto vices which [guilt not thou thy owne chaynes & scorne to fetter thyself *written above*] though *Beginning on f. 65*: Though bad [Long *written above*] habits bee dangerous [leaue deepe dyes *written above*] & hee washeth [. . .] a blackmore [& tis next to washing a blackmore *written above*] that can gett

232. 15–30. Confound . . . infirmities of it] *In R, f. 39.* Confound . . . twenty.] *minor variants on f. 39.* 23–29. He who . . . confusion] *omitted on f. 39* anticipate . . . infirmities of it] *as follows on f. 39*: Anticipate the virtues of old age before the caracters of it, so liue that thou mayst bee long old not in the [?stalenesse] of age butt the laudable att⟨r⟩ibutes thereof

of it *yong men who haue [forstall *written above*] the vices of age growe intolerable in gray hayres & twere better for themselues & the good of the world if they neuer attayned vnto them† *also on f.* 40^{v} *as follows*: Anticipate the virtues of age & bee happy without its infirmities. liue long old and [*space*] be old without [before *written above*] the infirmities of age 25–27. disproportionately . . . Wisdom] *In R, f.* 40^{v} *as follows*: irregularly diuides his dayes [life *written above*] crowds up his dayes & leaues to small a corner for the years of prudence. 30–32. so may'st thou . . . contemporaries] *In R, f.* 49^{v} *as follows*: so mayst thou bee coetaneous unto elder & liue bee a father longer then thy contemporaries

233. 13–30. Self conversation . . . his Sons] *In R, f.* 43^{v}, *as follows*: Self conuersation is better then such consortium [? some] buisie heads & who are in a hurry within are fayne to retire into company to bee out of the crowd of themselues Some schoolmen tell us Hee may bee properly alone with whom in the same place there is no other of the same species Nabuchodosor was alone though among the beasts of the fei[ld] & a wise man may bee sayd to bee alone though with a rabble of people litle better then Beasts about him. He that must needs haue company must needs haue sometimes bad company bee thou able [*rest of version varies but slightly from the printed version*]

234. 26–35. the Circle . . . invisible] *In R, f.* 53^{v}, *as follows*: The sunne of our felicitie setts at right Angles & makes butt short arches. In euery clyme wee are in a periscian state wherein our shaddowe & darknesse walk about us. *There is no happinesse without an eye of vnhappinesse† and while our feliciti⟨e⟩s stand upon the poynts of pyramids in the insecurity thereof there is a degree of vnhappinesse which leauens our tranquillities. our feliciti⟨e⟩s haue hollows inside and stand like the great Colossus noble & magnificent without butt full of rubbish & fals metall within [*rest of version virtually the same as printed version except that the following is added*: *farre remoued from eyes & dwells in a light inaccessible.†]

235. 31–**236.** 6. If thou must . . . inability] *In S47, f. 227; only the following variants noted*: **236.** 1. Taught from Heaven] *S47 adds*: nor to bee learnt elsewhere 2–3. make not . . . behind them.] quiet one partie butt leaue vnquietnesse in the other of a seeming friend making butt close aduersaries. *S47*.

236. 40–**237.** 2. Live . . . denomination *and* (237. 26–27) that triple . . . Beasts] *In R, f. 39, as follows*: Liue vnto the dignitie of thy nature and Leaue it not disputable at last whether thou hast been a man or whether a brutish [? turne] may not challenge the denomination & since thou art a composition of man & beast whether the brutall life may not challenge the denomination at least what ranck thou hast maintained in the triple diuision of man that of Heroe man or beast

237. 15–27. Let thy thoughts . . . Beasts] *Partly drafted in S48, f.* 146^{v}.

237. 36–**238.** 4. But . . . Friends] *Partly drafted in S48, ff.* 149^{v}*–150.*

239. 2–17. If thou . . . consolation.] *In R, f. 27, with the following chief*

variants: 2. Traytor] adulterer 5. shame,] shame, bid adieu vnto worth noble] worthy

240. 33–**241.** 7. Rest not . . . Notions] *In R, f. 65*[v], *as follows*: Vnderstand the rules butt sweare not vnto the doctrines of Zeno or Epicurus bee not ignorant in the rules of Antoninus butt acquiesce not in them butt looke beyond them [Antoninus *written above*] Lett Pythagoras bee thy remembrancer not thy [& sett not downe or conclude not with his morallity terminate *written above*] textuarie or finall instructor learne the vanity of all things in this world rather from Solomon then phocilides. sett not downe in the dogmas of the peripatus Academie or porticus bee a philosopher of the mount an Epictetus in the fayth & Christianise thy morallitie actions. [*line space*] Rest not in philosophicall paradoxes built upon [upon the stilts *written above*] the strength of naked reason & the hopes of mortall felicities butt labour after [in *written above*] the Ethicks of fayth & the maxims of Christian Truth [verity *written above*] under the aduantage of heuenly assistance & the happinesse of both beings without end. *reioyce [boast *written above*] not in lowe beatitudes & the summum bonum of earth consider the beatitudes of the mount what [examine well *written above*] concerne & interest thou hast in them what pretence vnto any or all, to establish thee in a tossing world to afford thee a glymps [some *written above*] of tranquillitie heare & [. . .] herafter†

242. 27–38. Bear not . . . in vain] *In R, f. 50, as follows*: Carry no slack reine upon pleasures and lett not complexion or contagion betraye thee vnto the inordinacy of delights. make pleasure thy recreation or intermissiue relaxation, not thy Diana, life and profession. The hard entrance into this world, the miserable going-out of it the sicknesses disturbances and sad Rencountres in it, do lowdly tell us, wee come not into the world to bee merry, or to runne a race of delight: butt to performe the sober acts of Righteousnesse, true Reason and the serious purposes of man. which to neglect [*the rest as printed*]

244. 24–37. For if . . . tell us.] *This passage (see note on 225. 37) is evidently related in part to the following, quoted by Wilkin as from S 74 (where it is not now to be found)*: If God had not determined a settled period unto the world, and ordered the duration thereof unto his merciful intentions, it seems a kind of impossibility that he should have thus long continued it. Some think there will be another world after this. Surely God, who hath beheld the iniquity of this, will hardly make another of the same nature. And some wonder why he ever made any at all, since he was so happy in himself without it, and self-sufficiently free from all provocation, wrath and indignation, arising from this world, which sets his justice and his mercy at perpetual contention. [*K, i, p. 161; cf. K, v, p. 224.*]

246. 12–28. The created World . . . same thing.] *The evolution of this paragraph is shown in R, ff. 35*[v]*–36, beginning with* the world it self is not old [*erased*] *continuing with some isolated sentences, and completed as follows (omitting some alterations)*: If this world bee butt a small parenthesis in aternity & a state of creation, but an interposition for a time in the line of the inuisible world between such a state as was before it & will bee after it & if diuers haue thought the same shal last butt 6 thousand yeares it cannott well bee calld old or long since one man hath liued the sixt part thereof. And in this short world men complayne of the shortnesse of life to palliat the shortnesse of our dayes tis good to knowe what wee can of times [what is *written above*] past & in some way as though wee had beheld it And surely whosoeuer hath taken a thoughtfull vewe of times past & well considerd the world & how therin things present [past *written above*] haue been answered by times [past *erased*] present how matters of one age haue been acted ouer in others and that there is nothing new vnder the sunne may conceaue himself in a manner [*rest as printed*.] *From l.* 22, He who, *the passage is repeated, with virtually no variation from the printed text, in* R, *f.* 64[v], *where, after a space, there is also the following sentence*: *A man may be weand of the world [earn an happy *written above*] at least find nothing to tempt him vnto the desires of the ages of the old world† *With this cf. the following isolated sentence in* R, *f.* 36[v]: Though most complayne of the shortnesse of human dayes yet vnto considerate minds [? length] may bee satietie. in life & euen in our happy and vnwearying days not to enuy the longeuity of our first fathers

246. 30–**247.** 1. Lastly . . . of it. *LF*, 195. 30–196. 4.

Additional Note

The following passage, unpublished hitherto, appears not to be closely related to any part of CM. That it was, however, at some time intended for that work is suggested by its style and by its occurrence in R, in which so many portions of CM are found. It is on f. 52 of the MS., in two drafts, of which the revised draft is given here.

*To bee metaphysically good, that is conformable vnto the Intellect of god is common with us vnto other creatures To bee morally good & conformable vnto his will [is that blessed goodnesse *written above*] which makes the will of god to bee done on earth as it is in heauen & our dayly petition our enioyment. The fall of bad [sinning *written above*] Angells hath cleared heauen of sinners. The sunne obeyeth his will the creatures on earth transgresse not man is the sinning animal. & therefore his dayly prayer [paternost *written above*] must bee his heauenly [daily *written beneath*] [? petion *read* petition], & wee hope of the blessed spirits for him us. *Followed by incomplete sentence thus*: made to serue god butt the first day offending of him. if not in the first day yett soon after offending of him [fallen from him *written beneath*]†

COMMENTARY

RELIGIO MEDICI

Engraving. The engraver was William Marshall (see p. xv). For Marshall see *DNB* and Bryan, *Dictionary of painters and engravers*.

1. 2–3. *greedy of life . . . an end.* Seneca, *Thyestes*, 883–4:

> vitae est avidus quisquis non vult
> mundo secum pereunte mori.

Also Seneca, *Troades*, 162–4.

8–10. *the name of his Majesty . . . imprinted.* In this general reference to the propagandist pamphlet-literature developed during the Civil War it is difficult to define the exact meaning of 'anticipatively, counterfeitly'; but the kind of publication which Browne had in mind was strikingly exemplified in December 1643, when a notoriously counterfeit document was put out to support the charge that two years earlier the king had incited the Catholics in Ireland to rise in his defence. See Gardiner, *The Fall of the Monarchy of Charles I*, ii, p. 341, and cf. *Mercurius Aulicus*, 51st week, ending 23 Dec. 1643 (pp. 723–4): 'Tuesday, *Decemb.* 19 . . . . Nor doth their forgery reach onely to their fellowes, His Sacred Majesty hath tasted as deepe of it as any Prince under heaven; more particularly this weeke, wherein the faction have dared to put in print a most malicious forged *Commission*, pretended to be granted to the Roman Catholicks in *Ireland*, the first day of October 1641. then when His Majesty was last at *Edenburgh*: whereby the Forger would fain teach the people, that the *Great Seale* of *Scotland* was really imployed (by some about His Majesty) to give life and encouragement to the Irish insurrection. . . .' (*SC* contains *Mercurius Aulicus* '1642', ?1643.)

3. 3. *scandall of my profession.* In MS. Sloane 1869, f. 93 (*K*, v, p. 283), Browne notes that 'Though in poynt of deuotion & pietie physitions do meet with common obloquie, yet in the Roman Calendar wee find no lesse then 29 Saints & Martyrs of that profession, in a small peece expressely discribed by Bzovius'; in whose *Nomenclator sanctorum professione medicorum* (1623) the number of such persons described is 33. Keck records the 'common speech (but onely amongst the unlearned sort) *Vbi tres medici, duo Athei*'. The copy of *42b* used by Keynes in reproducing the engraved title-page (*Bibliography*, facing p. 9) has the following manuscript insertion at the foot: 'Religiosus Medicus θαῦμα οὕτως θαυμαστόν.'

3. *naturall.* Scientific.

25. *distinguished not onely.* For other instances of 'only' separated from the word or words it qualifies see 33. 17, 34. 40, &c.

28. *the name.* Protestant.

33. *hand.* Assistance; cf. 58. 22.

35–36. *low . . . on foot.* Luther's father was a miner.

4. 4. *Resolutions*. 'Resolvers' in *42*; but Browne had a special liking for such abstract usages, e.g. 'zeales', 5. 9.

32. *memory*. Memorial (*OED*, s.v. Memory, 11).

5. 39. *disproving*. Disapproving (*OED*, s.v. Disprove, 3).

6. 8–9. *Venice . . . dayes*. As recounted, for instance, in P. Servita (Sarpi), *Interdicti Veneti historia* (*SC*, 1626).

23–26. *I could never . . . selfe*. Keck suggests that Browne here had in mind a passage in Montaigne, ii. 12, and finds the same influence elsewhere in *RM*. Browne refers to this in MS. Sloane 1869, f. 20, where he observes that similarities of thought and expression in different authors can come about by coincidence or 'concurrence of imagination': 'In a peece of myne published long agoe [sc. *RM*] the learned commentator [Annotator *written above*] hath paralleld many passages with others of Mountaignes essaies whereas to deale clearly, when I penned that peece I had neuer read 3 leaues of that Author (& scarce any more euer since.' For the sentiment cf. *PE*, vi. 6 (end).

7. 26. *Platoes yeare* (*and note*). *Timaeus*, 39; Augustine, *De civ. Dei*, xii, 13, 'De revolutione saeculorum'. (*SC* contains Healey's translation of *De civ. Dei*, 1620.) See also *K*, v, p. 224.

32. *that of the Arabians*. Rejected by Augustine, *De haeresibus*, i. 83 (Migne, *PL*, 42, col. 46), and, as pointed out by Greenhill, also (with 'that of *Origen*') in *The Forty-two Articles of Religion*, 1553, art. 40: 'The soulles of them that departe this life doe neither die with the bodies nor sleep idle.' Milton entertained the heresy thus condemned; see *Par. Lost*, x. 792 and *Christian Doctrine*, i. 13.

8. 5. *that of Origen*. Attributed to Origen. See Augustine, op. cit. i. 43 (*PL*, 42, cols. 33. 34). Rejected in *The Forty-two Articles*, 1553, art. 42: 'All men shall not bee saved at the length'. The manuscript readings (p. 261) introducing the word 'Chiliast' suggest that for a time Browne confused the opinions condemned in arts. 42 and 41; 41 is headed 'Hereticks called Millenarii.'

39. *the prophecy of Christ*. Matt. xxiv. 11. Cf. 1 Cor. xi. 19.

9. 2. *Arians . . . divided*. Augustine, op. cit. i. 50–52, describes varieties of Arianism.

12. *his own*. For other instances of anomalous or ambiguous pronominal usages see 32. 11, 56. 9–10, 58. 2–3, 68. 29–30, *H*, 84. 35–85. 1, &c.

14–15. *there is . . . many*. For other instances of 'singular' verbs with plural nouns see 20. 2, 40. 33, 59. 18 and note.

26. *oh altitudo*. Rom. xi. 33: 'O the depth (Vulg. *O altitudo*) of the riches', &c. See note to 11. 15.

30–31. *Certum est, &c*. Tertullian (*Opera*, *SC*), *De carne Christi*, v (*PL*, 2, col. 761): '. . . et sepultus, resurrexit; certum est, quia impossibile.'

10. 11. *a Buckler*. Eph. vi. 16.

15. *Platonick*. Derived from the Platonists.

16. *That allegoricall description of Hermes* (*and note*). Cf. *CM*, iii. 2 (229. 20–

21). On the origin of this description see F. L. Huntley, *Sir Thomas Browne*, 1962, pp. 109 and 262, and the authorities there listed; also A. Lefranc, *Grands écrivains français de la Renaissance*, 1914, pp. 172 sqq. The sentence has been traced back by C. Bäumker to the pseudo-hermetic twelfth-century *Liber xxiv philosophorum* (ascribed to Hermes), comprising 24 definitions of God (Bäumker, *Studien und Charakteristiken z. Gesch. d. Philos. insbes. des Mittelalters*, 1928, pp. 194–214). The second of these definitions runs 'Deus est sphaera infinita, cuius centrum est ubique, circumferentia nusquam.' The sentence does not occur in the Neoplatonic *Hermetica*, though some approach is made to it in *Poimandres* xii. 14: *και ὁ μὲν θεὸς περὶ πάντα καὶ διὰ πάντων* (repeated in xii. 20; cf. Eph. iv. 6). There are also anticipations in Dionysius Areopagitica (*Opera*, *SC*, 1644), e.g. *De mystica theologia*, iv. 571 (*PG*, 3, cols. 1045–6): 'Deus autem qui ubique praesens est, et implet omnia, a nullo continetur.' After the twelfth century the sentence, often without the ascription to Hermes, became a commonplace and is found in several *SC* books, e.g. Bovillus, *De intellectu*, &c. (1510, f. 69); Ficino, *Theologia Platonica*, xviii. 3 (1559, p. 326); Mersenne, *Quaestiones in Genesin* (1623, col. 57; cf. cols. 56, 85, 87, 88). It is cited as from Hermes by Rabelais, *Pantagruel*, iii. 13. Browne refers to *Pantagruel* in another connexion in 22. 28. In the definition, 'sphaera infinita' was sometimes replaced by 'sphaera intelligibilis *or* intellectualis' (= spiritual, non-material), whence Browne's reference in *GC*, 171. 26, to 'that intelligible sphere'. (See *OED*, s.v. Intellectual, *a.* 2.)

19–20. *anima . . . perspicui.* Paracelsus, *Philosophia sagax*, ii (*Opera*, *SC*, 1603–5, x, p. 274): '. . . Vnde anima bono iure spiritus, & spiritus ex Deo angelus hominis idonee vereque vocari potest.' (Marginal note: '*Anima Angelus hominis. . . .*' '*Entelechia*' is the Aristotelian term for essence, as in *De anima*, ii. 1 (412a). With '*Lux est umbra Dei*', cf. Ficino, *De lumine*, iv (*Opera*, 1561, p. 977): 'Deus certe . . . lux est inuisibilis, infinita, ueritas ipsa ueritatis cuiusque, rerumque omnium causa. Cuius splendor imò potius umbra, est lux ista uisibilis atque finita, causa uisibilium.' Browne's sentence appears in Ralegh's *History of the World*, I. i. 11, 'Of Fate' (1614, p. 15), with '*Lumen*' for '*Lux*': '*Lumen est Vmbra Dei, & Deus est lumen luminis.*' Ralegh gives marginal references to Plato, *Republic*, vi [508–9], and to Ficino's comments on *Republic*, vii [514–18]. Ficino there (ed. cit., pp. 1408–12) expounds the doctrine of shadows and realities but does not employ the sentence in question. See *GC*, 167. 16–17 and note; and cf. H. Vaughan (who was acquainted with Ralegh's *History*), 'The Dawning', ll. 17–18 (*OET*, p. 452):

> The whole Creation shakes off night,
> And for thy Shadow looks⟨,⟩ the light.

'actus perspicui', actual transparency, is again from Aristotle, *De anima*, ii. 7 (418ᵇ): *φῶς δέ ἐστιν ἡ τούτου ἐνέργεια τοῦ διαφανοῦς ᾗ διαφανές.*

28–29. *plants . . . earth.* The reference is in part to Gen. ii. 4–5, which was commonly taken as supplementary to the story of the third day's creation (i. 9–12). Water and plants were then created, but the plants could not grow until rain began to fall. The provision for this is described in ii. 6, which, according to the commentators, meant that the water on the earth was drawn up in 'mist' and could then come down as rain. Browne appears to forget this verse, which, as then usually understood, removes his difficulty. See *CE*, p. 94. Cf. *K*, v, p. 197, where Browne does refer to the 'mist'.

30–32. *the Serpent . . . curse.* It was sometimes supposed that the serpent went upright before the curse pronounced in Gen. iii. 14. See *PE*, i. 7 and *CE*, p. 116.

32–33. *triall . . . fallible.* Deut. xxii. 13–21.

11. 4. *retired imagination.* Miss Sanna records that some manuscripts read 'imaginations' and that 'retired imaginations' occurs also in 69. 20. Cf. 69. 28–29.

4–5. *Neque . . . mihi.* Horace, *Sat.* i. 4. 133–4 ('lectulus aut me porticus excepit . . .').

15. *Saint Pauls Sanctuary.* The marginal note in *P* and *L* 'o altitudo' suggests that Browne is again (see 9. 26) referring to Rom. xi. 33. The baffled reason takes refuge in St. Paul's words about God's unsearchable wisdom and knowledge.

18. *I am that I am.* Exod. iii. 14.

20. *have and shall be.* This form of sentence appears again in the heading to the address by 'A.B.' on p. 79: 'To such as have, or shall peruse. . . .'

24. *prescious.* Foreknowing. Cf. 'prescience', *CM*, 236. 18, &c.

25. *blast.* Cf. 16. 8, and see 2 Sam. xxii. 16; also Ps. xviii. 15.

28. *Peter.* The mistake, 'Paul' for 'Peter', in all the manuscripts was probably of Browne's own making. 2 Pet. iii. 8.

30. *instances.* For this word in the sense of 'instants' see *OED*.

31. *thousand.* Cf. 46. 4. The usage without 'a' occurs elsewhere, as in *2 Henry VI*, v. i. 85 and *Henry VIII*, IV. ii. 89.

38–39. *Aristotle . . . eternall. De coelo*, i, 10–12.

39. *two eternities.* The visible world as well as the invisible.

11. 40–**12.** 4. *similitude . . . substance.* The similitude occurs in *De anima*, ii. 3, where Aristotle says that as in geometry the more complicated figure of a square implies the existence of the simpler triangle, so the sensitive element in the soul implies the more rudimentary vegetative element. Browne goes on from this to suggest that the concept of the triangle is apposite to the tripartite nature of the soul, which unites the three faculties of vegetative, sensitive, and rational; and that this triangular constitution of the soul parallels the triple unity of God. Cf. *CE*, pp. 77–78.

12. 9. *secret Magicke of numbers.* As explored at large in *GC* (especially ch. v) with reference to the number five.

10. *Beware of Philosophy.* Col. ii. 8: 'Beware lest any man spoil you through philosophy and vain deceit' (A.V.). Cf. *PE*, iv. 13, 1646, p. 232): 'because the Apostle bids us beware of Philosophy, heads of extremity will have none at all.'

11. *a set of things*, &c. Cf. the references to the doctrine of signatures in 57. 7, &c.

17–18. *Hermes . . . invisible.* The reference is probably to the sentence 'Quod est inferius est sicut quod est superius' in the 'Smaragdine Table', attributed to Hermes Trismegistus (see *Alchemiae Gebri Arabis . . . Libri*, 1545, p. 294). Browne quotes the opening words of the Table in *CM*, 220. 1–2. Cf. Rom. i. 20.

34–35. *the Devill . . . at Delphos.* Cf. 30. 25–27, 44. 3–4, and *PE*, i. 11 (1646, p. 47): 'sometimes wee meet with wholesome doctrines from hell, *Nosce teipsum*: The Motto of Delphos was a good precept in morality.'

36. *to know him. I know he is.* The confusion ('him' = Satan, 'he' = God) is occasioned by the insertion, first in *43*, of ll. 27–36. But Browne is careless elsewhere about personal pronouns. See note on 9. 12.

39. *backparts.* Exod. xxxiii. 23.

13. 7. *make but.* With 'are not', the reading of three manuscripts, the passage supposedly means that consultation and election, or choice, have no place, or very little, in the mind of God; 'make but' or, as in the other manuscripts and *42*, 'are but', implies that the two processes are fused; and seems preferable.

14–15. *contemplated by man.* Cf. *Hermetica*, *Poimandres*, iv. 2 (Moltke).

13. 41–**14.** 1. *And then . . . hive.* Possibly a reminiscence of George Herbert, 'The Starre', ll. 29–32 (*Works*, ed. Hutchinson, p. 74):

Sure thou wilt joy, by gaining me
To flie home like a laden bee
Unto that hive of beams
And garland-streams.

The passage 13. 24–14. 12 was added in *43*. *SC* includes a copy of *The Temple*, 1641.

14. 14. *foure second causes.* Efficient, material, formal, and final. See *OED*, s.v. I. i. 5.

30. *Suarez Metaphysicks. R. P. Francisci Suarez* [1548–1617] . . . *metaphysicarum disputationum . . . tomi duo* (1605).

35. *Natura . . . frustra.* Aristotle, *Pol.* i. 1. 10. Cf. *De coelo*, i. 4 (271a, 34); *De partibus animalium*, iii. 1 (661b. 20), iv. 12 (694a. 15), &c.

14. 37–**15.** 1. *imperfect creatures . . . Sun is.* It was commonly held that small animals, such as flies and mice, were spontaneously generated by the action of the sun on decaying matter; and consequently these animals had not to be included in the six-days creation. See, e.g., Augustine, *De civ. Dei*, xv. 27. Cf. *PE*, iii. 27 (1650, p. 152).

15. 4. *Bees, Aunts, and Spiders.* Prov. vi. 6–8 (ants) with addition in Septuagint, 'Or go to the bee, and learn', &c.; ibid. xxx. 24–25, 28 (ants and spiders).

11. *Regio-Montanus.* Johann Müller of Königsberg (1436–76). He constructed an iron fly and a wooden eagle, both of which made celebrated flights. See P. Ramus, *Scholae mathematicae*, 1569, p. 65, and Du Bartas, i, 6. (Keck.)

12. *two soules.* Referring to the scholastic distinction of vegetative, sensitive, and rational; animals have the first two.

15. *encrease of Nile.* Cf. *PE*, vi. 8 (1646, pp. 315–19).

15–16. *conversion of the Needle.* Cf. *PE*, ii. 2, 3.

30. *its supernaturall station.* Josh. x. 12–13.

37. *the principle of motion and rest.* Aristotle, *Physics*, ii. 1 (192b. 13–15).

16. 1. *because that.* The elliptical usage, instead of 'because it is that', is paralleled at 16. 35: 'there was no deformity, because no forme', and at 57. 22, 'because delineated'. Cf. also *H*, 97. 40–98. 1, 'because no medal . . . enclosed'.

7. *sweetneth . . . wood.* Exod. xv. 25.

9. *God . . . Geometrician.* Cf. Plutarch, *Symposiacs*, viii. 2 (trans. Holland, 1603, p. 767): '*How* Plato *is to be understood, when he saith: That God continually is exercised in Geometry.*' ('. . . Written it is not in any place of all his books; howbeit held to be a saying of his. . . .') (Gr.)

17. *she only.* See note to 3. 25.

26. *formes.* 'Form' in scholastic logic is the essential inward character which determines the outward shape (the 'matter'). Cf. 57. 13.

40–41. *nature is the Art of God.* Cf. Hobbes, *Leviathan*, Introduction: 'Nature, the art whereby God hath made and governs the world.' (Wilkin.)

17. 19. *convert a Stoick.* See 20. 41.

23. *Fougade.* Or *fougasse*, a mine.

23. *miscarriage in the letter.* Miscarriage of the plot by means of the letter (sent anonymously to Lord Monteagle).

26–28. *King Philip . . . winds.* F. Strada, *De bello Belgico*, ii. 10 (1647, p. 436): '. . . cedere ad extremum non tam hostium virtuti . . . quam ventis tempestatibusque Anglorum loco præliantibus, coacti sint.' But the words are not here attributed to Philip.

34. *writing upon the wall.* Dan. v. 5.

35–39. *The successe . . . Sea.* The possibility of inundating the Low Countries by breaking the dykes, whether for offence or defence, had been considered already in the sixteenth century. When Leyden was besieged in 1574, the citizens surrounded their town with water in this way, with much resulting damage to the neighbouring districts. Requesens, who succeeded Alva in the charge of the country, wrote to Philip II that apparently the people would rather drown themselves and their property than submit, and that had the besieging army been Turkish they would already have done this; to which Philip replied that it would be easy to submerge Holland but also impolitic because too devastating. (See L. P. Gachard, *Correspondance de Philippe II sur les affaires des Pays-Bas*, 1858, iii, pp. 175–6.) No record of any such saying by the Sultan as Browne reports has been found.

18. 4. *intelligences.* See 32. 1–10 and notes.

24. *fooles . . . fortunate.* See *Oxford Dict. of Eng. Proverbs*, 'Fortune favours fools' and note to 18. 39.

25. *a wise man . . . fortune.* Cf. Juvenal, xiii. 20: 'Victrix fortunae sapientia.'

26–27. *opprobrious Epithets, &c.* E.g. *King John*, III. i. 61: 'That strumpet Fortune', and *Hamlet*, II. ii. 515.

39. *let providence . . . fooles.* See *Oxford Dict. of Eng. Proverbs*, 'God sendeth fortune to fools.'

19. 5–6. *judiciall Astrology.* The kind that judges and forecasts the future. *SC* contains 'W. Ramsey's Judicial Astrology Vindicated' (1651).

16. *Homers chaine. Iliad*, viii. 18–26. With the rest of the sentence, 'There is . . . God' (ll. 15–18), cf. Macrobius (*SC*), *In Somn. Scip.* i. 14–15 (on the unity of all things): 'inuenietur pressius intuenti a summo deo usque ad ultimam rerum faecem una mutuis se uinculis religans et nusquam interrupta conexio. et haec est Homeri catena aurea, quam pendere de caelo in terras deum iussisse commemorat.' See also note 29. 24.

36. *Faith.* The corrupt reading 'reason' seems to have entered the text at an early stage, as the obviously correct 'Faith' occurs only in *P* and, as a marginal conjecture, in *N*. Cf. 64. 15.

20. 10–11. *Archidoxis . . . Sympathies of things.* There are two works by Paracelsus with the title *Archidoxis*. Here the reference is to *Archidoxis Magica*, containing instructions how to prepare various amulets or sigils (occult devices) intended to cure specific diseases (Paracelsus, *Opera*, *SC*, xi, 1605, pp. 111–60). Cf. MS. Sloane 1848, f. 270ᵛ (*K*, v, p. 226): 'If you haue a mind to proceed farther, you may trie amuletes & transplantation. . . . And may also consider of the Sigill of paracelsus.' Cf. *LF*, 181. 17. In *PE*, i. 11 (1646, pp. 45 and 47) Browne observes that 'Charmes, ungrounded Amulets', &c. can be delusive. He refers to the other *Archidoxis* in *PE*, ii. 1 (1646, pp. 50–51).

12. *Brazen Serpent.* Num. xxi. 9.

15. *having read . . . of Naptha.* E.g. in Pliny, *HN*, ii. 108–9.

16. *fire of the Altar.* Lev. vi. 13; 2 Macc. i. 19–36.

17–18. *Elias . . . water.* 1 Kings xviii.

21–22. *Asphaltick . . . Gomorrha*). Cf. Pliny, *HN*, ii. 106: 'Nihil in Asphaltite Iudaeae lacu qui bitumen gignit mergi potest.' See *PE*, vii. 15 (1646, pp. 369–71) for a discussion '*Of the Lake Asphaltites*'.

22–23. *Manna . . . in Calabria.* G. Sandys, *A relation of a Journey begun . . . 1610* (1621, iv, p. 250), referring to the silk-industry in Calabria, adds that 'from the leaues of those [sc. mulberry trees] that grow higher on the mountaines . . . they gather plentie of *Manna*, the best of all other: which falls thereon like a dew in the night time.'

23. *Josephus. Antiq. Jud.* (*SC*), iii. 1. 6.

37. *inductive.* Arguable, reasonable, persuasive. Cf. 45. 23.

37. *That doctrine of Epicurus.* Diogenes Laertius, x. 139. 1.

20. 42–**21.** 1. *Those . . . holy Ghost.* Sc. the Macedonians.

21. 6. *the three Impostors.* There was a widespread belief in the seventeenth century that an anonymous book so entitled was or had been in existence, and various well-known writers were named as its possible author, including Boccaccio, Aretino, Giordano Bruno, and Campanella.

Digby, *Observations*, 1643, p. 12, assumes that the author was Bernardino Ochino. Burton (*Anatomy*, 3. 4. 2. 1, 1638, p. 690) mentions the book without showing clearly enough that it was distinct from *Cymbalum Mundi*, by Des Périers, which he mentions in the same sentence. Burton cites Mersenne, *Quaestiones in Genesin* (*SC*), where again no particular author is specified: 'Adde librum illum impium, quem à nescio quo Atheo de tribus impostoribus scriptum aiunt, in quo tam horrenda continentur, vt vir doctus me certiorem fecerit, se, cùm titulum vidisset, horrore correptum fuisse, & librum statim proiecisse' (1623, c. xvi, col. 533).

It is difficult now to believe that the book ever really existed, but the opinion it was supposed to advocate had been heard of long before the sixteenth century, for according to Matthew Paris (under year 1238) the Emperor Frederic II was accused of having said that there were three deceivers who had led the world astray, Moses, Christ, and Mahomet. The Emperor denied this accusation, but once it had been realized that such a view could be entertained it would be easy to conceive also of a book written to recommend it. Much later, apparently in the eighteenth century, an incomplete treatise *De tribus impostoribus* was published with the false date of 1598. The whole subject is discussed by P. G. Brunet in *Le traité des trois imposteurs* [the spurious work] . . . *precédé d'une notice philologique et bibliographique par Philomneste junior* (1867). The volume in *SC* (p. 49, no. 40), 'Hist. of the 3 late famous Impostors' (1669), has no connexion with the book referred to here.

17. *Galen . . . doubt thereof.* Galen, *Works* (*SC*), ed. Kühn, iv, pp. 772 sqq.: '*Quod animi mores temperamenta sequantur*', 3. (Gr.)

20. *Seneca. Troades*, 397, 401–2 ('nec parcens'), 378–9 ('an toti morimur').

30–31. *carry the buckler unto.* Hold a candle to.(?) Stand up to as an adversary, or assist as an armour-bearer.

22. 11–13. *left side . . . Nature. PE*, iv. 5 (1646, pp. 186–93): '*Of the right and left Hand.*'

14–15. *who shall arise . . . Resurrection.* Pererius, *Comment. in Genesin* (*SC*), iv. 2, § 202, p. 152 (1622), cites the question from Tostatus: 'In resurrectione, inquit, vtri Adamone, an Euae reddetur ea costa quae detracta est Adamo. . . .' (See *CE*, p. 90.)

15. *Whether Adam was an Hermaphrodite.* A common supposition, partly based on the words 'male and female created he them', which were taken to mean that individuals at first combined the two sexes. Cf. also Plato, *Sympos.* 189 sqq. (*CE*, p. 92.)

19–24. *whether the world . . . part thereof.* In *PE*, vi. 2, '*Of mens Enquiries in what season or point of the Zodiack it* [sc. the world] *began. . .* ', § 1 (1646, p. 283), Browne quotes this passage. Cf. *CE*, p. 63.

28–29. *Pantagruels Library. Pantagruel*, 7.

29. *Tartaretus.* Pierre Tartaret published his commentaries on Aristotle in 1494.

35. *Deucalion.* See *CE*, pp. 213–14. Cf. Ralegh, *History of the World*, I. vii. 3 (1614, pp. 86–88), *Of Deucalions Floud.*

36–37. *not to mee . . . alwayes.* Browne accepts the belief that water is a lighter element than earth. Various theories had been put forward to explain why portions of the world remain unsubmerged. (*CE*, p. 56.)

22. 37–**23.** 2. *How all . . . foesible.* Augustine enlarges on this in *De civ. Dei*, xv. 27, 'Of the Arke, and the deluge', &c. (trans. J. H[ealey], 1620, p. 536).

23. 3–6. *honest Father, &c.* Augustine, *De civ. Dei*, xvi. 7, gives several explanations, including the miraculous one that the animals could have been transported by angels. Cf. J. de Acosta, *De natura Novi Orbis* (1589), trans. (1604) *Natural & Moral History of the Indies*, Hakluyt Soc., 1880, i. 21, pp. 61–64, '*By what meanes tame Beasts passed to the Indies.*'

10–11. *Creatures there . . . Continent.* Acosta, op. cit. iv. 36, ed. cit. i, pp. 277–9, '*How it should be possible that at the Indies there should be anie sortes of beasts, whereof the like are no where else.*'

16–19. *I can make it probable, &c.* Browne attempts this in *PE*, vi. 6 (1646, pp. 294–305). Cf. Augustine, *De civ. Dei*, xv. 8 (trans. cit., p. 512), and *CE*, pp. 148–9.

23. *postulate.* Assumption. Gen. v. 27. Cf. *PE*, vii. 3, '*That Methuselah must needs be the longest liver of all the posterity of Adam.*'

26–30. *That Judas . . . overthrow it.* Matt. xxvii. 5 and Acts i. 18. The 'doubtful word' in Matthew is ἀπήγξατο, which could mean both 'was strangled' and 'hanged himself'. See *PE*, vii. 11 (1646, pp. 360–1).

30–33. *erected the Tower . . . Scripture.* Gen. xi. 4. Josephus, *Antiq. Jud.* i. 4. 2, adopts this unscriptural explanation. Cf. *PE*, vii. 6, where other motives are also considered.

39–40. *when Peter . . . Angel.* Acts xii. 15 (ἄγγελος).

24. 1. *Families.* Family appears here to have the obsolete sense, 'the servants of a house'. *OED*, s.v. 1.

2. *answered.* Sc. taking part in a *disputatio* or examination.

11. *Ptolomy.* Philadelphus, King of Egypt (283–247 B.C.). Josephus, op. cit. xii. 2, describes the negotiations.

12. *the Alcoran.* See B. Moran, 'Browne's reading of the Turkes', *N. and Q.*, 30 Aug. and 13 Sept. 1952.

19. *Philo. Life of Moses*, ii. 3 (14).

24. *Zoroaster.* 'Who by report, was five thousand yeeres before the warre of *Troy*' (Plutarch, *Isis and Osiris*; *Morals*, transl. Holland, 1603, p. 1306). The commentators on Genesis generally held that Moses was the first author (*CE*, p. 25).

24–25. *divers that writ before Moses.* Cf. Augustine, *De civ. Dei*, xv. 23 (see note to 24. 37).

36–37. *perished leaves of Solomon.* 1 Kings iv. 32–33, and Josephus, op. cit. viii. 2. 5.

37. *Enochs Pillars.* On which the discoveries and inventions achieved up to his time were supposed to have been written. The pillars were attributed by Josephus, op. cit. 1. 2. 3, to the descendants of Seth, and were believed to have survived the flood. Augustine, op. cit. xv. 23, alludes to divine writings left by Enoch, and identifies these with the prophecies of

Enoch referred to in Jude 14–15; but also gives reasons for doubting the authenticity of extant writings sometimes ascribed to Enoch.

25. 2. *Pineda.* Juan de Pineda, of Medina del Campo (d. 1593). *SC* contains his *Monarchia Eclesiástica, ó Historia Universal del Mundo*, 1620 (first published in 1588).

3. *those three great inventions.* See note, p. 263; also *PE*, ii. 2, '*Concerning the Loadstone.*' (1646, pp. 56–65; 'gunnes, printing' mentioned on p. 65).

15. *exceptions.* Arguments against the opposing view (*OED*, s.v. 5*a*).

25–26. *obstinacy . . . good.* Cf. Sterne, *Tristram Shandy*, i. 17: ''Tis known by the name of perseverance in a good cause, and of obstinacy in a bad one.'

35. *those foure.* Pagan, Jewish, Mohammedan, and Christian.

26. 22. *which Aristotle requires. Nicom. Eth.* iii. 6–9; but Browne may have been thinking especially of ii. 7. 2, where it is observed that confidence in excess becomes rashness.

39–40. *neither the one nor the other.* Since, in Browne's view, the opinions debated were not sufficiently 'fundamental'.

27. 2–3. *Socrates . . . Unity of God.* Plutarch (?), *De placitis philosophorum*, i. 7 (*Morals*, trans. Holland, 1603, p. 812): 'Socrates and Plato doe hold, that he [God] is one. . . .' Although, according to Plato, *Apology*, 26 sqq., the charge actually brought against Socrates was rather that of introducing new deities of his own, Browne's statement that he suffered in the cause of monotheism is not too wide of the mark.

4. *the miserable Bishop.* Burton, 2. 2. 3 (1638, p. 246): 'Virgil, sometimes Bishop of *Saltburge* (as *Aventinus* Anno 745. relates) by *Bonifacius* Bishop of *Mentz* was therefore called in question, because he held *Antipodes* (which they made a doubt whether Christ died for) and so by that meanes tooke away the seat of Hell. . . .' By a misunderstanding Boniface supposed Virgilius to have believed that there was another world, with sun and moon, and reported this to the Pope, with the result that Virgilius was called upon to explain himself; but there is no reason to suppose that he 'suffered' any sort of martyrdom. As observed by Greenhill, the reading 'living' in *43*, as against 'life' in the manuscripts and *42*, suggests that Browne had become more correctly informed. See Milner, *History of the Church of Christ*, 1812, iii, p. 189.

27–28. *Miracles in the Indies.* A number of these are described by E. Acosta, *Rerum a Societate Iesu in Oriente gestarum Volumen*, 1574.

33. *would . . . done.* See Textual Notes, p. 263. Emendation is not required. Cf. Defoe, *A new voyage round the world* (*Romances*, ed. Aitken, xiv, p. 140): 'My men would fain have had me gone ashore again.'

27. 35–**28.** 1. *Though indeed . . . transcend her.* Cf. Augustine, *De civ. Dei*, x. 12 (trans. Healey, 1620, p. 359): 'is not the world a miracle? yet visible and of his making. Nay; all the miracles done in this world are lesse then the world it selfe, the heauen and earth, and all therein. . . .' Cf. Augustine, *Serm.* 37, '*De verbis Apostoli*': 'Plus est enim facere quod nunquam fuit, quam reparare quod fuit.'

28. 19–23. *the Crosse . . . his hands.* Browne could have read in, for instance, Nicephorus (Callisti filius), *Eccl. Hist.* viii. 29 (*PG*, 146, pp. 110–11), about the miracle of healing done with the cross found by Helena, and also how Constantine had a nail of the cross put into the harness of his horse, 'ut in certaminibus tutus a vulneribus illaesusque maneret'.

24–25. *consecrated swords.* Described by 'A' [*recte* F]. Schott, *Itincrarium Italiae*, ii. 13 (1655, pp. 481–9).

25. *Baldwin.* First King of Jerusalem (1100–18).

34. *Antient of dayes.* Dan. vii. 9.

28. 40–**29.** 2. *cessation of Oracles . . . for it. PE*, vii. 12, '*Of the cessation of Oracles*' (1646, pp. 361–3). *Miscellany Tracts*, xi (*K*, v. 113–21). Plutarch, *De defectu oraculorum.*

29. 5. *his death.* Sc. Jesus'. Luke xxiii. 44–45.

5–6. *this . . . confessed it.* Browne quotes the confession in *PE*, vii. 12, as follows:

Me puer Hebræus Divos Deus ipse gubernans
Cedere sede jubet, tristemque redire sub orcum;
Aris ergo dehinc tacitus discedito nostris.

See H. W. Parke, *The Delphic Oracle*, 1956, ii, p. 209.

9. *Megasthenes.* Fl. *c.* 300 B.C. An authority on ancient India. Fragments on the chronology of Persia were (wrongly) attributed to him.

11. *a piece of Justine.* Justinus, xxxvi. 2. 12: 'Sed Aegyptii, cum scabiem et vitiliginem paterentur, responso moniti eum [sc. Moses] cum aegris, ne pestis ad plures serperet, terminis Aegypti pellunt.'

19. *as some . . . death also.* Deut. xxxiv. 5–8. Cf. Philo, *De vita Mosis*, ii. 291.

22. *doubtfull conceit of.* Sceptical opinion regarding.

24. *Ladder and scale.* Cf. 19. 15–18, 32. 13–20, 33. 17–22; also *CE*, p. 64 and pp. 182–3; and A. O. Lovejoy, *The Great Chain of Being.*

25–26. *and doe now know . . . Witches.* Browne gave his views on witchcraft more fully at Bury St. Edmunds on an occasion described in *A Tryal of Witches . . . 1664. Before Sir Matthew Hale Kt . . . 1682* (reprinted 1838; also in Cobbett and Howell, *State Trials*, 1816, vi, pp. 687–702). The two women accused were found guilty and hanged; but Browne's part in the inquiry appears to have been greatly misrepresented (especially by Edmund Gosse, *Sir Thomas Browne*, 1905, pp. 147–9, following too trustfully the account in F. Hutchinson's *Historical essay concerning witchcraft*, 1718). According to the earlier account, furnished by an anonymous witness of the proceedings, Browne's evidence was not given, as it was subsequently said to have been, right at the end of the trial, with the effect of turning the scales against the accused, but earlier. Moreover, so far as can be judged from the same report, Browne, while believing that the alleged victims had been bewitched, expressed no opinion as to the guilt of these particular women, but tried rather to explain the nature and processes of witchcraft: 'Dr Brown of Norwich, a person of great knowledge . . . was clearly of opinion that the persons were bewitched; and said, That in Denmark there had been a great discovery of witches, who used the very same way of afflicting persons, by sticking pins into them.... And his opinion was, That the devil in such cases did work upon the bodies of men and women, upon a natural foundation, (that is) to stir up, and excite such humours super-abounding in their bodies to a great excess . . . for he conceived, that these swooning fits were natural, and nothing else but that they call the mother, but only heightened to a great excess by the subtilty of the devil, cooperating with the malice of these which we term witches, at whose instance he doth these villanies.' (As in Cobbett and Howell.) See Dorothy Tyler, *Anglia*, 54, 1930, pp. 179–95, 'A review of the interpretation of Sir Thomas Browne's part in a witch trial in 1664'. Browne himself writes further on witchcraft in MS. Sloane 1869 (*K*, v, p. 252).

36. *power to transpeciate.* Denied also by Augustine, *De civ. Dei*, xviii. 18. Cf. J. Bodin, *De magorum daemonomania* (*SC*), ii. 6 (1581, p. 178).

30. 1–2. *Spirits . . . carnality.* Cf. Augustine, op. cit. xv. 23, Bodin, op. cit. iii. 7 (1581, pp. 203–4), and *PE*, vii. 16. 1 (1646, p. 371).

7. *Tribe of Dan . . . Devill.* Moltke cites Augustine, *De Antichristo*, § 2 (*PL*, 40, col. 1131), where conjunction with the devil is denied; nevertheless: 'in ipso vero conceptionis ejus initio diabolus simul introibit in uterum matris ejus.' The theory was based on the words about Dan in Gen. xlix. 17 and on the omission of Dan from the list of the tribes in Rev. vii.

12. *Maid of Germany* (*and note, p. 263*). Eva Flegen, of Meurs. The story of her alleged abstinence over many years was well known and generally believed. See, e.g., N. Wanley, *Wonders of the little world*, 1678, pp. 589–90. W. Fabricius Hildanus, however, heard in 1628, on what he considered very good authority, that the girl had been an impostor. See his *Observ. medic.* v. 33 (in *Opera*, *SC*, 1646). It would be easy for Browne to hear of this during his medical studies on the Continent, if not before. See *TLS*, 24 July and 21 Aug. 1948.

18–26. *who having . . . Magicke.* Cf. *PE*, i. 10 (1646, p. 41): 'Beside being a naturall Magician he [sc. the Devil] may performe many acts in wayes above our knowledge, though not transcending our naturall power, when our knowledge shall direct it; part hereof hath been discovered by himselfe, and some by human indagation which though magnified as fresh inventions unto us, are stale unto his cognition. . . . Many secrets there are in nature of difficult discovery unto man, of naturall knowledge unto Satan, whereof some his vain-glory cannot conceale, others his envy will never discover.'

19. *betrayed.* Sc. to them.

21. *actives . . . passives.* Cf. *PE*, I. 2 (1646, p. 44): '. . . the effects of naturall and created causes, and such as upon a due conjunction of actives and passives, without a miracle must arise unto what they appear.' T. Norton (fl. 1477), *Ordinal of Alchemy*, quoted in *OED*, s.v. Active, observes that 'Heate, and Cold be qualities Active; Moisture, and Driness be qualyties Passive'.

27. *good and bad Angels.* Cf. Paracelsus, *De origine morborum invisibilium*, v (*Opera*, 1603–5, i, p. 247): 'Is quicquid praeterea Diuis suis imperat, hoc fiat et gratum sit, siue ab hoc, siue illo, siue a spiritu, siue Angelo, siue Diabolo praestetur. Hoc enim modo spiritus etiam iussi sunt, ut docerent & iuuarent: quo nimirum beneficia ad nos redundarent tam ab inimicis, quam amicis.' See D. P. Walker, *Spiritual and demonic magic from Ficino to Campanella* (1958).

29–30. *Ascendens . . . Dei (and note).* This sentence has sometimes been attributed to Paracelsus, *De imaginibus*, apparently in error. A very similar sense is found, however, in Paracelsus, *Philosophia sagax*, i. 3 (*Opera*, 1603–5, x, p. 126): 'Astrum ducit hominem ad sublimem sapientiam, prudentiam, scientiam, vt in lumine admirabilis fiat, atque mysteria miraculorum Dei splendida & luculenta manifestentur.' It may be that Browne meant simply to give the gist of this passage. The association of the 'ascendens constellatum' with 'our good Angel' in the note is elucidated by a passage in MS. Sloane 1869, f. 17 (*K*, v, p. 246): 'Whether wee are vnder the care of our mothers good Angell in the womb or whether that spirit [sc. our guardian angel] vndertakes us when the starres are thought to concern us that is at our natiuitie men haue a libertie & latitude to opinion.' Moltke refers to Censorinus, *De die natali*, iii: 'Genius est Deus, cuius in tutela, utquisque natus est, vixit.' (The note by Lindenbrogius to this chapter in the edition of Censorinus of 1614 (*SC*) lists discussions of the subject by philosophers and theologians.)

33. *fellow-natures on earth.* Cf. Augustine, *Solil. animae ad Deum*, 27 (*PL*, 40, col. 885): 'Diligunt nempe concives suos.' Also *De civ. Dei*, viii. 25; and Paracelsus, *De fundamento scientiarum & sapientiae* (*Opera*, 1603–5, x, p. 67): 'Nam & nos angeli sumus.'

31. 3. *Plato. Timaeus*, 41 d–e; cf. Proclus, *Platon. Theol.* i. 13. (Moltke.) Also Porphyry, *Vita Pythagorae*, 19: ὅτι πάντα τὰ γινόμενα ἔμψυχα δεῖ νομίζειν.

3–4. *is yet . . . Philosophers.* E.g. Thomas Vaughan in his *Anima magica abscondita or a discourse of the universal spirit of nature* (1650).

11. *know not . . . Sunne.* Cf. 15. 1 and 70. 17. Spirits are generated without concoction from the sun.

32. 2–3. *not only . . . persons.* Cf. Clement Alexand. (*SC*), *Stromata*, vi. 294 (*PG*, ix, col. 390): 'per gentes et civitates sunt distributae angelorum praefecturae: fortasse autem ex iis sunt deputati singulis.' See also *CM*, 215. 8–14.

4–5. *Pythagoras and Plato.* Diogenes Laertius, viii. 32, attributes a doctrine of advisory spirits to Pythagoras. Cf. Plato, *Phaedo*, 107e, and *Timaeus*, 90a. Other observations by Browne on guardian angels in MSS. Sloane 1848 and 1869 are given in *K*, v, pp. 200 and 246. *SC* contains a copy of Apuleius, *De Deo Socratis*, 1625. See also *PL*, 219, cols. 43–44: 'Index de angelis custodibus.'

11. *their . . . them.* Their, sc. the angels'; them, sc. my opinion and metaphysics.

14. *Staire, or . . . Scale.* See 29. 24 and note.

21. *definition of Porphyry.* The note 'Essentia rationalis immortalis' in three of the manuscripts resembles Porphyry's definition of the soul in *De occasionibus* (ed. 1607, p. 285): 'Anima est essentia inextensa, immaterialis, immortalis'; there is no reference here to the difference between angels and men, but the author of the note may also have had confusedly in mind Porphyry's definition of man in *Isagoge*, iii. 6: 'animal rationale mortale.'

23. *man also was immortall.* Cf. Augustine, *De civ. Dei*, xiii. 1 (trans. Healey, 1620, p. 446): 'For God made not man as he did his Angels, that though they sinned yet could not dye; but so as hauing performed their course of obedience, death could not preuent them from partaking for euer of blessed and Angelicall immortality: but hauing left this course, death should take them into iust damnation.' See also *CE*, pp. 104–5.

30. *forms . . . properties.* See note to 16. 26. Browne supposes that the angels perceive at once the essential determinant qualities of any phenomenon and by their power of insight can define such qualities in terms of species or kind and not merely of individual or accidental properties. They can see farther than we can into the reasons why things are as they are.

33. *numericall.* Particular.

35. *Hypostasis.* Person.

39. *Habakkuk . . . den.* Bel and the Dragon 36 and 39.

40. *Philip to Azotus.* Acts viii. 39–40.

33. 7. *Angels of heaven.* Luke xv. 7, 10.

7–9. *I cannot . . . Angels.* 'those in' appears first in *43*. The Father is apparently Augustine, who in *De civ. Dei*, xi. 9, advocates, though not quite positively, the theory that 'Fiat lux' refers to the creation of the angels. Later, ibid. 32, he speaks of possible opposition to this view and says he would not contest the point. The order of the words in Browne's sentence, as altered, makes its meaning ambiguous, but probably he means 'I agree with the theologians mentioned by Augustine who were not sure that "Fiat lux" refers to the angels.' Augustine's theory was not favoured in the seventeenth century (*CE*, pp. 52–53).

11. *accident.* A non-essential quality, as at 32. 31.

16. *best part of nothing.* Creation *ex nihilo* was the orthodox view. Cf. 34. 41–35. 1.

17. *we are onely.* We only are. See note to 3. 25.

19. *linkes those two together.* Cf. Pererius, *Comment. in Genesin*, § 168, 1622, p. 53: 'homo est ligamen & vinculum & nexus Vniuersi, in eo enim consociantur inter se atque conjunguntur res incorporeae cum corporeis, & immortales cum mortalibus.' (*CE*, p. 69 n.) Also George Herbert, 'Mans medley', 7–12 (*Works*, ed. Hutchinson, p. 131).

36–37. *whereof.* Sc. the invisible world.

37. *noe description.* The negative, supplied by *P* alone, is essential. Many of the scriptural commentators point out that Moses did *not* write about *invisibilia*. (*CE*, p. 48.) M. Denonain noted that *P* has 'noe', but Miss Sanna was the first to restore the negative to the text.

37. *the other.* Sc. the visible world. For the form of the whole sentence

'to have left no description, and of the other so obscurely' cf. 34. 31–32: 'hath not beene able to prove it, and as weakely. . . .'

38. *parts . . . controversie (and note, p. 264)*. Why Moses failed to mention 'the element of fire' was still debatable (*CE*, pp. 176 and 194).

34. 3–4. *mysticall . . . Egyptians*. Acts vii. 22.

19. *ministring spirits*. Heb. i. 14.

28. *to repent*. Gen. vi. 6.

29–30. *would not destroy it*. Sc. by flood. Gen. ix. 9–17.

30. *that there is . . . faith*. Cf. Augustine, *Contra Academicos*, iii. 10. (Moltke.)

30–32. *Aristotle . . . world was eternall*. See notes to 11. 38–39.

38. *distinction*. Difference or qualification. Cf. 76. 24.

39–40. *generation not onely*. Not only generation. See note to 3. 25.

40. *but also creation*. Cf. 60. 24–25, 65. 9–13 and Augustine, *De civ. Dei*, xi. 18: '. . . contrariorum oppositione saeculi pulchritudo componitur.'

35. 4–5. *at the blast . . . made*. See note to 11. 25.

7. *as the text describes it*. Gen. ii. 7. See *CE*, p. 68.

12. *affections*. Properties. *OED*, s.v. 12.

14. *affirmative of Plato*. *Phaedrus*, 245c; cf. *Phaedo*, 105 sqq.

14. *not a negative from Aristotle*. See *De anima*, ii. 2–4 and iii. 5; also *De generatione animalium*, ii. 3.

15. *concerning its production*. Whether by infusion or by traduction. See Augustine(?), *De eccles. dogm.* 18 (*PL*, 42, col. 1216, and *CE*, pp. 78–79).

18–19. *Paracelsus . . . man*. Paracelsus, *De natura rerum*, i, 'De generationibus rerum naturalium' (*Opera*, 1603–5, vi, pp. 203–4).

22. *Antimetathesis*. Browne seems to intend the sense of a *chiasmus*, or inversion in a second phrase of the order followed in a first. 'Antanaclasis', the reading of the manuscripts and *42*, has a different meaning, incorrectly defined in the marginal note (see *OED*, s.v.).

22–23. *Creando . . . creatur*. Augustine(?), *De eccles. dogm.* 18 (*PL*, 42, col. 1216): 'Anima humana non cum carne moritur, quia non cum carne . . . seminatur, sed formato in ventre matris corpore Dei judicio creatur et infunditur.'

28. *equivocall*. Nondescript.

28–29. *monstrous productions*. G. B. della Porta, *Magiæ Naturalis Libri Viginti* (*SC*), ii. 12, '*Variæ hominis cum feris misturæ*' (1650, p. 77), gives instances from Plutarch, &c. Porta's work is mentioned favourably in *PE*, i. 8. (1646, p. 34).

37. *Crasis*. Blending, composition.

40. *and that the hand of reason*. And the soul the instrument or agent of reason (as the body the instrument of the senses). The reading of the manuscripts and *42*, 'the nearer ubi', in the sense of location, is paralleled in 38. 23 and 49. 12.

36. 14–15. *All flesh is grasse*. Isa. xl. 6.

26. *Lots wife*. Gen. xix. 26. Cf. *PE*, vii. 11 (1646, p. 360).

32. *contrary*. Aquinas, *S.T.* (*SC*) i, Quaest. lxxv, Art. 6, '*Utrum anima*

humana sit corruptibilis': 'Non invenitur corruptio nisi ubi invenitur contrarietas.'

37. 1. *world. That.* The punctuation of *43*, &c. allows the reader temporarily to suppose that the construction beginning 36. 29, 'I beleeve that', is being continued, whereas a new sentence begins after 'world'.

1–5. *those phantasmes . . . Adam.* Browne rejects Plato's explanation in *Phaedo*, 81d, that ghosts haunting cemeteries are the souls of the wicked showing their unwillingness to leave the material world.

8. (*O*) *Adam, quid fecisti?* 2 Esdras vii. 48.

21–22. *of a spirit.* Sc. of being a spirit.

38. 2. *Adam 30. yeares old.* This estimate was commonly accepted, though other ages between 20 and 50 were conjectured (*CE*, p. 80).

10. *sleepe within the bosome of our causes.* Cf. 48. 29–33 and Carew, 'Aske me no more', 3–4 (*Poems*, ed. Dunlap, p. 102):

'*For in your beauties orient deepe,*
These flowers as in their causes, sleepe.

Carew's *Poems* were first published in 1640. See also *H*, 124. 34–35 and *GC*, 166. 37 sqq. and cf. Ps. cxxxix. 14–15.

15. *yet.* However.

23. *that ineffable place.* 2 Cor. xii. 4.

23. *ubi.* See note to 35. 40.

25. *exaltation of gold.* The reading 'god' found in five manuscripts instead of 'gold' is adopted by M. Denonain. It is hard, however, to see what 'god' could mean in this context, whereas 'exaltation' was a common term for the refining or sublimating of metals. The process might not merely purify the metal but lead to its transmutation into something else, here identified by Browne with the philosophers' stone. The 'Divinity' which Browne has learnt from this process, by analogy, is that the soul cannot realize itself or transcend its earthly being until its carnal dross has been shed. In 38. 25 'something more then' replaces 'nothing else but' in the manuscripts and *42*; and it seems very unlikely that while making this change Browne would fail to correct 'gold' if it had been an error for 'god'. That it was not an error seems to be confirmed by the passage following 'discover' (38. 33) in *P*, wherein Browne gives his own 'hermiticall' definition of death (see p. 264).

29–30. *transmigrations . . . Silkeworms . . . Divinity.* Cf. H. Vaughan, 'Resurrection and Immortality', *Silex Scintillans*, 1650 (*Works*, O.E.T. 1957, p. 400). See also notes thereto and note to *RM*, 46. 2.

39. 5. *quantum . . . illo.* Virgil, *Aen.* ii. 274.

21. *Register of God.* Rev. xx. 15, &c.

22. *Testament of Diogenes* (*and note*). Cicero, *Tusc. Quaest.* i. 43.

24. *Coelo . . . urnam.* Lucan, vii. 819.

30. *Crowes and Dawes.* See *PE*, iii. 9 (1646, pp. 125–6). (Gr.)

32–33. *Jubilee . . . Saturne.* See p. 264.

33–34. *excepting one.* Christian IV of Denmark (1588–1648).

35. *three Emperours.* Sc. of Germany: Rodolph II (1576–1612), Matthias (1612–19), and Ferdinand II (1619–37).

35–36. *foure Grand Signiours.* The Sultans Ahmed I (1604–17), Mustafa I (1617–18 and 1622–3), Othman II (1618–22), and Murad IV (1623–40).

36. *as many Popes.* Leo XI (1–27 Apr. 1605), Paul V (1605–21), Gregory XV (1621–3), Urban VIII (1623–44). Leo XI thus died nearly six months before Browne was born; but see 38. 3–17 and cf. *PE*, iv. 12 (1646, p. 218).

40. 7–8. *that age . . . to dye.* Often reckoned to be 33, but other ages, from 30 to 46, had been conjectured.

26–27. *like figures . . . before it.* As in 56. 5–10, Browne is probably thinking of a numeration-table such as is described in R. Recorde's *Ground of arts* and illustrated on p. 23 of the edition published in 1632. There the line for units is the highest, with the lines for tens, hundreds, &c. following successively below, so that the value of figures placed on a lower line is always ten times that of figures on the line immediately above.

30–31. *Cicero's ground . . . well. De Senectute,* xxiii (84): 'neque me vixisse paenitet; quoniam ita vixi, ut non frustra me natum existimem.' (Gr.)

41. 4. *whole bookes.* E.g. Paracelsus, *De vita longa* (*Opera*, 1603–5, vi, pp. 106–58).

5. *balsome.* An oily essence supposed to pervade organic bodies. *sulphur.* One of the supposed ultimate elements of all material substances.

6–7. *glome or bottome.* Ball or clew (of thread).

16. *six thousand.* See 44. 1 and note.

26–27. *Victurosque . . . mori.* Lucan, iv. 519–20.

42. 3. *Curtius, Scevola, or Codrus.* Marcus Curtius (Livy, vii. 6), armed and on horseback, rode into a chasm in the Forum, as the soothsayers had declared that Rome's chief strength must be sacrificed before the chasm would close. C. Mucius Scaevola (Livy, ii. 12) made his way into the camp of Lars Porsena, meaning to kill him, and when discovered thrust his right hand into the fire, to show his indifference to death. Codrus, the legendary king of Athens, was said to have sacrificed himself for his country when an invasion was threatened (Cicero, *Tusc. Quaest.* i. 48; Justinus, ii. 6. 19).

4. *to.* Compared to. See note to 73. 10.

6. *Emori . . . curo.* Cicero, *Tusc. Quaest.* i. 8, quotes this line of Epicharmus.

8. *goe off at one blow.* Suetonius, *Caligula*, 30.

17. *accuse.* Perhaps in the sense of reveal, display. See *OED*, s.v. 6.

20–22. *though . . . death.* Seneca, *Phoenissae*, 152–3:

> Eripere vitam nemo non homini potest,
> At nemo mortem. (Gr.)

22. *from that.* Sc. from death. The rest of the sentence expands this thought: God, who was immortal, though he lived in the flesh, did not undertake the misery of doing so for ever.

30–31. *Hee forgets . . . our owne.* Browne may have intended a lighter punctuation after 'right', as the new sentence expounds not his but the Stoic's doctrine, as in Seneca, *De providentia*, vi. 7.

42. *affections*. See note on 35. 12.

43. 9. *Radamanth*. There is manuscript support for the more correct form 'Rhadamanth', but apparently 'Radamanth' was current. See *OED*, s.v. Rhadamanthus.

11–12. *prophesy . . . fire*. Plutarch (?), *De placitis philosophorum*, i. 3 (*Morals*, trans. Holland, 1603, p. 807): '*Heraclytus* and *Hippasus* . . . were of opinion, that Fire was the principle and beginning of all . . . againe, the whole world, and all the bodies therein conteined, shall be one day consumed by fire in that generall conflagration and burning of all.'

14. *Communis . . . Misturus*. Lucan, vii. 814–15.

18. *decayed*. As it was commonly supposed to be. Browne here agrees with the drift of Hakewill's *Apologie . . . Or an examination and censure of the common errour touching Natures perpetuall and universal decay* (1627, &c.). Cf. A. O. Lovejoy et al., *History of primitivism* (1935), and Cicero, *Academica*, ii. 37–38 (119).

21. *mutation*. See 48. 11–19 and note.

23. *Some beleeve*. 'Some' for 'I' in the manuscripts and *42*. Browne is discreet because the belief was not orthodox and most of the commentators on Genesis rejected it. It is more Platonic than scriptural. (*CE*, pp. 43–44.)

31–34. *unspeakable . . . understood*. Cf. *PE*, i. 9 (1646, p. 35): 'a loose and popular delivery will serve oftentimes in Divinity; as may be observed even in holy Scripture, which often omitteth the exact account of things, describing them rather to our apprehensions, then leaving doubts in vulgar minds, upon their unknowne and Philosophicall descriptions.' Cf. Augustine, *De civ. Dei*, xx. 21 (trans. Healey, 1620, p. 767). See *CE*, pp. 176–7.

34. *notwithstanding*. Parenthetical, as at 64. 9.

44. 1. *Elias 6000. yeares*. See *PE*, vi. 1 (1646, pp. 277–8) and iii. 3 (p. 134); also *RM*, 41. 16, *H*, 120. 10–11, *CM*, 221. 19, 246. 15–16. Pererius, op. cit. 1622, p. 59b, refers to the statement in Génébrard, *Chronologia*, 1570, p. 3: 'Mundum sex mille annis duraturum . . . Eliæ Rabbini Iudæorum Cabbalici commentum, in Talmud.' Cf. *Talmud*, ed. Epstein, VI, 'Sanhedrin', ii, p. 657: 'The Tanna debe Eliyyahu teaches: The world is to exist six thousand years.' See also *PL*, 219, cols. 49–52: 'Index de duratione mundi et ejus fine.'

2–3. *denyed unto his Angels*. Matt. xxiv. 36.

10. *old prophesies*. Illustrated in the marginal note. Cf. Matt. xxiv. 11 and 24; Mark xiii. 22.

11–12. *In those . . . of warres*. Brackets for inverted commas. As in the marginal note Browne seems to be quoting from memory. Cf. Matt. xxiv. 6; Mark xiii. 7; Luke xxi. 9. Moreover, as Moltke observes, this particular prophecy refers not to the Last Day but to the destruction of the Temple and the fall of Jerusalem. See Augustine, *Epist.* 80 (199), to Hesychius (*PL*, 33, col. 914).

13. *There shall be signes, &c.* Luke xxi. 25.

14–15. *like . . . night.* 1 Thess. v. 2.

16. *revelation of Antichrist.* 1 John ii. 18; 2 Thess. ii. 3 sqq.

18. *halfe of opinion.* The manuscripts have 'Paracelsus' before 'opinion'. In his *Liber Philosophiae*, 'De votis alienis' (*Opera*, 1603–5, ix, p. 146), Paracelsus affirms that Antichrist 'nunquam aperte monstrabitur'.

25. *Quousque Domine?* Rev. vi. 9–10.

36. *hath onely.* Alone hath. See note to 3. 25.

37. *Ipsa sui, &c.* In the errata of *43* 'sui' is incorrectly emended to 'suæ'; 'sui' in all manuscripts, *42* and *43*. It is just possible that Browne himself made the error (cf. 'Strebæus' altered in his hand to 'Stebæus', *GC*, 131. 17). For the sentiment, which was almost proverbial but expressed variously, see Seneca, *De vita beata*, 9. 4, and Claudian, *Panegyricus Manlio Theodoro*, l. 1: 'Ipsa quidem Virtus pretium sibi. . . .'

45. 1–4. *artifice . . . friends.* Seneca, *Ep.* 25, where Epicurus is quoted: ' "Sic fac", inquit, "tanquam spectet Epicurus" ' [*v.l.* aliquis]. (Gr.)

3–4. *deare and worthiest.* For the form of phrase cf. 'To the Reader', 2. 7.

7–8. *That great resolution.* Seneca, *Ep.* 113. 31: 'Hoc ante omnia sibi quisque persuadeat: me iustum esse gratis oportet.'

15–16. *those impieties.* It had often been supposed (on quite insufficient grounds) that Lucian must have had Jesus Christ in mind when in *The Lover of Lies* he mentioned a Syrian in Palestine who exorcised devils for a fee. Lucian's plain allusions to Christianity are not so objectionable. Perhaps Browne was thinking also of Lucian's disrespectful attitude to the Greek immortals. *Euripides.* E.g. *Orestes*, 418; Frag. of *Bellerophontes*, 288. *Julian.* The Apostate.

29–30. *shall . . . returne.* Cf. Augustine, *De civ. Dei*, xxii. 20.

31–41. *As at . . . single individuals.* The sentence beginning at l. 34, 'As at the Creation', is an expansion of that beginning with the same phrase at l. 31; and it may be that Browne intended to delete the first and shorter sentence but failed to make this clear enough in his manuscript.

46. 2. *millions.* The doctrine in the passage which originally followed here and was omitted in *43* (see p. 265), is paralleled in H. Vaughan's 'Resurrection and Immortality', especially ll. 25–37. For some 'Hermetic' parallels see the notes to that poem in Vaughan's *Works*, O.E.T., 1957, pp. 729–30.

2–5. *I have . . . selfe.* Browne alludes to the combination of mercury with other elements to form amalgams, from which it can be recovered in its 'numerical' (cf. 32. 33 and 36) or individual condition. *mortified. OED* cites J. Harris, *Lex. Tech.* (1704), i, s.v. Mortify: 'The Chymists say a thing is Mortify'd when its outward Form is altered or destroyed, as particularly when Mercury, or any other metal is dissolved in an Acid Menstruum.'

6–8. *the formes . . . parts.* See note on *GC*, 166. 36–167. 1; cf. Macrobius, *In Somnium Scipionis*, ii. 12: '. . . nihil intra uiuum mundum perire, sed eorum, quae interire uidentur, solam mutari speciem, et illud in originem suam atque in ipsa elementa remeare, quod tale, quale fuit, esse desierit.'

15–17. *made good . . . again.* Helmont, *Pharmacopolium*, 13 and 14 (*Opera*, 1707, p. 438), describes how Quercetanus, having noticed the appearance of foliation on the side of a vessel exposed to frost and containing a weak solution of plant-ashes, drew the conclusion that the plant was being resuscitated. Helmont explains that the foliation would have showed itself if the vessel had contained nothing but water. Browne may be referring to Quercetanus, who is mentioned in a letter of Browne's friend, Henry Power (10 Feb. 1647; *K*, vi, p. 280), asking for further guidance on this subject; Browne's reply is apparently not extant, but he seems to have said later (ibid., p. 282) that the leaves of the plant could at least be seen 'shadowed in glaciation'. See also Moltke, p. 276.

22. *Ezekiel.* xxxvii. 1–14.

30–31. *Which neither . . . man.* 1 Cor. ii. 9.

31–32. *translated . . . expresse it.* 2 Cor. xii. 1–4.

33. *Saint Johns description.* Rev. xxi. 19–21.

47. 4. *its owne soule . . . Creator.* Cf. 49. 3–4.

5–6. *whether . . . Heaven.* 2 Cor. xii. 2–4.

11–12. *Moses . . . Egyptians.* Acts vii. 22. Cf. 78. 10–12.

13–14. *desired to see God.* Exod. xxxiii. 18–23.

20–21. *if . . . objects.* Cf. Augustine, *De civ. Dei*, xxii. 29.

22. *species.* The outward appearances of things.

24. *Aristotles philosophy. De anima*, ii. 7.

33–34. *flame . . . soule.* Cf. Augustine, *De civ. Dei*, xxi. 9, 10.

34–35. *flames of sulphure.* Rev. xxi. 8.

36. *this present Hell.* See Section 51.

39. *textuarie.* Authoritative, as a text-book should be.

48. 1. *bodies that persist invincible.* Cf. *PE*, iii. 14 (1646, pp. 138–40), '*Of the Salamander*'.

5. *burnt the golden Calfe into powder.* It is not stated (Exod. xxxii. 20) that Moses did exactly this, but that 'he took the calf . . . and burnt it in the fire, and ground it to powder'. Cf. Deut. ix. 21.

7. *consumeth not.* Cf. Pliny, *HN*, xxxiii. 3 (trans. Holland, 1634, p. 465): 'it alone of all things in the world, loseth nothing in the fire.'

13–14. *not onely . . . beginning.* The saying in Mark xiii. 31 'Heaven and earth shall pass away', had to be reconciled with the tradition, stemming from Aristotle, that the heavens were incorruptible and eternal (see 11. 38–39 and note); hence the distinction here. The difficulty was usually met by references, e.g. Rev. xxi. 1, to a new heaven and a new earth, implying that the heavens will be renovated but not destroyed. (*CE*, p. 187. Cf. Augustine, *De civ. Dei*, xx. 24.)

21–22. *some . . . glasse.* E.g. in *Operum mineralium M. Ioannis Isaaci Hollandi, sive de lapide philosophiae*, i. 86; ed. L. Zetznerus, *Theatrum chemicum*, 1602–22 (*SC*), iii, p. 513: 'vitrum omnium extremum est, ac post iudicium quicquid sub firmamento comprehensum est, omne in vitrum diuina ordinatione conuertetur.'

22. *reverberated.* Fused as in a reverberating furnace (i.e. with the heat forced back or concentrated on the object).

36. *little compendium.* Man, the microcosm.

49. 9. *Anaxagoras.* Browne may have confused Anaxagoras with Anaximander. The former is ambiguous about the possibility of more worlds than one (see Kirk and Raven, *The Presocratic philosophers*, 525 and 526). But Anaximander was credited with this belief; see Kirk and Raven, 103a and pp. 121–3. Cf. Plutarch (?), *De placitis philosophorum* (*Morals*, trans. Holland, 1603, pp. 805–6): 'Anaximander . . . holdeth: that Infinitie is the principle of al . . . & therefor there be engendred infinit worlds'; and Augustine, *De civ. Dei*, viii. 2.

12. *ubi.* See note to 35. 40.

50. 38–40. *hard . . . for these.* Dante, *Inferno*, iv, places them in the outermost circle of Hell.

51. 9–10. *Shall . . . thus?* A telescoping of Rom. ix. 20–21.

24–25. *Aristotle . . . Ethicks.* Various charges had been brought against Aristotle; probably the reference here is to his friendship with Hermeias, tyrant of Atarneus, which could seem inconsistent with his reflections on tyranny in *Nicom. Eth.* viii. 10. 1–3. (Moltke.)

26. *Phalaris.* A Sicilian tyrant of the sixth century B.C., who roasted his victims in a brazen bull. Cicero has a number of references to this, e.g. *De Off.* ii. 7. 18.

27. *Scepticks.* Aulus Gellius, xi. 5. 8, distinguishes the Sceptics or Pyrronians from the Academics: 'quod Academici quidem ipsum nihil posse comprehendi quasi comprehendunt, et nihil posse decerni quasi decernunt, Pyrroni ne id quidem ullo pacto verum videri dicunt, quod nihil esse verum videtur.'

31. *refusing all honours.* Refusing perhaps in the sense of despising. Diogenes Laertius, vi. 72, records Diogenes's ridicule of good birth, fame, &c., but the reference may be chiefly to Lucian, *Dialogues of the Dead*, xiv, 'Diogenes. Alexander.'

37. *the Philosopher . . . avarice.* This is told of Crates, the Cynic, in Philostratus, *Life of Apollonius*, i. 13, and in W. Burley's *De vita et moribus philosophorum*, ch. xix.

52. 10–11. *know . . . evill.* Rom. vii. 19; Ovid, *Met.* vii. 20–21:

video meliora proboque,
deteriora sequor. (W. P. Smith, in *RM*, 1874.)

19. *desire with God.* 1 Tim. ii. 4.

19–21. *few shall . . . life.* Matt. vii. 14 (A.V.): 'strait is the gate, and narrow is the way, which leadeth unto life, and few there be that find it.'

26. *Strabo's cloake.* Strabo, ii. 5. 14, compares the shape of the inhabited world to a cloak.

26. *restraine it unto Europe.* Burton, 2. 2. 3 (1638, p. 246), describing the charge against Bishop Virgilius (see above, 27. 4–5) that he believed in the existence of the antipodes, adds '(which they made a doubt whether Christ died for)'.

38–39. *number of Elect.* Mark xiii. 20.

53. 2. *Atomist, or Familist.* (*a*) (probably) follower of Mrs. Atomy, leader of the sect described by T. Edwards in *Gangræna*, 1646, pp. 87–88. (See *RM*, ed. Denonain, 1953, p. xxxix.) (*b*) belonging to 'the Family of Love'. E. Pagitt, *Heresiography*, 2nd ed., 1645, has a section (pp. 81–91) 'Of the Familists'.

10. *on.* For 'one': 'on another' occurs in Browne's hand in MS. Sloane 1848, f. 161. See p. 272, note to 204. 2, l. 7.

21. *sentence Solomon.* Augustine, *Enarrationes in Psalmos*; on Ps. cxxvi. 2 (*PL*, 37, cols. 1667–8).

35. *Hierarchies.* Dionysius Areopagitica, *De coelesti hierarchia*, 6–8.

54. 15–16. *true . . . of my selfe.* Cf. *CM*, 244. 7–16.

27–28. *onely . . . Midianites.* Judges vii. 4–7.

33. *object.* Place before, present. Matt. xvii. 20.

55. 24. *Climate.* A belt of the earth's surface contained between two parallels of latitude.

39. *set downe by Solomon.* Prov. i. 7, 22, 32, &c.

56. 5–10. *as, in casting . . . feet.* See note to 40. 26–27.

57. 8–11. *characters . . . Physiognomy.* See note to *CM*, 224. 2–5.

10–13. *Phytognomy . . . formes.* Browne probably refers especially to G. B. della Porta's *Phytognomonica . . . in quibus nova facillimaque affertur methodus, qua plantarum . . . ex prima extimae faciei inspectione quivis abditas vires assequatur* (*SC*, 1588). Browne refers to this work in *GC*, 156. 18 and in *PE*, ii. 6 (1646, p. 93).

17–18. *cals . . . by their names.* Ps. cxlvii. 4.

18–19. *Adam . . . name.* Gen. ii. 19–20. See *CE*, pp. 80–81.

25–26. *booke of Physiognomy.* No longer attributed to Aristotle.

26. *Chiromancy. SC* contains (p. 28, no. 17) 'Indaginis, J. Introductiones in Chiromantiam . . . &c'. (1522.)

57. 42–**58.** 1. *the patterne . . . in that kind.* Anything we set before us to copy represents perfection because of its uniqueness. Cf. Cicero, *Orator*, ii. 8–9 and *PE*, vii. 19 (end).

58. 3. *herein.* By going beyond it, viz. the thing copied.

3. *it is wide.* 'it' now means the copy made, which distorts even when it idealizes.

59. 1–3. *I cannot . . . affection.* Moltke refers to Seneca, *De ira*, i. 14. 2: 'Non est autem prudentis errantis odisse.'

12. *party.* Part (of a subject treated).

17. *Βατραχομυομαχία.* The title of the mock-heroic poem formerly attributed to Homer, on a war between frogs and mice.

17. *S. and T. in Lucian.* The arraignment of Tau by Sigma in *Judicium Vocalium.*

18. *How doth.* There are several instances in *RM*, 1643, of plural nouns with 'singular' verbs (see note to 9. 14–15); and if, as is suggested by the

manuscripts (p. 266), Browne originally wrote 'do', he may not have seen enough reason to alter 'doth', which the printer could have adopted from *42*. See also Abbott, *Shakespearian Grammar*, 1870, 332–5 (pp. 234–9), 'Third person plural in -s.'

19–20. *breake . . . Priscian.* To break the head of Priscian (the grammarian) was to violate the rules of grammar. See *OED*, s.v. Priscian.

19. *Jupiter. Addition in manuscripts and 42, see p. 266.* In Lily's *Grammar* 'Regulae generales propriorum' (1681, p. 12) begin:

Propria quae maribus tribuuntur, mascula dicas.

20. *Si foret, &c.* Horace, *Epist.* ii. 1. 194.

24. *Actius his razor (and note).* Livy i. 36.

26. *Basilisco.* A large cannon. Cf. *Henry V*, ii. 17.

30. *their writings.* Sc. those of the scholars. The personal pronouns in the next sentence all refer to the princes.

36. *to.* Compared to, as in 42. 4.

60. 7–11. *Le mutin . . . yurongne.* H. G. Ward in *RES*, v (1929), pp. 59–60, pointed out that these lines are based on parts of Sonnet lxviii in Du Bellay's *Les Regrets*, 'Ie hay du Florentin l'vsuriere auarice', &c. The four lines distinctly drawn upon are 8–11:

Et le poltron Romain pour son peu d'exercise:
Ie hay l'Anglois mutin, & le braue Escossois,
Le traistre Bourguignon, & l'indiscret Francois,
Le superbe Espagnol, & l'yurongne Thudesque:

There is nothing of 'le larron de Gascongne' in the sonnet and nothing clearly corresponding to 'Le bougre Italien'. *SC* contains '*Les Œuvres Francoises de Joachim Du Bellay*' (1569).

12–13. *Saint Paul . . . Poet.* Titus i. 12, quoting Epimenides.

14. *as Neroes was.* Wilkin was probably right in supposing Browne's memory at fault, as it often was, the reference being seemingly not to Nero (see Suetonius, *Nero*, 38) but to Caligula who (*Caligula*, 30) exclaimed 'Utinam populus Romanus unam cervicem haberet'.

22–23. *Wisedome . . . vertuous.* Cf. Matt. xi. 19 and Luke vii. 34–35; also Juvenal, xiii. 26, 'Rari quippe boni.'

24. *contraries . . . another.* See 34. 40 and note.

30. *persists . . . inundation.* Cf. 69. 8 and *CM*, 207. 10–12.

61. 5. *ray . . . species.* See 47. 22 and note.

61. *substance . . . accidents.* Cf. 32. 30–31.

6. *formes.* Essences. See 16. 26 and note.

16–18. *how . . . selves.* Cf. Augustine, *Serm.* 304 (supposititious, *PL*, 39, col. 2329): 'Quomodo in aliis est misericors, qui in se ipso crudelis est?'; also *CM*, 236. 6–7.

18. *Charity . . . home.* Cf. 62. 18.

33. *impostures.* The manuscripts except *W* read 'impostours', but 'imposture' was a current form of 'impostor'; as in *PE*, 1646, p. 11.

61. 40–**62.** 1. *runnes . . . is.* As Browne was not always careful of his syntax the reading 'runnes' for 'runne' must remain doubtful.

62. 4–5. *not indivisible.* Aristotle, *Physics*, vii. 2 (233b): φανερὸν οὖν ὅτι οὐδέν ἐστι τῶν συνεχῶν ἀμερές. Cf. Bodin, *De magorum daemonomania*, *Praef.*, 1581, sig. **iij^{v}: 'Mathematicus, docens . . . quodcunque minimum corpus in orbe terrarum exstiterit id posse in infinita corpora dividi.' There appears to be no need for the emendations which have been suggested for 'indivisible', viz. 'divisible' or 'invisible'.

7. *discusse.* Disperse.

9. *entreate.* Deal with.

11–12. *fictions of what should be.* Cf. Sidney, *Apologie for Poetrie* (ed. Collins, p. 11): 'the diuine consideration of what may be and should be'; Aristotle, *Poetics*, ix. 1.

28–29. *I never yet . . . Woman.* Browne was married in 1641.

33. *Two natures in one person.* Divine and human in Christ.

33–34. *one soule in two bodies.* Cf. Augustine, *Conf.* (*SC*, 1650) iv. [6] 11: 'ego sensi animam meam et animam illius unam fuisse animam in duobus corporibus'. Cf. also Cicero, *De amicitia*, xxi. 81. (Moltke.)

63. 33. *the Italian. PE*, vii. 19 (1646, p. 384): 'who after he had inveigled his enemy to disclaime his faith for the redemption of his life, did presently poyniard him, to prevent repentance, and assure his eternall death.' Cf. Bodin, *De Republica*, v. 6 (1586, p. 608b). *SC* has the translation of Bodin by R. Knolles, 1606.

64. 2. *no such injury.* Sc. to oneself.

9. notwithstanding. See note to 43. 34.

13. *buffet Saint Paul.* 2 Cor. xii. 7.

13. *playes . . . at sharpe.* Fights with sword unbated.

15. *battell of Lepanto.* Browne refers to this again in his 'Observations on Naval Fights', MS. Sloane, 1827 (*K*, v, p. 211).

15–16. *passion . . . all.* Cf. 19. 4–6.

16. *conscience against all.* Even combating the faith which offers him comfort.

25. *generall.* From the errata-list, which is thus used here not to correct a misprint but to qualify a statement.

32–33. *that Lecher . . . Statua.* Pliny, *HN*, xxxvi. 5 (trans. Holland, 1601, ii, p. 566).

33. *Nero.* Tiberius (son of Titus Claudius Nero). *in his Spintrian recreations.* Tacitus, *Ann.* vi. 1; Suetonius, *Tiberius*, 43.

65. 9–13. *Antipathies . . . ruine of all.* See 34. 40 and note.

38. *Poynters.* The stars α and γ in the Great Bear, alined towards the pole-star.

66. 2. *Country.* ? County; *OED*, s.v. Country, 2.

4. *Cheap-side.* As a market-place.

7–8. *opinion of Socrates.* Plato, *Apology*, 21d.

9. *Homer . . . Fisherman.* The story is told in the lives of Homer attributed to Herodotus and Plutarch, one or other of which was included in early editions of Homer's works, e.g. Leyden, 1715, p. 569 (§§ 35–36). The fishermen had taken no fish and after giving up had spent their time

delousing themselves instead. The riddle was 'What we have caught we have thrown away and what we have not caught we have with us.' 'Herodotus' does not think that Homer died of chagrin because the riddle baffled him, as he was already ill at the time. Browne refers to the story again in *PE*, vii. 13 (1646, pp. 366–7), there rightly giving the plural, fishermen.

10–13. *Aristotle . . . Euripus.* Discussed at length in *PE*, vii. 13 (1646, pp. 363–6), 'Of the death of Aristotle'.

16. *sects.* 'sorts' in *42/43*, 'sects' or 'sexts' in the manuscripts. In some seventeenth-century hands 'e' approximates to 'o' and 'c' to 'r'. *OED* records the form 'sextes'.

20. *on.* For 'one'. See note to 53. 10.

23–24. *Solomon . . . knowledge.* Eccles. viii. 16–17.

36. *I was never yet.* See note to 62. 28–29.

66. 39–**67.** 1. *The whole world . . . woman.* Cf. 34. 16–17. With the manuscript reading 'woman' for world cf. 1 Cor. xi. 9: 'Neither was the man created for the woman; but the woman for the man.'

67. 17–19. *musick . . . full of harmony.* Cf. Addison, 'An Ode' ('The spacious firmament on high'), ll. 17–22:

> What though, in solemn silence, all
> Move round the dark terrestrial ball?
> What though nor real voice, nor sound,
> Amidst their radiant orbs be found?
> In reason's ear they all rejoice,
> And utter forth a glorious voice . . .

32–33. *Plato . . . musicke. Phaedo*, 86b–d; *Timaeus*, 47d. Cf. Ficino, *Comm. in Timaeum*, xxxii (*Opera*, 1561, pp. 1458–60), '*De harmonica Animae compositione*'. See *H*, 113. 28–32 and note.

36. *Tacitus. Ann.* i. 1.

37. *Cicero. Pro Archia*, i. 1.

39. *I feele not.* The abrupt transition suggests that a new section may have been intended here. The numbering of sections in *43* goes from 9 to 11, 10 being omitted. The evidence of the manuscripts is not in favour of introducing the 10 at this point, but Browne may well have originally meant to do so.

68. 20. *general Councells may erre. B.C.P.* Article xxi.

23–24. *oft-times . . . predecessours.* 'the 4th figure', in the manuscripts and *42*, refers to *Prior Analytics*, i. 23 (41b).

26–27. *sinne . . . Ghost.* Matt. xii. 31; Mark iii. 29.

30–31. *they . . . precepts.* The vicious contemn the precepts of the divines.

37. *like the Sunne's, &c.* Miss Sanna refers to Matt. v. 45.

39. *the worst best.* Cf. 69. 2 and *CM*, 206. 17.

69. 2. *Magnæ . . . vitia.* Mr. J. F. Soutter kindly refers me to Livy xxi. 4. 9 (on Hannibal): 'Has tantas viri virtutes ingentia vitia aequabant.'

5. *Antiperistasis.* Contrast.

8. *persist . . . corruption.* See 60. 30 and note.

11–12. *poysons . . . Antidote.* Cf. G. Herbert, 'Providence', l. 87:

Since where are poysons, antidotes are most.

17. *man without a Navell.* See *PE*, v. 5 (1646, p. 239), '*Of the Picture of Adam and Eve with Navells.*'

17. *yet lives in me.* Rom. vi. 6 and *De imitatione Christi*, iii. 34. 3: 'vivit in me vetus homo.' (Gr.)

19. *Defenda me Dios de me.* E. Bensly in *N. & Q.* 28 Oct. 1922, traces this saying to Antonio de Guevara, *Epistolas familiares* (Valladolid, 1541, f. lxxix^r). It is the last of four lines introduced by the sentence 'El buen marques de Santillana dezia . . . en una su copla'; and the reading is 'Defienda me Dios de mi'. Browne, however, may have derived the sentence from P. Camerarius, *Operae subcisiuae* (*SC*), iii. 26 (1609, pp. 97–98); the reading there is 'Defienda me Dios di mi'. *SC* contains a copy of this work dated 1599.

22. *Nunquam . . . cum solus.* Cicero, *De Off.* iii. 1. 1: 'P. Scipionem . . . dicere solitum scripsit Cato . . . nec minus solum, quam cum solus esset'.

35–37. *In briefe . . . many.* Cf. *PE*, i. 5 (1646, p. 19): '*Nos numerus sumus* is the motto of the multitude', &c., and L. de Morainvillier, *Examen philosophiae Platonicae* (*SC*), ii. 4. 2. 2 (1650, pp. 292–3): 'Multitudo, quò propior est vni, eò perfectior est eius potentia' (with reference to Proclus, *Elementa*, prop. 95).

70. 7. *above Atlas his shoulders.* Cf. *CM*, 211. 32–36 and 213. 40–214. 4.

10–11. *that surface . . . end.* The limitation of the earth is shown by the round surface it presents to the heavens.

12. *three hundred and sixty.* The number of degrees in the circle of the earth.

12–13. *number of the Arke.* Arke (arc) is here used for the whole circumference of the 'microcosm'.

16. *peece of Divinity.* See *CM*, 237. 13 and note.

17. *owes . . . Sun.* Cf. 15. 1 and 31. 11.

21. *Ruat . . . tua.* Possibly Browne's own modification of 'Fiat justitia et ruant coeli', *Oxford Dict. of Quotations*, 1953, p. 561. 2 (from William Watson's *Quodlibets of Religion and State*, 1602).

40–41. *slumber . . . soule.* Cf. Cicero, *De Sen.* xxii (81): 'Atqui dormientium animi maxime declarant divinitatem suam'; and Paracelsus, *De philosophia*, v (*Opera*, 1603–5, ii, p. 54): 'Corpore enim dormiente, Spiritus vigilat.'

41. *ligation of sense.* Cf. Burton, 1. 1. 2. 7 (1638, p. 24): 'This ligation of Senses. . . .'

42. *reason.* Of which the soul is the agent. See 83. 12 and note.

71. 2. *watery.* Corrected from 'earthly' in the *errata*. Scorpio belonged to the watery triplicity of the heavens, with Pisces and Cancer.

12–14. *Aristotle . . . defined it. De somno et vigilia*, i. 454b (ἀκινησία τις).

14–15. *Galen . . . corrected it. De motu musculorum*, ii. 4: 'Non igitur ne dormientis quidem omnes penitus otiosos musculos habent. . . .' (Moltke.)

32. *Themistocles.* As pointed out by Greenhill, the story is told of

Iphicrates by Frontinus, *Strategematon*, iii. 12. 2–3, where it is observed that the same story is told of Epaminondas. There appears to be no reason to connect it with Themistocles.

34–35. *Lucan and Seneca.* Who were made to commit suicide, but allowed to choose the way of death. See *CM*, 227. 8 and note.

36. *die daily.* 1 Cor. xv. 31.

72. 36–37. *The method . . . both.* See Aristotle, *Nicom. Eth.* v. 3. In *commutative* justice (concerned with transactions) an equality is aimed at between the value of the thing exchanged and the payment made for it, like the equality of the steps in an arithmetical progression; *distributive* justice (concerned with rewards or sharings out) is not a matter of strict payment, and the person receiving what is allotted to him is apt to get more than he has actually earned, perhaps double or treble—hence the reference to *geometrical* proportion. Browne indicates that in his commutative business he is apt to give more than commutative justice would demand.

39–40. *Doe unto others . . . selfe.* Matt. vii. 12; Luke vi. 31.

73. 5. *Hellebore.* Supposed to cure madness. Browne remembers Horace's association of avarice with madness in *Sat.* ii. 3. 82:

Danda est ellebori multo pars maxima avaris. (Gr.)

8. *Snow is blacke.* Cf. *PE*, i. 11 (1646, p. 47): 'if Anaxagoras affirme that Snow is black. . . .' See also ibid., p. 26. According to Cicero, *Academica*, ii. 31 (100), Anaxagoras not only denied that snow was white, but said it did not even appear so to him, because he knew it was water solidified and water is black.

8–9. *the soule is ayre, fire, water.* Aristotle, *De anima*, i. 2 (405a, b), quotes Diogenes for air, Democritus for fire, and Hippon for water.

10. *speculate.* The word 'to' following 'speculate' in *P* has the meaning 'compared to' as in 42. 4 and 59. 36. 'Speculate' is used transitively in *CM*, 233. 30.

10–12. *To that . . . an Atheist.* Cf. *LF*, 192. 10–13, and *CM*, 205. 31–34; also Col. iii. 5: 'covetousness, which is idolatry'.

18–19. *Aristotle . . . fortune; &c.* In *Nicom. Eth.* i. 8. 15 Aristotle suggests that possessions are necessary to happiness, since without them it is not easy to show generosity. Later on, iv. 1. 19, Aristotle observes that a small gift may show more liberality than a large one, according to the means of the giver.

35–36. *Hee that . . . Lord.* Prov. xix. 17.

74. 9–10. *not understanding only.* Not only not understanding.

10–11. *the prophecy of Christ.* With the marginal note (see p. 268) cf. Matt. xxvi. 11, Mark xiv. 7, and John xii. 8, in none of which is the future tense used. But cf. also Deut. xv. 11: 'the poor shall never cease out of the land.'

75. 3. *Crambe.* Staleness; alluding to the phrase 'crambe repetita' (Juvenal, vii. 154), a cabbage served again, applied to any tiresome repetition. Cf. *GC*, 173. 41.

4–5. *All is vanitie . . . spirit.* Eccles. i. 14.

6. *Aristotle . . . Plato. Nicom. Eth.* i. 6. 1 sqq.

7. *his summum bonum. Nicom. Eth.* i. 7 sqq.

13. *neat.* Pure.

15. *thy selfe and.* Not in MSS. and *42*. The insertion may be due to Digby's comment (*Observations*, 1643, p. 41) that 'this love must be imployed upon the noblest and highest object; not terminated in our friends . . .'.

20–21. *Thy will . . . undoing.* Cf. Job xiii. 15: 'Though he slay me, yet will I trust in him.'

77. 39. *unequall congress.* Virgil, *Aen.* i. 475, 'impar congressus Achilli'. (Gr.)

79. 3–4. *Cui . . . facilis.* Politian, 'Epitaphion Iocti Pictoris', l. 2 (Gruterus, *Delitiae CC. Italorum poetarum*, 1608, ii, p. 364).

HYDRIOTAPHIA AND THE GARDEN OF CYRUS
(*Dedications*)

83. 2. *Thomas Le Gros.* Son of Sir Charles Le Gros, of Crostwick Hall, near Norwich. Sir Charles had been a patient of Browne. See H. Mackinnon, *Bull. Hist. Med.* xxvii (1954), pp. 503–11, 'An unpublished consultative letter of Sir Thomas Browne' (Brit. Mus. Add. MS. 46378, B). Thomas Le Gros was admitted (aged 15) to Christ's Coll., Camb., 29 Apr. 1631, and to Gray's Inn 5 Aug. 1632 (*Alumni Cant.*).

12. *these.* The relics found in Norfolk.

13. *may . . . far.* On the assumption that the relics were Roman. See note to Plate facing 89.

20. *Theatrical . . . Urnes (and note).* See Vitruvius, *De architectura*, i. 1. 9, v. 3. 8, v. 5. Vitruvius, however, does not mention the Hippodrome; and the urns, or 'echeia', which he describes were meant to amplify the voices of the actors, not the applause of the audience. Kircher, *Musurgia Vniversalis*, ix. 4 (1650, p. 289), observes that the noises of the Hippodrome (as opposed to a theatre) would hardly need to be amplified, and suggests that the urns found there had an architectural, not an acoustic, function.

26. *noblest pyle (and note).* Raynham Hall. For Sir Horatio Townshend see *DNB*.

84. 1–2. *living . . . Antiquities.* Cf. note on *CM*, 228. 10–40 (10).

6. *Ægyptian account.* Cf. *PE*, vi. 1 (1646, p. 274). Diodorus, i. 23, quotes Egyptian estimates of 10,000 or 23,000 years for the period from Isis and Osiris to Alexander. Donne, *Essayes in Divinity* (1651, ed. E. Simpson, 1952, p. 18), cites 100,000 as an Egyptian estimate. For the shorter duration which Browne has in mind see note to *RM*, 44. 1.

24. *a new Britannia (and note).* Browne's extant correspondence with Sir William Dugdale is given in *K*, vi, pp. 331–58.

32. *one handsome Venus.* 'Venus' for Helen. Cicero, *De inventione*, ii. 1.

33. *bones of King Arthur (and note)*. Camden, *Britannia* (*SC*, 1637), Somersets.

37. *their predecessors . . . their mercies*. As Greenhill observes, it would improve the sentence to read 'our' for 'their' in both places. For similar obscurity in the use of pronouns see note to *RM*, 9. 12.

85. 3. *pisse . . . ashes*. Horace, *Ars Poetica*, 471.

11. *Gemme of the Old Rock (and note)*. A. Boetius de Boodt, *Gemmarum et lapidum historia*, ii. 3 (1609, p. 60), refers to diamonds found in India and Malacca 'qui vulgo de rupe veteri vocantur'. Browne mentions this work several times in *PE*, e.g. ii. 3 (1646, p. 70). See notes to 138. 9–10 and 141. 28–32.

86. 2. *Nicholas Bacon*. Son and heir of Nicholas, fourth son of Sir Nicholas, who was created premier baronet in 1611. Born 1623; Gray's Inn 1639; created a baronet 1661; d. 1666. (*Complete Baronetage*, iii.) Mentioned in Wood, *Athenae Oxonienses*, ed. Bliss, iii, p. 530. Related as follows to the Sir Edmund Bacon referred to in the note to 88. 4:

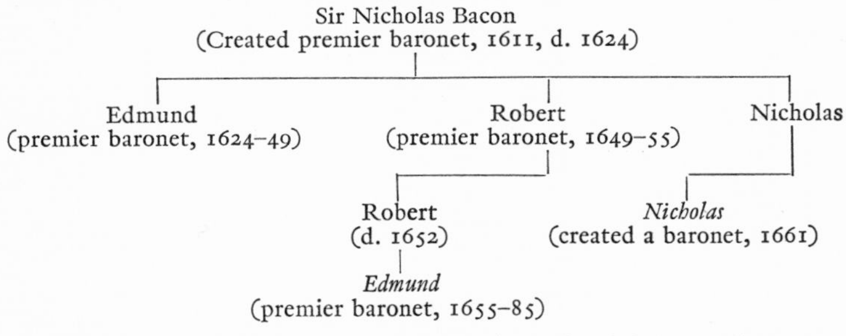

4. *Purblinde (and note)*. V. Plempius, author of *Ophthalmographia*, 1632, &c. (*SC*). ('Mihi nunquam videre licuit.', ed. of 1659, p. 29.) N. Cabeus, *In libros meteorologicorum Aristotelis commentaria et quaestiones*, 1646 (*SC*), iii. 8, Qq. 1–10, pp. 71–127.

5. *without issue (and note)*. Harvey's *Exercitationes de generatione animalium* (*SC*) was published in 1651.

8. *Dioscorides*. There was a long-standing confusion between Dioscorides Pedanius, author of *Materia medica*, who lived in the first century A.D. and another physician, Dioscorides of Phocas, who lived a hundred years earlier. Thus the edition of *Opera* by Dioscorides Pedanius published in 1598 (*SC*) quotes (sig. B4) the statement of Suidas 'Vixit cum Cleopatra Antonii temporibus'; and Browne accepts this, fusing with it Dioscorides' own statement (ibid., p. 2): 'terras multas obiuimus (nec enim militarem vitam egisse nos ignoras). . . .'

9. *Theophrastus*. *Enquiry into plants* and *Causes of plants*.

12. *the massiest*. Besler's massive volume was first published in 1613.

12. *three Folio's (and note)*. There is confusion here between C. Bauhin's one-volume *Pinax theatri botanici* (*SC*, 1623) and J. Bauhin's three-volume *Historia plantarum* (*SC*, 1650).

13. *New Herbals . . . America.* Browne may have been thinking of F. Hernandes' *Nova plantarum, animalium et mineralium Mexicanorum historia* (*SC*, 1651).

21. *Hippocrates the Circulation.* J. A. Van der Linden affirms this in *Selecta medica*, 1656 (*SC*), xiii. 232 and xvi. 53.

29. *great example (and note).* Hippocrates, in *De superfoetatione*, discusses sexual intercourse, and in *De dentitione* treats also of tonsilitis.

87. 6. *V finita's (and note).* The concluding rule in Lily's *Grammar* (under 'Prosodia') is that all final u's are long: '*v* finita producuntur omnia'. (Gr.) For the double plural (*finita's*) cf. *arcana's* (88. 8) and *Tartara's* (115. 21).

6–7. *Scaliger . . . Theophrastus.* J. C. Scaliger in his commentaries (*SC*) on Theophrastus, *De causis plantarum*, and on the *De plantis* attributed to Aristotle.

18. *venemous Vegetables.* See 131. 10–12 and note.

19. *Cato. De agri cultura*, 106 sqq.

20. *Tulipists . . . Professors (and note).* P. Lauremberg, *Apparatus plantarius primus*, i. 24 (1632, p. 117): '*Petrus Hondius* vocat *Tulpel*: quo nomine solemus per ignominiam appellare homines inurbanos & rusticos. *Narrencruijd*: quia in nullo flore ita insanitur, vt in Tulipa: nataque inde est *Tulipomania*.'

32–34. *ancient . . . garlands.* See note to 104. 25–26.

35. *Nullum . . . eloquium.* Seneca, *Ep.* 114. 12 ('placuit ingenium') (Mr. D. A. F. M. Russell).

37. *Apelles.* Pliny, *HN*, xxxv. 36. 12. (Gr.)

88. 3. *candour.* Kindness.

4. *Noble Family (and note).* See note on 86. 2.

8. *arcana's.* For the double plural see note on 87. 6.

9. *maniples.* Handfulls.

HYDRIOTAPHIA

89. *Plate opposite.* 'For the modern antiquary, a glance at the Plate . . . suffices to show that they [the urns] were of Saxon origin' (Sir John Evans in his edition of H, 1893, p. xx). See 95. 10 sqq. and 99. 21–25.

En sum . . . onus. Propertius, iv. 11. 14.

89. 10. *Potosi (and note).* Browne could read about the Peruvian silver-mines in A. de Herrera's *Novus Orbis* (*SC*, 1622), to which was attached *Brevis . . . Americæ descriptio.* This included (f. 9) '*Descriptio argenti-fodinarum Potosi*'.

18. *Adam . . . Earth.* Alluding to the tradition that Adam was formed of dust (Gen. ii. 7) taken from the four quarters of the earth. See *CE*, pp. 70–71.

20. *then . . . receive them.* Sc. from the things growing on the surface of the earth which nourished them.

90. 7. *Abraham.* Gen. xxv. 9.

9. *Adam . . . Calvary*. Adrichomius, *Theatrum terrae sanctae* (*SC*), 1600, p. 29, no. 145: '. . . licet quidam suspicentur Adam conditum esse in monte Caluariæ'; also N. Abram, *Pharus Veteris Testamenti*, 1648 (*SC*), ii. 20, pp. 60–62.

10–13. *God . . . Moses*. Deut. xxxiv. 6 and Jude 9.

15. *Hercules*. Kirchmann, *De funeribus Romanorum* (*SC*, 1625), i. 1 (1661, pp. 3–5), tells, out of Andron, the story about the cremation of Argeus by Hercules after Argeus had been killed in battle.

16–17. *Patroclus and Achilles*. *Iliad*, xxiii. 161 sqq.; *Od*. xxiv. 65 sqq.

18. *Meneceus and Archemorus*. Statius, xii. 60–104 and vi. 1–248.

20. *Hector*. *Iliad*, xxiv.

26. *West* (*and note*). Arnoldus Montanus, annotating Caesar, *De bello Gallico*, i. 26, 'propter sepulturam occisorum', refers to the practice of cremation. L. G. Giraldi, *De sepulchris*, 1539, pp. 64–65. Kirchmann, *De funeribus Romanorum*, 1661, p. 12.

30. *Pliny*. Kirchmann, op. cit. i. 2 (1661, p. 9), quotes Pliny, *HN*, vii. 54; 'ipsum cremari apud antiquos non fuit veteris instituti' and expresses surprise at that opinion.

31–33. *Table Laws . . . wine* (*and note*). Browne here refers to, and quotes in the footnote, two of the laws under Part i, 'De jure sacro', of the XII Tables, viz. nos. 2 and 4 ('tom.' for tomus, section). He refers to and quotes a third, no. 11 in the footnote to 18. 20. The law about not sprinkling the pyre with wine was attributed to Numa Pompilius. Browne could find all four of these laws in Kirchmann (ii. 20, iii. 1, iii. 7, and iii. 24), but may also have consulted Rosinus, *Antiq. Rom.*, ed. Dempster (1613, pp. 605–7), which he mentions in the footnote and with which he is in closer agreement in quoting no. 11. *SC* contains two copies of Rosinus (1583 and 1640). It also contains Vigenère's annotations on Livy (*Les decades*, '1573', ?1583), referred to again in the footnote to 99. 7, and Alexander at Alexandro, *Geniales dies*, 1651, both of which are mentioned in the footnote to 90. 31.

33–34. *Manlius . . . Son*. Titus Manlius Torquatus, who had his son executed for disobeying a military order. Livy, viii. 7. 22: '. . . structo extra vallum rogo cremaretur.'

34. *Numa . . . buried*. Kirchmann, i. 2: 'Sed et Plutarchus author est, eundem Numam testamento cavisse, ne corpus suum post mortem combureretur.' (*Numa*, xxii. 2.)

91. 1–2. *Remus . . . Ovid* (*and note*). Kirchmann, i. 2: 'hic vero sub ipso nascentis Reipub. exordio Remum hoc modo tradit libr. iv. Fastor. [l. 856].' In the note Browne specifies the edition by Carolus Neapolis, *Anaptyxis ad Fast. Ovid* (*SC*. 1638).

3. *Cornelius Sylla*. See note to 91. 27–29.

7. *even Crows*. Kirchmann, Appendix, 6 (1661, p. 706): '*Sepulturae honorem exhibitum etiam bestiis, puta Equis, Canibus, Corvis, Cornicibus, Anseribus. . . .*'

7–8. *Poppæa . . . enterment*. Mentioned by Kirchmann, i. 2. Tacitus, *Ann*. xvi. 6.

11–16. *Thales . . . Heraclitus.* Kirchmann, i. 1: 'Arguunt . . . non obscurè veterum Philosophorum de utroque sepulturae genere discordes sententiae, quas Servius annotavit in lib. xi Æneid. *Heraclitus* qui omnia vult ex igne constare, dicit debere corpora in ignem resolvi. Thales verò qui confirmat omnia ex humore procreari, dicit obruenda corpora, ut possint humore resolvi.'

20–22. *Some . . . in it.* Kirchmann, i. 1: '. . . multi . . . existimantes animam non nisi hoc modo à corporis sordibus purgari & ad suam naturam reverti posse.'

22–23. *such as . . . all things.* Cf. *RM*, 43. 10–16.

27–29. *Sylla . . . own.* Kirchmann, i. 2, quotes Cicero, *De leg.*, ii. 22. 56: 'C. Marii sitas reliquias apud Anienem dissipari jussit Sylla victor. . . . Quod haud scio an timens, ne suo posset corpori accidere, primus è patriciis Cornelius igne voluit cremari.'

35–37. *according to . . . Immortall (and note).* Cf. Giraldi, *De sepulchris*, 1539, p. 50: 'Nicolaus Damascenus . . . scribit a se uisum Zarmanochegan Indum, qui satis fortunatus Athenis se cremauit, quod abunde uixisset: in cuius tumulo ita inscriptum fuit . . . Zarmanochegas Indus . . . iuxta patrios Indorum mores seipsum immortalem faciens hic iacet.' Cf. Perucci, *Pompe funebri*, 1639 (*SC*), vii, i, p. 84.

92. 1–2. *the Chaldeans . . . Deity.* Giraldi, op. cit., p. 55: 'Quod autem Persae suorum cadauera non cremarent ut Graeci, in promptu causa est, quod deum ipsi ignem arbitrantur, eumque colunt, & propterea nefas illis uidentur deum hominum cadauera depasci.'

2–4. *The Persian . . . Dogges.* Giraldi, op. cit., p. 54: 'D. Hieronymus ait non prius cadauera humare, quàm aut ab alite, aut à cane traherentur.' Cf. Kirchmann, Appendix, 2 (ed. cit., pp. 696–7).

5–6. *the Persees now in India . . . Vultures.* J. A. v. Mandelslo, *Travels into the Indies* (during 1638–40), translated J. Davies, 1662, p. 76: 'Over the graves there are barrs laid cross like a grate, upon which they lay the body, there to remain till the Crows and other devouring Birds have consumed them.' Cf. Kirchmann, Appendix, 2 (p. 678); Agathias, *Historiae*, ii. 23; and Perucci, *Pompe funebri*, vii, p. 87.

6. *endure not . . . Beers of Wood.* H. Lord, *The Religion of the Persees*, 1630, viii, p. 39: 'they then carry him on an Iron Biere, for the lawe forbiddeth that the body of the dead should touch wood, because it is a fuell to the fier they accompt most holy.'

8–9. *Germans . . . Herthus.* Tacitus, *Germania*, 27 and 40.

11–13. *The Ægyptians . . . of them.* Giraldi, p. 42: 'Aegyptii, inquit [Herodotus, iii. 16] persuasum habent ignem animatam quandam esse belluam, quae, quaecunque nanciscitur, deuorat atque consumit: at cum est expleta, ipsam et quae ab ea uorata sunt, unà emori.'

13–15. *depositure . . . conservation.* Giraldi, p. 46: 'Alij sunt Aethiopes, qui uitreis uasis conclusos mortuos suos conseruant, ut nepotibus & posteris eorum sint notae effigies . . . Herodotus [iii. 24] tamen rem ita explicat: Posteaquam, inquit, Aethiopes . . . mortuum arefecerunt, totum gypso inducunt . . . dein sepulchrum ei è uitro . . . circundunt, in cuius medio defunctus interlucet . . . omnia penè uiuo assimilis.'

16. *imbibed by Pythagoras.* Kirchmann, op. cit. i. 2: 'Hos secutus Pythagoras. . . .'

18. *winde and sword.* Lucian, *Toxaris*, 38.

20. *graves in the ayr.* Kirchmann, Appendix, p. 680: 'Similem autem ritum Scythis quibusdam attribuit Statius [*read* Silius Italicus] lib. xiii [486–7]

At gente in Scythicâ suffixa cadavera truncis,
Lenta dies sepelit putri liquentia tabe.

Cf. Giraldi, p. 45.

20–23. *the Ichthyophagi . . . bodies.* These are mentioned by Kirchmann, Appendix, p. 697, who first calls them 'Æthiopes', and also by Giraldi, p. 46, who explains the habit of giving the dead a watery grave 'ea ratione . . . ut à piscibus cadauera uorentur, quod piscibus ii uictitent.'

23–28. *old Heroes . . . Oileus* (*and note*). Cf. Synesius, *Epist.* 4: 'Me autem in illo periculo . . . Homericum perturbabat illud, ne forte verum esset, mortem in aqua interitum & exitium esse etiam ipsius animi.' Synesius then quotes *Od.* iv. 511, with the reading cited in Browne's note instead of the usual one, *ἀπόλωλεν*:

Αἴας δ'ἐξαπόλωλεν, ἐπεὶ πίεν ἁλμυρὸν ὕδωρ,

adding 'mortem in mari perpetuum quendam interitum esse statuens'. Browne, however, mentions not Synesius but 'Magius', presumably Hieronymus Magius, among whose works the quotation has not yet been found. Another reference to the Greek fear of death by drowning occurs in *Iliad*, xxi. 281–3, where Achilles speaks of it as *λευγαλέῳ θανάτῳ.*

29–32. *The old Balearians . . . upon them* (*and note*). Giraldi, p. 57: 'In insulis quae Balearides a nostris . . . uocantur, illud quidem moris fuit, ut eius qui esse desiit, lignis quibusdam corpus membratim in frusta conciderent, et mox concisum in uas componerent, tum demum saxorum et lapidum aceruo accumularent, id quod Diodorus Siculus scriptum reliquit.'

32–36. *the Chinois . . . over it* (*and note*). Perucci, *Pompe funebri*, 1639, vii, p. 90: 'portono il Cattaletto alla Campagna . . . e quivi lo sepelliscono, ponendoli vn Pino appresso . . . in fine abbruggiano sopra il sepolcro molte carte dipinti con Schiaui, Caualli, e lauore diuersi. . . .' Perucci has a note: 'Ramus. nauig.'

38–40. *Christians abhorred . . . death.* A. Bosio, *Roma sotterranea* (*SC*), IV. i (p. 593c): '. . . Li Christiani però abborrirono sempre tal impietà.'

93. 4. *some have suffered . . . thereof* (*and note*). A. Bosio, op. cit. IV. i, 1632, p. 594c: 'Habbiamo diciò vn esempio notabile, riferito da S. Cipriano, di vn certo Martiale, il quale fù deposto dal Vescouato, perche hauea communicato con Gentili; & hauea sepellito li suoi figliuoli ne' sepolchri delli medesimi.' Bosio quotes Cyprian and gives a marginal reference 'S. Cipr. op. 68.', viz. Cyprian, *Epist.* 67. 6, where the subject is the defection of the two bishops Basilides and Martialis.

7–9. *For they hold . . . knees.* Cf. G. Sandys, *A relation of a iourney begun . . . 1610*, i, 'Of the Turkes . . . etc.' (1621, p. 71): 'The sides and bottome of the graue are boorded, and a boord laid ouer the corse to keepe the earth from it, leauing a sufficient compasse to kneele in. For they are of opinion that two terrible Angels called *Mongir* and *Guanequir*, do presently repaire vnto the graue, and put the soule againe into the body . . . and . . . demand of him in particular how he hath behaued himselfe in this life.' Cf. Belon, *Observations de plusieurs singularitez*, iii. 5 (1588, p. 384); and Burton, 3. 4. 1. 2 (1638, p. 647).

12. *Jabesh . . . Saul.* 1 Sam. xxxi. 12.

14–17. *And when . . . Asa.* Kirchmann, op. cit. iii. 6: 'Nam apud illos etiam super lectis Regum defunctorum aromata ac unguenta fuisse combusta, citra tamen cadaveris cremationem discimus ex lib. II. Paralip. cap. XVI ubi de Asa Rege mortuo sic legimus: [2 Chron. xvi. 14]. . . .'

16. *Jehoram.* 2 Chron. xxi. 19.

16. *Sedechias.* Jer. xxxiv. 5.

25. *hottest use.* Most violent treatment.

27–28. *not see corruption.* Ps. xvi. 10; Acts ii. 31.

28. *bone . . . not be broken.* John xix. 36.

31. *not corrupt on the Crosse.* Lipsius, *De cruce*, ii. 15 (*Opera*, *SC*, 1637, iii, p. 644): '*Corrumpi in Cruce passi sunt, & nefas sepelire.*'

33–34. *Jewish . . . Malefactors.* No reference to any such Jewish custom has been found, but see Frazer, *The Golden Bough*, xi (*Balder the Beautiful*, ii), p. 158 (on removing the hair of witches and wizards to destroy their maleficent powers).

94. 2–3. *deeply slashing . . . entrails.* Casalius, *De profanis et sacris veteribus ritibus*, Part I, *De profanis Aegyptiorum ritibus* (*SC*, 1644), vii.

4. *subject.* Substance, material. *OED*, s.v. *sb.*, 5.

4–5. *nor fully answered . . . Jonah.* The correspondence with Enoch, &c., as types of the Resurrection (see 106. 7–12 and note), would have been incomplete.

17. *treble calling out.* See 113. 13–16.

20. *Civilians.* Authorities on Civil Law.

21. *naturally found it.* Base it on nature.

22. *credit . . . the Phœnix.* E.g. Alexander Ross, *Arcana microcosmi*, ii. 21 (1652, p. 201). See *PE*, iii. 12 (1646, pp. 131–6).

24–25. *Elephants . . . Bees.* Kirchmann, op. cit., Appendix i (1661, p. 661): '*Bruta esse sepulturae studiosa, probatur exemplo Apium, Hirundinum, Formicarum, Gruum, Elephantorum, Delphinorum, Accipitrum, Leonum.*'

25–26. *which civill . . . interrments.* Kirchmann, loc. cit. (p. 662): 'Apibus id tribuit Plinius libr. XI. c. xviii. *Defunctas progerunt, funerantiumque more comitantur exsequias. . . .*'

Aræ . . . above it. The ancient distinction was between *altaria* for gods and *arae* for demi-gods or Heroes.

95. 1–3. *Besides . . . Opale.* Expanded 98. 32–37.

10. *Vrnes of Romanes.* See note to 89, plate.

12–16. *Brancaster . . . Burnham.* Brancaster, on the north coast of Norfolk, is rightly identified with Branodunum, for which see *Notitia vtraque dignitatum* under 'Comes littoris Saxonici per Britanniam'. See note on 95. 24. But Browne's derivation of Burnham has of course to be rejected.

22. *Institution of Constantine.* See Camden, *Britannia*, trans. Holland, 1610, pp. 76–77.

23. *Count of the Saxon shore.* See note on 95. 12–16.

24. *Dalmatian Horsemen.* See note on 95. 12–16. The *Notitia* (Lyons, 1608, p. 161), under sub-heading '*Sub dispositione viri spectabilis Comitis littoris Saxonici per Britanniam*' includes 'Praepositus equitum Dalmatarum Branodunensis, Branoduno'.

27. *a great overthrow.* Tacitus, *Ann.* xii. 31–32.

30. *Prasutagus . . . Paulinus.* Suetonius Paulinus. Tacitus, *Ann.* xiv. 31–38.

38. *Name of Walsingham.* It is not clear why this name should be cited unless Browne supposed it to be a Saxon perversion of 'Vespasian'.

95. 38–**96.** 2. *Now if . . . Icenia.* Greenhill cites a note on Ezek. xxvii. 11 ('the Gammadims were in thy towers') by Grotius, *Annotata ad Vet. Test.* (*SC*, 1644), ii, p. 366, which runs 'Probabilis est eorum sententia, qui intelligi putant habitatores Anconis Phoenices: nam Ancon est כמד. . . .' On this theory Anconia is derived from ἀγκών, bend of the arm, or elbow. Browne suggests a further etymological connexion, between Anconia and the Iceni, whereby Norfolk could claim the distinctive ('emphaticall') name of Icenia.

96. 5. *Seventy Thousand.* Tacitus, *Ann.* xiv. 33.

9. *Castor.* Venta Icenorum or Caistor St. Edmunds, three miles south of Norwich.

16. *high.* Early.

16–18. *Thetford . . . London (and note).* The Roman place-names mentioned are all taken from Antoninus' *Itinerarium*, route from Venta to London (1618, p. 30). Saxon counterparts, usually more than one each, have been more or less credibly found for all of them, Sitomagus being identified with Stowmarket, for instance, Combretonium with Ipswich, Adansam with Dedham, Canonium with Kelvedon, and Caesaromagus with Chelmsford (see the edition of the *Itinerarium* by G. Parthey and M. Pinder, 1848, p. 229). Browne rightly equates Venta with Caistor St. Edmunds, but seems to be led astray by identifying Sitomagus with Thetford. How he understood the other names listed in his note is uncertain but it looks as if he wished to derive Bretenham (presumably the place between Stowmarket and Lavenham) from Combretonium ('no very different sound' as he says in 95. 14–15 about Burnham and Branodunum). This Bretenham is very nearly on a straight line from Thetford to Coggeshall.

note 5. [*note*] *Sir Ralph Hare.* Of Stowe, Norfolk. Matric. from Magdalen

Coll., Oxford 1638, aged fourteen. Created baronet 1641. M.P. for Norfolk, &c. Died 1672. (*Alumni Oxon.*).

22. *Matilda* (*and note*). As remarked by Evans (*H*, 1893, pp. xix and 105), the meaningless 'Elle n'a elle' cannot be defended. Probably the object was not a coin but a reckoning counter such as were made first in the thirteenth century for use on a counting-board. See F. P. Barnard, *The casting-counter and the counting-board*, 1916. These counters were made to resemble coins and carried sometimes a text or maxim, occasionally the maker's name. 'Maud' may be a guess from a counter having a woman's head for device.

25. *Ic. Duro. T.* Browne's interpretations of these can be accepted. *Tascia*, 'a tribute Penye' (Camden, *Britannia*, 1610, p. 97); but more probably (? read 'Tascio') for Tasciovanus, father of Cymbeline. See Evans, *The coins of the ancient Britons*, 1864, pp. 220–2.

97. 5. *Norwich arose . . . Venta.* In the sense that Norwich replaced the Roman Venta, not that it was on the same site.

9–12. *Sueno . . . Navy* (*and note*). *Chronicon Johannis Bromton Abbatis Jornalensis*, in R. Twysden, *Historiae Anglicanae*, 1652, col. 885.

18–19. *Spartans . . . vinegar* (*and note*). According to Plutarch the money was iron, not copper. Browne writes of 'Iron money' in the same connexion in MS. Sloane 1869, f. 80 (*K*, v, p. 277).

20. *iron.* Caesar, *De bello Gallico*, v. 12 (where other metals also are mentioned).

97. 40–**98.** 6. *A great obscurity . . . wanting* (*and note*). Stow, 1603, p. 170: 'Spittle field . . . about the yeare 1576, was broken vp for Clay to make Bricke, in the digging whereof many earthen pots, called *Vrnae*, were found full of Ashes, and burnt bones of men, to wit, of the Romanes that inhabited here . . . euerie of these pots had in them with the Ashes of the dead, one peece of Copper mony, with the inscription of the Emperour then raigning: some of them were of *Claudius*, some of *Vespasian*, some of *Nero*, of *Anthonius Pius*, of *Traianus*, and others: besides these *Vrnas*, many other pots were there found . . . diuerse vials and other fashioned Glasses, . . . lampes of white earth and red . . . three or foure Images. . . .' On 'lachrymatories' see 103. 3 and note.

97. 40–**98.** 1. *because . . . enclosed.* See note to *RM*, 16. 1.

98. 8–10. *Macrobius . . . Antonini.* Kirchmann, op. cit. i. 2: 'Nam ab Antoninis illam abrogatam, ut quidam volunt, néque fictum, néque scriptum, néque pictum usquam memini legere . . . Macrobius quidem disertè scribit, morem illum suo jam tempore planè exolevisse, lib. vii, cap. vii. . . .'

14. *Severus.* See 102. 25 and note.

18–20. *after Tertullian . . . burning* (*and note*). Kirchmann, i. 2: 'ita existimamus, politiam religionis Christianae ritum hunc gentilem paulatim sustulisse, strenuè laborantibus in eo sanctis Patribus, ut ex Tertulliani scriptis passim videre est. Quod cum Paganus illis vitio verteret apud Minutium Felicem [*Octavius*, 11] his verbis: ***Inde videlicet & execrantur rogos & damnant ignium sepulturam....***'

39. *things wherein . . . dear unto them.* Kirchmann, iii. 5: '. . . quicquid preciosum habebant veteres, aut quae cara fuisse vivis non ignorabant, ea omnia soliti erant conjicere in rogum ejus, quem honore ibant affectum.'

99. 3–4. *Gemme . . . Propertius.* Kirchmann, i. 5, quotes the line in Propertius, iv. 7. 10:

Et solitum digito beryllon adederat ignis.

6–10. *that Romane Urne . . . Nuts of Crystall (and note).* This is a selection from the list given in the edition of Livy, with commentary, by B. de Vigenère (*SC*), *Les decades*, ii (1617, col. 868). The nearest approach to Browne's 'Crystall Ball' is 'deux pommes de crystal; vne autre moindre'.

11. *Monument of Childerick.* J. J. Chifflet, *Anastasis Childerici I. Francorum Regis, sive Thesaurus Sepvlchralis Tornaci Neruiorum effossus* (*SC*, 1655).

13–14. *Sword . . . Bees.* Chifflet, p. 38.

15. *bones and horseshoe.* Chifflet, p. 225.

16–17. *barbarous . . . Obsequies.* Chifflet, p. 76: 'Capvt v. *Childericus Rex sepultus est Tornaci in Neruijs, ritu barbarico.*'

19–20. *treasure of David.* Chifflet, p. 53, citing Josephus, *Antiq. Jud.* vii. 15. 3.

20. *Circumcision . . . buried.* Septuagint (see l. 18), Joshua xxiv. 31 (30): 'there they put with him into the tomb in which they buried him, the knives of stone with which he circumcised the children of Israel in Galgala. . . .'

29–30. *that Letter . . . Quintus.* Cicero, *Letters to Quintus*, ii. 15.

31. *Scribonius Largus. c.* A.D. 1–50. Author of *Compositiones medicae* (*SC*, 1655).

33. *that frugall Bit (and note).* Dio Cassius (Epitome), lxxvii, 12 ('Severus'): 'Certum cibi genus parant ad omnia, quem si ceperint quanta est unius fabae magnitudo, minime esurire aut sitire solent.'

35–36. *Druids . . . Pomponius.* Giraldi, op. cit., p. 64, refers to Pomponius Mela, *De situ orbis*, iii, 2 (on *Gaul*): 'Itaque cum mortuis cremant ac defodiunt apta viventibus olim.'

37. *Polydorus.* Polydore Vergil's *English History*, Camden Soc., 36, 1846, pp. 46–47.

37 (*note*). *Amandus . . . Pineda.* There is a slight inaccuracy here. Pineda, in the work referred to (see note to *RM*, 25. 2), xxvii. 11. 6, 1620, f. 216ᵛ, mentions the cremation of Belinus and, a little further on, has a marginal reference to Amandus Zierixensis, who, in his *Chronica compendiosissima*, 1534, ff. 39ʳ and 40ᵛ, gives a few facts about Belinus and Brennus, but says nothing about the cremation.

In *Scriptores ordinis minorum*, 1806, by Fr. Lucas Waddingus, p. 11, it is stated that Amandus called his *Chronica* '*Scrutinium, vel Venationem veritatis historicae*', and Greenhill, p. 184, gives this as if it were the published title.

100. 1. *That they held . . . delivereth.* Giraldi, p. 64: 'Gallorum in sepeliendis cremandisque cadaueribus ritus his propè uerbis à C. Caesare sexto belli Gallici commentario [vi. 16] refertur. . . .'

7. *Tacitus. Agricola*, xxi.

12–29. *That burning . . . slain by him.* In this passage Browne draws liberally on Olaus Wormius, *Danicorum monumentorum libri sex*, 1643, which he mentions in 101. 8.

12–13. *used in Sarmatia . . . Gaguinus.* Olaus Wormius, op. cit. i. 7, quotes Alexander Guagninus' *Sarmatiae Europeae descriptio* (1578) to this effect, *not* Robertus Gaguinus' *Compendium de . . . Francorum gestis.* Browne again writes 'Gaguinus' for 'Guagninus' in *Miscellany Tracts* (*K*, v, p. 27).

13–14. *Sueons . . . Olaus.* Olaus Wormius, loc. cit. (p. 46): 'Olaus Magnus lib. 16, cap. 37 [*History of the Goths*, &c., *SC*, 1658]. Sueonum & Gothorum principes . . . igne crematos asserit.' For Saxo see note to 100. 24–27.

15. *Tacitus.* Olaus W., p. 45, quotes Tacitus to this effect.

20–21. *Jutland . . . not many years before us.* Olaus W., p. 44, quotes Adolphus Cypraeus 'lib. 1. Annal. Eccles. Slesvicens, cap. 2' to this effect, with mention of the year 1588. (See note to 100. 32.)

20. *Anglia Cymbrica.* Camden, *Britannia* (trans. Holland, 1610, pp. 130–1): 'The Iutae . . . did for certain inhabite the upper part of Cimb⟨r⟩ica Chersonesus, which still the Danes call *Iuitland*. . . . But, in what place the Angles were seated, it is a question. . . . Now seeing that between Iuitland and Holsatia the ancient country of the Saxons, there is a little Province in the Kingdome of Dania, named at this day *Angel*, beneath the citie of *Flemsburg*, which Lindebergius in his Epistles calleth *Little Anglia*, I dare affirme, that now at length, I have found the place of our Ancestors habitation.'

22–23. *the Danish . . . dead* (*and note*). Olaus W., p. 40: 'Tres numerari solent hominum aetates qvae ab inferiarum modo denominationem acceperunt. Prima *Roisold* / secunda Høigold / tertia Christendomsold.' Olaus explains that in the earliest period the ashes left after cremation were covered with mounds called *Roiser*. *Brendetyde* and *Ildtyde* are further names for the 'prima aetas', both signifying the age of burning. See Olaus W., p. 45.

24–27. *Some deriving . . . enterrment.* Olaus W., pp. 50–51, mentions the claim for Unguinus to have instituted cremation and the statement of Saxo ('lib. 5.') that cremation laws were promulgated by Frotho the Great much earlier. Olaus quotes the passage from Saxo, which includes the words 'Ducem quempiam aut regem interfectum . . . concremari. Tam scrupulosam . . . observationem praestari voluit, ne promiscuos exseqviarum ritus existere pateretur.'

27. *Starkatterus.* Olaus W., pp. 32–33 and 53.

28. *Ringo . . . Harald.* Olaus W., p. 53 quotes Saxo, viii, for 'ritus . . . quibus Ringo, occisi a se Haraldi corpus rogo imponi curavit'.

32. *Ansgarius.* There is an account of his life in Cypracus, *Annales Episcoporum Slesvicensium*, i–iii (1634, pp. 7–28).

101. 8. *Wormius.* See note to 100. 12–29.

8–10. *in no ordinary number . . . Countreys.* The passage quoted by Browne in his note from Cypraeus is given by Olaus W., p. 48, as from 'Johannes

Adolphus Cypraeus Annalium Eccles. Slesvic. l. 1. c. 2': '. . . urnas . . . qvibus adeò abundabat collis. . . .'

10–12. *many other substances . . . Jewes-harp.* Olaus W., pp. 42–50. The 'Jewes-harp' is on p. 48: 'In Norvegia . . . instrumentum musicum Danis *en Mundharpe* [a mouth-harp] ex cupro deaurato nitidissimo, suo splendore omnes in admirationem trahens.'

14. *placed . . . circle.* Olaus W., pp. 62–67, 'De lapideis monumentis Danicis.'

16. *Rollrich stones (and note).* These are mentioned, with a reference to Camden, by Olaus W., p. 67: 'prope Burfort, Rolvonis saxa dicta.' Camden, *Britannia* (tr. Holland, 1610, pp. 374–5) suggests that the stones were erected by '*Rollo*, the Dane, who afterwards conquered Normandie.'

19–20. *large Vrne . . . Buckler (and note).* Browne's account of the find at Ashbury does not correspond with Twyne's in *De rebus Albionicis* (1590, p. 153), which tells of a monument and a body ('in leuissimos cineres redactum') together with a golden collar, &c.—no urn or mighty bones or buckler. Browne has evidently confounded this with Twyne's account (p. 75) of a discovery in Kent: 'ingens vrna cinere ossiumque maximorum fragmentis plena, cùm galeis ac clypeis. . . .' Browne himself refers to this discovery in *Miscellany Tracts* (*K*, v, p. 102), quoting the passage from Twyne.

21. *little Massingham (and note).* The note as given in *58* is misleading. 'In Norfolk' applies to Little Massingham (the reference being to a find for which Browne himself is the authority) and '*Hollingshead*' applies to the Anglesea urns.

21–22. *why the Anglesea Urnes . . . undiscovered.* Holinshed, *Chron.* i. 'The description of Britaine', i. 8 (1577, p. 16): 'sundry earthen pottes are often founde there [Anglesea] of dead mens bones conuerted into ashes, set with the mouthes downeward contrarie to the use of other nations.' In *Brampton Urns* Browne explains the inverted position 'as being less subject to have the Earth fall in, or the Rain to soak into them'.

102. 2. *Casalius. De urbis ac Romani olim Imperii splendore*, II. xxi (1601, p. 350).

2. *Bosio.* (Antonio.) *Roma sotterranea*, iii. 23 (1632, pp. 197–201).

15. *Pliny. HN*, xxxv. 49.

19–20. *Jupiter . . . Hercules.* Pliny, *HN*, xxxv. 45.

22. *mode of Pythagoras . . . Varro.* Pliny, *HN*, xxxv. 46 (Marcus Varro).

25. *Severus (and note).* Dio Cassius (Epitome), lxxvii. 15.

32. *Buxton.* See 96. 10.

35. *Patroclus. Iliad*, xxiii. 254 (ἑανῷ λιτὶ κάλυψαν).

103. 3. *Lachrymatories, or Tear-bottles.* Perucci, *Pompe funebri*, ii, p. 34: '*riponeuano vn Ampolla piena di lacrime. . . .*'

11. *retaining a Vinosity.* Lazius, *Comm. Reipublicae Rom.* (*SC*, 1551), iii. 18: 'Erat liquor is uino rubro quàm simillimus: quem unus ex rusticis qui simul aderant, paulo audacior, cùm gustasset, generosissimi uini gustum referre asseuerabat.'

15. *periods of Kingdomes (and note)*. Browne is apparently thinking of Plato, *Republic*, viii (546), where it is observed (Jowett, ii, p. 411) that 'A city which is thus constituted can hardly be shaken; but, seeing that everything which has a beginning has also an end, even a constitution such as yours will not last for ever, but will in time be dissolved.' There follows the notoriously obscure passage on two numbers, one pertaining to divine and the other to human births or begettings; and Browne (or his authority) seems to have got 'five hundred years' from the second number, which is 'oblong' and consists of 'a hundred numbers squared upon rational diameters of a square, the side of which is five ...' (ἑκατὸν μὲν ἀριθμῶν ἀπὸ διαμέτρων ῥητῶν πεμπάδος, δεομένων ἑνὸς ἑκάστων . . .).

16. *Opimian Wine*. A.U.C. 633, when Opimius was Consul.

19–20. *gold . . . teeth (and note)*. See note to 90. 31–33.

20. *this Urne*. One of those found in Norfolk.

20. *Opaline stone*. See 95. 3 and 98. 36–37.

26–27. *Box . . . Eternal (and note)*. Pliny, *HN*, xvi. 78: 'cariem vetustatemque non sentiunt.'

29–30. *Bay-leaves . . . years (and note)*. Casalius, *De veteribus sacris Christianorum ritibus* (*SC*, 1644), lxvi (1681, pp. 335–6): 'De corpore S. Umberti confessoris reperto 150. ann. post ejus obitum illaeso, inquit Surius tom. 5. 6. Septembris. Sed & herbae à sepulturae ejus die appositae fuerant . . . adeo virides sunt repertae . . .' Cf. A. Bosio, *Roma sotterranea*, I. xx (1632, p. 20 c).

32. *Temple of Diana*. Pliny, *HN*, xvi. 215, says that the cypress-wood used for this had lasted for 400 years.

32. *wood of the Ark*. Heb. ix. 4 &c.

34–35. *Ark of Noah . . . Josephus. Antiq. Jud.* i. 3. 5; xx. 2. 2.

103. 37–**104.** 2. *undated . . . position (and note)*. Goropius, *Origines Antwerpianae* (*SC*, 1569), iii, 'Niloscopium' (p. 320): 'siluae omnes partim ventorum procellis, partim violenta aquarum irruptione, procubuerunt. Harum igitur reliquiae quamobrem locis depressioribus inueniantur, & omnes ad eandem caeli regionem spectent; istis explicatis, non est obscurum.'

104. 7–8. *metall . . . Temple*. Pliny, *HN*, xxxvi. 14, says that charcoal was used for the foundations.

8–10. *lasting tests . . . years (and note)*. V. Biringuccio, *Pirotechnia*, 1558, iii. 10, p. 62, observes that architects sometimes use coal for the foundations of buildings, that pieces of coal are sometimes set up as boundary-marks, and that coal has been reckoned to last, in certain conditions, for over four hundred years. *SC* contains an edition of this work dated 1559 and also a French translation of 1556.

13–14. *Childerick . . . peeces*. Chifflet, op. cit. (note to 99. 11), p. 38: 'Effossa multa ferramenta, vetustate exesa & consumpta propter loci nonnihil humecti vitium.'

25–26. *Urne . . . it self*. Kirchmann, *De fun. Rom.*, iv. 3: 'Plutarchus in

Philopaemene [xxi. 3] auctor est, ejus urnam taeniis ac coronis adeo fuisse coopertam, ut vix conspici potuerit.'

27. *Olive and Myrtle.* Giraldi, De *sepulchris*, pp. 53–54: 'Lycurgum . . . ita instituisse . . . puniceo tantum amictu uelatum, & oleae fronde. . . .'

28. *Democritus . . . honey.* Kirchmann, op. cit. i. 8: 'Democritum mortuos in melle servandos, autor Varro' [*Sat. Men.*, 81].

30–33. *Plato . . . sepulture. Laws*, 958e. Cicero, *De leg.* ii. 27. 67–68. Giraldi, op. cit., pp. 4 and 11: 'Tituli enim qui Epitaphia dicuntur, autore Platone, quatuor uersiculorum numerum excedere non debent, ut transiens uiator facile perlegat . . . Plato etiam in illis suis legib. agros et in primis steriles sepulturis destinauit.'

33–34. *that sepulchrall . . . Judas.* Matt. xxvii. 5–8.

105. 3–7. *abject . . . Malefactors.* Kirchmann, ii. 24, quotes a comment on a reference by Horace to the Esquiline: '*ubi certus erat locus sepulchrorum ad corpora pauperum aut sceleratorum viliumque comburenda, aut canibus projicienda.*'

5. *contriued.* This is a pen-and-ink correction in one copy of *58*. The correction is not in Browne's hand but is nevertheless probably authoritative. See Introduction, p. xx and the edition of *Urne-Buriall* by Mr. John Carter, 1932, pp. 144–5; 'contriue' in Browne's hand could resemble 'continue' as 'continue' could resemble 'containe'. See textual notes to 122. 30, 136. 28, and 139. 7.

5–7. *Tiberius . . . Malefactors* (*and note*). Suetonius (*Tiberius*, 75. 3) says that the Emperor was in fact cremated according to plan, although at the funeral the cry was raised that a half-burning at Atella (where farces were performed) would be enough for him: 'Atellam . . . deferendum et in amphiteatro semiustulandum.' Casaubon's note adds 'ut fiebat in mendicis [not 'malefactors'] qui . . . raptim in Esquilliis cremabantur.'

7. *Nero.* Suetonius, *Nero*, 49. 4.

12–13. *Achilles . . . Patroclus.* Homer, *Od.* xxiv. 76–77.

20. *family Urnes* (*and note*). Marcus Aurelius, *Meditations*, trans. M. Casaubon, 1635 (2nd ed.), Notes, pp. 30–37 (on iv. 48, τάριχος ἢ τέφεα, and referring to urns found at Newington, Kent): '. . . One great urne was appointed to containe the bones and ashes of all one, either houshold or kindred.'

25. *Anatomies* (*and note*). Petronius, 34 ('dum licet esse bene').

106. 3. *Jewish Hypogæum.* A. Bosio, *Roma sotterranea*, ii. 22 (1632, p. 143).

7–12. *cemiteriall Cels . . . Resurrection.* Towards the end of A. Bosio's *Roma sotterranea* there are separate chapters on all the 'flourishes' and 'figures' listed by Browne, with the exception of Enoch, who is, however, mentioned with Elijah as an image of the Resurrection (Bosio, iv. 16; 1632, p. 613d). Cf. 94. 4–5, 124. 2, and *LF*, 189. 24.

20–22. *which makes . . . differences.* 'resented' has the obsolete sense of 'felt'. The tragical ends are less painfully felt by compassionate readers, who are consoled by thinking that the divine will does not ordain the same fate for everyone (trusting that theirs will be more fortunate). The thought is expanded in *CM*, 225. 21–31.

29. *Severus* (*and note*). Kirchmann, iii. 27: 'Simile quid de Alexandro tradit Lampridius: "*Cenotaphium in Gallia, Romae sepulchrum amplissimum meruit.*" ' Lampridius (*Historia Augusta*), *Severus*, lxiii. 3.

31. *a golden Urne*. Kirchmann, iii. 8: 'Eutropius de Trajano Imp. libro viii [5]. *Solus omnium Imp. intra urbem sepultus est, ossa ejus collocata in urnâ aureâ in foro, quod aedificavit sibi.*' (*Not* in Dio Cassius.)

106. 37–**107.** 6. *Rhetorick . . . possessor* (*and note*). Kirchmann, iii. 24, quotes from Cassiodorus, *Variae*, iv. 34, Theodoric's pronouncement as follows: '*Prudentiae mos est, in humanos usus terris abolita talenta revocare, commerciumque viventium non dicere mortuorum. . . . Ædificia tegant cineres, columnae vel marmora ornent sepulcra; talenta non teneant, qui vivendi commertia reliquerunt. Aurum enim sepulcris justè detrahitur, ubi dominus non habetur. . . . Non est enim cupiditas eripere, quae nullus se dominus ingemiscat amisisse.*'

107. 7. *terra damnata*. Or *caput mortuum*; the residue after calcination &c. in alchemy or chemistry.

10. *treasures of old Sorcerers*. Kirchmann, iii. 23: 'cadavera mortuorum amputare, & praesegminibus istis inimicos suos defigere solebant.' See also ibid. 24, 'De spoliatione cadaveris.'

15. *Plato's historian*. Er; *Rep*. x. 614b.

16–18. *How to keep . . . art*. Casalius, *De profanis Rom. ritibus* (1644, p. 248): '. . . referam fuisse apud eruditos dubitatum, quomodo cadavera ante combustionem octo diebus sine corruptione servarentur absque viscerum extractione: sed difficultas à Plinio tolli videtur lib. 22. cap. 24 dum ait: *Mellis quidem natura . . .*'

22. *Pyrrhus his toe* (*and note*). Pliny, *HN*, vii. 2. Cf. *PE*, iii. 14 (1646, p. 140), and Browne's verses on the subject, *K*, v, p. 238.

24–25. *And . . . ground*. Parenthetical, referring again to the discovery in Norfolk.

27. *lamp of Galuanus* (*and note*). F. Licetus, *De lucernis antiquorum reconditis* (*SC*), vi. 4 (1653, p. 599): 'De Lucerna Galvania mortuales ritus antiquorum mirifice representante.'

27. *Marlianus* (*and note*). *Urbis Romae topographia* (?1544), p. 8.

29. *Esquiline Field*. See note to 105. 3–7.

30–34. *that remarkable . . . incommixed*. *PE*, iii. 14 (1646, p. 140) refers to Pancirollus, *Rerum memorabilium*, &c., 'the chapter of *Linum vivum*' (i. 4, Frankfort, 1646, p. 16): 'De lino vivo aut asbestino': '. . . Regum quoque funera in eiusmodi adurebantur tunicis, ne corporis favillia cum reliquo misceretur cinere.'

108. 12. *Some . . . Skeletons* (*and note*). Lyserus, *Culter anatomicus* (1653), v, Praeloquium: 'Notandum autem uti . . . non quaevis Ossa . . . accipienda, sed ea, quae ab annosis desumuntur animantibus, quae ob siccitatem, majorem sunt adepta soliditatem. Contrarius quidem est *Columbus* & cadaver juvenis non obesi pusillâque staturâ praediti eligit.' *SC* contains two copies of R. Columbus, *De re anatomica* (1559 and 1593), but they had not to be consulted on this occasion.

13–14. *Hydropicall Heraclitus.* Diogenes Laertius, ix. 3, records details of Heraclitus's death from dropsy, and these are repeated in Marcus Aurelius, *Meditations*, iii. 3. See Heraclitus, *The cosmic fragments*, ed. G. S. Kirk, 1954, pp. 4–5.

16–17. *Saracens . . . sufficeth (and note).* Laurentius Valla, *Hist. Ferdinandi, Regis Aragoniæ*, iii (1521, f. 22v).

18. *pyre of Patroclus (and note). Iliad*, xxii. 52.

19. *Pompey.* Plutarch, *Pompey*, 80.

19. *burthen of Isaac.* Gen. xxii. 3.

25–26. *Metropolis of humidity (and note).* Hippocrates, *De carnibus* (*Opera*, 1595, iii, p. 30): 'At verò cerebrum frigidi & glutinosi sedes est & matrix (μητρόπολις τοῦ ψυχροῦ καὶ τοῦ κολλώδεος) . . . Atque idcirco cerebrum, quòd minimum pinguis, plurimum verò glutinosi habeat, à calido exuri nequit. . . .'

32–33. *to drink . . . prodigality (and note).* Valerius Maximus, iv. 6, Externa 1, refers to the tradition that Artemisia tried in this way to become 'Mausoli vivum ac spirans sepulchrum.'

109. 2. *copels, and tests.* Cupels, vessels made of bone-ash and used for the refining of gold and silver. For tests, meaning cupels in their iron containers, see *OED*, s.v.

9–10. *where no . . . them.* Kirchmann, ii. 27, gives evidence to the contrary: 'Graecos . . . ipsis Deorum templis fanisque mortuos suos humasse. . . .'

12. *Canaanites.* Gen. xxiii. 5–20.

12. *Family of Abraham.* Gen. xlix. 29–32.

12. *Josua.* Jos. xxiv. 30.

15. *memento's.* Kirchmann, ii. 22: 'ut viatores mortalitatis admonerentur.'

16–17. *whom . . . them.* Kirchmann, ii. 22: 'Pertinent huc antiquae inscriptiones, quibus Viatores vel hospites solent compellari: ut, ASPICE VIATOR. CAVE VIATOR. & similes.'

21–23. *Constantine . . . Porch.* Kirchmann, ii. 27: 'ille Constantinopoli in porticu templi Apostolorum humatus legitur.'

24. *Cuthred.* Overlord of the West Saxons, 740–54. The reference is to the burial in 758 of Cuthbert, Archbishop of Canterbury, in the cathedral. (Gr.)

25–32. *Christians . . . West (and note).* The note may be a little misplaced as Kirchmann does not discuss the Christian disputes. He does, however (iii. 8), refer to the conflicting views of historians about the orientation of corpses as practised by Athenians, Megarians, and Phoenicians. The different accounts could arise from the fact that a head pointed to the west would look to the east.

32–33. *Beda . . . Saviour.* Casalius, *De vet. sac. Christ. ritibus*, lxvi, 'De funeribus priscorum Christianorum': 'condebantur corpora . . . supina, respicientia etiam Orientem, sicuti Redemptorem nostrum fuisse sepultum, refert Beda in Marcum cap. 16. lib. 4. tom. 5.' (*PL*, 92, col. 295c). Cf. Adrichomius, *Theatrum Terrae Sanctae*, 1628, p. 175.

40. *gnaw'd*. As *58* reads 'knav'd' (corrected to 'gnawd') the printer's copy probably read 'knawd', 'knaw' being a form of 'gnaw' recorded in *OED*.

110. 10–13. *In an Hydropicall . . . fat*. This phenomenon was afterwards observed in a Paris cemetery and named 'adipocire'. (Wilkin.)

13. *castle-soap*. Castile soap.

14–16. *After a battle . . . uncorrupted*. Ammianus Marcellinus, xix. 9. 9. (Murison.)

18–20. *Marquesse of Dorset* (*and note*). W. Burton, *The description of Leicestershire*, 1622, p. 51. (Not an exact quotation.)

25. *Ortelius* (*and note*). *SC* contains *Theatrum orbis terrarum*, 1574. The map of Russia shows in the east a group of natives who had been turned into stone.

26–27. *Alexander . . . Cyrus*. Arrian, *Anabasis*, vi. 29.

34. *Cariola* (*and note*). Described in C. Ruini, *Anatomia . . . del Cavallo*. 1598, pp. 282–3 (*SC*, 1618).

111. 16–17. *the Saints . . . arose*. Matt. xxvii. 52–53.

18. *Patriarchs*. Gen. xlix. 29.

23. *where . . . remain*. See next note.

26–27. *Ezechiel's vision . . . Jehosaphat* (*and note*). Ezek. xxxvii; Joel iii. 2. *SC* contains *Biblia magna*, Paris, 1644, with commentary by various scholars, including Jacobus Tirinus, who annotates Ezek. xxxvii. 1 as follows: 'Ex hoc loco vult Dominicus Soto . . . omnium mortuorum ossa ex toto orbe in hunc campum per angelos sub tempus iudicij transferenda, vt vno eodemque loco omnes simul homines reuiuiscant. Sed verisimilius est quod Richardus, Suarez & alij docent, quemque resurrecturum vbi fuerit cuiusque eadauer, vel maior illius pars: indeque singulos rediuiuos manu angelica transferendos in vallem Iosaphat ad tribunal Christi.'

111. 30–**112.** 1. *take of*. Do away with.

112. 2–4. *ashes . . . field*. Lev. iv. 12.

8–9. *the Greek devotion*. Goar, *Euchologion* (or *Rituale Graecum*), 1647, pp. 525–38, 'Officium exequiarum'.

17. *Phocyllides . . . Lucretius* (*and notes*). Both the quotations are given by Vigenère in his commentary on *Les decades* of Livy, ii (1617, cols. 838 and 853. *SC* contains the edition of '1573' (?1583). For the passage in Phocylides see Bergk, *Poetae lyrici Graeci*, v. 104. Lucretius, ii. 999–1000.

19. *wings in Homer*. Od. xi. 222.

19. *which fell not*. Plato, *Phaedrus*, 246.

22. *Lucian*. *Hermotimus*, 7.

24. *Socrates* (*and note*). See note on 117. 30.

27. *Diogenes*. Diogenes Laertius, vi. 79.

29–31. *Stoicks . . . moon*. Tertullian, *De anima*, 54: 'Stoici, suas solas, id est sapientum animas, in supernis mansionibus collocant . . . sub lunam.' Cf. Lipsius, *Physiologia Stoicorum*, iii. 14 (*Opera*, 1613, pp. 878–9).

113. 1–2. *tedious . . . revolution.* Referring to the Platonic year. See *RM*, 7. 26 and note.

7–8. *aversly . . . ministration.* Kirchmann, iii. 2: 'vultu & capitibus aversis. . . . Et causa erat, ut id officium necessitatis esse ostenderent, non voluntatis.

8–11. *washed . . . nourishment.* Kirchmann, iii. 6: 'Denique ossa collecta vino, lacte, . . . imò etiam lacrymis fuisse irrigata. . . . Seneca in Consolat. ad Helviam. cap. 11. *Modò in eundem sinum, ex quo tres nepotes emiseras, ossa trium nepotum recepisti.*'

11. *opened . . . heaven.* Kirchmann, iii. 2: 'Tum iterum . . . oculos mortuo reseratos adapertosqúe fuisse. . . . Plinius monet lib. xi. cap. 38.'

13–14. *Their last . . . attendants (and note).* Kirchmann, iii. 9, refers to this threefold utterance as described by Servius on *Aeneid*, ii. 64, and adds, also out of Servius (on *Aen.* iii. 68): 'Soliti autem ad postremum Vale plerunque subjungere haec verba: *Nos te ordine, quo natura permiserit, cuncti sequemur.*'

17. *Romans . . . myrtle.* Kirchmann, iv. 3: 'Romani verò *Rosarum* adeo fuere studiosi, ut iis post mortem monumenta sua spargi supremo judicio nonnunquam jusserint . . . Apud Graecos tamen *Amarantho* potissimum sepulchra solita . . . Invenio & Myrti ramos sepulchris impositos apud Eurip. Electra [324]. . . .'

18–19. *Cypresse &c.* Kirchmann, iii. 1.

28–32. *Musick . . . descended.* Giraldi, *De sepulchris*, p. 25: 'Fuit enim opinio, ut scribit Macrobius [*In Somn. Scip.* ii. 3. 6], mortuos ad sepulturam cum cantu prosequi, quoniam animae ipsae post corporis uincula ad originem dulcedinis musicae, id est, ad coelum ipsum redire creditum est antiquis. [Quotation from Macrobius ends here.] Sunt qui ideo factum putent quod anima ipsa à plerisque harmonia existimata est. . . .' Cf. Kirchmann, ii. 4, and *RM*, 67. 32.

32–34. *Which . . . Capricornus.* Macrobius, *In Somn. Scip.*, i. 12: 'per has portas [sc. the two constellations mentioned] animae de caelo in terras meare et de terris in caelum remeare creduntur. ideo hominum una, altera deorum uocatur: hominum Cancer quia per hunc in inferiora descensus est, Capricornus deorum quia per illum animae in propriae immortalitatis sedem et in deorum numerum reuertuntur.' Cf. Ficino, *De immortal. animorum*, xviii. 5 (*Opera*, 1567, p. 405).

35–38. *burnt not children . . . combustion.* Kirchmann, i. 3. 'De Infantibus Plinius lib. vii. cap. xvi. Hominem prius quàm genito dente cremari, mos gentium non est. . . . Fulgentius Pla⟨n⟩ciades: Suggrundaria . . . quae nec Busta dici poterant, quia ossa, quae comburerentur non erant. . . .'

38. *kindled not fire.* Kirchmann, iv. 11: 'ne focum quidem lugentes instruebant.'

114. 1–2. *excessive . . . ghosts (and note).* Kirchmann, iv. 10: 'existimabant Manes immoderato luctu & lesso offendi.' Ibid., quotation of Tibullus: 'Tu manes ne laede meos. . . .'

3–4. *supine position.* Kirchmann, iii. 8: 'His . . . addo, Cadavera etiam supina in sepulchris fuisse posita.'

5. *Nor unlike.* Browne may have intended to write '*and* unlike' or 'Nor like' (see 102. 7–9) and was perhaps confused by the context.

6. *Diogenes.* Diogenes Laertius, vi. 31–32.

15. *heads forward.* Giraldi, op. cit. p. 67: 'Efferunt uero Turcae cadauera in caput, ut Hebraei quoque, non in pedes, ut nos.'

17. *They closed.* Kirchmann, i. 6: '*Oculi morientibus clausi. . . . Pupillas morituris albescere.*'

18–20. *iterated . . . affection.* Kirchmann, i. 13: 'clamorem . . . fuisse excitatum: Eo scilicet fine, ut vel exeuntem animam retardarent, vel in corpore adhuc delitiscentem expergefacerent.'

25–29. *That they suck'd . . . own (and note).* Kirchmann, i. 5: 'morientem solebant osculari . . . donec animam exhalaret. . . . An verò exeuntem animam hoc modo excipere & in se transferre voluerunt?' Cf. Perucci, *Pompe funebri*, p. 22: '*prima perche pensauano, che l'anima vscisse dalla bocca . . . secondo perche credendo Pittagoricamente la transmigratione dell'anima, gli offeriuano il proprio corpo.*'

30. *powred oyle . . . pyre.* Kirchmann, iii. 5: 'Quid jam de odoribus loquar, quos acervatim in rogum fuisse conjectos ex innumeris autorum locis videre est.'

31–33. *sacrifice unto the windes.* Kirchmann, iii. 2: 'Rogo jam incenso ventos optabant, qui flammam ardentiorem suscitarent alerentque, & ita cadaver . . . facilius citiusque absumeretur.'

35–36. *The Archimime . . . deceased.* Kirchmann, ii. 7: '. . . scurras & mimos, qui exsequiis interdum solebant adhiberi: ut patet ex Suetonio in Vespasiano capit. xix. *Sed in funere Paro archimimus personam ejus ferens, imitansque, ut est mos, facta & dicta vivi. . . .*'

114. 39–**115.** 1. *That they buried . . . Ferriman.* Casalius, *De profan. Rom. ritibus*, ii. 26: 'Mortuo composito in ipsius ore stipem ponebant, Charonti Portorium, & Naulum, quod est pretium solvendum pro vectura Navis. . . .'

115. 8–9. *persons Planet-struck . . . Heaven.* Kirchmann, i. 3: '*Infantes & Fulguritos cremari fas non fuisse.*'

9–10. *No Reliques . . . Malefactors.* Kirchmann, Appendix, 4: '*Sepultura quibus denegata . . . Atheniensium* [severitas] *in Sacrilegos & Proditores. . . .*' Ibid. 5: '*Sepulturâ prohibiti Suspendiosi & Αὐτόχειρες.*'

11. *Tartara's.* For the double plural see note to 87. 6.

17–19. *unto eight . . . combustion.* Kirchmann, iii. 2: '. . . morem fuisse antiquitus, ut si quando plura cadavera simul comburenda essent, . . . denis virorum corporibus singula muliebria apponerentur.' Kirchmann quotes Macrobius to the effect that this, in the ancient opinion, would make for a quicker burning: '*Ita nec veteribus calor mulierum habebatur incognitus.*' Symmachus, however, explains: '*non caloris erat, sed pinguis carnis & oleo similioris.*'

20. *Clarianders Wife.* Herodotus, v. 92.

21. *cold.* As in Milton, *Paradise Lost*, ii. 600–3.

24–25. *Female . . . spirits. Od.* xi. 225 sqq.

25–26. *Psyche . . . masculine (and note).* ψυχή with ἔχων.

27–28. *Egges . . . Lettuce.* Kirchmann, iv. 7: '*De cibis Feralibus, ut sunt Faba, Apium, Lactuca . . . Ova. . . .*'

31. *Morta.* One of the Fates. Aulus Gellius, iii. 16. 11.

34–35. *drink bloud. Od.* xi. 141–54.

35. *life of man.* Lev. xvii. 11 and 14. (Murison.)

36. *chirped like bats. Od.* xxiv. 6–9.

37–38. *a flock of birds. Od.* xi. 605.

116. 1–2. *departed . . . present.* Dante, *Inferno*, x. 97–103. (Gr.)

2–4. *Agamemnon . . . Son. Od.* xi. 444–61. See note to *CM*, 219. 17–36.

4. *afraid of swords. Od.* xi. 48–50.

4–6. *Sybilla . . . weapons. Aen.* vi. 290–4.

7. *Caesar and Pompey. Aen.* vi. 827 ('concordes animae nunc').

7–8. *Ajax . . . Ulysses. Od.* xi. 543–64.

8. *Deiphobus. Aen.* vi. 494–7.

11–14. *Charon . . . of the dead.* Charon, in Lucian's dialogue so named, does not specifically applaud the condition of Achilles among the dead, but shows himself unmoved by the supposed glories of human existence. In *Dialogues of the dead*, xv, Antilochus reproaches Achilles for disparaging death (*Od.* xi. 467 sqq.).

14. *Hercules. Od.* xi. 601–5.

15. *Julius.* Horace, *Odes*, i. 12. 46–48. Virgil, *Aen.* vi. 826 sqq.

16–18. *Images . . . simulachrum.* Murison cites Homer, *Iliad*, xxiii. 103–4.

23. *Platoes denne. Rep.* vii. 514 sqq.

25. *Pythagoras . . . Dante (and note).* Pythagoras is passed over.

27. *Cato.* Dante, *Purgatorio*, i. 31 sqq.

39–42. *Machiavel . . . exalted. Discorsi*, ii. 2.

117. 15. *Epicurus . . . hell. Inferno*, x. 13–15.

30. *Socrates.* In *Phaedo* (called 'the immortality of *Plato*' below).

31. *Cato.* Plutarch, *Cato Minor*, 68, 70.

118. 17. *three conquests.* English, Danish, Norman (on the supposition that the urns were Roman).

26–28. *old Philosophers . . . bodies (and note).* The work referred to in the note is *Oracula magica Zoroastris cum scholiis . . .*, 1599 (*Pselli scholia*, pp. 94–95).

33. *If we begin . . . live.* Cf. Manilius, iv. 16: 'Nascentes morimur. (Murison.)

119. 1. *work for Archimedes.* Referring to his treatise, *Arenarius*, estimating the number of grains of sand in the universe.

4–5. *not one little finger (and note).* Pierius, *Hieroglyphica* (*SC*), 1595, illustration on p. 352.

10. *David . . . cruell.* As in 2 Sam. viii. 2.

10–11. *Solomon . . . men.* 1 Kings xi. 1–8.

12–13. *Alcmenas nights.* Alluding to the story that Zeus turned one night into three while he was with Alcmena. Lucian, *Dial. deorum*, x, 'Mercury and Helios'. Cf. Lucian, *The Dream*, 17: τριέσπερος ὥσπερ ὁ Ἡρακλῆς.

15. *never to have been.* Sophocles, *Oed. Col.*, 1224: μὴ φῦναι τὸν ἅπαντα νικᾷ λόγον.

15–19. *Job . . . abortion.* Job iii. 1–16. Cf. *CM*, 243. 38–40.

21. *Questions (and note).* Marcellus Donatus, *Scholia*, 1604, pp. 420–1, on the passage in Suetonius, observes that according to Hyginus Achilles was known as Pyrrha at the time referred to.

120. 5. *probable Meridian of time.* The year 3000 from the creation of the world, on the theory (see below) that the world would last for 6,000 years altogether, 4,000 years B.C. and 2,000 after.

10–11. *Prophecy of Elias . . . Hector (and notes).* See note to *RM*, 44. 1. Charles V, born in 1500, would on this reckoning (see note above) have only 500 years in which to be famous. Hector had already had more than twice 969 before Charles was born.

16. *Janus.* Cf. *CM*, 236. 35.

17. *The great mutations of the world.* This phrase (with 'in' for 'of') occurs in a book known to Browne (see 142. 34 and note), J. Gaffarel's *Vnheard-of Curiosities* (translated from the French by E. Chilmead, 1650). Gaffarel indicates how the fall of great empires has been foretold by the stars, and then (p. 429) deals with objections: 'The First is, that if so be, by this *Writing*, all the Great Mutations in the World may be known; it is possible then, that the End of the World may in like manner be found out by It . . . which is Contrary to the Holy Scriptures.'

19. *whose death . . . pray for.* Thy Kingdom come.

28. *Circles and right lines.* See *GC*, 132. 34–37 and note; cf. 156. 27 and 168. 28–29.

28–29. *mortall . . . circle (and note).* Θ, for θάνατος. Cf. *CM*, 211. 14 and Martial, vii, 37.

35. *Gruter (and note).* See note to 123. 32–33.

121. 4–6. *To be content . . . Cardan (and note).* Cardan, *De propria vita*, ix (1614, p. 42), where C. nevertheless greatly modifies the statement.

6–7. *disparaging . . . himself.* In *In Cl. Ptolomaei De astrorum ivdiciis . . .*, iv (1578, pp. 629–80), Cardan gives a full account of his own character and circumstances in relation to his horoscope.

8. *Achilles horses. Iliad*, xvi. 149.

10. *Entelechia.* See *RM*, 10. 19–20 and note.

11–12. *The Canaanitish woman.* Matt. xv. 22–28.

18. *he is almost lost.* Chersiphron. Strabo, xiv. 1. 22; Pliny, *HN*, xxxvi. 14.

19. *Epitaph of Adrians horse.* Kirchmann, *De fun. Rom.*, Appendix, vi, quotes Xiphilinus (Dio Cassius, *Epit.* lxix. 10): 'Adrianus . . . Boristheni equo . . . mortuo & monumentum aedificavit, & columnam erexit, inscripto epigrammate.' The epitaph appears to have been lost, but Browne probably refers to one on Borysthenes which was published in

1599 by P. Pithou (*Epigrammata*, i, p. 145). A part of this epitaph was found a little later on a broken stone at Apt; but the genuineness of this has been much doubted. See *Corpus inscript. Lat.* xii, p. 144, no. 1122.

22. *Agamemnon.* Horace, *Odes*, iv. 9. 25.

122. 2. *Pagans could doubt* (*and note*). Euripides, fragm. from *Polyidus*, quoted by Plato, *Gorgias*, 492e:

> τίς δ' οἶδεν, εἰ τὸ ζῆν μέν ἐστι κατθανεῖν,
> τὸ κατθανεῖν δὲ ζῆν;

3–4. *right descensions . . . winter arches.* The arc of 'the longest sun' (i.e. at the summer solstice) thereafter loses height ('sets') from day to day 'at right descensions' (vertically) until about the time of the winter solstice, when the arc is lowest.

5. *light in ashes* (*and note*). Leon Modena, *Istoria de riti Hebraici*, v. 8 (Eng. transl., 1650, p. 233): 'When the Breath is now gone out of the Body . . . they set up, at the Head, a Waxe Light, placed in an Earthen Pitcher, or Vessel, full of Ashes.'

6. *brother of death.* See *LF*, 34–36, and note.

32. *feeding the winde* (*and note*). Drusius, *Annotationes in Coheleth*, 1635 (*SC*), p. 12 (on Eccles. i. 14): *νομὴ ἀνέμου*. Sic Aquila olim vertit . . . Idem significare voluit Symmachus, cum verteret *βόσκησις* (with the same meaning as *νομή*, feeding).

33. *Cambyses.* Herodotus, iii. 16.

33. *Mummie.* As a drug.

34. *Mizraim.* Son of Ham (Gen. x. 6); for an Egyptian (sc. mummified).

123. 5. *Osyris . . . Dogge-starre* (*variant reading on p. 269*). In *RM*, 22. 34–35, Browne mentions the common association of Noah with Deucalion, and is here perhaps confusing the 'shipp of Argos' with Deucalion's ark.

6. *incorruption in the heavens.* See note to *RM*, 48. 13–14.

8. *perspectives.* Telescopes.

11–13. *There is . . . destruction* (*additional passage on p. 269*). On the reference to Aristotle see note to *RM*, 48. 13–14.

11–16. *whatever hath . . . power of it self.* Editors have been troubled by this sentence, finding a contradiction between 'All others . . . within the reach of destruction' and 'which is the peculiar of that necessary essence that cannot destroy itself'. Accordingly some have put the first of these two sentences after 'power of it self'; others have left the first where it is but have enclosed it in brackets (in this following the edition of 1669), so as to make 'which is' &c. refer to being confident of no end. But emendation can be avoided if 'destruction' is taken in an active, not a passive sense—the power to destroy. God can destroy all others than himself, and he alone has the power to destroy. Cf. l. 19: 'God who can only [sc. who alone can] destroy our souls'; and *RM*, 48. 18–19: 'annihilation, which is beyond the power of sublunary causes'; ibid. 43. 19–23.

30. *Sardanapalus.* Athenaeus, xii. 38.

30–32. *funerall Laws . . . sober obsequies.* Cicero, *De leg.* ii. 23. 59.

32–33. *wood . . . Urne (and note)*. The epitaph quoted from Gruterus in the note is in *Inscriptiones antiquae totius orbis Romani* (*SC*), 1603, 'Spuria ac supposititia', p. xiv. 8. The words preceding the extract are 'P. Atilio Rufo et Atiliae Beronicae vx. vixer. ann. xxiiii sed Pvbl. men. x ante natvs est et eadem hora fvngorum esv ambo mortvi sunt. ille acv ista lanificio vitam agebant'. The penultimate word in Gruterus is 'vrna' not 'olla', and 'empta' is followed by the words 'atq. indvlgentia Pontific. locvs datus est'.

34. *Gordianus*. Emperor of Rome A.D. 238–44; Julius Capitolinus (*Historia Augusta*, *SC*), as quoted by Kirchmann, iii. 20, lists the five languages thus: '*Graecis & Latinis & Persicis, & Judaicis & Ægyptiacis literis*.'

34–35. *The man of God*. See note on 90. 10–13.

124. 5–6. *a late part yet to act*. According to the tradition which identified the 'two witnesses' of Rev. xi. 3 sqq. with Enoch and Elijah. Augustine, *De Genesi ad Litteram*, ix. 6 (*PL*, 34, col. 397). See also *CE*, pp. 149–50, and *PE*, vii. 10 (1646, p. 356).

6. *decretory*. Having to do with judgement.

12. *second . . . death*. Rev. xxi. 8.

13–14. *coverings of Mountaines*. Rev. vi. 16.

20. *stones thrown*. Dio Cassius, Excerpt of lxxviii (lxxvii), 13. 7, records how Antoninus searched for the tomb of Sulla and repaired it.

34–35. *Chaos of pre-ordination . . . fore-beings*. See *RM*, 38. 10 and note.

36–38. *Christian annihilation . . . divine shadow*. For the kind of mystical phraseology here illustrated Browne could have been indebted to various authorities, ancient and modern. It is well represented, for example, in the works of St. John of the Cross, whose *Opera mystica* were translated into Latin in 1639, and in those of St. Teresa, especially her autobiography, translated into English in 1642 as *The Flaming Hart*.

38. *divine shadow*. See *RM*, 10. 19–20 and note.

125. 9. *Sands of Ægypt*. See *H*, 13–15 ('depositure in dry earths', &c.) and note.

12. *Lucan*. vii. 809–10.

THE GARDEN OF CYRUS

126. *Engraving*. The diagram, together with the quotation from Quintilian (viii. 3. 9), occurs in B. Curtius, *Horti* (1560, p. 268) and G. B. della Porta, *Villa* (1592, pp. 196–7); and Browne is apparently indebted to these works (both are in *SC*) in several other places as well. Details of this relationship were first given by Dr. J. S. Finch in *Studies in philology*, xxxvii, 1940, pp. 274–82, and are also given in the notes below. They include certain classical references which Browne seems to make for himself but which are also made by Curtius or Porta or both; and Browne here, as elsewhere, becomes open to the charge of trying to seem more learned than he was. But, as on some other occasions, carelessness or laziness, 'the inactivity of my disposition' (*RM*, I. 13–14), seems a more likely explanation than dishonesty. Browne was indeed usually content with laconic documentation, if any, but as Dr. Finch himself observes, he does at least mention both these authorities (131. 33 and note), which he would hardly have done if he had meant to deceive.

129. 3–4. *Quincunciall . . . Ancients.* MS. Sloane 1875, f. 100 (Browne's autograph): 'In the ordering of trees the ancient & moderns much commended the Quincunx or disposure of trees that one stands betwixt 4 whereby 2 ways are cleere vnto viewe & passage. & this seemd very proper for affording a dewe nourishment, & conuenient distance.'

7–8. *Vulcan . . . Theology.* Hyginus, *Fabulae*, 140: 'Latona . . . parit Apollinem et Dianam, quibus Vulcanus sagittas dedit donum. post diem quartam quam essent nati, Apollo . . . Pythonem sagittas interfecit.' (The fullstop after 'donum' was not always accepted.)

10. *the diffused light.* Created on the first day. Cf. *Paradise Lost*, vii. 243–9. See *CE*, pp. 52–53.

18–19. *story . . . conservation.* How the supply of vegetable food was to be maintained is described in Gen. i. 11, 'the herb yielding seed, and the fruit tree yielding fruit after his kind, whose seed is in itself'.

21–23. *Chirurgery . . . Adam (and note).* Almost exactly repeated in *Miscellany Tracts*, 1683; see *K*, v, p. 4.

24. *Paradise . . . creation.* Gen. ii. 8 sqq. Pererius, *Comm. in Genesin*, iii (1622, pp. 88–89), is in favour of this view. *CE*, p. 94.

26. *Gardens were before Gardiners.* Porta, *Villa*, i (1592, p. 2): 'Arborum, herbarumque fructibus vescimur, . . . iccirco plantas ante omnia animalia mundo natas Theophrastus, Porphyrius, & Eusebius enunciarunt, & ante eos verissimus Moses. . . .' Also Curtius, *Horti*, i. 2 (1560, p. 3).

30. *seated in the East (and note).* See *CE*, p. 95. Cf. N. Abram, *Pharus Veteris Testamenti* (*SC*), ii. 3 (1648, p. 41).

130. 4. *Zoroaster . . . Mizraim.* Bidez et Cumont, *Les mages hellénisés*, 1938, i, p. 43: 'Parfois, ils se sont embrouillés dans les généalogies de la Genèse [Gen. x. 6] et au lieu de Nemrod, c'est son père, Chous, son oncle Misraim, ou son grand-père Cham que l'on trouve confondus avec Zoroastre.'

5–6. *a work of Agriculture.* Pliny, *HN*, xviii. 3, mentions several early writers on agriculture including Mago the Carthaginian, whose work was translated into Latin; but not Zoroaster. Browne's statement would be explained if 'Mago' had become confused with 'magus' and 'magus' understood to mean Zoroaster. On Zoroaster as *magus* see Ralegh, *History of the World*, I. xi. 1 (1614, pp. 169–70).

8. *if made by Semiramis.* Curtius, vi. 12, p. 149: 'Diodorus Siculus Semiramidem horum autricem extitisse, memoriae mandauit. Receptior tamen opinio est vt Cyrus hos eleuandos curauerit.' See note on 130. 16–18.

10. *raised upon pillars.* Strabo, xvi. 1. 5. Curtius, vi. 12, p. 150: 'Strabo vero pilas concauas, & terra plenas fuisse dicit. Quo profundius arbores radices agerent. . . .'

14. *Paradise . . . elevated.* See *CE*, p. 97. Cf. N. Abram, op. cit., ii. 4 (1648, p. 42), 'De loco Paradisi variae doctorum sententiae.'

16–18. *Syrian King . . . gardens (and note).* Diodorus, ii. 10, observes that the Hanging Garden was made by a Syrian king later than Semiramis. Josephus, *Antiq. Jud.* x. 11. 1.

26–27. *name of Paradise.* Julius Pollux, *Onomasticon* (*SC*), ix. 3 (13): 'Sed paradisi, Barbaricum nomen videtur: consuetudine autem, in usum Graecum pervenit, sicuti & multa alia Persica.'

30–31. *garden . . . Buckler.* גַּן and מָגֵן.

32. *Woods and Mountains.* Herodotus, i. 110.

35. *hanging Gardens . . . authour thereof.* Curtius, vi. 12, p. 149, 'De hortis apud Babylonem pensilibus: . . . de illorum conditore . . . Is autem fuit Cyrus, probabiliore opinione.'

37–40. *Ahasuerus . . . thereof.* Esther i.

37–38. *Artaxerxes Longi-manus.* Artaxerxes I, son of Xerxes.

131. 1–2. *Artaxerxes Mnemon.* Grandson of Artaxerxes I.

3. *second Brother (and note).* In *58* this note has no asterisk or raised number. It is placed against the beginning of the paragraph. In some editions it has been attached to the word 'opinion', thus wrongly linking the opinion with Plutarch. Browne seems merely to have wished to cite Plutarch for the relationship between Artaxerxes and Cyrus. The note has therefore here been attached to the word 'Brother'. *second.* Next younger.

4–5. *work . . . of Xenophon. Anabasis.*

7–8. *Lord . . . ordination.* Curtius, vi. 8, p. 143: 'Is enim vbicunque aut ageret vel diuerteret, hortos constituebat, rebus omnibus, quae terra ferebat, ornatos, ac refectos. . . . elegantiamque arborum in quincuncem ordinem positarum. . . .'

9. *Laertes. Od.* xxiv. 223–31.

10–12. *Attalus . . . Paradise.* Plutarch, *Demetrius*, 20.

13. *many of the Ancients.* E.g. Hyacinth, Narcissus.

17. *Strebæus.* The correct reading, but altered by Browne in two copies to 'Stebæus' (perhaps by temporary confusion with Stobaeus). The reference is to Xenophon, *Oeconomicus*, translated by Strebaeus in Xenophon, *Opera*, 1561, p. 354: 'arbores . . . ordines, et omnia in quincuncem pulchrè directa.'

19–20. *most elegant of the Latines (and note).* Porta, *Villa*, iv. 13, p. 196, refers to Cicero, *De Sen.* 17: 'et proceritates arborum et directos in quincuncem ordines.'

20. *Varro. De re rustica*, i. 7. 2. Mentioned by Porta, p. 196.

24. *figure . . . number.* Porta, iv. 13, p. 197: 'si X literam per medium seces, relinquitur V. . . .' Cf. Curtius, *Horti*, p. 268.

26. *Emphaticall decussation.* Decussation *par excellence.*

33. *footnote. Curtius . . . Porta.* See note to 128.

132. 5–6. *those of Constantine . . . Sky.* Representing the cross which

Constantine saw in the sky while marching against Byzantium, and which he incorporated also in his standard, or 'labarum'. See note to 132. 21–29.

11. *right*. Vertical, without cross-piece, as illustrated in J. Lipsius, *De cruce*, i. 5 (*Opera*, *SC*, 1637, iii, p. 647).

13. *mysticall Tau*. T; see note to 169. 1–6.

15. *Empedon*. Or 'tabella suppedanea', for the feet of the crucified to rest on. Discussed by Lipsius, op. cit. ii. 10 (ed. cit. iii, p. 661), and by G. Bosio, *La trionfante croce*, i. 6 (1610, p. 22).

16–19. *Lipsius . . . sword*. Lipsius, op. cit. i. 7 (ed. cit. iii, p. 649): 'Haec est quam Andreanam hodie dicimus. . . . Anne verâ? facit me vt ambigam Martyrologium Romanum: in quo hoc saltem legas, *in Cruce suspensum.* & magis Hippolytus, qui scribit *Crucifixum Patris in Achaiâ, ad arborem oliuae rectum*.' If this was the passage in Lipsius that Browne was thinking of he seems to have forgotten what Hippolytus is there said to have written.

21–29. *labarum . . . hit on* (*and note*). This passage follows closely parts of A. Bosio's *Roma sotterranea*, iv. 31 (1632, p. 629c), '*Del* X': Fv' espresso ancora il nome di Christo con quella cifra, composta dalle due lettere parimente greche *X*, & *P*. . . . La qual cifra, se bene sappiamo che fù vsata da Costantino e fatta porre da lui nel Labaro, ò Stendardo doppo che la fù mostrato il segno della Croce; . . . ne sacri Cimeterij si trovane innumerabili sepolcri antichi con questo segno, come si può vedere in alcuni epitaffi . . . e particolarmente in quello di Mario sotto Adriano; di Alessandro sotto Antonino . . . anzi la medesima fù parimente vsata da' Gentili; si bene in altro senso; e fù ancora questa trà li Ieroglifici de gli Egitti; Onde si vede vna medaglia di Tolomeo con l'istesse lettere; alle quali però state date varie interpretationi. . . .'

30–31. *crosses . . . heads. Cruces ansatae*; see 169. 7–13, 'handed crosses' and note.

32. *character of Venus*. ♀ (astronomical sign).

34–37. *Egyptians . . . intersection*. A. Kircher, *Obeliscus Pamphilius* (*SC*), iv, Hierogrammatismus 20 (1650, p. 371), marginal note 5: 'Per circulum & lineas rectas omnia in mundo explicant Aegyptii.' Marginal note 6: 'Quid per Crucem ansatam.' Text: 'Circulo igitur Orbes Coelestes, quibus se spiritus Mundi primò, ijs suam communicando virtutem, immiscet; per Crucem quatuor elementorum in sublunarem Mundum, virtutem . . . notabant.' Ibid. p. 366: 'processumque naturae in rebus sub ipso [charactere] symbolicè repraesentarunt, vehiculumque dixerunt Spiritus Mundi.'

38. *plain crosse* (*and note*). The discussion of *crux plana* by Nicolas Upton in his *De studio militari*, 1654, pp. 210–11, includes the statement (under 'De Cruce equali', p. 211) that in *crux plana* 'pes ejus est pars longior si bene fiat'. Upton's work is followed in the volume of 1654 by Iohan. de Bado Aureo, *Tractatus de armis*, and *Henrici Spelmanni Aspilogia*, the whole volume edited by Edoardus Bissaeus. (See note on 138. 5–8.)

132. 38–**133.** 4. *plain crosse . . . Altar* (*and notes*). Described in Casalius, *De vet. Rom. ritibus*, 1644, i, pp. 10 and 7, and reproduced thus:

The illustration of the 'Altar' as given by Casalius is adapted, rather than copied, from the 'Table'. It is given similarly by G. Bosio, *La trionfante croce*, 1617, p. 472.

133. 4–5. *Table of Bembus.* This is an elaborate assemblage of hieroglyphics in bronze. It was formerly possessed by Cardinal Bembo (1470–1547) and is now at Turin. It is assigned to the reign of Claudius or a little later. See E. Scamuzzi, *La 'Mensa Isiaca' del Regio Museo di Antichità di Torino*, Rome, 1939. The Table is also described in Kircher, *Oedipus Aegyptiacus*, 1652 (*SC*), iii, pp. 80–160.

7–9. *ceremony . . . cross.* Ezek. xlviii. 10.

11–13. *Oyle . . . X. Talmud*, Kerithoth, 5b: 'In anointing kings one draws the figure of a crown [sc. a circle], and with priests in the shape of the letter *chi*.' Cf. Horayoth, 12a. (*The Babylonian Talmud*, ed. I. Epstein.)

27–28. *from Abydenus . . . decussation (and note).* This is misleading because there is nothing about decussation in Curtius (*Horti*) at this point, or in Abydenus as quoted by Eusebius. The actual words of Curtius (vi. 12; 1560, p. 149) are: 'Abydenus (referente Eusebio) de praeparatione euangelica, scribit Nabuchodonosorem Babylonem triplici muro munijsse, atque in regia hortos pensiles plantasse.' Much follows, without reference to Abydenus or Eusebius, between this and Curtius's mention of decussation on p. 150 (see footnote, 'Decussatio ipsa, &c.'). The relevant passage in Eusebius, *Praeparatio evangelica*, is in ix. 41 (*PG*, 21, cols. 762–3).

29–30. *Alcinous . . . Paradise.* Curtius, vi. 14, p. 152: 'Homerum ipsum in illorum descriptione . . . paradisi simulacrum & historiam retinere voluisse.'

31. *Eustathius . . . word. Od.* vii. 112 (ὄρχατος). Eustathius, *Comm.* (*SC*) ad loc.: Ὄρχατος δὲ, δένδρα ἐπίστιχα κατὰ φυτείαν ἀμπέλου.

31. *emphatical.* Important.

32–33. *Diomedes . . . planted. Iliad*, xiv. 123: Πολλοὶ δὲ φυτῶν ἔσαν ὄρχατοι ἀμφὶς.

34. *Ulysses. Od.* xxiv. 341–2.

37. *Theophrastus. Enquiry into plants*, iv. 4. 8 and iv. 7. 7–8.

134. 9. *Varro.* See 131. 20 and note.

9. *Quintilian*. See 128 and note.

10. *Virgil (and note)*. The lines from Virgil are quoted by Curtius, x. 13, and Porta, p. 196, beginning 'Nec secius'.

14–17. *Saturn . . . Noah*. Bochart, *Geographia sacra*, 1646 (*SC*), i. 1: '*Historia de Noa & tribus filiis acuratè confertur cum fabula & Saturni tribus liberis.*'

29. *first sinne . . . world*. Gen. ix. 21.

135. 6–9. *Targum . . . Siloah*. P. Costus, *Targum Koheleth, hoc est, Caldaica Paraphrasis Ecclesiastis, Latine versa*, 1554, p. 10: 'herbas quoque olfactu nobiles adieci; item & arbores steriles & aromata ferentes, quas ad me daemones & nocentes angeli ex India, detulerant: omnes item arbores fructiferas. Horti autem termini erant à muro Ierusalem vsque ad littus aquarum Siluah.' (Expansion of Eccles. ii. 5.)

10–14. *And if Jordan . . . hinteth (and note)*. N. Abram, *Pharus Veteris Testamenti*, ii. 16 (1648, p. 56): '*Probatur Iordanum esse fluvium Paradisi, ex nomine Iarden, Eden, Genesar.*'

20–22. *so methodicall . . . relations*. Vitruvius, iii and iv.

29–31. *number . . . horses . . . Seasons*. Fulgentius (Planciades), *Mythologicon* (in *Mythologici Latini*, 1599, p. 166, on Apollo as the sun): 'Huic quoque quadrigam scribunt . . . quod aut quadripartitis temporum varietatibus anni circulum peragat' (or because of the four divisions of the day).

29–30. *strings of his Harp . . . orbes of heaven*. Natalis Comes, *Mythologia* (*SC*), iv. 10, '*De Apolline*' (1641, p. 361): 'Huic citharae inuentionem tribuerunt, quae septem chordis priùs muniebatur. . . . Qui chordarum numerus planetarum numero conueniebat.'

136. 6. *Vitruvius. De architectura*, vii. 1. 3–4.

10. *sculpture draughts*. Engraved drawings.

13. *Laureat draughts*. Laurel patterns.

18. *(note) five parts*. Sir Henry Wotton, *Elementa architecturae*, 1624, &c. (in Vitruvius, *De architectura*, 1649, p. 9): 'Omnes partes structurae, ad quinque capita reduci possunt. quam divisionem accepi *à Baptista Alberti*, ut ipsi suum tribuam. Suntque, *Fundamentum, Parietes, Aperturae seu lumina, Compartitio, Tectum*.' Alberti, however, in *De re aedificatoria*, i, divides a building into *six* parts, from which he expressly excludes the *fundamentum* (1512, f. xxxii).

22–23. *what figure . . . Leo the Third*. There is some ambiguity here, and perhaps some inaccuracy; but it seems more likely that the reference is to Pope Leo III (795–816) than to the Emperor Leo III ('Isauricus', 717–40), crowned by Germanus, Patriarch of Constantinople. If this is so 'Anastasius' can be identified with the 'Bibliotecarius' who wrote a history of the popes (*PL*, 127–8). In his life of Leo III Anastasius lists at great length the embellishments by Leo of various churches, but gives no details of his coronation, and mentions no coronal 'figure' or shape placed at any time on his head. Among improvements at the Lateran Church, however, he speaks of a *triclinium* with an apse decorated with mosaics; and other historians record that these represented St. Peter (seated above) handing down insignia to two kneeling figures, a banner to Charlemagne and a pallium to Leo III; and if Browne had seen, for instance, the engraving of this in *De Lateranensibus parietinis* (Rome, 1625) by N. Alemannus (who refers to Anastasius in this connexion), he could have been misled by the appearance of the pallium, for the middle part of this is caught into a loop and held over Leo's head in a way that might suggest, to a casual observer, that a rather formless sort of crown or 'diadem' is being conferred on him. (See Alemannus, pp. 70–72.) It would then be natural to ask what shape the crown was intended to have; though exactly why Browne should associate it with Anastasius remains unclear. It may be that as in other places (e.g. 149. 29, 156. 15–16, and *RM*, 11. 28) Browne was relying too much on his memory.

24–28. *That of Charles . . . this order* (*and note*). J. J. Chifflet, *Anastasis Childerici I*, 1655, p. 2: 'In Bibliothecâ Regiâ Bruxellensi seruatur magnae molis membraneus codex M.S. continens Historiam Caroli Magni, elegantissimis imaginibus illustratam; quarum vna exhibet antiquiores Franciae Reges.' This illustration is reproduced on p. 3 of Chifflet's volume, with Charlemagne's crown differing from the rest, as in Browne's description. The 'f.' before 'Stradæ' in the note may be a misreading or misprint for 'J.' (See next note).

25. *closed Crown*. J. Strada, *Imperator. Romanorum . . . Imagines* (*SC*), 1559, plate 82.

28. *continued*. Here, as in 139. 7, 'continue' may be used in the obsolete sense of 'contain'; but in Browne's handwriting 'containe' might look like 'continue'.

30–31. *radiated . . . Augustus*. As in Strada, op. cit., plate 2.

32. *Armenians*. A. Agostino (Agustin), *Dialoghi . . . intorno alle medaglie* (*SC*), 1625, p. 101.

34. *Diadems*. Ibid., p. 182: 'vna fascia, o benda . . . che portauano i Re. . . .'

36–37. *too upright . . . Aaron*. As portrayed in Genevan Bibles, at Exod. xxviii.

137. 1. *two Crowns . . . Ptolomy*. 1 Macc. xi. 13.

2–3. *historians . . . diadems*. P. Camerarius, *Operae subcisivae* (*SC*), lxi (1624, pp. 274–5), '*Diadema & Citaris qualia ornamenta regia fuerint* . . .', cites Justinus, xv. 3. 13, on the wounding of Lysimachus in the forehead by Alexander, 'ita . . . ut sanguis aliter claudi non posset, quam diadema sibi demptum rex alligandi vulneris causa capiti eius imponeret', and Plutarch, *Lucullus*, 18, describing how, when Mithridates bade his wives and sisters kill themselves, Monima, a wife, 'diadema capiti detractum collo circumposuit, seque suspendit, eoque celeriter rupto, ô execrandum, inquit, pannum, ne ad hunc quidem vsum aptus es?'

8. *Blancanus* (*and note*). *Aristotelis loca mathematica*, assembled by J. Blancanus, 1615 (*SC*), includes the spurious *Quaestiones mechanicae*. Of these no. 26 (Blancanus 25) is 'De Lecto' and Blancanus (p. 190) provides a diagram showing the diamond shapes made by the oblique cording.

12. *Cestius.* Agostino, op. cit., p. 90, no. 7.

19. *fenestræ reticulatæ.* Ezek. xli. 16. *θυρίδες δικτυωτάι* ('fenestrae in modum retis factae', 1628); 'fenestras obliquas', Vulg.; 'the windows were covered', A.V.; 'windows of fixed lattice-work', R.V.

20. *Greek expression.* Septuagint, *διὰ τῶν δικτυῶν.*

25–26. *reticulate . . . ground.* 1 Kings vii. 17–20.

27. *Craticula or grate.* Exod. xxvii. 4.

32. *Conopeion.* Isidore, *Origines* (*SC*), xix. 5. 5: '*Conopeum* est rete . . . contextum propter muscas & culices excludendos, quo magis Alexandrini utuntur. . . .'

33. *rushey labyrinths.* Theocritus, xxi. 11: *ἐκ σχοίνων λαβύρινθοι.*

34–35. *nosegaynets . . . Princes.* Browne may have been vaguely remembering the passage in Cicero, *In C. Verrem*, ii. 5. 11, where it is alleged that Verres, after the manner of the old Bithynian kings, used to be carried by eight bearers in a litter, with garlands round head and neck and an open-work bag or reticule containing rose-petals, which he occasionally moved to his nostrils. Where Cicero got this information about the kings of Bithynia is not known, but he probably did not mean the comparison with them to go beyond the litter. In Browne's sentence the kings have replaced Verres altogether.

35–36. *Reticulum . . . liver* (*and note*). Cf. Exod. xxix. 13.

138. 3–4. *why Vulcan &c.* Discussed by Leo Hebraeus, *De amore*, ii, in J. Pistorius, *Artis Cabalisticae* . . . i, 1587, pp. 419–21. (Gr.). *De amore* is mentioned in *PE*, vi. 11 (1646, p. 332).

5–8. *Heralds . . . method* (*and note*). The varieties of heraldic pattern mentioned in the note, check, mascle (lozenge), vair (cup-shaped check), and fusil (elongated lozenge), qq.v. *OED*, are described by Upton (see note to 132. 38), pp. 245, 251, 231, and 249–51 respectively. For saltyre see ibid., p. 251, and for ermines arranged quincuncially see ibid., p. 245 and the notes by Bissaeus, p. 83.

9–10. *cut . . . pyramidally.* A. Boece de Boot, op. cit. in note to 141. 28–32, p. 173: 'L'on a aussi coustume de tailler les diamans en forme de pyramide, croissant d'vne base quadrangulaire.'

12. *Rhomboidall decussations.* Made by the crossed lines used in shading.

12. *Sculptors.* In the obsolete sense of engravers.

13. *double Haches.* Double strokes forming angles.

14–15. *Americans . . . textures.* Possibly referring to the representations of 'decussated' designs in Mexican garments appearing on the half-title of A. de Herrera's *Novus Orbis* (*SC*, 1622; see note to 89. 10), especially 'Deus mortuorum' and 'Acamapich primus Rex Mexici'.

16–19. *Spider . . . Textury.* Moufet, *Insectorum . . . theatrum* (*SC*), ii. 13 (1634, p. 232): 'Et profecto hoc ipso Ægyptios, Lydos, Penelopem, Tanaquillida, Amestrim . . . superant, quòd (praeter vulgarem rationem & artem) nullis filis per transversum actis ex arctissima quadam villorum in longum continuitate solidam tenacemque telam componunt.'

26. *Dodder.* Cf. 160. 9. '*Cuscuta sive Cassutha*', 'a strange herbe, altogether without leaues or root, . . . groweth vpon sundry kindes of herbes . . .'.

Gerard, *Herbal*, 1633, ii. 577–8. (Henry Power to Browne, 15 Sept. 1648, *K*, vi, p. 282: 'I have . . . Gerard, with Johnson's addition [1633, &c.] . . . I shall embrace Gerard above all because you pleased to honour him with your approbation.') '*G*' in the following notes.

26. *Tetter*. Evidently not tetter-wort, or the great Celandine, but a botanical application, not recorded in *OED*, of the medical term for a skin-eruption.

27–28. *chalked Tile . . . fields. Constantini Caesaris* [IV *or* VII] . . . *de agricultura libri xx* [*Geoponica*], 1540 (*SC*), ii. 40, p. 69: '*De herba leone, quam & orobanchen uocant. Sotionis. . . . Si uero uelis hanc herbam in toto non apparere, quinque testas accipito, & in ipsis cum creta . . . Herculem leonem suffocantem pingito: easque testas ad quatuor angulos, et in medium arui deponito.*' *Orobanche*, lit. the vetch-choker; broomrape.

33. *Pentalithismus*. This form appears to be a coinage. Meineke, *Fragmenta*, ii, records τὸ πεντελιθίζειν (Hermippus, θεοί, 9).

139. 1–4. *played at Penelope . . . game* (*and note*). Eustathius, note on *Odyssey*, i. 401, with reference to Athenaeus, i. 16–17.

5. *Tables*. Backgammon. See next note.

5–10. *Tables . . . Moon*. Suidas (*SC*), iii (1705, p. 423): *Τάβλα*. Tabula. Nomen lusus quem Palamedes . . . invenit . . . tabula est mundus terrestris . . . Fritillus [dice-box] & in eo septem tesserae, septem stellae planetarum, Turricula vero, altitudo coeli; ex quo multa [& bona] & mala omnibus rependuntur. Alii vero [aliter] dicunt.'

7. *continue*. See note to 136. 28.

8–9. *Hermes . . . Osyris*. Diodorus, i. 16. 2 (ἱερογραμματεύς).

8. *Hermes* (*and note*). Referring to *Phaedrus*, 274c–d, where Theuth (Hermes) is credited with the invention of draughts and dice.

16. *illustrable from Aristotle*. See note to 137. 8. In the spurious *Quaest. Mechan.* Blancanus' no. 22 is 'Aristotle's' no. 23, 'De instrumento nucifrago'; and Blancanus (p. 185) again provides the text with an illustration.

139. 22–**140.** 9. *The Roman Batalia . . . Elephants* (*and note*). Most of this passage (including the reference to Virgil, *Georg.* ii. 279–81, and the diagram) is derived from the two works by Salmasius (*SC*) mentioned in the note. Salmasius, *De re militari Rom.*, 1657, pp. 21 and 25, also supplies references to Polybius [xv. 2] and Appian [viii. 124–6]. The 'battle of *Africa*' at Zama is described by Livy, xxx. 33.

140. 10–15. *Cuneus and Forceps . . . both sides*. F. Vegetius Renatus, *De re militari* (*SC*), iii. 19 (1553, p. 99): 'Cuneus dicitur multitudo peditum quae iuncta cum aciè primo angustior, deinde latior procedit, & aduersariorum ordines rumpit . . . Contra quem ordinatio ponitur quam forficem vocant. Nam e lectissimis militibus confertis in V literam ordo componitur: & illum cuneum excipit.'

11. *half a Rhombus*. Aelian (Tacticus), *De instruendis aciebus* (with Vegetius, &c., 1553, p. 254): 'Rhombum dimidiatum & iam transformatum in triquetrum, Cuneum seu rostrum vocamus.'

19–24. *The Rhombus . . . Angle* (*and note*). Aelian, op. cit., 'De Acie

Equestri' (1553, pp. 252–3): 'Aciebus ad Rhombi similitudinem formatis Thessalos primos vsos comperimus . . . equites enim constituti in hac forma vertere sese in quemvis prospectum possunt. . . . Quippe cum prestantiores, Rhombi latera teneant, & principes, angulos regant . . . ducem seu ductorem . . . Cvneatis Scythę vtuntur & Thraces. Quinetiam Macedones vsi sunt suadente rege Philippo.'

25. *Macedonian Phalanx . . . invincible.* Aelian, op. cit., p. 251: 'Macedonica phalanx inexpugnabilis & intoleranda hostibus habita est. . . .'

29. *Quincunciall quadrate of Curtius.* Benedictus Curtius, *Horti* (see note to 128), x. 13, '*De arborum ordinibus*', pp. 267–8 (diagram on p. 268). Cf. 142. 8.

30–33. *Thucydides . . . tile (and notes).* Virgil, ed. Guellius (*SC*), 1575, p. 85 (on *Georg.* ii. 278, 'secto via', &c.): '. . . docet poëtam alludere ad Graecorum τὸ πλαίσιον, & πλινθίον, quod est lateris forma, & militaris ordo quadrangulari forma: Thucyd. ἐν πλαισίῳ τεταγμένοι.'

36. *Babylon . . . square.* Herodotus, i. 178.

37. *holy City.* Rev. xxi. 16.

38. *pillars of Seth.* See note to *RM*, 24. 37.

141. 11. *Infants.* Jonah iv. 11 and Deut. i. 39.

13. *monument . . . furlongs.* Diodorus Siculus, ii. 7. 1.

20. *the elegant medall (and note).* Agostino, *Dialoghi* (see note to 136. 32), illustration (1625, p. 85).

23. *figure of the Ark.* Gen. vi. 15.

23–24. *table of the Shew-bread.* Exod. xxv. 23.

24–25. *stone . . . row.* The reference is apparently to Exod. xxviii. 17–21 (not 9–10); in either case 'stones' would be the more correct reading.

28–32. *Lapidaries . . . subtending.* A. Boece de Boot, *Le parfaict ioaillier, ou histoire des pierreries* (*SC*), 1644, ii. 7, p. 173, '*De quelle facon l'on taille le Diamant.* Le diamant se taille en diuerses figures. La plus noble est creuë estre la quarrée; c'est a dire lors que la superficie est reduite en tables quarrées. Mais lors que le diamant est faconné en telle forme, l'on doit obseruer a ce que les deux tables laterales ne fassent que la superieure, & que celles qui sont entre les laterales & la superieure constituent l'hypoteneuse d'vn angle droict. De plus il est necessaire que la table superieure soit vn parallellogramme longuet.'

141. 33–**142.** 4. *Tables of the Law, &c.* Exod. xxxii. 15.

142. 8. *note. Aristot. Mechan.* No. 26. See note to 137. 8.

9–10. *bed of Og . . . length.* Deut. iii. 11 (A.V., 'nine cubits *was* the length thereof').

11–13. *Funeral bed . . . measure.* G. Sandys, *A relation of a iourney* (1627, p. 130): 'Athwart the roome . . . there standeth a tombe, vncouered, empty, and all of one stone: brest high, seuen feete in length, not foure in breadth. . . . In this (no doubt) lay the body of the builder [Cheops].'

17. *Amazonian tomb (and note).* Browne seems to identify this with Τὸ Ῥομβοειδές, mentioned by Plutarch (*Theseus*, 27). But this was probably not a tomb. 23 sqq.

25. *naturall examples.* Chapters iii and iv of *GC* contain many references to Browne's own observations of nature, and in general no attempt has been made to annotate these.

33. *Musick of the Spheres.* Cf. *RM*, 67. 17–19.

33–34. *sevenfold Pipe of Pan.* Virgil, *Ecl.* ii. 36-37. Illustrated in Kircher, *Obeliscus Pamphilius*, 1650 (*SC*), p. 222.

34. *Gaffarell. Curiositez inouyes*, by Jacques G., was translated into English by E. Chilmead and published in the same year with title *Vnheard-of Curiosities.* Part iv, ch. 13 (p. 382) shows 'That the Starres, according to the Opinion of the *Hebrew* Writers, are ranged in the Heavens, in the forme of Letters: and that it is Possible to reade there, whatsoever of Importance is to happen, throughout the Universe.' Browne refers to this work again in *PE*, vi. 14. See note to 120. 17.

142. 37–**143.** 1. *remarkable Crusero.* G. Bosio, *La trionfante croce*, ii. 3, p. 137: 'Il mirabile Segno della Croce, di ch'io ragiono, pose il grande Iddio nel Firmamento, vicino al Polo Antartico. Ed è da' Piloti, e da Marinari, con vocabolo corrotto, chiamato Crusero.'

143. 6. *Julus.* Iulus, catkin.

11. *Calamus Aromaticus. Acorus calamus*, or sweet flag. *G*, i. 63–64.

12–13. *Petasites.* Or butter-bur. *G*, ii. 813–14.

13–15. *Blattaria . . . Barbatus. Verbascum blattaria* and *Verbascum thapsus* are two kinds of mullein, the 'moth' and the 'great' respectively; but Browne does not make clear what he means by 'our best spread Verbascum'; there are several common varieties.

19. *squamous.* Scaly.

19–20. *Knapweed . . . Jacea Pinea. G*, ii. 727–32, identifies knapweed with iacea, and describes a number of iaceas, as does J. Bauhin, *Historia Plantarum*, 1650 (*SC*), xxv (iii, pp. 27–34); but neither mentions one called *Jacea Pinea.*

20. *Oak-Rose* (*and note*). J. Bauhin, vii (I. ii, p. 86) 'Quercvvm Capitula Squammata'. (Illustration on p. 87.)

26–27. *Fathers of their Mother* (*and note*). Browne gives the last of the four lines on the artichoke, referring to the core, i.e. the seed (which will generate future matrices).

30. *Aaron.* Arum; Cuckow pint, or wake-Robin, *G*, ii. 833–5. *dragons. Dracontium*, *G*, ii. 831–3; *Arum Dracunculus.*

33. *Spongy leaves . . . Net-work* (*and note*). Bauhin, op. cit. xxxix (iii, p. '809' [*read* 799]): 'Alga marina πλατύκερως porosa . . . cum striis obliquis quasi texturam demonstrantibus.' Bauhin refers to F. Imperato, *Historia naturale*, 1599 &c., xxvii. 3, where the plant is called 'Poro ceruino', from the shape of its branches. The note could therefore be amended as follows: '. . . *porus cervinus* Imperati; *Porosa*, or Alga πλατύκερως Bauhini.'

144. 7–8. *Seraglio of Solomon.* There would be room for 1,000 maggots (the 700 wives and 300 concubines of 1 Kings xi. 3). The maggot in the teazel-head is referred to in *G*, ii. 1169. Cf. Pliny, *HN*, xxv. 239.

8–10. *uncous . . . abstersion.* The shafts are hooked or bent-up and thus suitable for scouring.

11. *Borith.* A cleansing herb, translated 'sope' in Jer. ii. 22 and Mal. iii. 2 (A.V.).

19. *milk-Thistle. Carduus Mariae*, Ladies thistle, *G*, ii. 1150.

20. *globe-thistle. Carduus globosus*, *G*, ii. 1150–2.

25. *Mercurie.* Good Henrie, *G*, ii. 329.

25. *weld. Lutea*, Weld, or Dyers weed, *G*, ii. 494–5.

27. *Santfoyne. Onobrychis*; red Fetchling, Medick Fetch, or Cockes-head, *G*, ii. 1245.

27–28. *French honey suckle. Hedysarum clypeatum*, *G*, ii. 1235.

29–31. *Jupiters beard . . . thunder. Sempervivum maius* or *barba Iovis*, *G*, ii. 509–12. Greenhill cites Brand's *Popular Antiquities*, iii, p. 317 (1849).

31. *Fenny Sengreen (and note). Stratiotes aquatilis*, or *Stratiotes potamios*, or *militaris aquatica*; Water Sengreen or Fresh-water Soldier, *G*, ii. 825–6.

32–33. *the Roman order.* Apparently referring to the 'ordination' described in 139. 22 sqq.

38. *from.* Judging by.

145. 8–9. *single . . . fearn.* Fuchsius, *Hist. plant.* (1542), 225, p. 595, has an illustration of the male fern showing an unfolded cluster of five fronds. For the form 'masle' see *OED*, s.v. Male, *a* and *sb*[2].

9. *Gramen Ischemon. Ischaemon vulgare*, cocks-foot grasse, *G*, i. 27–28.

10. *Sachell palme. Palma saccifera.* The reticulation on the cod or bag containing the fruit is illustrated in Bauhin, *Historia*, iii. 176 (i, p. 383); also in *G*, ii. 1554.

16–17. *pellitorye. Parietaria*, Pellitorie of the wall, *G*, ii. 330–1.

17. *Ragweed. Iacobaea*, Saint Iames his Wort, *G*, ii. 279–81.

146. 33. *Cummes.* Coombs or comes; the radicles of barley, &c. developed in malting.

147. 32. *findes.* Devises, invents (*OED*, s.v. 15).

39. *Stramonium.* Thorne-apple or apple of Peru, *G*, ii. 347–9.

148. 3. *bodies are first spirits.* Paracelsus, *Philosophia sagax*, i. 3 (*Opera*, x, 1605, p. 123), margin: 'Corpus omne initio est spiritus.'

5. *Aristotle. Meteor.* iv. 3 (380[a], 23–24). Cabeus, *Commentaria*, 1646, iv, p. 102.

14. *surcles.* small shoots.

23. *the four kinds.* See footnote to 169. 32. The sufficiency of the division into two kinds, Herb and Tree, is discussed again by Browne in *Miscellany Tracts*, i, 'Observations upon several plants mention'd in Scripture', no. 41 (*K*, v, pp. 42–43).

36. *Julus.* See note to 143. 6.

36. *pill.* Shell or peel.

148. 36–**149.** 1. *foraminous . . . leaf.* Bauhin, vii (1. ii, p. 87): 'Gemmae Foraminvlatae Qvercus.'

149. 3–5. *not only . . . Fly.* T. Moufet, *Insectorum . . . theatrum* (*SC*), ii. 4

(1634, p. 192): 'Nec tamen omnes Erucae in aurelias convertuntur, sed aliae contractae . . . putrescunt, é quibus nonnunquam tria quasi ova nigricantia excidunt, muscarum vel Cantharidum matrices.'

7. *Bees out of . . . Heifers.* Moufet, op. cit. i. 3, p. 12, '*De creatione, generatione, & propagatione Apum*', refers to Aristotle (*De gen. anim.* iii. 10) and adds 'Secuti eum philosophi, earum generationem ex alterius corporis corruptione provenire, rectè mea quidem sententiâ constituerunt: nempe ex tauro, bove, vacca, vitulóve putrefacto. . . .'

8–9. *Eeles . . . Perches (and note).* Schonevelde, *Ichthyologia*, 1624 (*SC*), p. 71, 'De Spirincho': 'Post aequinoctium vernum . . . Spirinchi & anadromi in mare remeant, anguillarum molestia, quae dorsi carnibus paulatim innascuntur, compulsi.'

13–14. *seeds . . . eyes (and note).* P. Lauremberg, *Horticvltvra*, i. 17 (1632, p. 84): '. . . huius generis semina quaedam, adeo exilia sunt, vt visu deprehendi difficulter possint . . . *Rapunculi . . . Cupressi. . . .*'

15. *disputed . . . Harts tongue. Phyllitis, G*, ii. 1137–9 ('a plant consisting only of leaues, bearing neither stalke, floure, nor seed'. Also Bauhin, xxxvii. 9 (iii, p. 756).

15. *Maidenhair. Trichomanes mas, G*, ii. 1143–6. This also, according to *G* (p. 1145), is 'without seed'.

29. *Tulip-Fly.* This has not been identified, but may represent Browne's imperfect memory of 'tipula' (q.v. *OED*) or 'tipalus', the insect described by Moufet, op. cit., pp. 69–70. Moufet has just spoken of a fly alluded to by Cardan, 'animal . . . quod non faetet'. Cf. the apparent lapse of memory referred to in the note to 156. 15–16.

29. *Goat-Beetle (and note).* Moufet, op. cit., p. '134' (recte 150): 'Cerambyces. . . . Alterum habemus, extra viridem, supinè fuscum. . . . Tertium huic concolorem ipse primus Pennio dedi, nucem moschatam & cynamum verè spirantem.'

150. 2–3. *Hippocrates . . . root.* Hippocrates, *De natura pueri* (*Opera*, 1595, iii, p. 22).

7. *Gallatures and treddles.* Both words denote the germ in the egg.

16. *Swallows Egges (and note).* Cornelius Agrippa, *De occ. phil.* ii. 2, 'De quinario': 'Hirundo non nisi quinque pullos parit.'

18. *Gentianella.* Felwort, *G*, ii. 436–7.

19. *Bell-flowers. Viola mariana* or *trachelium campanula*, *G*, ii. 447–53.

20. *cockle. Pseudomelanthium, G*, ii. 1086–7. (*Lychnis Githago.*)

20–21. *mullein and Blattaria.* See note to 143. 13–15.

30. *five Brethren.* The five leaves of the calyx. Cotgrave, 1611, 'Le gobelet d'une Rose, The fiue-leaued Cap or huske thereof; called, by some, the fiue brothers of the Rose.' (*OED*, s.v. Brother, 7b.)

151. 8–16. *five . . . equall circle.* This paragraph is apparently indebted to Bovillus, *De intellectu*, &c., 1510 (*SC*), to which Browne refers in 168. 13. One of Bovillus' treatises printed with *De intellectu* is *De dvodecim numeris*, which has a section 'De penthade', ff. 152–3. In the first chapter of this section he expounds the traditional doctrine that both 5 and 6 are 'spherical numbers', in that when they are multiplied by themselves the resulting figures are always rounded off by 5 and 6 respectively: 5, 25, 125, &c.; 6, 36, 216, &c.: 'In semetipsis quantum libet seipsis aucti redeunt.' Cf. 171. 20–23. Chapter 2 in Bovillus begins as Browne's paragraph does: 'Penthas sicut primus orbicularis numerus est: ita & orbicularium lationum euadit mensura.' and proceeds 'Quicquid enim in orbem con-

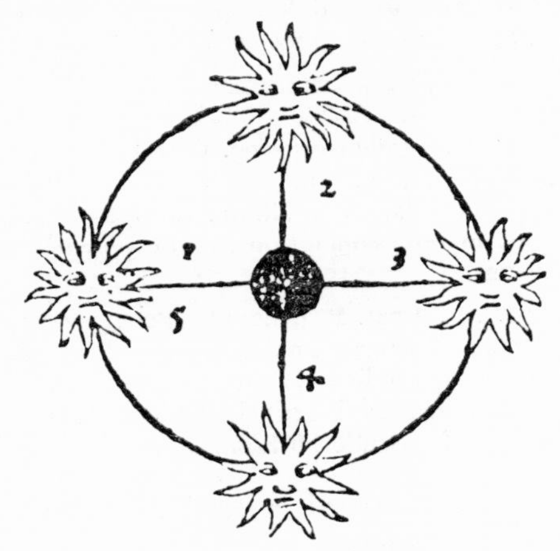

uertitur: quinto demum loco ac puncto in seipsum redit eique quo digressus est copulatur initio.' This is illustrated from a diagram representing the motion of the sun through its four quarters (points of rising and setting *both* counted). Browne's words about globular figures 'placed upon a plane in direct volutation' are explained in Bovillus' chapter 3, in

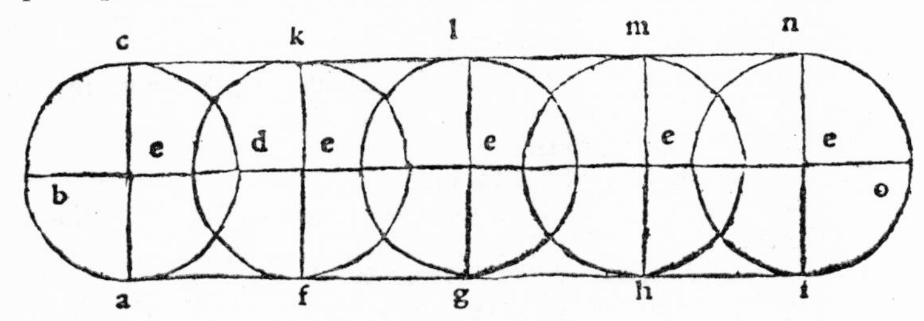

which he shows that when a circle or sphere is rolled forward on a plane it covers its own area five times by the time it regains its original position. Bovillus uses the diagram reproduced, wherein first 'd' is rolled on to 'f', then 'c' on to 'g', and so on. The doctrine of spherical numbers and motion is also set forth in Kircher, *Oedipus Aegyptiacus*, ii, pars altera, 32–33.

34. *Ajax . . . Delphinium.* There was much discussion about the identity of the flower which Ovid connected with the deaths of Hyacinthus and

Ajax (*Metamorphoses*, x. 164–6 and 206–19; xiii. 395–8); but Browne doubtless meant the larkspur or larkheel (*Delphinium Ajacis* or *Consolida*). Bauhin, *Hist. Plant.* xxvi. 89 (iii, pp. 210–12) describes the marking on the flower of *Consolida regalis*: 'folium corniculo annexum si pandatur A.I.A.I.A. literas inscriptas ostendat.' Cf. *G*, ii. 1081–3. For an illustration see Whibley, *A companion to Greek studies*, 90.

35. *Aarons Mitre in Henbane.* Referring to the shape of the flower in *Hyoscyamus niger*. See Josephus, *Antiq. Jud.* iii. 7. 6. (Gr.)

152. 3. *Aurelian.* From *aurelia*, a chrysalis.

8. *Weazell.* Also called sea-cat.

32–33. *experiment of Gomesius (and note).* Described in *De sale (SC)*, iii. 3 (1579, pp. 292–3). When the bee was pressed in the middle, 'rupta posterioris partis pellicula; ecce album, siue croceum, caput bouis, cartilaginea ferè ex materia concretum . . . de repentè erupit . . . mira quasi arte formatum.'

153. 19–21. *plainest . . . Bever.* P. Bellonius (Belon), *De aquatilibus*, 1553, pp. 28–29: 'In maiori Castore [cauda] sesquipedalis est, senos digitos lata . . . membrana glabra, ac liuida, contecta, super quam lineae quaedam squamas dimentientes incredibili artificio depictae sunt.'

23 (*note*). *Goshonder.* Goosander. *Weasell.* Smew. Not, as in 152. 8, the sea-cat.

41. *neatest Mummies.* Illustrated in Kircher, *Oedipus Aegyptiacus*, iii, pp. 412, 417, and facing p. 428.

154. 1. *Bembine table.* Illustrated in Kircher, op. cit., facing p. 78. See note to 133. 4–5.

2–3. *Orus . . . foot.* Illustrated in Kircher, op. cit. i, p. 40 and ii (pars altera), p. 101.

4. *cruciated . . . Trismegistus.* The letter X, which was among the letters supposed to have been invented by Hermes or Mercurius Trismegistus. See notes to 168. 19–23 and 169. 7–13.

5. *handed crosses (and note).* Crosses with handles (♀). See note to 169. 7–13. For hand = handle see *OED* s.v. hand, *sb.* 24.

6. *Isiacæ.* Of or relating to Isis.

7–8. *Jacobs Crosse.* Gen. xlviii. 13–14.

18. *curiously embroydered me.* Ps. cxxxix. 14 ('fashioned' B.C.P., 'curiously wrought' A.V.).

23. *phantastical Quincunx, in Plato. Symposium*, 189–91.

34. (*note*) In the edition of 1545 Gaza's translation of Aristotle, *De partibus animalium*, iii. 14, reads 'uenter, arsineum siue reticulum, omasum, abomasum.'

155. 14–15. *Greek translation . . . Fee.* στηθύνιον (Septuagint), a diminutive of στῆθος, breast. Lev. vii. 31. Browne points out that the diminutive sense is lost in the English translation.

16–18. *Rhomboidal . . . discovered.* G. Rondeletius, *De piscibus marinis*, (*SC*), iii. 11 (1554, p. 62).

24. *fech.* Vetch.

31. *seases.* Greenhill notes that this word 'is not to be found in any Dictionary, but a correction would be mere guess-work'. Mr. Carter emends to 'creases'. The corresponding words in *PE*, iii. 26 (see footnote) are 'folds and courses' (see *OED*, Course, *sb.* 29). But the meaning apparently intended for 'seases' (shaped containers, 'like honey-combs') agrees very well with that of *OED*, Sess, *sb.*[2], a term used in soap-manufacture ('origin obscure'): 'Each of the sections composing the frame or mould into which the soap is thrown to cool and solidify. . . .' The one example given is from 1854. For the verb 'Sess' *OED* gives no related meaning, but records several seventeenth-century spellings, including 'sease'.

156. 1–2. *legges of Castors horse.* Right forefoot raised high, right hind-hoof just pawing the ground; both left legs on ground. See Piranesi, *Vedute di Roma* (Campidoglio).

13. *Granadilla.* Bauhin, *Hist. Plant.* xv. 9 (ii, p. 114): 'in cujus foliis alique veluti passionis Christi figure delineatae conspiciuntur.'

15–16. *crucifixion . . . Pine.* Cf. R. Ligon, *A true & exact history of the Island of Barbadoes* (*SC*, 1657), 1673, p. 82 ('the Bonano'): '. . . and though her fruit be not so useful a food for the belly, as that of the Plantine, yet she has somewhat to delight the eyes . . . and that is the picture of Christ upon the Cross; so lively exprest, as no Limner can do it . . . more exactly; and this is seen, when you cut the fruit just cross as you do the root of Ferne, to find a spread Eagle: but this is much more perfect, the head hanging down, the armes extended to the full length, with some little elevation; and the feet cross one upon another.' Browne's confusion of the banana with the pine may be due to a lapse of memory or to a careless inspection of the page; the pine is the next tree that Ligon discusses. Cf. the difficulty referred to in the note on 149. 29.

18. *Porta.* Referring to his *Phytognomonica* (*SC*, 1588). See note to *RM*, 57. 10–13.

18. *the man Orchis* (*and note*). F. Columna, *Minus cognitarum stirpium . . . Ἔκφρασις*, cxlvi (*SC*, 1616, pp. 318–19): 'Haec autem nudi hominis, aut potius mulieris, effigiem integram veluti vmbram imitare videtur. . . .'

21. *plain crosse.* See note to 132. 38.

25–26. *Aiaia, &c.* Dr. Henry Power wrote to Browne on 9 Nov. 1958 (*K*, vi, p. 288) about 'the peculiar signature of Aiaia Viviu lilil. In what plant these tearmes are Inscribed, I would gladly know, though I have narrowly search'd very many yet either my fancy was not so active or else my enquiries not so [?] as to light of any plant, where I could [? even] rudely imagine any such characters.' Unfortunately Browne's reply seems not to be extant, but apparently he was referring to 'the common marsh sedge', which he classes in MS. Rawlinson D 109, f. 24 with other plants having 'hidden figures in the rootes under ground or inward parts above it'. This sedge has 'neat circles poynted like needleworke'. Wilkin, iii, p. 421, quotes a similar passage as from MS. Sloane 1847, attributing to 'the sedge a neate print'.

27. *Right lines and circles.* See note to 132. 34–37.

29. *frustums of Archimedes.* Referring to Archimedes on conic sections.

157. 5. *telarely.* In the fashion of a spider's web.

7–8. *That the colour . . . allowable.* Moufet, *Insectorum theatrum*, i. 14 (1634, p. 88): 'Omnes à sua eruca colorem habere Aristoteles affirmat: verum (ut hoc concedam) praeter illos colores alios obtinent.'

33. Aurelian. See note to 152. 3.

158. 4. *sesqui-tertian proportion.* Moufet, op. cit. ii. 13 (1634, p. 227): 'Hi etiam proportione constant . . . ita ut licet posteriora [sc. crura] primis semper breviora sint, tamen inter se mutuam qualitatem non amittunt.'

10 sqq. *Apophyses, Gomphosis, &c.* The anatomical terms employed here are defined by Galen in *De ossibus ad tirones* (*Opera*, ed. Kühn, ii, pp. 733–8).

32. *Summer-worm.* Moufet, op. cit. ii. 42 (1634, p. 325), '*De Lumbricis Aquaticis*': '. . . vibratili quodam modo sese arcuatim promovent . . . Angli *Sommer-wormes* vocant.'

35. *tiring.* Drawing, pulling (*OED*, Tire, *v*²).

159. 7. *rule of Solon.* Plutarch, *Solon*, 23.

15. *plane Tree in Pliny. HN*, xii. 5. 9.

160. 9. *Epithymum. Cuscuta epithymum.* The kind of dodder or *cuscuta* which grows on thyme. See note to 138. 26 above.

16. *scordium.* Water-germander, *G*, ii, 660–1.

23. *Poplars . . . Trees.* Homer, *Od.* x. 509–10.

161. 5. *Theophrastus. Enquiry into Plants*, I. x. 1.

8. *both motions of the Sunne.* Wilkin cites Browne's note in S. 47, f. 195ᵛ: 'flectit ad Aquilonem et declinit ad Austrum is Solons description of the motion of the sunne.' Allusion not traced.

15. *Theophrastus. De causis plantarum*, ii. 3 [4], on the influences upon vegetation of the various winds.

25. *Varro. De re rustica*, i. 7. 2. Cf. 131. 20.

162. 24–26. *Fenny waters . . . Arsmart. G*, i. 45: 'Dioscorides saith [of *calamus aromaticus*], the roots haue an heating facultie.' For similar observations on *cyperus*, water-crowfoot, and arsmart see *G*, i. 24, ii. 302 and ii. 114. Cf. G. Herbert, 'Providence', l. 129 (*Works*, ed. Hutchinson, p. 120).

38. *Harpalus... grow.* Theophrastus, *Enquiry into plants*, iv. 4.1; Plutarch, *Alexander*, 35.

42. *Splenetick medicine* (*and note*). Galen in the work referred to (ix. 2) gives a prescription for splenetic patients which includes 'corymborum hederae nigrae grana xxv.'

163. 10–11. *Clusius . . . Hierusalem.* Clusius gives both these observations (his own and that of Bellonius) in *Rariorvm Plantarvm Hist.* i. 17 (*SC*, 1601, p. 26), though without Browne's appreciation of 'the delightful view' presented by the red berries.

18–19. *horns . . . Goa* (*and note*). Linschoten, *Discours of Voyages*, i. 61 (1598, p. 110): 'These hornes hauing layne there a certaine time, doe sticke fast in the earth, (I meane the inner part of the horne) and there it taketh roote as if it were a tree, as I my selfe haue seene . . . which was neuer seene in any place of the world.'

164. 13. *Archimedes.* See note on 156. 29.

15–16. *Alexander . . . Navy.* Arrian, vii. 19.

17–18. *Tree . . . Camphire.* A camphor-yielding tree. Song of Sol. i. 14 and iv. 13; 'cypress' in margin of A.V. Since, as in R.V., identified with the henna-plant.

165. 6. *dipteros.* A building having two pillared sides or wings.

6. *hypæthros.* Open to the air. Cf. 'subdialia' below.

8. *Cavedia.* The inner halls or courts of Roman houses.

10. *Exedræ.* Halls or arcades, with recesses.

13. *Vitruvius . . . Pine. De architectura,* v. 1.

15. *Areostylos.* With columns thinly spaced out. See footnote to 136. 18. Most of the architectural terms in this paragraph are employed by Vitruvius.

17. *Court of the Tabernacle, &c.* Exod. xxvii. 9–11.

21. ἐπισκιασμός. Shade.

30. *colours of mediocrity.* Colours between the extremes of black and white. Beyerlinck, *Magnum theatrum,* 1678, iii, p. 304. (Gr.)

166. 5. *uliginous coats.* Slimy coverings for the seeds.

5. *Acari.* Mites.

12. *Helmonts tree.* Helmont, *Complexionum atque mistionum elementalium figmentum,* 30 (*Opera,* 1707, p. 104), describes at length how he planted the stem of a willow-tree weighing five pounds in sterilized earth moistened with rain-water or distilled water, and how the tree grew for five years until it weighed 169 pounds.

15. *Asarum . . . vomiting. Asarum,* asarabacca or hazel-wort. Burton 2. 4. 2. 1 (1638, p. 372) refers to it as a well-known emetic.

166. 36–**167.** 1. *Darknesse . . . Jove (and note).* Hippocrates, in *De dieta,* or *De victus ratione* (*Opera,* 1595, iv, 1, p. 8), arguing against popular notions of 'birth' and 'death', maintains that it would be more accurate to think in terms of increase and diminution, rising and falling, joinings and separations: 'Nihil quidem omninò perit, neque oritur quod priùs non erat, verùm inuicem commixta & discreta alterantur. At homines existimant quod ex orco in lucem augetur, oriri, quod verò ex luce ad orcum imminuitur, perire, magisque oculis quam rationi fidem esse adhibendam.' The changes and alternations in Nature are illustrated by 'Lux Ioui, tenebrae orco. Lux orco, tenebrae Ioui' (p. 9).

38. *seminall Idæa's . . . Orcus.* See note to *RM,* 38. 10.

167. 1–3. *They that held . . . upper heaven.* Hippolytus, *Refutation of all heresies,* i. 6. 4–5, attributes this view to Anaximander. See Kirk and Raven, *The Presocratic philosophers,* 1957, 127, pp. 135–6.

3. *took of.* See note to 111. 30–112. 1.

4. *shadows of stars.* Eclipses or occultations. According to Anaximander

these were caused by complete or partial blocking of the perforations, but no explanation of this was given.

4. *polary life (and note)*. Hevelius, c. xii, 1647, pp. 293–4.

12–13. *adumbration*. Luke i. 35: 'the power of the Highest shall overshadow thee.'

16–17. *The Sunne . . . God*. See note to *RM*, 10. 19–20 and cf. Ficino, *Liber de sole*, xiii (*Opera*, 1561, p. 975): '. . . aliquid admodum excelsius affirmamus, à quo quidem Sol coelestis longissimè distat, ut umbra quaedam illius esse iudicetur potius quam imago.'

20. *Pyramidal rayes*. See note to 167. 33.

24. *dark chamber*. *Camera obscura*.

25. *hornycoat*. *Cornea*.

25. *Christalline humour*. Crystalline lens.

27–30. *ancient Anatomy . . . decussation*. This view is referred to and rejected by Cabeus, *Comm. in Aristotelis Meteor.* (*SC*), 1646, iii, p. 72b, l. 18, and by Plempius (see note to 86. 4), *Ophthalmographia*, i. 19 (3rd ed., 1659, p. 29): '*De Nervis Opticis . . . Nervi uniuntur per contactum, non per intersectionem.*' According to the intersection or decussation theory the nerves arising on the right side of the brain connect with the left eye, and vice versa.

31–38. *reflected rayes . . . water*. Browne is thinking of a Y-shaped figure employed in Renaissance optical treatises to show how higher and lower objects seen in reflection reverse their relative positions (cf. Euclid, *Catoptrica*, 16). In the example given here, from Vitellio, *Perspectiva*, 1535, v. 53 (f. 136), A, B, and C are objects, D a beholder, and E–I a reflecting surface. The angle (or 'v') of incidence AHE–I = the angle of reflection DHE–I, and similarly with B and C. The lines of reflection D–H, &c., produced (or 'continued') to the place where A, B, and C are seen, show their reflections as M, L, and K respectively. Cf. Cabeus, op. cit. iii, 1646, p. 151.

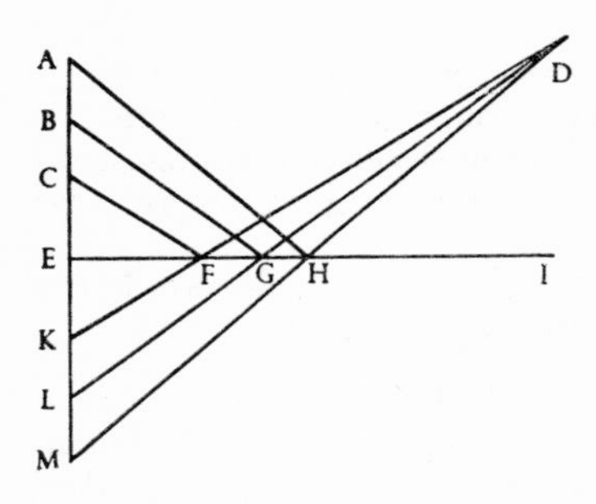

33. *visuall raye returneth*. Browne seems here to adopt the ancient theory of sight by extramission, though elsewhere he expresses doubt regarding it (*PE*, iii. 7, 1646, p. 120; see also *CM*, 225. 23–24 and note). According to this theory objects are seen, whether directly or through reflection, by means of rays sent out from the eye.

39. *moved bodies*. Bodies moved by a force strong enough to make them rebound. K. Digby, *Two treatises*, 1644, i, *A Treatise of Bodies*, xiii, p. 106, '*Of three sorts of violent motion, Reflexion, Vndulation, and Refraction*', instances the progress of a tennis-ball, which when struck to the ground observes (theoretically) the laws of equality between the angles of incidence and reflection.

167. 39–**168.** 8. *sounds . . . nature*. Reflected sounds in nature (echoes) and in buildings suitably constructed, e.g. with 'elliptical arches' (arcs), are elaborately described and illustrated by A. Kircher in *Musurgia Universalis*, 1650, ix, part 4, '*Magia Phonocamptica*', pp. 237 sqq. See also *K*, v, pp. 198–9.

168. 7. *well dividing*. Skilfully executing a succession or 'run' of short notes (as if made short by the division of longer ones).

9. *animall*. Having to do with the mind or spirit.

10–13. *Things entring . . . Bovillus* (*and note*). See note on 151. 8. The passage referred to here is in *De intellectu*, xiv. 8 (1510, f. 18): 'A mundo ad intellectum vna fit pyramis sensibilis: ab intellectu vero ad memoriam reliqua intellectualis. . . . A mundo itaque et memoria ad intellectum: fiunt in vtramque partem due pyramides. sensibilis vna: cuius basis mundus | alia intellectualis: cuius basis memoria.' Cf. the diagram in Bovillus, f. 85.

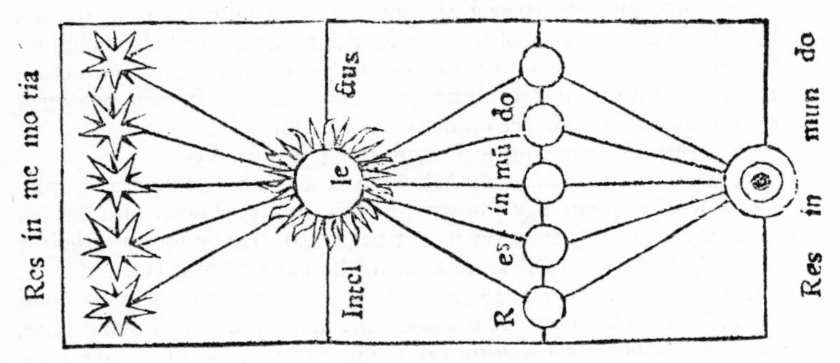

19–23. *Ægyptian . . . Character*. The stork's 'open Bill and stradling Legges' as the source of the letter X are well illustrated in Kircher, *Obeliscus Pamphilius*, 1650, p. 131, where X is included in a list of characters in the Egyptian and Greek alphabets. See note to 154. 4. Kircher, p. 385, explains the symbolism of this letter in a way which partly agrees with Browne's account: 'decussis illa celebris & mysteriosa quâ processum Spiritus Mundi ἄνω καὶ κάτω aptè innuebant.'

24. *Plato*. *Timaeus*, 36b. See note to 169. 1–6.

28–29. *circle . . . right lines*. See note to 132. 34–37; cf. 120. 28 and 156. 27.

31–33. *double aspect . . . it self*. This appears to be translated from Bovillus, op. cit., *De sensibus* (1510, f. 24^{v}): 'Anime duplex est aspectus: alius rectus quo despicit in corpus aut in mundum. Alius orbicularis & reciprocus: quo seipsam intuetur.' See also note to 132. 34–37.

39–41. *three substances . . . those two*. *Timaeus*, 35.

169. 1–6. *Justin . . . X for T* (*and note*). Justin Martyr, *First Apology*, 77 (93), alludes to the passage in *Timaeus* in which the Creator is said to have divided the World-Soul into four parts crosswise (although the words translated into 'Decussavit eum in universo' are not in the traditional text). The division into four is represented by Justin ('obscurius paullo', Lipsius, *De cruce*, i. 7, 1637, iii, p. 649) as an unconscious prefiguration of the Christian Cross and as having been suggested to Plato by the story of the brazen serpent which, held up on a pole, had the virtue of healing persons bitten by the fiery serpents (Num. xxi. 8–9). The letter Tau (T) was used as a symbol both of the brazen serpent and of the Cross. See also Casalius, *De vet. Rom. ritibus*, i (1681, p. 13). One form of T was + (see Kircher, *Obeliscus Pamphilius*, 1650, p. 132). Justin does not in fact say that Plato confused T with X.

7–13. *he learned . . . Countrey.* The passage in Justin referred to in the preceding note is quoted and discussed by Kircher, op. cit., p. 385 (and again in *Oedipus Aegyptiacus*, 1652 (*SC*), ii, pars altera, pp. 98–99). Kircher maintains that Plato undoubtedly took the figure of decussation from the Egyptians rather than from the brazen serpent, mentioning its derivation from the stork and its special significance (see note to 168. 19–23). Kircher speaks also (p. 439) of X as giving rise to other symbols, including the 'handed cross', ♀ (see note to 154. 5): 'crux ansata . . . amuletum contra aduersas potestates omnium efficacissimum . . . indicat praetereà processum animae mundi per omnia mundi membra.'

17. *yet cannot.* For the elliptical usage cf. 84. 35–36, &c.

17–19. *five . . . Nine (and diagram).* Five as a symbol of Justice occurs in several works apparently known to Browne, e.g. Theon Smyrnaeus, *Mathematica*, 1644 (*SC*), note on p. 283 to p. 159, 'De Quinario': 'dicitur quoque a Pythagoricis Iustitia quae in medio extremorum iacet.' Cf. N. Abram, *Pharus Vet. Test.* 1648 (*SC*), x. 29, p. 176: 'Nicomachus apud Photium . . . πεντάδα vocat . . . δικαιοσύνην, iustitiam. . . .' Browne's use, however, in his note of the form δίκη suggests that he may have been drawing rather upon L. C. Ricchieri (Rhodiginus), *Lectionvm antiq. libri xxx* (*SC*, 1599), xii. 10, '*Quinarij numeri potentia* (1517, p. 622): 'dicitur & numerus hic δίκη, id est Iustitia, quia denarium ex aequilibrio secet.' The number of Justice was sometimes given as four or as eight. See Macrobius, *In Somn. Scip.* i. 5 *ad fin.* (ed. W. H. Stahl, 1953, pp. 98–99).

23. *that common game.* Presumably ninepins, in which the pins were commonly arranged diamond-wise. Greenhill refers to the game of τὸ πεσσόν as described by Julius Pollux, IX. vii. 97–98.

169. 30–**170.** 3. *the Divisive Number . . . fingers.* Plutarch, *De defectu oraculorum* (*Morals*, transl. Holland, 1603, p. 1341): '. . . that in this number there is a naturall vertue and facultie of dividing, and that nature divideth many things by this number. For even in our owne selves she hath placed five exterior senses . . . likewise so many fingers in either hand.'

30. *justly dividing the Entities.* Plutarch (?), *De placitis philosophorum*, ii. 6 and 7 (*Morals*, 1603, p. 819): '*Empedocles* saith, that the first thing separate apart, was the skie or fifth essence, called *Aether*; the second, Fire; after which, the Earth; of which . . . sprang Water, from which Aire did evaporate.'

170. 14. *glasses.* Telescopes.

14. *the optick doctrine.* See 167. 20–38 and notes.

14–15. *wherein . . . loligo.* The connexion of this with the context is not obvious, but Browne may be alluding incidentally to the physical similarity between the human eye and that of the cuttle-fish (or *loligo*).

17. *wedding number.* Plutarch, *Quaest. Rom.* 2.

20. *allegoricall sence . . . Hesiod (and note).* See note to 169. 17–19. The passage from Rhodiginus quoted there is preceded by the following: 'Quintas porrò esse fugiendas, Hesiodus praecipit, quod inquiunt graeci Interpretes, allegorice signat, Nuptias multas. Quinarius enim γάμος dicitur, ex binario nanque pari consurgit, & impari ternario. . . .' The Hesiod reference is to *Works and Days*, 802:

πέμπας δ' ἐξαλέασθαι, ἐπεὶ χαλεπαί τε καὶ αἰναί.

24. *five . . . Virgins.* See note to 172. 8–20.

25–28. *Conjugall Number . . . Societies.* Plutarch, *Of Ei at Delphi* (*Morals*, 1603, p. 1357): 'Now the beginning and ground of even numbers is Two, and of odde, Three is the first: of which being joined together is engendered Five, which by good right is highly honoured as being the first compound of the first simple numbers, whereupon it is worthily named *Γάμος*, that is to say, Mariage; because the even number hath some resemblance to the female, and the odde, a reference to the male.'

33–34. *Quintuple . . . generation.* Perhaps referring to the division into five books of Aristotle's *De generatione animalium.*

171. 1–11. *Cabalistical accounts . . . was He (and note).* From *Cabalistarvm selectiora, obscvrioraqve dogmata, a Ioanne Pico ex eorum commentationibus pridem excerpta, et ab Archangelo Bvrgonovensi Minoritano, nunc primùm luculentissimis interpretationibus illustrata* . . . 1569, f. 74: 'Nisi nomini Abraham litera he ה addita fuisset, Abraham non generasset.' The comment on this gives both of Browne's reasons: the addition of 5 (he = 5) raised Abraham's number from 243 to 248, the number of the affirmative precepts in the Mosaic law (which Abraham would now be able to observe, having been made 'perfect'); also (ff. 76v–77r), 'sicut in creatis est masculus & fæmina; ita & in Diuinis . . . mater est binah . . . à binah omnes animae scaturiunt. Quoniam igitur ה h [for he] . . . est sigillum binah: Idcirco Deus volens Abraham multarum gentium patrem constituere, voluit ipsum conformem binah fieri, concedendo illi eius sigillum. . . .'

12–13. *measure and mansion in the Archetype.* Archangelus, op. cit., f. 67v: 'Sicut in domo eterni patris mansiones multe sunt, varij scilicet gradus gloriae attributorum & proprietatum . . .' and f. 74r: 'coeli materiales vim suscipiunt à coelis archetypis, ibi enim Abraham fauorem super coelestium amplissimum sensit.'

14–15. *ten of Sarai . . . five.* Archangelus, f. 76, also explains why Sarai became Sarah, h = 5 taking the place of i or Iod = 10; woman was not to share in the 'perfection' conferred on man. There are other discussions of these changes in the two names, as in N. Abram, *Pharus Vet. Test.* vii. 12 (1648, p. 176).

20. *unto none (and note).* Clusius, in his *Cvrae Posteriores*, 1611, p. 46, gives an illustration of 'Phalangium *Americanum*, showing ten legs. Cf. J. de Laet, *Novus Orbis*, 1633, p. 570.

21–23. *sphericity . . . account.* See 151. 8–16 and note.

24–25. *Name of God . . . six.* In יהוה, י = 10, ה = 5, ו = 6, the Hebrew letters being used also as numerals.

26. *Trismegistus . . . Sphere.* See *RM*, 10. 16 and note.

31. *the fifth yeare.* Lev. xix. 23–25.

34–35. *Feminine . . . masculine.* See note to 170. 25–28. Gen. i. 8, 10, 12. Caryl, *Comm. on Job*, iii. 6, cites an explanation of the discrepancy. See Herrick, *Poetical Works*, *OET*, 1956, p. 578.

4–5. *five golden mice.* 1 Sam. vi. 4, 18.

172. 6. *five . . . hundred.* Lev. xxvi. 8.

8–20. *Saint Paul . . . Pagan Champion.* N. Abram, *Pharus Vet. Test.* vii. 8 (1648, p. 174): 'Dauid eligit de torrente quinque limpidissimos lapides in Goliath pugnaturus. Nota sunt in Euangelio quinque talenta, quinque prudentes virgines, panes hordeacej quinque, quibus hominum quinque millia saturantur. . . . Paulus in Ecclesia quinque verba suo sensu loqui desiderat [1 Cor. xiv. 19].'

14. *radicall Letters.* Consonants in the roots of Hebrew words.

14–16. *radicall . . . Tribes.* N. Abram, op. cit. x. 18 (§ 78), discusses with reference to 1 Kings vi. 1 the length of the Captivity in Egypt and incidentally (p. 270) alludes to and illustrates the industry of the Masoretic commentators in their scrutiny of the Biblical texts, one instance (under marginal caption 'Quot literę in Pentateucho') being that they counted up the (radical) letters in the Pentateuch and arrived at the figure of 600,045. Browne erroneously equates this figure with the number of the Israelite soldiery recorded in Num. i. 46 and ii. 32, which is 603,550. The figure 600,045 also disagrees with other estimates of population in Exodus and Numbers.

23–24. *Criticall Physician . . . Quinque (and note).* J. C. Scaliger, *De causis linguae Latinae* (*SC*, 1580), 1584, xxviii, p. 67): 'Quinque deduxêre: vt esset, & unum praeter quatuor, κὶ ἕνκε.' The note seems to obscure the etymological point by omitting κὶ.

24–25. *five or three.* Plutarch, *Symposiacs*, iii. 9 (*Morals*, transl. Holland, 1603, p. 695: '*What is the meaning of the common proverbe: Drinke either five or three, but not fower?*'

25–27. *Hippocrates . . . Dysenteries.* In Hippocrates, *Epidemics*, vii. 3 (*Œuvres*, ed. Littré, v, pp. 370–2), a case of dysentery is described in which the patient took milk and water, the water making up one-sixth of the draught.

33–37. *Cabalisticall . . . fifth string.* This topic is discussed at some length in Mersenne's *Quaestiones celeberrimae in Genesin*, 1623 (*SC*), pp. 1705–8), where, with reference to what is said about Jubal in Gen. iv. 21, a general theory of music is expounded. Mersenne, who clearly thinks very little of the cabbalists' views concerning David's harp, emphasizes their conjectural and unscientific nature: 'Citharam Dauidicam 10 neruis instructam fuisse Cabalistae supponunt . . . Illi volunt Sephiroth omnes, & emanationes diuinas citharae Davidis praeesse. . . .'

The cabbalists assumed also that the notes and intervals on David's harp corresponded to ten notes of the Greek system as formulated by Aristoxenus, a two-octave scale represented roughly by A–*á* on the white notes of the pianoforte. In this scale the note 'Parhypate [*not* Perihypate] Meson', corresponding to the lower F, was so-called because it was the lowest note but one in the second of the tetrachords into which the two-octave scale was divided. The same note came to be called 'si fa ut' with reference to the triple hexachord system devised by Guido d'Arezzo in the eleventh century, in which the sequence 'ut re mi fa sol la' could begin at G or C or F (running G–E, C–A, or F–D). Later two of these hexachords were dropped, leaving only C–A, which with the addition of a seventh note 'si' (for B) constitutes the modern major scale; but the influence of the triple hexachord system remained in the sol-fa notation; and F, being 'si' in the sequence G–G, 'fa' in C–C, and 'ut' in F–F, could be referred to, as here, by all three names. Similarly C could be designated 'sol fa ut'.

In their efforts to assimilate the ten harp-strings to the Aristoxenian 15-note scale the cabbalists disregarded the five lowest notes of that scale and began with Parhypate Meson (F or 'si fa ut'); and the ten notes thus arrived at were made to correspond to the ten *sephiroth* or divine emanations. Each of these had its special character and meaning, *Tiphereth*, the fifth from the lowest, having the name and associations of 'Pulchritudo'. Browne's question is rather vaguely put, but he seems in effect to be asking why it was arranged that *Tiphereth*, and not another of the emanations, should correspond to C ('sol fa ut') on the fifth string. Perhaps a partial answer can be seen in a more extended description of *Tiphereth* given in Kircher's *Oedipus Aegyptiacus*, ii (1652, p. 294), where among other things it is said to represent 'linea media' and 'arbor in medio Paradisi plantata'.

173. 4–6. *cure . . . Eyes*. Greenhill refers to Gruterus, *Inscriptiones . . . Rom.* (see note to 123. 32–33). The inscription about the cure of the blind man is lxxi. 1 (ex Smetio): 'Tabella . . . quae putatur olim stetisse in Insula Tiberina . . . .' Inscription in Greek, translated: 'Hisce diebus Caio cuidam caeco, oraculum edidit. Veniret ad sacrum altare: & genua flecteret; à parte dextra veniret ad laeuam & poneret quinque digitos super altare; & eleuaret manum, & poneret, super proprios oculos. Et rectè vidit, populo praesente . . . sub Imperatoro nostro Antonino.' Cf. *PE*, i. 11 (1646, pp. 45–46).

7. *Comœdy . . . four parts (and note)*. Cf. J. C. Scaliger, *Poetices libri septem*, i. 9 (1586, p. 35): 'Veræ & primariæ [Comœdiæ partes] sunt quatuor, protasis, epistasis, catastasis, catastrophe.'

9–10. *five acts*. Horace, *Ars poetica*, 189–90.

15. *one leaf . . . have it (and note)*. This is misleading because J. C.

Scaliger, *De subtilitate*, clxxviii. 2 (1615, pp. 456–9), ‘*Henophylli historia*’, rejects Cardan’s concept of a plant with one leaf only (*unifolium*), but points out that some plants have no leaves at all.

22–23. *distract their verticities*. Turn away their vertices (*OED*, Verticity, ii. 3), sc. so as to point north again, avoiding the decussation.

23–26. *Geomancers . . . Beetle*. See, e.g., the configurations illustrated in *The Geomancie of Maister Christopher Cattan*, 1591, where, on p. 12, *acquisitio* is figured thus: * * * * * *

26–27. *Chiromantical . . . decussations*. See J. Indagine, *Introdvctiones apotelesmaticae* (*SC*, 1522), ‘Introductio in Chyromantiam’. Indagine does not ‘decry’ all crossings of lines in the hand, but some he does, e.g. (transl. F. Withers, 1598, f. C 3^{v}): ‘If you find a cross in this sort about the upper corner, . . . it signifieth a libidinous and an unshamefaste woman.’

28. *decussated . . . Great*. Shown in A. Agostino (Agustin), *Dialoghi . . . intorno alle medaglie*, 1625, pp. 140 and 167. The ‘figure’ in the coin,  , is set in isolation before the seated figure of Alexander. It has no mysterious meaning but is simply a control-mark attached to this particular issue, as was frequently done.

30–31. *Juno . . . Hercules*. Ovid, *Met*. ix. 298–300. Cf. *PE*, v. 219 (1646, p. 266).

32–34. *Amphidromicall . . . Cuttle-fishes*. Athenaeus, ix. 370. The feast was so-called because the newly born child was carried round the hearth. Suidas says that the ceremony took place on the fifth day after the birth.

34–35. *five . . . Cadmus*. See, e.g., Ovid, *Met*. iii. 126.

35–36. *Proteus . . . the Symbole of the first matter*. Eustathius, *Comm. in Odysseam*, on iv. 417–18, refers to those who have thought of Proteus in this way, because of his changeable nature; saying that he is the primal matter, the repository of the forms (τὴν πρωτόγονον εἶναι ὕλην, τὴν τῶν εἰδῶν δεκάδα.)

37. *by fives*. *Od*. iv. 412.

37. *fifth years Oxe*. *Il*. ii. 403; vii. 315.

39. *soul . . . Rhombus*. Marcus Aurelius, *Meditations*, xi. 12.

41. *nauseating*. Nauseated by.

41. *crambe*. Stale. See note to *RM*, 75. 3.

174. 4. *quaternio’s*. Referring to the ‘quaternary of numbers’, 1+2+3+4 = 10, and to the mystic significance attached by the Pythagoreans to this relationship: quaternio, for quaternion or quaternary, is here used generally for the undiscovered evidences of design in nature.

14. *Quincunx of Heaven* (*and note*). Greenhill observes that ‘in our latitudes, the Hyades are near the western horizon at midnight at the beginning of March’.

19. *the Oneirocriticall Masters* (*and note*). *Artemidori . . . & Achmetis . . . Oneirocritica. Astrampsychi & Nicephori versus etiam Oneirocritici*. Paris, 1603. Achmet was also known as Apomazar.

19–20. *frigid Interpretations*. E.g. Achmet, ed. cit. i. 70, p. 58: 'Legumina omnia mala sunt. . . .' Cf. *LF*, 187. 9–11 and notes.

23–24. *Bed of Cleopatra* (*and note*). The reference may be to the strewing of roses at Cleopatra's banquet described in Athenaeus, iv. 148.

26. *Pagan Theology*. Hesiod, *Theognis*, 123.

32. *Somnus in Homer*. Zeus, in the passage referred to, beginning of *Iliad* ii, sends not Sleep, but a dream (ὄνειρος, somnium). Browne may have taken the mistake from Natalis Comes (Conti), *Mythologia* (*SC*), 1641, p. 232, '*De Somno*': '. . . Illud verò quod scribitur ab Homero . . . non facilè intelligo, cur Somnus scilicet à Ioue mittatur ad excitandum Agamemnonem, quo armari iuberet multitudinem, cùm sit Somni munus vel magis etiam opprimere somno grauatos, quàm excitare: nisi tamen pro Somno Somnia intelligantur.'

34–35. *Huntsmen are up in America*. It is difficult to account for this statement save as evidence that 'the drowsy approaches of sleep' were having their effects. 'India' would be more suitable geographically, but less rhythmically pleasing. See *PE*, vi. 2 (1646, p. 283).

175. 2–4. *that time . . . awake again*. Cf. Wernerus Abbas S. Blasii, *Deflorationes SS. Patrum*, i. 2 (*PL*, 157, col. 750): 'Qua hora fiet judicium? Media nocte qua hora angelus Ægyptum devastavit [Exod. xii. 29], et Dominus infernum despoliavit, ea hora electos suos de hoc mundo liberabit.' Cf. H. Vaughan, 'The Dawning' (*OET*, pp. 451–2).

A LETTER TO A FRIEND

179. 6. *Ad portam . . . extendit*. Persius, i. 105. (Gr.)

18–19. *the great Antonio was dead*. W. Aldis Wright, *N. & Q.*, 7th ser., iv, 12 Nov. 1887, p. 386, cites G. Sandys, *A relation of a Journey begun . . . 1610*, iv (1621, pp. 248–9): '*Strombolo* . . . doth burne almost continually. . . . These places . . . are commonly affirmed by the Romane Catholickes to be the iawes of hell: and that within, the damned soules are tormented. It was told me at *Naples* by a country man of ours . . . who was a youth in the dayes of King *Henry*, that it was then generally bruited throughout England, that master *Gresham*, a merchant, setting saile from *Palermo*, (where there then dwelt one Anthonio called the Rich . . .) being crossed by contrary winds was constrained to anchor vnder the lee of this Iland. Now about mid-day, when for certaine houres it accustomedly forbareth to flame, he ascended the mountaine with eight of the sailers: and approaching as neare the vent as they durst; amongst other noises they heard a voice crie aloud, Dispatch, dispatch, the rich *Antonio* is a coming. Terrified herewith they descended . . . returned to *Palermo*, and forthwith enquiring of Antonio, it was told them that he was dead; and computing the time, did finde it to agree with the very instant that the voyce was heard by them.'

29. *Plautus*'s *sick Complexion*. *Captivi*, 647–8:

Macilento ore, naso acuto, corpore albo, et oculis nigris,
Subrufus aliquantum, crispus, concinnatus.

29–30. *an Hippocratical Face. Prognostics,* 2: 'sharp nose, hollow eyes', &c.

37. *Grashopper.* Cf. Juvenal, ix. 69. (Gr.)

180. 10. *Nitre.* In the obsolete sense of 'a supposed nitrous element in the air or in plants' (*OED*). *SC* contains '*W. Clar⟨k⟩e's* Natural Hist. of Nitre—1670', in which *inter alia* it is alleged that air containing nitre is conducive to health and longevity.

15. *Daw's Claw* (*and note*). Littré, in his edition of Hippocrates, refers to Hesiod, *Works and Days,* 679–80. See illustration, Appendix I, p. 250.

28. (*note*) *Bellonius de Avibus.* This note probably refers simply to the mention of 'passager . . . Birds', as Bellonius (Belon) in *Histoire de la nature des oyseaux, SC,* 1555, pp. 11 and 43–44, refers in a general way to such birds without giving the details (Greenland, &c.) supplied at the end of Browne's sentence.

31. *salient Point.* The heart as first seen in embryos.

34–35. *Death . . . Eye-lids.* Aristotle, *Problemata,* iv. 1.

35. *strift.* Striving.

181. 5. *Juno.* See note on *GC,* 173. 30–31.

7–8. *Monsters . . . happen* (*and note*). The quotation in the note has not been found in Hippocrates. A very similar sentence is attributed to Averroes by Cardan, *In Cl. Ptolemaei . . . de astrorum iudiciis,* iv. 74 (1554, p. 348): 'ut bene dixit Auerroës, contingunt monstra in omni arte.' Cardan's *Opera,* 1663, are in *SC.*

14–16. *Sigils . . . Paracelsus.* See note to *RM,* 20. 10–11.

34–36. *Nox . . . Genealogy.* Hesiod, *Theognis,* ll. 123, 212, 758. (Gr.)

182. 1. *about . . . unto it.* See *GC,* 175. 2–4 and note.

2–4. *Cardan . . . my own.* The observation has not been found in Cardan, and the reference should perhaps be to the standard work on palmistry by J. Rothman, translated in 1652 by Sir George Wharton as *XEIPOMANTIA or, The Art of Divining*; Wharton, *Works,* 1683, p. 532: 'He who is Born in the day time, and hath a *Masculine Planet* [the *Sun, Saturn, Jupiter, or Mars*] Lord of his *Geniture,* bears the more remarkable *Signs* [sc. the deeper, more noticeable lines] in his *Right Hand,* especially when the *Sign Ascending* is also *Masculine.* The contrary befalls those that are Born by *Night,* so oft as a *Feminine Planet* predominates, and the *Sign Ascending* is *Feminine.* If both hands agree, it must needs be, that in a *Day-Nativity* the *Feminine Planets* rule: Or that there falls out a *Mixture* of *Masculine* and *Feminine.* So in the *Night,* by the contrary Reason.'

10. *contingent.* Accidental.

14–17. *Charles the Fifth . . . that day.* Prudencio de Sandoval, *Hist. de Carlos V,* 1600, &c., xii and xviii, where the dates given are February 25th 1500, 1525 (battle of Pavia), and 1530 (crowning at Bologna).

18. *Antipater.* Pliny, *HN,* vii. 51 [52]. Cf. 253. 10 below.

20–22. *When . . . end.* See *RM,* 7. 26 and notes.

31–32. *before . . . them.* See *RM,* 30. 29–30 and notes.

35–36. *Tail of the Snake . . . mouth* (*and note*). Pierius, *Hieroglyphica,* 1631

(*SC*), xiv. 2 (p. 167): 'Serpens igitur caudam depascitur suam, vt generum immortalitatem . . . ostentet: vt principium ad finem directum esse, finemque ad principium reflecti doceat.'

183. 5–6. *Duke John Ernestus Mansfield (and note).* This telescopes the names of two persons, who died within a few days of each other in 1626, as recorded in Knolles, *The generall Historie of the Turkes*, 5th ed., 1638, p. 1471: Count Ernestus Mansfelt and Duke John Ernestus. It is of the latter that Knolles says: 'His body was opened, and not one drop of bloud found, but his heart withered to the smalnesse of a Nut.' See *Camb. Mod. Hist.* iv, p. 98.

9. *Bouffage.* 'Any meat that (eaten greedily) fils the mouth, and makes the cheeks to swell' (Cotgrave in *OED*).

10–11. *Characters of Dante (and note).* See *H*, 111. 3–4 and footnote.

14. *sextâ cervice.* Carried by six. Juvenal, i. 64.

17–18. *Ferrarius . . . Ear (and note). De arte medica infantium* (*SC*), iv. 9 (1605, pp. 227–8).

19–20. *Cardan . . . Thumb.* Cardan, *De rerum varietate*, xv. 79 (*Opera*, 1663, iii, pp. 286–7): '*Vnguium maculae quid significent.* . . . Thenar ignis pericula nuntiat.'; and ibid. viii. 43 (iii, p. 161): '. . . eorum, quae mihi euentura sunt, . . . vestigia in vnguibus apparent.'

25. *last Face of Hippocrates.* See note to 179. 29–30.

29. *backward.* Retrogressively. Greenhill (Glossary) compares Seneca, *Epist.* 122. 18; but the corresponding phrase in Seneca bears a different sense.

31. *Ulmus (and note). Physiologia barbae humanae*, 1602, iii. 3, pp. 199 sqq. and iii. 7, pp. 283 sqq. The note is out of place in *90*; Ulmus makes no reference to Louis II.

33. *Lewis . . . King of Hungary.* 1506–1526. A. Bonfinius, *Rerum Vngaricarum decades*, 1581, Appendix . . . per J. Sambucam, pp. 754–5, records that Louis II was born 'sine extrema cute' and that 'adolescens canos aliquot alebat capillos.' Cf. M. Fumée, *The Historie of the Troubles of Hungarie* (translation), 1600 (*SC*), p. 32: 'when he was newly borne, he had no skinne that couered his bodie, which he neuerthelesse recouered. . . .'

184. 5–7. *that Endemial Distemper . . . Backs.* This subject is fully discussed by G. E. Kellett in *Annals of Medical History*, vii (1935), pp. 467–79. Although the existence of the disease as described by Browne may be doubted, the symptoms were several times recounted in the sixteenth and seventeenth centuries by respectable medical authorities. Perhaps the version nearest to Browne's is that in a work by J. Guillemeau translated as *The Nvrsing of Children*, xxxix (1635, p. 116): '*Of the breeding and comming foorth of Haires on children's backs and raines, called in Languedocke Masquelon, and of the Latines,* Morbus pilaris.' H. Montuus, *De infantum febribus* (1558), also associates the disease with Languedoc. The word for it was variously spelt, 'masquelons', 'masclous', &c., and Browne seems to give a roughly phonetic rendering of the name as he may have heard it at Montpellier. There are, however, books in *SC* in which the subject is treated: Schenckius, *Observationes medicae rarae* (1610, v. 8), and Borelli, *Observ. medico-physicae* (1656), i. 80 ('Vermes in dorso—Masclous dicti'). Schenckius cites both Montuus and Guillemeau.

8. *Coughs and Convulsions.* Guillemeau, loc. cit.: 'this disease drawes along with it Epilepticall convulsions.'

12–13. *one Man . . . single parts.* Herodotus, ii. 84.

16. *Pyrrhus (and note).* Plutarch, *Life of Pyrrhus*, 3, says that he had few teeth and that the upper ones formed a single continuous bone.

16–19. *Bannyans . . . Flesh.* 'that for superstitions sake never eat flesh nor fish all their lives' (Burton, 3. 4. 13; 1638, p. 669). Cf. Herodotus, iii. 100.

22. *(note) See Picotus de Rheumatismo.* This note is evidently misplaced in *90* (against ll. 5–6) as there is nothing in *De Rheumatismo* (1577) on the 'Morgellons'. But Picotus (Pichot) devotes several pages to dental disease as a form of rheumatism, enumerating (p. 13) 'dentes erosi, forati, rubiginosi, dolentes' among the phenomena.

31. *Disease of his Country.* F. Glisson, *De Rachitide . . . qui vulgo The Rickets dicitur* (*SC*, 1650) (2nd ed. 1660, p. 3): 'Innotuit autem primum hic morbus . . . in occidentalibus Angliae tractibus triginta circiter retro ab hinc annis.'

33. *scarce so old.* John Graunt, *Observations upon the Bills of Mortality*, 3rd ed., 1665, 19, p. 46, notes that no cases were recorded before 1634. (Gr.)

184. 37–**185.** 2. *Inhabitants . . . halted.* Du Loir, *Les Voyages*, 1654 (*SC*), pp. 357–8, 'Relation du Voyage de Levant': 'Rouigno . . . Iamais ie ne fus si surpris que d'abord y voir boiter presque tous les habitans. . . . plusieurs personnes . . . m'asseurerent que de neuf mille habitans qui sont dans Rouigno il y en a sept mille de boiteux.'

184. 37–**185.** 1. *twenty Years ago.* See Introduction, p. xxii.

185. 2. *Rickets encreaseth.* Graunt, op. cit., p. 49: 'the Rickets were never more numerous than now, and . . . they are still increasing.'

13. *Plato. Rep.* iii. 405d (καταρρους).

15. *Polydore Virgil. Hist. Angl.* xxvi (1570, p. 611, l. 41): 'facile in morbum incidit, quem pleuresim vocant, qui cùm apud Anglos rarus sit. . . .'

28. *Kell.* The membrane investing the intestines; *omentum.*

33. *(note). So A.F.* Not explained.

38. *brake the Rule of Cardan (and note).* Cardan, *Podagrae encomium*, in Dornavius, *Amphitheatrum sapientiae*, ii (1619, p. 218): 'illius peculiaria . . . dona . . . lapidem in vesica generari prohibet, & pulmonem vlcere affici. . . .'

186. 1. *Aristotle. Problemata*, x. 1. Cf. *PE*, i. 6 (1646, p. 21).

5. *Vegetius.* (Renatus, Publius.) *Mulomedicina*, iii. 61–65 (1574, pp. 157–60): 'De tussi.'

9. *Arrianus . . . Coughs of Hawks.* 'Arrianus' looks like an error for 'Aldrovandus', as Arrian (*De venatione*) has nothing on hawks or other birds, and is concerned only with ground-hunting. Aldrovandus, how-

ever, in his *Ornithologia* (*SC*, 1610), deals at length with hawks, including their diseases. In particular, in I. iv (1599, p. 322), he describes several remedies under the marginal captions 'Si pulmonibus laboret' and 'Ad Asthma'.

18–40. *Hippocrates . . . good signification* (*and notes*). Material for this passage is derived from the Conclusions (ἀποτελέσματα) in *De insomniis* as follows: *Dreams . . . Diseases*, Apotelesma, no. iii; *Diet*, *Exercise*, *Sweating* and *Vomiting*, no. vii; *Prayers . . . Heroes*, no. xxvii; *healthful . . . Stars*, no. viii; *Flying*, no. xxi; *Limpid Fountains*, no. xxviii; *white Vestments*, no. xxxix; *fruitful green Trees*, no. xxviii; *not in dark Habits*, no. xliii; *take nothing away from us*, no. xliv. With 'Limpid Fountains' cf. also Astrampsychus (see note to *GC*, 174. 19), 1603, p. 7.

41. *Cardan. De vita propria*, xxxvii.

187. 9–10. *dream of Lettuce . . . Disease*. Achmet (see note to *GC*, 174. 19–20), i. 70, p. 58: 'Lenticula luctum praesagit.'

10–11. *Figs . . . foolish Talk*. Astrampsychus, 1603, p. 1.

11. *Eggs . . . Trouble*. Astrampsychus, p. 9: 'certus dolor.'

12. *dream of Blindness*. Astrampsychus, p. 9: 'Caecum videri, omnium optimum est.'

13. *Nicephorus*. See note to *GC*, 174. 19.

33–34. *Marriages . . . Candle*. Referring to the kind of auction-sale in which bids were received while a small piece of candle continued to burn. See *OED*, s.v. Candle, *sb*. 5.d.

188. 1. *this serious Person*. The subject of the *Letter*.

5. *Petrarcha*, *Dante*, *and Ariosto*. See Paulus Jovius, *Elogia doctorum virorum*, 1571 (*SC*), pp. 22, 20–21, and 188–9.

8. *Ciceronian Poets*. Cf. *RM*, 67. 37.

18. *Decipiency*. Greenhill points out that this, by etymology, should be 'desipiency' (*desipientia*); but in the manuscript (see 254. 33) Browne himself writes 'dicipiency'.

28–32. *where good Wishes . . . Heaven*. Cf. *RM*, 73. 23–24.

189. 14. *second Life of Lazarus* (*and note*). Baronius, *Annales ecclesiastici*, 34. 4 (1738, i, p. 118): 'Epiphanius . . . testatur Lazarum post resurrectionem annos vixisse triginta.'

15. *Tears of his Saviour*. See *RM*, 40. 7–8 and note.

24. *Enoch or Elias*. Gen. v. 24 and 2 Kings ii. 11. See *H*, 106. 7–12 and note.

190. 32. *climacterically old*. Old at 63.

191. 2–3. *Jewels . . . Cloud*. A. de Boot, *Le parfaict ioailler*, *SC*, 1644, p. 169 (on the diamond): 'S'il est teint de quelque couleur . . . s'il est nuageux; s'il cache quelque fente, grain, ou poil . . . il en doit perdre la moitié' (sc. of the standard price).

193. 28. *Recipiscency*. Greenhill notes the incorrectness of this form (from *resipiscentia*); but see note to 188. 18.

The paragraphs of LF from 'Tread softly' *to the end are almost wholly repeated in various sections of CM, and are annotated at the relevant points below.*

CHRISTIAN MORALS

201. 1–2. *David, Earl of Buchan.* Son of Henry, third Lord Cardross . . . married first, in 1697, Frances, daughter and heiress of Henry Fairfax of Hurst, Berkshire, by [Anne,] daughter of Sir Thomas Browne of Norwich. . . . She died 31 July 1719. (*Scots Peerage*, 1905, ii, p. 275.)

26. *Elizabeth Littelton.* Elizabeth Browne married in 1680 George, youngest son of Sir Thomas Littelton. (Wilkin, i, liii, &c.)

202. 12. *Arch-Bishop of Canterbury.* Thomas Tenison, 1636–1715. Archbishop, 1694. See *DNB.*

17. *John Jeffery.* 1647–1720. Archdeacon of Norwich 1694–1720. See *DNB.*

203. 9. *Cebes*'s *Table.* The short work known as *Κέβητος Θηβαίου Πίναξ* was probably written in the first century A.D. but was for long attributed to Cebes the pupil of Socrates. *SC* contains '*Epicteti Enchiridion & Cebetis Tabula*' (Greek and Latin), 1651.

11–14. *narrow Gate . . . Erudition. Cebetis Thebani Tabula*, 12 (1670, p. 41): 'Videsne januam parvam & viam quandam ante januam, parum frequentem . . . ut quae & praeceps & aspera & praerupta esse videatur? . . . Haec igitur . . . via est, quae ad Veram Eruditionem ducit' and p. 43: '. . . ad Eruditionem ubi quis pervenerit, ea curat illum, suamque illi vim propinat, ut ante omnia expurget . . . mala quae secum attulerat omnia.'

23. *in lyons Skins.* 'In armour, in a state of military vigilance' (Gr.). Tilley, *The proverbs in England*, gives, from Erasmus, *Adagia*, the saying 'Si leonina pellis non satis est, vulpina addenda.'

35–36. *Lapithytes . . . Centaurs.* Ovid, *Met.* xii. 210 sqq. (Lapithae.)

204. 1. *be Cæsar.* As a conqueror.

2. *within thy self. Addition on p. 272: poppies . . . garden.* Livy, i. 54. 6.

6. *Cato.* Of Utica. Plutarch, *Cato minor*, 25.

9. *Sisters.* For daughters. See Introduction, p. xxiii.

10. *Origen's (and note).* Eusebius, *Ecclesiastical History*, vi. 8.

36–38. *there may . . . poor. Variant on p. 272: they haue no pleasure in them.* Eccles. xii. 1.

39. *Irus.* The beggar in Homer, *Od.* xviii.

205. 2. *Give . . . unto eight.* Eccles. xi. 2.

12–13. *he who . . . Rewarder.* Prov. xix. 17.

14. *Ides.* The day for paying back loans. Cf. *Hor. Ep.* ii. 69.

19. *Ax of the Prophet.* 2 Kings vi. 5–7.

32–33. *Thou art my Confidence . . . Sun.* Job xxxi. 24; 26–27.

206. 7. *magnetically.* Fixedly.

17. *best . . . Good (and note).* Quotation not identified. Cf. *RM*, 53. 37–39, 68. 39–69. 4, and *PE*, i. 5 (1646, p. 19), '*vltimus bonorum*'.

32. *Gamaliel.* Acts v. 35–39.

207. 6. *follow . . . evil.* Exod. xxiii. 2.

7. *Pompey*'s *Pillar.* At Alexandria. Celebrating the capture of Alexandria

by Diocletian. The association with Pompey has not been convincingly explained.

32. *Socrates*. Cf. Burton, 2. 3. 7 (1638, p. 351). Aelian, *Varia historia*, ii. 13.

208. 9. *Diabolism*. Calumny (διάβολη). Cf. Job i and ii.

13. *noble Christian*. Referring perhaps to Rom. xii and xiii.

31–32. *Stars . . . Orbs*. Cf. *GC*, 167. 4.

209. 4. *Adraste and Nemesis*. Greenhill conjectured 'Adrastean Nemesis' since A. and N. were not separate deities; but in MS. Rawlinson D. 109, f. 21v, 'Adraste and Nemesis' is plainly written in Browne's own hand.

15–16. *think . . . suffer them*. Cf. the proverb (of uncertain authorship): 'Solamen miseris socios habuisse doloris.'

37. *Zeno*'s *King*. Cicero, *De fin*. iii. 22 (on the Stoic concept of the Wise Man and his self-command): 'Rectius enim appellabitur rex quam Tarquinius qui nec se nec suos regere potuit.'

210. 10. *wise man's wax*. Homer, *Od*. xii. 173.

32. *Memory of Seneca*. (The elder.) *Controversiae*, i (Preface), 1–3. (Gr.) *or Simonides*. Cicero, *De oratore*, ii. 87 (357). (Gr.)

211. 14. *Theta's*. θ, initial letter of θάνατος, signifying punishment by death. Martial, vii. 37. 2. Cf. *H*, 120. 28–29.

14–15. *no nocent . . . himself*. Juvenal, xiii. 2–3. (Note in *CM*, 1756.)

31. *Sons of Jupiter* (*and note*). Plutarch, *Alexander*, 2 and 3.

35. *Periœci*. People living in the same latitude, but opposite meridians. See *PE*, vi. 2, p. 283.

212. 3. *wild Horses of Plato*. *Phaedrus*, 246, 253–4. But only one of the two horses was 'wild'.

9. *Lipara: Vulcan's Art*. 'Vulcani domus', Virgil, *Aen*. viii. 417–22. Vulcan's abode was on Hiera, one of the Lipari Islands.

24–32. *Let not . . . indited them. Addition on p. 275: pythagoras in the Moone*. No reference to this has been found in the lives of Pythagoras. Lucian's Icaromenippus visits the moon and is there met not by Pythagoras but by Empedocles, who instructs him how to perceive the earth therefrom. The visitor describes the various sins and follies of mankind which are thus seen by him. (*Icaromenippus*, 15–19.)

26. *Oedipus*. Cf. *RM*, 7. 3.

30. *Laconism on the Wall*. Dan. v. 25–28.

213. 6. *Affectation . . . Money*. Cf. *RM*, 51. 37.

6–8. *reject . . . World*. Cf. *RM*, 51. 29–32.

10. *stand out of my Sun*. Plutarch, *Alexander*, 14.

15–16. *Bias . . . Wise-man*. Of Priene, one of the seven wise men of Greece. Cicero, *Paradoxa Stoicorum*, i. 8, attributes to him the saying 'Omnia mecum porto mea.' Cf. Valerius Maximus, vii. 2.

214. 11–12. *Poysons . . . bad*. Cf. 69. 11–13.

15. *King Demetrius*. Demetrius I (Poliorcetes), of Macedonia, 336–283 B.C.

27–29. *So that . . . Mankind.* Cf. *H*, 84. 28–32.

37. *Tycho.* The god of chance, τύχη; or (with derivation from τεύχω) the maker.

215. 2–3. *Andreas Doria.* 1466–1560; Genoese patriot and admiral. See E. Petit, *André Doria*, 1887. The incident referred to is described by Cardan, at the end of his *Encomium podagrae.*

5–8. *Cato . . . design.* Plutarch, *Cato minor*, 68, 70.

13. *Socrates.* Plato, *Apology*, 37 c–d. See notes to *RM*, 30. 27 and 32. 4–5.

13. *Cardan. De vita propria*, xlvii, 'Spiritus'.

19. *Tropicks and Deflexions.* Turnings back and turnings aside.

20. *Asphaltick Lake.* See *RM*, 20. 21–22 and note.

25–26. *like Vulcan. Iliad*, i. 592.

34. *tract.* Course, drift, tendency.

216. 9. *Orontes into Tiber.* Juvenal, iii. 62; of foreigners coming into Rome. (Note in *CM*, ed. of 1756.)

25–26. *the Lazy of Brazilia.* The sloth. Clusius, *Exotica* (1605), v. 16, pp. 110–12.

29. *solemn.* Ordinary.

35–36. *a Lyon in the way.* Prov. xxii. 13.

36. *Leaden Sandals.* Hippocrates, *Articulationes*, 62 (*Œuvres*, ed. Littré, iv, p. 266) refers to a leaden sandal for surgical use. (Gr.) But Browne may be alluding to the proverb recorded by Tilley in *The Proverbs in England*, L 136, 'To have Lead on one's heels.'

38. *Hercules . . . breath.* Allusion not traced.

217. 15. *uncharitableness. Addition on p. 277*: (*a*) *Solon . . . dead.* Plutarch, *Solon*, 21. (*b*) *to looke euerlastingly backward.* Dante, *Inferno*, xx. 13–15.

21. *Athens* (*and note*). Xenophon, *Memorabilia*, iii. 5. 3 (Socrates' praise of the Athenians).

35. *Astræa* (*and note*). Cf. Ovid, *Met.* i. 149–50.

218. 3. *Laërtius.* Diogenes Laertius, *De vitis &c. philosophorum.*

6. *a Hand to burn.* Referring to Mutius Scaevola; Livy, ii. 12. See note to *RM*, 42. 3.

23–24. *delight . . . rarity.* Juvenal, xi. 208.

31. *Jupiter's brain* (*and note*). Athenaeus, xii. 514e and xiv. 642f. (Gr.)

32. *Cytheridian Cheese.* The reference is to Diogenes Laertius, x. 6. 11, but the meaning of 'Cytheridian' is uncertain (? from κυθρίδιον, a small cup or pot). The reading τυροῦ Κυθνίου seems preferable as the island of Cythnus was known for its cheese. See Aelian, *On animals*, xvi. 32.

32. *Tongues of Nightingals.* Lampridius (*Historia Augusta*, *SC*), *Elagabalus*, xx. 5: 'comedit saepius . . . linguas pavonum et lusciniarum.'

218. 37–**219.** 2. *Nero . . . Calda* (*and note*). Suetonius, *Nero*, 48. 4: 'fame et iterum siti interpellante panem quidem sordidum oblatum aspernatus est, aquae autem tepidae aliquantum bibit.' See also ibid. 27. 2. Cf. Pliny, *HN*, xxxi. 23.

219. 14. *candid.* Favourably disposed (*OED*, s.v. 4).

17–36. *Quotation . . . fly from it. Variant on p. 278:* (*a*) *Aginour.* For Agamemnon. See note on *H*, 116. 2–4. (*b*) *Machiauell . . . Italie. Il Principe*, 7, &c.

21. *Cicero.* The mistake (in the lost *De gloria*) is pointed out by Aulus Gellius, xv. 6. (Gr.)

23–24. *Plautus . . . conception.* In the latter part of *Amphitruo* Plautus makes Alcmena seem to bear Hercules the day after he had been begotten by Jupiter. 'Plautus tempora & rem commiscuit' (*Comoediae*, ed. Taubman, *SC*, 1621, p. 2, Argument to *Amphitruo*, by J. Camerarius).

25. *Apollinaris Sidonius.* The first mistake referred to occurs in his *Carmina*, ix. 25, where he speaks of Babylon drinking the Tigris: 'inclusum bibit hinc et inde Tigrim.' The second, in *Carmina*, xvi. 18–21, turns on a confusion of 1 Sam. v and vi (about the Philistines and the Ark) and 2 Sam. vi. 2 sqq. (about David fetching the Ark from Kirjath-jearim).

32–33. *Commodus after . . . Severus.* In *Il Principe*, xix. Machiavelli gives the emperors from Marcus to Maximinius in their correct order, but discusses the characters of some in the order Severus, Caracalla, Commodus, and Maximinius.

220. 1–2. *Trismegistus . . . est* (*and note*). See note to *RM*, 12. 17–18.

5. *Cardan. De subtilitate*, x (*Opera*, 1663, iii, p. 544).

5. *Scaliger. De subtilitate ad Cardanum*, ccxxxvi, 1 (1615, p. 575).

6–7. *Compage.* Structure.

10. *Delphian Blade.* Erasmus, *Adagia*, ii. 3. 69: '*Gladius Delphicus.* De re dicebatur ad diversos usus accommodabile.' (Gr.)

14. *Royal Vein.* 'The *vena basilica* in the arm, one of the veins opened in bloodletting'. (Gr.)

20. *Sibyls leaves.* Virgil, *Aen.* iii. 444.

27–28. *genealogy of Hector.* 'Quae mater Hecubae?' was one of the puzzling questions asked by Tiberius (cf. *H*, 119. 21 and footnote; Suetonius, *Tiberius*, 70). (Gr.)

28. *King of France.* Louis XI, father of Charles VIII. See Aemilius Paulus, *De rebus gestis Francorum*, under heading Carolus VIII (1569, p. 589). (Gr.)

31. *Ergotisms.* Strictly logical arguments.

221. 6–7. *Eluctation.* Struggling forth.

12. *Exantlation.* Drawing up, as from a well.

13. *half out of the Pit.* See *Oxford Dict. Eng. Proverbs*, 'Truth lies at the bottom of a well'.

19. *six thousand.* Although MS. Sloane 1885 also (see p. 279) omits 'years' it seems hardly possible that Browne meant 'days'. See notes to *RM*, 44. 1 and *CM*, 241. 9–242. 23.

19. *make out.* Either understand or, more probably, accomplish.

31. *sing the same Song.* See *Oxford Dict. Eng. Proverbs.*

222. 4. *Diogenes . . . Money.* Diogenes Laertius, vi. 20–21.

6–7. *Some Negros . . . white* (*and note*). J. A. v. Mandelslo, *Travels into the*

Indies (*translation*), iii, 'Capo Verde' (1662, p. 264): 'They believe the dead will rise again, but that they shall be white, and trade there as the *Europeans* do.'

26. *the first . . . last* (*and note*). Greenhill gives the reference to Seneca.

30–31. *capitulation.* Agreement.

39. *in the World. Addition on p. 280: persius . . . extra.* Persius, 1. 7.

223. 6. *particle . . . Man.* See note to 237. 13.

40. *extract of the World.* See note to *H*, 89. 18.

224. 2–5. *Men . . . Physiognomy.* Fully illustrated in G. B. della Porta, *De humana physiognomonia* (1586, &c.).

24–25. *uncomely . . . moles.* Cf. Swift, *Gulliver's Travels*, ii, 'A voyage to Brobdingnag', 5 (ed. Davis, 1941, p. 103): 'Their Skins appeared so coarse and uneven, so variously coloured when I saw them near, with a Mole here and there as broad as a Trencher, and Hairs hanging from it thicker than Pack-threads.'

32–33. *Pompey . . . Great.* Plutarch, *Pompey*, 13. 4–5.

225. 2. *beginnings. Addition on p. 281: Lucan, 7, &c.* viii. 27–32.

13. *Bellisarius. PE*, vii. 17 (1646, p. 375): 'We are sad when wee reade the story of Belisarius that worthy Cheiftaine of Justinian; who, after the Victories of Vandals, Gothes, and Persians . . . had at last his eyes put out by the Emperour, and was reduced to that distresse, that hee beg'd reliefe on the high way. . . . And this we do not only heare in discourses, Orations and Themes, but finde it also in the leaves of *Petrus Crinitus* [*De honesta disciplina*, ix. 6], *Volateranus* [*Commentarii*, 1559, pp. 15–16] and other worthy Writers. But . . . wee doe not discover the latter Scene of his misery in Authors of Antiquity, or such as have expresly delivered the story of those times.'

13. *Beggers bush.* See *Oxford Dict. of Eng. Proverbs*, s.v.

13. *Bajazet in the grate.* The story that Tīmūr, or Tamburlaine, after defeating Bajazet I, the ruler of the Ottomans, had him put into an iron cage, first appears in Pope Pius II's *Asiae Europaeque elegantissima descriptio.* See Marlowe, *Tamburlaine*, ed. V. Ellis-Fermor, 1930, pp. 29 sqq. Browne's most likely source was R. Knolles, *The Generall historie of the Turkes* (3rd ed. 1621, p. 227): '*Baiazet* . . . did violently beat out his braines against the barres of the yron grate wherein he was inclosed, and so died about the yeare of our Lord 1399.'

23–24. *extramission . . . self-reflexion.* In *PE*, iii. 7 (1646, p. 120) Browne refers to the opinion of 'Aristotle [*De sensu*, 438a] . . . and others; who hold that sight is made by Reception, and not by Extramission, by receiving the rayes of the object into the eye, and not by sending any out'. See note to *GC*, 167. 33.

226. 10. *second Death.* Rev. ii. 11, xx. 14, &c.

28. *perspectives.* Magnifying glasses.

227. 8. *Lucan and Seneca.* Tacitus, *Ann.* xv. 63 and 70. (Gr.) See *RM*, 71. 34–35 and note.

12. *the old Heroes.* See *H*, 92. 23–28 *and note.*

22. *Socrates in Plato. Phaedo*, 117–18.

24. *poyniards.* A *sword* in Plutarch, *Cato minor*, 70.

25–26. *pummel of his Sword (and note).* Thomas Ross, *Continuation of Silius Italicus to the death of Hannibal* (*SC*), iii (1661, pp. 75–76, marginal note on p. 75): 'he took Poison, which he alwaies wore about him (some say, in the Pommel of his Sword)'. According to Juvenal, x. 165–6, the poison was carried in a ring.

30–31 *Emperour . . . sleep (and note).* Referring to Solyman, who accused Abraham Bassa of misgovernment and treachery. R. Knolles, *The generall historie of the Turkes* (5th ed., 1638, p. 654h): 'All which the Bassa . . . humbly confessed & . . . craued of him pardon. But his hard heart was not by any tears to be mooued: for the same night as he was slumbring . . . an eunuch cut his throat with a crooked knife, which *Solyman* had deliured vnto him. . . .' Cf. *RM*, 71. 32–33.

228. 15–17. *So that . . . any one.* See 214. 27–29 and note.

229. 13. *counterfeited Thunder.* Salmoneus. Virgil, *Aen.* vi. 585–6. (Gardiner.)

20. *Trismegistus his Circle.* See *RM*, 10. 16 and note.

31–32. *Guardian Spirits.* See *RM*, 32. 4–5 and note.

230. 14. *bid early defiance.* Cf. 209. 7.

25. *Tree of Goa (and note).* Theophrastus, *Enquiry into plants*, i. 7. 3. Cf. Gerard, iii. 1. 35 (1636, pp. 1513–14).

34–35. *Rake not . . . others.* Cf. 207. 17–19.

231. 4. *that inhumane Vice (and note).* Aristotle, *Nicom. Eth.* ii. 6. 18 and 7. 15.

23. *Diogenes . . . Statues.* Diogenes Laertius, vi. 49.

232. 8–9. *Wise men . . . Stars (and note).* Cf. Burton, 1. 2. 1. 4 (1638, p. 57), where the same Latin text is quoted; also Helmont, *De vita*, 31 (*Opera*, 1707, i, p. 119): 'Tuentur autem se Scholae per illud: Sapiens dominabitur Astris.' Ralegh, *History of the World*, 1. i. 11 (1614, p. 14), quotes as from Ptolemy '*Sapiens, & omina sapientis medici dominabuntur astris.*'

29. *anticipate . . . Age.* Cf. *RM*, 40. 1–2.

31. *Adams (and note).* See note to *RM*, 38. 2.

233. 1. *intend.* Intensify. (*OED*, s.v. i. 4.)

7. *Attalus His Garden (and note).* Cf. *GC*, 131. 10–12.

13. *black Sails.* Plutarch, *Theseus*, 17. (Gr.)

29–30. *Pompey . . . Sons (and note).* As also in *H*, 83. 11.

234. 1. *Covarrubias (and note).* This emblem may be the source of the poem attributed to Herrick 'Vpon a Cherrystone sent to the tip of the Lady Jemmonia Walgraves eare' ('a deaths head on the one side & her face on the other', Sloane MS. 1446, f. 62v); Herrick, *Poetical Works*, *OET* 1956, pp. 417 and 495. The work by Covarrubias is in *SC* (Madrid, 1610).

26–27. *short Arches.* Cf. *H*, 122. 3–4, 'winter arches', and note.

27. *periscian.* Inhabiting the polar regions, where the sun can be seen through the day to cast shadows (σκιάι) in all directions.

31. *Colossus . . . within.* Pliny, *HN*, xxxiv. 18. (Gr.)

37. *old Dictates.* Plutarch, *Solon*, 27.

235. 4. *Swims in Oyl.* Cf. *PE*, vii. 15 (1646, p. 370).

12. *Historia Horribilis (and note).* The reference is to *Tragica, Seu tristium historiarum De Poenis Criminalibus et Exitu Horribili . . . Libri II. Islebiae* 1597. *Procurante & sumptum faciente Henningo Grosio.*

12–13. *Flay not . . . Glass.* Alluding to the servant of Vedius Pollio, who for this offence was thrown into a pond to feed the lampreys. (Gr.)

13–14. *nor pound . . . offendeth thee.* Alluding to the death of Anaxarchus as told by Diogenes Laertius, ix. 10. 59. (Gr.)

16. *Stoically mistaken . . . sins.* Cicero, *Paradoxa Stoicorum*, iii, 'Aequalia esse peccata et recte facta.'

17. *commutatively.* See note to *RM*, 72. 36–37.

17. *iniquous.* Unfair.

20–21. *Arrows . . . of Jonathan.* 1 Sam. xx. 20.

22. *a Dead Enemy smells well.* Suetonius, *Vitellius*, 10. (Gr.)

29. *Homerican Mars (and note).* 'Gradivus' was a surname of Mars. Juvenal's reference is to *Iliad*, v. 858. (Gr.)

29–30. *Women . . . Revenge.* Juvenal, xiii. 191–2. (Gr.)

236. 10. *Scorpions.* 1 Kings xii. 11, 14.

12. *Regulus.* Whom the Carthaginians were said to have tortured by keeping him awake. See e.g. Aulus Gellius, vii. 4.

18. *In contingences . . . Tempers.* In judging what a person may do from the study of his character. Cf. 241. 37–242. 2.

25. *Whispering-places.* See *GC*, 167. 39–168. 8 and note.

36. *David's Servants.* 2 Sam. x. 4.

37. *the expected Elias.* See note to *H*, 124. 5–6.

237. 13. *Divine particle.* Horace, *Sat.* ii. 2. 79:

atque adfigit humo divinae particulam aurae.

17. *Choragium.* χορηγεῖον, the place where the chorus was trained in its movements.

33. *Crystalline.* See note to *GC*, 167. 25.

238. 9. *not an Eye.* Cf. *GC*, 167. 11–12.

39. *inclination not coaction.* See note to 232. 8–9.

40. *Stygian Oaths.* Oaths 'by the Styx', which could not be broken. *Iliad*, xv. 38; *Od.* v. 185.

239. 32. *Olybius his Urn (and note).* Licetus, *De lucernis antiquorum reconditis (SC)*, 1621, pp. 8–9, says that this lamp, unearthed about A.D. 1500, had supposedly been alight for about that number of years: 'dum foderetur a rusticis terra solito altius, reperta est vrna fictilis, & in ea altera vrnula; in qua erat Lucerna adhuc ardens inter duas ampullas . . . purissimo quodam liquore, plenas; Cuius virtute lucerna illa per tot annos arsisse creditur; & nisi retecta fuisset, perpetuo arsura.'

36. *Jove . . . Stone (and note)*. Polybius, iii. 25; Aulus Gellius, i. 21. 4. The person making the oath would throw the stone away, wishing he too might be cast out if the oath was not kept.

240. 2–3. *Urn of the Prætor*. Receptacle for votes of condemnation or acquittal.

4. *swear as Osman (and note)*. Knolles, 1638, p. 1383 (for year 1619): 'The Great Turks oath to Bethlem Gabor, Prince of Transylvania. [promising to defend him in all circumstances] Sultan Osman . . . *sweares by the Highest, Almightiest, and Almighty Gods Holinesse, by his Kingdome, by the substance of the Heauens, the Sunne, the Moone, and the Starres, by the earth, and by all under the earth, by the braines and all the hairy scalpe of my mother, by my head, and all the strength of my soule and body, by the holy Great Mahomet, and by my Circumcision*, That I thee. . . .'

27. *Elater*. Driving force (ἐλατήρ).

30. *Vulcans*. Alluding to Vulcan's lameness.

241. 1. *Antoninus*. Marcus Aurelius.

2. *Pythagaras*. Referring to the rules of conduct ascribed to Pythagoras in Diogenes Laertius, viii. 17–18.

4. *Phocylides*. See *H*, 112. 17 and note.

241. 9–**242.** 23. *In seventy . . . Heaven (Section 22)*. In this section a distinction seems to be made between the degrees of knowledge and wisdom attainable by the age first of 70 or 80 (§ 1) and then of 100, the 'sixtieth part' of time according to the estimate, referred to elsewhere by Browne, that the world would last 6,000 years altogether (see *RM*, 44. 1, and note). One hundred years is also the length of a man's life assumed by Er in Plato, *Republic*, x. 615. Browne, however, does not make the distinction of the two ages very clear and it is arguable that he has 70 or 80 in mind throughout the section. Support for this can be found in the fact that in addition to the estimate of 6,000 years for the duration of the world there is another and shorter estimate put forward in the Talmud (translation, ed. Epstein, vi, 'Sanhedrin', ii, p. 658): 'Elijah said . . . "The world shall exist not less than eighty-five jubilees, and in the last jubilee the son of David will come." ' As a jubilee is a period of 50 years the resultant figure, after multiplying by 85, is 4250; and this divided by 60 gives just under 71. But Browne does not mention this estimate.

241. 35. *Orbity*. Bereavement.

38–39. *Judge . . . outside*. See note to *RM*, 32. 30.

242. 30. *Diana . . . Profession*. Referring to the words of Demetrius, who made silver shrines for Diana at Ephesus, to his fellow craftsmen: 'by this craft we have our wealth' (Acts xix. 25).

243. 36–38. *Cicero . . . cradle again. De senectute*, 23 (1754).

244. 5. *are only*. See note to *RM*, 3. 25.

13–16. *Though . . . present*. Cf. *RM*, 54. 12–21.

245. 10–13. *the prayer . . . to come*. Cf. *RM*, 44. 24–26.

28–30. *Nero's mind . . . perish*. Suetonius, *Nero*, 38. (Gr.)

246. 15–16. *Six Thousand years.* See note on 241. 9–242. 23.

23–24. *things long past . . . acted over.* Cf. *RM*, 7. 28–30.

31. *think . . . last.* Horace, *Epist.* i. 4. 13.

247. 1–7. *And if . . . unto them.* See *H*, 124. 36–38 and note.

NOTES ON THE PASSAGES IN *LF* NOT PUBLISHED IN 1690

251. 17. *st Innocents churchyard.* Cf. *H*, 125. 9 and footnote.

252. 20–21. *double chinnd (and note).* Aristotle, *Hist. Animal.* iii. 11, 518b, 20. The sense of Gaza's rendering, double-chinned, is contradicted by J. C. Scaliger in his translation and commentary, 1619 (*SC*), p. 348: 'qui *non* sunt mento bipartito' (μὴ διγένειοι). The accepted text of Aristotle has μαδιγένειοι, smooth-chinned.

21–23. *varices . . . baldnesse.* Aristotle, loc. cit. 25.

36. *mosse. OED*, s.v. *sb.*[1], 3a, cites Chambers, *Cycl.* 1727–41: 'There is also a kind of greenish moss growing on human skulls that have long been exposed to the air, called *usnea humana*, or *muscus calvarius*. The antients made a deal of use of it as an astringent, &c.'

253. 34. *Virbiusses.* Persons who have come to life after seeming to be dead. Ovid, *Met.* xv. 544. *Jonsonus Virbius, or The Memory of Ben Jonson Revived* was published in 1638.

39. *Nonnus . . . feuer.* D. Heinsius refers to this in his *Aristarchus sacer* (*SC*, 1627), 1639, ix, p. 783.

254. 7. *liued . . . after.* See note on *LF*, 189. 14.

7–9. *pursued . . . others.* Baronius, *Annales ecclesiastici*, 35. 5 (1738, i, p. 225).

255. 22. *nimio de stamine.* Juvenal, x. 252.

INDEX OF AUTHORS CITED OR REFERRED TO IN THE FOOTNOTES AND COMMENTARY

(Excluding the Bible and modern authorities. Page and line-numbers in italics refer to footnotes in which the mention or citation of an author is not enlarged upon in the Commentary.)